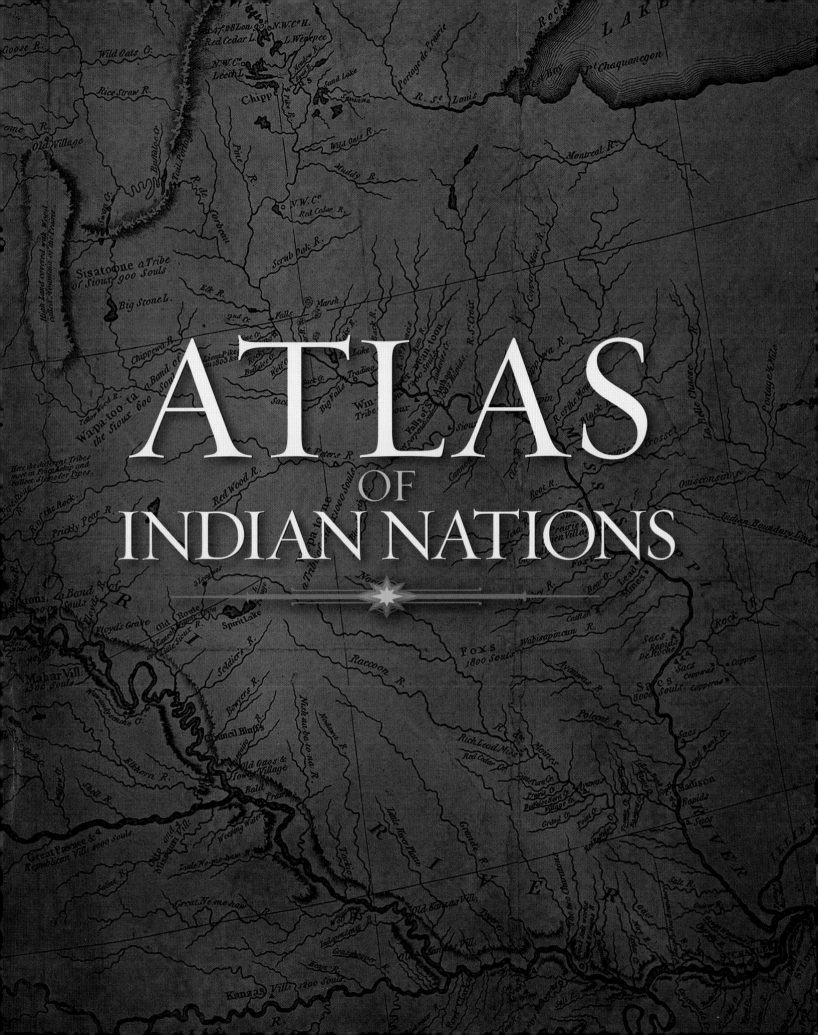

ATLAS
OF
INDIAN NATIONS

ATLAS
OF
INDIAN NATIONS

ANTON TREUER

NATIONAL GEOGRAPHIC

WASHINGTON, D.C.

CONTENTS

INTRODUCTION | 8
FEATURED MAPS:

PALEO-INDIAN MIGRATION AND SITES • MISSISSIPPIAN MOUNDBUILDERS

NATIVE LANGUAGES • ESTIMATED NUMBER OF INHABITANTS AT TIME OF CONTACT • EUROPEAN SETTLEMENT AT A GLANCE

EPIDEMICS • RELIGIOUS MOVEMENTS • SHRINKING INDIAN TERRITORIES

THE ATLAS OF INDIAN NATIONS | 20

CHAPTER 1
NORTHEAST | 22
FEATURED MAPS:

NATIVES AND PURITANS • THE EUROPEAN INVASION • THE FUR TRADE • EARLY CONTACT IN THE NORTHEAST

BATTLE OF THE MONONGAHELA • THE IROQUOIS LEAGUE • THE BLACK HAWK WAR

TRIBAL HISTORIES | 50

CHAPTER 2
SOUTHEAST | 58
FEATURED MAPS:

MOUNDVILLE • THE SECOTAN AND THE LOST COLONY • THE FIVE CIVILIZED TRIBES

THE TRAIL OF TEARS • LAND GRABS AND RESISTANCE

TRIBAL HISTORIES | 84

CHAPTER 3
ARCTIC AND SUBARCTIC | 88
FEATURED MAPS:

FIRST ARCTIC ENCOUNTERS • FINDING THE NORTH POLE • HUDSON BAY FUR TRADE

RUSSIAN AMERICA: COMPANY CONTROLLED

TRIBAL HISTORIES | 110

CHAPTER 4
PLAINS | 114
FEATURED MAPS:

THE HORSE IN NORTH AMERICA • MAPPING INDIAN LANDS • WARS FOR THE PLAINS

THE SAND CREEK MASSACRE • THE QUEST FOR MÉTIS INDEPENDENCE IN CANADA • BATTLE OF THE LITTLE BIGHORN

WARS FOR THE BLACK HILLS • THE WOUNDED KNEE MASSACRE • DWINDLING BUFFALO HERDS

TRIBAL HISTORIES | 148

Preceding pages: In the spring, the Menominee and neighboring tribes speared fish by torchlight at night, harvesting about 85 percent male fish with efficiency and sustainability. Native nations developed numerous unique and vibrant cultures over centuries of life on the continent before European arrival.
Opposite: A Menominee warrior with head roach, war paint, and feathers

ELEVENTH CENSUS OF THE UNITED STATES.
ROBERT P. PORTER, SUPERINTENDENT.

INDIANS.

MAP OF
LINGUISTIC STOCKS
OF
AMERICAN INDIANS
chiefly within the present limits of the United States.
From Annual Report of Bureau of Ethnology Vol. 7.
by J. W. POWELL.

CHAPTER 5

SOUTHWEST | 164

FEATURED MAPS:

THE PUEBLO REVOLT OF 1680 • HOPI RESISTANCE • THE SANTA FE TRAIL • CHACO CANYON

MEXICO, AMERICA, AND THE APACHE • THE TREATY OF GUADALUPE HIDALGO

APACHE RESISTANCE • THE LONG WALK OF THE NAVAJO

TRIBAL HISTORIES | 192

CHAPTER 6

GREAT BASIN AND PLATEAU | 198

FEATURED MAPS:

JEDEDIAH SMITH • FATHER PIERRE-JEAN DE SMET • FLIGHT FOR FREEDOM

CONFLICTS IN THE GREAT BASIN AND PLATEAU • BATTLE OF FOUR LAKES

TRIBAL HISTORIES | 222

CHAPTER 7

NORTHWEST COAST | 228

FEATURED MAPS:

THE BATTLE OF SITKA • CREATING BORDERS • THE OREGON TRAIL

NORTHWEST GOLD RUSHES • WHALING IN THE NORTHWEST

TRIBAL HISTORIES | 250

CHAPTER 8

CALIFORNIA | 256

FEATURED MAPS:

FRÉMONT EXPEDITIONS • THE CALIFORNIA GOLD RUSH • KLAMATH RIVER TRIBES

THE MODOC WAR • CALIFORNIA MISSIONS

TRIBAL HISTORIES | 280

APPENDIX | 287

MAP OF ALL U.S. RESERVATIONS | 288

LIST: ALL FEDERALLY DESIGNATED TRIBAL ENTITIES | 290

MAP OF ALL ALASKA NATIVE LANDS | 294

LIST: ALL ALASKA NATIVE ENTITIES | 296

MAP OF ALL CANADIAN FIRST NATIONS RESERVES | 298

LIST: ALL FIRST NATIONS | 300

MAP SOURCES | 303 • ILLUSTRATIONS CREDITS | 304 • LIST OF THE MAPS | 306 • INDEX | 308

Opposite: North America was home to more than 500 distinct tribes, speaking more than 300 distinct languages from 29 different primary language families, as shown on this map. The linguistic diversity of North American tribes is astounding. By contrast, European languages have three major classifications, broken into several families. The largest tribal language families in the United States and Canada are Athabascan (Na-Dené), Uto-Aztecan, and Algonquian (Algic). In Mexico, some tribal languages are quite vibrant. Quechua has six to seven million speakers. But most indigenous languages of the Americas are extremely endangered.

Plate 150

From Copyright Photograph 1908 by E.S.Curtis

Photogravure John Andrew & Son

BEAR'S BELLY – ARIKARA

INTRODUCTION

The land made the first people of North America. More than 500 distinct tribes lived in North America, speaking more than 300 languages from 29 language families. They built massive metropolitan complexes at Cahokia (Illinois) and Tenochtitlan (central Mexico), formed powerful confederacies in the Great Lakes, developed complex social, religious, and political systems, and occupied every corner of the continent not sheathed in ice. The cultural and linguistic diversity of the indigenous peoples of North America dwarfs that of Europe and many other places. Eight major regions of North America each had a distinct cultural evolution, informed and shaped by the land itself. From long-established urban centers in the Southeast to tiny sedentary villages in California and the Northwest Coast, from seasonally nomadic family groups in the Arctic to large nomadic tribes on the Plains, the land shaped the people. Sometimes tribes that had well-established cultures in other regions abandoned older religious practices when they moved into new areas, as happened with many tribes from the Southeast and Northeast that moved to the Plains. The cultures of North America were dynamic and changing long before European contact. The complexities of tribal culture, geography, and historical experience demonstrate a myriad of experiences, ways of knowing, art forms, societies, and political systems. The beauty and depth of the first people of the land continue to amaze.

Nature infuses Indian art and culture. A depiction of the sun dominates this Hopi kachina mask (above). An Arikara man (opposite) poses with a tanned bear hide.

COMING TO AMERICA

Indians are indigenous to the Americas. Although many people examine the prevailing theories of Paleo-Indian migrations from Asia to North America and end up thinking, "We are all immigrants here," the fact of the matter is that Indians arrived in the Americas and developed a diverse array of cultures and languages, inhabiting the entire hemisphere before there were any humans living in what is now England (the British Isles were entirely encased in ice until 12,000 years ago) and many thousands of years before the emergence of ancient Chinese, Egyptian, or Phoenician civilizations.

Nobody knows the details of exactly when or how the first Americans arrived. It is geologic certainty that there were extended periods of time from 45,000 to 11,000 years ago when vast quantities of the Earth's water were sucked into massive glaciers and Asia and North America were connected by land (not just ice). The footprints of prehistoric camels and horses that traveled from the Americas to Asia have been found on that land bridge, confirming beyond doubt that such crossings were possible.

Geologists and archaeologists have long suspected that humans made the trip, too, but from Asia to the Americas. This theory has changed and evolved dramatically over the past 20 years as new archaeological evidence at Monte Verde (Chile), Meadowcroft Rock Shelter (Pennsylvania), and other places has pushed the dates back further and further. Although there is undisputed evidence of humans in Clovis (New Mexico) about 11,000 years ago, that is no longer the earliest evidence of human habitation in the Americas. New theories, supported by linguistic, genetic, and archaeological evidence, suggest multiple migrations from Asia, probably by land and water—and much earlier than previously imagined. The oral histories of the tribes in North America make their indigenous status paramount, and everything in the scientific record supports that view.

A Caribou Inuit woman and her children. Because of the small size of traditional Inuit communities, extended family and kin networks remain a vital part of the social fabric.

NATIONS ON THE MOVE Opposite: Archaeologists, linguists, and geneticists have all studied the early arrival of humans in North America, and they are starting to agree more and more with tribal oral histories. People came to the Americas earlier than previously imagined. And they likely came multiple times and in many different ways. This map shows the prevailing assumed land migration pattern from Asia to the Americas.

LAND SHAPED THE PEOPLE

The land shaped Native American cultures. Most were farmers. In the Southwest, the Hopi farmed corn on arid slopes with an innovative system of rain-capture irrigation. In the Northeast, many tribes farmed corn, beans, and squash in a balance that produced high yields without depleting soil fertility or requiring crop rotation. In the Plains, numerous tribes thrived by hunting the 30 million buffalo that lived there. In all regions, tribal peoples picked berries and gathered tubers, nuts, and regionally specific crops such as the wild rice of the Northeast. In the Northwest, Arctic, and Northeast, fishing was critical to survival.

The different paths to sustenance and prosperity shaped political and cultural institutions. The Sun Dance of the Plains tribes was infused into the tribal religious and ceremonial repertoire for most tribes that moved there, regardless of where they came from originally. Lifeways and religious practices were rooted to place and formed by the land even more than by ancestral history.

But tribes shaped the land, too. Controlled burning extended the range of the buffalo all the way to New Jersey. Great moundbuilding civilizations built earthen pyramids still standing today at Cahokia and other places. At Chaco Canyon, nine miles of structures align in perfect symmetry, built by people who had no wheel or transit but amassed a highly developed knowledge of astronomy, solar cycles, weather, and Earth movements through the seasons. Each tribe has its own linguistic and cultural history, but the eight major geographic regions in which they lived were indelible parts of their formation.

DISEASE PANDEMICS

Although the tribes of North America and the regions that shaped them vary greatly, there are common elements to their histories. The most devastating of those shared experiences came through the

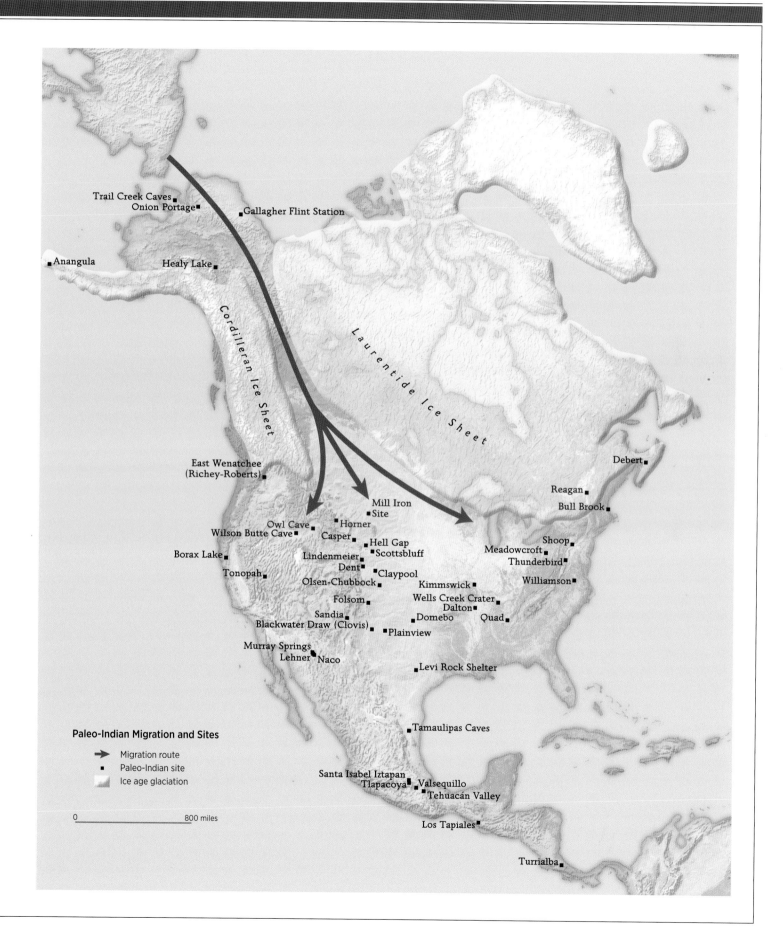

Paleo-Indian Migration and Sites

➤ Migration route
■ Paleo-Indian site
░ Ice age glaciation

0 ——————— 800 miles

Trail Creek Caves
Onion Portage
Gallagher Flint Station
Anangula
Healy Lake

Cordilleran Ice Sheet

Laurentide Ice Sheet

East Wenatchee
(Richey-Roberts)

Debert
Reagan
Bull Brook

Mill Iron
Site
Owl Cave
Horner
Wilson Butte Cave
Casper
Shoop
Hell Gap
Meadowcroft
Scottsbluff
Thunderbird
Borax Lake
Lindenmeier
Dent
Williamson
Tonopah
Claypool
Olsen-Chubbock
Kimmswick
Folsom
Wells Creek Crater
Dalton
Sandia
Domebo
Quad
Blackwater Draw (Clovis)
Plainview
Murray Springs
Lehner Naco

Levi Rock Shelter

Tamaulipas Caves

Santa Isabel Iztapan
Tlapacoya Valsequillo
Tehuacán Valley

Los Tapiales

Turrialba

CANADA

North Dakota

Minnesota

South Dakota

Nebraska

Kansas

Iowa

Missouri

Oklahoma

Arkansas

Texas

Louisiana

Wisconsin

Illinois

Cahokia

Michigan

L. Superior

L. Michigan

L. Huron

L. Erie

L. Ontario

Indiana

Ohio

Kentucky

Tennessee

Mississippi

Alabama

Georgia

West Virginia

Virginia

North Carolina

South Carolina

Florida

New York

Pennsylvania

Maryland

Delaware

New Jersey

Maine

Vt.

N.H.

Mass.

Conn.

R.I.

ATLANTIC OCEAN

Gulf of Mexico

Mississippian Moundbuilders, 900–1450
- Middle Mississippian
- South Appalachian
- Caddoan
- Plaquemine
- Oneota
- Fort Ancient

0   200 miles

Map shows present-day boundaries.

introduction of European diseases to which Indians had no natural immunity. The peoples of the Middle East and Europe domesticated sheep, pigs, and chickens, and their sustained daily exposure to the animal population along with crowded and usually unsanitary city conditions exposed them to many diseases. Their populations were periodically hit with terrible plagues. But the diseases in Europe came in spurts, and the populations had a chance to recover before the next major plague. The survivors developed immunities to many of those diseases, and their impact lessened over time to become chicken pox, measles, and other renditions of more serious plagues. In North America, all of those diseases were unknown by Indians. They got them all at the same time. As a result, in most areas, around 95 percent of the tribal population died during the early contact period. Making matters worse, those deaths often occurred at the same time that Europeans came to take their land or enslave their people. The combination crippled resistance and toppled many tribal political systems.

COLONIAL REGIMES

Europeans came to North America to seek better lives, escape religious persecution, and pursue a host of ambitions. Indians were often seen as obstacles to those ambitions, especially when European empires were engineering new colonial regimes in North America. Those empires fought one another for rights to the land and resources, but they all seemed to assume that what was in North America was theirs for the taking despite the long histories and human rights of the first peoples of the land.

The Spanish were interested in gold and precious metals, and they relied heavily on slave labor to engineer their empire. Their relations with tribes in North America often focused on access to slaves and resources. They encouraged tribes to fight one another, raid one another, and sell their tribal captives to the Spanish Empire. They established a mission labor system in the Southeast, Southwest, and California. In California, the missions controlled the army as well as the clergy, and they worked together to subjugate numerous tribes. By the time the Mexican government secularized those missions, many tribes no longer had any functional political systems. Some no longer even had living tribal languages. Most were landless in their own land and relegated to a feudal labor system throughout the Mexican and early American periods. Resistance to the Spanish Empire was crushed.

In California, the Northwest Coast, and the Arctic, the Russian Empire also wanted tribal resources. The Russians were less concerned with gold and mining than the Spanish. They wanted furs, especially sea otters. Here, too, the financial imperatives of empire dictated policy, and the Russian-American Company controlled the Russian navy and army. The Russians traded with tribal peoples, but they also took land and conscripted labor around their forts and trading posts. Many indigenous women were raped or forced to marry Russian men. They brought missionaries, who worked to systematically change tribal religion and language. Once again, resistance was brutally suppressed.

In the Southeast and Northeast, it was the French who sought to expand their empire. Like the Russians, they wanted furs, but they also wanted colonies, land, and religious converts. Uncharacteristically, their missionaries worked in tribal languages, so even today there are some entirely Christianized areas in northern Canada with a 100 percent fluency rate in the tribal language. The French formed alliances with some tribes, such as the Ojibwe, Ottawa, and Potawatomi. But they fought any opposed to their

The creators of Cahokia had a highly evolved culture. This deer mask was unearthed at the Cahokia excavation site in southern Illinois, directly across the Mississippi River from St. Louis, Missouri.

THE GREAT MOUNDBUILDERS Some of the tribal peoples of North America built massive earthen mounds. At Cahokia they were part of a sophisticated political, religious, and social order. In other places, they served ceremonial or funerary purposes. Some were geometric, pyramid-shaped, or made to resemble animals, birds, or serpents. Some shapes are obvious only when viewed by helicopter or airplane, designed to get the attention of spirits.

NATIVE LANGUAGES

RUSSIA

ICELAND

0   400   800
statute miles

0   400   800
kilometers

Beaufort Sea

Alaska (U.S.)

Baffin Bay

GREENLAND (DENMARK)

Gulf of Alaska

YUKON

N.W.T.

NUNAVUT

Labrador Sea

PACIFIC OCEAN

BRITISH COLUMBIA

ALBERTA

Hudson Bay

NFLD. & LAB.

QUEBEC

SASK.

MANITOBA

ONTARIO

P.E.I.

N.B.

N.S.

CANADA
U.S.

ME.

WASH.

MONT.

N.DAK.

MINN.

WIS.

N.H.
MASS.

VT.

N.Y.

R.I.
CONN.

OREG.

IDAHO

WYO.

S.DAK.

Lake Superior

MICH.

PA.

N.J.

OHIO

N.Y.

DEL.

NEV.

UTAH

COLO.

NEBR.

IOWA

KANS.

MO.

ILL.

IND.

KY.

W. VA.

VA.

N.C.

CALIF.

ARIZ.

N.MEX.

OKLA.

ARK.

TENN.

S.C.

MISS.

ALA.

GA.

TEXAS

ATLANTIC OCEAN

MEXICO
U.S.

FLORIDA

Gulf of Mexico

BAHAMAS

CUBA

Map Key

③ Language family

35 Language or dialect

Languages

1 Eskimo-Aleut
2 Algic
3 Na-Dené
4 Haida
5 Wakashan
6 Chimakuan
7 Salishan
8 Tsimshianic
9 Chinookan
10 Alsean
11 Siuslaw
12 Coosan
13 Takelman
14 Wintuan
15 Maiduan
16 Utian
17 Yokutsan
18 Plateau Penutian
19 Karok
20 Chimariko
21 Shastan
22 Palaihnihan
23 Pomoan
24 Yana
25 Salinan
26 Cochimí-Yuman
27 Seri
28 Washoe
29 Yukian
30 Esselen
31 Chumashan

Languages

32 Uto-Aztecan
33 Kiowa-Tanoan
34 Keresan
35 Zuni
36 Guaicura
37 Otomanguean
38 Coahuilteco
39 Comecrudan
40 Cotoname
41 Aranama
42 Solano
43 Maratino
44 Quinigua
45 Naolan
46 Karankawa
47 Kootenai
48 Cayuse
49 Siouan-Catawba
50 Tonkawa
51 Caddoan
52 Adai
53 Atakapan
54 Chitimacha
55 Tunica
56 Muskogean
57 Natchez
58 Yuchi
59 Timucuan
60 Calusa
61 Iroquoian
62 Beothuk

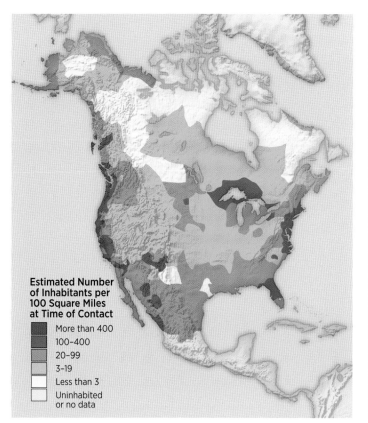

Estimated Number of Inhabitants per 100 Square Miles at Time of Contact
- More than 400
- 100–400
- 20–99
- 3–19
- Less than 3
- Uninhabited or no data

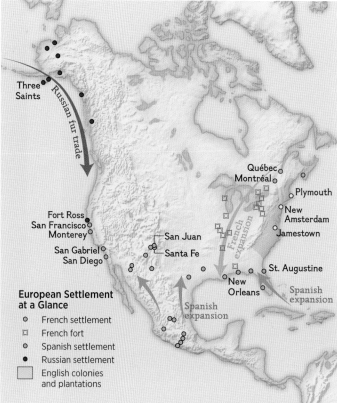

European Settlement at a Glance
- ○ French settlement
- ⊡ French fort
- ◎ Spanish settlement
- ● Russian settlement
- ▢ English colonies and plantations

ambitions. They even issued a genocidal edict against the Fox, refusing to accept their surrender after a series of punitive wars. The Fox who were not killed or sold into slavery sought refuge with other tribes, eventually merging with the Sac.

The Dutch, and soon after them the British, had colonial aspirations as well. They came after the land and all its resources—furs, deerskins, slaves, mineral wealth, farmland, and converts. The British sought allies among the Iroquois Confederacy and used those allies to dispossess other tribes and spar with the French over colonial rights. Some tribes were toppled, and most were irrevocably changed.

Indians were not passive players in this history. They developed strategies for dealing with European empires and settlers. In the Southeast, some tribes actively evolved their cultures to become more like that of the British. They developed slave-based plantation-style economies and, like the British, started to rely on black slaves more than Indian slaves as a labor force. They created representative structures of governance, written laws, and sophisticated political policies. Other tribes retreated west to avoid the encroachment of European empires, while some actively resisted the most onerous intrusions into the land and lifeways.

There were even a few notable cases of multitribal resistance. In the Great Lakes, Ottawa chief Pontiac brought more than a dozen tribes together in 1763, burning down 9 of the 11 British forts there and putting the others under siege. He hoped for French support, which never came, and eventually his warriors had to return to provide for their families and sieges were broken. During the early 1800s, Shawnee chief Tecumseh led another pan-Indian resistance with major support from several tribes, only to lose his life in a battle during the War of 1812. In the Plains, the Lakota, Cheyenne, and Arapaho

POPULATION COLLISION North America was densely inhabited prior to European contact. Although precise data is not available, we do know village sizes and tribal population information in many places and can accurately extrapolate from that information. The map above (left) shows the varied densities of the tribal populations at the time of European contact. As seen on the map (right), the Russians, French, Spanish, and English converged on North America from multiple directions, reconfiguring the tribal populations of the continent.

LANGUAGES OF THE INDIAN NATIONS The Indian nations of North America were exceptionally diverse. They spoke more than 300 distinct languages. Those languages have been grouped into 29 primary language families, as seen on this map (opposite). The tribes within any given language family shared certain linguistic and cultural roots, but those commonalities did not equate to political or social cohesion. Just as the British and German people spoke tongues in the same language family but had separate political and social histories, so too did Indian tribes with shared linguistic roots.

often worked in concert against American invasion. Other tribes, such as the Apache, fought alone against the Mexican and American militaries.

Tribal resistance, accommodation, and retreat were the strategies employed by tribes. But these rarely did more than buy their people a little extra time before European expansion engulfed them. In the end, they had to deal with new languages, customs, religions, and political systems not of their making and not within their realm of control.

The tribes gave much to the rest of the world. Many kinds of food—corn, beans, squash, vanilla, chocolate, maple, tomatoes, potatoes, and chilies—dominate the list of contributions. But Indians also changed the nature of European farming and introduced the obsidian scalpel, knowledge of trephination surgery, the birth of corporate enterprise, and enough gold to make that system work.

AMERICAN PERIOD

When the United States of America was born, tribal peoples had to confront a whole new reality—one that was little interested in respecting Indian lives or lifeways. Manifest Destiny—the idea that the United States was destined to spread from Atlantic to Pacific and subordinate any land or people in between—was the dominant paradigm. Through encroachment and squatting, military action, and negotiated treaties, the tribes of North America were deliberately dispossessed. They descended into abject poverty, a condition that has yet to be overcome by most. When the U.S. government stopped making treaties in 1871, the process

Epidemics Among
Indians, 16th–20th Centuries

Cholera
1831–38   Disease name and date(s) of epidemic

DISEASE EPIDEMICS Diseases brought by Europeans ravaged the tribal populations of the Americas. This map shows some of the most debilitating disease outbreaks in North America. Diseases traveled far faster than colonial regimes. Sometimes entire tribes were wiped out by European diseases before most tribal members had seen a white man.

continued through executive orders from the President and acts of Congress.

Many tribes resisted their dispossession. Some, like the Lakota, had initial success, but most were eventually defeated. Some, like the Yahi, were annihilated; others came very close. Genocide happened in many places. Some of the most horrific acts in human history were perpetrated by the U.S. Army or local militias.

The war on tribal cultures and languages was carried on long after the physical genocide stopped. More than 20,000 Native American children were removed from their homes and sent to residential boarding schools every year. In those government-run schools, children were beaten for speaking the only languages they knew, forced to pray in the Christian tradition, and torn from the social fabric of tribal communities. Today, as a result, many North American tribal languages are extinct. Most are threatened.

The U.S. government passed legislation called the Dawes Act in 1887. That enabled the government to allot the Indians reservations—to break up the communal land that had been held in common for all tribal members. Instead, each family got a private allotment and two-thirds of the reservation land was opened for white settlement. Most Indians lost their private allotments over the years to land speculators and outright fraud. On Leech Lake (Minnesota), the tribe owns 4 percent of its own reservation. In California, Indians are often minorities in their own communities. The government terminated some reservations and relocated many tribal people to urban areas. Education and social service policies and practices have also undermined the rights of Native peoples to raise their young according to tribal custom. Bitterness and pain remain in Indian country, as justice, remedy, reconciliation, and even truth remain elusive for many Indians.

MODERN ERA

Things are changing quickly for Indians today. Tribal governments in the United States and Canada have been trying to reclaim their sovereign power and rights. It can be contentious, but more and more, tribal peoples are engaged in a growing empowerment of their new political structures. Some tribes, such as the Florida Seminole, have eliminated poverty for their citizens. Their story is an exception, though, rather than the rule. Economic opportunity is still a major problem in Indian lands, with half of the children in poverty. Still, tribes are increasingly finding ways to make a brighter future.

Some tribes are also making great strides to preserve and revitalize tribal language and culture. Immersion programs and scholarly work among the Ojibwe, Mohawk, Crow, Blackfoot, and other tribes are showing true promise. Although the future vitality of tribal languages and cultures is not guaranteed, it is possible. And through those emergent efforts comes an opportunity to preserve the knowledge and ways of knowing that connected human beings to the diverse landscape of the North American continent in the first place and gave birth to its first peoples. With that comes the potential for all of us to better understand and appreciate the spirit of the land itself.

**Religious Movements,
17th–20th Centuries**
○ Location of selected movement

Indian Shaker Church 1881
Feather Religion 1904
Dreamer Cult
c. 1850
Drum Religion
c. 1880
Handsome Lake
Longhouse Religion
1799
Earth Lodge Religion
c. 1872
Dream Dance
c. 1900
Winnebago Prophet
(Black Hawk War)
1832
Delaware Prophet
(Pontiac's Rebellion) 1763
Bole Maru
Religion 1890s
Ghost Dance
1889
Shawnee Prophet
(Tecumseh's Rebellion) 1811
Popé (Pueblo Rebellion)
1680
Native American
Church 1918
Quanah Parker
Peyote Religion c. 1900

INTERTRIBAL RELIGIOUS MOVEMENTS
Most religious belief systems in North America were specific to each tribe and not evangelized from one tribe to another. But some beliefs captivated people from many different tribes, such as the Ghost Dance of the later 19th century. This map shows some of the major regional religious movements in North American tribal communities.

SHRINKING INDIAN TERRITORIES

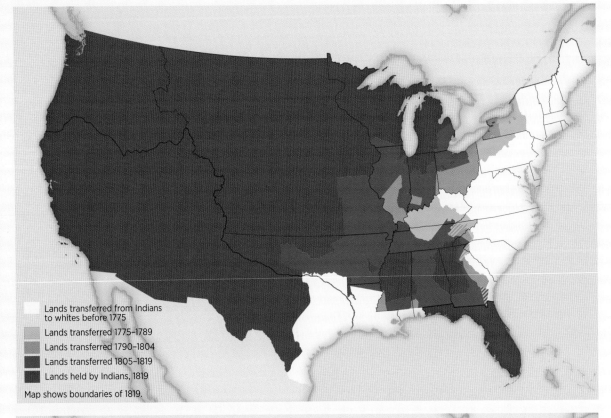

1775–1819

In 1775, most of the United States was still Indian land; however, even George Washington acknowledged that it would require a "great wall" to restrain European settlers from moving into Indian lands. Through 200 years of land transfers—in which lands previously inhabited by Indians became official property of non-Indians—the Native population was gradually confined to small areas within the United States.

Lands transferred from Indians to whites before 1775

Lands transferred 1775–1789

Lands transferred 1790–1804

Lands transferred 1805–1819

Lands held by Indians, 1819

Map shows boundaries of 1819.

1820–1864

By 1820, settlers had moved well into the Midwest, pushing into Indian lands and displacing Native inhabitants through conflict or the simple pressure of their presence. By 1834, Indians had ceded large swaths of land as far west as Kansas. In one astonishing 14-year period starting in 1850 and motivated by mid-century gold finds, nearly the entire west coast of the United States transferred from Indian to American hands. The only state still almost entirely in Native hands was New Mexico.

Lands held by non-Indians, 1820

Lands transferred 1820–1834

Lands transferred 1835–1849

Lands transferred 1850–1864

Lands held by Indians, 1864

Map shows boundaries of 1864.

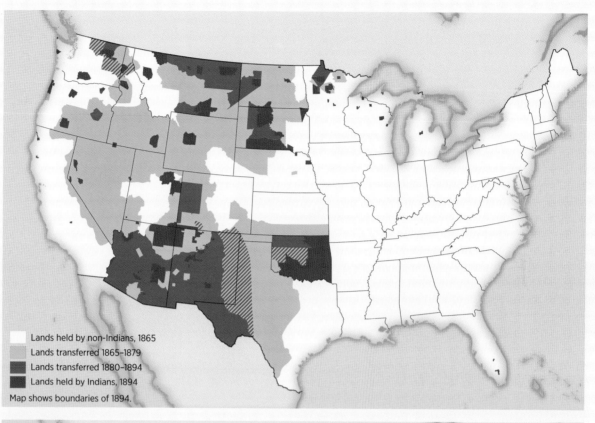

1865–1894

By late 1865, with the end of the Civil War, 20,000 soldiers were manning western forts. The Department of War struggled against the Apache and Navajo in New Mexico, and conflicts raged across the West. Between 1865 and 1879 vast areas of land transferred out of Indian hands, including about one-third of Texas; the rest of Kansas; most of North Dakota, Wyoming, and Idaho; and nearly all of Nevada. During the following 14 years, other cessations, treaties, and deals continued to chip away at Indian lands until tribal lands amounted to what they are today, with the exception of Oklahoma—though the 1887 Dawes Act would soon change that.

Lands held by non-Indians, 1865
Lands transferred 1865–1879
Lands transferred 1880–1894
Lands held by Indians, 1894
Map shows boundaries of 1894.

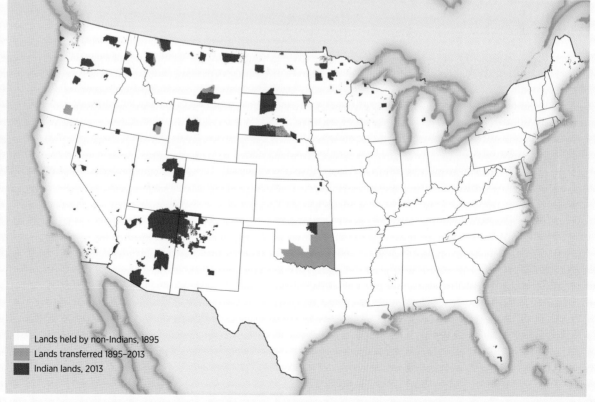

1895–2013

From 1895 to 1988, Native Americans lost another two-thirds of their land to non-Natives. The largest of these losses was nearly half of Oklahoma, previously known as Indian Territory. One major source of losses was the Dawes Act, eventually rescinded in 1934, which parceled out reservations to individual Indians, who then sold off parts of their land to non-Natives.

Lands held by non-Indians, 1895
Lands transferred 1895–2013
Indian lands, 2013

RUSSIA

*Bering
Sea*

*Beaufort
Sea*

ALASKA
(U.S.)

U.S.
CANADA

YUKON

N.W.T.

*Gulf of
Alaska*

BRITISH
COLUMBIA

ALBERTA

SASK.

NORTHWEST
COAST
PP. 228–255

CANADA
U.S.

PACIFIC

WASH.

MONT.

N.D.

OCEAN

OREG.

IDAHO

GREAT BASIN
AND PLATEAU
PP. 198–227

WYO.

S.D.

NE

CALIF.

NEV.

UTAH

COLO.

CALIFORNIA
PP. 256–286

ARIZ.

SOUTHWEST
PP. 164–197

N. MEX.

U.S.
MEXICO

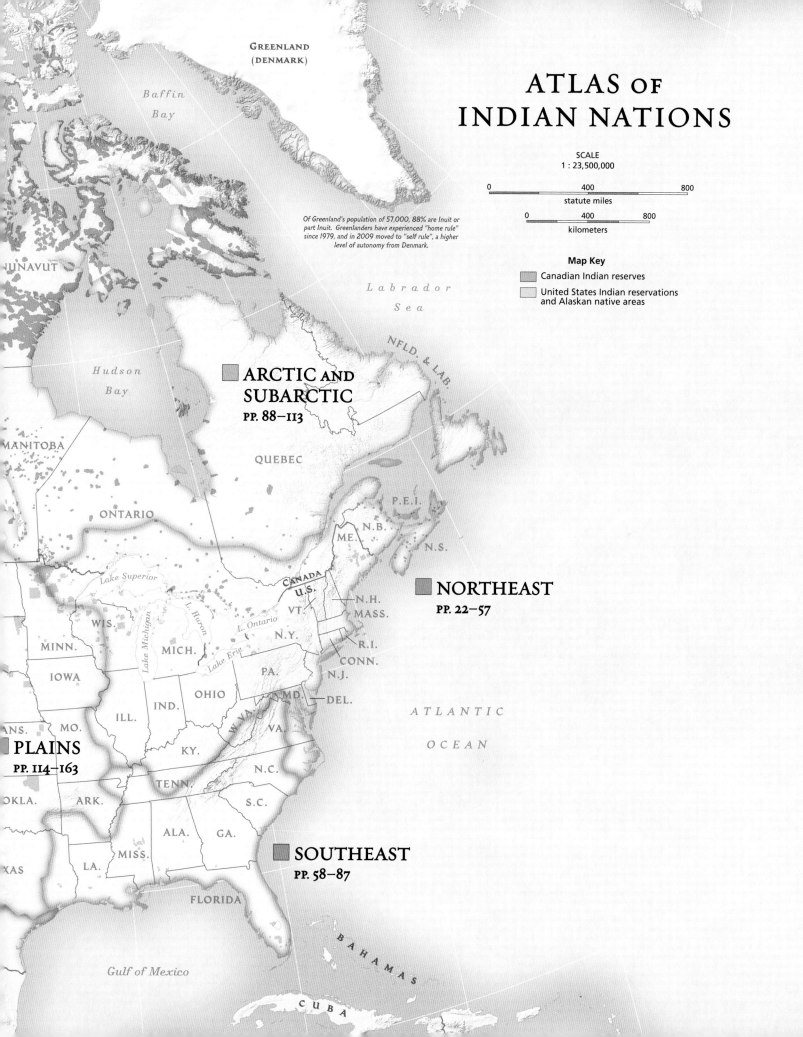

GREENLAND
(DENMARK)

*Baffin
Bay*

ATLAS OF
INDIAN NATIONS

SCALE
1 : 23,500,000

| 0 | 400 | 800 |

statute miles

| 0 | 400 | 800 |

kilometers

Map Key
Canadian Indian reserves
United States Indian reservations
and Alaskan native areas

*Of Greenland's population of 57,000, 88% are Inuit or
part Inuit. Greenlanders have experienced "home rule"
since 1979, and in 2009 moved to "self rule", a higher
level of autonomy from Denmark.*

NUNAVUT

*Labrador
Sea*

*Hudson
Bay*

NFLD. & LAB.

MANITOBA

ARCTIC AND
SUBARCTIC
PP. 88–113

QUEBEC

ONTARIO

P.E.I.

N.B.

ME.

N.S.

Lake Superior

CANADA
U.S.

NORTHEAST
PP. 22–57

N.H.

WIS.

L. Huron

L. Ontario

N.Y.

VT.

MASS.

MINN.

Lake Michigan

MICH.

Lake Erie

R.I.

CONN.

IOWA

PA.

N.J.

IND.

OHIO

MD.

DEL.

ILL.

W. VA.

ATLANTIC

ANS.

MO.

VA.

OCEAN

PLAINS
PP. 114–163

KY.

N.C.

OKLA.

ARK.

TENN.

S.C.

XAS

LA.

MISS.

ALA.

GA.

SOUTHEAST
PP. 58–87

FLORIDA

BAHAMAS

Gulf of Mexico

CUBA

NORTHEAST

CHAPTER ONE

CAYUGA

HO-CHUNK
(WINNEBAGO):
see listing in Plains

KICKAPOO

LENAPE
(DELAWARE):
see listing in Plains

MALISEET
(MALICITE)

MENOMINEE

MICMAC

MOHAWK

MOHEGAN

NARRAGANSETT

OJIBWE
(CHIPPEWA)

ONEIDA

ONONDAGA

OTTAWA (ODAWA)

PASSAMAQUODDY

PENOBSCOT

PEQUOT

POTAWATOMI

POWHATAN

SENECA

SHINNECOCK

TUSCARORA

WAMPANOAG

Tribes in the Northeast thrived on a mixed
economy of farming, fishing, hunting,
and gathering that allowed a population
density that rivaled that of western Europe.
Competition over land and resources was
intense, and the strongest leveraged even
greater strength through powerful alliances
with other tribes and with Europeans in
both trade and war.

INDIAN NATIONS
OF THE NORTHEAST

The Northeast is one of the richest places on Earth. Although Europeans would get rich by stripping away the largest copper, nickel, and iron ore deposits in the world, harvesting the largest virgin stands of white pine timber, and farming millions of acres of prime agricultural land, Native people saw a different kind of wealth. The region provided so much fish, wild game, wild rice, and arable land that it supported a substantial tribal population. The population density rivaled some of the more populated parts of Europe, which was a tremendous source of strength but also a weakness. Tribes with large villages were more prone to be ravaged by European disease. Because the Northeast was one of

the first parts of the continent continually colonized by Europeans, the sustained contact between whites and Indians made those disease outbreaks more frequent and disastrous. Most estimates place the Native death toll at 95 percent of the tribal population.

The tribes of the Northeast had highly developed political systems and networks of alliances. The wealth of the land led to competition over resources between tribes, and when the French and British entered the fray, the scale of conflict rose to epic levels. Both France and England issued genocidal edicts aimed at various tribes and nearly succeeded in completely eliminating some. But there was resistance and survival. The Northeast saw some of the most famous people and events in history: Hiawatha, Pocahontas, Tecumseh, Pontiac, the Iroquois League, and Thanksgiving, to name a few. Their stories are

Menominee diplomats from Wisconsin (left) display eagle feathers, each earned through bravery in war, but also carry pipes and blankets in preparation for diplomatic council. The Wampanoag of New England (above) were renowned peacemakers, although they were as skilled with the bow as with diplomacy.

legend, but legends are often deeply misunderstood and distorted.

CONNECTED BY WATER

All tribes in the Northeast traveled, traded, and warred on the waterways that dominate the landscape. The smallest advantage in water-related technology made all the difference in the dominance of certain groups. The Ojibwe birchbark canoe enabled them to defend and expand their territories at the expense of other tribes. The occupation of large islands (Manitoulin, Madeline, Isle Royal, Mackinac, Long Island) gave the tribes who lived on them major defensive advantages.

The birchbark canoe was one of the most critical inventions in the Northeast. The technology and expert craftsmanship behind the invention evolved among the Ojibwe, but

THE NORTHEAST

USING THE MAPS

An important distinction needs to be considered when utilizing this atlas. Our style is to label, on the large-scale regional maps, particular reserves in Canada and reservations in the U.S. The lists at the back of this book are of tribal entities. Reserves or reservations represent the modern geographic situation of a people, in many cases far from an ancestral homeland. A tribe embodies their cultural, linguistic, and traditional heritage. Our methodology in presenting this daunting subject, in a way befitting the scope of this book, was to limit our map coverage to those tribal entities given formal recognition by the governments of Canada or the United States.

Map Key

- Canadian Aboriginal Land
- Federal Indian Reservation *(occupied by one or more tribal entities)*
- ▲ Tribe receiving federal recognition but without a designated reservation
- ★ State or provincial capital
- • Selected city or town

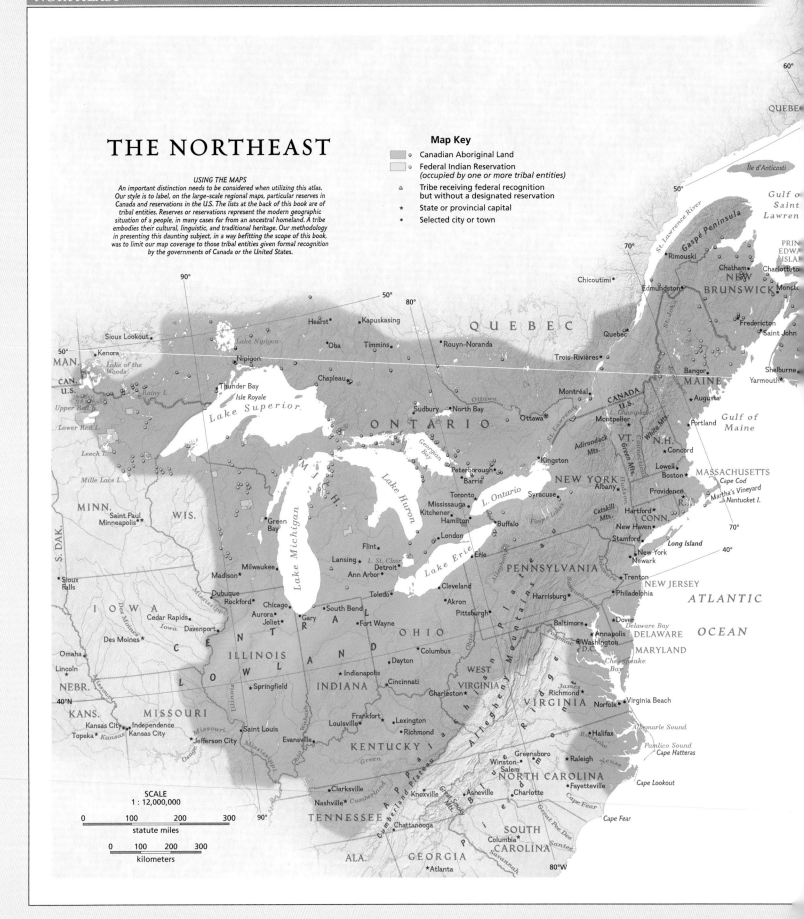

SCALE
1 : 12,000,000

0   100   200   300
statute miles

0   100   200   300
kilometers

L'Anse aux Meadows, St. Anthony
Lourdes-de-Blanc-Sablon, Roddickton
Gander
Grand Falls-Windsor, Saint John's
ISLAND OF NEWFOUNDLAND
Corner Brook
Jerseyside, Trepassey
Channel-Port aux Basques
Cape Breton Island
Sydney Mines
NOVA SCOTIA

was shared and mastered by their allies and immediate neighbors, including the Ottawa, Potawatomi, and Menominee. The Iroquois to their east and the Dakota to their west used wooden canoes dug out from tree trunks. Compared to dugouts, the birchbark canoe provided several benefits. It was lighter, faster, more buoyant, and easier to repair than other options, making it a tremendous advantage in war. On the edge of conflict zones, the Ojibwe often lived on islands like Madeline Island. They kept watch and, when enemies attacked, pushed out in canoes to face their foes on the water, quickly swamping the tippier and less buoyant craft of their foes and then clubbing their enemies in the water. When pursuing enemies, those using the birchbark canoe could overtake their foes most of the time. When escaping from enemies, birchbark again had the advantage of greater speed.

In diplomacy, the birchbark canoe made it possible for the Three Fires Confederacy to maintain a sophisticated political and cultural arrangement for generations across the largest confederated region in the Northeast. The canoes connected people, maintained communication, transported goods, and enabled hunters to trap prey over vast territories.

In trade, the birchbark had obvious and undeniable superiority. The speed and buoyancy of the craft made it ideal for bringing furs to market and for maintaining complicated networks of fur harvesters and traders. It powered the Three Fires Confederacy. Although most men in the confederacy trapped, the Ottawa used birchbark canoes to cover thousands of

---

CHRONOLOGY

500
Algonquian (Algic) westward migration from the Atlantic begins

1607
Jamestown settled by British

1630s
French and British colonists establish permanent communities in the Northeast; Pocahontas, Pequot War

1641–1701
Beaver Wars (Iroquois Wars): Ojibwe, Ottawa, and Potawatomi emerge victorious over Iroquois

1675
King Philip's War brutally crushes Wampanoag-led pan-Indian resistance

1713
Peace of Utrecht: France and England draw lines between claims in the Northeast

1754–1760
French and Indian War: Most tribes take sides with either French or British

1763
Pontiac's War: Ottawa and allies capture nine and besiege two British forts on Great Lakes

1776
American Revolution fractures Iroquois Confederacy

1812–15
War of 1812 removes British threat to American sovereignty, allowing the new nation to push west

1830
Indian Removal Act: Relocation of tribes from southern Great Lakes

---

The village was the nexus of social, economic, and political life for Indians in the Northeast, and every river, bay, and island had a distinct community and leadership structure. But the tribes with the most sophisticated alliances and confederacies, such as the Wabanaki in the Maritime Provinces, the Iroquois in New York, and the Three Fires in the Central Lakes, had the greatest success at protecting themselves in both conflict and diplomacy and even today hold some of the best real estate in their traditional homelands.

---

miles in bringing those furs to market on behalf of their allies. It gave them specialized skills and jobs, earning them the name "traders," from whence the tribal name Ottawa is derived. In turn, trappers were able to specialize and canoemakers to become skilled artisans. The entire population developed economic efficiencies that brought growth and an increase in the standard of living.

The structure of the birchbark canoe made it adaptable as well. Trees can get only so big, limiting dugouts' size. But birchbark can be sewn and sealed to cover much larger vessels. As French demand for furs escalated, the birchbark canoe was adapted for cargo use with ease. The French themselves abandoned every major type of craft technology they brought with them and adopted the birchbark canoe. And although construction materials have changed for modern canoemaking, the architectural design and use has remained constant—a testament to the enduring genius of the canoe and the people who invented it.

Waterways were the highways of the Northeast for trade, travel, and war. Every single major tribal village was immediately adjacent to water, not just because people relied on fishing and needed to drink, but because of water's strategic importance in connecting people to resources and to one another.

POLITICAL AND CULTURAL DIVERSITY

In the Northeast, it was not simply the strong individual tribes that survived—it was those who leveraged greater strength from alliances with other tribes and with Europeans who were able to dominate the territory and emerge from the colonial era intact. The Iroquois Confederacy, Three Fires Confederacy, Wabanaki Confederacy, and other tribal

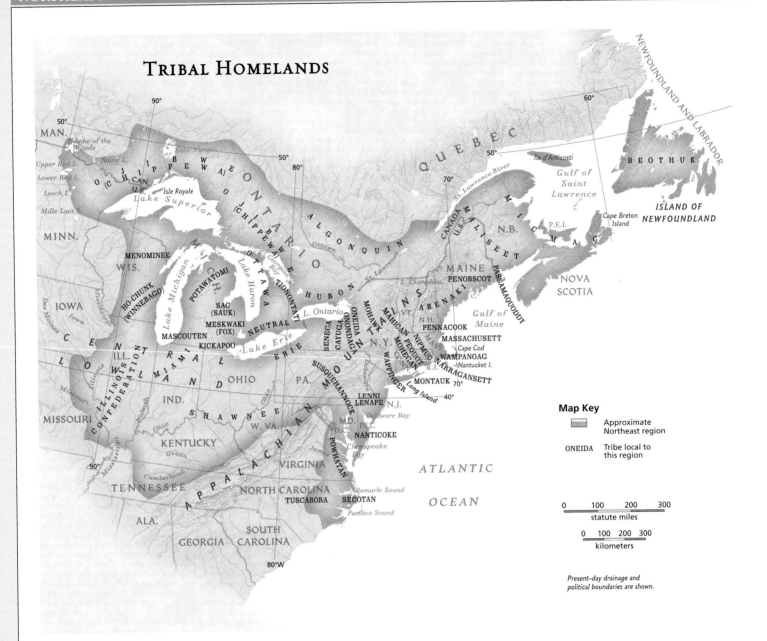

TRIBAL HOMELANDS

Map Key

▨ Approximate Northeast region

ONEIDA Tribe local to this region

|0   100   200   300|
statute miles

|0   100 200 300|
kilometers

Present-day drainage and political boundaries are shown.

alliances were the means to survival and, for some, an increasing territory and standard of living for a long time after European contact.

Almost every tribe in the Northeast originated from one of three mother groups: Algonquian, Iroquoian, or Siouan. The Algonquian (or Algic) people were at one time a single group with one language, but as they spread out throughout the Northeast and migrated west, they diversified in language and culture. Twenty-seven tribes trace their origins to this mother group, including the Ojibwe, Ottawa, Potawatomi, Menominee, Micmac, Wampanoag,

The territorial holdings of tribes in the Great Lakes shifted tremendously from 1600 to 1800. Tribes such as the Huron were depopulated by disease and Iroquois attacks. The Ojibwe expanded their territory 20-fold during the same time period, moving rapidly west into what is now Minnesota. These territorial lines reflect tribal lands right before the treaty period began, around 1800.

and Powhatan. Algonquian tribes typically built wigwams and other domed structures. They fished more than they hunted and farmed more than they fished. Even as the Algonquian tribes changed and diverged, several cultural commonalities remained, among them a strong, patrilineal clan system that was one of the primary determining factors in what kind of positions people assumed in life—political leadership, protection, medicinal practice, and so on. Although rapid geographic dispersal and marriage with Europeans challenged the clan system for many Algonquian

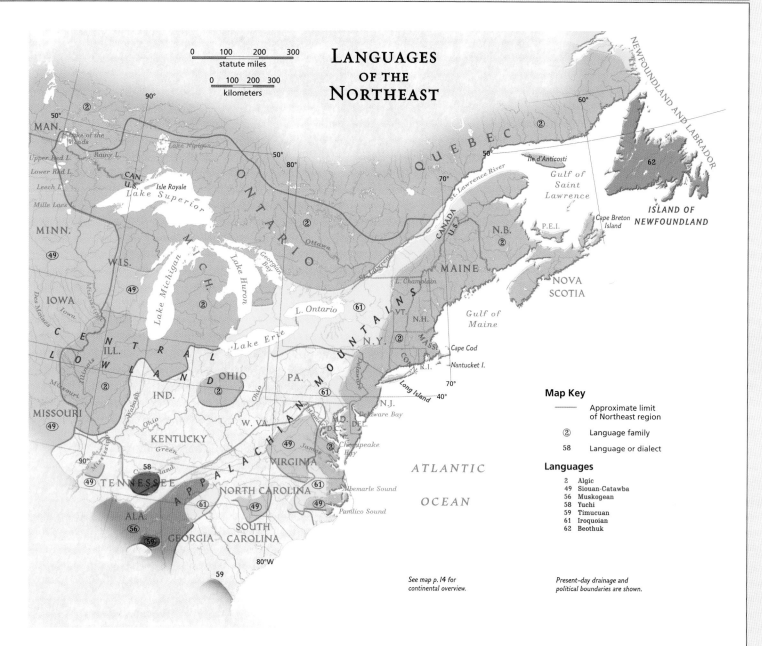

LANGUAGES OF THE NORTHEAST

0   100   200   300
statute miles

0   100   200   300
kilometers

Map Key

— Approximate limit of Northeast region

② Language family

58 Language or dialect

Languages

2 Algic
49 Siouan-Catawba
56 Muskogean
58 Yuchi
59 Timucuan
61 Iroquoian
62 Beothuk

See map p. 14 for continental overview.

Present–day drainage and political boundaries are shown.

peoples, clan remains an obvious surviving attribute of their culture.

The Iroquoian tribes formed the second largest group of Indians in the Northeast. Like the Algonquian tribes, they sprang from one mother group and diversified over time. They, too, maintained a sophisticated clan system. However, for Iroquoian tribes, clan was passed down matrilineally (through the mother), meaning Iroquoian women held a high degree of power. The longhouse dominated Iroquoian architecture, and many families shared a single longhouse, joining

There were more than a hundred tribes living in thousands of villages in three primary language groups in the Northeast. With time, the languages and cultures changed, but they can still be traced to these mother groups. The Algonquian tribes had patrilineal clans, the Iroquoian tribes had matrilineal clans, and the Siouan tribes had both clans and complicated kinship networks that governed social life.

whole communities together in everyday life with sophisticated kinship networks and ceremonial functions. Iroquoian people were famous for their agricultural innovations cultivating the three sister crops of corn, beans, and squash, and more than other tribes in the Northeast they relied on farming, with much less augmentation from gathering, fishing, and hunting.

The Siouan family of tribes included groups in the Northeast as well, such as the Ho-chunk (Winnebago). However, Siouan tribes in the Northeast were markedly different from Siouan groups

"Though it may cost me my liberty, it is my duty, and I will continue to speak and act also, till the wrongs of my people shall be righted."

—HOLE IN THE DAY (OJIBWE)

of the Plains. They maintained vibrant patrilineal clan systems, deeply relied on agriculture, and never adopted the horse as a primary tool in hunting. The Ho-chunk and other Siouan groups in the Northeast used domed lodges for ceremonial purposes and for their primary residences, but had tepee structures for travel and seasonal living.

CLANS: KEY TO CULTURAL COHESION

Every tribe in the Northeast had a vibrant clan system that defined social structure and often political leadership as well. A clan, or totem, was an emblem for one's family and could be represented by an animal, bird, or fish. Clan determined the kinds of positions people were expected to undertake in many tribes. Certain clans were responsible for protecting the people, for example. Others

were keepers of medicinal knowledge, oral histories, or spiritual leadership. Some clans were for political leadership as well. Entire tribes were named after the clan of their chiefs, like the Fox and Mohegan (Wolf).

Although the importance of clan was universal throughout the Northeast, the rules and culture around clans varied greatly from tribe to tribe. Most of the Algonquian-speaking tribes had a patrilineal clan system, passed down through the father's line. As such, hereditary chieftainships typically followed the male line from father to son through many generations. For Iroquoian-speaking tribes, the clan was usually passed down through the mother, and clan mothers could veto war decisions, appoint male chiefs, and maintain separate councils. The Siouan-speaking tribes in the Northeast had clans, too, and like their Algonquian neighbors, they normally passed down the male line. But the Siouan groups also had a complicated network of kin relationships overlapping clan that governed many dimensions of social life. There were some exceptions as well, such as the Potawatomi, among whom boys followed the clan of their father and girls followed the clan of their mother. For most tribes, marriage to someone of the same clan was considered strictly taboo and viewed as incest even if the people were of no biological relation.

The nature of the clan system shifted and changed over time. For groups that expanded territory very rapidly such as the Ojibwe, entire regions were settled by warriors and their families with no representation from customary

Many families in the Northeast held fast to traditions despite incredible poverty, dispossession, and change. Pictured here is a traditional Ho-chunk (Winnebago) family (above) and an Iroquois mask (top).

Map Key

Approximate cultural region boundary
(See pages 20–21 for North American
map showing all eight regions
depicted in this work.)

Canadian Indian Reserve
(occupied by one or more First Nations)

U.S. Federal Indian Reservation
(occupied by one or more tribal entities)

Federally designated tribal entity
with no land holding

Chapleau 61 Canadian Indian reserve name

Oneida U.S. Federal Indian reservation

190 Canadian first nation or
U.S. designated tribal entity
(Number correlates to Canadian
First Nations on pages 300–303
U.S. tribal list on pages 290–293.)

★ Provincial or state capital

• Selected city or town

Today, the Oneida, Mohawk, Seneca, Ojibwe, Ottawa, Potawatomi, and others live on Canadian First Nations reserves and U.S. reservations across the Great Lakes region.
Note that the numbers refer to tribal entity names.

chieftainship clans. As a result, some of the warrior clans like Bear and Marten came to dominate the ranks of Ojibwe leaders in Minnesota, which was very different from the dynamic in the central part of Ojibwe country. Among the easternmost tribes, Christian missionary work was so successful that the clan system faded from memory after many generations of sustained contact.

For most tribes, although changed and challenged, clan is still a primary marker of identity in the tribal cultures of the Northeast.

RESISTANCE

Many tribes in the Northeast resisted European pressure—and usually paid a very heavy price for it. The Wampanoag, Pequot,

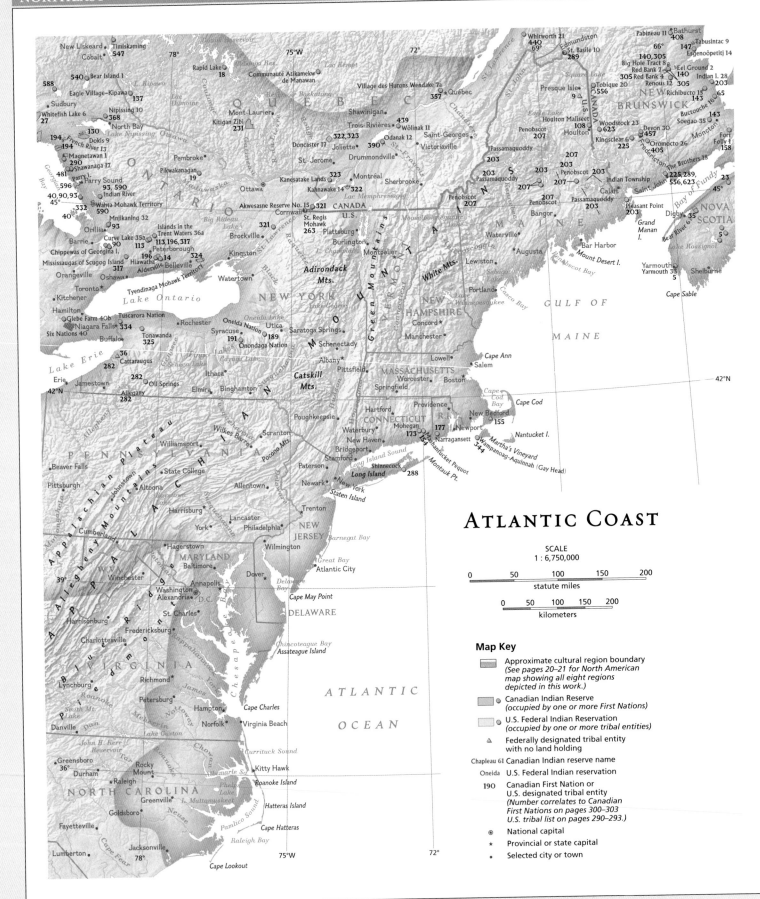

ATLANTIC COAST

SCALE
1 : 6,750,000

0   50   100   150   200
statute miles

0   50   100   150   200
kilometers

Map Key

Approximate cultural region boundary
(See pages 20–21 for North American
map showing all eight regions
depicted in this work.)

Canadian Indian Reserve
(occupied by one or more First Nations)

U.S. Federal Indian Reservation
(occupied by one or more tribal entities)

△ Federally designated tribal entity
with no land holding

Chapleau 61 Canadian Indian reserve name

Oneida U.S. Federal Indian reservation

190 Canadian First Nation or
U.S. designated tribal entity
(Number correlates to Canadian
First Nations on pages 300–303
U.S. tribal list on pages 290–293.)

◉ National capital

★ Provincial or state capital

• Selected city or town

Pressure from European colonists on tribal lands in New England was intense and was sustained longer than in any other part of the Northeast. Some New England tribes relocated north or west to Canada to seek refuge. Others stayed on what they retained of their ancestral lands. Today, there are numerous Canadian First Nations, some U.S. state–recognized reservations, and some federally recognized reservations, as noted on this map.

and Powhatan were all targeted by British colonists in brutal genocidal wars. The Fox suffered terribly at the hands of the French. Usually each tribe faced its political and military interactions with Europeans alone, but in a few cases, the Northeast generated some of the most famous instances of major pan-Indian resistance.

In 1763, Ottawa chief Pontiac united a massive coalition of tribal forces after the French lost the French and Indian War and were forced out of North America. Pontiac burned down 9 of the 11 British forts in the Great Lakes and put the others under siege. He called for French reinforcements, but none were sent. As the sieges dragged on, his ranks dwindled as warriors had to return to hunting and trapping to feed their families; eventually, the British sent reinforcements and broke the sieges. Pontiac carried on a guerrilla war for some time afterward. Although his resistance did not succeed in forcing the British out of the Great Lakes, it did succeed in showing Indians the power of their united resistance.

Shawnee chief Tecumseh was one of the most celebrated Indian leaders, uniting a coalition of numerous tribes in the southern Great Lakes to fight off American expansion during the early 1800s. He traveled tirelessly, using deft diplomacy, inspiring oratory, military action, and knowledge of several tribal languages to unite Native people in common purpose. He partnered with his brother, Tenskwatawa, a prophet who advocated for the people to abandon alcohol as well as the economic, cultural, and political influences of Europeans. Many Indians believed that both brothers had special powers.

In 1806, Indiana territorial governor William Henry Harrison challenged Tenskwatawa to demonstrate his spiritual power by making daytime turn to night, which was immediately followed by a dramatic solar eclipse. Tecumseh's name meant Shooting Star; a brilliant comet streaked through the night sky in 1811 when he was trying to persuade the Creek to join his confederacy. Later that same year, the New Madrid earthquake shook the entire Midwest

The birchbark canoe was one of the greatest advantages enjoyed by the Ojibwe in trade, travel, and war. It was lighter, more buoyant, and faster and had a larger cargo capacity than the wooden dugouts used by most tribes. Even the French abandoned other types of craft and adopted the birchbark canoe when they came to the Northeast.

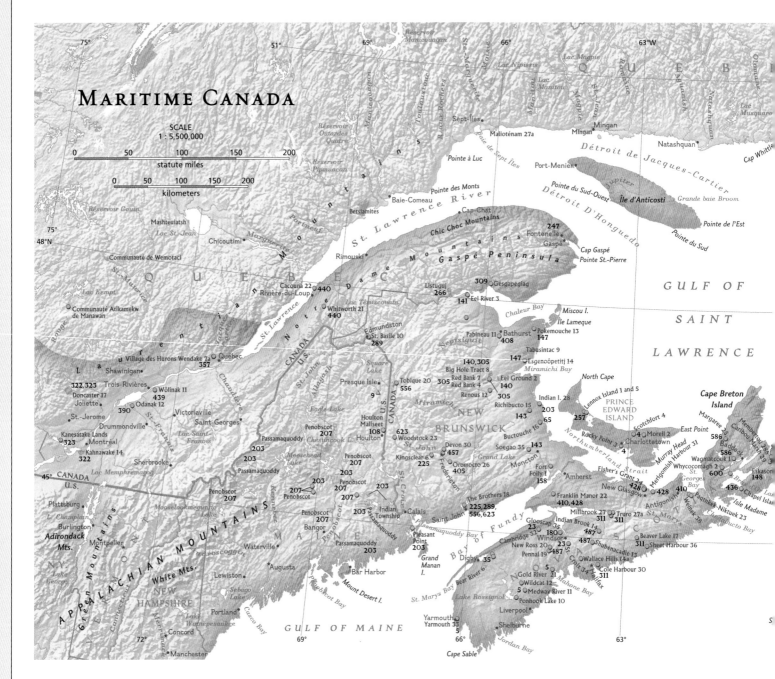

MARITIME CANADA

SCALE
1 : 5,500,000

0   50   100   150   200
statute miles

0   50   100   150   200
kilometers

and South, lending further credence to the claims of Tecumseh and Tenskwatawa that the Great Spirit blessed their efforts.

Tecumseh and his brother founded villages in Greeneville, Ohio, in 1805 and in Prophetstown, Indiana, in 1808, both of which were inhabited by several different tribes. In 1811, Harrison led a large U.S. force against Prophetstown while Tecumseh was away. In the ensuing Battle of Tippecanoe, the warriors of Prophetstown were forced to retreat and the village, along with all of its abundant food stores, was burned to the ground. It was a major setback for

Tecumseh, who united with the British during the War of 1812. British Maj. Gen. Henry Procter agreed to join Tecumseh in a combined attack on the Americans at the Battle of the Thames, but failed to appear, leaving the Indian force vulnerable. Tecumseh was killed, and his confederacy crumbled without him.

COLONIZATION AND SURVIVAL

Colonization was hard on the tribes of the Northeast. Some, such as the Pequot, emerged with only shattered remnants of their political

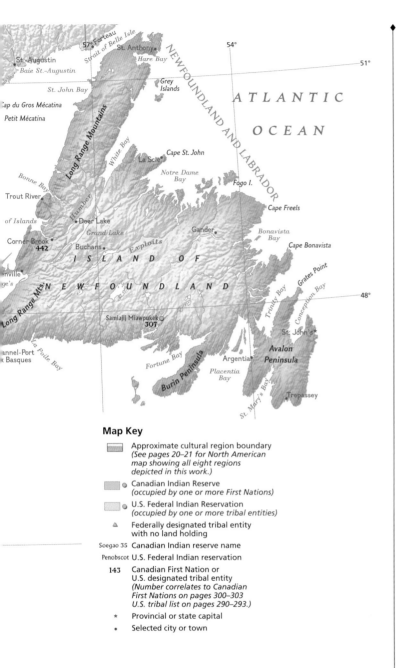

Map Key

◻ Approximate cultural region boundary
(See pages 20–21 for North American map showing all eight regions depicted in this work.)

◻● Canadian Indian Reserve
(occupied by one or more First Nations)

◻● U.S. Federal Indian Reservation
(occupied by one or more tribal entities)

△ Federally designated tribal entity with no land holding

Soegao 35 Canadian Indian reserve name

Penobscot U.S. Federal Indian reservation

143 Canadian First Nation or U.S. designated tribal entity
(Number correlates to Canadian First Nations on pages 300–303 U.S. tribal list on pages 290–293.)

★ Provincial or state capital

• Selected city or town

The Penobscot formed a powerful alliance with the Abenaki, Micmac, Passamaquoddy, and Maliseet, known collectively as the Wabanaki Confederacy, in New England and the Canadian Maritime Provinces. The Wabanaki usually supported the French-speaking Acadians in their conflicts with the British, and the British paid bounties for Penobscot scalps.

forms, and sovereign, growing tribal governments. Many tribes in the Northeast are realizing that their sovereign authority is vested in their languages and cultures, not just in treaties or a relationship with Canada or the United States. Immersion programs are springing up throughout the Northeast, with great strength being demonstrated by the Mohawk, Ottawa, and Ojibwe. The military battles that engulfed the tribes of the Northeast when Europeans first encountered them have been replaced by a new war—waged with pens, computers, and recording equipment—to maintain identity through revitalizing tribal languages and cultures. Although the future vitality of tribal languages and cultures in the Northeast is not certain, it is certainly possible. And the richness of the land and historical experience of the Northeast tribes make fertile soil for verdant growth and a bright future. ✈

Arrowmaker, a 20th-century Chippewa (Ojibwe). During the early contact period, the Ojibwe assumed a powerful and lucrative position as middlemen in trade between western tribes and the French.

structures, lands, and languages. Others, like the Mohawk, retained vibrant languages and cultural forms. Some of the large tribes such as the Ojibwe have no fluent speakers left in some communities and a 100 percent fluency rate in others. Each tribe and each community within each tribe has a unique and often complicated story.

Throughout the Northeast, the richness of the land was reflected in a cultural wealth of astonishing depth and breadth. Although much was lost in the struggle over the land, much was retained as well—land on all of the largest lakes in the region, vibrant cultural

a	Boston	1	Newport
b	Charles Town	2	Portsmouth
c	Cambridg	3	Taunton
d	Newton	4	Bridgwater
e	Watertown	5	Seaconk
f	Dedham	6	Woodcok
g	Medfield	7	Prudence I.
h	Roxbury	8	Patience I.
i	Dorchester	9	Swansey
k	Milton	10	Brokland
l	Braintre	11	Bushwick
m	Waymouth	12	Newtown
n	Winesemel	13	Flushing
o	Lim	14	Oyster Bay
p	Beverley		
q	Manchester		
r	Bradford		
s	Topsfield		

New Albanie

New Yorke

East Reach

Colo:

Johnsons Kil

nie

New York

Manhattens I.

West Chester

East Chester

Rye

Greenwich

Stratford

Newark

Fayrfield

Stratford

Milford

New Haven

Branford

Guilford

Saybrook

Eatons Neck

Sharp Po.

Ashford

Huntington

Hemsted

Flatlands

Gravesend

Jamaica

Dierfield

Hadfield

Northamton

Westfield

Winsor

Conecti

Wethersfield

cut

Midletown

Colonie

Squaheeg

Swamfield

Colonie

Hadley

Spring: field

Enfeild

Hartford

Uncas

Norwich

London

Lime

Malachsets

Squabaug

Glafs R.

Ruffels Delight

Indian R.

Lancaster

Nipnak

Uauer R.

Providence R.

Potuxet R.

Pequid Count

Stoniton

Naraganset Buls C.

Warwick

Wickford

Vishers I.

Gardners I.

Block I.

Montangh Po.

South Sand Beach

South Hamton

North Hamton

East Hamton

Long Iland

Connecticut R.

Martmake R.

Penicook

Dover

Pascataway R.

Exeter

Portsmouth

Chensford

Grotten

Billerita

Wochester

Woburn

Ridin

Shesheen

Andiver

Haveril

Wamsiek

Amsbury

Hamton

Salsbury

Newber

Rowley

Ipswich

Salem

Marbli

Boston Har:

Hull

Hinga

Greene

Marshfield

Daxbury

Plymouth

Mont Hope

Plymouth Colony

Pocasset C.

Elisabeths I.

Rode Iland

Providenti

Kenebu

New

Hadeck

York

NATIVES AND PURITANS
From Thanksgiving to Genocidal War

U nder Chief Massasoit, the Wampanoag in the early 1600s forged a peaceful relationship with English settlers in New England. Tisquantum (Squanto), a Patuxet Indian, lived with the Wampanoag at the time. His story has been embellished over the years, but the popular version does contain some truth. Massasoit, Squanto, and other Wampanoag taught the Puritans how to farm in the Americas by rotating crops to maintain soil fertility.

Although the romanticized version of the first Thanksgiving story so often taught to American children is frequently attributed to the Wampanoag–Puritan experience, archival records do not support that. The first clear evidence of a tribal–white harvest celebration appears after the Pequot War in 1637, rather than as part of the Wampanoag efforts to teach Puritans to survive their first winter in 1621.

The peaceful relationship deteriorated after the death of Chief Massasoit. His son Wamsutta (Alexander) died immediately after his first parley with the English as chief, and his people suspected that he had been poisoned. The relationship disintegrated even further in 1675, when the English hanged three Wampanoag men for a murder they did not commit. Wamsutta's brother, Metacom (Philip), rallied the remaining Wampanoag population, who numbered fewer than 1,000. Other tribes joined them and a confederation of tribes that once battled each other offered the English formidable resistance. The conflict, called King Philip's War, was brutal. The Indians burned 52 of the 90 English settlements in the area. Five percent of the white population was killed, as was 40 percent of the Indian population. The Wampanoag were reduced to only 400. Metacom's wife and children were sold as slaves. After the English killed him, the chief's head was displayed on a pike in the village of Plymouth for more than 20 years. ■

TRIBAL CONFLICT IN NEW ENGLAND Thanksgiving might dominate American thoughts of tribal–white relations in New England, but the reality was entirely different. The Pequot War of 1637–38 saw punitive raids of British settlements at Hartford ❶ and surrounding areas, shown on this 17th-century map. Tribal resistance was crushed at the Mystic Massacre, ❷ when British militia besieged a large Pequot village (right) while most of the warriors were away. From a precontact number of 16,000, the tribal population was reduced to just 500 by the end of the conflict. King Philip's War in 1675 also engulfed the region. The Wampanoag and their allies destroyed 52 of the 90 British towns across New England, and the conflict consumed villages from Dover ❸ to Greenwich ❹. In the end, Metacom (King Philip) was killed, his family sold into slavery, and his head displayed on a pike at Plymouth ❺.

Peter Minuit, Dutch West India Company's governor general of New Netherland colony, purchases Manhattan from the Indians for 60 guilders (roughly $25 in 1626 dollars) in 1626.

Assiniboine

Ft. Bourbon
Lake Winnipeg
Ft. Dauphin
Ft. Espérance
Ft. Maurepas
Ft. Bas de la Rivière
Ft. La Reine
Ft. Rouge
Ft. St. Charles
Ft. St. Pierre
Albany
St. Lawrence

Micmac
Ft. Gaspareaux
Ft. Beauséjour
Ft. St.-Jean
Ft. Menagoueche

Ft. Kaministiquia
Lake Superior
Ft. Témiscamingue

❸ Québec
New France

Pays d'en Haut
Nipissing
Sault Ste. Marie
St. Ignace
Michilimackinac
❷
Lake Huron
Menomini
Algonquin
Ottawa
Ft. de La Présentation
Ft. Richelieu
Montréal
Ft. Chambly
Ft. Ste. Anne
Ft. Boishébert

Abenaki

Yanktonai

Yankton
Ft. Beauharnois
Winnebago
Lake Michigan
Sauk
Prairie du Chien
Ottawa
Ft. Frontenac
Ft. Rouillé
Lake Ontario
Ft. Niagara
Mohican
Ft. Orange
Ft. St. Frédéric
Ft. Carillon

Dakota

Missouri
Platte

Iowa
Ft. St. Louis-Le Rocher
Ft. Crèvecoeur
St. Joseph
Ft. Detroit
Ft. St. Joseph
Lake Erie
Presque Isle
Ft. Le Boeuf
Wiltwyck
❶
Iroquois
Pequot
Ft. Hoop
Ft. Ninigret

Pawnee
Ft. de Cavagnial
Ft. Orleans
Miami
Ft. Miami
Kekionga
Ft. Sandoské
Machault
Ft. Duquesne
Ft.
New Amsterdam
Heemstede
❺
Illinois
Wabash
Ft. Ouiatenon
Shawnee
Ft. Wilhelmus
Delaware
Ft. Christina
Ft. Nassau

Missouri
Cahokia
Vincennes
Ohio

Kiowa
Ft. de Chartres
Kaskaskia
Ste. Genevieve
Zwaanendael

Fernandina
Osage
Ft. Massac
Yuchi

ATLANTIC OCEAN

L o u i s i a n a
Mississippi
Cherokee
Tennessee

Dutch and French Claims

□ French claim
□ Dutch claim
⊡ French fort
⊡ Dutch fort

0 ——————— 300 miles

Arkansas
Ft. Assumption
Chickasaw

Twin Villages
Arkansas Post
Red

Wichita
Caddo
Sabine
Ft. Tombecbe
Ft. Toulouse
Tombigbee
Alabama
Chattahoochee

Natchitoches
Ft. Rosalie
Choctaw
La Mobile
Ft. Condé
Tonkawa
Baton Rouge
Biloxi
Ft. Maurepas
New Orleans
❹
Ft. St. Louis

ERODING TRIBAL TERRITORY The Beaver Wars (Iroquois Wars) lasted from 1641 to 1701. The Iroquois Confederacy was encouraged to attack their neighbors by Dutch and then British allies who wanted to disrupt French trade and acquire more territory. The Huron (like the man at right, calling moose) were largely depopulated as a result. But the Three Fires Confederacy, allied with the French, beat back the Iroquois advances, absorbing Huron lands. Massive battles and large-scale loss of life disrupted political, economic, and social life for six decades. Throughout the tribal conflicts, the Dutch and English steadily eroded the tribal land base in New England, the Chesapeake, the Ohio River Valley, and Appalachia through treaties, conflict, and burgeoning European settlements. The French had a similar pattern in the Great Lakes and the Mississippi watershed.

THE EUROPEAN INVASION

Dutch, British, and French Ambitions in the Northeast

The Dutch and then the British forged powerful alliances with the Iroquois Confederacy (Cayuga, Mohawk, Oneida, Onondaga, and Seneca) ❶, using their Native allies to disrupt French trade and military alliances. The French in turn formed an alliance with the Three Fires Confederacy (Ojibwe, Ottawa, and Potawatomi) ❷. For decades, neither the French, Dutch, nor British could dominate the tribes in those confederacies. All the players needed things from one another, and the accommodations they all made forged a new culture in diplomacy, war, and trade. Explorer Samuel de Champlain actively encouraged French traders to marry Native women and cement those relationships with tribal pipes and mixed bloodlines.

As tribal control of the land and the importance of the beaver fur trade shifted, power dynamics also shifted. Eventually the British and Americans did what the Dutch and French could not: They overwhelmed and started to control tribal peoples in the Northeast. Treaties no longer cemented friendships. Instead, they chiseled land out of Indian hands in ever-escalating proportions. Eventually the tribes were so besieged by white settlers that they could not trap, hunt, and use resources around them at a level sufficient to sustain trade and support their families. They needed the money from land sales to buoy their declining living standards—which meant there was less and less land from which they could generate resources. In the end, white settlers and their governments in the United States and Canada ended up with most of the land, and the tribes fell into abject poverty.

When European governments one at a time were forced to relinquish their colonial ambitions in the Americas, they recalled their military and government officials, but left traders, citizens, and settlers. These became the French-speaking Quebecois in Canada ❸, French-speaking Cajuns in Louisiana ❹, the New York Dutch ❺, and the English-speaking settlers of Canada and the United States. Their ideas and languages would slowly permeate tribal communities—by proximity and association, formal education policies, and the efforts of numerous missionaries of many denominations.

The tribes survived, and against all odds many maintained vibrant cultures, religions, and languages. But the political and economic power of the tribes in the Northeast has not recovered to its pre-contact level. ■

Samuel de Champlain

Although the Battle of Bloody Brook during King Philip's War in 1675 (above) and other major battles and wars captured the attention of European immigrants to the Northeast, diplomacy was the real way that most Indians lost control of the land. Pictured here (right) is the René-Robert Cavelier de La Salle expedition on the Mississippi River bartering for Indian trade, exploration rights, and land.

THE FUR TRADE
Shifting Dependencies and Power

The fur trade caused Native Americans and Europeans to need one another in a way that no two peoples had experienced before. The European economic, political, and military mission in North America hinged on access to tribal resources and the specialized knowledge of Indian people. Indians needed European trading partners in order to stay technologically matched to their tribal enemies, defend their territories, and sell their furs to elevate and maintain their new standard of living. The mutual dependence brought power, but also intensified conflict, especially during the Beaver Wars (Iroquois Wars), where tribal confederacies with opposing European allies fought brutal campaigns.

While some tribes like the Ojibwe ❶ expanded their territory and standard of living, many smaller tribes could not withstand the onslaught, especially during repeated waves of disease. Smallpox and other diseases devastated entire regions. Those with strong allies and travel networks, such as the Michigan Potawatomi, maintained water and land routes to connect their furs to market ❷. But over time, the fur harvest intensity was not sustainable, creating shortages. Meanwhile, Europeans acquired more tribal land, further reducing Indian access to furs.

When tribes could not produce to demand, their importance to Europeans diminished. After the French lost the French and Indian War to Britain, tribes could no longer play European powers off one another. By the time the American nation was born, tribes were in a defensive position. The fur trade imploded soon afterward, as European fashion shifted away from furs. Many tribes sold their land to compensate for trade income lost to declining resources, demand, and land. It was a vicious cycle. ■

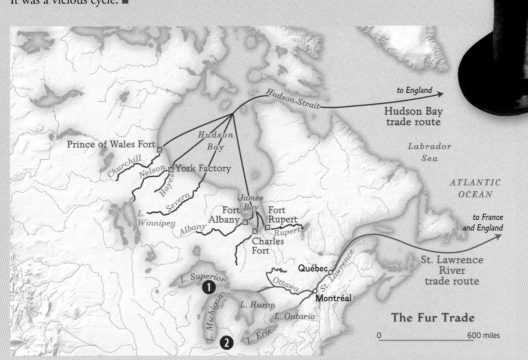

The Fur Trade

0   600 miles

THE MIGHTY BEAVER The abundance of beaver and other furbearing animals in the Great Lakes and Hudson Bay regions led to trade along the waterways leading into the area. Skins were shipped to France and England, where products such as this British beaver skin top hat (above) were made. The Three Fires Confederacy (Ojibwe, Ottawa, and Potawatomi) kept a strong alliance with the French that gave the tribes exclusive control over the vast territory and the French exclusive trading rights with them.

Le Beau port.

Les chiffres montrent les brasses d'eau.

tre bar-

G Cabanes des fauuages, & où
ils labourent la terre.
H Petite riuiere où il y a des
prairies.
I Ruiffeau.
L Langue de terre plaine de bois
où il y a quantité de fafrans,
noyers & vignes.

calfeu-

ffez haut

M La mer d'vn cul de fac en tour-
nant le cap aux ifles.
N petite riuiere.
O petit ruiffeau venant des pre-
ries.
P autre petit ruiffeau où l'on
blanchiffoit le linge.
Q Troupe de fauuages venant

pour n

R playe
S La cof
T Le fie
enbufc
8. arqu
V Le fieu
feuant

AMÉRIQUE DU NORD   ÉTATS-UNIS

CHAMPLAIN AND GLOUCESTER HARBOR Samuel de Champlain mapped "Le Beau Port,"
present-day Gloucester Harbor, Massachusetts, in 1605. He was astounded at the diversity of
the ecosystem and the way indigenous people shaped it, with selective cutting and burning to
elevate both sunlight and soil nutrients for extensive corn, bean, and squash fields. The port
had abundant fish and a natural barrier against storm surges. The harbor was highly prized by
Natives and Europeans, setting the stage for trade in agricultural goods and furs.

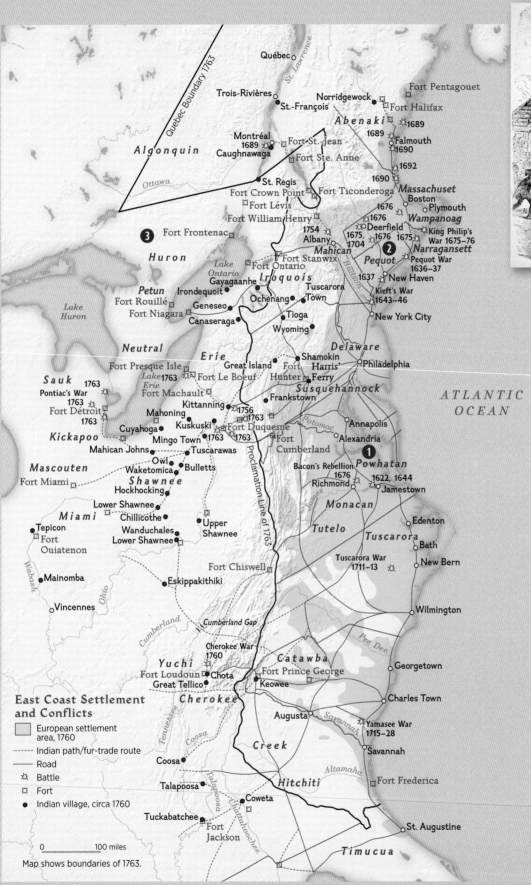

LAND AND LIFEWAYS For tribes throughout the Northeast, traditional land and lifeways were under immediate assault with the arrival of the first European immigrants. Europeans came to settle, and that required land. They also came with deep religious convictions, and that brought missionary activity. And they came for resources—timber, food, furs, metal, and slaves. Together, those pressures threatened the many tribes that called the Northeast home. Most sought diplomatic solutions, but the pressure was so unrelenting that conflict broke out as well, as seen in the conflict zones on the map (left) and in this depiction of King Philip's War (above).

East Coast Settlement and Conflicts

- ☐ European settlement area, 1760
- ⋯⋯ Indian path/fur-trade route
- —— Road
- ☆ Battle
- ☐ Fort
- ● Indian village, circa 1760

0 —— 100 miles

Map shows boundaries of 1763.

EARLY CONTACT IN THE NORTHEAST
Friendship, Then Conflict and Controversy

Indian–white relations were extremely complicated. There was initial diplomacy and even friendship following the first contact experiences in the Northeast, but there were also conflicts so bloody that their effects are still felt today. In a land of abundant resources, numerous languages, and competing ambitions, the early contact period involved not just cross-cultural sharing, but also misunderstanding and pain.

In the Chesapeake Bay region ❶, the British made their first real attempts at permanent colonies. Pocahontas was among the best known Indians of all time, and she figured prominently in that early experience, although her real story was one of adversity, disempowerment, and tragedy rather than one of unrequited love and intercultural harmony. Immediately after the establishment of Jamestown, Capt. John Smith was captured by Opechancanough, half brother of the principal Powhatan chief, Wahunsunacawh. Pocahontas, Wahunsunacawh's daughter, helped Smith escape, motivated by humanitarianism rather than romantic involvement. Smith wrote about his captivity in 1608, 1612, and 1624, embellishing the story with each new telling.

In 1614, Pocahontas was captured by the English and held for ransom. Wahunsunacawh agreed to peace in exchange for the return of his daughter, but the English did not uphold the bargain.

Pocahontas, still just a teenager, was baptized and married to English planter John Rolfe (not John Smith), even though she was already married to a Powhatan man. She was never granted the right to exercise her own free will and felt deeply conflicted over her obligations to her tribe, family, and Native husband on the one hand and a sense of obligation to her English husband on the other. She accompanied Rolfe to England, where her beauty made her a great curiosity, but she died before she could return home. Her son, Thomas Rolfe, survived and returned to Virginia, and many people today trace their lineage to him.

In New England ❷, the Pequot were subjected to a brutal genocidal conflict from 1637 to 1638 that reduced the tribal population from 16,000 to around 500. The English used slavery not just for forced labor but also to remove people from the land. Thousands of Pequot were sold into slavery, many sent to the Caribbean. King Philip's War in 1675 ended with 75 British settlements destroyed or severely damaged and the tribal population decimated, scattered, and dispossessed. Even pacifists like William Penn were not interested in holding back the land speculation and settlement pressure. Although Indians in Canada ❸ had a somewhat different historical experience, they lost most of their land there, too. ∎

Conflict between British settlers and the Powhatan in this depiction of a 1622 massacre (left) overshadowed the diplomacy and early peace overtures of the tribes in the Chesapeake. Further north, the Iroquois helped the British keep the French out of most of New England. An Iroquois (above) scalps a white man in this 18th-century color lithograph.

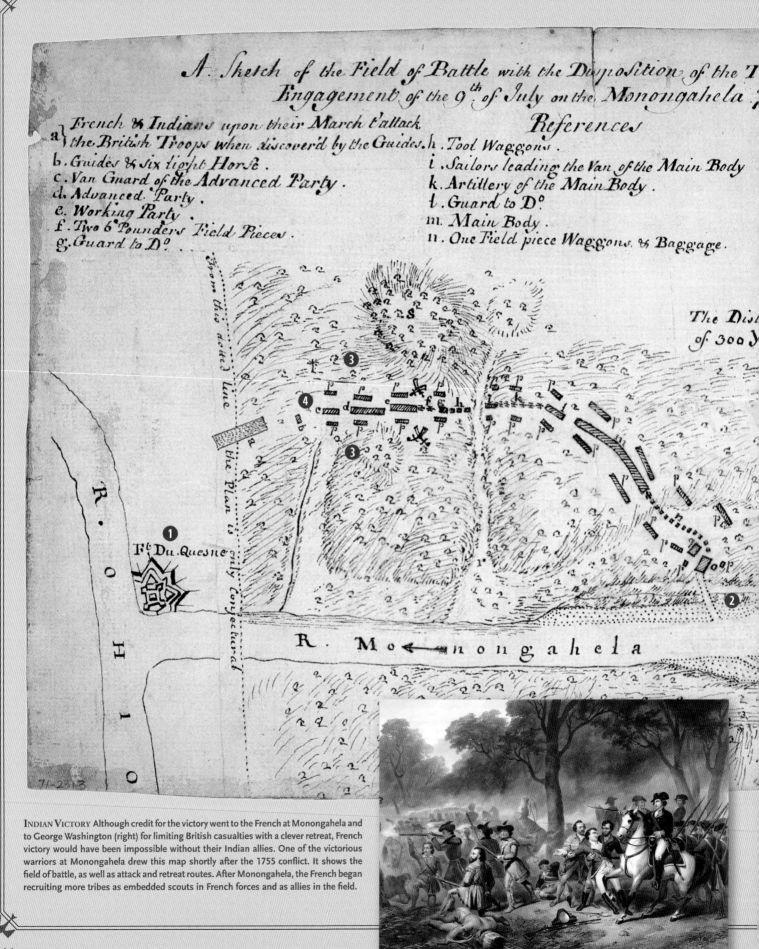

A Sketch of the Field of Battle with the Disposition of the T
Engagement of the 9th of July on the Monongahela ?

References

a} French & Indians upon their March t'attack the British Troops when discover'd by the Guides.
b. Guides & Six light Horse.
c. Van Guard of the Advanced Party.
d. Advanced Party.
e. Working Party.
f. Two 6 Pounders Field Pieces.
g. Guard to Do.

h. Tool Waggons.
i. Sailors leading the Van of the Main Body.
k. Artillery of the Main Body.
l. Guard to Do.
m. Main Body.
n. One Field piece Waggons & Baggage.

The Dist
of 300 Y

Ft. Du. Quesne

R. O H I O

R. Mo ← n o n g a h e l a

Indian Victory Although credit for the victory went to the French at Monongahela and to George Washington (right) for limiting British casualties with a clever retreat, French victory would have been impossible without their Indian allies. One of the victorious warriors at Monongahela drew this map shortly after the 1755 conflict. It shows the field of battle, as well as attack and retreat routes. After Monongahela, the French began recruiting more tribes as embedded scouts in French forces and as allies in the field.

BATTLE OF THE MONONGAHELA

Changing the Nature of War

French–British trade rivalry erupted into official war many times over the centuries. One such confrontation, the French and Indian War, forced the French to abandon their claims to North America. The British suffered terrible casualties and setbacks in the course of the conflict, most notably at the Battle of the Monongahela in Pennsylvania on July 9, 1755.

Gen. Edward Braddock had led a large force of 2,200 army and colonial militia into the Ohio River Valley, expecting to rout the French defenders of Fort Duquesne ❶. Braddock's expeditionary force had a terrible time cutting its way overland through the thick Pennsylvania woods and arrived on the banks of the Monongahela River ❷ exhausted, with an overstretched supply line. Eager for a quick victory, Braddock nevertheless ordered his troops to form ranks and move on the fort.

The French were garrisoned with a force about half the size of Braddock's, but they were reinforced by Ottawa and Potawatomi warriors, who introduced the British to a radically different style of fighting. Indian warriors set up snipers on both sides of the access road to the fort ❸ and started firing on the formed British ranks. The British were used to organized lines of soldiers marching at and firing on one another and so suffered significant casualties without inflicting much harm on the tribal force, which successfully halted the British advance ❹. French troops then marched in typical European fashion and engaged the British head-on.

The British were now flanked on two sides by Indians, with the advancing French force in front of them and the river behind them. They had no contingency plan nor any experience fighting warriors in concealed positions. The war whoops and eagle whistles of the warriors added to the terror of the fighting conditions for the British troops, who fell into disarray. Braddock had at least three horses shot out from under him, yet managed to rally a brave defense for a time. But when he received a mortal wound, the royal troops and colonial militia were routed. Col. George Washington tried with minimal success to cover the retreat and reduce the casualties. Despite his efforts, the casualty rate was 85 percent for the British force. Humiliated by their defeat, the British permanently changed the structure of their military, developing a new position of skirmisher and deploying skirmishers in every new conflict to counter the impact of concealed fighters and snipers. ∎

Although British regulars at Monongahela were well trained and well equipped with muskets and powder (see powder horn, above), their tactics (see battle plan, immediate left) were ineffective against the concealed tribal forces. Topography hampered their redeployment or retreat. Aided by sniper fire from the Ottawa and Potawatomi, the outnumbered French troops could fight the British effectively.

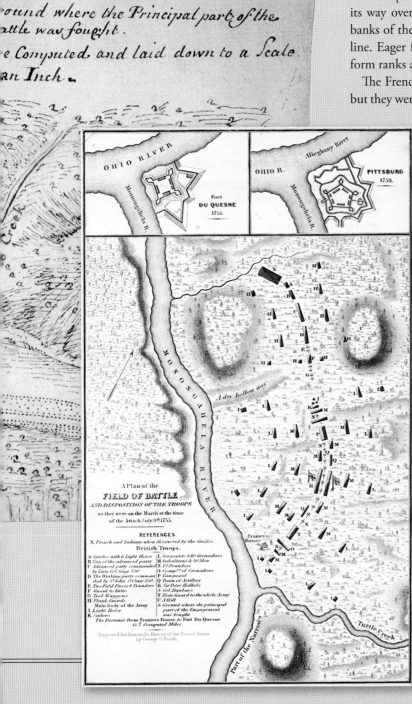

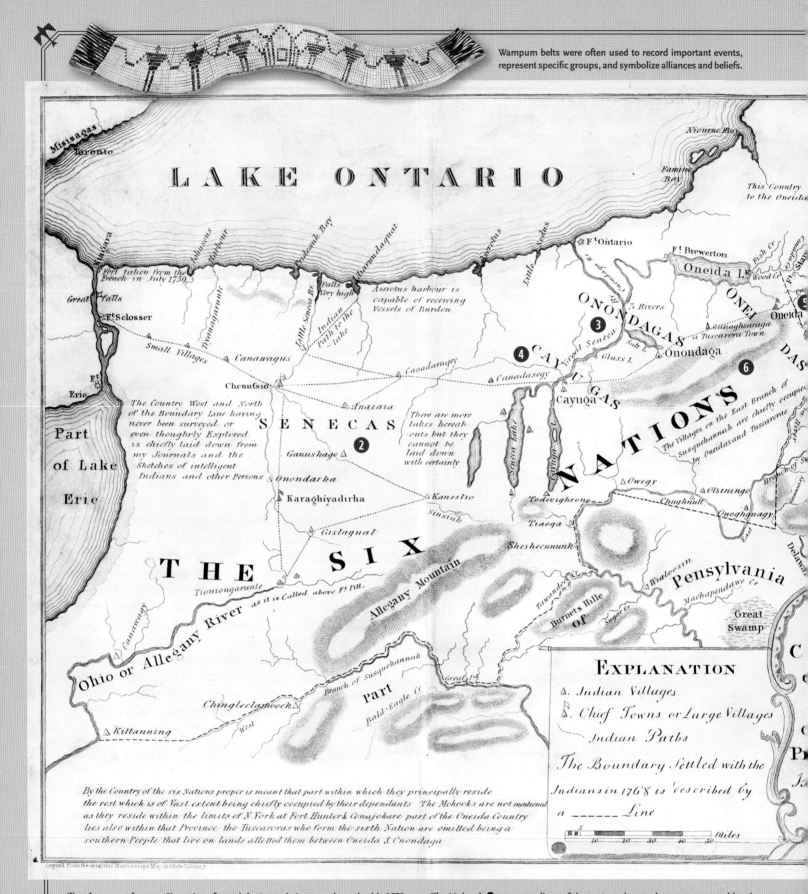

Wampum belts were often used to record important events, represent specific groups, and symbolize alliances and beliefs.

LAKE ONTARIO

Part of Lake Erie

SENECAS

ONONDAGAS

CAYUGAS

NATIONS

THE SIX

Pensylvania

Ohio or Allegany River *as it is Called above Ft Pitt.*

Allegany Mountain

Part of

Misisagas

Toronto

Niourne Bay

Famine Bay

This Country to the Oneida

Ft Ontario

Ft Brewerton

Oneida Lk

Oneida

Nitagara

Fort taken from the French in July 1750

Great Falls

Ft Slosser

Ft Erie

Aseroeus harbour is capable of receiving Vessels of Burden.

3 Rivers

Salt L.

a Tuscarora Town

Onondaga

Small Villages

Canawagus

Chenufsio

Canadaragey

Canadasegy

Cayuga

Owegy

Otsiningo

Onoghquagy

The Villages on the East Branch of Susquehannah are chiefly occupied by Oneidas and Tuscaroras

The Country West and North of the Boundary Line having never been surveyed or even thoughtly Explored is chiefly laid down from my Journals and the Sketches of intelligent Indians and other Persons

There are more lakes hereabouts but they cannot be laid down with certainty

Ganushago

Onondarka

Karaghiyadirha

Kanestio

Sisinink

Todevighrono

Tiaoga

Sheshecununk

Wialoosin

Burnets Hille

Machapendawe Cr

Great Swamp

Gistaquat

Tioniongarunte

Canaway

Chingleclamoock

Kittanning

Branch of Susquehannah

Bald-Eagle Cr

West

Great Isl.

EXPLANATION

Δ. *Indian Villages*

Δ. *Chief Towns or Large Villages*

Indian Paths

The Boundary Settled with the Indians in 1768 is described by a ------- *Line*

Miles
10   20   30   40   50

By the Country of the six Nations proper is meant that part within which they principally reside the rest which is of Vast extent being chiefly occupied by their dependants. The Mohocks are not mentioned as they reside within the limits of N.York at Fort Hunter & Conajohare part of the Oneida Country lies also within that Province the Tuscaroras who form the sixth Nation are omitted being a southern People that live on lands allotted them between Oneida & Onondaga

Copied from the original Manuscript Map in State Library

THE IROQUOIS LEAGUE Six nations formed the Iroquois League, shown in this 1771 map. The Mohawk ❶ were guardians of the eastern door and were represented by nine chiefs in the league. The Seneca ❷ guarded the western door and had eight council chiefs. The Onondaga ❸ kept the central fire for the entire league and were represented by fourteen chiefs. The Cayuga ❹ with ten chiefs and the Oneida ❺ with nine were also located centrally on either side of the Onondaga. A sixth tribe, the Tuscarora ❻, originally from North Carolina, joined the Iroquois League in the 18th century, but had no chiefs in the grand council.

THE IROQUOIS LEAGUE
Six Nations United

The Haudenosaunee (People of the Longhouse), or Iroquois, include six different tribes. Around 1450, five tribes organized the Iroquois League, a sophisticated ceremonial and cultural institution. The Iroquois League was created primarily to make peace and maintain stability between the member tribes.

The incredible military and economic power of the Iroquois was made possible by one of the most innovative and efficient agriculture systems in the world. The three sister crops—corn, beans, and squash—were cultivated in integrated fields, with bean vines growing up the cornstalks and the squash partially shaded underneath. It was a natural relationship that maintained soil fertility, moisture, the perfect combination of sun and shade, and a food yield per acre that was ten times what European farmers could achieve at home or on the same plots of land with Old World agricultural techniques.

For hundreds of years, the Iroquois dominated a vast swath of territory, annexed other lands, and exacted tribute from neighboring tribes. In 1677, the Iroquois Confederacy formed a long-lasting alliance with the British known as the Covenant Chain. They supported the British in most of their conflicts with the French and divided over support for the British during the Revolution.

In the second half of the 18th century, the Iroquois underwent a religious revitalization through a prophet named Handsome Lake. Handsome Lake preached temperance, monogamy, and aversion to gambling. Some of his ideas may have been influenced by Christian thinking, especially because polygamy and gambling were deeply entrenched cultural patterns for the Iroquois. However, his ideas had wide appeal and fused with longhouse tradition. ■

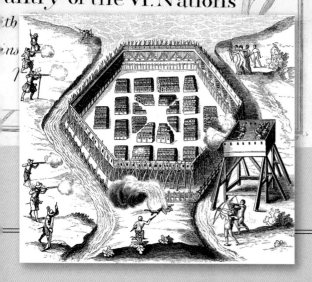

Iroquois chiefs (above) gathered in 1870 to read the images and messages depicted in numerous wampum belts of historical importance to their tribes. Strong palisades did not deter Samuel de Champlain from attacking this Onondaga village (left) in 1615. The Iroquois often constructed palisades, fortifications constructed by driving long, thick stakes vertically into the ground, to defend their villages.

THE BLACK HAWK WAR
Tragedy in the Western Great Lakes

BLACK HAWK

Black Hawk was not a hereditary civil chief, but a respected war leader who ascended to civil authority in his tribe, the Sac and Fox. He was 45 years old when the War of 1812 broke out. He allied with the British and distinguished himself by leading a sizable band of Sac and Fox warriors in at least eight major battles, including those at Forts Meigs, Stephenson, and Johnson. Their efforts were a major contribution to blocking American expansion up the Mississippi River.

After the Black Hawk War of 1832, he was taken prisoner by the United States. While in prison, he advocated for his right to petition the government. In an extended legal battle, he won his case and was allowed to travel to Washington, D.C. His case raised issues about whether Native people were U.S. citizens and about the rights of Indians within U.S. law. Black Hawk was released from custody in 1833, but not on his own terms or of his own accord; rather, he was released into the custody of a rival chief. In spite of this tremendous blow to his ego, Black Hawk lived to the age of 71.

When Black Hawk died, his gravesite was desecrated. Non-Native grave robbers dug up his bones and his chief medals. Black Hawk's bones and medals ended up in the hands of a collector, but the collector's house burned down, and no trace of the chief's remains or items could be found.

In 1832, Black Hawk led a substantial group of Sac and Fox across the Mississippi River east into Illinois to plant corn on land that had been used by his tribe for many decades ❶, shown in this map from the same year. More than two-thirds of the 1,500 people in his company were women and children. Nevertheless, U.S. settlers thought it was an attack. When approached by local militia, Black Hawk hoisted a white flag of truce, but was immediately fired upon. The Indians returned fire, routing the militia.

The U.S. government called 7,000 troops to the conflict. Against all odds, Black Hawk and his people avoided a direct confrontation or capture. He cleverly sent most of his people northwest toward the Black River Falls, Wisconsin (off the map near) ❷, and took a small group of warriors to make a diversionary attack near Milwaukee ❸. By the time U.S. troops reached Milwaukee, Black Hawk and his small diversionary force were gone. He repeated the strategy over and over in different places. But with 7,000 troops looking for the Sac and Fox, it would be impossible to maintain this illusion forever.

Eventually, Black Hawk and his people found themselves pinned against the Bad Axe River, in present-day southwestern Wisconsin (off the map near) ❹. Black Hawk pushed forward with his warriors in an attempt to buy time for their families to escape across the river to safety. Abraham Lincoln was a captain in the U.S. Army during this battle. Women, children, and elders were swimming for safety while their warriors pressed the attack against the U.S. troops that had engulfed their position. On the opposite bank of the river, a large force of Dakota led by Wabasha was waiting for those who swam across. They bludgeoned survivors as they crawled up the riverbank.

Of the 1,500 Sac and Fox who entered Illinois to plant corn, only 200 survived the carnage at the Battle of the Bad Axe River. Amazingly, Black Hawk and 40 others escaped and fled. Eventually, they sought refuge with the Ho-chunk (Winnebago), but their Indian friends turned them in to the U.S. government to avoid the wrath of the U.S. Army on their village ❺. ■

The Battle of the Bad Axe River was devastating for the Sac and Fox. Warriors fought with ferocious intensity against U.S. troops to protect their children, elders, and wives while they swam to safety, only to realize that a large Dakota force allied with the U.S. was positioned on the opposite bank. Hundreds were killed.

TRIBAL MILITARY GENIUS Black Hawk's genius as a military leader and his experience in the field proved vital to the survival of his people for months of pursuit. Outnumbered 15 to 1, the Sac and Fox warriors ran for miles to set up clever diversionary attacks or to raid for supplies, never exposing their small numbers or the direction of their travel. In the meantime, their families traveled in different directions to stay away from U.S. troops and conflict zones. Across Illinois and southern Wisconsin, U.S. troops were frustrated by the speed and unpredictability of Black Hawk's movements and attacks. Shown here are some of the major battle and raid locations during the conflict, including the crushing defeat for the Sac and Fox at the Battle of the Bad Axe River (left).

TRIBES OF THE NORTHEAST

The tribes of the Northeast had highly developed political systems and networks of alliances. When the French and British entered existing tribal conflicts, clashes rose to epic levels. Following are brief histories of select tribes of the region.

■ CAYUGA

Current Locations: Ontario; New York, Oklahoma
Language Family: Iroquoian

The Cayuga, or Guyohkohnyo (People of the Great Swamp), are one of the tribes of the Haudenosaunee (People of the Longhouse), often referred to as the Iroquois. Around 1450, the Cayuga and four other tribes (Mohawk, Oneida, Onondaga, and Seneca) organized a sophisticated ceremonial and cultural institution, the Iroquois League. The Cayuga held a large political, military, and geographic position just west of the Onondaga.

The Cayuga survived the early British period, but eventually warfare between their allies and the French-allied Ojibwe, Ottawa, and Potawatomi brought severe casualties and dislocation. Most Cayuga allied with the British in the American Revolution. U.S. troops then confiscated and burned Cayuga food, killed many people, and forcibly dispersed the survivors.

Some Cayuga and Seneca fled to the Ohio River Valley and others to Canada, where they received small land grants. Another group stayed in New York, even though the U.S. government did not recognize their right to do so at first. The fracture proved permanent. The Cayuga in the Ohio River Valley eventually were relocated to the Seneca-Cayuga Reservation in Oklahoma. Those in Ontario were incorporated into the Six Nations of the Grand River First Nation. The Cayuga in New York were pressured to sign the Treaty of Canandaigua in 1794, ceding most of their land in the Finger Lakes region. But the Cayuga endure in their homeland at Seneca Falls, New York, in addition to the recognized communities in Oklahoma and Ontario.

This Lenape bag is typical of the cross-cultural experience of Native people in the Northeast. European trade beads are incorporated into a buckskin bag with a traditional Lenape motif.

■ ■ HO-CHUNK (WINNEBAGO): *see listing in Plains*

■ KICKAPOO

Current Locations: Kansas, Oklahoma, Texas; Mexico
Language Family: Algonquian

The Kickapoo are closely related to the Mesquakie (Fox). The Kickapoo occupied a substantial territory along the Wabash River in Indiana when the French arrived. They subsequently formed a central part of Tecumseh's pan-Indian confederacy and actively participated in the War of 1812, including the Battle of Tippecanoe. After the war, the U.S. asserted military and political dominion over the Ohio River Valley and southern Great Lakes, and pressure mounted to relocate the Kickapoo. The tribe fractured during relocation, moving to different places, and never recovered cohesion.

One of the first permanent reservations established for the Kickapoo was in Kansas. Other Kickapoo tried to move out of the way of the encroaching white settlements east of the Mississippi. Some sought refuge in Texas prior to the state's independence. Afterward, the tribe split again, with some seeking refuge on the Chickasaw Nation Reservation and some on the Muscogee-Creek Reservation, both in Oklahoma. Another band moved to Mexico, near Nacimiento, after Texas statehood.

The Oklahoma Kickapoo were granted an independent reservation in 1883, only to have it allotted ten years later. Largely landless on their own reservation, the Kickapoo were terminated under the auspices of the Curtis Act in 1898, but were reinstated in 1936. The Kickapoo who stayed in Texas received state recognition in 1977.

■ ■ LENAPE (DELAWARE): *see listing for Delaware in Plains*

■ MALISEET (MALICITE)

Current Locations: New Brunswick, Quebec; Maine
Language Family: Algonquian

The Maliseet, or Wolastoqiyik, are indigenous to Maine, New Brunswick, and Quebec. They had early and sustained contact with the French, and as a result nearly a third of the Maliseet population today has French surnames and a significant percentage of the tribe is Catholic. When conflict escalated between the French and British, the Maliseet sided with the French. They formed even stronger alliances with the Abenaki, Penobscot, and Passamaquoddy, creating the Wabanaki Confederacy.

The Maliseet territory included much of the French-colonized area known as Acadia. Usually the Maliseet and their Wabanaki allies supported the French-speaking Acadians in their fights with the British. The Acadians lost the last of those wars in 1758, and Maliseet lands were overrun with British colonists. In the American Revolution, the tribe tried to stay neutral, but eventually Maliseet were drawn into the conflict on both sides, causing a major tribal rift.

The U.S.–Canada border crossed through Maliseet territory, and in spite of the 1794 Jay Treaty, which provided for their free trade and travel across the border, most of the Maliseet migrated to Canada. Today, the Maliseet live in six major First Nations in New Brunswick, one in Quebec, and several unofficial cultural enclaves elsewhere in the U.S. and Canada.

■ MENOMINEE

Current Locations: Wisconsin
Language Family: Algonquian

The Menominee call themselves Mamaceqtaw, meaning "the people," or Kiash Matchitiwuk, "the ancient ones." The name Menominee is derived from an Ojibwe word, meaning "people of the wild rice." The Menominee lived near Mackinac, Michigan, when Europeans encountered them. They avoided genocidal conflicts, maintaining territory in northeastern Wisconsin during the French and British regimes.

Through seven treaties between 1821 and 1848, the United States claimed title to Menominee lands in Wisconsin and designated the tribe for removal to Minnesota. Instead, they ceded their Minnesota reservation for a much smaller one on the Wolf River in northeastern Wisconsin. There they developed one of the world's first sustainable forestry programs, which provided jobs and revenue. By the 1950s, they had banked more than $10 million.

The Micmac have maintained many traditional lifeways, including vibrant hunting and fishing traditions. But they have been influenced by pan-Indian cultural movements, as well, such as the modern powwow. Pictured here is a Micmac powwow dancer in traditional men's dance regalia.

In 1954, the U.S. government developed the devastating Indian policy called termination, which disbanded tribal governments and converted tribal land to taxable status. The Menominee were terminated in 1961. In response, tribal members formed a corporation to own their land and look after their people as stockholders. To pay taxes, the Menominee sold pieces of their reservation to speculators. The tribe's forestry program was closed. Menominee activists persuaded the U.S. to reinstate the Menominee in 1973. The government had misplaced the $10 million the tribe had in trust, but the tribe eventually recovered most of it, and successfully re-formed its forestry initiative.

■ MICMAC

Current Locations: Labrador, New Brunswick, Newfoundland, Nova Scotia, Quebec; Maine
Language Family: Algonquian

The Micmac (Micmaq, Mi'kmaq) are indigenous to New England and the Maritime Provinces of Canada. Unlike most tribes, whose governance structures were built entirely around autonomous villages, the Micmac organized seven primary districts, each represented in a grand council. The sophistication of their political organization enabled the Micmac to deal with European intrusions more effectively than did many of their Native neighbors.

When the French came to Micmac territory, the grand council made peace with them, and in 1610, a number of prominent chiefs converted to Catholicism. The Micmac developed deep religious, personal, familial, and political ties with the French settlers in their area. They allied with the French Acadians throughout the French–British conflict in eastern Canada. When the Peace of Utrecht in 1713 drew lines between French and British land claims in North America, cutting through their land, the Micmac were furious that they had not been consulted by either side. The Micmac did trade and parley with the British, but never formed especially close or trusting relations with them, and in the Revolutionary War, a fair number of Micmac sided with the Americans.

After the Revolution, Micmac political and military power declined. The escalating pace of white settlement led to greater concentration of the tribal population on smaller and smaller tracts. The Aroostook Band of Micmac stayed on the U.S. side of the border, but the bulk of the Micmac population was in Canada. Today, the Micmac still have numerous First Nations scattered around Quebec and the Maritime Provinces.

■ MOHAWK

Current Locations: Ontario, Quebec; New York
Language Family: Iroquoian

The Mohawk, or Kanien'kehá:ka (People of the Flint), are one of the tribes of the Haudenosaunee (People of the Longhouse), also known as the Iroquois. Around 1450, the Mohawk and four other tribes (Cayuga, Oneida, Onondaga, and Seneca) organized the Iroquois League. The Mohawk held a large political, military, and geographic position in the Mohawk River Valley on the eastern edge of Iroquois lands. They were considered the guardians of the eastern doorway for the Iroquois Confederacy, a military union that overlapped the Iroquois League.

The Mohawk were strong in the early British period. They were at the forefront of major wars against the Pequot and Mahican that pushed those tribes east and south, gaining expanded territory for the Mohawk. Eventually, warfare between the Iroquois Confederacy and the French-allied Ojibwe, Ottawa, and Potawatomi brought severe casualties and dislocation to the Mohawk. There was a rift in the tribal population after 1666, when some left for French-influenced Montreal and others remained in New York.

Most Mohawk villages allied with the British in the American Revolution. After the Revolutionary War, the U.S. exerted pressure on Iroquois lands, paying veterans with grants of yet-to-be-obtained land there. The U.S. government assumed control of most Mohawk land with the Treaty of Canandaigua in 1794. The Mohawk now live in several First Nations in Ontario and Quebec as well as their reservation in New York.

■ MOHEGAN

Current Locations: Connecticut
Language Family: Algonquian

The Mohegan are an offshoot of the Pequot, indigenous to New England. The Mohegan split from the Pequot shortly before contact with Puritan settlers, and the tribes were often in conflict over the years. The Mohegan grew in numbers and power from their primary villages along the Thames River Valley in present-day Connecticut, but rapid British settlement in the 1600s brought disease that killed many.

The Pequot had a brutal conflict with British settlers in the 1600s, and the Mohegan were dragged in on the side of the settlers. When King Philip's War tore New England apart in 1675, the Mohegan again aided European settlers and suffered at the hands of other tribes. Due to the support the Mohegan provided for white settlers, they were not targeted by the British or U.S. government, but because they were at the center of many conflicts and disease epidemics, the tribe dwindled in numbers throughout the 18th century. The language died out, and Christianity replaced tribal religious forms. Most Mohegan eventually had more European blood than Mohegan.

The Mohegan had not signed treaties with the U.S. government, having lost much land to the British. Thus, they had to petition the U.S. government for formal recognition, which came in 1994 as the Mohegan Tribe of Connecticut.

■ NARRAGANSETT

Current Locations: Rhode Island
Language Family: Algonquian

The Narragansett are indigenous to present-day Rhode Island and vicinity. They were among the first in New England to encounter European explorers and to have sustained contact with British settlers. The tribe warred sporadically with the neighboring Pequot, and when the Pequot became embroiled in a war with European settlers, the Narragansett backed the settlers. War left the Pequot so depopulated and disempowered that the Narragansett and Mohegan fought over their territory.

The Ho-chunk (Winnebago) chief Du-cur-re-a and his family, in about 1830. The Ho-chunk thrived in the western Great Lakes, in what is now Wisconsin, even though they were a small tribe relative to the Three Fires Confederacy to their north and east and the Oceti Sákowin (Seven Council Fires of the Dakota, Nakota, and Lakota) to their west.

When King Philip's War broke out in the late 1600s, the colonists feared that the Narragansett would join other tribes allied against the settlers and so preemptively attacked them. The initial attack, often called the Great Swamp Fight, was devastating for the Narragansett, whose warriors were unable to regroup to defend their main villages, where women, children, and elders perished. In response, the Narragansett destroyed Providence. In the end, however, the tribe was significantly weakened.

The Narragansett never recovered numbers, territory, or diplomatic power. By the time of the American Revolution, the tribe was seen more as an ethnic enclave than a tribal nation, and they were not courted by either the British or the Americans. The Narragansett did maintain a strong sense of community, though, developing a tribal church and land plot. Eventually, in the 20th century, they built a ceremonial building and sought to revitalize vestigial remnants of their culture.

■ OJIBWE (CHIPPEWA)

Current Locations: Manitoba, Ontario, Quebec, Saskatchewan; Michigan, Minnesota, Montana, North Dakota, Wisconsin
Language Family: Algonquian

The Ojibwe are smaller than only the Cherokee and Navajo in the number of U.S. enrolled members. However, there are twice as many self-identified Ojibwe people as enrollees, plus 125 Ojibwe First Nations in Canada, making the Ojibwe the largest tribe in terms of geographic dispersal, land, and population. They were distinguished from other Algonquian tribes by language and by customs, including writing on birchbark scrolls, using birchbark canoes, and mining and working copper.

Conflict in the Northeast and prophecies by Ojibwe religious leaders led many Ojibwe to slowly migrate from their homeland on the Atlantic coast westward through the Great Lakes. They allied with the Ottawa and the Potawatomi, forming

This Ojibwe shirt exemplifies many traditional tribal motifs: the beaver fur lining, brain-tanned buckskin, and floral design pattern typical of the Northeast.

the strong Three Fires Confederacy. This enabled the Ojibwe to prosper in the French and British fur trade, fend off intrusions, and expand their territory.

The American period brought new challenges, because Ojibwe lands were rich in timber, iron, and farming potential. The U.S. government pressed them to sell, and over time, they did so. But tribal leaders insisted on keeping the largest lakes in Ojibwe hands. They also insisted that their people be allowed to hunt, fish, trap, and gather wild rice on all lands sold to the U.S. government.

These rights, called usufructuary rights, were written into treaties in Michigan, Minnesota, and Wisconsin. The treaties and their tribal land-use clauses became the basis for a number of legal claims in the 1980s and 1990s. Many whites thought the Indians were getting special new rights, when in fact they were exercising rights they had had before white men came and that were protected under the treaties.

■ ONEIDA

Current Locations: Ontario; New York, Wisconsin
Language Family: Iroquoian

The Oneida, or Onyota'a:ka (People of the Standing Stone), are one of the tribes of the Haudenosaunee (People of the Longhouse), often referred to as the Iroquois. They held a large political, military, and geographic position in central New York State as part of the Iroquois Confederacy.

The American Revolution shattered the Iroquois alliances and tore the Oneida apart. Other Iroquois communities allied with the British because of their trade and diplomatic relations. The Oneida, however, had strong ties to the colonists, including a Christian contingent of the tribe. Most eventually backed the colonists, even bringing critical reinforcements and supplies to George Washington at Valley Forge.

After the Revolutionary War, the bulk of the Oneida stayed in New York, where a substantial 300,000-acre reservation was established for them with the 1794 Treaty of Canandaigua, the first real U.S. Indian reservation. But a flood of white settlers and the New York state government eventually whittled the reservation down to just 32 acres. In the 1830s, a large group of Oneida relocated to Canada, and another group was relocated to Green Bay, Wisconsin. Their language is still spoken by a handful of elders, and there is an active effort to revitalize the language and culture, especially on the Wisconsin reservation.

■ ONONDAGA

Current Locations: Ontario; New York
Language Family: Iroquoian

The Onondaga, or Onönda'gega (People of the Hills), are one of the tribes of the Haudenosaunee (People of the Longhouse), often referred to as the Iroquois. Around 1450, the Onondaga and four other tribes (Cayuga, Mohawk, Oneida, and Seneca) organized a ceremonial and cultural institution, the Iroquois League. The Onondaga, who were strong through the early British period, held the spiritual and geographic center of the Iroquois League as well as a large territory in central New York State.

The American Revolution shattered the Iroquois alliance. Initially, the Onondaga remained neutral, while many other Iroquois communities allied themselves with the British. When the colonial military came to Iroquois lands, though, this mattered little, and the Onondaga were burned out of their primary village. The survivors sided with the British and their Iroquois brethren.

After the Revolutionary War, the U.S. exerted pressure on Iroquois lands, paying war veterans with grants of yet-to-be-obtained land there. Many Onondaga fled to Canada, while others stayed in New York, where the 1794 Treaty of Canandaigua set aside a small land tract for them. Today, the Onondaga live on a reservation in New York and two First Nations in Canada.

■ OTTAWA (ODAWA)

Current Locations: Ontario; Michigan, Oklahoma
Language Family: Algonquian

The Ottawa are a large tribe closely related to the Ojibwe and Potawatomi. When the French first encountered the Ottawa, the tribe controlled a large swath of territory in the central and eastern parts of the Great Lakes, primarily around Lakes Huron and Michigan. The Ottawa built and maintained a powerful trade and military alliance with the French. This alliance enabled the Ottawa to increase their standard of living, develop specialized skills in trapping and trade, and—with the benefit of the birchbark canoe and European

weapons—defend their growing territory.

When the Dutch and later British governments armed the Iroquois Confederacy to push the French and Indian allies out of the central Great Lakes, the Ottawa provided formidable resistance. Even after the French army pulled out of the region, Ottawa chief Pontiac formed a pan-Indian alliance that burned 9 of the 11 British forts in the Great Lakes area. When the French failed to reinforce Pontiac, the British broke sieges at the other two forts.

Many Ottawa communities sided with the British during the American Revolution and the War of 1812. After American sovereignty in the southern Great Lakes was assured, many Ottawa moved into Canada to avoid reprisals. Today, the Ottawa inhabit several reservations in Michigan and numerous First Nations in Ontario. The unceded Ottawa land on Manitoulin Island in Lake Huron has been a particular source of pride.

■ PASSAMAQUODDY

Current Locations: Maine, New Brunswick
Language Family: Algonquian

The Passamaquoddy, closely related to the Maliseet, are indigenous to present-day Maine and New Brunswick. The Passamaquoddy were primarily farmers. They had early and sustained contact with the French, and as a result many are Catholic. When conflict escalated between the French and British, the tribe

Many items of everyday use were infused with the deep artistic traditions of the Northeast. Pictured here is a beautifully worked pair of Iroquois moccasins.

usually sided with the French. Together with the Abenaki, Penobscot, Micmac, and Maliseet, the Passamaquoddy formed the Wabanaki Confederacy.

The Passamaquoddy territory included much of the French-colonized area known as Acadia. In conflicts with the British, the Passamaquoddy and other Wabanaki allies supported the Acadians. The French-speaking Acadians lost the last of those wars in 1758, and Passamaquoddy lands were soon overrun with British colonists. The tribe tried to stay neutral during the American Revolution, but eventually they were drawn into the conflict on both sides.

The U.S.–Canada border crossed right through the middle of Passamaquoddy territory. Today, the Passamaquoddy live in one First Nation in New Brunswick and one reservation in Maine, and they have several unofficial cultural enclaves elsewhere in the U.S. and Canada.

■ PENOBSCOT

Current Locations: Maine
Language Family: Algonquian

The Penobscot are indigenous to present-day Maine and the Maritime Provinces of Canada. They are an offshoot of the larger Abenaki group, and their language is sometimes classified as Eastern Abenaki, even though the two groups were politically distinct. The Penobscot were primarily farmers. They had early and sustained contact with the French, and usually sided with the French against the British. They formed an even stronger alliance with their

The birchbark canoe, developed by the Ojibwe and shared with their allies, was lighter, faster, more buoyant, and easier to repair than other watercraft.

Ojibwe harvest wild rice on the Leech Lake Indian Reservation in Minnesota. One harvester uses a push pole to move the canoe through the rice and the other knocks the grains into the canoe with sticks.

Abenaki cousins, as well as the Micmac, Passamaquoddy, and Maliseet, known as the Wabanaki Confederacy.

Penobscot support for the French was so strong that the British actually issued a bounty on Penobscot scalps in 1755, via the Spencer Phipps Proclamation, a genocidal edict. The tribal population dwindled from 10,000 to around 500 from disease, oppressive warfare, and the bounty on their tribal members. The American Revolution and War of 1812 posed profound challenges for the Penobscot. The U.S.–Canada border crossed Penobscot territory, but the tribe was so small and overwhelmed there was little to do but hold on. Today, the Penobscot live on a reservation in Maine and in several unofficial cultural enclaves elsewhere in the U.S. and Canada.

▥ PEQUOT

Current Locations: Connecticut
Language Family: Algonquian

The Pequot are indigenous to present-day Connecticut and occupied strategic territory. They had to balance conflicts with the Mohegan and Narragansett with the presence of European settlers. In 1637, the British colonists declared war on the Pequot, and the Mohegan and Narragansett sided with the colonists. Pequot warriors raided Hartford and other British settlements, but their villages were left vulnerable. The Pequot village at Mystic was attacked by British militia in 1637 while most of the warriors were gone, and the British embarked on a genocidal bloodbath, killing women, elders, and children. Even the Narragansett were taken aback by the Mystic Massacre. At the Great Swamp Fight near Fairfield, Connecticut, the Pequot endured another terrible setback.

Soon, most of the Pequot were dead and many others had been exiled to the West Indies as slaves. Only about 500 remained—a population so small that the Pequot were insignificant in King Philip's War, the American Revolution, and the War of 1812. The Pequot language and religion died out, although some of the people survived. Today, the Mashantucket Pequot are a federally recognized tribe and among the wealthiest gaming tribes.

▥ POTAWATOMI

Current Locations: Ontario; Kansas, Michigan, Oklahoma, Wisconsin
Language Family: Algonquian

The Potawatomi (spelled many ways) are closely related to the Ojibwe and Ottawa in language and culture. They had established numerous villages around Lake Michigan by the time the French arrived in the 17th century. The Potawatomi alliance with the Ojibwe and Ottawa put the Potawatomi in charge of the sacred fire and central diplomatic functions.

Along with their Indian allies, the Potawatomi formed close relations with the French and actively traded with them. Many joined the Ottawa chief Pontiac in his war against the British after the French lost the French and Indian War. The Potawatomi mended ties with the British afterward, and although most stayed neutral during the Revolution and the War of 1812, some sided with the British, and many joined Tecumseh.

Two major bands were relocated in the 1830s from Indiana and Illinois to a reservation in Kansas. The Mission Band ultimately sold its land in Kansas, signed a new treaty in 1867, and was relocated to Oklahoma, where its members acquired U.S. citizenship prior to most Indians; they have since been called the Citizen Band Potawatomi. The Prairie Band remained in Kansas. Others stayed near Lake Michigan, with current populations in Canada, Michigan, and Wisconsin.

▥ POWHATAN

Current Locations: Virginia
Language Family: Algonquian

The Powhatan were a confederacy of 30 closely related Algonquian tribes in present-day Virginia, including the Powhatan, Arrohateck, Appamattuck, Pamunkey, Mattaponi, Chiskiack, Kecoughtan, Youghtanund, Rappahannock, Moraughtacund, Weyanoak, Paspahegh, Quiyoughcohannock, and Nansemond. "Powhatan" has been used to refer to the largest tribe in the confederacy, the people of all the tribes, the principal village, and its primary chief.

The British first arrived at Jamestown in 1607 and expanded their colonies without Powhatan permission. Over the decades, the Natives and colonists battled. The English campaign from 1644 to 1646 proved especially devastating because it was accompanied by several outbreaks of disease. The confederacy fell apart afterward, as the Powhatan were outnumbered and overwhelmed. Many were forced into slavery in Virginia and the West Indies.

In 2009, Virginia recognized seven tribes that were formerly part of the Powhatan Confederacy. They have 3,000 tribal members, but only the Pamunkey and Mattaponi have retained tribal lands since the 1600s. All seven tribes are trying to get federal recognition, but old state records designated citizens as either white or colored, so proving Indian descent to the satisfaction of the government has been difficult.

■ SENECA

Current Locations: Ontario; New York, Oklahoma
Language Family: Iroquoian

The Seneca, or Onöndowága (People of the Great Hill), are one of the tribes of the Haudenosaunee (People of the Longhouse), often referred to as the Iroquois. Around 1450, the Seneca and four other tribes (Cayuga, Mohawk, Oneida, and Onondaga) organized the Iroquois League, in which the five original member tribes held essential positions and were represented by 50 traditional chiefs in joint council. The Seneca, who were numerous, strong, and stable through the early British period, guarded the western door of the Iroquois League and occupied a substantial territory in western New York State. On the western edge of Iroquois lands, they warred frequently with the adjacent tribes, including the Huron, Ojibwe, Ottawa, and Potawatomi.

Eventually, warfare between the Iroquois Confederacy and the French-allied Ojibwe, Ottawa, and Potawatomi brought casualties and major dislocation to the Seneca. The American Revolution then shattered the Iroquois alliance. Most Seneca actively allied themselves with the British, with whom they had long-standing trade and diplomatic relations. When the colonial military came to Iroquois lands, the Seneca suffered severe casualties.

After the Revolutionary War, the United States exerted great pressure on Iroquois lands, paying veterans with grants of yet-to-be-obtained land there.

This Tuscarora bag incorporates traditional Iroquois artistic design with European trade beads and American flags—symbols of the changing economy.

Some Seneca retreated into Pennsylvania with the Cayuga and were eventually relocated to Oklahoma. Others fled to Canada. But most stayed in New York, where by the treaties of Fort Stanwix in 1784 and Canandaigua in 1794, their land tenure was firmly established. Today, the Seneca live in New York, Oklahoma, and Canada.

■ SHINNECOCK

Current Locations: New York
Language Family: Algonquian

The Shinnecock are a small tribe indigenous to present-day Long Island in New York. They are linguistically and culturally related to the Pequot and Mohegan. During the height of Pequot power in Connecticut, the Shinnecock on Long Island were considered a subject tribal entity of the Pequot. European diseases ravaged the tribal population early on, and the high population density of the Shinnecock villages enabled by the abundance of fish and other food proved to be a disadvantage in weathering the virgin-soil epidemics.

Although not targeted as directly as the Pequot in warfare, the Pequot War and King Philip's War did claim casualties among the tribe and greatly increased the pressure on tribal land. By the 19th century, the small tribal enclave of Shinnecock people on Long Island was entirely Christianized and had lost most of its tribal language speakers and most of its land. Many Shinnecock married into the growing black community on Long Island in the late 1800s, and today the tribal population is entirely mixed black and Shinnecock. The tribal population has maintained a distinct sense of community through that time and, in recent years, has worked hard to revitalize ancient tribal customs and traditions. The tribe finally received federal recognition in 2010 as the Shinnecock Indian Nation. It maintains several businesses and has been actively pursuing a significant land-claim dispute.

Woven reeds form this domed house in a re-created Powhatan Indian village at the Jamestown Settlement, a living-history museum of life in 17th-century Virginia.

The Wampanoag have worked to revitalize critical aspects of their culture, with projects such as this replica of an authentic precontact lodge.

■ TUSCARORA

Current Locations: Ontario; New York
Language Family: Iroquoian

The Tuscarora are indigenous to North Carolina. Although closely related to the Iroquois in language and culture, they were an independent entity at the time of European contact. Warfare fractured the tribal population in the early 1700s, and the majority of the tribe moved north into present-day Pennsylvania and New York. Isolated in the middle of a conflict zone between the Three Fires Confederacy and the Iroquois Confederacy and in between the French and British, they needed allies to survive. The Tuscarora appealed to their Oneida cousins for help and, after a long diplomatic process, were adopted into the Iroquois Confederacy as a sixth nation.

Like the Oneida, the Tuscarora population split during the American Revolution. Some allied with the British or remained neutral; others sided with the Americans. The split became permanent afterward when the pro-British contingent moved to Ontario and eventually settled on the Six Nations First Nation there. The rest of the tribe in New York, like the Oneida, endured numerous encroachments on tribal land and lifeways by the New York government.

The Tuscarora Nation of New York is federally recognized. There was a smaller but substantial Tuscarora population remaining in North Carolina. Like the Lumbee, they were dispersed into the mainstream white and black populations of Robeson County. Although not federally recognized, the Tuscarora enclaves in North Carolina have formed a loose affiliation in the Tuscarora One Fire Council.

■ WAMPANOAG

Current Locations: Massachusetts
Language Family: Algonquian

The Wampanoag (People of the First Light) were sedentary farmers of corn, beans, and squash who augmented their diet with fish and game. Wampanoag women had a voice in political functions, and the tribe sometimes had female chiefs. Men hunted, fished, and fought; women produced 75 percent of the food. Land rights were passed down through the mother. The Wampanoag had a large territory in present-day southeastern Massachusetts and Rhode Island, with a precontact population estimated at 12,000. The Wampanoag were at the center of the story of the first Thanksgiving, as well as the brutal and devastating 1675 conflict known as King Philip's War, which forever altered the tribe politically and culturally.

Due to their frequent sustained contact with white settlers, the Wampanoag were more exposed than other tribes to virgin-soil epidemics, which wiped out as much as 90 percent of the population, bringing poverty, hunger, and political upheaval. Because the Wampanoag were hurt earlier than their Indian neighbors, they became more vulnerable to attacks than ever before. They suffered defeats at the hands of the Narragansett and were forced to cede territory.

Today, there are five distinct organized groups of Wampanoag. Although all have applied for U.S. government recognition, only two have federal status—the Wampanoag Tribe of Gay Head (Martha's Vineyard) and the Mashpee Wampanoag Tribe. There are more than 2,000 tribal members. The Wampanoag language was stamped out, but tribal members are trying to revitalize it from missionary documents, Bibles, and other sources.

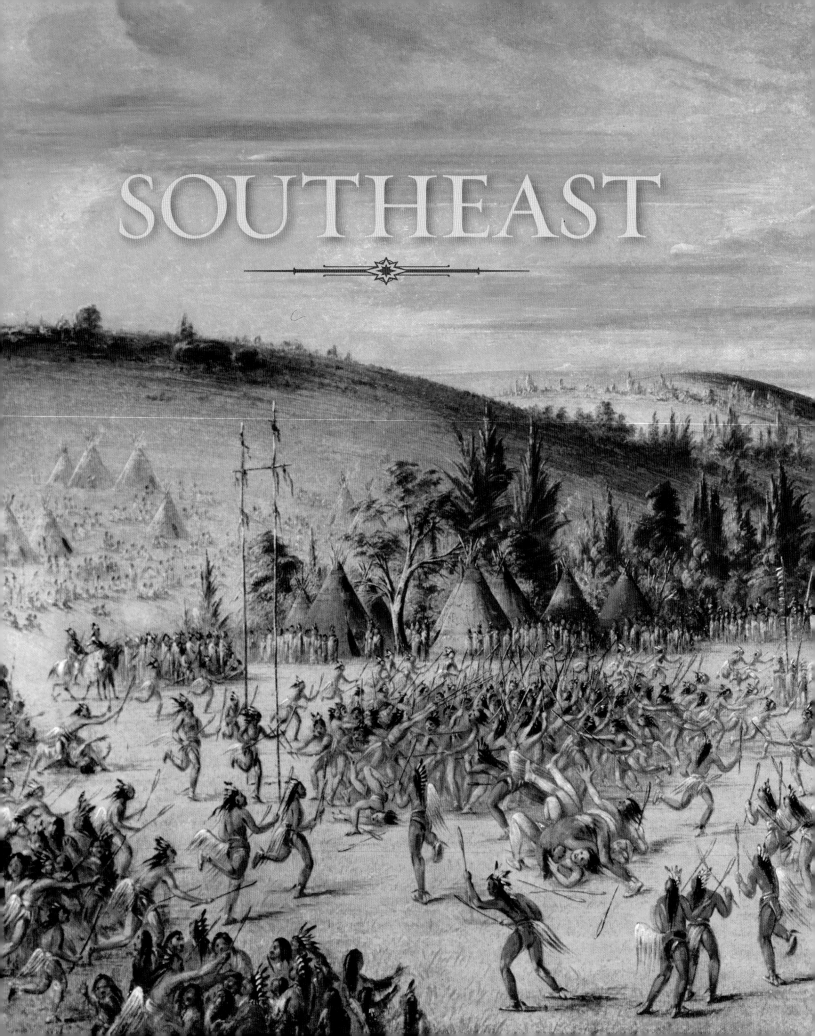

SOUTHEAST

·CHAPTER TWO·

BILOXI   CREEK (MUSCOGEE)

CATAWBA   MICCOSUKEE

CHEROKEE   SEMINOLE

CHITIMACHA   TUNICA

CHOCTAW

COUSHATTA

Tribes in the Southeast flourished with corn agriculture, sedentary villages, and highly structured political systems. Because of abundant food and stable leadership, the population density was high relative to most parts of the world, and social activities such as sports flourished, like this Choctaw stickball game, depicted in a painting by George Catlin from the 1830s.

INDIAN NATIONS OF THE SOUTHEAST

The Southeast is one of the most hospitable environments to human life in the world. The soil is exceptionally fertile. There is ample rainfall. Agriculture featuring corn (maize), supplemented with beans and squash, provided a well-balanced and easily maintained food supply for the many tribes that called the region home. The food that people grew added to the ready and variable food the region produced naturally—nuts, berries, tubers, fish, birds. The winters were colder 500 years ago than they are now, but still mild enough in the Southeast not to cause undue hardship. Travel was easy by both water and land. People flourished in the Southeast, generating a population density that rivaled the most populated parts of Europe. The great Mississippian moundbuilders constructed Cahokia, Moundville, and many other great urban centers all along the Mississippi River, its tributaries, and points eastward. When Hernando de Soto became the first European to see the inland life of the Indian nations in the Southeast, he was astounded at the myriad of cultures, the numbers of people, their wealth, and the flourishing arts and sports.

De Soto may have marveled at the tribal cultures of the Southeast, but he also plotted their destruction. His goal was to identify natural resources and help Europeans exploit them. In the process, he fought many of those tribes while he was there in 1540–41. Though it was a relatively short period of time in the overall history of the Native Americans, even this brief sustained European contact with

The Creek are descendants of the great Mississippian moundbuilders and, until the removal era, were one of the largest tribes in the region. Pictured left is Tchow-ee-put-o-kaw, a Creek woman painted by George Catlin. The arts flourished in the Southeast through the removal era, as seen in this elaborate basket (above).

Indians in the Southeast changed their world overnight.

FROM MISSISSIPPIAN MOUNDBUILDERS TO NEW NATIONS

Although much attention is given to assimilation and missionary efforts and the military campaigns that wrested the land from Native hands, nothing so changed the human landscape in the Americas as the disease pandemics that Europeans brought. Throughout the centuries in the Middle East and Europe, humans had domesticated pigs, sheep, and other livestock, and from that sustained contact erupted many deadly diseases. The urbanization of the European population accelerated the transfer of these infections. But over time, enough of the European population survived and passed on powerful antibodies to fight the diseases. When Europeans came to the Americas, the diseases came with them, but Native Americans did not have the same antibodies and the effects were devastating.

Measles, mumps, whooping cough, bubonic plague, and smallpox wiped out millions of people. The human tragedy was heightened because, while Europeans had been exposed to diseases in cycles over long periods of time, the tribal populations of the Americas were hit by many at the same time. Compounding the damage, the Europeans themselves came with military might and demands for land, slaves, and resources right in the midst of the debilitating pandemics. Entire tribes were depopulated. Leadership structures and social structures were shaken to their cores.

Some of the strongest tribes suffered the worst, because the more densely populated a region was, the more quickly the diseases spread. In addition, the more hospitable a climate was to food production and human life, the more hospitable it also was to everything in the germ pool. The Southeast consequently suffered a 95 percent mortality rate. The Hernando de Soto expedition in 1540–41 exposed most tribes in the Southeast to the disease vectors, and when the Spanish, French, and British came to colonize there decades later, some places where de Soto had seen settlements of 20,000 people or more were now vacant. The human landscape throughout the entire region had been forever altered. The Mississippian moundbuilders were no more. The population had imploded, and the highly structured and hierarchical political systems they built collapsed along with the population.

Early French, Spanish, and English colonists found instead many groups like the Choctaw and Creek, who were really remnant tribes of the Mississippians that had begun to coalesce and regroup. They were just starting to rebuild new nations in the Southeast when Europeans came to stay. The new tribal nations still farmed corn, beans, and squash. They still had vibrant cultures, and the arts

CHRONOLOGY

MID-1500s
Mississippian moundbuilding culture implodes as disease pandemics kill 95 percent of tribal population

1550–1700
New tribes coalesce from the Mississippian culture, building new nations and developing strategies for dealing with the French, Spanish, and British

1779–1811
Cherokee, Chickasaw, Choctaw, Creek, and Seminole embrace American ideas and come to be called the Five Civilized Tribes

1811
Creek join Tecumseh's alliance

1813–14
Red Stick War (Creek civil war): Upper Creek traditionalists (Red Stick) resist further assimilation, but are blocked by Lower Creek; America suppresses them, and most join the Seminole in Florida

1817
Seminole Wars begin

1830
Indian Removal Act paves the way for relocation of tribes from the Southeast to Indian Territory (Oklahoma)

1830–38
Trail of Tears: Most people in the Five Civilized Tribes get relocated to Oklahoma, many perishing on the way

1858
Seminole Wars end; some Seminole avoid relocation to Oklahoma and hide in Everglades

and sports were still a big part of them. But the people were changed. Their political systems were new and growing. The people were receptive to consciously evolving their ways of governing and economies. It was fertile soil for a colonial experiment.

STRATEGIES OF RESISTANCE: PRE-REMOVAL ACCOMMODATION

No peoples want to submit their governments or personal lives to outside power. Resistance to colonization was common in the Americas, as elsewhere, but it did not always take the form of war. The tribes of the Southeast were diverse and populous, and the means they pursued to protect their sovereignty and ways of life were equally diverse. The precolonial experience in rebuilding had left most of the tribes in the region open to new ideas and ways of doing things. When Europeans first came to their lands, the Indians saw just as much opportunity as threat.

The Cherokee, Choctaw, Chickasaw, Creek, and Seminole embraced trade with the British, Spanish, and French, often playing them off against one another for the best prices, terms, and relationships. When the British introduced the slave trade in the Americas, the largest tribes of the Southeast were willing to raid their smaller neighbors on behalf of the British. Tens of thousands of Indians were sold into slavery, and the Southeast became tenser, more violent, and less hospitable to smaller groups.

The British slave trade boomed in the Americas, starting with this attempt to enslave Native Americans before heavier reliance was placed on slaves imported from Africa. In a two-year slave raid in Florida, the British military under the command of James Moore took more than 10,000 Timucua and other Indians as slaves. Many of the Florida Indians were already being incorporated into the Spanish mission system for both acculturation and labor. The raid was a major encouragement to the English, who took hope

THE SOUTHEAST

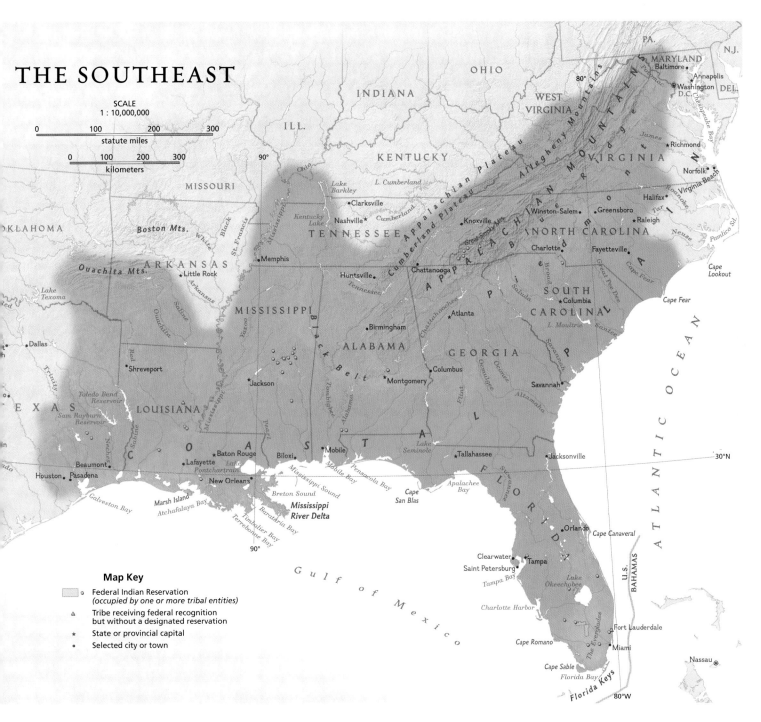

SCALE
1 : 10,000,000

0   100   200   300
statute miles

0   100   200   300
kilometers

Map Key

▫ Federal Indian Reservation
(occupied by one or more tribal entities)

△ Tribe receiving federal recognition
but without a designated reservation

★ State or provincial capital

• Selected city or town

in their ability to successfully conduct slave raids in Indian country and at the same time weaken the escalating strength of their Spanish economic and military rivals.

Afterward, the British actively recruited Native Americans to raid their Native neighbors for slaves and sell them to the colonists. This trade transformed the culture and level of violence in

Federally recognized tribes in the Southeast today. The demography bears a sharp contrast to the numerous, overflowing villages across the region reported by Hernando de Soto at first contact in 1540–41.

the Southeast. The Yamassee War of 1715–17 was largely a defensive measure against the slave raids. Many of the larger tribes actively raided their smaller neighbors, selling their Native captives as slaves to the British, with devastating effect. Eventually, however, the British realized that Indian slaves were so susceptible to disease that it was cheaper to acquire slaves in Africa and bring

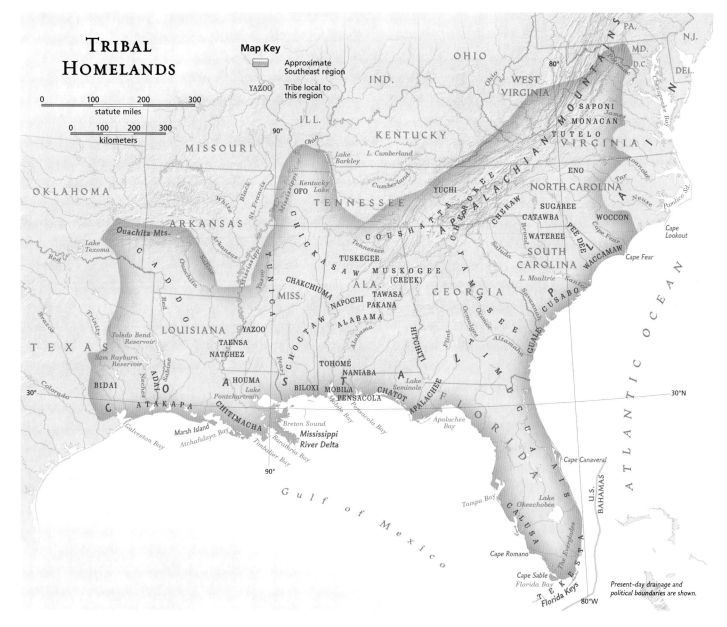

TRIBAL HOMELANDS

Map Key

▨ Approximate Southeast region

YAZOO Tribe local to this region

Present-day drainage and political boundaries are shown.

them to the Americas. The Indian slave trade declined, but the political and economic revolution it created endured.

The largest tribes flourished with new commerce, the slave trade, and new relationships. They diversified and expanded their economies and grew their political structures. Many were very open to European ideas and technologies.

By the middle of the 1700s, the tribes of the Southeast were being pulled in many directions. The French, Spanish, and English had all built forts on the edges of their territory. Each European power had

The Muscogean-speaking peoples of the Southeast were at one time a single people that spread out and diversified. Being in the same language family meant shared linguistic and often cultural foundations, but not necessarily shared political or military alliances. Other tribes, such as the Cherokee, came to the Southeast and, in spite of abundant resources there, clashed over territory.

opposing agendas and methods for achieving them. The various European governments, missionaries, and settlers pulled at tribal alliances with the lure of better trade terms and pushed at them with land-sale requests and slave raids. The tribes did their best to play the Europeans off against one another and actively traded with all of them, but their efforts at neutrality were constantly tested.

The political and economic stakes were incredible. The Creek were selling 50,000 deerskins every year out of Savannah alone. The trade proved profitable, and it transformed the large tribes from

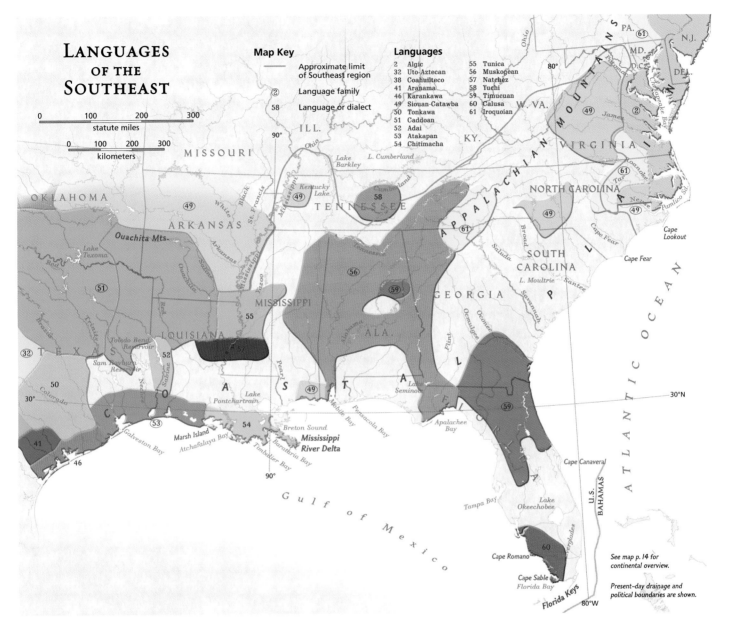

LANGUAGES OF THE SOUTHEAST

Map Key

— Approximate limit of Southeast region

② Language family

58 Language or dialect

Languages

2	Algic	55	Tunica
32	Uto-Aztecan	56	Muskogean
38	Coahuilteco	57	Natchez
41	Aranama	58	Yuchi
46	Karankawa	59	Timucuan
49	Siouan-Catawba	60	Calusa
50	Tonkawa	61	Iroquoian
51	Caddoan		
52	Adai		
53	Atakapan		
54	Chitimacha		

The Southeast is dominated by tribes from the Muscogean language family—Creek, Seminole, Choctaw, and others. The Cherokee are from the Iroquoian language family and likely migrated to the Southeast from the eastern Great Lakes a few centuries before European contact. There are a few tribes whose languages are classified as language isolates, as well as some from the Siouan language family.

See map p. 14 for continental overview.

Present-day drainage and political boundaries are shown.

self-sufficient farmers to increasingly diverse specialists in various aspects of trade, harvest, and diplomacy.

After the American Revolution, President George Washington embarked on a conscious assimilation plan that was quite different from the missionary assimilation work in most other places. Washington wanted to Americanize the tribes of the Southeast, not just convert them to Christianity. He appointed Benjamin Hawkins to work with the Cherokee, Chickasaw, Choctaw, Creek, and Seminole and teach them European–American ways. These tribes continued to evolve their farming practices, escalated their use of slavery, heightened hierarchical divisions within the tribes, and globalized their economies. The project was so successful that these five tribes were referred to as the Five Civilized Tribes.

The Five Civilized Tribes moved quickly to embrace American economic and political relations. They saw the power and rapid growth of the American nation and had little interest in fighting it. They accepted and actively participated in the plantation-style slave economy. Many of them owned black slaves, especially among the Cherokee Nation. By treaty provisions, many Cherokee, Creek, and Choctaw became U.S. citizens voluntarily in the early 1800s, a hundred years before most Native Americans. They actively participated in the American political process as citizens as well and viewed themselves as functional dual citizens of the United States and their respective Native nations. The tribes also embraced democracy internally and externally. They revolutionized their political systems, creating new, modern forms of government infused with democratic ideals. They modeled their systems on the American political structure, with a heavy emphasis on special power and privilege for landowners. The Cherokee in particular imbued their political institutions with American ideals.

Sequoyah, son of a Cherokee mother, Wurteh, and a white father, was a Cherokee silversmith who single-handedly developed the Cherokee syllabary. His system is still used today. Sequoyah saw the value of writing from watching European settlers use their "talking leaves." He worked on a system for Cherokee that had a unique symbol for each syllable in the language—86 characters. It took him from 1809 to 1821 to perfect the system. The Cherokee Nation had a massive land holding in the Carolinas and Georgia, but many Cherokee had moved to Arkansas and elsewhere in the Southeast. Sequoyah first tried his system with the Arkansas Cherokee with great success and astonishment. He introduced the system to the

Sequoyah's Cherokee syllabary, introduced in 1821, was a remarkable writing system developed by a previously nonliterate people. Within a couple of years, the Cherokee had a higher literacy rate than the British colonists around them and two newspapers being printed in the tribal language. The syllabary is still widely used.

Cherokee Nation with a formal letter from their cousins in Arkansas. It was officially adopted in 1825, and within a few years the Cherokee had a literacy rate higher than their white neighbors and were publishing two newspapers in the tribal language.

Sequoyah continued to work as a silversmith to support his seven children, but he grew so excited about writing indigenous languages that he spent the last several years of his life traveling throughout the Southeast, Texas, and Mexico to learn about other tribal languages and explore the possibility of other writing systems or even a universal Indian writing system. He died in Mexico around 1840 before he could finish the study. Sequoyah's writing system enabled the Cherokee to run their government with written laws and sophisticated political communication networks that kept their citizenry educated and engaged.

The accommodations made by the Five Civilized Tribes, and also by other tribes in the Southeast such as the Catawba, were never sufficient to sate the land lust of American settlers. The tribes accepted American nationhood, but they were not going to surrender their own nations or land. The government picked away at their holdings bit by bit. Some tribes, like the Creek, signed more than 20 land cession treaties before it was all over. Whatever hope the Southeast tribes had that accommodation would win favorable treatment were

"We can never forget these homes, I know, but an unbending, iron necessity tells us we must leave them. I would willingly die to preserve them, but any forcible effort to keep them will cost us our lands, our lives, and the lives of our children."

—MAJOR RIDGE (CHEROKEE)

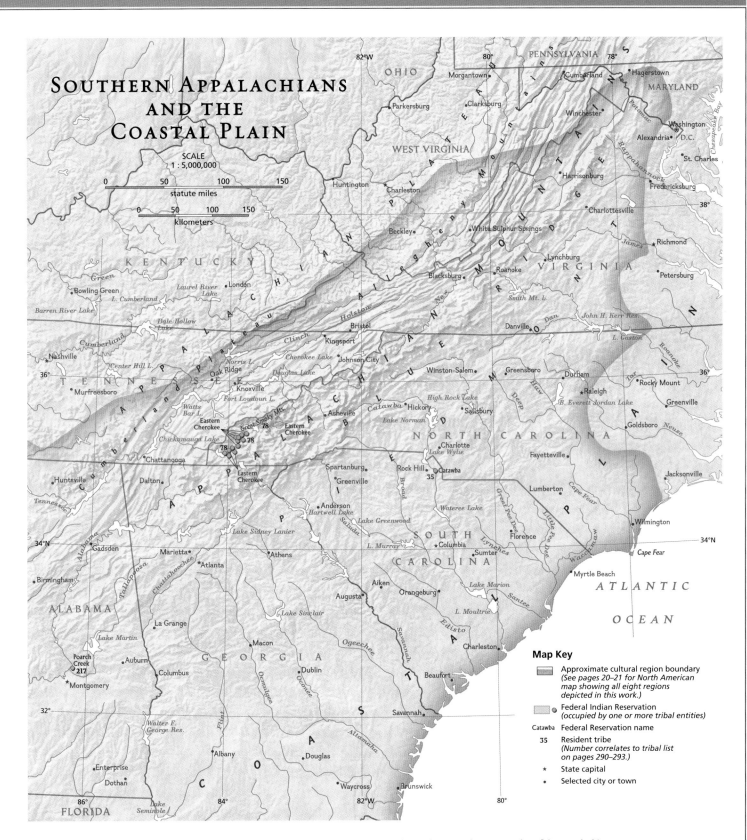

SOUTHERN APPALACHIANS AND THE COASTAL PLAIN

SCALE
1 : 5,000,000

0   50   100   150
statute miles

0   50   100   150
kilometers

OHIO

PENNSYLVANIA

82°W   80°   78°

Morgantown

CumberLand

Hagerstown

MARYLAND

Parkersburg   Clarksburg   Winchester   Washington D.C.

WEST VIRGINIA

Alexandria   St. Charles

Chesapeake Bay

Huntington

Charleston

Beckley

White Sulphur Springs

Harrisonburg   Fredericksburg

38°

Charlottesville

KENTUCKY

Green

Bowling Green   L. Cumberland   Laurel River Lake

London

Barren River Lake

Dale Hollow Lake

Cumberland

Center Hill L.

Nashville

TENNESSEE

Murfreesboro

Oak Ridge

Norris L.

Clinch   Kingsport

Holston   Bristol

Cherokee Lake   Johnson City

Douglas Lake

Knoxville

Fort Loudoun L.

Watts Bar L.

Eastern Cherokee

Great Smoky Mts.   78   Eastern Cherokee

Chickamauga Lake   78   78

78

Chattanooga

Eastern Cherokee

Dalton

Huntsville

Tennessee

Gadsden

ALABAMA

Birmingham

Lake Martin

Poarch Creek   217

Montgomery

Marietta   Atlanta

La Grange

Columbus

Auburn

GEORGIA

Macon

Dublin

Tallapoosa

Chattahoochee

Lake Sinclair

Flint

Ocmulgee

Oconee

Walter F. George Res.

Albany

Douglas

Enterprise

Dothan

Lake Seminole

FLORIDA

86°   84°   82°W   80°

Beckley

Blacksburg

New

Roanoke

Lynchburg

VIRGINIA

Richmond

Petersburg

Smith Mt. L.

Danville   Dan

John H. Kerr Res.

L. Gaston

Roanoke

36°

Winston-Salem   Greensboro   Durham

Rocky Mount

High Rock Lake   Raleigh

Haw   B. Everett Jordan Lake   Greenville

Asheville

Catawba   Hickory   Salisbury

Lake Norman

Deep   Goldsboro   Neuse

NORTH CAROLINA

Charlotte

Lake Wylie   Fayetteville

Spartanburg   Rock Hill   Catawba

Greenville   35

Broad

Anderson   Wateree Lake

Hartwell Lake

Lake Greenwood   Great Pee Dee   Cape Fear

Saluda   Lumberton

Little Pee Dee

Wilmington

34°N   34°N

SOUTH   L. Murray   Lynches   Florence   Waccamaw   Cape Fear

CAROLINA   Columbia   Sumter   Myrtle Beach

Athens   Aiken   Orangeburg   Lake Marion   ATLANTIC

Augusta   L. Moultrie   OCEAN

Santee

Edisto

Charleston

Ogeechee

Savannah

Beaufort

C   O   A   S   T

Waycross   Brunswick

Map Key

▭	Approximate cultural region boundary *(See pages 20–21 for North American map showing all eight regions depicted in this work.)*
▭◉	Federal Indian Reservation *(occupied by one or more tribal entities)*
Catawba	Federal Reservation name
35	Resident tribe *(Number correlates to tribal list on pages 290–293.)*
★	State capital
•	Selected city or town

It is not by accident that the federally recognized tribes in the Southeast cluster on the eastern edge of the Appalachians.
The terrain there offered a natural shelter and stronghold for those who resisted removal. During the Trail of Tears era, this became the most concentrated
holdout of Cherokee in the Southeast. Even today, outside of Oklahoma, this is the largest concentration of Cherokee people.

FLORIDA

SCALE
1 : 4,500,000

0   50   100   150
statute miles

0   50   100   150
kilometers

Map Key

Approximate regional boundary
(See pages 20–21 for North American
map showing all eight regions
depicted in this work.)

Federal Indian Reservation
(occupied by one or more tribal entities)

Federally designated tribal entity
with no land holding

Big Cypress   Federal Reservation name

277   Resident tribe
(Number correlates to tribal list
on pages 290–293.)

★   State capital

•   Selected city or town

---

completely dashed when the U.S. government passed the Indian Removal Act in 1830, paving the way for relocation to Oklahoma.

STRATEGIES OF RESISTANCE: PRE-REMOVAL CONFLICT

While most of the tribes in the region tried to accommodate European powers and the new American nation by adapting their political systems, economies, and culture, that strategy was not followed everywhere all the time. Some of the most famous Indian

The Miccosukee fared a little better than many other tribes in Florida, surviving diseases and invaders and holding on to reduced but important chunks of their homeland.

wars happened in the Southeast, including the Red Stick War, the Seminole Wars, and others.

Some tribes, like the Creek, embraced change and accommodation at first. But eventually many of the Upper Creek became disillusioned with the strategy because no matter how much the people changed and no matter how much land was given, the settlers always came asking for more. When the Shawnee leader Tecumseh came to them in 1811, with a comet blazing in the sky above him, promising change if they resisted the United States, the Creek were listening. And when he promised them a sign and the New Madrid earthquake shook their villages, they responded. Tragedy ensued as the Lower Creek maintained allegiance to the United States while the Upper Creek allied with Tecumseh and the British. It was a civil war among the tribe, and many people died. At Fort Mims in present-day Alabama in 1813, the Upper Creek, also known as the Red Stick, overran the Lower Creek and U.S. garrison, killing more than 500 people. There was retributive warfare afterward, and most of the Red Stick fled to Florida and joined the Seminole, tripling that tribe's population and fighting on for their freedom, land, and way of life.

The Seminole fought longer than any other tribe in the Southeast, from 1817 until 1858. The Seminole were changing quickly. Unlike most tribes in the Southeast, they had repudiated slavery and offered safe refuge to runaway slaves. When the Seminole were attacked by the U.S. government, the escaped black slaves, Red Stick Creek, and Seminole fought side by side to protect tribal lands and lifeways.

Some Seminole bands successfully outfought and outlasted the U.S. Army campaign, but most were forcibly relocated to Oklahoma. At the Treaty of Payne's Landing in 1832, a small group surrendered and relocated to Oklahoma; the U.S. government viewed that treaty as representing the entire Seminole population, even though most chiefs had never seen it. Osceola and others fought on until that chief's death in 1837. Again the Seminole fought on, and again another group surrendered in 1842. Whittled down and constantly harassed and harried, the Seminole quit fighting in 1858. Most had moved to Oklahoma by then. The remnant population in Florida hid in the swamps and isolated areas, and their status as legitimate residents was contested by the government until the middle of the 20th century.

Some of the smaller tribes that had suffered so much during the slave-raiding era now found themselves in a somewhat more advantageous position with regard to removal. They had been overlooked by the Army. Hiding out or living quietly, they lost most of their land, too, but some were able to hang on in the Southeast instead of marching on one of the trails of tears. Whether the strategy was accommodation or war, the tribes of the Southeast were not going

Billy Bowlegs was one of the last Seminole leaders to surrender. Seminole chief Wild Cat helped the U.S. persuade Bowlegs to surrender at the end of the Third Seminole War. He relocated to Oklahoma with 123 followers.

to keep their land, and removal engulfed most of them—with a few notable exceptions.

STRATEGIES OF RESISTANCE: POST-REMOVAL

The famous Trail of Tears was really numerous trails of tears, and the majority of the tribal population in the Southeast was relocated to Indian Territory (Oklahoma), with numerous casualties and heartrending injustice. Forging a path ahead would take time and often different approaches.

Major Ridge was an accomplished but controversial Cherokee diplomat. Ridge led Cherokee warriors in an alliance with American troops under Gen. Andrew Jackson's command against the traditionalist Red Stick Creek in 1814. He also led Cherokee warriors with Jackson against the Seminole in 1818. Ridge was made a chief at age 21 and, along with Charles Hicks and James Vann, advocated for close ties to the U.S. Ridge was well rewarded for his actions within the Cherokee Nation and by the U.S. He was wealthier than most rich white plantation owners in the South.

This Choctaw basket exemplifies typical Southeast style—tight fiber weaving, intricate artistic design, and highly practical for everyday use.

When pressure mounted for the Cherokee to sell all of their lands and relocate to Oklahoma, the tribe was deeply divided. Most refused to move, felt betrayed by the request, and even boycotted the negotiations. But Ridge strongly felt that the people would be killed and stripped of any land if he did not negotiate for a new home. He signed the Treaty of New Echota in 1835, knowing it would alienate and infuriate many of his people.

Ridge moved to Oklahoma in 1837 ahead of the main Cherokee move in the Trail of Tears. Two years later, Ridge, his son, and his nephew were assassinated under ancient Cherokee blood law, whereby an entire family could be held accountable for one person's wrongdoing. Ridge's sale of the land was a capital offense according to Cherokee law. Reprisals went back and forth for decades in Oklahoma after the assassination. It was a painful time.

Some tribes, like the Miccosukee and Florida Seminole, chose isolation. They avoided whites, hid in remote areas, and carried on their language, culture, and ways of survival. It wasn't until after World War II that they felt safe emerging from isolation and forged new governments with recognition and funding from the U.S. government.

The lower Mississippi River Valley sustained a dense tribal population. Disease thinned the numbers there after the Hernando de Soto expedition, but the Choctaw in present-day Mississippi rebounded until the American colonial period. Today, they still have several communities on their Mississippi reservation. Other tribes in the Delta region survived and adapted, as well.

Most tribes sought to engage the non-Native governments around them. Many sided with the Confederacy during the Civil War, hoping that allegiance would generate fair treatment for them in a new nation. Some tribes split their loyalties, and divisions were sometimes tragic. They went on to work within the evolving legal system in Oklahoma and the federal government to reassert self-governance, control of their land, and revitalization of their languages.

Another strategy was employed by some of the Indians in the Southeast, reminiscent of the Métis community in the Northeast and northern Plains. Many Indians from Southeast tribes had acquired U.S. citizenship via treaty. Many more had married white settlers. Some had moved out of tribal lands long before removal, forming separate tribal enclaves across the South or living in predominantly non-Native communities. When most of the Indians in the Southeast were being moved to Oklahoma and some were fighting the U.S. Army, these people simply stayed where they were. They didn't fight and they didn't move. Some maintained distinct tribal enclaves, a number of which were later recognized by the federal or state government, others not recognized by anyone but themselves. Some melded into the general non-Native population.

Regardless of the strategies used to survive the colonial era, relocation, and its aftermath, the tribes of the Southeast persevered. They did what their forebears did throughout time: they built communities and nations. Even today, that incredible effort continues. ✈

Seminole Indians spearing fish in the Florida Everglades. The Seminole are one of the most financially successful tribes, owning and operating businesses such as Hard Rock restaurants and casinos. But they have never forgotten the land, water, and lifeways that sustained their ancestors.

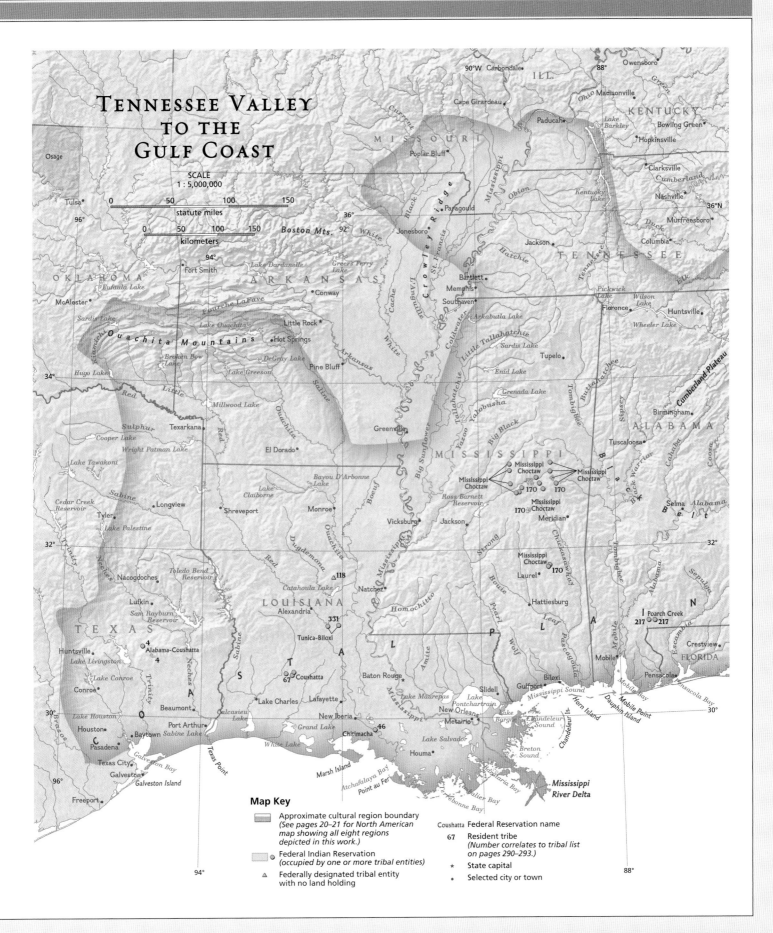

TENNESSEE VALLEY TO THE GULF COAST

SCALE
1 : 5,000,000

0   50   100   150
statute miles

0   50   100   150
kilometers

Map Key

Approximate cultural region boundary
(See pages 20–21 for North American
map showing all eight regions
depicted in this work.)

Federal Indian Reservation
(occupied by one or more tribal entities)

Federally designated tribal entity
with no land holding

Coushatta   Federal Reservation name

67   Resident tribe
(Number correlates to tribal list
on pages 290–293.)

★   State capital

•   Selected city or town

MOUNDVILLE
Mississippian Political and Cultural Center

From the 9th to 16th centuries, Indians in the Southeast built numerous large villages and small cities, dominated by massive earthen mounds that served political, social, and ceremonial functions. Scholars have called this society the Mississippian culture, and it gave birth to most of the tribal peoples of the Southeast. In the heart of the Mississippian region, Indians built Moundville in present-day Alabama, and it soon became one of the most important cities in the entire area.

Moundville was the second largest Mississippian urban center ever built, with only Cahokia (Illinois) its rival. The site covered more than 300 acres and included large wooden palisade walls and numerous mounds for political and social purposes that reinforced a highly evolved clan-based hierarchy. More than 1,000 people lived within the walled section of the city and another 10,000 in the immediately surrounding area. They thrived on corn agriculture and trade. Recent archaeological excavations have uncovered numerous precious metals, shells, pots, statues, and works of art.

Moundville swelled with residents and visitors for five centuries, longer than any city founded by European immigrants in America. The community found a way to sustainably harvest enough corn, wood, and game to maintain that population density—a remarkable accomplishment. Climate changes eventually pressured the sustainability of corn production at the same yield, and the population was forced to disperse, almost 100 years before the arrival of the first Spanish explorers in the region. Yet the ideas, knowledge, and culture of the great moundbuilders were sustained in the new tribal populations of the Southeast encountered by the Hernando de Soto expedition in 1540–41.

De Soto's expedition brought terrible disease outbreaks that dramatically reduced tribal numbers, and the moundbuilding era came to a close as the remaining members of the tribal population focused on survival and rebuilding. Today, Moundville is the site of a major archaeological excavation, museum, and cultural center. Two large mounds and several smaller ones and funerary sites have been excavated and cleared. Much of the material is presented in the museum, although the original site and mounds are impressive in their natural splendor. ∎

At Moundville, Indians from many Mississippian tribes converged for trade, diplomacy, ceremony, and the arts (above). It was a pre-Columbian metropolis (artist's rendering, left), and the mounds there served ceremonial, funerary, and political needs. Continuing major excavations that began in 1955 unearthed this cup (top) and many other artifacts, which encouraged political and social support for a new museum and cultural center.

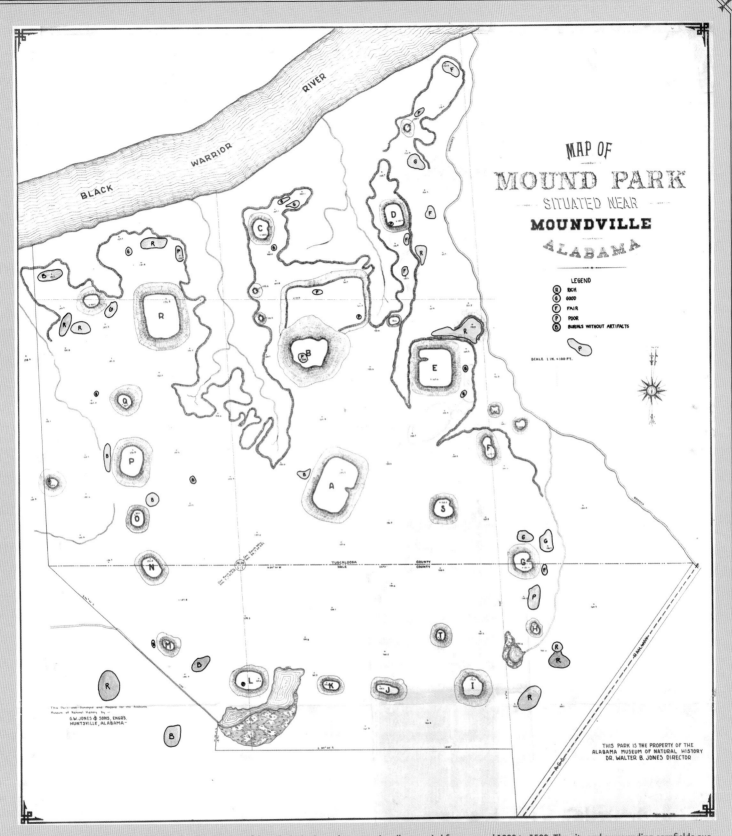

MAP OF
MOUND PARK
SITUATED NEAR
MOUNDVILLE
ALABAMA

LEGEND
R RICH
G GOOD
F FAIR
P POOR
B BURIALS WITHOUT ARTIFACTS

SCALE 1 IN. = 100 FT.

THIS PARK IS THE PROPERTY OF THE
ALABAMA MUSEUM OF NATURAL HISTORY
DR. WALTER B. JONES DIRECTOR

MOUNDVILLE, ALABAMA, is the site of a major center of the Mississippian culture, continually occupied from around 1000 to 1500. The city and surrounding cornfields sustained a population of about 10,000 people. The mounds themselves were political, social, and ceremonial in design and purpose, reinforcing the social and political hierarchy. Climate change reduced food production, and the population dispersed between 1450 and 1500. The culture continued in the rapidly evolving tribal groups of the Southeast, but disease pandemics and population decline after European contact ended moundbuilding. This site map for Moundville shows the locations of primary mounds, structures, and burial sites. The original site stretched more than 300 acres, and only a portion of it has been excavated.

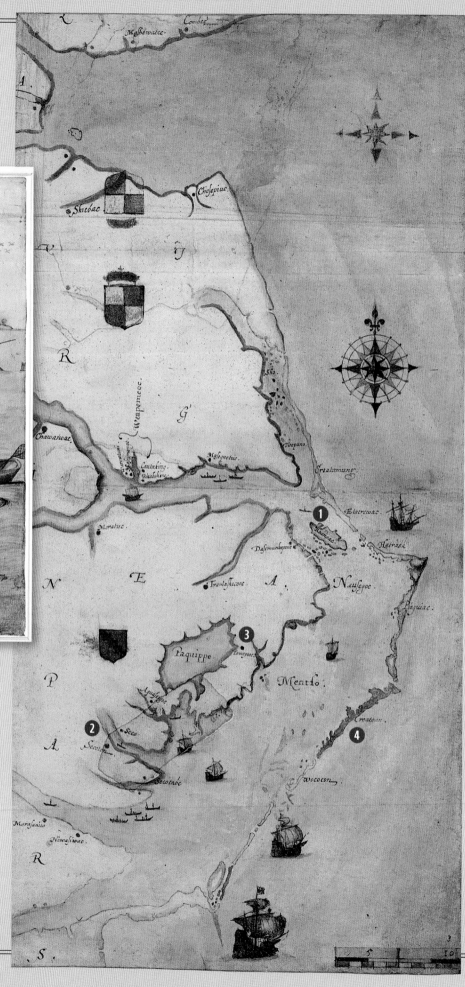

CAROLINA INDIANS actively harvested fish, especially in the summer when winter corn supplies ran out and the new harvest was not yet ripe. The Outer Banks protected a sheltered coastline where the Secotan and their neighbors could safely use nets, traps, spears, and hook fishing to sustain a large population (above). Wooden dugout canoes, often more than 35 feet long, dominated the water scene, as evidenced by a number that were found intact in later archaeological digs. Both the Spanish and British relied on the indigenous population to provide all of their food in the initial years of colonization. If the land had been vacant, neither European power could have survived. This watercolor map (right) shows the east coast of North America from the Chesapeake Bay in Delaware, Maryland, and Virginia to Cape Lookout in North Carolina. Elizabethan gentleman and artist John White, working with Walter Raleigh, produced the map between 1585 and 1593 as Raleigh attempted to establish a colony in the New World.

THE SECOTAN AND THE LOST COLONY
England's First Settlement in the Americas

Dispatched to the Americas by Sir Walter Raleigh in 1584, Philip Amadas and Arthur Barlowe were the first British explorers in the Carolinas. Based on their writings and maps, the British embarked on two major attempts to establish a colony in what was named Virginia, an area later separated into the modern states of Virginia, North Carolina, and South Carolina. In the first of these, the very next year, Ralph Lane established a colony at Roanoke Island ❶, but the attempt was a total disaster. Although the Secotan Indians, who had two large villages called Secotan ❷ and Pomeyooc (Pomeiooc) ❸ agreed to the British presence, the newcomers had little to offer in trade and made little diplomatic effort to establish a mutually beneficial relationship. Desperate for supplies and unable to fish or farm self-sufficiently, the British settlement was abandoned when Sir Francis Drake arrived, and all settlers went back to England.

John White led another settlement attempt at Roanoke in 1587. Like his predecessors, White was unable to make the colony self-sufficient, forcing him to make a three-month supply run to England that ended up taking three years. Upon his return, White found the word "Croatoan" (possibly for Croatoan Island) carved into a tree, a likely attempt by the settlers to communicate their destination when foraging for supplies ❹. None of the settlers survived, and no further details of their demise have emerged, earning that settlement the name the "Lost Colony."

White's drawings, paintings, and writings about the Secotan were engraved by Theodore de Bry and printed in four languages. They helped fuel the public and government push for British colonization. The Secotan were happy to trade with the British, not only because metal implements were highly practical and new but also because the Secotan had been involved in a long, brutal war with their Native neighbors, the Neiosioke. Trade with the British raised their standard of living and armed them like their enemies who traded with the Spanish. Although it took decades for the British to establish their later colony at Jamestown, the tribal–white relationship in Virginia and Carolina quickly deteriorated. When the British crushed the Powhatan resistance in Virginia, they turned on the Secotan in Carolina, and the tribe was so depopulated from disease and warfare that most of the people fled west to avoid the British. ∎

The Secotan depended on corn agriculture, fishing, and hunting to sustain their population. They actively traded and allied with the British in an effort not only to keep peace but also to gain access to European weapons and trade goods. They were engaged in a long-standing war with their neighbors to the west, the Neiosioke, who traded with the Spanish on a regular basis. Their village at Pomeyooc (Pomeiooc) was fortified by a large palisade to protect it from enemy attacks. A common council fire was kept in the center of the village and served as a political and social focal point, although each lodge had its own fire for heat and cooking.

THE FIVE CIVILIZED TRIBES

Culture in Motion, 1757

The Five Civilized Tribes were the Cherokee ❶, Chickasaw ❷, Choctaw ❸, Creek ❹, and Seminole ❺. The British and early American settlers called them "civilized" because they adopted European clothes, farming tools, and housing and because, in spite of some conflict during the early contact period, they maintained friendly relations with their white neighbors. Some owned black slaves and developed large forced-labor plantations. Benjamin Hawkins and others were appointed by the U.S. government to advance the civilization of the tribes, and their involvement was welcomed. In addition to the government agents, missionaries swarmed the tribes, sometimes competing over conversion territory.

The tribes saw the benefits of technological advancement in medicine, commerce, and war. They intentionally evolved their political structures to develop more European-style representative governance and formal processes. The Cherokee in particular used written law and documentation to further develop their politics and economy. The tribes believed that their accommodations would earn them acceptance by whites and enable them to stay in their homelands. The tribes never surrendered their tribal identities or their tribal nationhood, but sought simply to peacefully coexist with whites and prosper.

That hope was dashed when Andrew Jackson became President of the United States and actively sought to dispossess and relocate the tribes so white settlers could control the land. It was a bitter betrayal that divided the tribes from their non-Native neighbors and often divided the tribes internally as well. Many people advocated for continued peace and accommodation, but others felt that the betrayal was unforgivable and bound to impoverish and disempower them. The government resorted to force to get the land from the Indians, and tribes were relocated west of the Mississippi. The consequences were tragic. ■

The Seminole, like the men pictured here, had a slightly different perspective than the other members of the Five Civilized Tribes. They initially embraced policies of accommodation like the Creek, adopting European clothing and technologies. But when Benjamin Hawkins came to show the Creek how to farm European style, the Seminole were less interested in economic or political acculturation.

Chickasaw children in European-manufactured textile clothing. The Chickasaw, like other members of the Five Civilized Tribes, actively adopted many European technologies, clothes, and ideas, yet without subordinating their tribal identity or sovereignty as a Native nation.

THE CHOCTAW were considered one of the Five Civilized Tribes because of their willingness to acculturate and adapt to the new economy in the Southeast. The Choctaw were an especially numerous and proud people, and their accommodations to change came on their own terms. Tribal members were happy to use thatch-covered lodges and live as their ancestors had for centuries, but in order to increase their standard of living, safety, and ease of life with European tools and dwellings, they made careful choices. As a result, today the Choctaw still maintain a vibrant culture and living language.

THE TRAIL OF TEARS
The Cherokee Nation During the Removal Era

One at a time, the U.S. government isolated, pressured, negotiated, and if necessary fought the Five Civilized Tribes to acquire their land and assets. After the Indian Removal Act of 1830, the government set aside land for each tribe in present-day Oklahoma ❶. They called the removal location Indian Territory because it was the intent of those who devised the policy to concentrate all Native Americans there.

The Cherokee were the largest of the five tribes and also the most acculturated and prosperous. They made many accommodations to the government, ceding land numerous times to make room for white settlers and keep peace with them. The Cherokee fought alongside Andrew Jackson when he led U.S. troops against Red Stick Creek in 1814 and then against the Seminole in 1818. Many Cherokee had adopted European ideas and technologies, converted to Christianity, or intermarried with whites. Still, they had prime agricultural land in the heart of the South, and white settlers, plantation owners, and government officials wanted all of it.

After the federal government relocated most of the Choctaw—at a terrible cost in lives and livelihood to the tribe—it began to focus on moving the Cherokee. Some Cherokee chiefs, including Major Ridge, were willing to accept terms for immediate removal if the new land was suitable and the price was fair. But John Ross and other Cherokee leaders questioned the terms and the timing. The tribal government was so divided that factions began separate negotiations with the U.S. government. Ridge and others signed the Treaty of New Echota in 1835, granting the land and relocation terms requested by the Americans. Ross continued to oppose this treaty, even acquiring 15,000 Cherokee signatures on a petition protesting its terms and the manner of the negotiation. In spite of these objections, Ross could not persuade the U.S. Senate to nullify the treaty. It was ratified by a one-vote margin, and the Cherokee were forced to move. Cherokee plantations were given to white settlers in a lottery. Those who resisted evacuation were killed.

The main body of the Cherokee population was

This 1830s drawing of Andrew Jackson, who removed many Indians from the Southeast, mocked his professed compassion for Indians as the paternalistic "Great White Father."

In spite of bitter divisions among the Cherokee leadership about terms for land sale and removal of the Cherokee Nation to Oklahoma, John Ridge, Charles Hicks, James Vann, and some of the other Cherokee chiefs agreed to sign the Treaty of New Echota in 1835, which set terms for the sale of Cherokee land, establishment of a new reservation in Indian Territory, and relocation of the tribal population.

The count[...]
and that v[...]
was by th[...]
given to [...]

—WILLIAM M[...]
WAS CREEK AN[...]

American painter Robert Lindneux's "The Trail of Tears," created in 1942, was one of his most famous paintings. In it, the Cherokee move west by horse and covered wagon, bundled against the winter cold.

MAP

SHOWING THE LANDS

Ioways

assigned to

EMIGRANT INDIANS

WEST OF

ARKANSAS & MISSOURI

Camanches of Red River

Scale of 60 miles to 1 inch

The Trail of Tears

- Cherokee lands ceded with Treaty of New Echota
- ← Land route
- ← Water route

0   100 miles

Map shows boundaries of 1839.

TRAILS OF TEARS The Cherokee removal did not follow a single path west; there were at least three major routes from the Cherokee Nation. Many were forced into a concentration camp in Tennessee before marching the thousand miles west. In Illinois, at Berry's Ferry, the Cherokee were charged a dollar each to be ferried across the river instead of the normal rate of 12 cents. Most of the Cherokee removals converged at Tahlequah, Oklahoma, and started the painful process of rebuilding in Indian Territory.

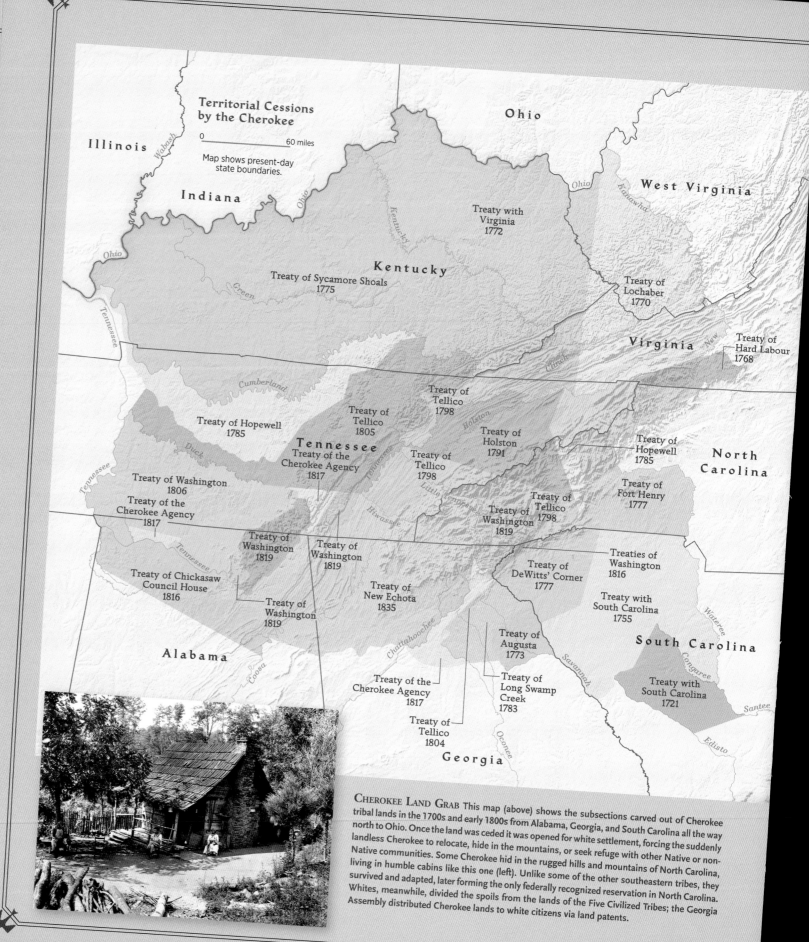

Territorial Cessions by the Cherokee

0 ——— 60 miles

Map shows present-day state boundaries.

Illinois

Indiana

Ohio

Kentucky

West Virginia

Treaty with Virginia 1772

Treaty of Lochaber 1770

Treaty of Sycamore Shoals 1775

Treaty of Hard Labour 1768

Virginia

Treaty of Hopewell 1785

Treaty of Tellico 1798

Treaty of Tellico 1805

Treaty of Holston 1791

Treaty of Hopewell 1785

Tennessee

Treaty of the Cherokee Agency 1817

Treaty of Tellico 1798

Treaty of Fort Henry 1777

North Carolina

Treaty of Washington 1806

Treaty of the Cherokee Agency 1817

Treaty of Tellico 1798

Treaty of Washington 1819

Treaty of Washington 1819

Treaty of Washington 1819

Treaties of Washington 1816

Treaty of DeWitts' Corner 1777

Treaty of Chickasaw Council House 1816

Treaty of Washington 1819

Treaty of New Echota 1835

Treaty with South Carolina 1755

South Carolina

Alabama

Treaty of Augusta 1773

Treaty with South Carolina 1721

Treaty of the Cherokee Agency 1817

Treaty of Long Swamp Creek 1783

Treaty of Tellico 1804

Georgia

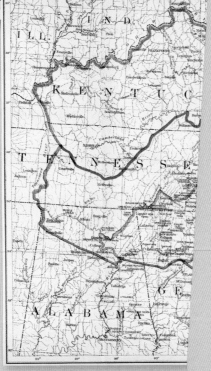

CHEROKEE LAND GRAB This map (above) shows the subsections carved out of Cherokee tribal lands in the 1700s and early 1800s from Alabama, Georgia, and South Carolina all the way north to Ohio. Once the land was ceded it was opened for white settlement, forcing the suddenly landless Cherokee to relocate, hide in the mountains, or seek refuge with other Native or non-Native communities. Some Cherokee hid in the rugged hills and mountains of North Carolina, living in humble cabins like this one (left). Unlike some of the other southeastern tribes, they survived and adapted, later forming the only federally recognized reservation in North Carolina. Whites, meanwhile, divided the spoils from the lands of the Five Civilized Tribes; the Georgia Assembly distributed Cherokee lands to white citizens via land patents.

The Seminole attack a U.S. Marine Corps supply train in Florida in an 1812 painting. Most of the tribes in the Southeast used strategies of accommodation, diplomacy, and voluntary acculturation to protect their nationhood, lands, and families. However, that did not save them or their lands from plunder by the government and their white neighbors. The Red Stick Creek and the Seminole fought to protect themselves.

· SOUTHEAST ·

LAND GRABS AND RESISTANCE
Accommodation and War in the Southeast

Most of the tribes in the Southeast tried to accommodate the British and then U.S. governments by adopting European economic and cultural trappings. In the end, the tribes were dispossessed and relocated, one treaty at a time. Some stayed on tiny fragments of their original land, but most ended up in Oklahoma.

Some tribes resisted. In the early 1800s, the Creek descended into civil war. Many of the traditionalist Red Stick Creek, who no longer wanted peaceful accommodation, joined the Florida Seminole in 1814, tripling the Seminole population. The U.S. government was intent on dispossessing the Red Stick, and Gen. Andrew Jackson led a large force of U.S. soldiers, White Stick Creek, and allied Cherokee to attack the Red Stick Creek and Seminole in Florida in 1817. The campaign solidified U.S. control over eastern Florida, but the Seminole protected most of their territory. In 1821, the U.S. assumed control over Florida from the Spanish by treaty, even though the Seminole were the sovereign rulers of much of the state and had never been consulted.

The Seminole harbored runaway slaves, and many whites felt that the Indians undermined the institution of slavery and wanted

Chief Billy Bowlegs

the Seminole to be taught a lesson. That set the stage for renewed conflict. In 1832, a few of the Seminole chiefs, such as Billy Bowlegs, agreed to the Treaty of Payne's Landing, which included terms for a massive land cession and removal to Oklahoma. Most of the Seminole leadership did not participate in the treaty. Nevertheless, the U.S. Army came in 1835, intent on seeing all the Seminole relocated.

Seminole chief Osceola rallied a fierce resistance. There were about 4,000 Seminole and several hundred allied black runaway slaves who mustered a force of around 1,000–1,500 warriors against a professional army of 9,000 troops. In spite of the overwhelming odds, for two years the Seminole harassed, harried, and raided their white pursuers and thus successfully protected their families while avoiding a head-on battle. When Osceola came to parley under a flag of truce in 1837, he was captured and imprisoned. The chief died in prison and was afterward decapitated and his body put on display. By 1842, most of the fighting was over. A group of 3,800 Seminole were forcibly relocated to Indian Territory, as were others who were captured or surrendered later. Only a fraction stayed on in Florida. ■

TRIBES OF THE SOUTHEAST

As the great Mississippian moundbuilding culture collapsed from devastating disease pandemics in the 16th century, new tribes coalesced and evolved in the Southeast. Following are brief histories of select tribes of the region.

■ BILOXI

Current Locations: Louisiana
Language Family: Siouan

The Biloxi are indigenous to southern Mississippi, Louisiana, and Texas. Although they first encountered Europeans in 1699, later than most tribes in the Southeast, the Biloxi were indelibly affected by European contact without ever seeing a white man because other tribes inadvertently brought the pandemics to the Biloxi.

The Biloxi were sedentary farmers who hunted deer, bear, and buffalo to augment their diet, accumulating large food supplies. Disease and raids weakened the tribe. The similarly depopulated Tunica and some isolated groups of Caddo and Choctaw united with the Biloxi for mutual protection and social cohesion even though they were from different language and cultural backgrounds. In 1981, they were formally recognized by the U.S. government as the Tunica-Biloxi Tribe of Louisiana.

■ CATAWBA

Current Locations: South Carolina
Language Family: Siouan

The Catawba are a small tribe, with an estimated precontact population of only about 5,000. The Catawba moved around quite a bit because their small numbers and exclusion from alliances with their larger neighbors left them quite vulnerable to attack. When Europeans arrived in the Southeast, the Catawba had several villages near the present-day border of North and South Carolina.

The Catawba entered into a number of treaties with the British, who eventually established a reservation for them in 1763. The state of South Carolina acquired the Catawba land in 1840 through a state treaty.

Older ways gave way to an assimilated lifestyle, Christian religion, and lots of intermarriage with white and black neighbors. The Catawba population fell as low as 200, and the tribal language died out entirely. Many joined the Mormon Church, and a significant number relocated to Utah. The Catawba are the only federally recognized tribe in South Carolina.

■ CHEROKEE

Current Locations: North Carolina, Oklahoma
Language Family: Iroquoian

The Cherokee are one of the only Iroquoian-speaking tribes of the Southeast. Most scholars and tribal elders agree that the Cherokee came to the Southeast from the Great Lakes, where conflict among tribes threatened their vitality. The Cherokee settled in a huge swath of territory that included parts of present-day Alabama, Georgia, Kentucky, North and South Carolina, Tennessee, Virginia, and West Virginia. There were almost 70 independent Cherokee towns, each with its own leaders but united not just by common language

This Calusa cat–man figurine was made around 1000. The Calusa were an independent tribe in central Florida, decimated by disease and warfare and later absorbed by the Seminole.

and culture but also by a diplomatic process that enabled the people to work together for their common defense and betterment. Other tribes frequently tested Cherokee power, and the Cherokee had intermittent and sometimes intense conflict with the Creek, Delaware, Shawnee, and other tribes. A smallpox epidemic in 1738–39 killed more than half of the population.

Through several treaties, the Cherokee agreed to accommodate white settlers, accepting payment for land and maintaining peace with Europeans most of the time. The Cherokee openly embraced many European technologies and ideas. They formed a modern government, evolving their matrilineal clan-based system into a representative council. They employed European farming techniques, and when the British slave trade expanded to Cherokee country, they accepted and participated in the slave trade as plantation and slave owners. The Cherokee were one of the first tribal groups to acquire U.S. citizenship in large numbers, enabled by a treaty provision in 1817, more than 100 years before most Indians were afforded citizenship through the Indian Citizenship Act in 1924. Because of the acculturation the Cherokee were willing to accept, they and their immediate neighbors the Chickasaw, Choctaw, Creek, and Seminole were called the Five Civilized Tribes.

The Cherokee controlled a diminished but still impressive territory in the heart of the Southeast. Eventually the U.S. government wanted it all, and passed the Indian Removal Act in 1830. The Cherokee story was especially heartbreaking, culminating in the Trail of Tears. Most Cherokee went on the forced march to Oklahoma, where they formed the Cherokee Nation. The United Keetoowah Band of Cherokee also resides in Oklahoma, primarily composed of Cherokee who moved to Arkansas or Oklahoma ahead of the Trail of Tears. The Eastern Band of Cherokee, primarily composed of those who withdrew from the Cherokee Nation before removal, still lives in North Carolina.

CHITIMACHA

Current Locations: Louisiana
Language Family: Isolate

The Chitimacha are a language isolate, unrelated linguistically to other tribes in the Southeast. The tribe has inhabited the Mississippi Delta region of Louisiana for at least 2,000 years. Prior to European contact, the Chitimacha had 15 major villages in four distinct groups with a total population of around 20,000. Among the cultural distinctions of the tribe were the customs of body tattooing and head flattening.

The Chitimacha were devastated by diseases brought by Europeans. The expansion of the slave trade in the South then brought other tribes such as the Creek to Chitimacha territory on slave raids for the British. Many Chitimacha intermarried with French colonists, converted to Catholicism, and lost their language and culture. By 1917, the tribe was largely landless, and the population was reduced to 51 at its nadir. The tribe has been rebuilding and now numbers 720.

CHOCTAW

Current Locations: Mississippi, Oklahoma
Language Family: Muscogean

The Choctaw are descended from the great Hopewell and Mississippian mound-building cultures. In the 17th century, the Choctaw coalesced from many different Muscogean groups. They covered a territory that included much of present-day Alabama and Mississippi and parts of neighboring states. The tribe had three distinct regions (east, west, and south), each with its own leadership structures and chiefs.

In 1786, a peace and friendship treaty between the Choctaw and the United

This Karl Bodmer painting from 1833 shows the temporary lean-to dwellings of a typical Choctaw camp. The Choctaw were sedentary farmers but took periodic extended trips to gather and hunt.

States inspired the Choctaw to adopt a number of American diplomats and perform elaborate ceremonies. Even as the government thereafter betrayed Choctaw loyalty with repeated land cessions and removal, the Choctaw never went to war with the United States.

Major land cessions in 1820 and again in 1825 did not satisfy white land hunger. In 1830, at the Treaty of Dancing Rabbit Creek, the Choctaw sold 11 million acres of land to the U.S. and agreed to relocation to Oklahoma. It was the single largest land cession from an Indian tribe that had never fought the U.S. in a war. Around 5,000 Choctaw stayed in Mississippi. The remaining 15,000 Choctaw were forcibly relocated on the first Trail of Tears in 1831–33; more than 2,500 people died on the trip.

The Choctaw Nation of Oklahoma endured land allotment and political maneuvers to divest them of their new lands. The Mississippi Band of Choctaw Indians was largely ignored by the government for generations except for continued pressure on relocation. Choctaw from both reservations served as the first U.S. Army experiments in "code talking" with the use

of tribal languages to communicate military intelligence. Tribal language revitalization has been a top priority for the Mississippi Choctaw in particular, and it has been having marked success in recent years.

COUSHATTA

Current Locations: Louisiana, Oklahoma, Texas
Language Family: Muscogean

The Coushatta are closely related to the Creek. They originally had villages along the Tennessee River Valley in Alabama, but moved south into Georgia and spread out through Alabama prior to European contact. The Coushatta were on friendly terms with their Creek cousins and were part of the Creek alliance for many years, but throughout much of the early contact period they were not under Creek protection. Eventually, the tribe shifted west into Mississippi, Louisiana, and Texas to avoid both the European conflict and the Creek civil war.

Today, the Coushatta have three small reservations. The Coushatta Tribe of Louisiana and the Alabama-Coushatta Tribe of Texas are independent reservations. The Alabama-Quassarte Tribal Town in Oklahoma is a recognized independent tribal entity that has dual membership with the Muscogee Creek Nation.

■ CREEK (MUSCOGEE)

Current Locations: Alabama, Oklahoma
Language Family: Muscogean

The Creek are one of the largest tribes in the Muscogean language family. At the height of the Mississippian culture, the ancestors of the Creek united the Mississippi River Valley and Southeast in a network of powerful confederacies and chiefdoms, building Cahokia and other great urban centers. The Mississippian culture imploded after contact with Europeans, not because of warfare but because of disease.

More than 20 loosely related groups of survivors regrouped in Tennessee, Georgia, and Alabama, forming the Creek or Muscogee people. Each Creek town has its own leaders, but they often coordinated diplomatic and military efforts.

Although the Creek did their best to play the French, Spanish, and British off against one another and actively traded with all of them in the 1700s, their efforts at neutrality were constantly tested. The Creek were selling 50,000 deerskins every year out of Savannah alone. The trade proved profitable and transformed the Creek from farmers to increasingly diverse specialists in various aspects of trade, harvest, and diplomacy.

The Creek made accommodations to American independence after the Revolution and willingly accepted Benjamin Hawkins, who was appointed by George Washington to "civilize" the Creek. The tribe began to adopt European technologies and ideas, even embracing the plantation economy.

Creek allegiances shifted when the Shawnee chief Tecumseh sought their alliance in 1811 against the Americans. Tecumseh had been chased out by the Choctaw. But when he came to Creek lands, a comet blazed in the night sky, and because Tecumseh's name meant Shooting Star, many took it as a spiritual sign. A large group of traditionalist Creek who had misgivings about the pace of cultural change in their land pledged support to Tecumseh. They called themselves the Red Stick.

Most of the Red Stick came from the Upper Creek towns, and they were immediately opposed by the White Stick from the Lower Creek towns. A brutal civil war erupted. The Red Stick War mainly

A woven beaded belt with tassels made by Creek Indians in about 1820

took place in 1813–14 and included a major Red Stick victory at Fort Mims. But Andrew Jackson led a large force of U.S. Army troops against them, supported by the Lower Creek and the Cherokee, which crushed the Red Stick in 1814. The Treaty of Fort Jackson forced the Creek to sell 20 million acres of land—more than half the Creek territory, including most of present-day Alabama. Many of the Red Stick fled south and joined their Seminole cousins, tripling the size of that tribe.

A treaty in 1825 sold most of the remaining Creek land. The terms were so unfair that President John Quincy Adams nullified the treaty and negotiated a new one in 1826 with provisions that the Creek did not have to relocate. But there was pressure on the government not to honor the renegotiated treaty. The Indian Removal Act of 1830 forced relocation of many tribes. Another treaty in 1832 established the process for Creek removal to Indian Territory in Oklahoma. It was the 20th major land cession treaty signed by the Creek.

Today, the Muscogee Nation of Oklahoma is home to most of the recognized Creek. There are three recognized tribal towns in Oklahoma with significant Creek populations—the Alabama-Quassarte, Kialegee, and Thlopthlocco. In Alabama, the Poarch Band of Creek Indians gained federal recognition in 1984.

■ MICCOSUKEE

Current Locations: Florida
Language Family: Muscogean

The Miccosukee, descended from the Mississippian moundbuilders, have

John White painted this image of Weroans, one of the principal chiefs at Secotan. White's work was widely published and helped fuel further British exploration and colonization in the region.

a small reservation in Florida. After the Mississippian disintegration, the Miccosukee established homes in the Tennessee Valley region of Georgia, then split into two groups, one moving into the Carolinas and the other into Alabama.

In the 18th century, the Miccosukee were besieged with white encroachment, the growth of the Creek political structure, and the unrest brewing among the tribes and Europeans. Many migrated south into Florida, becoming part of the Seminole group, although their Hitchiti dialect is not mutually intelligible with their Creek and Seminole cousins.

The Miccosukee participated in the resistance to American colonization during the Seminole Wars of 1817–1858. The Miccosukee were one of the most traditional groups of Seminole, long wary of the government and preferring to live as they had since the end of the Seminole Wars without any formalized relationship with the U.S. That changed as the Seminole Tribe of Florida pursued land claims and business development, inspiring the Miccosukee to pursue a new path. They were federally recognized in 1962.

▓ SEMINOLE

Current Locations: Florida, Oklahoma
Language Family: Muscogean

The Seminole are indigenous to present-day Florida. In the 18th century, the Seminole came into being through the arrival of several groups of Muscogean people in northern Florida. Most were Creek, but some were Choctaw. The Seminole were heavily influenced by the deeply agrarian culture of their Mississippian forebears, and even today the Green Corn Dance is one of their most prominent ceremonies.

The Seminole often absorbed runaway tribal slaves and mission Indians from elsewhere in Florida. They even gave refuge to runaway black slaves.

In the early 1800s, the Red Stick War among the Creek resulted in a civil war within that tribe. Many of the traditionalist Red Stick Creek joined the less

The Miccosukee were one of the most tenacious groups in the Southeast. They preserved many traditional lifeways in spite of constant pressure on their land and resources. Pictured here are Miccosukee children fishing.

numerous Seminole in 1814, spurring the U.S. government—who sought to dispossess the Red Stick—to take a mostly unsuccessful military action against the Seminole in 1817. When the U.S. Army tried to relocate the Seminole in 1835, Seminole chief Osceola led a spirited but ultimately failed resistance.

By 1842, most of the fighting was over. A group of 3,800 Seminole were forcibly relocated to Indian Territory. The Oklahoma Seminole are now the Seminole Nation of Oklahoma. Most of the Miccosukee and a small group of Seminole hid out in the Everglades; in 1957, one group got federal recognition and a small reservation as the Seminole Tribe of Florida. The Seminole Tribe of Florida was instrumental in transforming the economic landscape in Indian lands. The tribe opened a high-stakes bingo operation on the reservation, defying Florida state law. In 1981, the tribe won a landmark court case, *Seminole Tribe of Florida* v. *Robert Butterworth,* legitimizing its rights. Within a decade, more than a third of the tribes in the U.S. got into the gaming business, and it changed the economic picture of many tribes and the political trajectory of all.

▓ TUNICA

Current Locations: Louisiana
Language Family: Isolate

The Tunica are a language isolate, in other words, not linguistically related to other tribes in the Southeast. When the Hernando de Soto expedition came through their lands in 1541, the Tunica had more than a dozen large villages in Arkansas and Mississippi. There were intermittent conflicts between the Natchez and the Tunica, but Tunica numbers and strength were sufficient to deter raids or major wars until European diseases ravaged the tribal population. By the 1700s, the Tunica were much more vulnerable to raids and warfare, so the Tunica forged a friendship with the French against the Natchez. It helped for a time.

After the French were forced out of North America, the Tunica moved farther south to isolate their families from Spanish–British conflict. Between tribal warfare, entanglements in European wars, and continued epidemics, they were reduced to a population of hundreds. They bonded with other fragmented communities and survived, gaining federal recognition in 1981 as the Tunica-Biloxi Tribe of Louisiana.

ARCTIC
AND SUBARCTIC

•CHAPTER THREE•

ALEUT (UNANGAN)

ALUTIIQ

ATHABASCAN

CHUGACH

CREE

EYAK

HOLIKACHUK

INNU (MONTAGNAIS-NASKAPI)

INUIT (ESKIMO)

INUPIAT

OJI-CREE (SEVERN OJIBWE AND JAMES BAY CREE)

YUP'IK (ESKIMO)

The Arctic is a vibrant landscape, and it has sustained an amazing breadth of human and animal life. This copperware engraving shows Canadian Inuit with a kayak and igloo.

INDIAN NATIONS OF THE ARCTIC AND SUBARCTIC

The Arctic and subarctic have one of the most forbidding climates on the planet. Temperatures in many places stay subzero for months on end. Daylight is extremely limited in the winter and prolonged in the summer. Across the ice pack and tundra, there isn't an abundance of natural forage for humans. There are no large trees north of the subarctic boreal forest. And yet people have lived there for thousands of years. The Inuit, Athabascan, Algonquian, and other tribal peoples of this region found a way to live in harmony with the harsh environment—sustainable, vibrant life. It's an amazing testament to human fortitude and resourcefulness.

In the far northern reaches of the Arctic, indigenous peoples found a myriad of ways to harvest fish and animals on and through the ice. They hunted whales, seals, birds, and small game. They fished. And they used nearly every part of every animal they took. They manufactured waterproof clothing, built warm lodges and igloos, and domesticated dogs for travel and the transportation of goods.

Just south of the ice pack, thousands of square miles of tundra extend in all directions. Here, too, Native peoples hunted animals, gathered berries and tubers in the summer, and followed huge herds of caribou. South of the tundra there is another major topographical feature: the boreal forest—small trees, brush, and rushing rivers. Indigenous people here hunted, fished for salmon, and enjoyed a more diverse subsistence economy by gathering berries and nuts, hunting big and small game, and trapping furbearing animals.

The climate has changed significantly over time. Around 1350, there was a climatic event called the Little Ice Age, during which it was impossible for whales to traverse the water under the ice pack, forcing the Arctic peoples to adjust their harvests and relocate some villages. Today, the opposite is happening. Climate change is melting the polar pack ice. Although more open water makes access easier in general, the lack of ice has stressed some species such as the polar bear to the point where extinction is a real possibility.

Throughout all of the ecological transformation, there has been human transformation, as well—the arrival of Europeans, significant evolution of the tribal economy, and the relocation of numerous indigenous communities. But in spite of the human and environmental change,

People had to be resourceful to survive. This Inuit man wears a rainproof parka made of walrus intestine. The Inuit also domesticated dogs (above) and used them to travel and transport supplies. Even today, traditional clothing and travel by dogsled persist because they are often the most practical choices.

the peoples and their unique cultures and worldviews have endured.

ARCTIC MIGRATION

In some ways, archaeologists, linguists, and geneticists have produced as many questions as answers about human migrations to North America. But some information is clearer than ever now. We know that the peoples of the Eskimo-Aleut language family come from very different genetic stock than Native Americans who live in the lower 48 states, and those differences are reflected in their DNA and the linguistic underpinnings of their languages. It seems very clear that there were multiple migrations throughout the Americas over many thousands of years. Archaeologists can now confirm dates earlier than ever imagined for Native American habitation of the continent—at least 18,000 years ago and possibly earlier. The Eskimo-Aleut group came more recently, within the past 10,000 years.

Because the Arctic and subarctic areas were far less densely populated than the rest of North America, Eskimo-Aleut peoples and other indigenous peoples of the far north suffered less from the European disease pandemics that ravaged the Indian peoples of the rest of the continent.

Once humans established themselves in the Arctic and subarctic, they did not stay in one place. The Inuit spread out into Greenland and, once established, had sustained contact with Norsemen prior to the Columbus voyages to North America. Eventually, four distinct Eskimo-Aleut languages emerged in Alaska, as well as numerous dialects of Inuit languages. The Athabascan group diversified into a myriad of different tribes and languages across the western subarctic.

LIVING OFF THE LAND

In spite of the remarkably harsh and unrelenting climate, the indigenous people who

---

CHRONOLOGY

1576–78
Martin Frobisher maps Baffin Island; British open Arctic trade and exploration

1713
Peace of Utrecht: France and England delineate their land claims in the Arctic, igniting conflict in the Maritime Provinces

1742
Joseph La France opens trade route to Hudson Bay

1799–1867
Russian-American Company establishes Russian colonies in North America

1886–1909
Robert Peary's Arctic explorations search for the North Pole

1971
Alaska Native Claims Settlement Act establishes corporations to govern oil revenues for Alaskan Natives

1972
Molly Hootch prevails in Tobeluk v. Lind; Alaska forced to allow many Alaskan Natives to attend day schools instead of residential schools

1999
Nunavut created as Canada's largest province, populated by 30,000 Inuit

---

Even today, food remains more abundant in the water than on land throughout most of the Arctic. At Baffin Island, an Inuit hunter waits on an ice floe for ringed seal (opposite). In some regards, tribes in the Arctic and subarctic fared better than many elsewhere in North America due to their geographic isolation. The map on the following page shows the modern-day Native lands across Alaska and Canada. In Alaska, Native communities are referred to as villages, but Natives do not have sovereignty over their land. In Canada, the Native people—known as First Nations—live on reserves.

---

called the Arctic home survived and flourished there by whaling, hunting seals, trapping, and fishing. In the slightly more temperate subarctic, Native resourcefulness extended to gathering and the hunting of caribou, as well. The caribou are the most ubiquitous large game animals in the Arctic and subarctic, with several distinct herds from Alaska to Labrador in the North American Arctic and several smaller herds in Scandinavia and Russia. Caribou are versatile creatures and are able to thrive in both tundra, with its treeless frozen soil, as well as taiga, the environment dominated by coniferous boreal forest. Until habitat loss killed off the herds in Minnesota, northwestern Ontario, and Manitoba, there was a large woodland caribou population, too.

Some caribou herds rarely move. But those that inhabit the most frigid parts of the Arctic undertake some of the world's most incredible mammal migrations. The Porcupine Caribou, named after the Porcupine River in Alaska that dominates their calving grounds, travel 1,500 miles from their winter feeding area to their spring calving grounds—the longest migration of any land animal on the planet. The Gwich'in people (Athabascans) built their lives around the caribou, constructing homes, camps, and villages all along the lengthy migratory route and subsisting almost entirely on caribou. Even today, the caribou are the primary food supply for most Gwich'in.

Caribou are extremely sensitive to human encroachment and habitat loss. The George River Caribou in Quebec and Labrador declined 92 percent, from nearly a million animals to 72,000, primarily because of habitat loss from flooding for hydroelectric projects, the construction of power lines, and road and housing development. The current proposed oil extraction along the North Slope in Alaska is a source of great contention for Alaskan Natives who rely on the

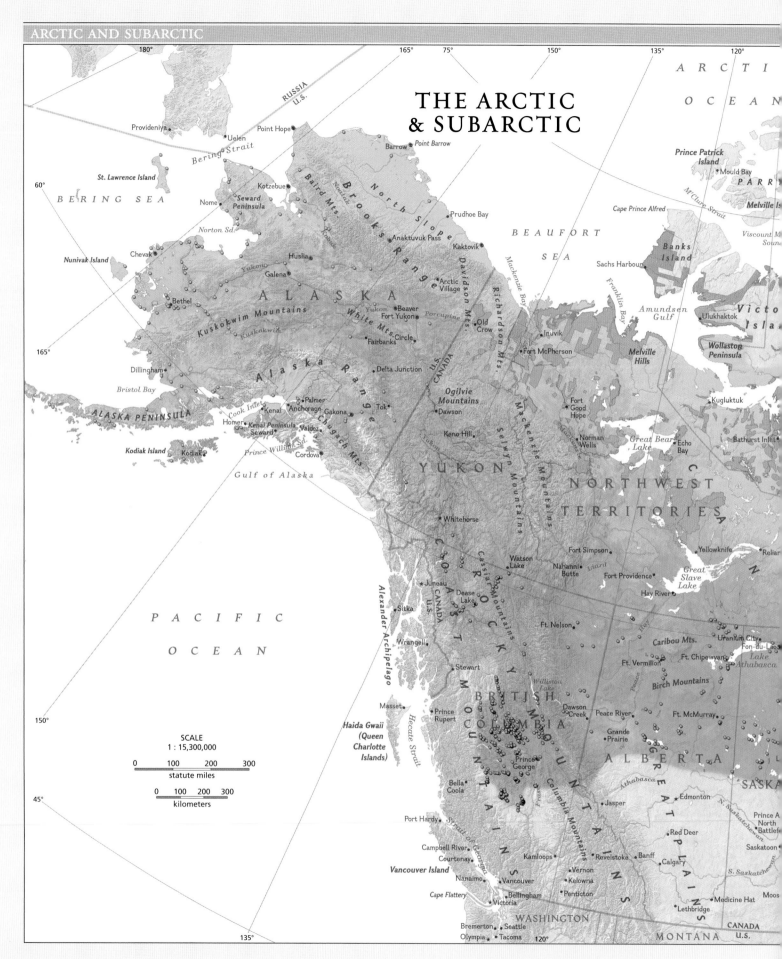

THE ARCTIC & SUBARCTIC

ARCTIC

OCEAN

RUSSIA
U.S.

*Prince Patrick
Island*

• Mould Bay

PARR

*Provid-
eniya*

• Uelen

Point Hope •

Barrow • Point Barrow

McClure Strait

Melville Is

Bering Strait

St. Lawrence Island

Cape Prince Alfred

*Banks
Island*

*Viscount M
Soun*

BEAUFORT

60°

B E R I N G   S E A

Kotzebue •

*Seward
Peninsula*

Nome •

North Slope

Prudhoe Bay •

SEA

Sachs Harbour •

*Amundsen
Gulf*

Ulukhaktok •

*Victo
Isla*

Anaktuvuk Pass •

Kaktovik •

Baird Mts.

Brooks Range

Nunivak Island

Chevak •

Norton Sd.

Davidson Mts.

Huslia •

Yukon

Galena •

*Arctic
Village*

Mackenzie Bay

Inuvik •

*Wollaston
Peninsula*

165°

Bethel •

A L A S K A

Beaver •

Fort Yukon •

White Mts.

Circle •

Porcupine

Old
Crow •

Fort McPherson •

*Melville
Hills*

Kuskokwim Mountains

Yukon

Kuskokwim

Fairbanks •

U.S.
CANADA

Franklin Bay

Kugluktuk •

Dillingham •

Alaska Range

Delta Junction •

*Ogilvie
Mountains*

Fort
Good
Hope •

*Great Bear
Lake*

Echo
Bay •

Bathurst Inlet

Bristol Bay

Tok •

Dawson •

Selwyn Mountains

Norman
Wells •

Palmer •

Gakona •

Keno Hill •

Mackenzie Mountains

Homer •

ALASKA PENINSULA

Cook Inlet

Kenai •

Anchorage •

Kenai Peninsula

Seward •

Valdez •

Chugach Mts.

Y U K O N

Kodiak Island

Kodiak •

Prince William Sd.

Cordova •

Yukon

N O R T H W E S T

Gulf of Alaska

Whitehorse ★

T E R R I T O R I E S

Yellowknife ★

Relian

P A C I F I C

Fort Simpson •

Liard

O C E A N

Watson
Lake •

Nahanni
Butte •

Fort Providence •

*Great
Slave
Lake*

Juneau ★

Cassiar Mountains

Dease
Lake •

Hay River •

Sitka •

C
O
A
S
T

CANADA
U.S.

Wrangell •

Ft. Nelson •

Bay

Uranium City

Caribou Mts.

Fon-du-Lac •

Alexander Archipelago

Stewart •

R
O
C
K
Y

*Williston
Lake*

Ft. Chipewyan •

*Lake
Athabasca*

Birch Mountains

Masset •

Hecate Strait

Prince
Rupert •

M
O
U
N

Dawson
Creek •

Peace River •

Peace

Ft. Vermilion •

Ft. McMurray •

150°

*Haida Gwaii
(Queen
Charlotte
Islands)*

B R I T I S H

T
A
I
N
S

Grande
Prairie •

SASKA

SCALE
1 : 15,300,000

Bella
Coola •

C O L U M B I A

Prince
George •

A L B E R T A

0   100   200   300

statute miles

Fraser

Athabasca

G
R
E
A
T

Edmonton •

Prince A
North
Battlefo

0   100 200 300

Port Hardy •

Jasper •

Columbia Mountains

Red Deer •

N. Saskatchewan

Saskatoon •

kilometers

45°

Campbell River •

Kamloops •

Revelstoke • Banff •

P
L
A
I
N
S

Calgary •

Vancouver Island

Courtenay •

Vernon •

Nanaimo •

Vancouver •

Kelowna •

S. Saskatchewan

Cape Flattery

Strait of Georgia

Bellingham •

Penticton •

Medicine Hat •

Victoria •

Lethbridge •

135°

Bremerton •

Seattle •

W A S H I N G T O N

120°

CANADA
U.S.

Olympia •

Tacoma •

MONTANA

GREENLAND
(KALAALLIT NUNAAT)
(DENMARK)

GREENLAND
Of Greenland's population of 58,000,
89% are Inuit or part Inuit.
Greenlanders have experienced "home
rule" since 1979, and in 2009 moved to
"self rule," a higher level of autonomy
from Denmark.

Map Key

Canadian Aboriginal Land

Alaskan Native Land or
Federal Indian Reservation

★ State or provincial capital

• Selected city or town

NUNAVUT
In 1999, after decades of lobbying,
debate, and planning, the new territory
of Nunavut was separated from the
Northwest Territories, giving the mostly
Inuit-populated area its own form of
government within Canada.

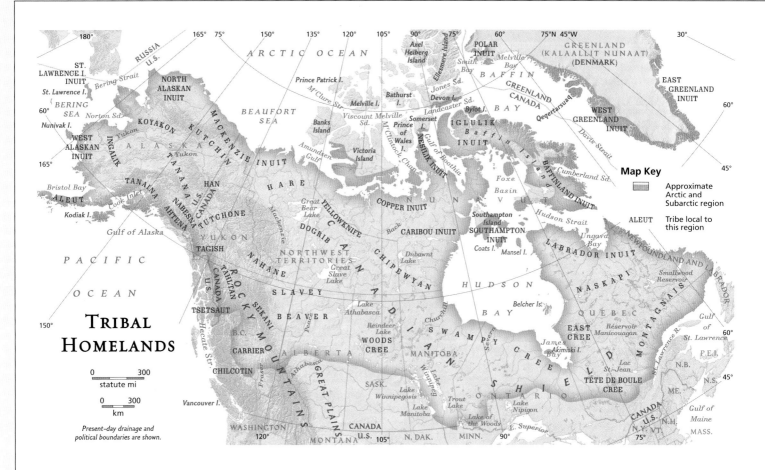

TRIBAL HOMELANDS

0 — 300
statute mi

0 — 300
km

Present-day drainage and political boundaries are shown.

Map Key

Approximate Arctic and Subarctic region

ALEUT   Tribe local to this region

---

caribou, as well as for environmentalists concerned about the Porcupine herd. There is a massive 5.7 billion barrel untapped oil deposit under the Porcupine herd's calving grounds.

INDIGENOUS RELATIONS WITH RUSSIA, DENMARK, ENGLAND, AND FRANCE

Although the people of the Arctic and subarctic did not have a united large-scale resistance to European encroachment like that of many Plains tribes, the arrival of Europeans challenged and changed the people in many ways. Europeans came to the frigid north to exploit resources such as furs and whales, and they sought a passage across North America. The early British expeditions of Martin Frobisher brought military conflict to some of the Inuit people. The Russians made a more concerted effort to control and colonize Aleuts in Alaska, relocating communities, committing massacres, raping many women, and pressuring the Native people to harvest sea otters to extinction in some areas. Russian colonization did not end until Alaska was sold to the United States in 1867.

The tribal lands in the Arctic and subarctic today are clustered around large inland bodies of water, rivers, and ocean coastlines because that's where the most abundant food, such as fish, and the birds and animals that fed on the fish, was found. Inland furbearing animals and caribou brought tribal peoples everywhere in the Arctic, but even the caribou needed water.

The French spent less time in the Arctic than the Russians and British, but they, too, wanted to find a Northwest Passage and to open valuable trade routes to the Arctic from the Great Lakes. Joseph La France was the son of an Ojibwe woman and a French fur trader in the central Great Lakes. He aspired to a position in the French fur trade, but in 1739 was denied a license by New France because he had violated Indian liquor law. La France then changed allegiance to the British. He traveled through the western French trade chain—Grand Portage (Minnesota), Rainy Lake, Lake of the Woods, and Lake Winnipeg—and used his Ojibwe language skills to partner with numerous Ojibwe and Cree trappers and traders, offering to get them higher prices for their furs from the British. He spent three years building relationships, acquiring birchbark canoes, stockpiling furs, and planning a route to the British forts in Hudson Bay.

La France eventually traveled via the Hayes River to Hudson Bay, arriving at York Factory in 1742. Traveling with him was a small armada of birchbark canoes full of beaver furs. La France's

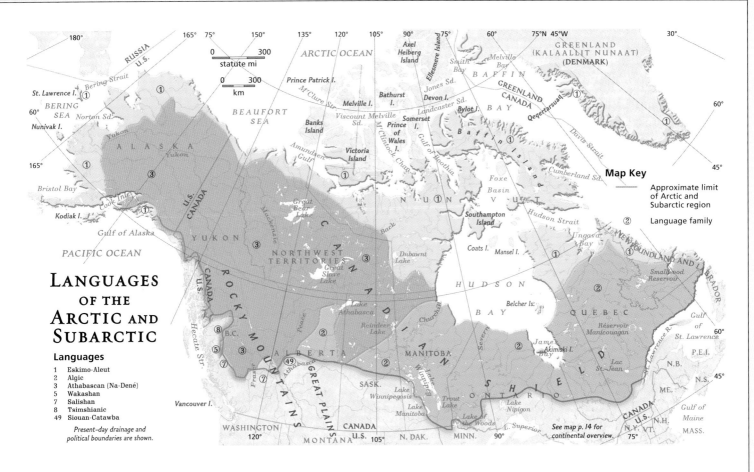

LANGUAGES OF THE ARCTIC AND SUBARCTIC

Languages

1   Eskimo-Aleut
2   Algic
3   Athabascan (Na-Dené)
5   Wakashan
7   Salishan
8   Tsimshianic
49 Siouan-Catawba

Present-day drainage and political boundaries are shown.

Map Key

—— Approximate limit of Arctic and Subarctic region

② Language family

See map p. 14 for continental overview.

successful mission opened the British fur trade with the subarctic on a level never before seen. Soon, numerous Assiniboine, Cree, Ojibwe, and Oji-Cree communities were traveling to Hudson Bay to trade. Within 20 years, the British had successfully bested the French in the French and Indian War and pushed their trade networks west.

In more recent years, the peoples of the Arctic and subarctic have had some success in asserting political positions, especially in Canada and Greenland. Inuit-dominated Nunavut, separated from the Northwest Territories in 1999, is Canada's largest province. Its capital, Iqaluit on Baffin Island, was chosen by plebiscite. Nunavut contains most of the Canadian Arctic Archipelago and all of the islands in Hudson Bay. The province is so vast that it is actually larger than all of western Europe. But Nunavut is also incredibly remote. It is the northern-most permanently inhabited place on Earth.

There are more than 40 tribal languages spoken in the Arctic and subarctic. Most belong to three language families: Eskimo-Aleut (including Inuit and Yupik), Na-Dené (including Athabascan groups), and Algonquian (including Naskapi and Cree). The Inuit languages are clustered in the Arctic, the Athabascan in the western subarctic, and the Algonquian in the eastern subarctic.

An Athabascan mask made in 1880 at the Anvik village site on the Yukon River. Masks have secular and ceremonial uses.

Archaeological evidence shows continuous human habitation in Nunavut for more than 4,000 years.

In spite of the immense size of the province, it is inhabited by only a little more than 30,000 people. Almost all of them are Inuit. That, in turn, has created some interesting new political realities in Canada. Because the population is overwhelmingly Inuit and most are speakers of their language, the province has declared Inuit an official language along with English and French, and its websites and political discourse often function primarily in the tribal language. There are routinely Inuit representatives in the Canadian Parliament now, and they are just as respected and powerful as any other Canadian representatives.

The people of Nunavut have been quite isolated from many of the developments of the modern world, but certainly not all. Missionaries came to Nunavut during the British colonial

ALASKA NATIVE CORPORATIONS

Arctic Slope Regional Corp.

NANA Regional Corp.

Bering Straits Native Corp.

Doyon Ltd.

Alaska (U.S.)

CANADA

See pages 294–295 for a detailed map of all native lands and tribal entities in Alaska.

AHTNA Inc.

Calista Corp.

Cook Inlet Region Inc.

Chugach Alaska Corp.

Sealaska Corp.

Bristol Bay Native Corp.

Aleut Corp.

Koniag Inc.

Map Key

Alaskan native lands

Corporation boundary

0   150
statute mi

0   150
km

Alaska (left) didn't become a U.S. state until 1959, and the legal status of indigenous people there remains very different from elsewhere. After passage of the Alaska Native Claims Settlement Act in 1971, Natives became shareholders in one of 12 corporate districts, with claims to money from resource extraction but not to sovereign rule of the land. First Nations dominate the tribal configuration for Arctic and subarctic tribes in Canada (right). Treaties, court cases, and acts of parliament determine their relationship with the government. But in Nunavut, 30,000 indigenous people occupy the largest Canadian province and have representation in parliament.

compelled to go to a residential boarding school. By 1972, the state of Alaska was sending more than 1,000 Alaskan Native youths to residential boarding schools—hundreds of miles from their homes and families—in Chemawa, Oregon, and Chilocco, Oklahoma. Hootch filed suit, claiming that Alaska discriminated against Native people based on race, because 95 percent of residential school attendees were Native and because only non-Native children had the choice of attending day schools in their home communities. Twenty-six other students from three villages in the Bethel area of southwest Alaska joined her, making it a class action lawsuit. As the case, *Tobeluk* v. *Lind,* progressed, the state of Alaska defended the residential schools, said that Hootch represented a minority of Alaskan Natives, and

period and converted most of the population. About 60 percent of the Inuit there are Anglicans, and most of the rest are Catholic. New technologies changed tribal life as well, including modern tools, snowmobiles, and boat motors. But the Native population still relies very heavily on fishing, hunting, and trapping for food and income. This makes the population of Nunavut one of the most self-sufficient in the world.

Greenland, to the east of Nunavut, is part of the Danish Commonwealth but independent. Of the 55,000 people in Greenland, 80 percent are Inuit. In 1979, Denmark granted Greenland home rule, which has kept the island excluded from the European Union.

REDRESSING WRONGS: RESIDENTIAL SCHOOLS, CORPORATIONS, AND LAND CLAIMS

A 16-year-old girl named Molly Hootch transformed the education system in Alaska in 1972. Hootch grew up in the village of Emmonak on the Yukon River, and like many Alaskan Natives, she had no option to attend school in or near her village but was instead

Sports and recreation have unique variations in the Arctic. The Eskimo seesaw and blanket toss send people flying high into the air.

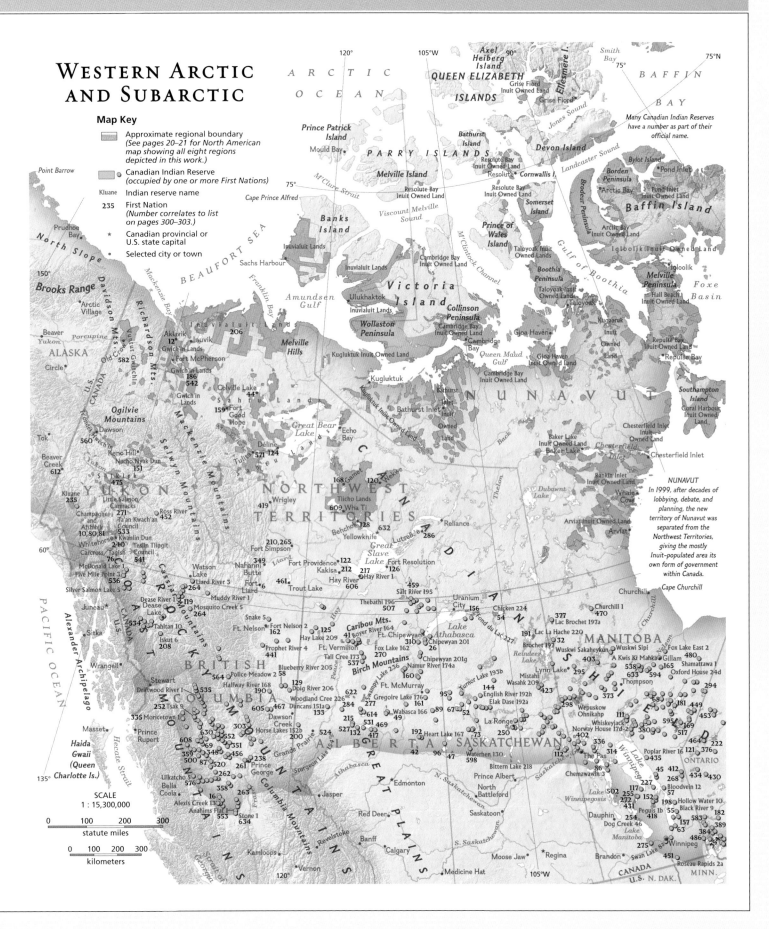

WESTERN ARCTIC AND SUBARCTIC

Map Key

Approximate regional boundary
(See pages 20–21 for North American
map showing all eight regions
depicted in this work.)

Canadian Indian Reserve
(occupied by one or more First Nations)

Kluane — Indian reserve name

235 — First Nation
(Number correlates to list
on pages 300–303.)

★ — Canadian provincial or
U.S. state capital

● — Selected city or town

Many Canadian Indian Reserves
have a number as part of their
official name.

NUNAVUT
In 1999, after decades of
lobbying, debate, and
planning, the new
territory of Nunavut was
separated from the
Northwest Territories,
giving the mostly
Inuit-populated area its
own form of government
within Canada.

SCALE
1 : 15,300,000

0   100   200   300
statute miles

0   100   200   300
kilometers

The Canadian First Nations around Hudson Bay are some of the most isolated in the Arctic. The Inuit and the Algonquian-speaking Cree, Oji-Cree, and Naskapi all rely on traditional hunting, fishing, trapping, and gathering for their diet and lifestyle. Missionaries worked actively in many of these communities, creating the great irony of widely practiced traditional harvesting techniques but very little adherence to traditional religious practices.

claimed that it would be too expensive to provide education in indigenous villages. However, the state soon realized that it was not likely to prevail and offered a settlement, opening day schools in many villages and enabling young Alaskan Natives to live at home and attend school.

In 1968, the Atlantic-Richfield Company discovered a vast oil reserve in Alaska. The company was faced with a dilemma, however, not just in extraction of the oil but also in bringing it to market. A proposed pipeline would cross thousands of miles of primarily Native land, and obtaining the rights-of-way would be time consuming, expensive, and not guaranteed. The Native peoples of Alaska had numerous unresolved land claims from encroachment by Russian, British, and American settlement and resource extraction. The transfer of jurisdiction from Russia to the United States had never involved proper diplomacy with or agreement from the people who actually occupied the land.

In 1971, with overwhelming private business and political pressure to get access to the oil, the Nixon administration pushed through the Alaska Native Claims Settlement Act. The act abolished Native title to all land in Alaska. It established 12 Native regional corporations, each covering a different region in Alaska, and later a 13th corporation to represent Alaskan Natives no longer resident in Alaska. The act also established more than 200 official village corporations. Alaskan Natives no longer held title to the land after the act, but each could have shares in both regional and village corporations. The corporations then received title to 44 million acres of land and compensation in the amount of

This Yup'ik finger mask was made out of polar bear fur and commonly used while dancing.

$963 million, prorated by shares. The remaining land was open for oil extraction and pipeline work.

Many Alaskan Natives were happy to see some acknowledgment of their previous land tenure and ownership and to receive some compensation for the land opened for white settlement and resource extraction. But the act was polarizing, divisive, and upsetting to many as well, because of the extinguishment of Native title to so much land, the fact that mineral and oil extraction was excluded from most of their shares, and the ongoing environmental concerns.

ENVIRONMENTAL LITMUS TEST

Today, the Arctic and subarctic regions are changing quickly. Climate change is challenging the ability of some species to survive and of indigenous people who rely on them to continue their traditional lifeways. Some of the most poignant reminders of environmental issues come from the Native people of the north. Sheila Watt-Cloutier, a Canadian Inuit, was named a finalist for the Nobel Peace Prize in 2007—the year that former vice president Al Gore won the prize—for her activism on climate change awareness.

Aleut women collect seal blubber and meat from a fresh harvest in 1892. Men typically hunted, and women cleaned and processed the game. Even today, seal harvesting is an active practice among the Aleut.

From 1576 to 1578, Martin Frobisher made three trips in search of the Northwest Passage. He is painted here with other Englishmen skirmishing with the Inuit.

· ARCTIC AND SUBARCTIC ·

FIRST ARCTIC ENCOUNTERS

The Search for the Northwest Passage

The long-sought Northwest Passage—a sea route from Europe across the top of the Americas to Asia—exists, but it wasn't until 2009 that climate change reduced the ice pack sufficiently to enable ships to travel across the Arctic. From 1497 to 1772, brutal competition among England, France, Spain, and Russia to find the fastest way across the Americas transformed the lives of many Inuit, Cree, and Athabascan people via disease, war, and upheaval.

The efforts started in the North Atlantic—John Cabot for England in 1497 and Esteváo Gomes for Spain in 1524. Neither got much farther than the outer banks of Canada's Maritime Provinces ❶. Martin Frobisher took three trips in 1576–78, mapping Baffin Island and Frobisher Bay ❷. He got side-tracked with mining and warred with the Inuit in his efforts to claim land and coerce labor. In 1772, Samuel Hearne traveled overland from Hudson Bay ❸ (labeled as Mar Christiano on the map) to the Arctic Ocean, proving that the Northwest Passage by water was not a practical route, and England finally abandoned its 300-year search.

The French searched for the Northwest Passage via the Great Lakes ❹. The Spanish tried to find it by coming from the Pacific, but they confused explorers for generations by thinking that California was an island ❺ and that the passage, which they called the Strait of Anián ❻, had been successfully traversed. That only served to fuel Russian, Spanish, and English exploration and conquest, with detrimental effect on the Aleut and Inuit peoples.

Expeditions from 1776 to 1793 by James Cook, George Vancouver, and Alexander MacKenzie confirmed the impossibility of ship travel via the Northwest Passage. ■

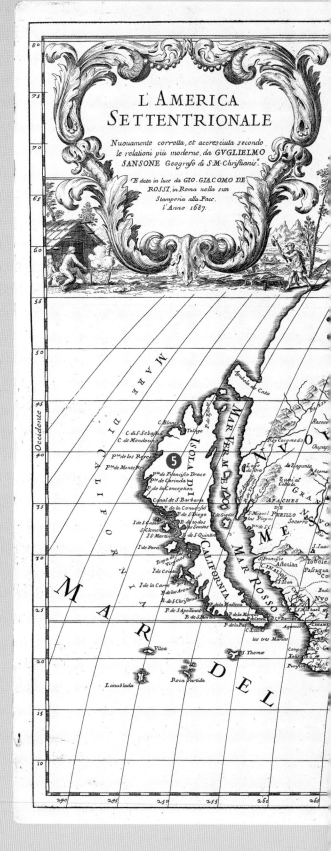

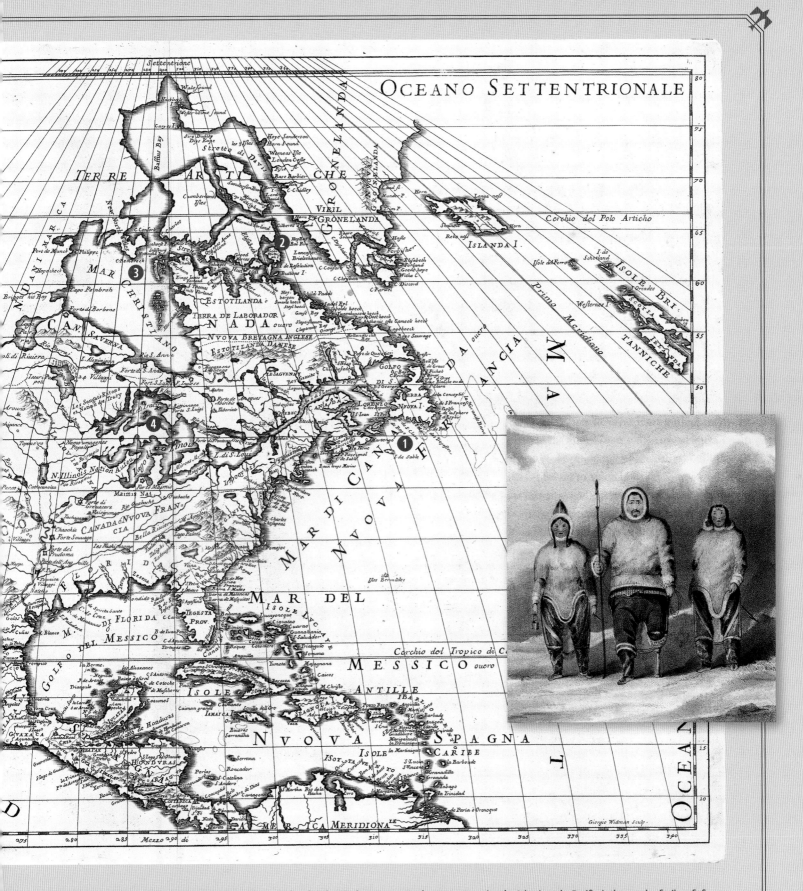

THE STRAIT OF ANIÁN It took a long time for Europeans to realize that the Northwest Passage, the route connecting the Atlantic to the Pacific, is thousands of miles of often impassable straits, ice floes, and land. As early as 1539, Hernán Cortés commissioned Francisco de Ulloa to find a western entrance through a fabled (and nonexistent) ice-free corridor called the Strait of Anián. This 1835 chromolithograph (above, right) shows three Inuit friends of explorer Sir John Ross: Shulanina, Tulluachiu, and Tirikshiu.

Robert Peary was one of the only white Arctic explorers to use Inuit clothes, food, and lodging. Ahhu, his Inuit seamstress (top right), crafted parkas from animal skins. Peary is pictured here distributing utensils to the wives of Inuit hunters who supplied his crew with food (above).

PEARY'S EXPLORATION

The frozen expanse north of Greenland is a vast landscape with few obvious landmarks and incredibly harsh weather. Robert Peary made several trips here in his Arctic explorations and searches for the North Pole. This map, published in 1907, shows the routes Peary took between 1892 and 1906. He was often more interested in his own fame than the welfare of the Inuit he relied upon. Peary misrepresented some claims and never made it to the North Pole, but his maps and journals did document the land and people with detail not seen from previous white expeditions.

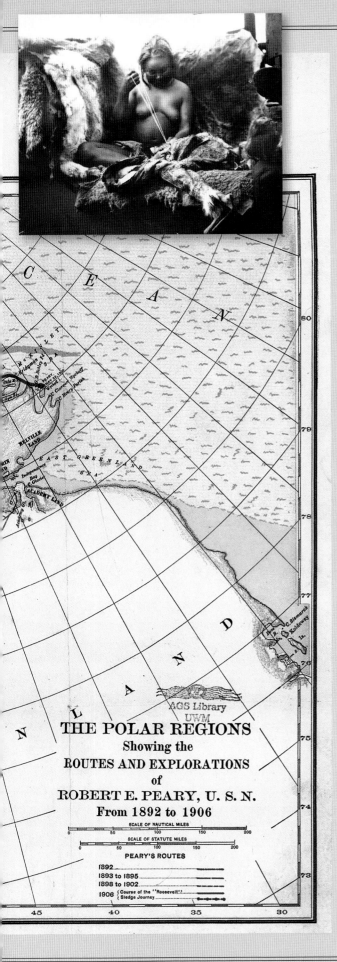

FINDING THE NORTH POLE
The Peary Expeditions

The North Pole is the northernmost point on the planet; it is in the Arctic Ocean, covered by ice. Robert E. Peary received wide acclaim for "discovering" the North Pole  in 1909, receiving a rear admiral's pension from the U.S. Congress. Several U.S. Navy ships have been named after him.

It is now widely known that Peary never actually made it to the pole, although he did get within five miles with the help of four Inuit guides—Ootah, Seegloo, Egingway, and Ooqueah. Another American, Frederick Cook, made it just as close a year before Peary with Inuit guides Ahwelah and Etukishook and competed unsuccessfully for similar fame and claim.

Peary made several Arctic exploring trips in the effort from 1886 to 1909. Those trips provided critical mapping information of the northernmost sections of the Arctic. Peary mapped areas north of Ellesmere Island ❷, and Cape Jesup ❸ during his 1889–1902 expeditions. During his 1891 expedition, Peary broke two bones, and his entire crew had to wait for him to recuperate in their winter camp in Greenland ❹ (Cook, a physician, was a member of Peary's exploring party and set the broken leg). The Inuit showed his crew how to hunt, dress, and travel. It transformed Peary's practice, as the explorer ever after adopted the use of igloos, Inuit clothes, and food while traveling in the Arctic.

In 1897, Peary brought six Inuit from Greenland back to the United States. Most of them died. He left a young boy named Minik Wallace in the U.S. with no assistance to return to his people. Peary was also criticized by the Inuit for stealing a number of meteorites they had acquired and kept for many years, which he later sold for $50,000. ▪

The flags of five nations at Peary's claim to discovery of the North Pole in 1909, held by Ootah, Seegloo, Egingway, Ooqueah, and Peary crew member Matthew Henson.

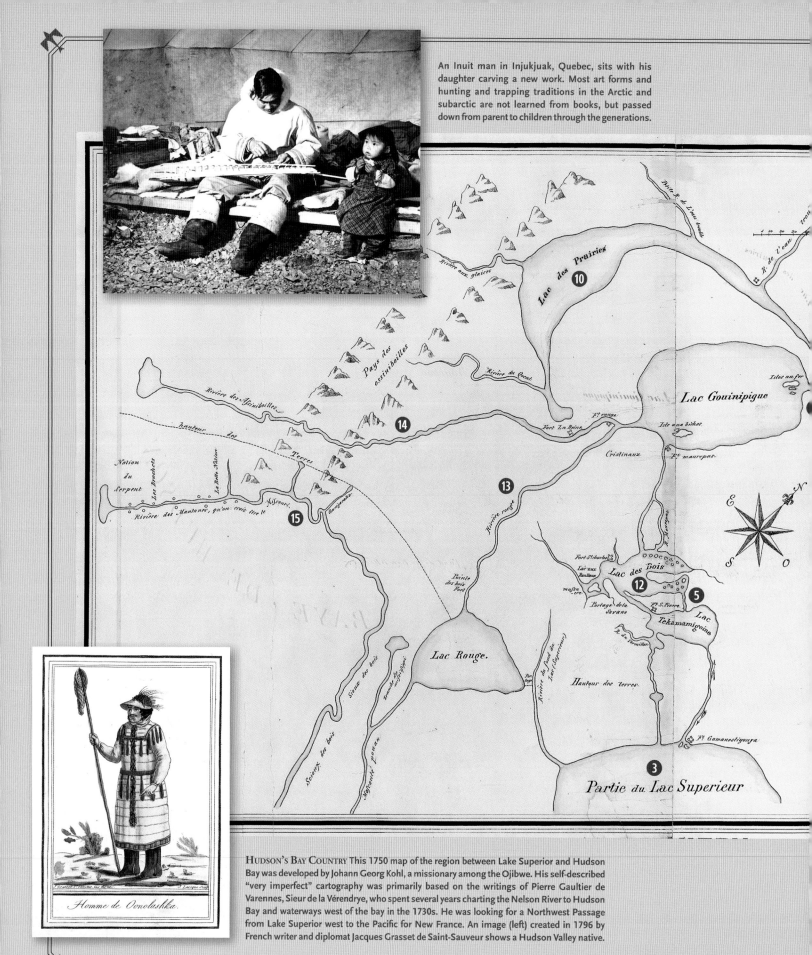

An Inuit man in Injukjuak, Quebec, sits with his daughter carving a new work. Most art forms and hunting and trapping traditions in the Arctic and subarctic are not learned from books, but passed down from parent to children through the generations.

Homme de Oonolashka.

HUDSON'S BAY COUNTRY This 1750 map of the region between Lake Superior and Hudson Bay was developed by Johann Georg Kohl, a missionary among the Ojibwe. His self-described "very imperfect" cartography was primarily based on the writings of Pierre Gaultier de Varennes, Sieur de la Vérendrye, who spent several years charting the Nelson River to Hudson Bay and waterways west of the bay in the 1730s. He was looking for a Northwest Passage from Lake Superior west to the Pacific for New France. An image (left) created in 1796 by French writer and diplomat Jacques Grasset de Saint-Sauveur shows a Hudson Valley native.

HUDSON BAY FUR TRADE

Global Corporate Enterprise at First Contact

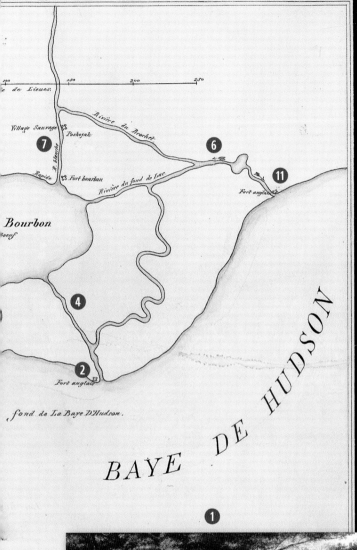

In 1610, British explorer Henry Hudson made it around Greenland and into Hudson Bay ❶. His ship was trapped in the ice, though, and he and his crew were forced to winter in James Bay, the southernmost section of Hudson Bay. After the spring thaw, he wanted to voyage further, but his crew was so set against further exploration that they mutinied, abandoning Hudson to his death.

In spite of the inauspicious beginnings of British exploration there, Hudson Bay proved to be the linchpin to British exploration and trade in the Arctic and subarctic. The British government gave a royal charter to the Hudson's Bay Company in 1670, and it soon became one of the biggest businesses in the world. From a base at York Factory ❷ in what is now Manitoba, the company established private land tenure for 15 percent of the entire acreage of North America, including much of the land west of Hudson Bay. Although none of those land claims were understood or agreed upon by the indigenous people there, "Rupert's Land," as it was called, was eventually sold in 1870 and formed the basis of British (now Canadian) claims over indigenous land there. That expanse included much of Canada and parts of four current U.S. states.

The Hudson's Bay Company acquired trade rival the Northwest Company in 1821 and dominated the fur trade from 1670 to 1870. Several trade routes were established to connect Native trappers, European fur traders, and the major posts on Hudson Bay, including chains of lakes and rivers from Lake Superior ❸ and major waterways, including the Nelson ❹, English ❺, Churchill ❻, and Saskatchewan ❼ Rivers. Also shown are Lakes Winnipeg (both basins) ❾ and Manitoba ❿, Fort Churchill ⓫, Lake of the Woods (Lac des Bois) ⓬, Red River ⓭, Assiniboine River ⓮, and the Missouri River ⓯.

Cree, Ojibwe, Oji-Cree, and Inuit trappers escalated trapping for 200 years. Most of their fur harvest was brought by canoe to Hudson Bay and sold to the British. Today, in the James Bay ❽ and Severn regions, the Cree and Oji-Cree rely on trapping, fishing, and gathering to feed their families. Most families also sell furs trapped over the winter. The northern reaches of Hudson Bay are dominated by the Inuit, who also subsist on natural resources and trap to raise money. Although snow machines have often replaced dogsleds as preferred transportation, the lifestyle is still more ancient than modern. ∎

The Arctic and subarctic fur trade brought incredible profit to the British, French, and Russians, who competed and sometimes warred with one another over rights to trade routes and relationships with the tribes there. In this painting, white traders and Indians move furs for the Hudson's Bay Company.

RUSSIAN AMERICA: COMPANY CONTROLLED
Trade, Empire, and Colonization

The Russian Empire empowered Grigory Shelekhov to explore, trade, and claim lands in North America in the 1780s. Shelekhov established the Shelekhov-Golikov Company and navigated, mapped, and colonized significant parts of the Alaskan coast. At Kodiak Island ❶, where the indigenous population resisted, his forces killed hundreds of Natives.

From 1783 to 1786, Shelekhov established the first Russian colonies, forts, and trading posts in North America. His company morphed into the Russian-American Company, an independent organization with incredible freedom and power to colonize, kill, trade, settle, and control Russian America on its own behalf, not just on behalf of the Russian Empire. Between 1799 and 1867, the Russian-American Company did exactly that, establishing 14 forts in North America, including on the Aleutian Islands ❷, and bringing 72 ships on numerous trips back and forth. Sitka ❸ became a thriving port.

Grigory Shelekhov

The Russian-American Company dispossessed the indigenous peoples of Alaska, established Russian Orthodox missions, and brutally suppressed resistance. Although the fur trade declined and Russia sold its interests in Alaska to the United States in 1867, the company endured for many years. Many of the indigenous peoples of Alaska today still profess the Russian Orthodox faith and carry the blood of Russian traders and company men. ▪

The Russian-American Company had exclusive trading rights and political and economic control of Russian colonies in Alaska, with its own military and flag.

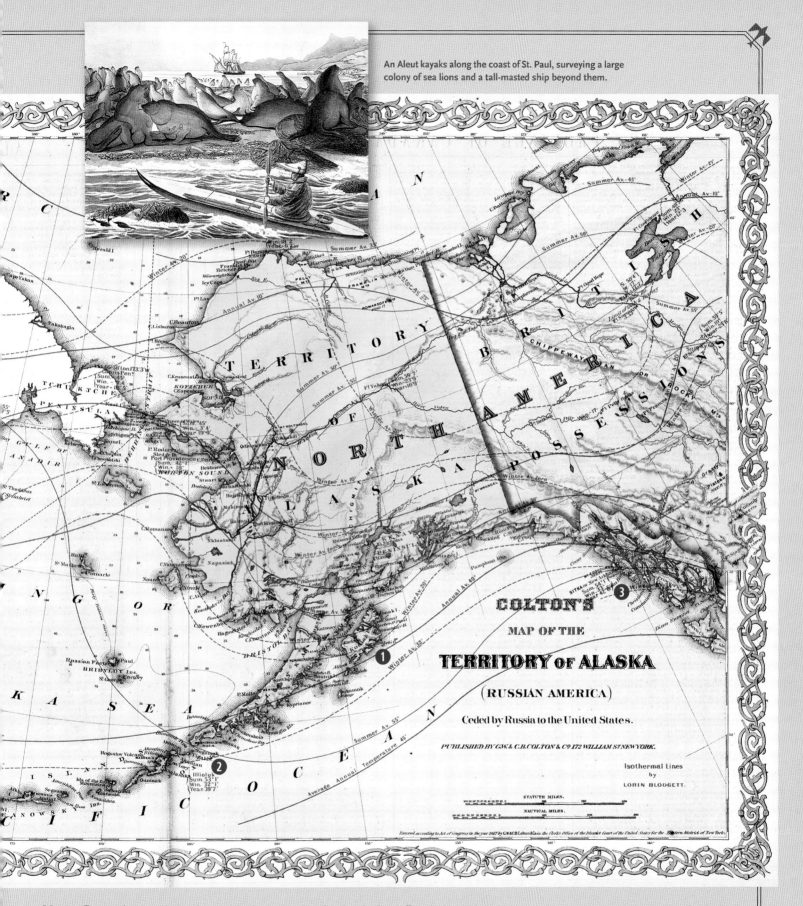

An Aleut kayaks along the coast of St. Paul, surveying a large colony of sea lions and a tall-masted ship beyond them.

COLTON'S

MAP OF THE

TERRITORY of ALASKA

(RUSSIAN AMERICA)

Ceded by Russia to the United States.

PUBLISHED BY G.W.& C.B.COLTON & C? 172 WILLIAM ST.NEW YORK.

Isothermal Lines
by
LORIN BLODGETT.

STATUTE MILES.

NAUTICAL MILES.

MAPPING RUSSIAN AMERICA The Russians sustained an economic, political, and military effort to colonize Alaska and monopolize its trade and natural resources from 1799 to 1867. This 1869 map shows the major connection point in the Bering Sea, trade outposts among the Aleuts, and the port of call in Sitka, managed through the Russian-American Company. The company was run with ruthless efficiency and complete disregard for indigenous land, life, and resources. Thousands of Aleuts were killed, raped, or dispossessed.

TRIBES OF THE ARCTIC AND SUBARCTIC

As the great ice ages retreated, bears, seals, and whales were able to thrive in the Arctic. Human beings followed, spreading out across the Arctic and subarctic. Following are brief histories of select tribes of the region.

ALEUT (UNANGAN)
Current Locations: Alaska
Language Family: Eskimo-Aleut

The Aleutian people call themselves Unangan, meaning "Original People." Most of the population lives in the Aleutian Islands of Alaska. The Russian-American Company colonized the islands in the late 1700s, sparking a significant and ultimately tragic tribal resistance. The Russians killed many Aleuts and for decades consistently raped the women, to the point where even today the entire Aleut population has at least some Russian blood running through their veins. In the 1820s, the Russian-American Company resettled a couple thousand Aleuts to Kamchatka Krai, Russia, and the Pribolov Islands, Alaska; the resettled population struggled and eventually dwindled to around 500 people. There are about 20,000 Aleuts now living in the Aleutian Islands.

ALUTIIQ
Current Locations: Alaska
Language Family: Eskimo-Aleut

The Alutiiq (Pacific Eskimo) are a tribe from the Yup'ik branch of the Eskimo-Aleut language family—their language is Sugcestan—indigenous to Alaska, north and east of the Aleutian Islands. They suffered terribly at the hands of the Russians, who massacred 500 Alutiiq in 1784, forcing the tribe to abandon a traditional village site and regroup. They hunted and trapped furbearing animals with great skill and were targeted by the Russian-American Company for labor in its fur empire. Even though most of the population was forced to convert to the Russian Orthodox Church and the Russians brutally suppressed tribal control of their communities for decades, tribal members did maintain many traditional lifeways even through those dark times.

This Yup'ik seal mask shows not just depth of artistic sense but resourcefulness. With wood, feathers, wool, and paint, the artist brings life into art.

ATHABASCAN
Current Locations: Alaska; British Columbia, Northwest Territories, Nunavut
Language Family: Athabascan (Na-Dené)

The Athabascan group is not really one people or one language, although all the Athabascan tribes were a single people long ago. As the Athabascan spread over most of inland Alaska and the western subarctic region, they diversified linguistically and culturally. Today there are 31 languages in the Athabascan family that form 7 distinct subgroups. Several Athabascan languages are recognized as official languages in Canada's Northwest Territories. The Athabascan are also related to the Tlingit and Eyak, and together those three groups form the Na-Dené language family.

The Athabascan tribes inhabit forbidding territory, and even today most of the tribal population maintains many traditional lifeways such as caribou hunting, trapping, gathering, and fishing. The Athabascan tribes of the subarctic were more dispersed and less densely populated than their counterparts in other parts of North America, and as a result they suffered less from European disease pandemics than many tribes. The relative geographic isolation of many of the tribes also made it possible for them to avoid direct military conflict with European powers during the colonial period.

CHUGACH
Current Locations: Alaska
Language Family: Eskimo-Aleut

The Chugach are an offshoot of the Alutiiq (Pacific Eskimo), indigenous to the Kenai Peninsula and Prince William Sound. They have always been expert hunters, trappers, and fishermen, skills that led the Russians to subjugate them and bend their labors to the Russian fur empire. The colonial period was especially brutal for them. The tribe rebounded, however, and carried on many traditional lifeways. New challenges arose for the tribe in 1964 when a tsunami leveled the main Chugach village, but again the people rebuilt and survived. The oil spill from the Exxon Valdez disaster in 1989 heavily affected the wildlife, fisheries, and environment around Chugach lands, as well.

CREE

Current Locations: Alberta, Manitoba, Northwest Territories, Ontario, Quebec, Saskatchewan (see also Cree entry in chapter 4, Plains)
Language Family: Algonquian

The Cree are one of the largest tribal groupings in the subarctic. There are more than 250,000 Cree who occupy 159 Canadian First Nations from British Columbia in the west to the Maritime Provinces in Canada. The Plains Cree are also numerous (see listing for Cree in Plains). The subarctic Oji-Cree and Naskapi are offshoots of the main body of Cree.

The Cree did not maintain a central government, but rather numerous villages over a huge territory, each with its own leaders. Land loss came hand-in-hand with poverty, political disempowerment, and devastating waves of disease. But the Cree had advantages in the treaty period in that their introductions to European disease did not coincide with massive military campaigns against them, with a few notable exceptions. That and the relative geographic isolation of many Cree communities in Canada helped them to retain their language and culture. Throughout much of the subarctic, fluency rates are still nearly 100 percent and much of the population still leads a subsistence lifestyle.

EYAK

Current Locations: Alaska
Language Family: Athabascan (Na-Dené)

The Eyak are a very small tribe from the Cordova area of Alaska. Culturally, they are very close to their more numerous Chugach neighbors, but linguistically the Eyak descend from the much larger Na-Dené language grouping. The Eyak inhabited four primary villages when the Russians first came to their land in the late

Sockeye salmon make an abundant and much appreciated catch at Bristol Bay. The bounty of the ocean was and remains the key to survival for many Native people in the Arctic.

1700s. Their tribal population decreased significantly throughout the contact period because of Russian colonization, disease, raids by other Native groups, and a decline in the standard of living that threatened many families. The Eyak adapted, although their last fluent language speaker passed away in 2008. The abundant salmon in their region have been a primary food source for generations.

HOLIKACHUK

Current Locations: Alaska
Language Family: Athabascan (Na-Dené)

The Holikachuk are a small tribe from the Athabascan branch of the Na-Dené language family. Indigenous to the Innoko River region of Alaska, the tribe flourished by hunting, fishing, and gathering, maintaining little contact with Europeans through the early fur trade and colonial period. The tribe was eventually targeted by

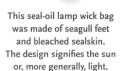

This seal-oil lamp wick bag was made of seagull feet and bleached sealskin. The design signifies the sun or, more generally, light.

missionaries, who converted much of the population. The language quickly started to decline afterward. The entire village was relocated in 1962–63 to Grayling on the Yukon River. Their last speaker died there in 2012.

INNU (MONTAGNAIS-NASKAPI)

Current Locations: Labrador, Quebec
Language Family: Algonquian

The Innu—not to be confused with the Inuit—are sometimes called the Montagnais or Naskapi. They are indigenous to the eastern boreal forest in the subarctic and have numerous First Nations in Labrador and Quebec. Samuel de Champlain sought the alliance of the Innu against the Iroquois early in the French colonial period. The tribe was also allied with the Maliseet against the Micmac.

In 1609, the tribe sent warriors to aid the French against

the Iroquois. Afterward, the Innu were frequently raided by the Iroquois, who took captives and sought to push their territory farther north and west. The debilitating warfare continued until 1701. The Innu later rebounded thanks to the abundant moose, caribou, deer, small game, and other natural resources for subsistence lifeways.

The Innu never ceded their traditional territory to the French or British, and their land claims remain a source of contention in Canada today. Catholic, Moravian, and Anglican missionaries worked extensively in Innu lands, and each denomination gained many converts. Today, the Innu remain culturally and politically active throughout Labrador and Quebec.

The arts and culture flourished in the Arctic. Pictured here is an elaborate Aleut basket collected at Attu Island in 1896.

▦ INUIT (ESKIMO)

Current Locations: Alaska; Labrador, Northwest Territories, Nunavut, Quebec, Yukon; Greenland; Russia
Language Family: Eskimo-Aleut

The Inuit are the largest subsection of the Eskimo-Aleut language family. Inuit people are indigenous to a vast territory that includes Little Diomede Island and the North Slope in Alaska, Big Diomede Island in Russia, most of the Canadian Arctic, and Greenland. The Inuit in Greenland migrated there from Canada by 1300. The name Eskimo is derived from a Cree word meaning "raw eater," a reference to the culinary practice (still followed in some places) of eating raw seal; Inuit (plural) and Inuk (singular) are the preferred terms.

The Inuit resourcefully domesticated dogs and pioneered their use for transportation of food, furs, and people. The Inuit had a diverse food supply in an incredibly harsh climate, gathering small berries on the tundra, whaling, fishing, and hunting. The people were tenacious. Around 1350, the

Little Ice Age brought a prolonged period of intense cold to the Arctic that prohibited most whales from swimming there, putting pressure on the Inuit who relied on them. The Inuit held on, and eventually the whales returned.

Many Inuit practiced open marriage. It was not sexual promiscuity or even a sexually derived practice, but a social one that served to unite disparate family groups and forge bonds of family and community. Open marriage and wife swapping largely died out in the 20th century.

The Inuit had many early encounters with Europeans. The Greenland Inuit had sustained interactions with Norsemen prior to Columbus's voyages to North America. Martin Frobisher mapped some Inuit

An interpreter at Kotzebue, Alaska. The Inupiat have lived in Kotzebue for at least 600 years. This picture was taken by Edward Curtis, who photographed Natives throughout North America in the early 20th century.

territory in 1576. The Inuit population was dispersed widely enough not to suffer as terribly from European diseases as many other North American indigenous groups, but epidemics still took a toll.

In the 1950s, the Canadian government actively sought to relocate many Inuit people from remote village sites and isolated family clusters to new locations. This disrupted tribal life, displaced people, and created dependency issues among one of the most self-sufficient groups in Canada. In the 1970s, many Inuit became more politically engaged, and their land claims in Alaska and Canada helped raise awareness and somewhat mitigate the poverty.

The political action of the Inuit population brought many other changes as well. In Greenland, all Inuit people had become citizens of Denmark. In 1979, Denmark granted Greenland home rule; the country is part of the Danish Commonwealth but independent, and therefore excluded from the European Union. Of the 55,000 people in Greenland, 80 percent are Inuit. In 1999, the Northwest Territories in Canada were divided into two territories, with Nunavut predominantly an Inuit province. As a result, the Inuit now have representation in the Canadian Parliament and much more autonomy for decisions that affect the people there.

▦ INUPIAT

Current Locations: Alaska
Language Family: Eskimo-Aleut

Although the Inupiat are closely related to the Inuit, their language, culture, and distinct historical experiences have led most historians to classify the group independently. Although often called Eskimo, from a Cree word, the Inupiat groups each have separate terms of self-reference. The Inupiat live on Alaska's North Slope, the northwest Arctic region of Alaska, and around Nome.

The Inupiat were expert whalers, hunters, and subsistence fishermen. That brought pressure on them from the Russians and

British during the height of the fur trade and whaling periods. Many Inupiat relocated from traditional villages in Alaska between 1890 and 1910 because of terrible influenza epidemics and food shortages. The disruptions hurt traditional harvesting in many places and created dependency on government programs for some Inupiat, although the indigenous languages and practices of the region have persisted.

OJI-CREE (SEVERN OJIBWE AND JAMES BAY CREE)

Current Locations: Manitoba, Ontario, Quebec
Language Family: Algonquian

The Severn area remains one of the most geographically isolated in the greater Hudson Bay area and subarctic. Many Oji-Cree communities there are accessible only by boat, float plane, or truck access across the ice in winter. Fluency rates in the tribal language remain high—close to 100 percent—but ironically, ancient religious traditions are not vibrant at all. Missionaries came to Oji-Cree country early and did prolonged work in tribal languages. In fact, at Bearskin Lake, the word doodem means "friend," where in other Algonquian-speaking areas it means "clan" and refers to an important cultural construct that is no longer evident in Oji-Cree territory. Most tribal members in this region practice traditional harvesting and rely very little on global economies or even welfare programs.

The James Bay area of Hudson Bay is home to the closely related James Bay Cree. Here, too, traditional lifeways and tribal language are still vibrant. Canadian hydroelectric projects have flooded huge portions of the tribal land base in recent years and forced thousands of people to relocate hundreds of miles. The heartrending moves have disrupted tribal food harvests, resources, and community structures.

YUP'IK (ESKIMO)

Current Locations: Alaska; Russia
Language Family: Eskimo-Aleut

The Yup'ik are indigenous to Alaska and the Russian Far East. New genealogical

An Inuit man stands near his igloo. In spite of the fur trade, missionaries, and political integration with the U.S. and Canada, indigenous people in the Arctic carry on many traditional lifeways.

research confirms that the Yup'ik are biologically quite different from other Native Americans, which likely means that they came to Alaska more recently, perhaps around 10,000 years ago. The Yup'ik suffered from European diseases, but the severity of the disease imprint on the Yup'ik population was much less pronounced than in many Native communities. Their relative geographic isolation also made it harder for diseases to spread rapidly.

The Yup'ik relied on a mixed subsistence economy of hunting, fishing, whaling, and gathering. Many suffered at the hands of the Russians, who brutally colonized Alaskan coastal communities. In 1867, however, Alaska transferred out of Russian jurisdiction and the pressure on Yup'ik lifeways subsided significantly.

Today Yup'ik communities continue to rely on traditional harvesting, but they are also integrated into the global economy for tourism, trade, and natural resource extraction. The Alaska Native Claims Settlement Act of 1971 also created a mechanism for the Yup'ik to benefit from some of the corporate exploitation of natural resources. In spite of that, the Yup'ik remain some of the greatest advocates for environmental awareness and sustainable harvesting.

PLAINS

·CHAPTER FOUR·

ALABAMA (CREEK)

ARAPAHO

ARIKARA

ASSINIBOINE

BLACKFOOT
(BLACKFEET)

CADDO

CHEYENNE

CHICKASAW

COMANCHE

CREE (PLAINS CREE)

CROW

DELAWARE

GROS VENTRE

HIDATSA

HO-CHUNK
(WINNEBAGO)

IOWA (BÁXOJE,
IOWAY)

KAW (KANSA,
KANZA)

KIOWA

MANDAN

MIAMI

MODOC

OMAHA

OSAGE

OTOE-MISSOURIA

PAWNEE

PEORIA

PONCA

QUAPAW

SAC AND FOX

SHAWNEE

SIOUX (DAKOTA,
LAKOTA, NAKOTA)

TONKAWA

WICHITA

WYANDOTTE

The land defined its people, and nowhere was
this more evident than the Great Plains, where
free-ranging buffalo sustained more than 30
distinct tribes and tens of thousands of people.

INDIAN NATIONS OF THE PLAINS

The land has always shaped people more than people shape the land. Nowhere was this more evident than in the Great Plains, a vast expanse from northern Saskatchewan to the tip of Texas, and from the Rocky Mountains to the Mississippi River. The Plains became habitable after the last ice age when a rapid explosion in animal and bird populations brought humans to the Plains from all over North America. Early tribal people from the Siouan, Caddoan, Algonquian, and Uto-Aztecan language families converged on the Plains, eager to reap the bounty of the land and build their families and communities.

In spite of the many differences among the groups that came to the Plains and the variations that emerged within groups, even those of the same language families, the land shaped them all. Immense herds of buffalo, around 30 million strong, roamed the Plains and Tallgrass Prairie. Among the planet's large mammal populations, only the wildebeest of Africa could compare in number to the North American bison. That one species would supply food, shelter, clothing, writing material for Winter Counts that document oral histories, and spiritual inspiration for countless thousands of tribal people.

WINTER COUNTS: HISTORY ON BUFFALO HIDE

Many Plains tribes, including the Lakota, Blackfoot, Mandan, and Kiowa, used detailed pictographs on animal skins called Winter Counts to record their history. They chronicled

The introduction of the Spanish horse revolutionized Plains hunting, war, and culture. Tribes like the Nez Perce developed distinct breeds such as the Appaloosa (above). Blackfoot chief Stu-mick-o-sucks (opposite) had many horsehair adornments when he was painted by George Catlin in the 1830s.

important astronomical phenomena such as the Leonid meteor storm of 1833, abundance or shortage of critical foods, and notable weather events. Tribes developed different patterns for recording their history. The Kiowa marked the passing of a year not just by winter but also by their summer Sun Dance ceremonies. The Lakota customarily referenced the first measurable snowfall as the dating point for Winter Counts. Although many Winter Counts archive important events over a year and also name that particular year, such as the "Year the Stars Fell," the culture of Winter Count recording did not limit the recording to a single year; some counts cover much longer periods of time.

Many scholars have studied the Winter Counts. Some, like Garrick Mallery of the Smithsonian Institution, built careers on that work. But to the tribes on the Plains, the Winter

Counts were not mysteries to be solved, but instead practical recording devices to aid tribal oral historians. The imagery on the Winter Counts served as a series of symbolic and practical reminders of the sequence of historical and astronomical events, enabling oral historians to tell complicated and detailed histories of their people going back decades.

The oral histories were not just people telling stories that could easily be distorted with time and repetition. They were told over and over in group settings, with prompters and the Winter Counts to maintain their validity. Only true elders who had heard the stories many times and were well acquainted with the Winter Counts became bona fide oral historians. Although the practice of maintaining Winter Counts evolved to paper and other materials and eventually faded, the respect for elders and the importance of oral history remain among many Plains tribes not as vestiges of the Winter Counts, but as continuous cultural belief and historical practice.

Horses Transformed Tribal Life

Many years later, as the Spanish horse proliferated through the region, the land and the animals transformed human life again. The horse enabled the Plains tribes to radically alter their hunting methods, changing from chasing herds off cliffs to direct pursuit of their prey on horseback. It gave the Plains tribes a more efficient way to acquire food, and that in turn enabled many tribes to sustain higher population densities, bigger and healthier families, and more reliable food resources in all seasons. The standard of living for the Plains tribes improved.

Life on the Plains was beautiful and by many standards very rich, but it was also filled with competition over territory and natural resources. The horse enabled Native people on the Plains to travel faster, farther, and more efficiently, making

---

CHRONOLOGY

8000 B.C.
End of the last ice age:
Buffalo and other animal and bird populations grow rapidly in the Plains, drawing humans

A.D. 1830
Indian Removal Act: U.S. government pressure on tribal people escalates, forcing the relocation of many tribes to Oklahoma

1851
First Treaty of Fort Laramie established territorial lines and heralded land loss for many tribes

1868
Second Treaty of Fort Laramie: After winning Red Cloud's War, the Lakota and Cheyenne dictate terms for a massive land reserve encompassing parts of five states

1876
Battle of the Little Bighorn: Custer's troops are annihilated after attacking a large Lakota, Cheyenne, and Arapaho village

1890
Wounded Knee Massacre: Government suppression of the Ghost Dance culminates in the slaughter of 300 Lakota men, women, and children, becoming a symbol of genocide

1898
Curtis Act brings allotment to many tribes in Oklahoma

1918
Native American Church is formed, combining pre-Columbian use of peyote with Christianity and spreading among many Plains tribes

---

The Plains remain home to numerous Native nations on reservations in the United States and First Nations in Canada (opposite). Despite terrible hardships, including land and culture loss, tribes held onto some of the best hunting and fishing grounds, often along the waterways shown on this map.

---

the nomadic groups more flexible, adaptable, and able to persevere. Riding also made it possible for the tribes to fight with one another more easily, more often, and with more devastating effect. Some tribes maintained agricultural pursuits in addition to hunting. Some kept the earth-covered lodge designs of their ancestors east of the Mississippi. But they all hunted, they all fought, and they all grew in numbers and knowledge.

Religion and the Land

The land also seemed to inspire all the people who came there with a profound respect for spiritual forces beyond humanity. All Plains tribes embraced vibrant religious beliefs that usually focused on a creator and a pantheon of helping spirits placed in the winds, the earth, the sky, and water—listening, helping, and keeping the world in balance. Great diversity emerged among traditions on the Plains, but some were shared across tribal lines, even between enemies. All the tribes used tobacco as a tool to show respect, a reciprocal offering that accompanied every harvest of plant or animal, every diplomatic foray, and every military endeavor.

Some ceremonies like the Sun Dance proliferated and dominated the religious experience of many tribes. For the Lakota, the sacred ceremony was one of the seven original ceremonies given to their people. For the Ojibwe at Turtle Mountain, it was a gift from the Lakota and is called the Thirsting Dance rather than the Sun Dance. Other tribes place the origin of the ceremony with their own tribes, and many variations abound in the stories and practice of the ritual.

Groups who had no knowledge of the Sun Dance in their original woodland homes rapidly adopted it as a primary centerpiece of their rituals once they moved onto the Plains. The Dakota who stayed in Minnesota and the Cree

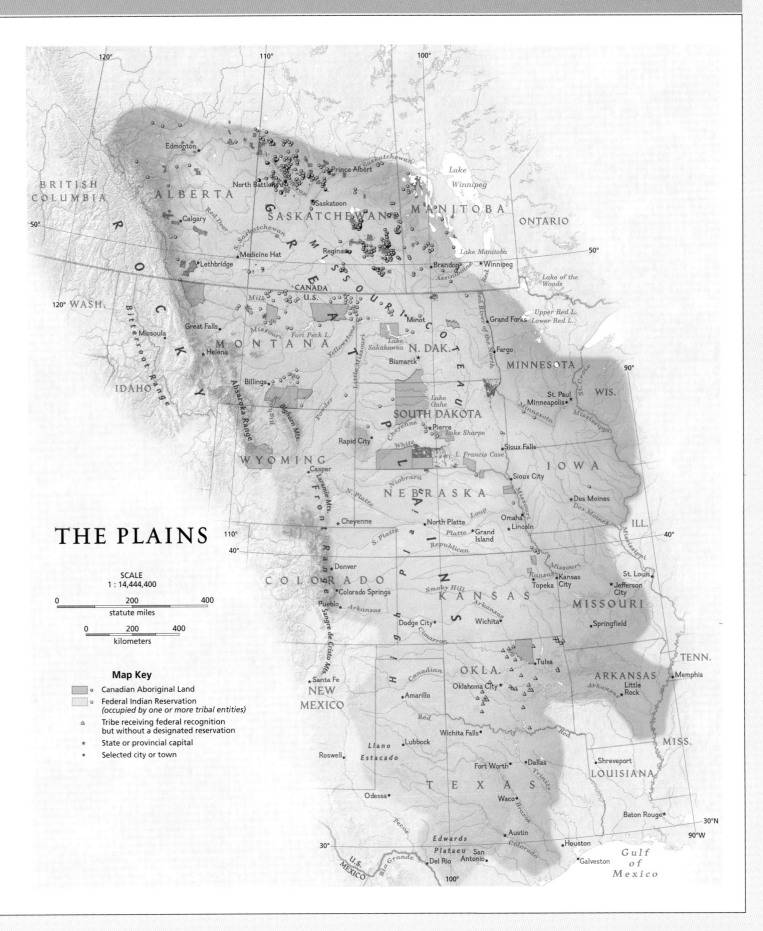

THE PLAINS

SCALE
1 : 14,444,400

0   200   400
statute miles

0   200   400
kilometers

Map Key

Canadian Aboriginal Land

Federal Indian Reservation
(occupied by one or more tribal entities)

△   Tribe receiving federal recognition
but without a designated reservation

★   State or provincial capital

•   Selected city or town

The Plains had abundant food in the form of large herds of buffalo. But the nomadic nature of the animals that sustained the people forced people to follow the herds and brought the tribes into constant contact and frequent conflict over territory and resources. Large groups such as the Lakota, or groups in powerful alliances such as the Cree, emerged as dominant in territorial clashes.

who stayed in the swamps and woodlands east of the Plains never acquired the Sun Dance, for example, but their relatives did so immediately upon establishing homes on the Plains.

Sun Dancers make personal sacrifices as spiritual payment in order to have their prayers answered. Those sacrifices always include a dedicated mental and spiritual focus on a very specific prayer and almost always involve giving up food and water. In many places, there may also be small offerings of flesh (tiny pieces cut from the arm or back) or piercing of the skin on the chest or back, usually to connect the Sun Dancer to the sacred tree in the center of the Sun Dance arbor or to buffalo skulls.

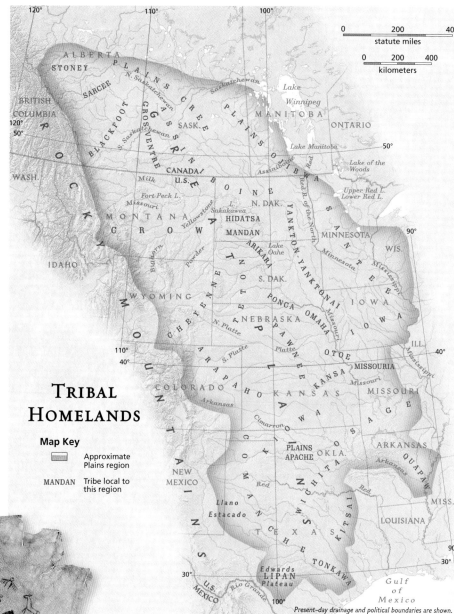

TRIBAL HOMELANDS

Map Key

▨ Approximate Plains region

MANDAN Tribe local to this region

Present-day drainage and political boundaries are shown.

Many Plains tribes recorded their history with Winter Counts, pictographs on animal skins. Lone Dog's Winter Count was made in the mid-19th century.

Sun Dancers typically pledge to fast, dance, and sacrifice for four days at the Sun Dance for four consecutive years, with focus on a prayer for their people, community, or family. Because Sun Dancers are sacrificing so much for the benefit of all, their families, community members, and supporters attend the ceremonies not just to watch but also to sing, dance, and pray around the outside of the Sun Dance arbor. Supporters usually refrain from eating or drinking near the dance arbor, and most participants use sweat lodge ceremonies, burn sage, and pray for the cleansing of bad thoughts to bend all those in attendance to the common effort of the Sun Dancers.

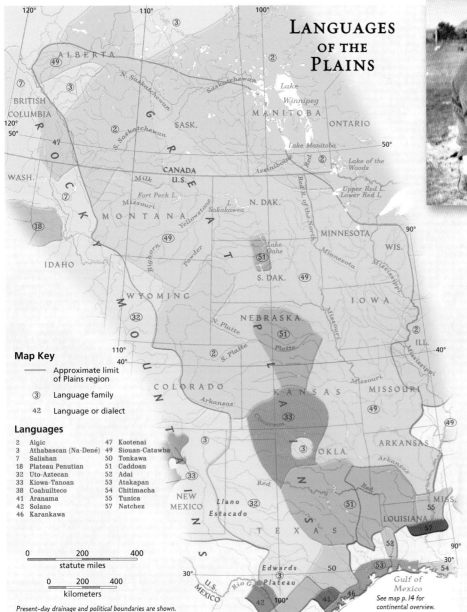

LANGUAGES OF THE PLAINS

Map Key

— Approximate limit of Plains region

③ Language family

42 Language or dialect

Languages

2	Algic	47	Kootenai
3	Athabascan (Na-Dené)	49	Siouan-Catawba
7	Salishan	50	Tonkawa
18	Plateau Penutian	51	Caddoan
32	Uto-Aztecan	52	Adai
33	Kiowa-Tanoan	53	Atakapan
38	Coahuilteco	54	Chitimacha
41	Aranama	55	Tunica
42	Solano	57	Natchez
46	Karankawa		

0 200 400
statute miles

0 200 400
kilometers

Present-day drainage and political boundaries are shown.

See map p. 14 for continental overview.

Wooden Leg (above) was a Cheyenne warrior who fought in the Battle of the Little Bighorn. In this photograph, he communicates in sign language. This map (left) shows the linguistic diversity of the Plains. There were more than 30 distinct tribes from several major language families. People relied on both sign language and multilingual tribal interpreters for intertribal diplomacy.

Usually, Sun Dance leaders have mastered pipe, sweat lodge, and other ceremonies before assuming leadership of the dance. Although participation had often been open to all people, in 2003 Arvol Looking Horse, keeper of the White Buffalo Calf Woman pipe, and other Lakota spiritual leaders agreed to limit the active participation of non-Native people, because so many had tried to participate for reasons other than community betterment.

THE GHOST DANCE

Few ceremonies spread so quickly among the Plains tribes or caused such a vehement reaction from the U.S. government as the Ghost Dance. A Northern Paiute medicine man named Wovoka envisioned and shared the Ghost Dance with many tribes in the Rocky Mountains and northern Plains in 1889 and 1890. He was probably born in 1856 in the Smith Valley region of Nevada and received instruction in tribal culture, especially by his father, who may have been a skilled medicine man himself. When Wovoka was only 14 years old, family tragedy left him an orphan, after which he was taken in and cared for by David and Abigail Wilson, ranchers in Yerington, Nevada. Wovoka assumed the name Jack Wilson while living with them, although he never forgot the language and teachings of his Paiute family.

As an adult, Wovoka returned to his people and developed a reputation as a powerful spiritual leader. He was reported to be able to perform levitation and to produce ice in his hands or summon it from the sky, even on a hot summer day. On many occasions, he demonstrated his invulnerability by being shot at and catching the bullets. Some have dismissed these demonstrations as parlor tricks, but others believed he had a divine power, and this later influenced

The Cree first entered the Plains by canoe along the Assiniboine and Saskatchewan Rivers, where many of their communities are located today. The land changed the people into horsemen and buffalo hunters. For all Plains tribes today, the First Nations in Canada are often clustered along rivers where food, water, trade, trapping, and travel opportunities were most abundant.

the Lakota belief that ghost shirts used in Wovoka's Ghost Dance could stop bullets.

During a solar eclipse on January 1, 1889, Wovoka had his famous Ghost Dance vision, and he worked for several years to share the ceremony and his teachings of peace with other tribes. Drawing on older beliefs and practices among many tribes about the importance of dance, ceremonial uses of drums, and the circle as a symbol of birth, life, and connection to the ancestors, the Ghost Dance invited participants to dance in circular fashion to special songs while praying. The dance served to unite the living with their ancestors and provide a path to peace, cooperation between peoples, and revitalization of the health, peace, and prosperity of Native nations. The Ghost Dance appealed to many tribes across the Plains at the end of the 19th century, when intense conflict, disease, and the eradication of most of the buffalo had decimated the tribal population and left many Native people without obvious options for sustaining their traditional lifeways. As the Ghost Dance spread, variations of the dance and specialized regalia were introduced, such as ghost shirts.

Although the Ghost Dance was entirely peaceful and even preached the importance of harmony and peace between races, many U.S. government officials and citizens feared the zeal of the dancers and the efficacy with which the ceremony seemed to unite tribal people in common purpose (even if that purpose was peace). Consequently, the Ghost Dance was outlawed by the U.S. government in spite of the country's constitutional protections of religious freedom. The dance was brutally suppressed by the U.S. Army, culminating in the infamous Wounded Knee Massacre of 1890.

In large part because of the U.S. government suppression of the dance, but also partly because tribal people in the Plains were so overwhelmed with the daily struggles of dealing with abject poverty and the problems that go with it, the Ghost Dance died off

The hawk on this Brulé Lakota shield was a symbol of power and protection in war, and the image and feathers evoked spiritual help.

almost as quickly as it started. Wovoka lived on until September 20, 1932, but was never able to see his vision fully enacted or his ceremony thrive beyond the first few years. There have been a few attempts to revitalize the dance and the vision of Wovoka, including by the American Indian Movement during the takeover of the Wounded Knee Trading Post in 1973. Some have been well supported, but none has generated the pan-Indian movement the Ghost Dance first conjured in 1889.

TERRITORIAL PRESSURE BEFORE EUROPEANS

The Great Plains had abundant food resources in birds, small game, and big game—especially buffalo. Those resources attracted lots of people to the Plains from other parts of North America. As Indians moved in, they established homes where there was access to water, wood for cooking and heating, and easily defended homelands, but

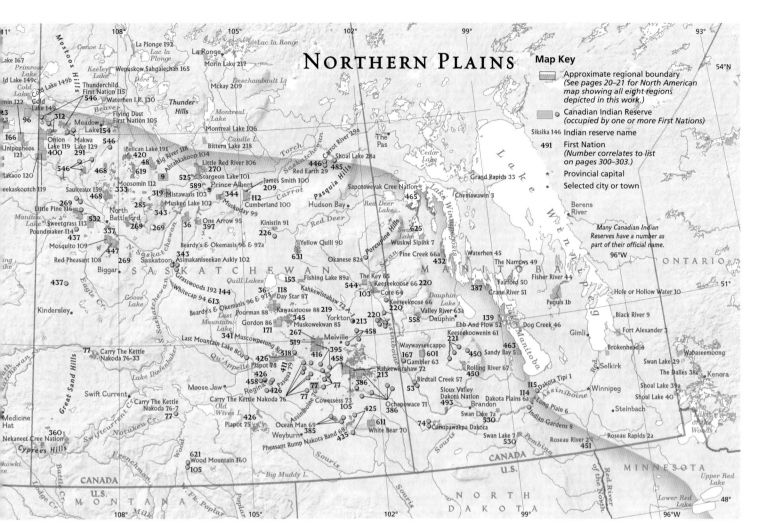

NORTHERN PLAINS

Map Key

Approximate regional boundary
(See pages 20–21 for North American
map showing all eight regions
depicted in this work.)

Canadian Indian Reserve
(occupied by one or more First Nations)

Siksika 146   Indian reserve name

491   First Nation
(Number correlates to list
on pages 300–303.)

★   Provincial capital

•   Selected city or town

*Many Canadian Indian
Reserves have a number as
part of their official name.*

they also ranged far and wide to follow the buffalo herds. The constant movement created conflict, and the tribes on the Plains often battled one another.

Some tribes expanded their territory at the expense of other tribes both before and after the arrival of Europeans. The Cree, for example, expanded their territory from Quebec in eastern Canada to Alberta. Even today, they have more than 150 Cree First Nations in Canada. Other groups, like the Blackfoot and Sioux (Dakota, Lakota, and Nakota), expanded as well, changing rapidly as they did. The westernmost group of Sioux, the Lakota, was the smallest of the seven original Sioux bands. But throughout the 1700s and 1800s they expanded their territory and increased their population so much that they formed seven new bands of their own and today outnumber the other Sioux groups. Territorial expansion often enabled population expansion and stabilization. Territorial declension could spell disaster for a tribe on the Plains.

The Lakota and Cree assumed powerful military positions. But it came with a price. The Plains offered very little geographical separation between tribal areas and very little natural protection for tribal populations. Everyone was vulnerable in times of war. Although the smaller tribes on the Plains were often displaced, all tribes that engaged in war suffered loss of life, grief, and sometimes profound tension over core values and worldview. The struggle for survival in the harsh climate of the Plains was hard, but sometimes compounded tremendously by intertribal conflict.

At the same time that the Cree and the Sioux were expanding rapidly across the Plains, other tribes had a hard time fending off attacks and maintaining the integrity of their social and political structures. The Arikara, Hidatsa, and Mandan, for example, each had a very difficult time because they were surrounded by powerful enemies. When disease epidemics came to their communities, they became so depopulated and weakened that they were forced to

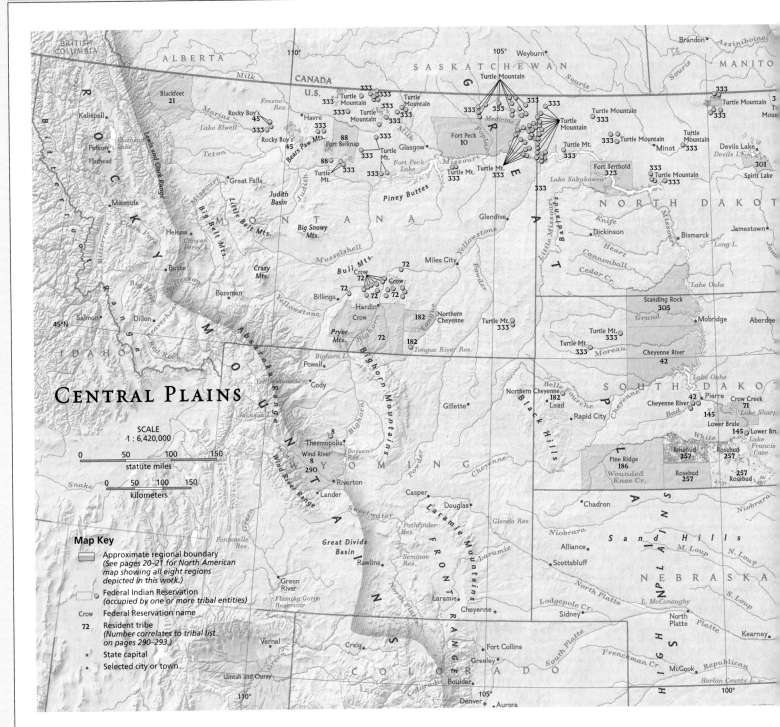

CENTRAL PLAINS

SCALE
1 : 6,420,000

statute miles

kilometers

Map Key

Approximate regional boundary
(See pages 20–21 for North American map showing all eight regions depicted in this work.)

Federal Indian Reservation
(occupied by one or more tribal entities)

Crow   Federal Reservation name

72   Resident tribe
(Number correlates to tribal list on pages 290–293.)

★   State capital

•   Selected city or town

band together for mutual protection, which realigned their political systems and social structures. They survived and adapted.

INDIAN TERRITORY

The central Plains area was eventually designated by the U.S. government as a major removal destination for all tribes in the United States. At first, this place called Indian Territory meant any U.S. lands west of the Mississippi River—Kansas, Nebraska, and Oklahoma. But as it became clear that there was land that white people wanted even in those remote places, Indian Territory started to shrink in the eyes of the government to present-day Oklahoma.

Tribes were moved there from all over. The Modoc were forced to Oklahoma from California. Several tribes, such as the Creek, were moved there from the Southeast. From the Ohio River Valley and

This map shows today's Indian reservations on the Plains. Numerous political and economic forces deprived the tribes of prized territory, including the discovery of gold in the Black Hills, the construction of transcontinental railroads, and the success of initial Indian resistance to white intrusions. In the end, the intentional slaughter of the buffalo weakened the Plains tribes enough to enable the U.S. to wrest away the land.

Through allotment, the U.S. government took reservation land that was held in trust for the benefit of all tribal members and chopped it up into individual parcels, giving some to tribal members and opening the rest to further white settlement. Most of the land, including that allotted to Indians, went out of tribal hands in a short time. Indians became minorities on their own reservations in some places.

There were many tragedies, but once again, the tribes of the Plains adapted. The Native American Church was born in Oklahoma and flourished among many tribes there as it still does today. Others held on to

southern Great Lakes, the Miami, Delaware, Peoria, and others were relocated. Other tribes from throughout the Plains were concentrated there as well. Some, like the Comanche, had been among the most numerous and powerful tribes on the continent. Some of the tribes were nomadic, accustomed to hunting buffalo on horseback; others were sedentary farmers. In Oklahoma, tremendous pressure was exerted on their lifeways and religions and on their lands.

This 1900 portrait of Turning Bear, a Lakota warrior, shows the evolution of war culture into stylized regalia. The buffalo skull (above) was likely ceremonial.

> "The White Man goes into his church and talks about Jesus.
> The Indian goes into his tipi and talks with Jesus."
>
> —QUANAH PARKER (COMANCHE),
> FOUNDER OF THE NATIVE AMERICAN CHURCH

ancient beliefs and ways. Oklahoma is still Indian Territory, and the meaning of that name is shifting yet again, as the tribes and people who live there exert greater control over their own affairs and futures.

STRUGGLE ON THE PLAINS

The Plains tribes shared many common struggles. They had to contend with harsh winters, and only those with tenacious spirit and deep knowledge survived. All tribes on the Plains also contended with devastating, debilitating disease pandemics brought by Europeans. In Europe, people had domesticated animals and suffered through the transfer of diseases from the animal to the human population intermittently for many generations, slowly building immunities to those diseases. But in the Americas, the

dog, turkey, and llama were the only domesticated animals, and they didn't have the same diseases as pigs and sheep. The germ pool from Europe worked like a toxic soup, and some tribes were reduced by as much as 97 percent.

The diseases weakened the tribal populations right at the height of both intertribal conflict on the Plains and the concerted efforts of the United States and British Canada to acquire tribal land. The pressures compounded with devastating effect. Some of the largest tribes also had some of the most densely populated villages and tended to suffer more than other groups from disease. Some tribes merged to survive; others relocated away from conflict zones. All had to decide how to face the European settlers and their armies.

In facing European expansion, all Plains tribes shared a common struggle, and a common goal: resistance. A few chose to resist not with military force but instead with cultural force, maintaining tribal languages, customs, and belief systems, sometimes against overwhelming odds. Others maintained cultural resistance and used military force as well. Some of those groups, especially the Cheyenne, Comanche, and Lakota, had very successful wars, at least for a while. But all the Plains tribes, whether they resisted militarily, culturally, or by other means, eventually had to contend with land loss, and it was heartrending.

One key strategy used by the U.S. government was to slaughter the buffalo population to starve the tribes into submission. Vestigial herds survived in Yellowstone, parts of North Dakota, and Manitoba, but the animal that had sustained the entire human population of the region would never be able to do so again.

A 1915 photograph of a Blackfoot family shows their wagon and hide-covered tepee, as well as the patriarch's World War I–era hat, vest, and buttoned shirt.

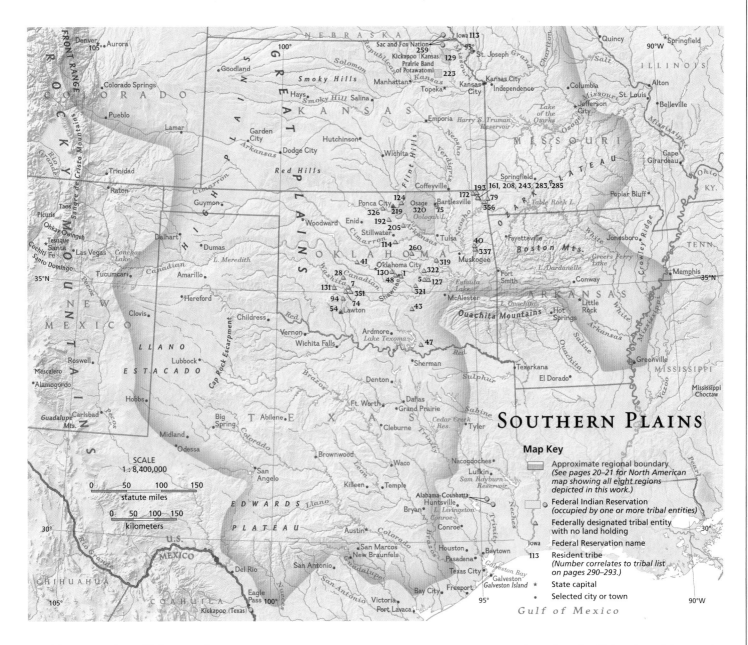

SOUTHERN PLAINS

Map Key

▭ Approximate regional boundary
(See pages 20–21 for North American map showing all eight regions depicted in this work.)

◦ Federal Indian Reservation
(occupied by one or more tribal entities)

△ Federally designated tribal entity with no land holding

Iowa Federal Reservation name

113 Resident tribe
(Number correlates to tribal list on pages 290–293.)

★ State capital

• Selected city or town

Gulf of Mexico

Land loss meant loss of lifeways, adaptation to fewer resources, less access to whatever resources remained, and a declining standard of living. Poverty came to the Plains tribes, far beyond the wishes or expectations of even the cruelest invaders. In the center of the Plains was Indian Territory—a physical place. The injustice of government policy, ecological catastrophe, and human cruelty assailed all groups that were moved there.

In spite of the ugliest chapters in the history of the Plains tribes, there was something else that united them. Over the many

In the 1830s, the U.S. government called all lands west of the Mississippi River "Indian Territory" and designated that as land for removal of all tribes from east of the river. A few decades later, Indian Territory was reduced to present-day Oklahoma. A few tribes remain in Kansas and Nebraska, but most were relocated to Oklahoma.

generations that the Plains shaped its people, the land endowed those tribes with gifts stronger than all the cruelties and misfortunes of the human condition. The indigenous people of the Plains kept their beliefs in spiritual force, with respect for the natural world and all its inhabitants. They found ways to adapt, survive, rebuild, and thrive. Today, the Plains are home to thousands of Native people with growing populations, vibrant cultural traditions, and sovereign governments, represented by many inspiring leaders and citizens—praying, working, and building for a brighter future. ✈

The Horse in North America

→ Diffusion route of horses

0   200 miles

Map shows present-day boundaries.

Sarcee   Plains Cree   1750

1730

Blood

Blackfeet

Piegan

Palouse 1730

Nez Perce

Cayuse

❹

1710

1690–1700

Rocky

Columbia

Snake

Assiniboine

Plains Ojibway

1770

Gros Ventre

Missouri

1720

Crow

1730

Hidatsa

Mandan

Arikara

1750

Sioux

1770

Cheyenne

Sioux

Ponca   Missouri

❸

Shoshone

1720–25

Omaha

Ioway

Pawnee

1770

Illinois

Great Salt Lake

Arapaho

Otoe

Missouria

Kaw   1724

1775

Colorado

Ute

Arkansas

Osage

Mississippi

Miwok

1659

Rio Grande Pueblos

Kiowa

1719

Quapaw

Navajo

Kiowa-Apache

Yokut

Western Pueblos

1600

Apache

Apache

Comanche

❷

Wichita   1690

Caddo

Kichai

Tawakoni

Tonkawa

Rio Grande

1690

❶

THE SPANISH HORSE When the Spanish came to Mexico in the 16th century, they brought horses with them for transportation and war. Many escaped and in the wild grew in numbers and spread out through the Plains. Although some Mexican tribes and even the Pueblo were introduced to the horse directly by the Spanish, most of the tribes on the Plains saw large herds of horses long before they ever saw a white man. Independently of Europeans, the Plains tribes domesticated the feral herds, developed specialized breeds, and incorporated the horse into the fabric of social, cultural, military, economic, and political life.

THE HORSE IN NORTH AMERICA
Transformation of Tribal Life, Hunting, and Warfare

The common understanding of the history of the horse on the American Plains is full of misconceptions. Both horses and camels actually evolved in North America long before they inhabited other parts of the world. Consistent archaeological evidence of horses in the Americas can be found from 3.5 million years ago. It was from North America that the horse migrated to the Eurasian land mass and eventually spread throughout the rest of the world. But the North American horse died off around 12,000 years ago and was reintroduced to North America in 1493 by the Spanish in mainland Mexico ❶. Feral herds quickly spread throughout the continent again, and these wild horses completely changed tribal life.

On the Great Plains of North America, the wild Spanish horse was domesticated by many Indian tribes. It revolutionized hunting, warfare, and even spiritual perspective. The Comanche, who first and most successfully mastered the horse on the southern Plains, completely dominated the area ❷ because of their horses. Prior to the reintroduction of the horse, buffalo hunting often involved chasing herds off cliffs or less efficient stalking with bows and arrows or spears. But after the horse was domesticated on the Plains, tribal hunters could close the distance from their prey with speed and precision, more carefully choose their kills, and damage less meat in the process. The horse was a powerful advantage in warfare as well, not just because warriors could use them in light cavalry charges but also because they speeded up communication and transportation. Horses also enabled the use of controlled fire against opponents on foot without endangering the warriors who were on horseback. The Lakota and Nakota were especially adept at this military tactic ❸.

Some tribes, such as the Nez Perce, developed their own specialized breeds of horse ❹. The horse became interwoven in the lives and spiritual practices of many Plains tribes, and the artistic and spiritual imagery of the horse dominates Winter Counts and personal spiritual items such as drums and pipe bags. Aside from the buffalo that sustained tribal populations on the Plains, the horse was culturally and practically the most important animal in the region. ▪

The horse dominates this Winter Count (below), painted with natural pigments on elk hide. It shows the centrality of the horse in the culture and the glory of the hunt. Lakota men (right) display the evolved war regalia of Plains tribes in the height of the horse culture, including tall eagle staffs and eagle feather war bonnets, as well as adornments on the horses themselves.

MAPPING INDIAN LANDS
The Lewis and Clark Expedition

After France ceded the Louisiana Purchase to the United States in 1803, the political and economic landscape changed dramatically for the Plains tribes. President Thomas Jefferson launched the Corps of Discovery Expedition, led by Meriwether Lewis and William Clark. Although the American explorers succeeded in reaching the Pacific Ocean and defining the country's territorial ambitions, their scientific, mapping, and political accomplishments and even their survival depended entirely on the help they received from the Indians of the Plains.

A Blackfoot chief named Ackomock-Ki (The Feathers) drew and presented the expedition with a detailed map of the Upper Missouri River. (Note: North is roughly to the right.) The map shows numerous tributaries of the Missouri River that were not known to American cartographers at the time ❶. It also depicts and names 12 peaks in the Rocky Mountains ❷. Knowledge of the topography was critical to the success of the expedition in reaching the Pacific Ocean. The map key lists the number of tents of each Indian group, the number of nights the Indians took to travel between points, and the Indian names for each place.

Lewis and Clark negotiated with many tribes, dealt with horse raids by the Crow and Blackfoot, and very narrowly avoided becoming embroiled in inter-tribal warfare between the Lakota and Omaha. One of the saddest ironies of the expedition was that the often marginalized Indian guides and allies of Lewis and Clark equipped the U.S. government with the maps, tools, and information that would lead settlers and soldiers to the region. They had no way of knowing how much this would contribute to tribal land loss and colonization. ◼

GUIDED BY INDIANS An 1850 painting by Thomas Mickell Burnham depicts the Lewis and Clark expedition. Expedition members created the most comprehensive and detailed maps to date of the geological, environmental, and human landscape in North America. The efforts of the expedition would never have been possible without Indian guide Sacagawea and the help, supplies, and guidance of many tribes along the way.

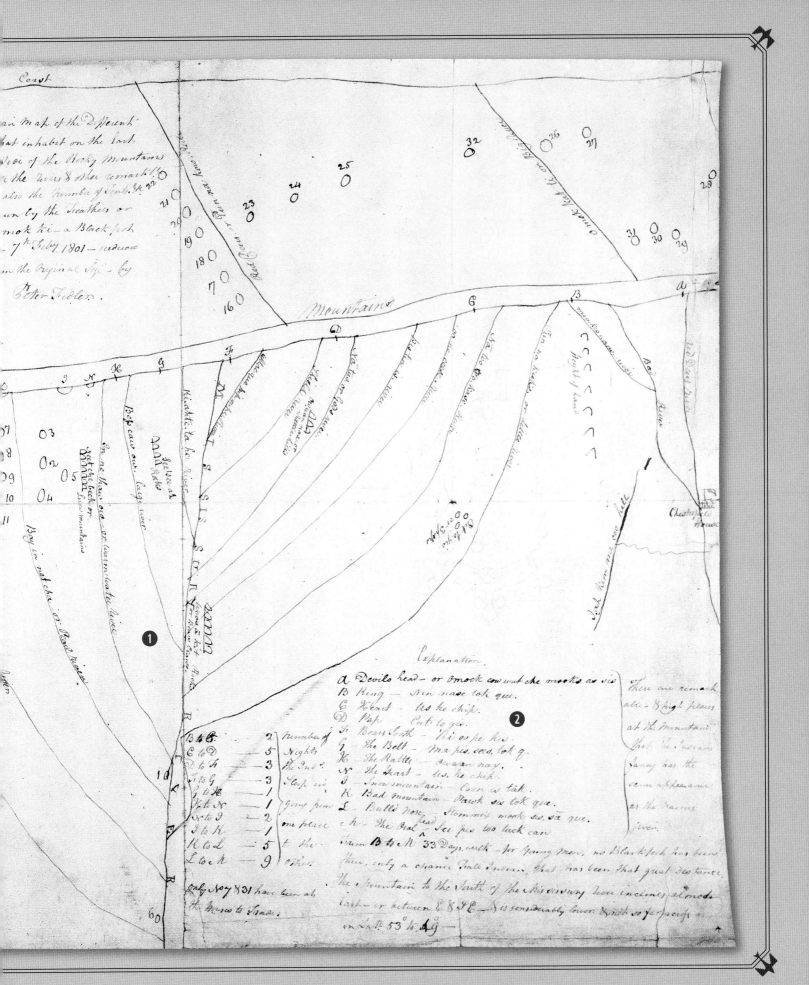

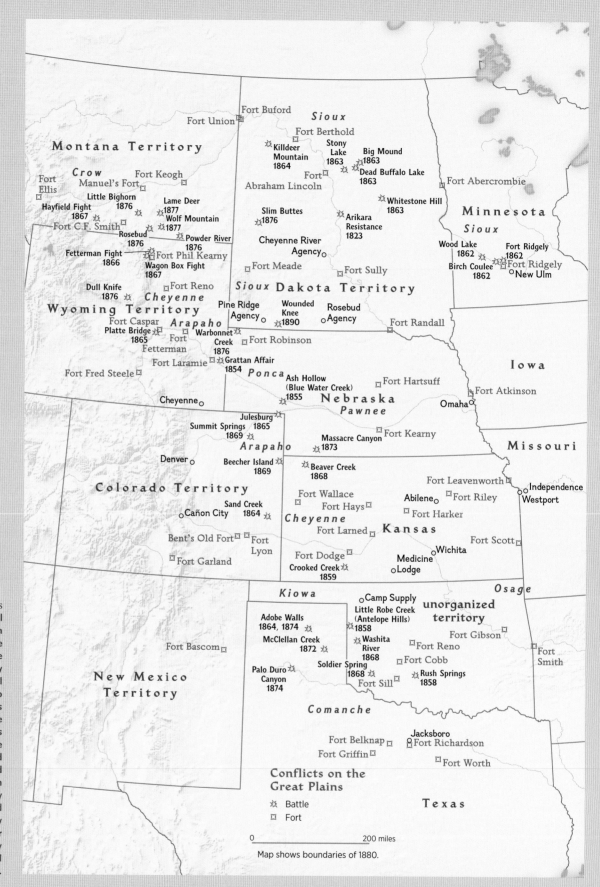

Montana Territory

Fort Union
Fort Buford

Sioux

Fort Berthold
Killdeer Mountain 1864
Stony Lake 1863
Big Mound 1863
Dead Buffalo Lake 1863

Fort Abercrombie

Crow
Fort Ellis
Manuel's Fort
Fort Keogh

Fort Abraham Lincoln

Whitestone Hill 1863

Minnesota

Sioux

Little Bighorn 1876
Hayfield Fight 1867
Lame Deer 1877
Wolf Mountain 1877

Slim Buttes 1876

Arikara Resistance 1823

Wood Lake 1862
Fort Ridgely 1862

Fort C.F. Smith
Rosebud 1876
Powder River 1876

Cheyenne River Agency

Birch Coulee 1862
Fort Ridgely
New Ulm

Fetterman Fight 1866
Fort Phil Kearny
Wagon Box Fight 1867

Fort Meade

Fort Sully

Sioux **Dakota Territory**

Dull Knife 1876
Fort Reno

Cheyenne

Wyoming Territory
Fort Caspar

Pine Ridge Agency
Wounded Knee 1890
Rosebud Agency

Fort Randall

Iowa

Platte Bridge 1865
Arapaho
Fort Fetterman
Warbonnet Creek 1876
Fort Robinson

Fort Laramie
Grattan Affair 1854
Ponca
Ash Hollow (Blue Water Creek) 1855

Fort Hartsuff
Fort Atkinson

Fort Fred Steele

Nebraska

Cheyenne
Pawnee
Omaha

Julesburg 1865
Fort Kearny

Missouri

Summit Springs 1869
Arapaho
Massacre Canyon 1873

Denver
Beecher Island 1869
Beaver Creek 1868

Fort Leavenworth
Independence
Westport

Colorado Territory

Fort Wallace
Fort Hays
Abilene
Fort Riley

Sand Creek 1864
Cañon City
Cheyenne
Fort Harker

Fort Larned
Kansas

Bent's Old Fort
Fort Lyon
Fort Dodge
Medicine Lodge
Wichita
Fort Scott

Fort Garland
Crooked Creek 1859

Kiowa
Camp Supply
Little Robe Creek (Antelope Hills) 1858

Osage

unorganized territory

Fort Gibson

Adobe Walls 1864, 1874
McClellan Creek 1872

Washita River 1868
Fort Reno
Fort Cobb

Fort Bascom

Palo Duro Canyon 1874
Soldier Spring 1868
Fort Sill

Fort Smith

Rush Springs 1858

New Mexico Territory

Comanche

Jacksboro
Fort Richardson
Fort Belknap
Fort Griffin
Fort Worth

Conflicts on the Great Plains

✳ Battle
◻ Fort

Texas

0 ——————— 200 miles

Map shows boundaries of 1880.

SETTLEMENTS AND FORTS
The long history of tribal conflicts over territory on the Plains left many Native nations with little tolerance for intrusions, especially the kind that hurt critical resources like the buffalo herds. When white settlers came to stay, building the settlements and towns shown here, conflicts broke out. Settlers often had little regard for tribal land rights or people, but even when whites violated treaty stipulations that protected tribal land, the U.S. Army invariably came to their rescue, building the many forts on this map, to control the Indians.

WARS FOR THE PLAINS

Protecting Land and Lifeways

Tribes used many tactics to protect their lands and lifeways. Some acculturated and appeased whites, some used diplomacy, some avoided contact as much as possible, and some actively resisted intrusions. On the Plains, tribal cultures evolved in a world where nomadic groups often followed huge herds of buffalo across extensive hunting grounds, and the human movement created territorial conflict. Groups such as the Comanche, Cree, and Lakota expanded their territory at the expense of other tribes. That left most tribes with little tolerance for getting pushed around. Most of the best known conflicts between Native nations and the U.S. government occurred in the Plains. These include those of the Lakota known as Red Cloud's War, the War for the Black Hills, and the Battle of the Little Bighorn. They also include some of the most despicable atrocities in human warfare at the Sand Creek and Wounded Knee massacres.

The human cost of America's colonization of the Plains was incredible. Thousands of Indians were killed in conflicts across the region. Hundreds of white soldiers and civilians were killed as well. The U.S. government expended vast financial resources to control the land and its people, building numerous forts throughout the Plains and staffing and supplying them for generations.

When the wars were over, the U.S. government did little to build bridges or rectify wrongs with the defeated. Even today, the tribes of the Plains remain some of the most impoverished communities in the United States. The standard of living, quality of life, and peace and prosperity of the Native nations of the Plains were in many ways higher before contact with whites than they are now. Awareness is improving, though, and with it the hope that the conflicts over the Plains and their enduring impact can be rectified for the benefit of all. ■

On November 27, 1868, George Armstrong Custer and the U.S. Seventh Cavalry attacked Black Kettle's Cheyenne camp on Washita Creek, as shown in this 19th-century engraving. Some warriors had raided white settlements against the directions of the chiefs. The attack went forward despite diplomatic efforts of tribal leaders. Twenty-one soldiers and 100 Indians (mostly children, elders, and women) were killed. Crazy Horse (top) led the Lakota and Northern Cheyenne who killed Custer at Little Bighorn in 1876.

THE SAND CREEK MASSACRE
Col. John M. Chivington's Great Plains Attack

On November 29, 1864, John M. Chivington, a colonel in the Colorado militia, engineered one of the most atrocious massacres in the Plains. Chivington hated Indians, saying, "Damn any man who sympathizes with Indians . . . I have come to kill Indians, and believe it is right and honorable to use any means under God's heaven to kill Indians."

Black Kettle, a chief well respected among the Cheyenne, had gone to Fort Lyon and arranged what he believed would be a lasting peace for his people with the U.S. government. The Cheyenne had been pressured through a series of treaties to give up vast tracts of land, and Black Kettle's diplomacy was critical to avoiding a broad regional conflict between the Cheyenne and the United States. Black Kettle set up a camp with about 800 Cheyenne and Arapaho on Sand Creek, just 40 miles from the fort. He flew an American flag and a white flag of truce over his tepee lodge pole in the center of the camp. Feeling secure after the diplomacy, the Cheyenne men went buffalo hunting en masse, leaving only 60 men in camp.

Chivington had no regard for the peace or for the Cheyenne and Arapaho. He brought 700 Colorado militia and ordered a surprise attack. Although estimates of the actual number of people killed vary, at least 4 soldiers and around 150 Indians were killed, mostly women and children. The soldiers proceeded with callous disregard for human life and the role of innocents in the event. Most of those killed were horribly mutilated. Many soldiers cut the genitalia off women and wore them for hatbands or on their saddle-bows. White Antelope's scrotum was cut off and made into a tobacco pouch. Soldiers made sport of kicking human fetuses. Some of the fetuses and genitalia were displayed at the Apollo Theater and various saloons in Denver after the event.

Capt. Silas Soule and one other officer refused the order to attack children and afterward offered testimony about the atrocities. Soule was murdered in Denver a few weeks later. There were three investigations, which produced lots of corroborating testimony about how events unfolded, but nobody was ever charged and there were no formal repercussions. Chivington defended his actions and those of his men in killing children by saying, "Nits make lice." ∎

CAUGHT BY SURPRISE The Cheyenne and Arapaho were caught by surprise when Colonel Chivington attacked because they had so recently arranged a permanent peace and were flying the U.S. flag and white flag of truce. Most of their men were away hunting. An artillery barrage inflicted most of the casualties. Then, the militia charged through the village, with cavalry on both flanks of the village, enveloping those who could not flee on horseback.

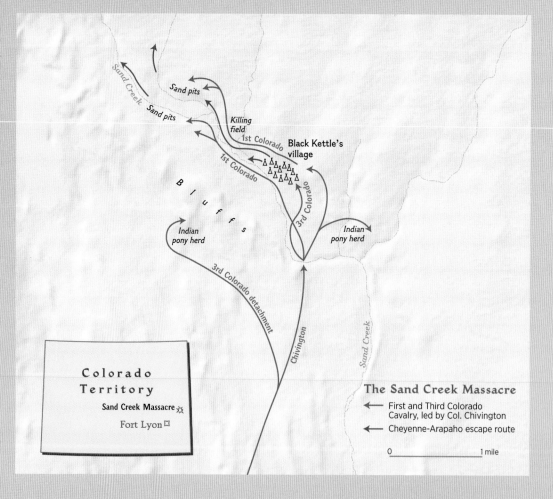

Sand Creek
Sand pits
Sand pits
Killing field
1st Colorado
Black Kettle's village
1st Colorado
Bluffs
3rd Colorado
Indian pony herd
Indian pony herd
3rd Colorado detachment
Chivington
Sand Creek

Colorado Territory
Sand Creek Massacre ✡
Fort Lyon ⊡

The Sand Creek Massacre
← First and Third Colorado Cavalry, led by Col. Chivington
← Cheyenne-Arapaho escape route

0 ———————— 1 mile

Col. John M. Chivington led the massacre at Sand Creek. Because of his hatred of Indians, he ignored the peace brokered by the government, codified in treaty, and renewed by his superior officers. He also would not listen to the objections of his subordinate officers who refused to kill children.

This 19th-century drawing (right) by an unknown artist and early 20th-century painting (above) by Robert Lindneux show the vulnerability of the Indian camp. Sand Creek was a slow and winding waterway, easily crossed on foot or by horse. There were no major ravines or hills to provide cover or to slow the advance of the cavalry. The initial artillery barrage killed many people, and escape was difficult without a horse, although some Indians survived in sand pits on a knoll near the river.

Sand Creek

Sand Pits

THE BATTLE OF BATOCHE, 1885 Métis dreams of independence died at the Battle of Batoche. Thousands of Métis people had flocked to Batoche, which served as a bastion of cultural strength, especially after Louis Riel's return to Canada from exile. But the Métis were not prepared for a long military campaign against well-trained British regulars. They had hastily prepared, insufficient fortifications and numerous civilians to protect. When they ran out of ammunition after a few days, British forces stormed the settlement and rounded up the Métis.

The Riel Rebellions

→ Canadian military column

☒ Battle

⌂ Fort

0 —————— 100 miles

Map shows boundaries of 1885.

Peace

Lake Claire

Lake Athabasca

Wollaston Lake

Cree Lake

Southern Indian Lake

Churchill

Hudson B

District of Athabasca

Reindeer Lake

Nelson

District of Keewatin

Lesser Slave Lake

Athabasca

Beaver

Athabasca Landing ○

Peter Pond Lake

Lac la Ronge

District of Saskatchewan

Severn

Fort Saskatchewan

Frog Lake Apr. 1885

Loon Lake June 1885

☒ Fort Pitt

Frenchman's Butte May 1885

N. Saskatchewan

Edmonton ○

Battleford

Saskatchewan

Cedar Lake

Duck Lake, Mar. 1885

Prince Albert

Fort Carlton

☒ Batoche ②

Batoche, 1885

Lake Winnipeg

District of Alberta

Strange

North-West Rebellion 1885

Cut Knife Creek, Apr. 1885 ☒

Battleford Mar. 1885

☒ Fish Creek Apr. 1885 ④

Lake Winnipegosis

Saskatoon ○

Middleton

Banff ○

Canmore ○

Calgary ○

Canadian Pacific Railway

Otter

S. Saskatchewan

Northcote May 1885

District of Assiniboia

Moose Jaw

Regina ○

Qu'Appelle ○

Manitoba

Lake Manitoba

Selkirk Incident 1816

Red River Rebellion 1869

Lac Seul

British Columbia

Fort MacLeod ⌂

⌂ Fort Whoop-Up

Medicine Hat

⌂ Fort Walsh

Cypress Hills Massacre 1873

Swift Current

Maple Creek 1882

Moosomin ○

Wood Mountain ○

Estevan ○

Brandon ○

Portage la Prairie

Courthouse Rebellion 1849

① Winnipeg

Fort Garry 1869

Lake of the Woods

Canadian Pacific Ra

Ontari

Pembina ③

Red

Sup

Montana Territory

Missouri

⌂ Fort Buford

Dakota Territory

Minnesota

Mississippi

St. Paul ○

After the rebellion failed, some Métis sought refuge with their Cree or Ojibwe relatives. A few tried to maintain culturally independent Métis communities in Canada, but over time were largely absorbed into the general population. Pictured here are Métis and Native prisoners in 1885.

THE QUEST FOR MÉTIS INDEPENDENCE IN CANADA
Louis Riel and the Rebellions of 1869 and 1885

By the middle of the 19th century, a new people emerged in Canada: the Métis. Most had mixed European (mainly French or Scottish) and indigenous (Cree and Ojibwe) ancestry. They had a distinct language, Michif, which incorporated French nouns and Ojibwe verbs, that was widely spoken across the Canadian Plains. Fort Garry ❶, Batoche ❷, and many other Métis settlements dominated the landscape in Manitoba and Saskatchewan. The Métis did not identify themselves as Native or British. They were culturally independent and wanted true political independence as well.

In 1869, the Hudson's Bay Company sold Rupert's Land to the British government. It was a vast stretch of territory that included much of present-day Manitoba and Saskatchewan. The British then appointed William McDougall as governor and sent him to assert British control. The Métis, led by Louis Riel, rebelled, forcing McDougall's troops to seek refuge in Pembina, North Dakota ❸. Riel pursued a diplomatic path rather than a military one, establishing a Métis-dominated provisional government for what is now Manitoba.

The Métis occupied Fort Garry and tried in court and then summarily executed Thomas Scott, a British subject vehemently opposed to the Métis. Manitoba became a province in 1870, and Riel's efforts seemed to have paid off. But Canada's Anglo population was incensed over the execution of Scott, and the Wolseley Expedition soon threatened Métis dreams. Riel fled to the United States. He was exiled for five years, being elected to parliament every year while in exile but never taking his seat.

Riel returned to Canada in 1885, determined to establish an autonomous Métis government. Operating out of Batoche, Riel drew Métis supporters from all over Canada. The Métis had two early victories at Duck Lake and Fish Creek. At Fish Creek ❹, the Métis cleverly deployed 200 men in concealed areas, cutting the 900 British troops arrayed against them into two sections and inflicting severe casualties. The British besieged Batoche, and when the Métis ran out of ammunition, the soldiers routed them. Riel surrendered and was executed, and the Métis scattered. Some tried to maintain independent communities, others took refuge in Native communities, and most blended into the non-Native population. Michif, the Métis language, is threatened now, but still spoken in a few places. ■

Louis Riel, an uncompromising idealist, led the Métis quest for independence.

The Battle of Fish Creek, depicted in this 1885 artwork, was a remarkable military accomplishment for the largely untrained Métis militia. The Métis occupied strategic positions along the creek banks and ravine, using only 20 cavalry as a diversion. They split the 900 British troops into two unfortified positions and used sniper fire and artillery to inflict heavy casualties, forcing their retreat.

BATTLE OF THE LITTLE BIGHORN
Custer's Last Stand

Lt. Col. George Armstrong Custer and a large detachment of the U.S. Army Seventh Cavalry were annihilated by Lakota, Cheyenne, and Arapaho forces on June 25, 1876, at the Battle of the Little Bighorn—a seminal event in both U.S. military and Plains Indian history. Numbered circles in the text correspond to key points on both the hand-drawn map (right) and the map on the following page. In 1874, Custer had led U.S. troops into the Great Sioux Reservation. The action inflamed the Lakota because it violated terms of the 1868 Treaty of Fort Laramie, which required tribal permission for anyone to enter their land. Custer had political and financial interests in the action because he aspired to run for political office. If he succeeded in opening Lakota land to railroad interests, he would have the support he needed. From 1874 to 1876, the U.S. Army presence on the Great Sioux Reservation grew, and there were several skirmishes and some significant battles. As part of a three-pronged march through Lakota land designed to engage and defeat the Lakota, Custer stumbled into one of the largest Plains Indian encampments in history, misjudged the strength of the Native force, and brought the U.S. Army its most infamous defeat at the hands of Indians.

The Lakota, Cheyenne, and Arapaho had congregated on the banks of the Little Bighorn River ❶ in unprecedented numbers in the summer of 1876. (Note: North is to the left.) With considerable numbers of U.S. Army troops established on Lakota land and the history of brutal massacres at Sand Creek and other places, the Lakota and Cheyenne had worked together for several years to protect their families with joint actions and increased protection in sheer force of numbers. There were spiritual reasons for the huge Indian encampment, too. Sitting Bull had had a series of visions about the Sun Dance, which all three tribes were participating in before the Army arrived. He also had a vision that the tribal force would have a great victory, which swayed some Indians to stick together beyond practical considerations.

On June 25, Custer's scouts warned him about the size of the tribal gathering, but Custer was undaunted. As his force approached the battle site, he feared that he would lose the element of surprise and so launched an ambitious and ultimately reckless attack. Custer divided his force into three detachments. He sent Capt. Frederick Benteen and one detachment to cut off the most likely escape route for the Indians along the riverbank. Then

Custer (left) was a shrewd tactician, but he met his match at the Little Bighorn, not just because of the size of the Indian force but also because of the military genius of tribal leaders, such as Sitting Bull (right) and Chief Gall.

Haⁿ hoⁿ Ska. a Kew.

3

Gall wakiⁿ Tⁱ G. A. Custer Battle Field
June 25 aⁿd 26. 1876

2

Iⁿkpa'a
Arate...
hiⁿtemato
hⁿya wowⁱya
papa Coⁿtⁱⁿlⁱa
Ka ⁱⁿya ⁱeepⁱ
Ska
pawaⁿⁱⁱya
ⁱⁱⁱ aⁿpⁱⁱ ⁱⁱa
kⁱⁱⁱ aⁿ ya ⁿaⁱⁱ
aⁿwⁱⁱⁱ ⁱⁱota ⁱⁱⁱⁱⁱ
...a ⁱⁱⁱⁱⁱa ⁱⁱⁱⁱⁱⁱⁱ
Ko waⁿⁱⁱ

1

BATTLE TACTICS A topographical map (above), drawn, in charcoal and ink, shows the Battle of the Little Bighorn. Gall led Lakota warriors across the flatland on the riverbank as soon as Reno's detachment attacked. He pinned down and then routed Reno's force. Simultaneously, Crazy Horse formed a pincer that forced Custer into a running fight. The tribes enveloped and destroyed Custer's detachment. Mounted Sioux Indians (left) attacked with arrows during the battle.

Maj. Marcus Reno

MAP OF CUSTER BATTLEFIELD

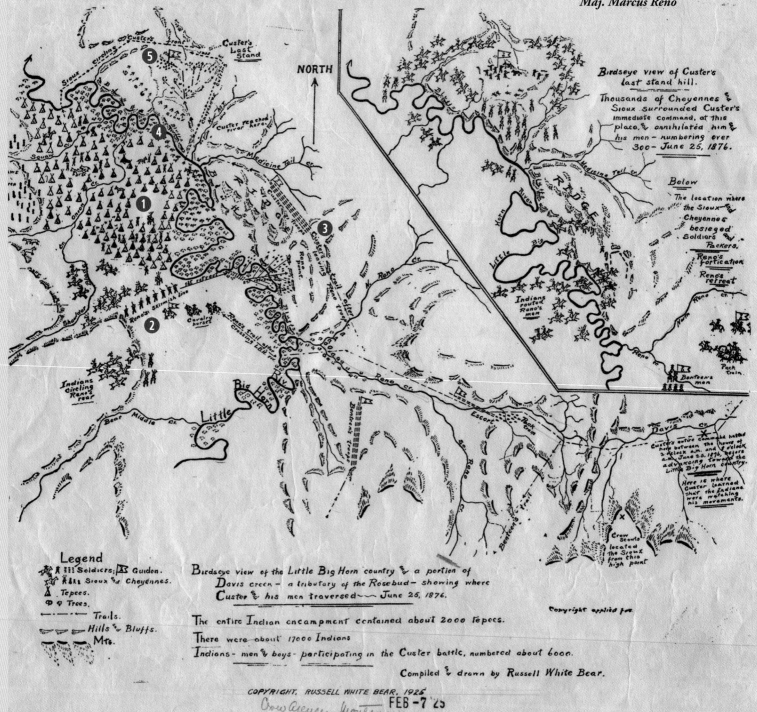

> "It is not necessary for Eagles to be Crows.
> We are poor…but we are free. No white man controls our footsteps.
> If we must die…we die defending our rights."
>
> —SITTING BULL

he ordered Maj. Marcus Reno to take 175 soldiers across the river and attack the Indian camp head-on ❷. Custer himself took the remaining 210 soldiers under his command along the river to flank the tribal encampment ❸.

Reno's force immediately ran into trouble. He had his men dismount and form a skirmish line, firing into the Indian camp and killing the wife of prominent Hunkpapa Lakota chief Gall and several other Indians, primarily women and children. Gall rallied a furious Indian defense that overwhelmed Reno's detachment. Cheyenne warriors joined the Hunkpapa pursuit of Reno's men and killed a fair number as they retreated across the river.

Simultaneous to Reno's rout, Custer's detachment was detected by the Oglala Lakota on the opposite bank. Crazy Horse and other Lakota leaders crossed the river ❹ and pressed the attack, forming a pincer movement around the U.S. troops there and enveloping the entire force. Custer fought for higher ground and eventually ordered his forces to shoot their own horses to provide cover from bullets and arrows, but it was too little too late. The Indian encampment was more than 20,000 strong, with at least 3,500 warriors. Surrounded and eventually overwhelmed, Custer and his troops made their last stand on high ground east of the river ❺. All troops and scouts in his detachment were killed. Reno and Benteen later rejoined forces, and as Army reinforcements started to converge on the Little Bighorn, the tribal force packed up their families and evacuated.

In the eyes of the American public and the government at the time, the defeat of the Seventh Cavalry and Custer's death were viewed as a massacre and a tragedy. But to the Lakota, Cheyenne, and Arapaho, it was the fitting end of a man who killed children and violated treaties.

The military campaigns against the Plains tribes continued after the Battle of the Little Bighorn, but with a major shift in strategy. Greater resources were devoted to the eradication of the buffalo in order to starve the Plains tribes into submission. Military engagements were more carefully chosen by officers to divide and conquer, with odds that overwhelmingly favored the U.S. Army. ∎

Native Americans' oral accounts and paintings like this one of U.S. troops being driven across the river eventually got a broader audience and helped provide critical details and perspective on the battle.

Captain Keogh's horse Comanche was the sole survivor from Custer's entire detachment. The 21-year-old mixed-breed gelding was found, injured, two days after the battle. He was nursed back to health and given special stabling and honors for the remaining eight years of his life.

SITTING BULL

Sitting Bull, a Hunkpapa Lakota Sioux, was born in 1831 in the Dakota Territory (what is now South Dakota), and became a spiritual leader at the forefront of his tribe's resistance to white settlers.

In his native language his name, Tatanka-Iyotanka, loosely translates to a buffalo bull stubbornly resting on its haunches. His calm fearlessness in battles against other tribes (such as the Crow, with whom he first fought in a raid at age 14) as well as the U.S. Army earned him the respect of his own people and his enemies. In a move that might seem reckless to some but calculated and nervy to others, he once calmly smoked a pipe while soldiers shot at him; they all missed and he cleaned his pipe and walked away. His stubbornness in not yielding to the U.S. government would become one of the great legends of the Old West.

His first encounter with U.S. soldiers occurred in the summer of 1863, when soldiers attacked Sitting Bull's people in retaliation for the Santee Rebellion in Minnesota. His fortitude in other encounters with their adversaries caused his people to make him head chief in about 1868.

Sitting Bull's most famous campaign was against George Armstrong Custer, whom he defeated at Little Bighorn in 1876. The U.S. Army was eventually successful in corralling all of the Lakota onto reservations. Sitting Bull lived at the Standing Rock Reservation in North Dakota, where he was killed in a shoot-out with Lakota police officers in December 1890.

WARS FOR THE BLACK HILLS
Red Cloud, Sitting Bull, Crazy Horse, and the Lakota Resistance

When the U.S. Army came to take the Black Hills ❶ away from the Lakota, they underestimated the power of the tribal resistance. From 1866 to 1868, the Lakota won a series of impressive victories with a massive resistance led by Red Cloud that united most of the Lakota. Crazy Horse became famous among his own people as a battle tactician, and after the Fetterman Fight ❷, he became famous among non-Natives, too. Reeling from its defeats, in 1868 the U.S. government signed the second Treaty of Fort Laramie ❸, with terms largely dictated by Red Cloud, including the requirement for written permission for any white man to come into Lakota land, the abandonment of all forts on the Bozeman Trail ❹, and the largest reservation in U.S. history, with five current states for the exclusive use of the Lakota.

When Custer led troops into the Black Hills again a few years later, Red Cloud continued to trust the government, and the Lakota fractured over the issue. Red Cloud, Spotted Tail, and other chiefs refused to fight, believing that Custer's trespasses would be rectified. But Crazy Horse and Sitting Bull knew better. They chose the path of resistance that brought Custer to his death at the Battle of the Little Bighorn ❺.

Realizing that defeating the Lakota and their allies militarily would be costly, U.S. generals and politicians advocated the annihilation of their food source—the buffalo. Crazy Horse eventually surrendered, undefeated. But those who fought the Lakota had no love for their chiefs. Both Sitting Bull and Crazy Horse were eventually assassinated, and the Lakota resistance ended. ∎

At the Fetterman Fight, Crazy Horse engineered a daring bait-and-ambush plan at Fort Phil Kearny: He staged a small raid on the fort, and when the soldiers sallied out, he lured them into a ravine where 81 soldiers were killed by more than 2,000 Lakota, Arapaho, and Cheyenne warriors.

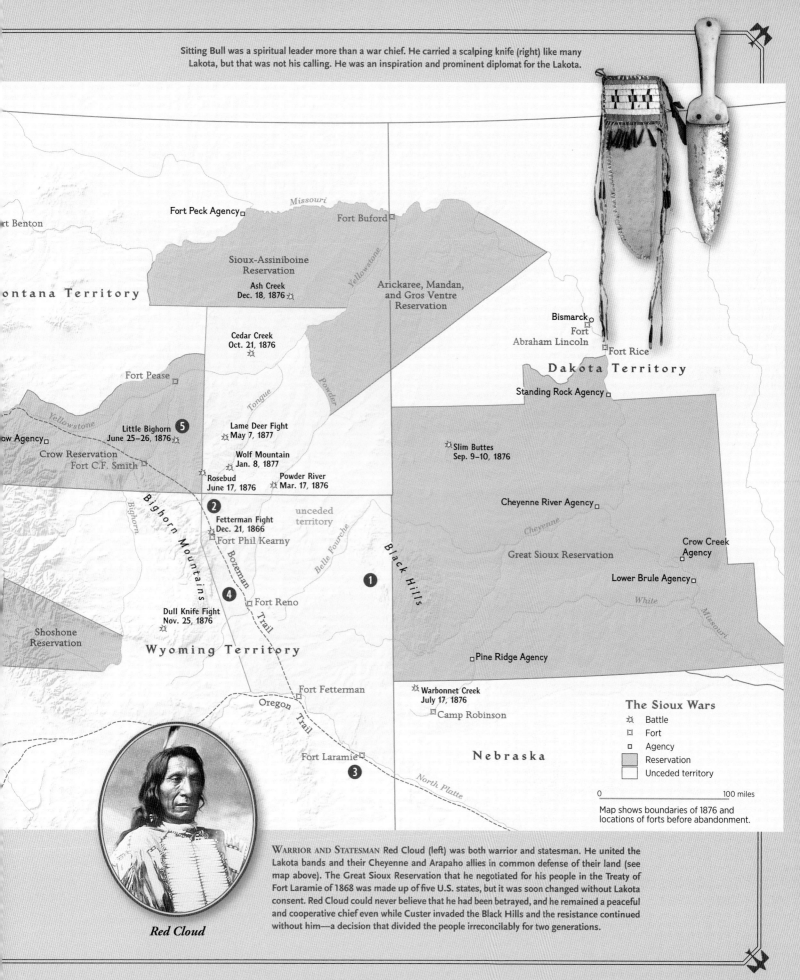

Sitting Bull was a spiritual leader more than a war chief. He carried a scalping knife (right) like many Lakota, but that was not his calling. He was an inspiration and prominent diplomat for the Lakota.

t Benton

Fort Peck Agency □

Missouri

Fort Buford

Sioux-Assiniboine
Reservation

Ash Creek
Dec. 18, 1876 ☼

ntana Territory

Yellowstone

Arickaree, Mandan,
and Gros Ventre
Reservation

Cedar Creek
Oct. 21, 1876
☼

Bismarck
Fort
Abraham Lincoln
□ Fort Rice

Dakota Territory

Fort Pease □

Powder

Tongue

Standing Rock Agency □

Yellowstone

Little Bighorn
Lame Deer Fight
June 25–26, 1876 ☼ **5** ☼ May 7, 1877

ow Agency □

Crow Reservation
Fort C.F. Smith □

Wolf Mountain
☼ Jan. 8, 1877

Slim Buttes
☼ Sep. 9–10, 1876

Cheyenne

Rosebud ☼ Powder River
June 17, 1876 ☼ Mar. 17, 1876

2

unceded
territory

Bighorn

Fetterman Fight
☼ Dec. 21, 1866
□ Fort Phil Kearny

Belle Fourche

Black Hills

Cheyenne River Agency □

Great Sioux Reservation

Crow Creek
Agency
□

Bighorn Mountains

Bozeman

4

Dull Knife Fight
Nov. 25, 1876
☼

□ Fort Reno

Trail

1

Lower Brule Agency □

White

Missouri

Shoshone
Reservation

Wyoming Territory

□ Pine Ridge Agency

Fort Fetterman

Oregon *Trail*

Warbonnet Creek
☼ July 17, 1876
□ Camp Robinson

Nebraska

The Sioux Wars
☼ Battle
□ Fort
□ Agency
▨ Reservation
☐ Unceded territory

Fort Laramie □

3

North Platte

0   100 miles

Map shows boundaries of 1876 and
locations of forts before abandonment.

Red Cloud

WARRIOR AND STATESMAN Red Cloud (left) was both warrior and statesman. He united the Lakota bands and their Cheyenne and Arapaho allies in common defense of their land (see map above). The Great Sioux Reservation that he negotiated for his people in the Treaty of Fort Laramie of 1868 was made up of five U.S. states, but it was soon changed without Lakota consent. Red Cloud could never believe that he had been betrayed, and he remained a peaceful and cooperative chief even while Custer invaded the Black Hills and the resistance continued without him—a decision that divided the people irreconcilably for two generations.

THE WOUNDED KNEE MASSACRE
Religious Persecution and Revenge

The Ghost Dance spread across the Plains in the late 1800s, as the vision of Paiute medicine man Wovoka inspired the Lakota and others to unite in common spiritual purpose. The unity that the peaceful dance generated terrified the U.S. government. They feared the military power of the Lakota and used the U.S. Army to stop Indians from conducting the ceremony.

The U.S. government's suppression of the Ghost Dance came to a brutal climax on December 29, 1890, at Wounded Knee Creek on the Pine Ridge Reservation in South Dakota. The day before, a group of 350 Miniconjou and Hunkpapa Lakota had been intercepted by Maj. Samuel Whiteside and a detachment of the U.S. Seventh Cavalry at Porcupine Butte and brought to Wounded Knee. The Lakota, led by Spotted Elk, set up camp at the base of a ravine ❶, close to the U.S. troop encampment. (Note that the numbered circles correspond to both the modern and archival maps.) Tensions were high because Sitting Bull had been assassinated two weeks before, and the Army unit in charge of the action was George Armstrong Custer's former unit, still seething at the Lakota from memory of their defeat at the Battle of the Little Bighorn. Col. James Forsyth and the rest of the Seventh Cavalry joined the camp later on December 28, bringing with them four multibarrel rapid-fire Hotchkiss guns.

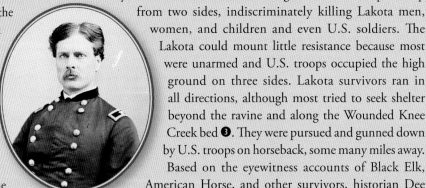

Col. James Forsyth was promoted for his leadership of U.S. troops after the massacre.

On the morning of December 29, U.S. troops disarmed the Lakota, but Black Coyote, a deaf Lakota man, could not hear the call for surrender and his rifle accidentally discharged when grabbed by U.S. soldiers. The Hotchkiss gun batteries ❷ opened up from two sides, indiscriminately killing Lakota men, women, and children and even U.S. soldiers. The Lakota could mount little resistance because most were unarmed and U.S. troops occupied the high ground on three sides. Lakota survivors ran in all directions, although most tried to seek shelter beyond the ravine and along the Wounded Knee Creek bed ❸. They were pursued and gunned down by U.S. troops on horseback, some many miles away.

Based on the eyewitness accounts of Black Elk, American Horse, and other survivors, historian Dee Brown estimated that 300 of the 350 Lakota were killed or wounded. The Army commissioned civilian help with burial at the massacre site three days later, which placed the frozen bodies of 84 Lakota men, 44 women, and 18 children in a mass grave ❹. They also found four live Lakota infants wrapped in blankets next to their dead mothers. Other Lakota were buried elsewhere or simply unaccounted for. Twenty-five U.S. soldiers died, most from friendly fire. U.S. soldiers were awarded 20 Medals of Honor, and Forsyth was later promoted to major general. ■

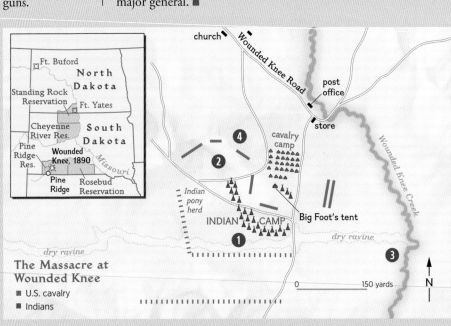

The Massacre at Wounded Knee

- ■ U.S. cavalry
- ■ Indians

HOW THE MASSACRE UNFOLDED The Lakota camp at Wounded Knee was adjacent to the water, on the lowest point of land (left). U.S. troops occupied the high ground on three sides. The Lakota were not expecting an attack. The Hotchkiss batteries tore through the Lakota camp, and most casualties were immediate. Those who tried to escape up the creek bed or through holes in the U.S. lines were pursued by cavalry; some were killed miles away.

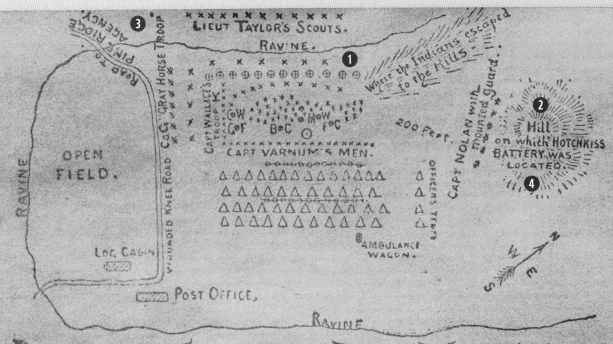

DIAGRAM OF THE SITUATION AT THE BATTLE OF WOUNDED KNEE AT THE TIME THE INDIANS OPENED FIRE.

Map labels:
- LIEUT TAYLOR'S SCOUTS.
- RAVINE.
- ROAD TO PINE RIDGE AGENCY.
- "GRAY HORSE TROOP" CoG.
- Where the Indians escaped to the Hills.
- CAPT WALLACE'S TROOP.
- CoW
- GoF
- BoC
- MoW
- FoC
- CAPT VARNUM'S MEN.
- OPEN FIELD.
- RAVINE.
- WOUNDED KNEE ROAD
- LOG CABIN.
- POST OFFICE.
- 200 Feet.
- OFFICERS TENTS
- CAPT NOLAN with mounted guard.
- Hill on which HOTCHKISS BATTERY WAS LOCATED.
- AMBULANCE WAGON.
- RAVINE.
- N S E W (compass)

····· SOLDIERS.
····· INDIANS.
△△△△ SOLDIERS TENTS.
⊕⊕⊕⊕ INDIAN TEPEES.
⊙ BIG FOOT'S TENT.
BoC THE BEE CORRESPONDENT.
GoF GENERAL FORESYTHE.
MoW MAJOR WHITESIDE.
CoW CAPTAIN WALLACE.
FoC FATHER CRAFTS.
·· TWO INTERPRETERS.
⊕⊕⊕⊕ CAVALRY HORSES tied together.

HAND-DRAWN DIAGRAM In this map of Wounded Knee (above) by "B-C The Bee Correspondent," the directional compass is incorrect; north is to the bottom of the map. The U.S. Army buried 146 men, women, and children in a mass grave at the massacre site (left), but total Indian fatalities were likely twice as high. A snowstorm descended, and many people received no burial other than a heavy blanket of snow. Some survivors took refuge in a nearby church. The event was significant not just for its brutality and unnecessary nature but also for its impact on the Lakota and other tribes, who felt truly persecuted for their religious beliefs and race. It was the final chapter in the wars for the Plains, and its mark is still felt throughout Indian country.

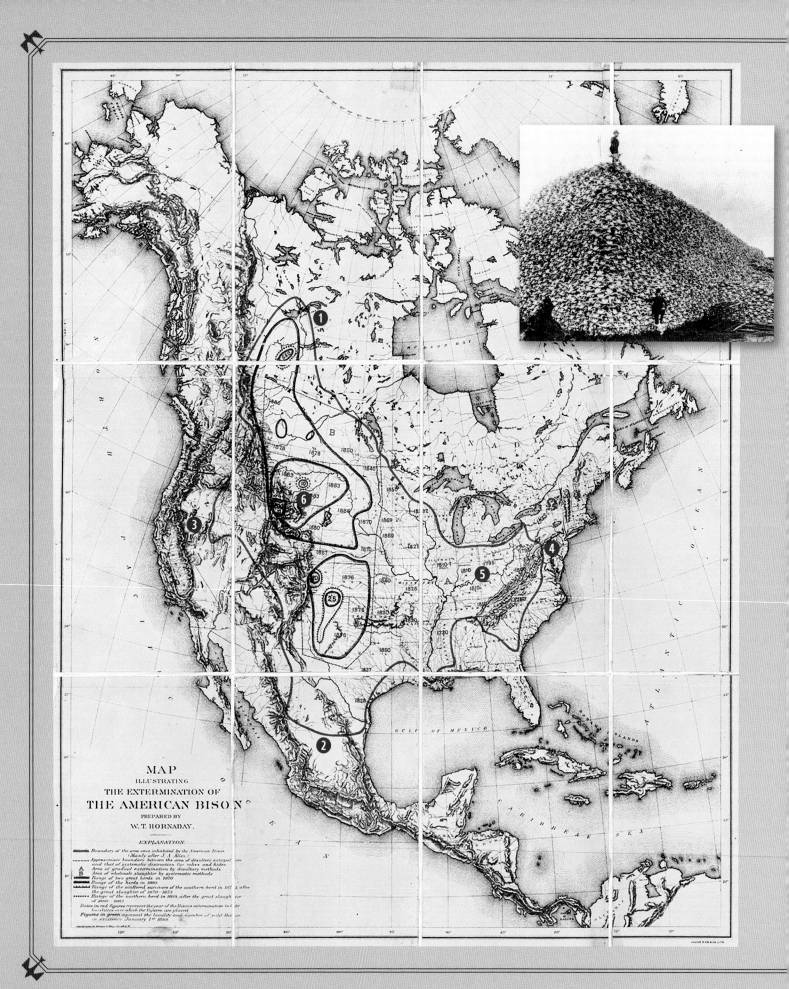

MAP
ILLUSTRATING
THE EXTERMINATION OF
THE AMERICAN BISON
PREPARED BY
W. T. HORNADAY.

EXPLANATION.

Boundary of the area once inhabited by the American Bison
(Mainly after J. A. Allen.)
Approximate boundary between the area of desultory extirpation
and that of systematic destruction for robes and hides
Area of gradual extermination by desultory methods
Area of wholesale slaughter by systematic methods
Range of two great herds in 1870
Range of the herds in 1880
Range of the scattered survivors of the southern herd in 1875, after
the great slaughter of 1870-1873
Range of the northern herd in 1884, after the great slaughter
of 1880-1883
Dates in red figures represent the year of the bisons extermination in the
localities over which the figures are placed
Figures in green represent the locality and number of wild Bison
in existence January 1st 1889

JULIUS BIEN & CO LITH.

DWINDLING BUFFALO HERDS
Ecological Genocide

The American bison was the most numerous large mammal in the Americas before European contact. More than 30 million buffalo roamed a territory that covered the entire Great Plains from Great Slave Lake ❶ in northern Canada to central Mexico ❷ and from California ❸ in the west to Appalachia and New Jersey ❹ in the east. Indians used fire to reduce underbrush throughout the Ohio River Valley ❺ to extend the buffalo range and maintain feed for the herds.

The Plains tribes can be thought of as buffalo people because the animal was so important for them in so many ways. The buffalo sustained tribes all across the Plains. It was the primary source of food, lodge coverings, and clothing. The land and the buffalo dictated where people would live. Many tribes on the Plains were at least somewhat nomadic because they followed the buffalo. That in turn meant that the buffalo shaped the social and political structure of the Plains tribes. It also caused frequent shifts in human territory and sometimes terrible conflicts over land and hunting rights. The buffalo inspired many

spiritual beliefs and practices, as well. The beasts were incorporated into prayers, art, and dance in many different ways.

When Custer was killed at the Battle of the Little Bighorn ❻, he had foolishly attacked a camp of nearly 20,000 Lakota, Cheyenne, and Arapaho. That fact that 20,000 people could camp in the same place and have enough to eat was truly astounding. The fact that they relied entirely on the buffalo for food says a lot about the abundance of the bison and the way the animal enabled Indians to come together for ceremony, politics, trade, and military protection. Once the U.S. government realized how the buffalo helped Indians to maintain not just freedom but also power, it embarked on a genocidal war on the buffalo. Slaughtering buffalo was easier and less costly than fighting Indians. The government planned to starve the Plains tribes into submission.

Army units and civilians were tasked with killing off the buffalo. They were paid bounties for each animal killed. In the 1870s, as many as five million buffalo were killed in some years. Piles of skulls were collected as evidence for bounties. Eventually—weakened, starving, and dispirited—numerous Indians came into Army forts to surrender. Some, like Crazy Horse, were actually undefeated in battle. ■

Protection of the few wild buffalo herds, such as those at Yellowstone National Park, has helped increase their numbers. As demand for buffalo meat has increased, more people have established ranches. But the population is held in check because beef cattle and buffalo do not coexist well. Cattle are susceptible to bovine tuberculosis carried by bison.

THE AMERICAN BISON

PREPARED BY

W. T. HORNADAY.

EXPLANATION

Boundary of the area once inhabited by the American Bison (Mainly after J. A. Allen.)

Approximate boundary between the area of desultory extirpation and that of systematic destruction for robes and hides

A Area of gradual extermination by desultory methods
B Area of wholesale slaughter by systematic methods

Range of two great herds in 1870

Range of the herds in 1880

Range of the scattered survivors of the southern herd in 1875, after the great slaughter of 1870-1875

Range of the northern herd in 1884, after the great slaughter of 1880-1883

Dates in red figures represent the year of the Bison's extermination in the localities over which the figures are placed.

Figures in green represent the locality and number of wild Bison in existence January 1st 1889.

STARVED INTO SUBMISSION The bounty system on buffalo was so effective that white civilians and soldiers killed 30 million animals, mainly in the 1870s. Piles of skulls like these at the Michigan Carlson Works in Detroit (opposite, top) in about 1880 showed the level of carnage. The slaughter of the buffalo was designed to starve the Indians into submission, and it worked. Many Indians became dependent on government rations, their self-sufficiency stripped away, and have recovered only slightly in recent years.

TRIBES OF THE PLAINS

The Plains buffalo were in never-ending motion, and the people there moved with them, competing with one another for territory. Following are brief histories of select tribes of the region.

▨ ALABAMA (CREEK)

Current Locations: Oklahoma
Language Family: Muscogean

The Alabama are an offshoot of the Creek tribe that inhabited many villages along the Gulf Coast states of Florida, Alabama, and Louisiana. The Alabama descended from the great Mississippian culture and are linguistically similar to the Chickasaw, Choctaw, Seminole, and other Muscogean tribes. The Alabama contended with European invaders early, when Hernando de Soto's expedition came through their territory in 1539. In addition to direct military action, the expedition exposed the Alabama to devastating disease epidemics that ravaged the population, killing as many as 95 percent of the tribe over the next few decades.

The Spanish and English sparred for control over the region many times before American independence, sometimes directly involving the Alabama and other nearby tribes. The Alabama adapted to European influence and presence, developing modern economic and political institutions, which brought them recognition, along with the Cherokee, Chickasaw, Choctaw, and Seminole, as one of the Five Civilized Tribes. Adaptations and acculturation did not spare the Alabama from American imperialism, though. In 1830, President Andrew Jackson signed the Indian Removal Act, which authorized the U.S. government to relocate the Southeastern tribes to west of the Mississippi River.

The move was physically, financially, and politically disempowering, but the Alabama adapted to their new home in Oklahoma. They succeeded at farming their reservation and stabilizing their standard of living until

The eagle feather headdress, like this one belonging to Arapaho chief Yellow Calf, was not just ornamental. It symbolized political and military power.

the general allotment of their reservation. Again, tribal members had to rebuild livelihoods with diminished resources, but they preserved their sense of community and many dimensions of tribal culture.

▨ ARAPAHO

Current Locations: Oklahoma, Wyoming
Language Family: Algonquian

The bounty of food on the Great Plains enabled some tribes to grow rapidly, and around 1700, one of the largest got too big to avoid depleting nearby wood supplies and other resources, so they amicably split into two groups. The Gros Ventre went north into Canada, and the Arapaho stayed in the western Great Plains as one of just a few major tribes in the Algonquian language family there. The Arapaho further split into different bands. Their allies on the Plains included the Kiowa and Comanche. They had periodic conflict with the Lakota, Pawnee, Shoshone, and Ute, although the disagreements between the Arapaho and Lakota were permanently laid to rest by the mid-1800s.

A treaty in 1851 assigned a substantial reservation to the Arapaho and Cheyenne in Colorado, but settlers immediately swarmed the tribal lands. The northern band of the Arapaho retreated to Wyoming. New treaties were negotiated in 1865 and 1867, but the terms were not favorable to the Arapaho, and many tribal leaders refused to sign. Some elements of the treaties were contested through 1903.

Most of the northern band settled on the Wind River Reservation in Wyoming along with their hereditary enemies the Shoshone. A majority of the southern band was, along with many Cheyenne, pushed into Indian Territory and, by 1935, settled at Concho, Oklahoma. The land swindles and allotment fraud they endured were some of the most egregious in Oklahoma, but they adapted and forged new livelihoods.

▨ ARIKARA

Current Locations: North Dakota
Language Family: Caddoan

The Arikara or Ree, who call themselves Sahnish, are one of the few primarily agricultural tribes of the Plains. They farmed corn, beans, and squash and kept permanent villages with log and earthen lodges. The Arikara are of the Caddoan language family, along with the Pawnee and Wichita, although those languages are quite distinct from one another. The Arikara hunted bison, antelope, and small game in addition to farming, and their diverse food supply generated not just health but also a population density higher than in many other Plains tribes.

Density made the Arikara population especially susceptible to European disease pandemics, with losses of nearly 95 percent of the tribal population. The dramatic decline in population challenged the very structure of their communities. As the Arikara sought to rebuild, they were pressured and raided repeatedly by other tribes, especially the Lakota. They moved north and established villages close to the Hidatsa and Mandan along the Missouri River. No sooner had the Arikara become settled and acclimated to their new home, however, than did the U.S. government establish the Fort Berthold Reservation in 1851, consolidating most of the Arikara, Hidatsa, and Mandan population there.

The U.S. government relentlessly whittled away at the tribal land at Fort Berthold with the use of executive orders, allotment, and Indian Agency enabling of land fraud. Then in 1954, the government dammed the Missouri River and flooded most of the lush lowland the Arikara farmed at Fort Berthold, forcing them to much higher and drier surrounding areas, dramatically reducing the arable farmland and making the people abandon their homes, graveyards, and former village sites. The Arikara language is in a tragic state of decay, with a tiny handful of speakers remaining, but tribal members have a vibrant participation in cultural activities.

ASSINIBOINE
Current Locations: Saskatchewan; Montana
Language Family: Siouan

The Assiniboine are an offshoot of the Nakota, one of the central groups sometimes labeled as Sioux. They are linguistically and culturally similar to their Nakota cousins, but political and military alignment was a different matter. The separation from the Nakota occurred around

Many tribes recorded events and histories with Winter Counts, pictures on hides. Here, a Blackfoot historian writes a Winter Count around 1901.

1600 over a quarrel between two men who courted the same woman. One won the woman's heart, and the other killed his rival. The dead man's family retaliated, and many lives were lost until a faction of the tribe split off. The splinter group took refuge among the enemies of the Nakota, the Cree. For many years, the Cree and Assiniboine warred against the Nakota and their Dakota and Lakota relatives. The name Assiniboine is derived from the Ojibwe Asiniibwaan, which means "Stony Sioux" and most likely

referred to the culinary practice of using heated rocks to boil water. Today, most Assiniboine people live at Fort Peck or Fort Belknap in Montana or in Saskatchewan.

BLACKFOOT (BLACKFEET)
Current Locations: Alberta; Montana
Language Family: Algonquian

The Blackfoot are one of the most prominent tribes of the western Plains and, along with the Arapaho and Cheyenne, one of just a few tribes in the Algonquian language family there. Four distinct bands of Blackfoot—the Northern Peigan, Southern Peigan, Blood, and Blackfoot—formed the base of a powerful confederacy created long before European contact. Blackfoot is the name of one band, although Blackfeet is the name of their reservation in Montana; both terms have been somewhat erroneously, although not offensively, applied to the entire confederacy. For significant periods in the 1800s, two non-Blackfoot tribes—the Sarcee and Gros Ventre—were also part of the confederacy.

The confederacy dominated a swath of territory on the eastern edge of the Rocky Mountains across the Plains in present-day Alberta, Montana, and Saskatchewan. The Blackfoot shared cultural connections and military allegiance, but rarely came together aside from their annual Sun Dance. The bands followed a seasonal round that focused heavily on hunting buffalo, augmented with small-game hunting, fishing, and gathering chokecherries. The Blackfoot quickly adopted use of the Spanish horse into their culture for hunting and war. Although they had intermittent conflict with other tribes on all sides of their territory, their most prolonged territorial conflicts were with the Lakota, and later the Assiniboine and Cree. In spite of the pressure from other tribes, harsh winters, and introduction of sometimes terrible disease pandemics after European contact, the Blackfoot flourished throughout the 1800s, keeping military control of their territory and developing war societies, kin networks, and ceremonies.

The treaty period brought profound challenges for the Blackfoot. The U.S.–Canada border was drawn through the middle of their territory with no consideration for tribal rights or lifeways. As both the British and U.S. governments pursued land acquisition and cultural assimilation, the Blackfoot suffered significant political disempowerment and poverty on both sides of the border. In the U.S., several treaties signed in the 1850s and 1860s directly affected the Blackfoot, defining their territory, ceding land, and eventually establishing the Blackfeet Reservation at Browning, Montana, out of a portion of their original land. In Canada, Treaty 7, signed in 1877, established four First Nations (called reserves at the time) for the member bands of the original Blackfoot Confederacy.

The concentration of the Blackfoot on smaller land parcels made them much more susceptible to smallpox epidemics in the later 1800s. Disease and eradication of the buffalo herds brought appalling living conditions and starvation. Yet the Blackfoot survived and endured. Land claims and a complicated relationship between the Blackfoot Reservation and Glacier National Park have sometimes been ongoing issues of contention. In recent years, the Peigan Institute was created and still serves as a national model for tribal language revitalization.

CADDO

Current Locations: Oklahoma
Language Family: Caddoan

Prior to European contact, the Caddo were a large group of diverse tribal bands and villages that inhabited a substantial territory in present-day Arkansas, Louisiana, Oklahoma, and Texas. The Caddo descended from the great Mississippian moundbuilding

Hidatsa-Mandan Indian Black Horse or Arlie Knight readies himself for prayer at the Fort Berthold Indian Reservation in North Dakota. He sits in a traditional earth lodge that he built on his property. With an earth roof and constructed with cottonwood and ash timbers, the lodge is 60 feet in diameter and about 16 feet tall. Earth lodges are used for prayer and other ceremonial purposes.

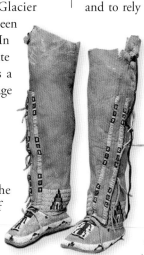

Beaded child's moccasins, probably Cheyenne, made in the late 19th or early 20th century

culture. Their villages were large and sedentary, focused primarily on agriculture, augmented with gathering and hunting. In the 13th century, drought forced the Caddo peoples to adapt and spread out and to rely more on hunting and gathering. The Pawnee and Wichita likely diverged from the main body of Caddo at this time.

The larger sedentary villages were advantageous for the Caddo in most regards, but as the Plains tribes grew in number and acquired the Spanish horse, the Caddo communities became susceptible to raids. When the Hernando de Soto expedition came through their territory in 1541, engaging the Tula band of Caddo in a fierce military action, the Caddo population was exposed to diseases brought by the invaders. Their villages were devastated in many areas, and the population loss accelerated their vulnerability to raids.

Both Spanish and French missionaries actively tried to convert and assimilate the Caddo, with some success. Once Texas became a state in 1845, pressure to take their land became overwhelming. Within two decades, most of the Caddo were forcibly relocated and concentrated on a reservation at Binger, Oklahoma. The diversity within the Caddo peoples prior to contact faded fast, both through the mingling of the Caddo communities concentrated at Binger and through relentless acculturation pressure.

A Caddo medicine man named John Wilson introduced the Ghost Dance to the tribe in the 1890s as it spread across the Plains. Wilson (not to be confused with Wovoka, also known as Jack Wilson, the Paiute prophet and founder of the Ghost Dance) was also a fervent believer in the Native American Church, which combined pre-Columbian use of peyote with

Christianity. Many Caddo still participate in the Native American Church. In spite of pressure on Caddo land, they adapted, and by the 1970s had developed a well-designed modern tribal government.

▦ CHEYENNE

Current Locations: Montana, Oklahoma
Language Family: Algonquian

The Algonquian tribes, including the Cheyenne, were a single people that diversified culturally and linguistically as they spread out from the Atlantic seaboard centuries before European contact. When the La Salle expedition first encountered the Cheyenne in 1680, they had villages in the Mississippi headwaters region of northern Minnesota and had developed a distinct culture and language. By the 1730s, when the French established permanent trading posts in parts of Minnesota, the Cheyenne had moved out of the woodlands and onto the Great Plains. They were pulled by the lure of better hunting, especially of buffalo, and also pushed by powerful enemies—Cree to the north and Dakota to the southeast.

The Cheyenne found friends among the Arapaho and by the 1830s settled in parts of Colorado and Wyoming. They often fought with the Assiniboine, Cree, and Lakota, but in 1840 the Cheyenne forged a lasting peace with the Lakota, which stabilized their territory. The 1851 Treaty of Fort Laramie drew territorial lines around their peoples and restricted their free movement. When the Cheyenne then defended their reserved lands and families, the U.S. Army intervened. From 1857 to 1879, the Cheyenne repeatedly fought U.S. troops.

The Cheyenne had two major bands that did not always coordinate their activities. Black Kettle and the Southern Cheyenne were attacked in 1864 while flying the U.S. flag and a white flag of truce over their camp at Sand Creek, Colorado. Many Cheyenne, including elders, women, and children, were massacred. The Northern Cheyenne fought along with the Lakota at the Battle of the Little Bighorn in 1876 and other battles in the U.S. wars for the Black Hills. In 1877, most of the Southern Cheyenne were forcibly moved to a new reservation in Oklahoma. Many of the Northern Cheyenne eventually settled on a reservation in Lame Deer, Montana. There is an adage among the Cheyenne that the Crow got the land, the Lakota got the glory, but the Cheyenne did the fighting.

▦ CHICKASAW

Current Locations: Oklahoma
Language Family: Muscogean

The Chickasaw are originally from the American Southeast in present-day Alabama, Kentucky, Mississippi, and Tennessee. Like many tribes in the region, they

A spirit design decorates the top of this Assiniboine hand drum.

encountered the Hernando de Soto expedition in 1540, which exposed them to European peoples, technology, and diseases. Despite population loss to pandemics, for the next 200 years the Chickasaw retained control over their land, economy, and political structures. Like the Cherokee, Choctaw, Creek, and Seminole, the Chickasaw saw certain advantages in the economic and political structures of their new European neighbors. They developed a sophisticated plantation-style economy, embraced education, and evolved their political system to include representative governance and law.

Along with many other tribes in the area, the Chickasaw were subject to President Andrew Jackson's removal order in 1830. They were forcibly relocated to Oklahoma. The tribal economy was crushed, and many people died. The U.S. government intended for the entire tribe to be absorbed into the new Choctaw reservation, but persistent advocacy enabled the Chickasaw to establish an independent reservation in Oklahoma in 1856.

The Atoka Agreement of 1897 forced the Chickasaw to endure allotment and severe land loss within the boundaries of their reservation, eventually losing more than 75 percent of their land. The U.S. government tried several times to terminate the tribe altogether, but the people and their government endured. Today, the Chickasaw are one of the larger tribes in the U.S., with nearly 40,000 enrolled members.

▦ COMANCHE

Current Locations: Oklahoma
Language Family: Uto-Aztecan

The Comanche were one of the largest and most powerful tribes in the southern Plains when Europeans first arrived. Unlike many tribes in the Uto-Aztecan language family, they had long ago abandoned corn as a primary food source and instead relied on hunting, gathering, and sometimes raiding to gather resources. The Comanche are closely related to the Shoshone, from whom they diverged in the late 17th century. Around the same time, they acquired horses.

The Comanche were certainly one of the first Plains tribes to adopt the horse into their culture, travel, and hunting methods. They may also have been the primary conduit through which other Plains tribes acquired the horse. The use of horses transformed the Comanche, allowing them to grow in numbers through both high birth rates and the addition of numerous captives acquired while raiding other tribes. The Comanche had more than 40,000 people and at least one horse for each Native person in their territory, with access to another two million feral horses. They soon controlled a huge swath of territory that included much of present-day southern Oklahoma, northern Texas, and parts of New Mexico and Colorado.

The Comanche did not maintain a central government, but rather a dozen distinct bands, each with its own leadership. The loose affiliation among the bands was cultural, linguistic, and sometimes military, but rarely political. The Comanche raided their neighbors in all directions, forming an alliance with the Kiowa and other tribes intermittently in the 19th century. When white settlers came to the southern Plains, the Comanche traded with them, but suffered no trespasses on their land. The tribe was so powerful that after the creation of the Republic of Texas, Sam Houston negotiated a territorial line between the white and Comanche parts of Texas with the full understanding and agreement of the Comanche. Houston was much chagrined when the Texas legislature voted it down.

Diseases crushed the tribal population, reducing their numbers from more than 40,000 to less than 3,000 between 1817 and 1867. At the same time, the buffalo herds of the southern Plains were almost annihilated. At the Treaty of Medicine Lodge in 1867, the Comanche were offered a reservation in Oklahoma in return for annuities, infrastructure development, and (most important to Comanche leaders at the time) a promise to stop the wholesale slaughter of the buffalo by white settlers. The Comanche surrendered 60,000 square miles of territory.

In 1874, a large group of Comanche rode off the reservation to stop the continued killing of the remaining buffalo herds, attacking a white hunting party and bringing the wrath of the U.S. Army upon themselves. The Army pressed all Indians off the reservations, and many people were killed. Quanah Parker and the last remaining band of Comanche surrendered a year later at Fort Sill, Oklahoma. There were a few other military engagements, but the Comanche never regained control over their homeland. The Comanche were crammed together with the Kiowa on the Fort Sill Reservation.

The population has rebounded from its low of around 1,500 in 1890 to more than 15,000 tribal members today. The Native American Church and Christianity are both practiced on the reservation. The tribal language is spoken only by a handful of elders now, although many cultural traditions remain strong.

■ CREE (PLAINS CREE)

Current Locations: Alberta, British Columbia, Manitoba, Saskatchewan; Montana, North Dakota (see also listing for Cree in Chapter 3, Subarctic)
Language Family: Algonquian

The Cree are one of the largest tribal groupings in North America. They number more than a quarter of a million and occupy reservations in Montana and North Dakota as well as First Nations reserves in Canada. For more information on the Subarctic Cree, the relatives to the north, see chapter 3. The Cree are part of the Algonquian language family, like the Ojibwe, Ottawa, and Potawatomi. Although the original Cree homeland is along the Atlantic coast, they split off from the main group as they started to migrate west many years before European contact. They settled thousands of villages in much of Canada and parts of the northern United States. When the Cree had established themselves in northern Minnesota, they formed a powerful alliance with the Assiniboine and eventually with the Ojibwe. Together with their allies, they expanded their territory on the Plains at the expense of other tribes, especially the Dakota and Nakota.

By the time Europeans sought Cree land, the tribe controlled a huge section of land from the Canadian Rockies east. In Canada, the British government pushed for land cessions starting in the early 1800s, but it was almost 1900 by the time it got all of the treaties signed to wrest land from the powerful Cree tribes. The Cree did not maintain any kind of central government, but rather had numerous groups over a huge territory. Even the primary culture areas inhabited by the Cree contained many different villages, each with its own leaders. Land loss came hand in hand with poverty, political disempowerment, and devastating waves of disease. But the Cree were fortunate during the treaty period in that their introductions to European disease did not coincide with

Sioux warriors perform a war dance before departing for battle in this 1888 chromolithograph. The ceremonies preceded battle and usually lasted for four days; some were thought to induce a state of self hypnosis.

concerted military campaigns against them. In addition, their relative geographic isolation helped many of them to retain their language and culture. In the Severn region, for example, language fluency rates are still nearly 100 percent and much of the tribal population still leads a subsistence lifestyle.

In the United States, the Cree fared quite differently. The U.S. government used a heavy hand in dealing with many Plains tribes, and it became obvious to the Cree that they would not be treated fairly. Many simply walked across to Canada, but not all. Those who stayed were largely ignored by the U.S. government in numerous treaty rounds even though they still occupied large tracts of land. The government stopped making treaties with Indians altogether in 1871 and still had not addressed the land tenure of the Cree.

Some Cree shared a large region in North Dakota with the Ojibwe. In 1882, the U.S. government established the Turtle Mountain Reservation, and the Cree and Ojibwe in the region were collectively concentrated there. Today, there are more than 30,000 enrolled members there, of which Cree are a significant minority group. A group of Cree and Ojibwe splintered off from the main community at Belcourt on the Turtle Mountain Reservation and moved west into Montana, where they remained officially landless despite their continued habitation of a large area. Many other Cree were allowed to take up residence at other reservations. One band moved to the Flathead Reservation, and another settled on the Blackfeet Reservation.

In 1908, Frank Churchill was sent to Montana to negotiate with the Cree chief Rocky Boy for settlement of his people on a reservation. In deft diplomacy, the chief communicated a fairly sophisticated understanding of the Cree land

An illustration created in about 1900 of an Arapaho Ghost Dance, based on a photograph by James Mooney

tenure to the American diplomat, including the fact that the Cree were composed of many bands in different places across Montana and Idaho, often in predominantly white towns. Churchill requested that Valley Country be set aside as a permanent home for the Cree and that white settlement there cease. The Cree hung in limbo for several more years, but in 1916 an executive order confirmed the status of Rocky Boy's Reservation as a permanent home for the Cree and Ojibwe. Several small bands of Cree voluntarily moved there, while others were involuntarily diverted there. After the Indian Reorganization Act, the Cree established a modern tribal government on the reservation, where they uphold ancient traditions and culture.

CROW

Current Locations: Montana
Language Family: Siouan

A Dakota wooden frame drum, dating to the 19th century

The Crow, or Apsáalooke in their own language, are closely related to the Hidatsa. Their own oral histories record a time when they lived in the southern Great Lakes, near Lake Erie. Eventually, they were driven out by powerful enemies to the east and settled in the Lake Winnipeg region of the Canadian Plains. The Cheyenne, and eventually the Ojibwe, Cree, and Lakota, all in turn pressured the Crow in their new home, and they retreated farther west. By the time Europeans encroached on the Plains, the Crow occupied a large territory along the Yellowstone River in Montana and Wyoming.

The Treaty of Fort Laramie in 1851 established borders around Crow land, which significantly reduced the size of the ancestral territory. The treaty also affirmed the rights of the Crow to exclusive occupancy and use of their newly defined land. But the Lakota and Cheyenne had little regard for either the territorial rights of the Crow or the U.S. government's map of Indian domains. Both the Cheyenne and Lakota encroached on Crow lands and hunting grounds, overwhelming the Crow with sheer numbers. The Crow were forced to withdraw their families in spite of the treaty protections.

The Lakota victories in Red Cloud's War in 1868 and the Battle of the Little Bighorn in 1876 emboldened the Lakota and Cheyenne to press their claims against the Crow, who eventually lent their support to the U.S. in hopes that it would help protect their families and land. Many Crow served as scouts in the U.S. Army. But the war against the buffalo did more to pacify the Lakota and Cheyenne than American or Crow military actions.

When the pressure on Crow land was somewhat relieved, the Crow, like the other tribes, still had to contend with poverty. Their reservation was larger on a per capita basis than many others, but the Crow still felt the sting of not just poverty but also the impact of the eradication of the buffalo on their lifeways. Today, the Apsáalooke language is undergoing a concerted revitalization effort that shows great promise to protect the language and the traditional culture.

■ DELAWARE
Current Locations: Ontario; Oklahoma, Wisconsin
Language Family: Algonquian

The Delaware lived in present-day New Jersey and New York when British settlers arrived. Theirs is a story of numerous displacements and relocations. They were peaceful and friendly toward the colonists, but that did not prevent their displacement when the pace of white settlement overwhelmed them. Before the Revolutionary War, the tribe splintered into several groups. Some sought refuge with other tribes in New York, Ohio, and Pennsylvania. Others remained in New Jersey and southern New York, but were unable to maintain community land tenure, language, or cultural traditions; over a few generations, they were almost entirely absorbed into the non-Native population.

Some Delaware moved into Canada and, in spite of land loss and cultural pressure, still have three recognized First Nations there. Yet another group moved to upstate New York and merged with the Mahican. Together they were relocated to Shawano County, Wisconsin, where they have a small reservation adjacent to the Menominee. They successfully preserved their sense of community, although the tribal language faded and missionaries converted the entire population.

A somewhat smaller group of Delaware endured a number of relocations by the U.S. government, moving from Pennsylvania to Ohio to Missouri, then to a reservation in Kansas and then another at Bartlesville, Oklahoma. The largest group of Delaware succeeded in maintaining a distinct community, moving like the smaller group to Pennsylvania, then Ohio, and eventually to present-day Missouri in 1793. In Missouri, this group of Delaware had to contend not only with the rapidly expanding American nation but also with British and Spanish traders, diplomats, and armies. In 1820,

This traditional woman's dance dress displays elaborate beadwork, brain-tanned hide, and jingles.

the Delaware accepted a land grant from the Spanish government and relocated to present-day eastern Texas. They were eventually forced from there, too, as many retreated from Texas in 1854 to settle at the Wichita Agency.

The Wichita had terrible pressure on their lands, especially through the allotment process, and most Delaware were enrolled and allotted as citizens of the Wichita or Caddo tribes. Culture and language loss accentuated the assimilation of the Delaware,

and for years they were unable to legally document their distinct community identity to the satisfaction of the U.S. government in appeals for federal recognition. The Oklahoma Indian Welfare Act of 1936 enabled Delaware at Anadarko, Oklahoma, to organize, although federal recognition was not affirmed until 1958.

■ GROS VENTRE
Current Locations: Montana
Language Family: Algonquian

The name Gros Ventre is derived from the French for "big bellies"; in their own language, the tribe referred to themselves as A'aninin, the People of the White Clay. Like the Arapaho and Cheyenne, their historic homes were on the east coast of North America, although they had settled in the central Great Lakes region as early as 3,000 years ago. By the time the French made it to the Mississippi headwaters, Rainy Lake and Lake of the Woods in what is now the Minnesota-Ontario border region, the Gros Ventre had emerged as a distinct people, with numerous villages along the Red River Valley in the eastern Plains. European diseases spread ahead of white men as they came to the Plains, and the extent of the damage to the Gros Ventre tribal population is not fully known, although most estimates are that more than half of their people perished.

The western Great Lakes and Plains were tense places to live. The winters were extreme, and survival was never guaranteed. The Gros Ventre abandoned their agricultural traditions as they moved onto the Plains because the soil was not well suited for traditional corn agriculture and because hunting proved to be a more reliable method of obtaining food. To maintain their standards of living, tribes competed over territory on the Plains. The Assiniboine and Cree constantly pressed the Gros Ventre, and through the advantages those tribes had in being upriver from their enemies and having reliable sources of guns and ammunition, the Gros Ventre were eventually forced to evacuate their homes in the Red

River Valley and move farther west, eventually into Montana. Resident tribes did not take kindly to their intrusion into new territory, however, and the Gros Ventre had to contend with new enemies on many fronts.

When the U.S. government, making way for white settlers, tried to draw lines between tribes on the Plains and establish reservations for many of them in the Treaty of Fort Laramie in 1851, the Gros Ventre were pressured to settle near U.S. military forts. They came to rely heavily on government rations to replace the food supplies lost to them when they were denied access to their historic territory and when the Plains buffalo were slaughtered wholesale.

Even after settling at the forts and Indian agencies, tribes competed over resources, and by 1871, the U.S. government had to relocate the Gros Ventre to Fort Belknap in north-central Montana. The Gros Ventre reservation was further reduced in 1895 to accommodate mining interests. A substantial group of Assiniboine—historic enemies of the Gros Ventre—was eventually settled at Fort Belknap, as well. The Gros Ventre formed strong friendships and family ties with the new arrivals, even absorbing some Métis and Cree when they sought refuge from conflict in their home communities. The Fort Belknap Indian Reservation became a cultural melting pot in some ways, but the Gros Ventre preserved their traditions and language, even though they embraced powwow customs in the 20th century.

HIDATSA
Current Locations: North Dakota
Language Family: Siouan

The Hidatsa, who are related to the Crow, were actually just one of three separate bands that called themselves Hiraacá, but the three groups merged and the name Hidatsa was applied to all. The Hidatsa trace their migration back to a homeland in central Minnesota, then along the Red River Valley, Lake Winnipeg, and Devil's Lake (North Dakota). The Dakota, Lakota, and Nakota eventually drove the Hidatsa out of Devil's Lake. The outnumbered

A Pawnee family poses next to their earth lodge in Loup, Nebraska, in this photo by William Henry Jackson taken in the late 19th or early 20th century.

Hidatsa then allied with the Mandan.

Smallpox epidemics devastated the tribe in the 1830s, and the Hidatsa and Mandan joined their villages for mutual protection and preservation of their social order. The Arikara, who had similar problems with both disease and stronger enemies, joined the alliance a few decades later.

The U.S. government reserved territory for the three tribes with the Treaty of Fort Laramie in 1851 and consolidated the Arikara, Hidatsa, and Mandan population to this much smaller tract of land. The Fort Berthold Reservation was created by executive order in 1870. The U.S. government relentlessly whittled away at the tribal land at Fort Berthold with the use of executive orders, allotment, and Indian Agency–enabled land fraud.

In 1954, the government dammed the Missouri River and flooded most of the lush lowland areas the Hidatsa farmed at Fort Berthold, forcing most of the tribe to the much higher and drier surrounding areas, dramatically reducing the arable farmland, and destroying homes, graveyards, and former village sites. Today the Three Affiliated Tribes, as the Arikara, Hidatsa, and Mandan are called, are growing in number and working to improve their standard of living and to revitalize tribal traditions.

HO-CHUNK (WINNEBAGO)
Current Locations: Nebraska, Iowa
Language Family: Siouan

Archaeological evidence confirms that the Ho-chunk (Winnebago) lived in Wisconsin by the year 500. In southern Wisconsin, the Ho-chunk maintained a sophisticated clan system and kinship network across multiple villages. Unlike many tribes in the Great Lakes and the Plains, they did not experience constant territorial pressure from their Native neighbors.

When the Americans came after Ho-chunk land, the tribe chose passive resistance. They simply avoided diplomatic and military encounters, not fighting but also not complying with removal orders. Treaties in 1825, 1832, and 1837 called for land cessions, removal, and new reservations, but with limited effect. The 1837 treaty created a reservation in the far southeastern corner of Minnesota, but no one moved until 1842, and even then most stayed in Wisconsin.

A treaty in 1846 ceded the largely unused reservation for a new one at Long Prairie in central Minnesota. The government was able to relocate less than half of the population to Long Prairie. The Ho-chunk were unhappy there because the land was not suited to their accustomed type of farming and because Dakota and Ojibwe war parties often traveled through their new villages en route to fighting one another.

In 1855, the Ho-chunk ceded Long Prairie and moved to a smaller but more fertile reservation at Blue Earth in southern Minnesota, although most of the tribe continued to squat on their former homeland in Wisconsin. The Ho-chunk at Blue Earth flourished for a time, but after the U.S.–Dakota War of 1862, they were forcibly relocated to Nebraska, even though they had nothing to do with the conflict. Today, the Wisconsin Ho-chunk assist the Nebraska community with language and culture revitalization. Gaming revenue has accelerated efforts to revitalize the tribal language.

IOWA (BÁXOJE, IOWAY)
Current Locations: Kansas, Nebraska, Oklahoma
Language Family: Siouan

The Iowa splintered off from the Ho-chunk in Wisconsin and settled in the present-day state of Iowa long before European contact. They had a mixed economy that relied on both farming and hunting. The tribe successfully negotiated its way through steady pressure from larger Indian neighbors who wanted to claim their territory, as well as French, British, and Spanish explorers. But the United States brought overwhelming pressure on tribes after the Revolutionary War, steadily pushing west through the southern Great Lakes. One by one, tribes were forced west of the Mississippi. The Sac and Fox relocation pushed more and more Indians to the edges of their lands, and by the time the Americans came after Iowa land, it was very difficult to sue for decent land terms.

Most of the Iowa were relocated west of the Mississippi in 1824, to a new reservation on the Kansas–Nebraska border. Another group of Iowa avoided the new reservation by moving into Missouri, but white settlement there quickly forced them out. In 1883, a new reservation was established for them in Oklahoma. Today, both the Iowa Tribe of Oklahoma and the Ioway Tribe of Kansas and Nebraska are working hard to strengthen their respective communities, which at the lowest point had been reduced to just a couple hundred people.

Dr. Charles A. Eastman (1858–1939), wearing a feather headdress, heavily fringed and beaded shirt, leggings, and moccasins enters a decorated, brightly lit tepee of the Wahpeton Sioux.

KAW (KANSA, KANZA)
Current Locations: Oklahoma
Language Family: Siouan

Unlike many tribes in the Siouan language family, the Kaw were not nomadic, but rather sedentary farmers who lived in earthen lodges. Although the Kaw can trace their roots to the Ohio River Valley, by the time Europeans encountered them, they occupied a large territory that covered parts of present-day Iowa, Missouri, Nebraska, and much of Kansas. They maintained a strong military presence to protect themselves from raiders.

The Kaw successfully kept control over most of their territory until 1825, when they signed a treaty that surrendered more than 18 million acres for less than one-third of a cent per acre. The U.S. government soon started using former Kaw land as relocation space for other tribes, and the influx of new neighbors coupled with the land loss impoverished the Kaw. Land and railroad speculators preyed on Kaw land holdings.

A federal act in 1872 established a reservation for the Kaw in Kay County, Oklahoma, with the expectation that the entire population would be forced to relocate. In spite of tremendous pressure on the remaining Kaw lands through allotment and on their culture through residential boarding schools, the Kaw adapted. Today, the Native American Church, which incorporates pre-Columbian use of peyote with Christianity, is widely practiced, as is Christianity.

KIOWA
Current Locations: Oklahoma
Language Family: Kiowa-Tanoan

The Kiowa are related to the Pueblo of New Mexico, a connection that was only firmly established in the 20th century. By the time Europeans came to the southern Plains, the Kiowa controlled a large territory in present-day Oklahoma and Texas. They were friendly with their Comanche neighbors and followed a similar seasonal round, reliant primarily on hunting. When conflict in the northern Plains pushed the Cheyenne and other tribes south, however, it created territorial competition with the Kiowa. The Kiowa were accomplished warriors and raiders, and they fought with the Arapaho, Cheyenne, Osage, Pawnee, and even the Sac and Fox. As Mexican and American settlers encroached on tribal land in the southern Plains, the Kiowa again rallied to their own defense.

The first half of the 19th century was filled with conflict as the Kiowa defended their villages and raided white and Native communities throughout New Mexico,

Texas, and Mexico until well after the Civil War. Early peace treaties produced little effect, because white settlers did not respect the sovereignty of the Kiowa, and the Kiowa had no tolerance for intrusions on their land or livelihoods. The Treaty of Medicine Lodge in 1867 did more to reconfigure the dynamic on the southern Plains because it had strong terms of support for tribal territorial control, but that treaty also brought the Kiowa their first reduction in territory as well as reliance on government annuities to compensate for loss of access to natural resources. The vicious spiral brought poverty and erosion of political structures. The treaty was broken a year later, and the Kiowa resumed raiding in Texas. But after the massacre at Washita Creek in 1868, the Kiowa realized that raiding would only bring horrendous consequences upon their families.

The Kiowa were settled on a smaller reservation in Oklahoma contemporaneously with the Comanche and some Apache who had allied themselves with the Kiowa. The Kiowa intermittently left the reservation to hunt or raid throughout the 1870s. Many Kiowa picked up the Ghost Dance and the Native American Church. The pow-wow proliferated in the 20th century and remains a vibrant part of tribal culture.

MANDAN

Current Locations: North Dakota
Language Family: Siouan

The Mandan, closely related to the Ho-chunk (Winnebago), built large wooden lodges covered with earth and lived in large villages in the eastern Plains. Like the Ho-chunk, they probably farmed more than they hunted originally. But as the Mandan migrated farther west and onto the Plains, they came to rely more on the seasonal cycle of hunting and gathering, although their lodges and more densely populated villages date to their roots as agricultural people.

Disease pandemics hit the Mandan harder than many other Plains tribes, killing

Sioux female doll made from deerskin and canvas in about 1890, wearing deerskin dress with bead and cowrie shell decoration

as much as 98 percent of the tribal population, because they lived so close to one another in traditional villages.

By the time Europeans came onto the Plains, the Mandan were in close alliance with the Siouan-speaking Hidatsa and the Caddoan-speaking Arikara. Over time, those three tribes came to rely on one another for mutual protection. The clan relationships and inter-marriages connected their tribes in perpetuity.

The Mandan had early encounters with the Lewis and Clark expedition, George Catlin, and other European explorers. The U.S. government reserved territory for the three tribes under the Treaty of Fort Laramie in 1851 and consolidated the Arikara, Hidatsa, and Mandan population there. The formal Fort Berthold Reservation was created by executive order in 1870. The U.S. government then relentlessly whittled away at the tribal land at Fort Berthold with the use of executive orders, allotment, and Indian Agency enabling of land fraud.

In 1954, the government dammed the Missouri River and flooded most of the lush lowland areas the Mandan farmed at Fort Berthold, forcing 80 percent of the tribal population to move to the much higher and drier surrounding areas, reducing the arable farmland, and forcing tribal members to abandon homes, graveyards, and former village sites.

MIAMI

Current Locations: Oklahoma
Language Family: Algonquian

The Miami are originally from the Atlantic coast. By the time the French established fixed posts and forts in the southern Great Lakes, though, the Miami had several substantial bands in Indiana, southern Michigan, and Ohio. They had come to the southern Great Lakes from Wisconsin in large part because of sustained conflict with the Iroquois Confederacy in the eastern Great Lakes. The Miami worked cooperatively with the French, and some Miami

A 19th-century battle between the Sioux and the Sac and Fox, re-created on canvas by George Catlin joined Pontiac during his war against the British in 1763. But soon afterward, most Miami bands accepted British trade and political position in the region.

The relationship between the Miami and the Americans was much more contentious. Most Miami sided with the British during the Revolutionary War. Afterward, the new American nation sought to expand its control over Miami territory. Miami chief Little Turtle led large war parties against American troops and won a couple of major battles.

The tide of battle shifted dramatically in 1794, after the Shawnee, Miami allies, were defeated at the Battle of Fallen Timbers. Pressure mounted on all tribes in the southern Great Lakes, and the next year, many were forced to sign the Treaty of Greenville or to retreat into Canada. The Miami signed, and it was the beginning of a series of horrible land transactions that soon disempowered and impoverished most of the tribal population. The Indian Removal Act of 1830 increased pressure on the Miami to relocate west of the Mississippi. In 1840, a reservation was established for them in Kansas. Even there, the Miami would not be permitted to rest. The new Kansas reservation was ceded in 1867 and the remaining tribal population relocated once again, this time to Oklahoma.

Today, the Miami Tribe of Oklahoma is the only federally recognized Miami tribal community, although many Miami refused to relocate and either took refuge in other tribal communities or squatted in their original homelands, mixing with the European population. Today, some of those Miami descendants have sought to recreate cultural enclaves and even

A 19th-century pouch, made from leather, porcupine quills, and duck skin. The design depicts three thunderbirds, bringers of lightning, wind, and rain.

sought recognition as a tribe, so far without success.

■ MODOC

Current Locations: Oklahoma, Oregon

Language Family: Penutian

The Modoc are originally from what is today the Oregon–California border region, where they followed a seasonal cycle of gathering, fishing, and hunting. Although their band was very small, they successfully defended their territory from other tribes, including the Klamath, for many years.

Modoc life changed quickly after the arrival of Europeans. Tribal members made many adaptations—from clothing to naming traditions. That still would not spare them a brutal colonial experience during the early American period. In 1864, the large non-Native population demanded formal acquisition of the entire 5,000 square miles of Modoc land. The tribe was vastly outnumbered and overpowered and had no choice

but to sign the proffered treaty, which required them to settle on the Klamath Reservation with their former enemies.

The move to Klamath was a disaster for the Modoc. Poverty, high mortality rates, and disempowerment were heart-rending. With a small band of followers, Modoc Chief Captain Jack left the reservation and returned to the ancestral Modoc homeland. The U.S. Army and local militias pursued and attacked Captain Jack's band. The event came to be known as the Modoc War. Facing complete annihilation, the band had no choice but to surrender in 1865. But they broke free from the Klamath Reservation again as soon as the Army left. They maintained a guerrilla war and avoided capture from 1865 to 1873. Again with little hope of victory and facing dismal living conditions, the Modoc surrendered. The U.S. government hanged all the Modoc leaders.

The remnants of Captain Jack's band were exiled to Oklahoma, but arid conditions on the tract eventually set aside for them meant it was ill suited for agriculture and devoid of fish or game. The population dwindled to 68 people by the time their lands were allotted in 1891. Some Modoc stayed at

Sioux Indians playing lacrosse in 1851, as depicted by Seth Eastman. The game was much rougher than today's version, doubling as training for combat. Games sometimes involved hundreds of players and lasted for days.

Klamath. Many married and were absorbed into the Klamath community there. As the living conditions in Oklahoma improved somewhat in the early 1900s, some voluntarily migrated to Oklahoma, although the U.S. government refused to acknowledge them as Modoc rather than Klamath.

The Modoc of Oklahoma were terminated as a federally recognized tribe in the 1950s, although after a long legal battle, successfully reinstated in 1978. The tribe's language has been totally lost, but its sense of community and distinct governance persist. There are around 200 people on the tribal rolls today.

OMAHA

Current Locations: Nebraska
Language Family: Siouan

The Omaha are closely related to the Kansa, Osage, Ponca, and Quapaw. Before 1600, those tribes were one people, but they separated and developed distinct language and cultural differences over time. The Omaha migrated from the Ohio Valley to the Tallgrass Prairie near the mouth of the Missouri River. They established large semipermanent villages, grew corn, and ranged west through the Tallgrass Prairie and Plains to hunt buffalo. The Dakota, Lakota, and Nakota raided Omaha villages, and tensions remained high through much of the early 1800s. They did not war with the United States, in spite of many encroachments.

In the 1831 Treaty of Prairie du Chien, the Omaha ceded their lands east of the Missouri but retained hunting rights. Pressure on their lifeways and land mounted, and the Omaha signed additional treaties in 1836 and 1854, the latter of which established the current Omaha Reservation in Thurston County, Nebraska. The last treaty was highly contentious, and the large Omaha delegation that went to Washington felt deceived by the treaty process and the result. The tribe has made a concerted effort to preserve tribal culture and practice. In spite of a long-standing effort by Quaker and other missionaries, assimilation never fully succeeded.

In 1908, long after the heyday of war parties and inter-tribal conflicts, Gros Ventre warriors reenacted a war party for photographer Edward S. Curtis.

OSAGE

Current Locations: Oklahoma
Language Family: Siouan

The original homelands of the Osage were in present-day Kentucky. After decades of warfare and territorial pressure from the powerful Iroquois Confederacy, they migrated out of the Ohio River Valley and west to the Tallgrass Prairie and eventually the central Plains. The Osage flourished and controlled substantial territory in parts of present-day Arkansas, Kansas, Nebraska, and Oklahoma. When the French arrived in the 1600s, they actively traded with them and formed an alliance when the French fought Algonquian tribes in the southern Great Lakes. The French even brought a delegation of Osage chiefs and warriors to Paris in 1725.

As the French and Spanish were replaced by Americans, the Osage–French relationship worked to the business advantage of the Osage because French traders remained after their government sold the Louisiana Purchase. However, their friends in the fur trade had no power to protect the Osage. Treaties in 1808, 1818, and 1825 forced the Osage to sell their land in Arkansas, Oklahoma, and Kansas. They were promised a reservation in Oklahoma, only to find

out that it was a removal location for the Cherokee and other members of the Five Civilized Tribes. Forced onto a less desirable location in Kansas, the Osage suffered from extreme poverty and harsh conditions. They were pressured for further land cessions by treaty in 1865.

In 1870, the Osage agreed to move to Oklahoma, using the proceeds from the sale of their Kansas reservation to buy their new land in Oklahoma. Despite enduring allotment in Oklahoma, the Osage successfully retained their mineral rights on the new reservation, and when the oil boom came, many Osage were able to benefit financially. However, between various types of property swindles and federal legislation requiring those who were half Osage to have guardians exercise a durable power of attorney over their finances, many Osage were defrauded. Today, there are nearly 15,000 tribal members, most of whom live on or near the reservation.

OTOE-MISSOURIA

Current Locations: Oklahoma
Language Family: Siouan

Although one people long ago, the Siouan group diversified culturally and linguistically as it spread from east to west through

Oglala Sioux perform the Sun Dance on the Pine Ridge Reservation in South Dakota in the mid-20th century. Two men and a woman hold up wreaths toward a tree adorned with ceremonial objects.

explorers and traders, and eventually the full force of the American expansion. Epidemics wreaked havoc on the population contemporaneously with relentless attacks from the Cheyenne and Lakota.

During this difficult period, the U.S. pressed the Pawnee for land cessions. From 1818 to 1875, the Pawnee were forced into treaties and endured executive orders that obliterated their traditional territory and left them with just a fragment of their land in the form of a reservation at Nance County, Nebraska. The Lakota continued to raid the Pawnee on their reservation, the confines of which made them predictable targets.

Due to the Lakota raids and loss of life as well as white encroachment, the Pawnee agreed to move to Oklahoma in 1875. Their lands were allotted in 1892, and by 1900 the population had been reduced to less than 1,000. Throughout the transition to reservation life, Pawnee men signed up for the U.S. Army as scouts, especially during the campaigns against the Lakota. The tradition of military service continued with each American war, even to the present day, when the Pawnee still serve in higher numbers per capita than the general population.

the central United States. The Otoe were living in the present-day Minnesota–Iowa border region and the Missouria in present-day Missouri when the French encountered them in the 1600s. By 1800, pressure from the Sac and Fox and other tribes coupled with disease to reduce the numbers of the Missouria to the breaking point. Some tribal members sought refuge with and were absorbed by the Osage and Kaw, but a larger group unified with the Otoe.

Although explorer George Catlin estimated that there were at least 1,200 Otoe-Missouria when he encountered the tribe in 1833, a tribal census in 1886 found only 334 tribal members, as warfare and disease took their toll. Severely weakened, the tribe signed treaties with the U.S. in 1830, 1833, 1836, and finally 1854. The last treaty established a reservation for the Otoe-Missouria on the Kansas-Nebraska border.

The tribe split into two main bands. A missionized group assumed the name Quaker Band, while those who followed traditional religious practice called themselves the Coyote Band. Between 1876 and 1881, tribal lands on the reservation were sold and a new reservation established in Oklahoma. The Quaker Band moved

there, but the Coyote Band was sent to the Sac and Fox Reservation. Eventually, many Coyote Band members migrated to the Otoe-Missouria Reservation. The Curtis Act abolished their tribal government, and the tribe was not federally reinstated until 1984.

▓ PAWNEE

Current Locations: Oklahoma
Language Family: Caddoan

The Pawnee may have been one of the first tribes to settle on the Plains. They had a mixed economy, reliant on both farming and hunting. The Plains were heavily contested, and many powerful tribes sparred for land and resources. The Pawnee had four independent bands and a population of more than 12,000. Through the strength of their numbers and long experience defending their lands, they maintained control over a substantial territory in the present-day states of Kansas and Nebraska. The Pawnee encountered Spanish conquistadors, numerous French and British

Calumet, or ceremonial pipe made from wood and feather, in about 1875. The pipe was not smoked but displayed in ceremonies.

▓ PEORIA

Current Locations: Oklahoma
Language Family: Algonquian

The Peoria are an offshoot of the large Algonquian group, closely related to the Miami. The Peoria had historic homelands on the Atlantic coast, although they had been long established in the southern Great Lakes when the French encountered them. Most Peoria rapidly converted to Catholicism through the work of French Jesuit missionaries. In the mid-1700s, at least one band of Peoria moved to present-day Missouri, while another stayed on the south shore of Lake Michigan.

By treaties in 1818 and 1832,

the Peoria ceded their lands in Illinois and Missouri for a reservation in Kansas along with the Kaskaskia, Piankeshaw, and Wea, who were all subsumed under the tribal designation Peoria. The tribe signed the Omnibus Treaty in 1867 and was again relocated, this time to Oklahoma. They endured allotment through the Curtis Act and continual pressure to assimilate. Their tribal government was disbanded and terminated, but finally reinstated in 1978.

PONCA

Current Locations: Nebraska, Oklahoma
Language Family: Siouan

The Ponca migrated from the Ohio River Valley to the Upper Missouri River prior to European contact. The Lewis and Clark expedition noted that the Ponca farmed corn in addition to hunting—a somewhat anomalous development in that area. That they had established farms suggests a sustained period of habitation to keep sufficient seed on hand through droughts and raids.

The Ponca signed treaties with the U.S. in 1817, 1825, 1858, and 1865, ceding their territory for a substantial reservation on the Niobrara River, a location of their own choosing. When the Lakota defeated the U.S. Army and dictated terms at the Treaty of Fort Laramie in 1868, the treaty created competing claims for the long-established Ponca reservation, which the Lakota wanted. To avoid a war between the tribes, the U.S. government coerced the Ponca into moving to Oklahoma.

The Ponca refused to move, however, and were relocated by force by the Army in 1877. Standing Bear, a Ponca chief, left the reservation, was detained by U.S. officials, and filed a legal protest in U.S. court. He said that he could not be detained as a prisoner of war because his tribe had never been at war with the U.S. He ultimately won, although the victory came with an assumption that he relinquished his tribal status by seeking rights common to U.S. citizens. The case did raise awareness of the

unfair treatment of his people, though, and in 1881, the U.S. government established a second reservation for them in Nebraska. About half of the tribe moved there, while the rest stayed in Oklahoma. The Nebraska Ponca were terminated in 1966, but reinstated in 1990.

Twentieth-century Mandan-Hidatsa woman sews a box at the reconstructed 1575–1781 Indian village at modern-day Fort Abraham Lincoln State Park in North Dakota.

QUAPAW

Current Locations: Oklahoma
Language Family: Siouan

The Quapaw migrated out of the Ohio River Valley around 1200 to present-day Arkansas. Although a smaller group than many of their Native neighbors, the Quapaw flourished with a highly developed agricultural economy and close-knit clan and kin network. The Hernando de Soto expedition in 1541 exposed the tribe to European diseases, which ravaged their population. The French had decades of sustained contact with the Quapaw and, through both missionary work and intermarriage, introduced most of the tribe to Catholicism and European value systems. Although they ceded most of their land in

three major treaties, it was the treaty of 1834 that established the Quapaw Reservation in Oklahoma and required their relocation there. The tribe moved and adapted, even though their tribal language and many cultural customs were lost.

SAC AND FOX

Current Locations: Iowa, Kansas, Nebraska, Oklahoma; Mexico
Language Family: Algonquian

The Sac (Sauk) and Fox are two distinct tribes of the Algonquian language family. The Fox emerged as a well-defined people in the eastern Great Lakes, and by the time the French arrived there early in the 1600s, they had moved west into what is now Michigan's Upper Peninsula. The Dakota and Ojibwe warred with the Fox, and so the Fox moved south toward Green Bay, Wisconsin, where they held a dominant position on the trade route that the French used to connect their colonies in Louisiana with the Great Lakes.

The French eventually issued a genocidal edict against the Fox. From 1690 to 1733, the French took no prisoners and encouraged their Indian trading partners to exterminate the tribe. The weakened Fox sought refuge among their cousins, the Sac, and over the next several decades the tribes slowly merged their bloodlines and customs.

By 1800, the merged Sac and Fox had moved to southern Wisconsin, northern Illinois, and Iowa. Some bands allied with the British during the War of 1812, while others remained neutral. After that war, the U.S. ramped up pressure on the pro-British bands to cede land. Most Sac and Fox were unaware that the treaty they signed in 1825 included land cession clauses rather than simple peace and friendship language, so the rapid influx of settlers to the newly available land caught them by surprise.

The Black Hawk War erupted in 1832, when 1,500 Sac and Fox crossed into Illinois to plant corn and were fired upon by the local militia. Warriors returned fire. With only 500 warriors and twice as many children and elders, their leader Black Hawk eluded capture, fighting a brilliant guerrilla war against more than 7,000 U.S. soldiers. With the help of Dakota reinforcements, the U.S. eventually pinned the Sac and Fox near Madison, Wisconsin. The resulting treaty forced the tribe to surrender all remaining land and move west of the Mississippi.

Ten years later, the tribe was removed from Iowa to a new reservation near Topeka, Kansas, although numerous Sac and Fox fled or hid. In 1859, the tribe fractured as some went to Mexico with the Kickapoo to elude the Americans. Some returned to Iowa, squatting in their former homeland. They eventually saved enough money by selling crafts to purchase land, which many years later received federal recognition as a reservation. The rest of the Sac and Fox stayed in Kansas, but after ten years, the government moved the tribe again, this time to Oklahoma. There the tribe lost more land through allotment in 1891, with only 1.3 percent of their reservation left in Indian hands.

The Fox people, whose numbers swelled as high as 20,000 prior to conflict with the French, numbered only 500 at the population's lowest point. Although scattered today, the population is back to its precontact level, and at the reservation in Tama, Iowa, the language and culture remain especially strong.

■ SHAWNEE
Current Locations: Oklahoma
Language Family: Algonquian

Although the Eastern Shawnee Tribe of Oklahoma has only about 2,500 citizens today, as recently as 1800 they were one of the largest and most powerful tribes in the southern Great Lakes. Two major bands flourished on both sides of the Appalachians from Tennessee to South Carolina when British settlers first encountered them in the 1600s. The Shawnee put up a fierce resistance to the

encroachment of Europeans starting around 1690. Pressure from the British colonists and other tribes, especially the Cherokee, eventually forced both bands north into the Ohio Valley and Pennsylvania.

Shawnee chief Tecumseh forged a pan-Indian alliance to resist further intrusion on Shawnee lands during the War of 1812. His brother Tenskwatawa, a spiritual leader, united their people at Prophetstown and for a long time commanded a huge swath

A Blackfoot brave stands in the doorway of a tepee in an encampment near Calgary, Alberta, in this 1889 photo.

of territory along the southern Great Lakes. American attacks at Prophetstown did not kill many Indians, but did destroy large amounts of stored food, which weakened the tribal resistance. In 1811, future U.S. President William Henry Harrison led a successful engagement against Tecumseh and the Shawnee at Tippecanoe, and the tribe never fully recovered.

Many Shawnee, fearing retribution, sought refuge with other Great Lakes tribes in the U.S. and Canada. The Shawnee who remained in the Ohio Valley were forced to sign a treaty in 1831 by which they surrendered their remaining land and

moved to a much smaller parcel in Ottawa County, Oklahoma. Some allied Seneca were relocated with the Shawnee. Pressure on Shawnee land continued through the allotment period, but the Indian Reorganization Act of 1934 enabled the tribe to establish a modern tribal government.

■ SIOUX
(DAKOTA, LAKOTA, NAKOTA)
Current Locations: Alberta, Manitoba, Saskatchewan; Minnesota, Montana, Nebraska, North Dakota, South Dakota
Language Family: Siouan

The Sioux are one of the largest and most powerful tribal groups on the Plains. They are not really one homogenous tribe, but rather a large and diverse alliance among many different bands that the Sioux themselves originally called the Oceti Sákowin, or Seven Council Fires: Mdewakanton, Sisseton, Teton, Wahpekute, Wahpeton, Yankton, and Yanktonai. All bands in the Seven Council Fires shared certain commonalities in language and culture, but not uniformity.

Four of the seven major bands were Dakota and occupied the eastern section of Sioux territory. Their dialect used a *d* in many places where the Nakota used an *n* and the Lakota used an *l*. The eastern Dakota did not practice the Sun Dance, but actively maintained the Wakan Dance as their central religious society. They also relied for food on farming corn, harvesting wild rice, and fishing, whereas other bands of Sioux to the west relied much more on hunting.

By the 1800s, the western Lakota had grown greatly in numbers, spreading through present-day Nebraska, North Dakota, South Dakota, and parts of Montana and Wyoming, occupying new territory claimed at the expense of other tribes. The Lakota further diversified into seven more bands: Blackfoot, Brulé, Hunkpapa, Miniconjou, Oglala, Sans Arc, and Two Kettles.

The name Sioux is really a corruption of the Ojibwe word naadowesiwag, a species of snake. The "siw" root morphed into

Sioux. That has left many Dakota, Lakota, and Nakota unhappy with the term Sioux, although it has persisted simply because writing out all the diverse groups who fit under the grouping gets cumbersome and the original name Oceti Sákowin does not really accurately encompass the organization of Sioux communities today.

All Sioux groups had to defend themselves from brutal military actions by the U.S. Army. The most well-known conflicts are the U.S.–Dakota War of 1862, Red Cloud's War, the Battle of the Little Bighorn, and the Wounded Knee Massacre. The Lakota have had a powerful impact on the culture of many other tribes because they have actively shared their teachings and ceremonies about sweat lodges and the Sun Dance, leading to the proliferation of Lakota customs beyond their immediate region. The Lakota have also often been the subject of movies and books, capturing the imagination of many non-Native people. Today, there are Sioux communities in several U.S. states and Canadian provinces.

Ogala Lakota tribesman Stanley Goodvoice Elk burns sage and prays to prepare for a kettle dance to thank the thunderbeings (thunderstorms) as they leave for the summer. Elk wears the mask of a heyoka, a receiver of spiritual visions.

■ TONKAWA

Current Locations: Oklahoma
Language Family: Isolate

The Tonkawa spoke a unique language that is now extinct. They had an ancestral homeland in Oklahoma and Texas, perhaps numbering as many as 5,000 people at the height of their power. Even with numbers like those, the Tonkawa were vastly outnumbered by the Apache, Comanche, and other Plains tribes to their north. The Tonkawa were greatly affected by both warfare and disease prior to the American period. They sided with the Confederacy during the Civil War and afterward were heavily persecuted, losing as much as half of the remaining tribal population in conflicts with the United States. In 1884, the survivors were forcibly relocated from Brazos, Texas, to Oklahoma. Their reservation lands were allotted in 1891.

A leather amulet of the 19th-century Plains Indians, with bead decoration, contains an umbilical cord.

■ WICHITA

Current Locations: Oklahoma
Language Family: Caddoan

The Wichita are indigenous to the lands that are now Kansas, Oklahoma, and Texas. Four major groups of Wichita, including the Taovaya, Tawakoni, Waco, and Wichita, covered the extent of this large territory when Europeans first encountered them.

The Wichita had many encounters with early Spanish conquistadors and French explorers and traders. Disease took its toll on the tribe, which maintained fairly dense villages for purposes of protection, enabled by their mixed agricultural and hunting economy. For this lifestyle, they constructed large earthen lodges, which they covered in grass, quite distinct from their more nomadic Comanche neighbors.

Wichita bands were significantly weakened by disease and sporadic warfare by the time the Americans came after their land. A permanent reservation was established for them in 1872 in Oklahoma.

■ WYANDOTTE

Current Locations: Oklahoma
Language Family: Iroquoian

The Wyandotte (Wyandot), indigenous to Ontario and Quebec, were attacked and pursued by the Iroquois Confederacy in the 1600s. By the late 1700s, the weakened tribe had regrouped in the southern Great Lakes. Many bands allied themselves with the British during the Revolutionary War.

After they lost the Battle of Fallen Timbers in 1794, the Wyandotte were forced to yield territory. More land was lost by treaty in 1817 and 1843, when a reservation was established in Kansas. Some of the tribe voluntarily moved to Oklahoma after white settlers began encroaching on their Kansas reservation.

Both the Kansas Wyandotte and the Oklahoma Wyandotte were in legal limbo for many years. The Oklahoma Wyandotte eventually succeeded in getting a land grant and were joined by some Kansas and Michigan relatives, only to lose much land through allotment. They were formally recognized as the Wyandotte Tribe of Oklahoma in 1937. Other Wyandotte survivors are scattered throughout the Great Lakes, including Canada.

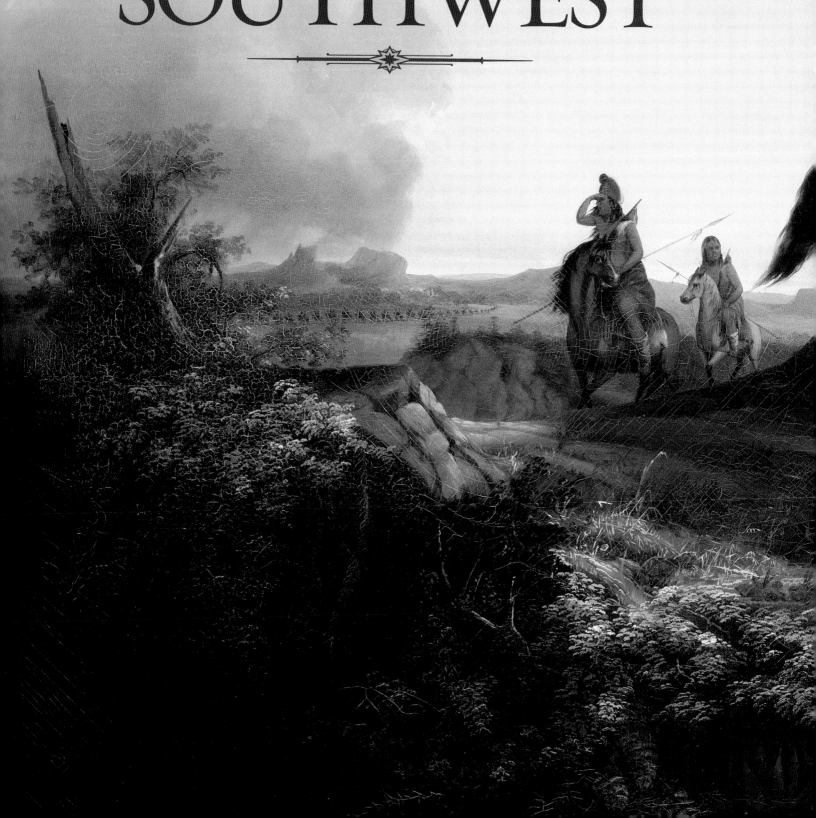

SOUTHWEST

· CHAPTER FIVE ·

APACHE

COCOPAH

HAVASUPAI

HOPI

HUALAPAI

MARICOPA

MOHAVE
(MOJAVE)

NAVAJO

PIMA

PUEBLO

QUECHAN (YUMA)

TIGUA
(YSLETA DEL SUR)

TOHONO
O'ODHAM
(PAPAGO)

YAQUI

YAVAPAI

ZUNI

Baishan (Black Knife) was a Chiricahua
Apache war leader and chief lieutenant
of Mangas Coloradas during the Apache
resistance in the 1830s and 1840s. The
Apache were among the most resilient
and tenacious tribes in the Southwest in
resisting intrusions into their land.

Indian Nations of the Southwest

T he Native nations of the Southwest have long achieved amazing, seemingly impossible, accomplishments. The Anasazi, predecessors to the Hopi and Pueblo, built an astounding nine-mile-long city at Chaco Canyon, with more than 70 satellite communities and a central building constructed with more than 50 million sandstone blocks and 5,000 trees. All the major structures at Chaco align perfectly at the summer solstice. And the Anasazi did it without human slaves, beasts of burden, compasses, transits, or wheels. The climate in the Southwest is harsh, and the people could be just as tough as the weather. No matter how hot and dry the deserts, no matter how cold the highest

peaks, the peoples of the Southwest found a way not just to survive but to thrive. Many of the tribes there farmed, but often by innovative means suited to their environments. Every year, Yuman-speaking peoples along the Colorado River watched for the sediment-filled spring thaw to overrun the banks of the river and immediately planted corn, beans, and squash in the floodplain, harvesting bountiful crops right before the landscape turned completely arid again. The Zuni, like the Anasazi before them, dug elaborate irrigation systems and diverted water to nurture their crops. The Pueblo of the Rio Grande Valley planted along the fertile riverbanks. The Hopi figured out how to divert captured rain to feed a large population in a very dry place. The tribes all gathered nuts, berries, cactus fruit, and many kinds of plants. Most hunted. Some, such as the Pueblo, merely augmented their farmed

Southwest tribes maintain an array of artistic, cultural, and religious traditions. They include pre-Columbian regalia and beliefs such as those of this Hopi Snake Clan priest (opposite), as well as distinctive art that fuses tribal art forms with modern items, as in turquoise and metalwork (above).

food supply; others, like the Apache, relied primarily on hunting. Some tribes fished, although many of the Apache and Yavapai bands eschewed it for cultural reasons.

The Spanish changed the lives of all the tribes in the Southwest, although not all by conquest. They introduced sheep, chickens, horses, and metal plows. The Navajo quickly seized upon ranching and maintained huge herds of sheep, as they still do. Even the sedentary farmers at Zuni eventually took up ranching. The Apache, who were never conquered by the Spanish even though they fought each other plenty of times, raided settlers' livestock and kept large horse herds. The Spaniards' introduction of the horse changed the nature of travel, war, and raiding, too. Mounted on horseback, people went farther to attack, moved more quickly, and surprised their enemies more often.

INDIGENOUS FOODS OF THE SOUTHWEST

Despite the unforgiving climate of the Southwest, the precontact Pueblo population was more than 40,000, and other tribes also had large populations and often high population densities. The size and splendor of Chaco Canyon and other ancient Anasazi sites also evidence a large indigenous population. That was possible only because of the abundance and diversity of food in the Native diet.

The Southwest is very dry, but there are places suited to rain capture, irrigation, and maintenance of soil moisture. The most sedentary tribes lived along riverbanks or mesas where irrigation and rain capture was easiest. At Hohokam, the Anasazi dug eight-foot-deep irrigation trenches 20 miles long. Many Indians successfully farmed corn, squash, pumpkins, sunflowers, beans, and chilies.

All tribes in the Southwest hunted elk, deer, antelope, rabbits, and other small game. Many fished, as well. People gathered foods that were closest to them, including piñon nuts, acorns, saguaro, cholla, prickly pear, mesquite beans, agave, and several kinds of berries.

Some tribes had cultural prohibitions against eating certain foods. Among the Apache, for example, most people abstained from eating bear and often fish. Each tribe had different rules. And sometimes within a tribe, individuals might have personal spiritual food prohibitions or requirements.

Although new foods such as fry bread have become a part of the tribal diet and today most Southwest Indians purchase much of their food in stores, many individuals and tribes are working to revitalize emphasis on healthy traditional indigenous food.

KACHINAS AND TRADITIONS

Kachinas are spirits in the cosmology of the Puebloan people, especially those at Acoma, Hopi, Isleta, Laguna, and Zuni. Many things

---

CHRONOLOGY

2000 B.C.
Anasazi, Hohokam, and Mogollon cultures emerge among Indians already established in the Southwest for hundreds and possibly thousands of years

A.D. 1130–1180
Great drought forces Anasazi to abandon Chaco Canyon and spread throughout the Southwest, settling many Pueblo village sites

1598
Juan de Oñate expedition heralds formal start to Spanish mission period

1680
Pueblo Revolt: Hopi, Pueblo, and Zuni unite to expel Spanish from Arizona and New Mexico

1821–1848
Mexican independence brings new government and settler pressures on tribes; altercations over Texas set the stage for a shift in colonial power

1848
Treaty of Guadalupe Hidalgo ends Mexican–American War

1848–1855
California gold rush brings hundreds of thousands of white prospectors through the Southwest

1853
Gadsden Purchase: America further expands its southern border

1886
Geronimo surrenders, ending the Apache Wars, but starting the longest prisoner-of-war experience in U.S. history for the Apache

---

Native nations in the Southwest flourished at the convergence of the plains, mountains, and desert. They sometimes resisted Spanish, Mexican, and American intrusions and, in spite of horrible treatment, fared better than tribes in other areas in holding onto their lifeways, languages, and land.

---

can be considered kachinas, including thunderbirds, the wind, special places, and even the souls of departed ancestors. Most kachinas, like people, have relationships to one another. There are more than 400 identified kachinas. For the Hopi, many of the kachinas live around the San Francisco Peaks near Flagstaff, Arizona. For the Zuni, many live in the water near their pueblo. Kachinas travel from their homes to the people to dance, eat, sing, and bring rain and gifts.

Many pueblos invoke the help of kachinas through ceremony. Elaborate dances appeal to the kachinas for rain, plentiful harvests, healing, fertility, and protection. Dancers dress in ornate regalia to symbolize the kachinas, and both the spirits and the dancers are called kachinas.

Among the Hopi in particular, the creation of dolls that represent the kachinas has evolved since the late 1800s into a highly specialized art form. The dolls are not designed to be toys or idols for worship, but rather teaching tools. The dolls are supposed to resemble the spirits so that they can be studied to better acquaint children with the nature of the spirits they represent. Usually made of cottonwood, the dolls are painted with colors, each a symbol for a cardinal direction or specific attribute. There are also unique symbols for different traits that describe a kachina's nature. Starting in the mid-1900s, the dolls became commoditized as well as symbolic; exceptional dolls can sometimes sell for as much as $10,000.

EUROPEAN INVASION

When the Spanish came to the Southwest, they were after resources—gold, silver, labor, food. At the sedentary pueblos, they established missions, as they had across Mexico. They didn't just try to convert the Natives; they also coerced their labor and took surplus food. That limited the

THE SOUTHWEST

SCALE
1 : 10,550,000

0	100	200	300

statute miles

0	100	200	300

kilometers

Map Key

⬜ ○ Federal Indian Reservation
(occupied by one or more tribal entities)

★ State or provincial capital

• Selected city or town

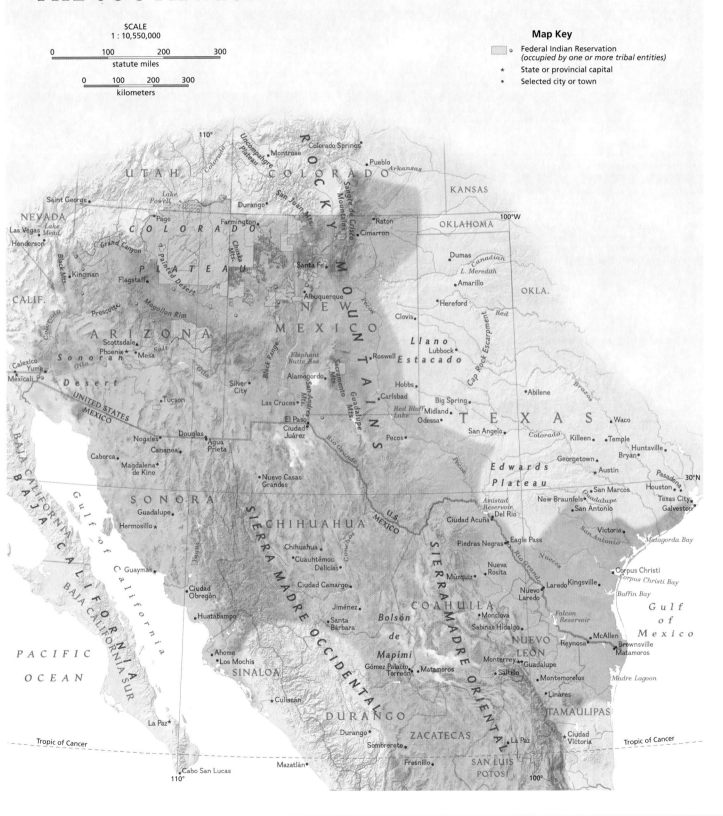

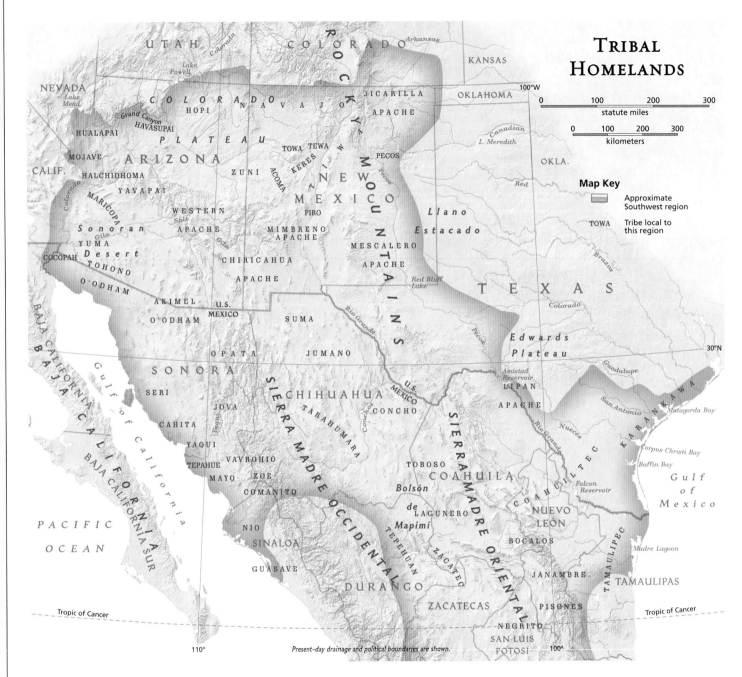

TRIBAL HOMELANDS

Map Key

Approximate Southwest region

TOWA — Tribe local to this region

Present-day drainage and political boundaries are shown.

---

ability of the farmers to trade, and raiding from the more nomadic Apache and Navajo increased after Spanish contact. The Spanish never could colonize the powerful Apache and had only limited success with the Navajo.

In 1821, Mexico won independence from Spain. The Mexicans had their own colonial ambitions, and for most tribes in the Southwest, it was resistance as usual. After Texas declared independence,

The hot, dry climate of the Southwest was not well suited to Euro-American agricultural techniques. Indigenous peoples had developed specialized knowledge of how to farm, gather, hunt, and later ranch in the region, and that—coupled with a tenacious attachment to place—helps explain how the tribes held onto much of their original homeland.

Mexico regarded it as a rebellious Mexican state. When the U.S. annexed that state, the Mexican–American War was on, and it ultimately led to America claiming title to the entire Southwest. But the 1848 Treaty of Guadalupe Hidalgo, which made that exchange, had no input from any tribe. Many tribes had never ceded an acre of land to the Spanish or Mexicans, and a few had never seen a white man. Then gold was discovered in California in 1848, and tribes across

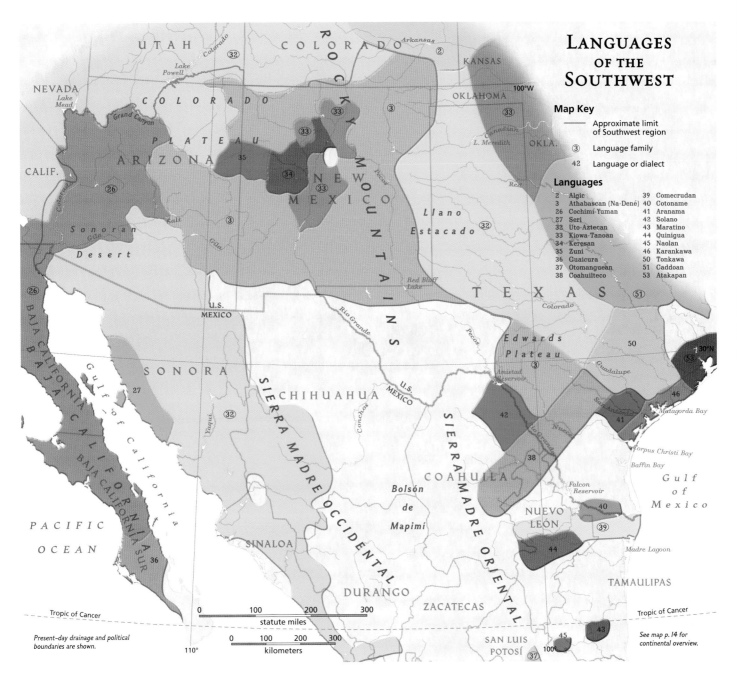

LANGUAGES OF THE SOUTHWEST

Map Key

—— Approximate limit of Southwest region

③ Language family

42 Language or dialect

Languages

2 Algic	39 Comecrudan
3 Athabascan (Na-Dené)	40 Cotoname
26 Cochimí-Yuman	41 Aranama
27 Seri	42 Solano
32 Uto-Aztecan	43 Maratino
33 Kiowa-Tanoan	44 Quinigua
34 Keresan	45 Naolan
35 Zuni	46 Karankawa
36 Guaicura	50 Tonkawa
37 Otomanguean	51 Caddoan
38 Coahuilteco	53 Atakapan

Present-day drainage and political boundaries are shown.

See map p. 14 for continental overview.

The Southwest is home to myriad languages and cultures, including the related Apachean and Navajo languages, the numerous Puebloan languages, and unrelated language isolates nearby. In spite of brutal conflict, relocation, and sustained pressure, the languages of the Southwest are in better health in many places than those of tribes elsewhere.

the Southwest were flooded with white travelers, prospectors, and settlers. Resisting the Americans would be the biggest challenge yet.

Indian Wars

Resistance took many forms through the Spanish, Mexican, and American eras. War was the most obvious, and the Southwest was full of dramatic clashes between powerful tribes and white military might. The Pueblo often made accommodations to the Spanish at first, but when the Europeans ramped up pressure on their religions and lifeways, the Spanish unintentionally united the tribes against a common foe.

The Pueblo Revolt of 1680 killed one-fifth of the Spanish in the Southwest and drove the rest through Texas to Mexico. It took the Spanish 12 years to reassert a presence in Pueblo country. The Apache, Navajo, Quechan, and Yavapai all resisted the Mexicans and Americans. For the first 250 years

> "I shall remain.
> I have nothing to lose
> but my life, and
> that they can come and take
> whenever they please,
> but I will not move."
>
> —MANUELITO

of European contact, they fought for their land and won.

The American period turned the tide for most tribes, and the results were heartbreaking and merciless. The tactics that secured government control over much of the region cost much more than Indian lives and tax dollars. It cost the new American nation moral authority and dignity.

TRIBAL PERSEVERANCE

Many tribes also resisted with adaptations to custom and tradition. Syncretism—the blending of traditions—sometimes enabled the preservation of cultural forms by appeasing Spanish demands for conversion to Catholicism, but this was done only for show. For example, some of the Pueblo accepted baptism and then took the baptized children into the kivas and removed their baptism by tribal rite.

The sheer perseverance of the tribes of the Southwest was resistance in and of itself. They simply outlasted all the invading armies. The Hopi and Pueblo tribes never moved most of their villages. They remained through the Spanish, Mexican, and American conquests—and they still stay. At Hopi and Taos, some live in

Culture and family flourished even in the harshest places. Pictured (left) is a Mohave (Mojave) doll, swaddled in a cradleboard. The map shows Indian reservations clustered along the Rio Grande and the Colorado, Pima, and Salt Rivers. Tribes held onto those homelands against overwhelming odds. They thrived where the environment sustained life with greatest ease, but also where there were spiritual incentives, such as, for the Navajo, a homeland within their four sacred mountains in the heart of the Southwest.

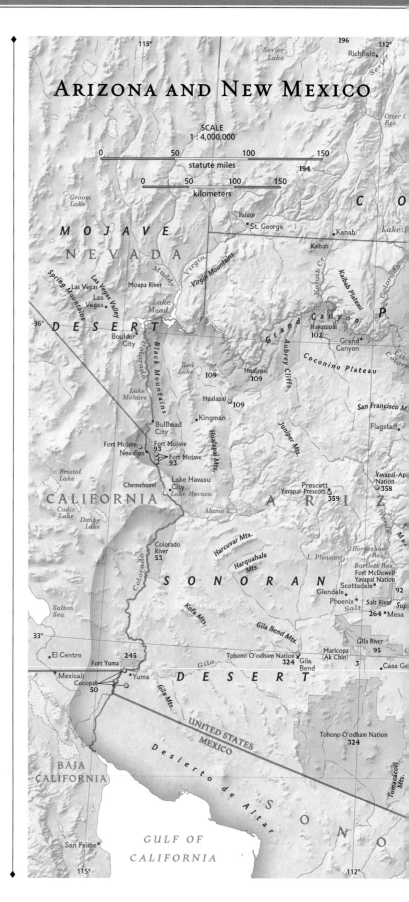

ARIZONA AND NEW MEXICO

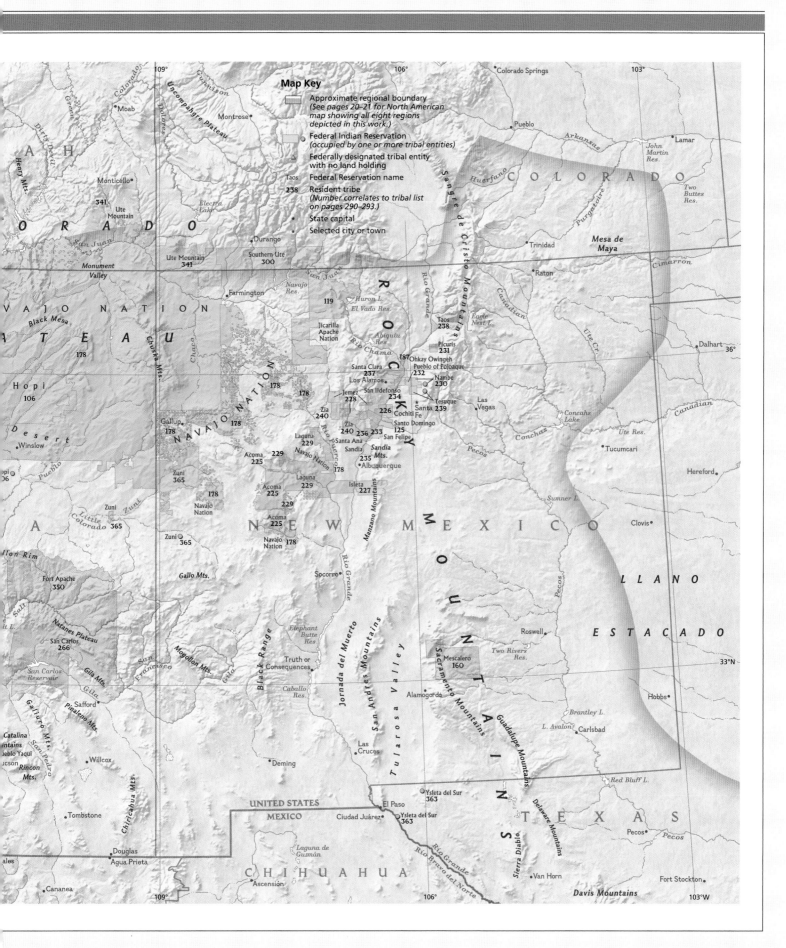

Map Key

Approximate regional boundary
(See pages 20–21 for North American map showing all eight regions depicted in this work.)

Federal Indian Reservation
(occupied by one or more tribal entities)

Federally designated tribal entity with no land holding

Taos   Federal Reservation name

238   Resident tribe
(Number correlates to tribal list on pages 290–293.)

★   State capital

•   Selected city or town

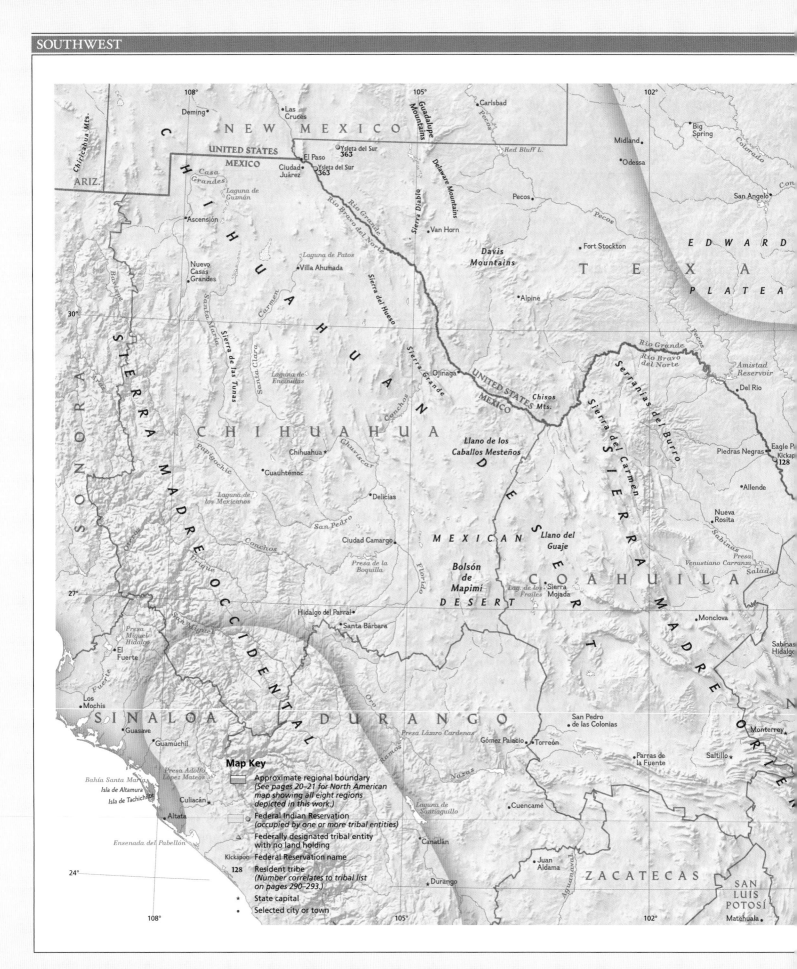

Map Key

▢ Approximate regional boundary
(See pages 20–21 for North American
map showing all eight regions
depicted in this work.)

○ Federal Indian Reservation
(occupied by one or more tribal entities)

△ Federally designated tribal entity
with no land holding

Kickapoo Federal Reservation name

128 Resident tribe
(Number correlates to tribal list
on pages 290–293.)

★ State capital

• Selected city or town

SOUTHERN TEXAS AND NORTHERN MEXICO

SCALE
1 : 4,500,000

0   50   100   150
statute miles

0   50   100   150
kilometers

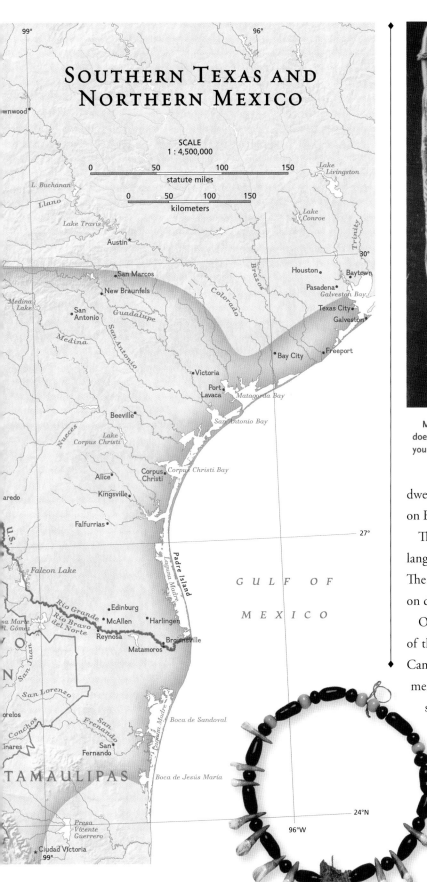

Many tribes used cradleboards to carry their infants, as this Apache woman does in 1903. The tight wrapping was believed to help promote good behavior in young children and good posture later in life. The canopy is a sunshade and also a security measure in case of tripping or dropping.

dwellings continually inhabited longer than almost any others on Earth.

The Havasupai still have a 100 percent fluency rate in the tribal language. Many other Southwestern tribes have high fluency rates. The artistic, musical, and cultural traditions of Native nations are on display everywhere in the region.

Over the centuries, everyone who bet against the Native nations of the Southwest has been wrong. From the wonders of Chaco Canyon to the wonders of cultural perseverance, the accomplishments of the tribes are truly astounding. And as they brace themselves in the fierce, hot wind, there is no reason to think that they haven't outlasted just the colonizers. They might just outlast everyone yet to come.

Southern Texas was the scene of territorial conflict between Mexican and American forces. In the Treaty of Guadalupe Hidalgo, most of the Southwest became part of the United States. Many Indians in the region retreated into Mexico or were relocated to Oklahoma. But the Kickapoo, the Pueblo of Ysleta del Sur, and several other tribal enclaves hung onto their lands along the Texas portion of the Rio Grande. Glass bead and teeth amuletic necklace (left) of an Apache medicine man.

THE PUEBLO REVOLT OF 1680
How Pueblo Unity Taught the Spanish Empire a Powerful Lesson

Juan de Oñate led the first Spanish colonization of the Pueblo in 1598. The Pueblo population was more than 40,000 strong then, although more than 15,000 died from European diseases to which the Pueblo had no natural immunity. The Spanish came to convert and sometimes enslave the Native population, harvest resources, and settle. At Acoma ❶, the Pueblo resisted, but after hundreds were killed, hundreds more enslaved, and many had their feet amputated, the resistance collapsed.

The Spanish met a mixed reception. The newcomers brought horses, sheep, chickens, peaches, watermelon, wheat, and metal plows, all of which were avidly incorporated into the Pueblo economy and lifestyle. But the Spanish also suppressed Pueblo religion, and that was a constant source of discontentment. Catholic priests confiscated masks, prayer sticks, and effigies, directly suppressing treasured ceremonies. The Spanish accused Pueblo men of witchcraft and hanged many, imprisoning others, including Ohkay Owingeh (Popé), an Indian from San Juan ❷.

The Pueblo marched on Santa Fe ❸ and successfully forced the release of the prisoners. Ohkay Owingeh moved from San Juan to Taos ❹ and plotted a resistance effort, securing the alliance of most of the 46 pueblos, plus Hopi and Zuni. When his plan was discovered, a spontaneous conflict erupted. Within three days, the Pueblo put Santa Fe under siege and destroyed every other Spanish settlement in the region. Antonio de Otermín, the governor of Santa Fe, staged a daring escape, but the Pueblo killed 500 Spaniards and chased the remaining 2,000 to Mexico.

Otermín returned in 1681, but was forced to retreat once more. For 12 years, the Pueblo were again masters of their own land. Ohkay Owingeh unsuccessfully tried to convince the Pueblo to cast aside all Spanish foods and tools as the Pueblo prepared for another major conflict.

In 1692, the Spanish returned again, but with a diplomatic solution instead of a military one. They offered formal land grants to each Pueblo community and appointed a public defender to argue Indian cases in Spanish courts. According to Joe Romero, a former lieutenant governor of Cochiti Pueblo, "We taught them a lesson. We killed them and chased the rest all the way through Texas to Mexico. They came back years later, but they came with a little more respect." ■

In 1675, Spanish suppression of Pueblo religious life became so oppressive that the Pueblo marched on the Palace of the Governors in Santa Fe (above), demanding the return of all captives. A San Juan Indian named Ohkay Owingeh (called Popé by the Spanish) was among those released, and he went on to orchestrate the Pueblo Revolt of 1680 from Taos (left). Taos was built in the 1500s and has been continually inhabited ever since.

NUEVO MEXICO This 1768 Spanish map shows a clear delineation of Pueblo country. Even more than 100 years after the Pueblo Revolt of 1680, the Spanish were careful not to inflame further pan-Pueblo military resistance. Note the clustering of pueblos along the Rio Grande, enabling access to water and fertile soil. Pueblo resistance and continued occupation of ancestral homeland was not just about religious freedom; it was about the land and resources, too.

HOPI RESISTANCE

De Vargas, Menchero, and the Reassertion of the Spanish Regime

From 1688 to 1704, Diego de Vargas served as captain general and then governor of Santa Fe de Nuevo Mexico, and in 1691–92 he led a bloodless repossession of New Mexico after the 1680 Pueblo Revolt. De Vargas then used brutal force after 1692 to suppress further Pueblo resistance.

Spanish control in Hopi lands in what is now northeastern Arizona was a different story. It took the Spanish longer to reach the Hopi than almost any other group in the Southwest, but by 1629 they were in Hopi territory in force, colonizing and setting up missions. The Hopi were especially resistant to conversion to Catholicism, and the Spanish in turn exerted tremendous pressure on the tribe, enslaving many people, using others for temporary forced labor, and exacting tribute in both goods and crops on one Hopi village after another. The Pueblo of Awatovi (Aguatuvi) was the only notable Hopi settlement that converted to Christianity.

In the Pueblo Revolt of 1680, the Hopi killed many Spanish missionaries and dismantled all the missions in their area stone by stone. Pueblo refugees from New Mexico sought refuge with the Hopi, and almost the entire Tiguex population was absorbed by the Hopi, as well. It took the Spanish 20 years to come back to Hopi land. In 1700, they tried to pick up where they left off, accelerating conversion at Awatovi and exerting powerful coercive military pressure on the traditional Hopi elsewhere. The Hopi took decisive action and destroyed the entire pueblo at Awatovi,

Diego de Vargas

killing most of the men and adopting the women and children into the main Hopi population. Without Hopi allies or converts, the Spanish were again forced to abandon their missionary work on the mesas in 1701.

In the 1740s, Fray Juan Miguel Menchero again attempted to reestablish the Spanish missions in Hopi country. He traveled throughout the region, taking inventory of and mapping the Spanish colonial effort, including pueblos along the Rio Grande. The effort made little progress in conversion of the tribal population, and once more the Spanish mission effort among the Hopi failed.

Menchero's map (opposite) shows some landmarks well known today. Rio Grande (also called the Rio Bravo del Norte), separating present-day Texas from Mexico ❶, Rio Pecos ❷, Gila River ❸, Rio Conchos in Chihuahua near the Big Bend (province Sonora labeled farther west) ❹, Colorado River ❺, San Juan River in northeastern Arizona ❻, Rio Puerco ❼, Albuquerque ❽, Santa Fe ❾, Taos ❿, Mission Acoma, New Mexico ⓫, Hopi Pueblo Tano/Tewa ⓬, Hopi Pueblo Walpi, Arizona ⓭, Zuni Mission ⓮, and Kykotsmovi Village, Arizona ⓯. ∎

MENCHERO'S MAP When Fray Juan Miguel Menchero tried to reestablish the Spanish missions in Hopi land in the 1740s, he took an inventory of the Spanish colonial effort and thoroughly mapped the tribal land and pueblo locations (opposite). Like his predecessors, Menchero was frustrated at the futility of the effort to gain converts. On the surface, some people converted to Catholicism, but kachina belief and practice still dominated the Hopi experience, and the Pueblo maintained most of their pre-Columbian dances and customs.

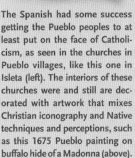

The Spanish had some success getting the Pueblo peoples to at least put on the face of Catholicism, as seen in the churches in Pueblo villages, like this one in Isleta (left). The interiors of these churches were and still are decorated with artwork that mixes Christian iconography and Native techniques and perceptions, such as this 1675 Pueblo painting on buffalo hide of a Madonna (above).

The Santa Fe Trail

0 ——————— 100 miles

Map shows boundaries of 1880.

THE ROAD WEST The Santa Fe Trail was the path that brought American settlers and military men to the Southwest from the American-controlled lands near the Mississippi River. Although the trail itself had been there since the 1700s, William Becknell's trade mission in 1821 opened American minds to colonizing the region. Within 25 years, the U.S. was fighting the Mexican government and Indian nations for control of the land and its resources.

WILLIAM BECKNELL

William Becknell, a white man, was born and raised in Virginia, but moved to Missouri in 1810. He fought in the War of 1812 under Daniel Boone, son of the famous frontiersman. Afterward, he had terrible financial struggles and was even jailed for failure to pay debts.

In 1821, after the Spanish lost control of their Southwest territory, including what's now New Mexico, Becknell set out on a high-risk trade mission over the Santa Fe Trail and became the first American to make that long trip from St. Louis to Santa Fe. He converted $300 of trade goods into a $6,000 purse on his first trip, and $3,000 of trade goods into $91,000 on his second trip. His ventures opened the American trade push into the Southwest, as well as the eventual U.S. military influx. Becknell became known as the Father of the Santa Fe Trail. He went on to serve in the Missouri and Texas state legislatures before his death.

Indians remember Becknell differently than do most Americans. For the Comanche, who controlled the land along the Santa Fe Trail, as well as for every tribe in the Southwest, he was the man who opened the door for American expansion to their detriment.

THE SANTA FE TRAIL

Opening the Way for the American Invasion of the Southwest

The Santa Fe Trail is an overland route from Franklin, Missouri (off the map; Missouri River shown at ❶), to Santa Fe, New Mexico ❷. It crosses parts of five states and spans 900 miles. The American invasion of the Southwest and the histories of Mexico and tribes in the region would have been entirely different without it. Although the Comanche and other tribes traveled its distance and controlled much of the route for generations before European contact ❸, the road itself was developed and maintained by the Spanish, who sought to connect the Southwest with their colonies on the Mississippi River and in the Southeast. This map (opposite), made in 1806, shows the Missouri River ❹, Rio Grande ❺, and "Mountains of New Mexico" ❻.

In 1821, Mexico gained independence from Spain and claimed dominion over Santa Fe and the Southwest—despite the fact that the tribes in the Southwest were far from conquered and had ceded little land to either Spain or Mexico. Soon the Santa Fe Trail was buzzing with commercial activity. The Comanche taxed the route, exacting tribute from travelers, but also actively trading with them.

It didn't take long for the U.S. government to set its expansionist ambitions on the Southwest. As trade and traffic grew along the Santa Fe Trail, territorial conflict between the U.S. and Mexico broke out, culminating in the Mexican–American War. The Santa Fe Trail was the primary military route that brought the U.S. Army to the Southwest in 1846. After the U.S. won generous terms with the Treaty of Guadalupe Hidalgo in 1848, the Army asserted a permanent presence in the Southwest.

The overland route brought not just the U.S. Army, but also a new flood of settlers who continued across the Santa Fe Trail until the close of the Indian wars in the Southwest. A railroad line, extended to the region in 1880, eclipsed the land route. ∎

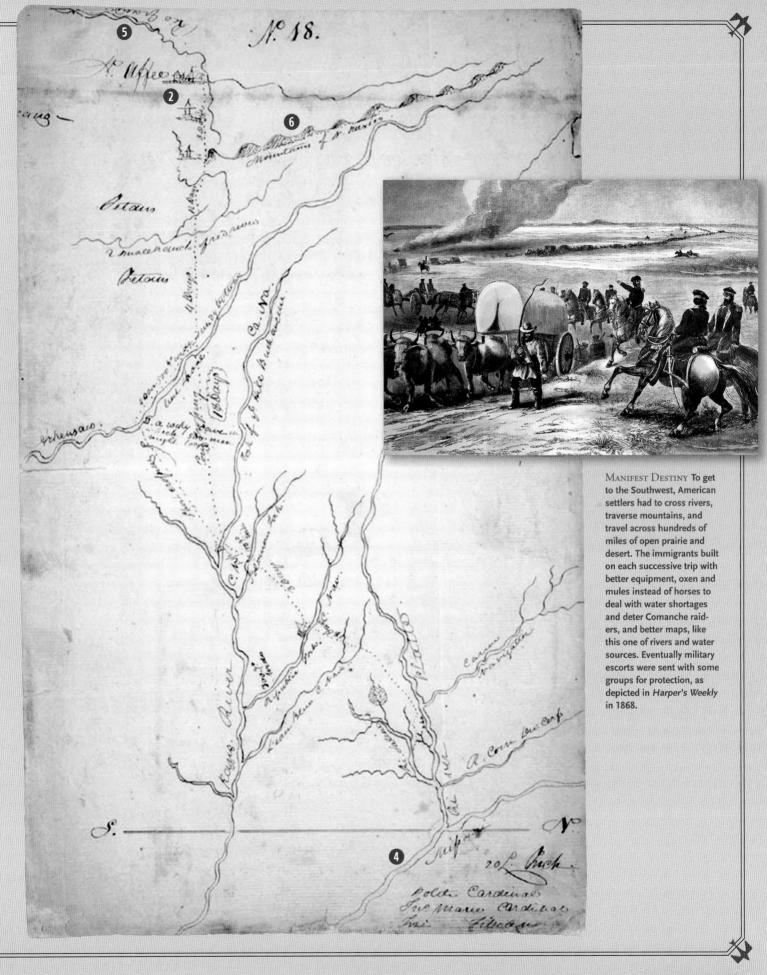

Nº 48.

MANIFEST DESTINY To get to the Southwest, American settlers had to cross rivers, traverse mountains, and travel across hundreds of miles of open prairie and desert. The immigrants built on each successive trip with better equipment, oxen and mules instead of horses to deal with water shortages and deter Comanche raiders, and better maps, like this one of rivers and water sources. Eventually military escorts were sent with some groups for protection, as depicted in *Harper's Weekly* in 1868.

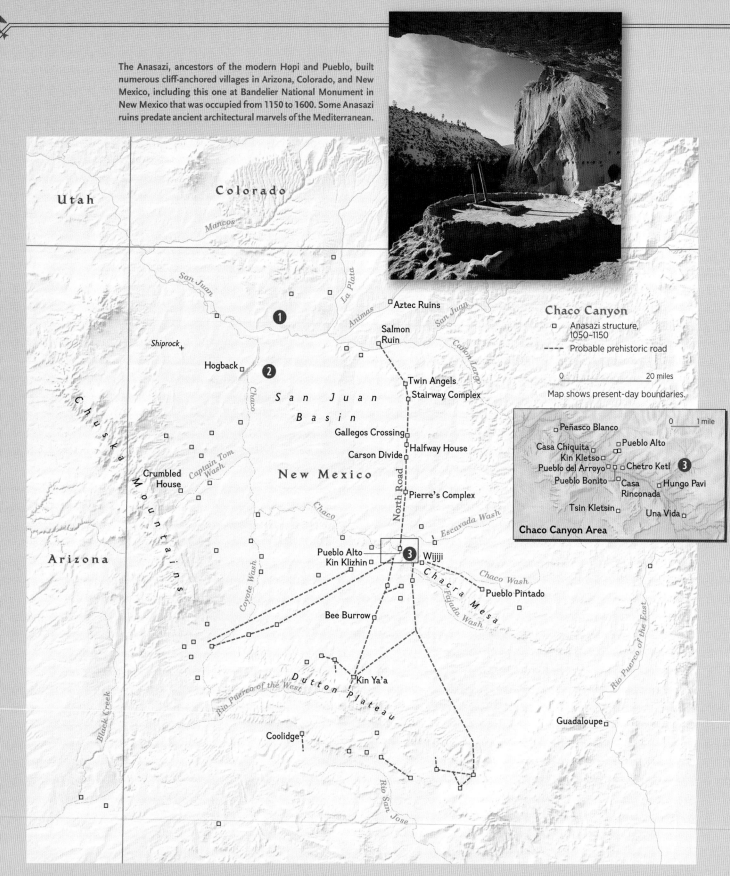

The Anasazi, ancestors of the modern Hopi and Pueblo, built numerous cliff-anchored villages in Arizona, Colorado, and New Mexico, including this one at Bandelier National Monument in New Mexico that was occupied from 1150 to 1600. Some Anasazi ruins predate ancient architectural marvels of the Mediterranean.

Utah

Colorado

Mancos

San Juan

La Plata

Animas

1

Aztec Ruins

Salmon Ruin

San Juan

Cañon Largo

Shiprock +

Hogback

2

Twin Angels

Stairway Complex

Chaco

San Juan Basin

Gallegos Crossing

Carson Divide

Halfway House

Captain Tom Wash

Crumbled House

New Mexico

Chuska Mountains

Arizona

Chaco

North Road

Pierre's Complex

Escavada Wash

Pueblo Alto
Kin Klizhin

3

Wijiji

Chaco Wash

Chacra Mesa

Fajada Wash

Coyote Wash

Pueblo Pintado

Bee Burrow

Black Creek

Kin Ya'a

Dutton Plateau

Rio Puerco of the West

Rio Puerco of the East

Coolidge

Guadaloupe

Rio San Jose

Chaco Canyon

▫ Anasazi structure, 1050–1150

---- Probable prehistoric road

0 —— 20 miles

Map shows present-day boundaries.

Chaco Canyon Area

0 —— 1 mile

Peñasco Blanco

Casa Chiquita   Pueblo Alto
Kin Kletso

Pueblo del Arroyo   Chetro Ketl   3

Pueblo Bonito   Casa   Hungo Pavi
                Rinconada

Tsin Kletsin

Una Vida

ANASAZI ARCHITECTS At Chaco Canyon, the Anasazi built along a nine-mile stretch of the canyon with many buildings aligned with the cardinal directions and others aligned with the 18.6-year lunar cycle. It must have taken many centuries to master the cycles and even longer to figure out instrumentation to align such massive buildings over so large an area with such precision. Mapped here are Pueblo Bonito, the largest of the intact complexes at Chaco; Chetro Ketl; and numerous smaller kivas, apartment complexes, and outlying structures. The builders did not have compasses, transits, levels, the wheel, or heavy machinery.

CHACO CANYON

Ruins Provide Clues to the Life the Anasazi Built, Then Abandoned

Today Chaco Canyon is home to the largest pre-Columbian ruin north of Mexico, and from 900 to 1150 it was the center of a major hub of economic and cultural activity. The Anasazi, ancestors of the Hopi and Pueblo, built the massive sandstone buildings at Chaco Canyon along a nine-mile stretch of the canyon where the San Juan ❶ and Chaco ❷ Rivers converge. More than 70 satellite communities farmed corn and hunted near the main citadel and urban center where they congregated for trade and ceremony. Basalt and obsidian artifacts, rock markings, and sophisticated analysis of construction techniques confirm that Chaco Canyon and other Anasazi sites throughout the Southwest were regional trade hubs that regularly interacted with numerous communities throughout the Southwest, the Plains, and Mexico.

Religious life was extremely important to the Anasazi, who built 15 massive kivas able to hold 400 people each, plus more than 100 smaller ones (see square symbols on the map). Chetro Ketl, one

The arts were important to the Anasazi, as seen in this elaborate pottery work.

of the numerous buildings at Chaco, took 50 million sandstone blocks and 5,000 trees to construct ❸. Many of the buildings were multistory, with more than 100 rooms. They were constructed in perfect alignment to one another. A bird's-eye view of the structures shows alignment and symmetry of unparalleled precision. Lunar and solar guides enabled the alignment and heightened its spiritual importance. The sophistication of Anasazi instrumentation and knowledge has never been fully determined.

Both the Hopi and the Pueblo tell histories of their ancestral occupation of Chaco Canyon. From 1130 to 1180, there was a debilitating drought that plagued the region and remains the most likely cause for Anasazi migration to new village locations along the Rio Grande and other parts of the Southwest. Crop failures and the depletion of animal and tree resources that could no longer sustain the large population at Chaco likely encouraged the residents to leave and spread out. Raiding from other tribes and periodic warfare may have contributed to the decision to move. ∎

Many of the buildings at Chaco Canyon, built by the Anasazi, were aligned to capture major solar and lunar events—a marvel of astronomical knowledge, design, and construction that took scientists decades to understand after the site was first excavated and studied in 1920. The ruins of Pueblo Bonito are pictured above. At left is an artist's rendition of life in an Anasazi cliff dwelling.

MEXICO, AMERICA, AND THE APACHE

Colonial Transition in the Southwest

In spite of the constant military pressure from the Spanish and then the Mexicans, the Apache never yielded. As the U.S. and Mexico fought for dominion of the Southwest, there would be a distinct difference between the regimes. The Spanish never sought treaties with Indians and never established reservations in the Southwest. Rather, they viewed the land as theirs as soon as they claimed it. The Mexicans claimed it from the Spanish when they won independence. For both, Indians were just sources of labor or, if resistant, impediments to efficient administration. But the Americans took a different approach, one forged by British treaty practice and a long history of conflict, dispossession, and relocation. They introduced the Apache to reservations, and it was a hard adjustment.

Some Apache agreed to peace and friendship with the Americans in 1846 and allowed them passage to fight the Mexicans ❶. The Mexicans had been hard on them, and it seemed wise to let someone else fight their enemies at first. But no sooner had the U.S. won the Mexican–American War than did the Southwest see a surge of white settlement, mining, and traffic.

Now the Apache were fighting Mexicans to the south and Americans to the north and east ❷. One band at a time, the Americans coerced or forced Apache groups to new reservations at San Carlos ❸ and elsewhere. In 1875, 1,500 Tonto Apache and Yavapai were forced to march to San Carlos in the winter, and nearly half died; only a small number returned many years later to their original homeland. U.S. efforts to concentrate other Apache bands, led by Cochise, Geronimo, Naiche, and Victorio, on reservations ignited resistance that would engage more than a fourth of the entire U.S. Army. ∎

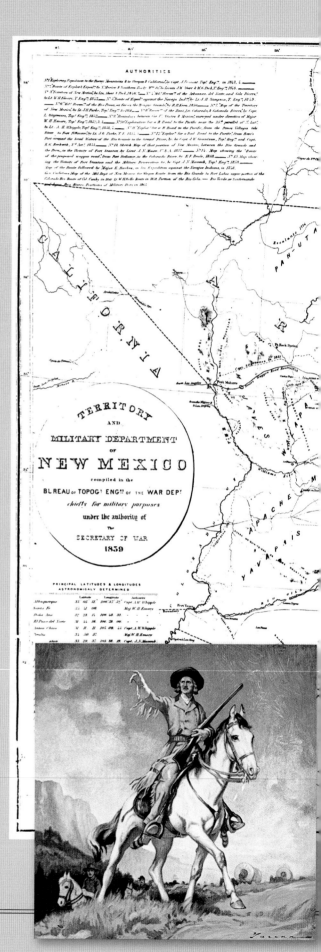

The U.S. Army established a powerful presence in the Southwest when it fought Mexico for control of the region. Many tribal leaders remained neutral or even allowed the Americans to pass through their land for a time. But when the Mexican–American War was over, the Army stayed at Fort Bowie (above) and other posts. Kit Carson (right) was Indian agent for the Jicarilla Apache and then an officer in Army campaigns against the Mescalero Apache and, even more famously, the Navajo.

Cochise was an uncommonly strong and imposing man. He kept his band of Apache at peace with the U.S. for a long time, but eventually led them in one of the longest episodes of Indian resistance.

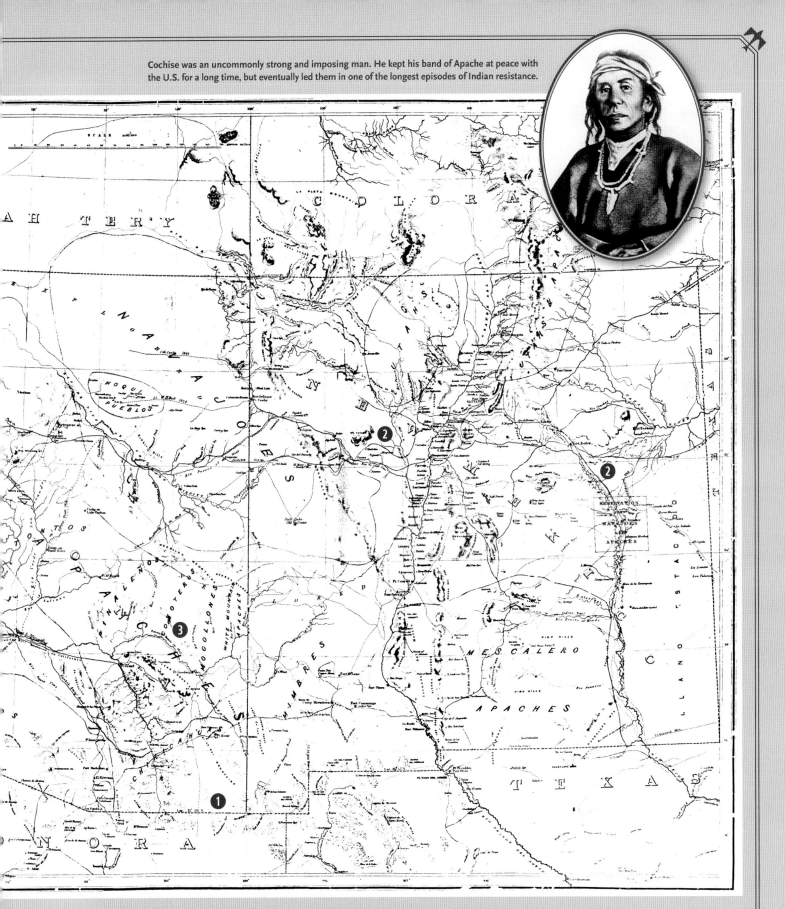

TRIBAL RESISTANCE Although the tribes of the Southwest were not quick to militarily engage settlers or the U.S. Army, when they did, the region became a tinderbox. Most tribes, whether they resisted or not, lost land and many lives. This map reveals the level of attention given to the area. Made in 1859, the map shows the "Territory and Military Department of New Mexico" and was made by the Bureau of Topographical Engineers of the War Department under authority of the secretary of war.

POLITICS AND WAR In 1847, when this map was drawn, Mexico claimed possession of all of the Southwest, the southern Rocky Mountains, and California. But after losing the Mexican–American War, Mexican authorities signed the Treaty of Guadalupe Hidalgo in 1848 (left) and the southern boundary of the U.S. was drawn pretty much as it is today. None of the tribes in the Southwest were included in the diplomacy, setting the stage for further conflict.

THE TREATY OF GUADALUPE HIDALGO

America Asserts Control of the Southwest, 1848

The Treaty of Guadalupe Hidalgo ended the Mexican–American War and transferred a vast territory from Mexico to the United States that would later become the states of Texas ❶, New Mexico ❷, Arizona ❸, Colorado ❹, Utah ❺, Nevada ❻, and California ❼.

After Mexico won its independence from Spain in 1821, the Mexican army was kept busy trying to colonize the Southwest, but repeated raids from the Apache and Comanche frustrated their advances. When Texas declared itself an independent republic in 1835, Mexico simply viewed it as a rebellious state of its own nation, not a threat to its sovereignty. That view held until the U.S. annexed Texas and granted it statehood in 1845. Now Texas was not a minor rebellion, but part of another country that could actually threaten Mexico. War ensued.

At the conclusion of the Mexican–American War, U.S. diplomat Nicholas Philip Trist negotiated the land transfer and other terms. No tribes were consulted in the talks, even though they had undisputed control of much of the land being transferred. The Treaty of Guadalupe Hidalgo made provisions for Mexicans within the new borders of the U.S. to become citizens and have their land and property protected. Indians had no similar protections, but were simply viewed as obstacles to American expansion.

In Article XI of the treaty, the U.S. pledged to stop Apache and Comanche raids into Mexico and return the Mexican captives of Indians to Mexico. Both the Apache and the Comanche, however, were simply too powerful for the U.S. to enforce the treaty provision. Mexico filed 366 claims for Indian raids, and the tension ultimately motivated the U.S. to make the Gadsden Purchase in 1853 ❽, which put more Apache territory within the borders of the U.S. ∎

After the Basilica in Mexico City fell to U.S. troops, Nicholas Philip Trist (above) successfully negotiated the Treaty of Guadalupe Hidalgo for the U.S. government, putting the states of Arizona, California, Colorado, Nevada, New Mexico, Texas, and Utah in U.S. hands.

MAPA de los ESTADOS UNIDOS DE MÉJICO,

Según lo organizado y definido por las varias actas del Congreso de dicha República, y construido por las mejores autoridades.

LO PUBLICAN J. DISTURNELL, 102 BROADWAY.

NUEVA YORK, 1847.

REVISED EDITION.

GERONIMO

Geronimo was one of the most prominent and iconic leaders of the Apache resistance to Mexican and American occupation of tribal land in the Southwest. He received little mercy from the Americans, Mexicans, or other Indians, but he was forgotten by none of them.

Geronimo was born in 1829 in a conflict zone where most Apache men had to become warriors to survive. His family was wiped out by Mexican soldiers in 1858—his mother, his wife, and all three of his children. After the massacre, Geronimo had little to lose, and his heart ached for revenge. He worked with the chiefs of the Chiricahua Apache, and although Geronimo is often referred to as a chief, he deferred to them throughout his life. Geronimo was a warrior, and when Mangas Coloradas asked him to help lead defensive attacks and raids in the 1860s, Geronimo was happy to do his part. Mangas Coloradas was captured, tortured, and killed by American soldiers in 1863. Geronimo then deferred to the chief's sons, Taza and then Naiche, in war and peace. Geronimo was a fearsome warrior and war leader, and he may have killed hundreds of Mexicans through the course of the Apache resistance.

Geronimo played a central role in Chiricahua Apache opposition under Naiche and, when the wars were over in 1886, was relocated to Florida, Alabama, and then Oklahoma. Geronimo attended the World's Fair in St. Louis in 1904 and marched in Theodore Roosevelt's Inaugural parade in 1905, but he was never free. On his deathbed in 1909, Geronimo said, "I should have never surrendered. I should have fought until I was the last man alive."

APACHE RESISTANCE
Impossible Choices and Tragic Endings

The Apache were hunters and raiders, more nomadic than other tribes in the Southwest and protective of their territory. None of that mattered to the Spanish or Mexicans, who continually encroached on Apache land. The Mexican government built up troop levels in Apache country and sought to displace the tribe, even issuing a bounty on Apache scalps in 1835. The Apache fought back, killing as many as 5,000 Mexicans and destroying more than 100 settlements.

The Americans assumed control over much of the Southwest after the Mexican–American War and the Treaty of Guadalupe Hidalgo in 1848. It didn't take long for American ambitions to pressure the Apache. Soon American settlers were acting like and then were treated like their Mexican counterparts. When Apache chief Naiche agreed to peace with the United States and brought his band into the San Carlos Reservation ❶, Geronimo followed. But conditions at San Carlos were unbearable. It was hot and dusty, unlike the homeland of the Chiricahua high in the Sierra Madre ❷. There was little food, and the government mismanaged rations.

When the government suppressed tribal ceremonies and killed a prominent medicine man, Geronimo and Naiche had had enough. Their 1885 breakout from San Carlos put thousands of U.S. soldiers in the field against them, and nearly as many from Mexico. But they avoided capture, raiding in Mexico. In 1886, Charles Gatewood, tasked by Gen. Nelson Miles, was finally able to barter terms from the Apache, and they surrendered at Skeleton Canyon, Arizona ❸. Geronimo believed there to be reasonable conditions attached to his surrender, but the government considered it unconditional. Geronimo, Naiche, and others were sent away as prisoners of war to Texas, Florida, Alabama, and finally Fort Sill, Oklahoma. Most, including Geronimo, would never return home. ■

The Apache were a large tribe and more nomadic than many others in the Southwest, which put them in conflict with other tribes and sometimes with each other. With the acquisition of horses, the Apache became skilled raiders and warriors. During the colonial era, they fought the Spanish, Mexican, and U.S. armies.

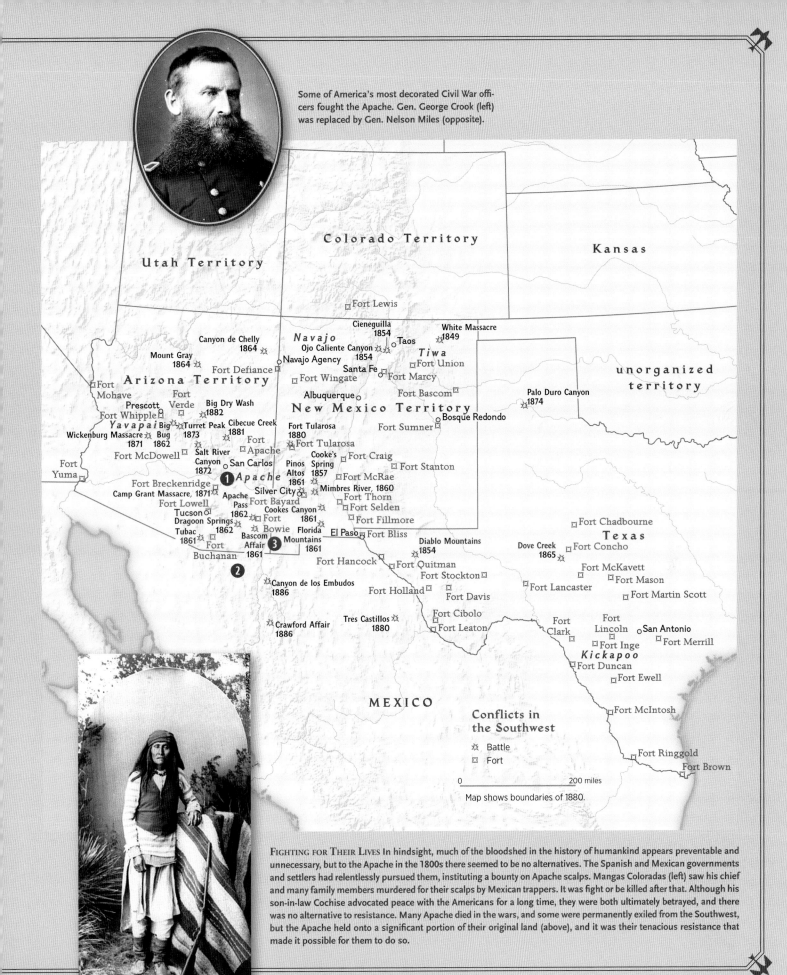

Some of America's most decorated Civil War officers fought the Apache. Gen. George Crook (left) was replaced by Gen. Nelson Miles (opposite).

Utah Territory

Colorado Territory

Kansas

unorganized territory

□ Fort Lewis

Cieneguilla 1854
☆ Taos
White Massacre 1849

Navajo
Canyon de Chelly 1864 ☆
Ojo Caliente Canyon 1854 ☆☆
Navajo Agency ○
Tiwa
☐ Fort Union

Mount Gray 1864 ☆
Fort Defiance □
Santa Fe ○
□ Fort Marcy
Fort Bascom ○

Arizona Territory
□ Fort Mohave
Fort Verde
Big Dry Wash 1882 ☆
Albuquerque ○
New Mexico Territory
Palo Duro Canyon 1874 ☆

Prescott ○
Fort Whipple □
Yavapai Big ☆☆ Turret Peak Bug 1873
Cibecue Creek 1881
Fort Tularosa 1880
○ Bosque Redondo

Wickenburg Massacre 1871 1862
☆ Fort Apache
☆ Fort Tularosa
Fort Sumner □

Fort McDowell □
Salt River Canyon 1872 ☆
San Carlos ○
Cooke's Spring
□ Fort Craig

Fort ○ Yuma
Fort Breckenridge □
Apache
Pinos Altos 1861 ☆
☐ Fort McRae
□ Fort Stanton

Camp Grant Massacre, 1871
Apache Pass
Silver City ○
Mimbres River, 1860 ☆
Cooke's Canyon

Fort Lowell □
Fort Bayard □
☐ Fort Thorn

Tucson ○
1862 ☆
Cookes Canyon 1861 ☆
□ Fort Selden

Dragoon Springs
Fort □
□ Fort Fillmore

Tubac 1862 ☆
☆ Bowie Florida Mountains 1861
El Paso ○
☐ Fort Bliss
□ Fort Chadbourne

1861
Bascom Affair 1861
3
Diablo Mountains 1854 ☆
Dove Creek 1865 ☆
Texas
□ Fort Concho

Fort Buchanan □
2
Canyon de los Embudos 1886 ☆
Fort Hancock □
□ Fort Quitman
□ Fort Stockton
□ Fort McKavett
☐ Fort Mason

Fort Holland □
□ Fort Davis
☐ Fort Lancaster
□ Fort Martin Scott

Crawford Affair 1886 ☆
Tres Castillos 1880 ☆
☐ Fort Cibolo
Fort ☐ Leaton
Fort Clark
Fort Lincoln
○ San Antonio
☐ Fort Merrill

□ Fort Inge
Kickapoo
□ Fort Duncan
□ Fort Ewell

MEXICO

☐ Fort McIntosh

Conflicts in the Southwest

☆ Battle
□ Fort

0 ————————— 200 miles

Map shows boundaries of 1880.

□ Fort Ringgold

Fort Brown

FIGHTING FOR THEIR LIVES In hindsight, much of the bloodshed in the history of humankind appears preventable and unnecessary, but to the Apache in the 1800s there seemed to be no alternatives. The Spanish and Mexican governments and settlers had relentlessly pursued them, instituting a bounty on Apache scalps. Mangas Coloradas (left) saw his chief and many family members murdered for their scalps by Mexican trappers. It was fight or be killed after that. Although his son-in-law Cochise advocated peace with the Americans for a long time, they were both ultimately betrayed, and there was no alternative to resistance. Many Apache died in the wars, and some were permanently exiled from the Southwest, but the Apache held onto a significant portion of their original land (above), and it was their tenacious resistance that made it possible for them to do so.

THE LONG WALK OF THE NAVAJO

Dispossession and Relocation in the Southwest

Raids on Navajo villages and farms by Mexican and American settlers and militia became common after the Treaty of Guadalupe Hidalgo in 1848, and the Navajo retaliated. As tensions escalated, the U.S. Army moved against the tribe. Col. Kit Carson was put in charge of a concentration effort, tasked with bringing the Navajo into Fort Wingate ❶ and other American forts to surrender. He embarked on a brutal military campaign. His troops killed Navajo civilians, burned crops, pulled out the Navajo peach orchards in Canyon de Chelly ❷ that had been cultivated since first contact with the Spanish, and destroyed thousands of herd animals. By 1863, the last bands of near-starved Navajo surrendered.

Then began the Long Walk of the Navajo. From 1864 to 1866, the U.S. Army forced the Navajo on 53 marches to the Bosque Redondo Reservation on the Pecos River in New Mexico ❸. Hundreds perished, although the government moved more than 9,000 Navajo there. Conditions at Bosque Redondo were terrible. A group of Mescalero Apache were settled there, too, which caused problems because of the war between the Apache and Navajo. The land was not well suited for agriculture.

Many Navajo could not abide the poverty, death, or dispossession. In 1865, Navajo chief Barboncito led 500 Navajo in a daring escape from the reservation, avoiding the pursuit of a large and determined New Mexico militia. It was costing the government more than $1.5 million to feed the Navajo at Bosque Redondo, eventually convincing the Americans to negotiate with Navajo leaders for a return to Dinétah, the sacred land of the Navajo. A treaty was signed in 1868, and the Navajo returned to a smaller reservation within their original homeland.

Manuelito, another important Navajo chief, organized Indian police to stop raids from 1872 to 1875. He and other Navajo leaders worried that the government would decide to move them again. Encroachments by white settlers, miners, and ranchers continued through the 1900s, but the Navajo remain in Dinétah. ▪

More than 8,000 Navajo surrendered to Kit Carson during his 1864 campaign preceding the Long Walk. Many Navajo were killed during the military action, and hundreds more died on the Long Walk and at Bosque Redondo.

YAQUI

Current Locations: Arizona; Mexico
Language Family: Uto-Aztecan

The Yaqui are indigenous to present-day Arizona and northwestern Mexico. Prior to Spanish contact, the Yaqui had a vast territory where they farmed along rivers, gathered desert foods, and hunted small game. Starting in 1617, the Spanish mission system forced their conversion and exploited Yaqui labor. But the system allowed relative peace and some tribal autonomy over their lands. As the Spanish tightened control and demanded more labor, there was a revolt in 1740 that was brutally suppressed. As many as 5,000 Yaqui were killed. Many fled north to the Tucson region.

After Mexican independence, some Yaqui sought their own independence. From 1825 to 1833, a group of Yaqui led by Juan Banderas fought unsuccessfully for a pan-Indian state. The Mexican army executed Banderas in 1833. After the Mexican–American War, more Yaqui settled north of the border. The city of Tucson grew up around the Yaqui, who were often trilingual speakers of English, Spanish, and Yaqui. The tribe was federally recognized in 1978 and received a small land grant, the Pascua Yaqui Reservation.

YAVAPAI

Current Locations: Arizona; Mexico
Language Family: Yuman

The Yavapai are closely related to the Havasupai and Hualapai in language. However, they lived more like the linguistically very different Apache than like their Yuman relatives, relying on hunting rather than farming. There were even mixed Yavapai–Apache bands.

Gold was discovered in California in 1848, and white migrants streamed west. In 1852, the Yavapai assisted the Quechan

Pueblo Indians near Taos, performing a ceremony. Traditional Pueblo rites often invoke the power of the sun as well as spirits and natural creatures.

in defending their ferry crossing on the Colorado River. When gold was discovered on Yavapai land in 1863, prospectors and ranchers flooded in. In 1864, the governor of Arizona declared all Yavapai to be hostile and called for the tribe's removal. A brutal military campaign ensued and, one at a time, Yavapai groups were forced to surrender. Although some were relocated, more squatted on their former lands, living as they always had, and it would take decades for the U.S. to deal with each band.

The Fort McDowell Reservation was established in 1903. In 1910, one band was granted land at Camp Verde and another at Middle Verde.

This Zuni chair was made in 1850. The Zuni made many adaptations after contact with the Spanish, but maintained deep connections to tradition.

The two merged at Camp Verde in 1937. Another band was established at the Yavapai Prescott Indian Reservation in 1935. In some ways, the persistence of the Yavapai paid off. They lost most of their land, but they maintained their lifeways.

ZUNI

Current Locations: Arizona
Language Family: Isolate

The Zuni are a language isolate, but closely related culturally to the Hopi and Pueblo. They emerged as a distinct people at least 7,000 years ago and established pueblos along the Zuni River 3,000–4,000 years ago. Zuni Pueblo was built around the year 1000 and has been inhabited ever since. Some families have lived in the same buildings for centuries.

Descending from the ancient Anasazi, Hohokam, and Mogollon, the Zuni were products of their environment. Dry upland irrigated farming maintained the supply of corn, squash, pumpkins, and beans. Lacking limestone, the Zuni built with mud bricks and stucco. Ceremonial life was rich, and the Zuni held dances and feasts to honor ancient spirits.

The Spanish came to Zuni land in 1539, earlier than elsewhere in the Southwest. They sought the lost cities of Cibola, and the beautiful sun-bathed Zuni pueblos fit their notion of the imaginary cities. The Spanish brought horses, sheep, chickens, plants, and metal plows. But the Spanish also suppressed Zuni religion, which was a constant source of bitterness. Catholic priests confiscated masks, prayer sticks, and effigies. The Zuni rose up with their neighbors in 1680 in the Pueblo Revolt, then abandoned all pueblos for a time and moved en masse to nearby high, defensible Corn Mesa; eventually, they moved back to the river but remained highly concentrated.

Today the population is about 12,000, and around 9,000 speak the tribal language. The artwork, dances, feasts, and customs are visible throughout the community.

GREAT BASIN
AND PLATEAU

·CHAPTER SIX·

BANNOCK

CAYUSE

COEUR D'ALENE

COLVILLE
(CONFEDERATED
TRIBES)

GOSHUTE

KLAMATH

KOOTENAI

NEZ PERCE

PAIUTE

PEND D'OREILLE
(KALISPEL)

SALISH

SHOSHONE

SPOKANE

UMATILLA

UTE

WALLA WALLA

WARM SPRINGS
(CONFEDERATED
TRIBES)

YAHOOSKIN

YAKAMA (YAKIMA)

Shoshone Indians ford a river on horseback. The Great Basin and Plateau regions of North America include a vast area from the deserts of Nevada in the south to the lush valleys of the Canadian Rocky Mountains in the north, where the Plains meet the mountains, and a myriad of indigenous peoples found diverse ways to survive every natural and human-induced challenge imaginable.

INDIAN NATIONS OF THE GREAT BASIN AND PLATEAU

The Great Basin and Plateau make a vast and remarkably diverse landscape with an equally diverse indigenous population. The people there were unbelievably resourceful, finding ways to thrive in the harshest of environments—hot, dry, salty basins; towering mountains; and windswept plateaus. Many tribes relied on the abundant salmon, trout, whitefish, and steelhead in the rivers of the Plateau. Most hunted every kind of major North American big game in their land—bison, elk, moose, antelope, mountain goats, mountain sheep, and bear. Some relied more on small game, and some even depended on snakes, lizards, and rodents. Every tribe gathered food, drawing in edibles available only to those who knew what to look for—pine nuts, camas bulbs, wild onions, seeds, and many kinds of berries. There was conflict over the land prior to the arrival of whites, but that conflict was usually far less pervasive and debilitating than the tribal wars on the Plains and in the Great Lakes region.

EARLY ENCOUNTERS AND THE GOLD RUSH

In 1776, the Spanish government wanted to find an overland route to connect its missions in New Mexico with those in California. However, the proposed route ran through some of the most forbidding natural terrain in North America and across the territories of powerful tribes like the Comanche and the Ute.

Franciscan priests Francisco Atanasio Domínguez and Silvestre Vélez de Escalante led an expedition to scout the route, making them the first white men to see the Colorado Plateau region. The Franciscans became hopelessly lost, but luckily for them, they first encountered the Ute from Lake Timpanog, who received them in friendship. The Ute were concerned that any attack on the Spanish by the Comanche might be blamed on them. The Ute ultimately sent three of their own people to guide the Spanish expedition, using smoke signals to communicate with other Ute and careful scouting to avoid enemies, who were often nearby.

Domínguez came down with rheumatic fever. After the Ute guides were released, the expedition had a terrible time finding potable water in the salt flats of Utah and turned south through Arizona. The report on the expedition was probably more important than their actual accomplishments.

The artistic traditions of the tribal peoples of the Great Basin and Plateau continue. Pictured here is an oil painting of a Nez Perce Indian (left) from the mid-19th century. Pictured above is Northern Shoshone tribal member Randy'l Hedow Teton, with beaded horse tackle in the Shoshone tradition.

It said that they found "lush, mountainous land filled with game and timber, strange ruins of stone cities and villages, and rivers showing signs of precious metals." This description would drive much of the subsequent exploration and colonization of the Great Basin.

Many tribes of the Great Basin and Plateau encountered Americans during the Lewis and Clark expedition. Sacagawea was a Shoshone woman who worked as a language interpreter for Lewis and Clark from 1804 to 1806. She was from the Lemhi River Valley in Idaho. At 12 years of age, she had been captured by the Hidatsa and brought to North Dakota. The next year, a French fur trader named Toussaint Charbonneau purchased and married her. When Meriwether Lewis and William Clark arrived in North Dakota, they hired Charbonneau as a guide and Sacagawea as an interpreter.

Sacagawea was not really an expedition guide, but she featured prominently in the journals. Her role as interpreter secured the assistance of the Shoshone. She reunited with her brother and other family members, from whom she had been separated since her capture. Their reunion was bittersweet, as Sacagawea was delighted to see them but never able to rejoin them, instead being obligated to her husband for the rest of her life. Among the many things noted about Sacagawea in the expedition journals was her role in saving the journals themselves from a boat accident and recommending the Yellowstone River crossing that went on to become the Bozeman Pass and the Northwest Railroad crossing.

Some tribes in the Great Basin and Plateau stayed relatively isolated from Europeans through the Spanish, Mexican, and British periods, but nobody could avoid whites when the Americans came to the region. The Oregon Trail was opened in 1842, creating an overland route to California and connecting

CHRONOLOGY

8000 B.C.
Plateau Penutian, Salishan, and Uto-Aztecan people spread out and diversify all over Plateau

A.D. 1750
Tribes of Great Basin and Plateau acquire horses

1805–06
Lewis and Clark expedition traverses Plateau

1842
Oregon Trail opens overland route to California

1849
California gold rush brings white settlers across Great Basin and Plateau

1855
Walla Walla Treaty Council establishes three reservations for dozens of Plateau tribes

1860–63
Gold discovered in several places in Plateau

1863
Bear River Massacre: 493 Shoshone killed by U.S. Army

1877
Nez Perce War and Chief Joseph's flight to Canada

1926–1957
Several dams on Columbia and other rivers block salmon runs, upsetting tribal peoples

1983
Uranium mine at Spokane Reservation and silver, lead, and zinc mine at Coeur d'Alene designated as major superfund cleanup sites

The Great Basin and Plateau region (map, opposite) is one of the most geographically and culturally diverse parts of North America, encompassing tribes that flourished in dry deserts, frigid mountains, windswept plains, and lush valleys.

the riches of the west to the populations of the east. The discovery of gold in California brought the 1849 gold rush, and tribal lands across the entire area were soon flooded with white prospectors, travelers, settlers, and ranchers. Many of the new immigrants had absolutely no respect for Indians or their land rights. They saw the west as vacant land, with resources free for those willing to take them. Conflicts broke out, and some grew to the scale of regional wars. Local militia and often the U.S. Army were called to the frontier to put down "Indian uprisings" and punish tribal people who defended their lands and lifeways.

The government began pressuring tribes for land cessions, establishing reservations, and consolidating the tribes on the new reservations. It was a painful time for Indians in the Great Basin and Plateau. Several tribes were sometimes forced into one reservation—even groups who had been at war with one another the previous year. In 1855, 14 tribes were put together on the new Yakama Reservation; then, when gold was discovered on the reservation later that year, the government started to dispossess the people of the little land they still had.

The encroachment of white settlers grew exponentially when gold was discovered within the boundaries of the Plateau itself in 1860, and for three years there was a frenzy of white settlement, mining, prospecting, and predation on tribal lands and people. The injustices were astounding. The Bear River Massacre saw the U.S. Army kill 493 Indians who defended themselves with spears against professional soldiers in skirmish lines with modern weapons.

ASSIMILATION

Assimilation by design took many forms in the Great Basin and Plateau. Missionaries came early and often. Belgian Jesuits like Pierre-Jean De Smet

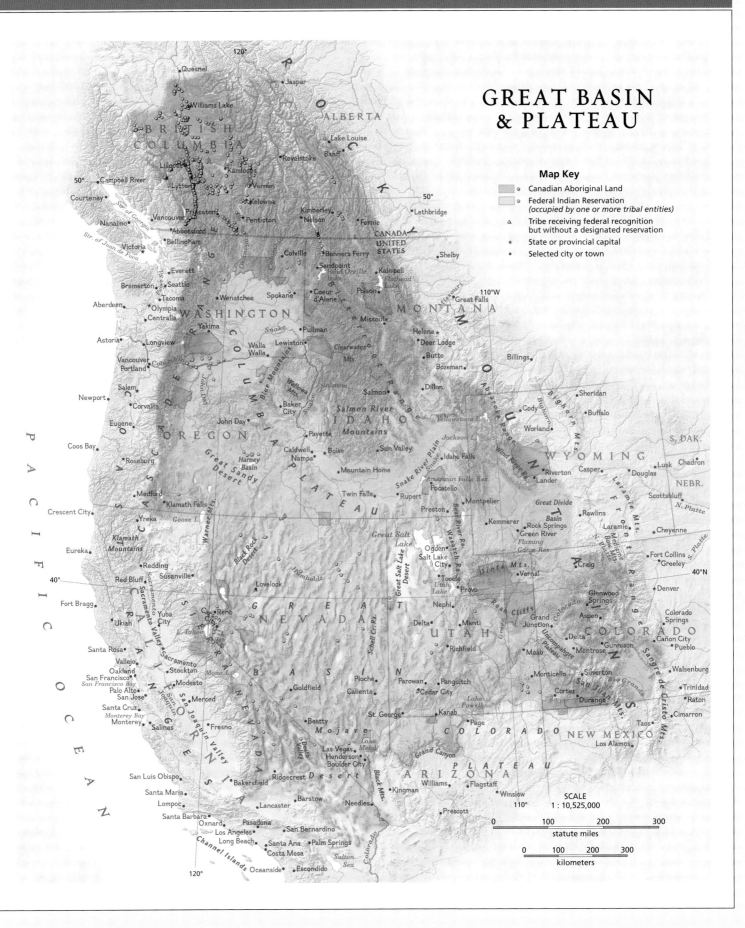

GREAT BASIN
& PLATEAU

Map Key

Canadian Aboriginal Land

Federal Indian Reservation
(occupied by one or more tribal entities)

△ Tribe receiving federal recognition
but without a designated reservation

★ State or provincial capital

• Selected city or town

SCALE
1 : 10,525,000

0   100   200   300
statute miles

0   100   200   300
kilometers

Many tribes of the Great Basin and Plateau were isolated from other groups because of the often rugged terrain. On the Plateau, some tribes were more nomadic, especially after acquisition of the Spanish horse. But boundaries between tribal territories shifted far less than on the nearby Plains, where intertribal warfare often changed the human landscape.

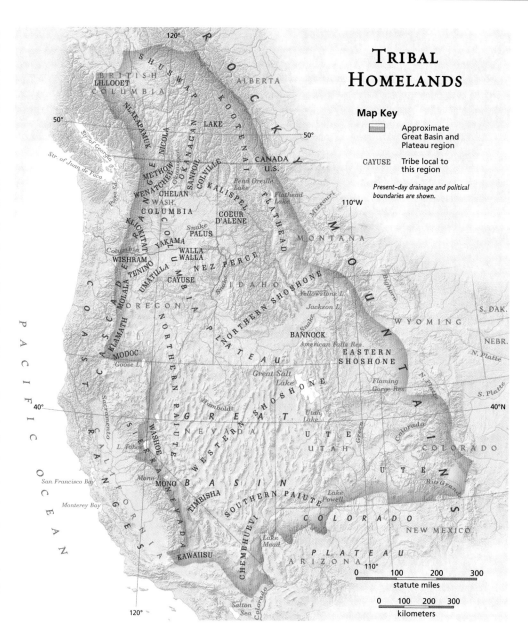

TRIBAL HOMELANDS

Map Key

Approximate Great Basin and Plateau region

CAYUSE   Tribe local to this region

Present-day drainage and political boundaries are shown.

devoted decades to cultivating relationships, gaining converts, and using their influence and trade connections to draw tribal peoples away from older worldviews and lifeways. Many tribes embraced the changes the same way they had embraced the fur trade and the opportunity to use specialized skills at trapping to buy things they needed instead of harvesting and making it all themselves.

Many American missionaries came, too, including Episcopalians, Lutherans, Methodists, and, in the Great Basin, lots of Mormons. Their influence on some tribes was profound. Even today, the largest religious groups on many reservations are Christian. Some are Mormon; some are Catholic—it all depended on who got there first and how long they stayed.

Pocatello was a Shoshone chief who led his people during the tumultuous transition to reservation life. He was born in Utah in 1815 and had lived to nearly age 50 when Brigham Young brought the first waves of Mormon settlers to the region. Pocatello pursued a diplomatic course with the Mormons, but in 1862 gold was discovered in Montana, and the travel routes through Shoshone land soon flooded with prospectors and settlers. Later that year, Abraham Lincoln sent a detachment of the U.S. Army to secure the overland mail route to keep California connected to the east and ensure its participation in the Civil War on behalf of the Union. Together, the military deployment and settler growth set the stage for a major confrontation with the Shoshone.

The Shoshone were wrongly accused of theft in 1862 in the Cache Valley, and four chiefs were executed, igniting a series of counterattacks. Pocatello heard that soldiers were coming for retribution and escaped with his band, barely avoiding the Bear River Massacre, which devastated a large group of Shoshone in January 1863. Pocatello signed the Fort Bridger Treaty in 1868, which relocated his people to the Fort Hall Reservation. In 1875, he led them off the reservation and sought refuge with the Mormons, but despite being baptized, they were forced back to Fort Hall by federal troops.

The government ran residential boarding schools at that time, while churches ran both day and boarding schools. Many Indians

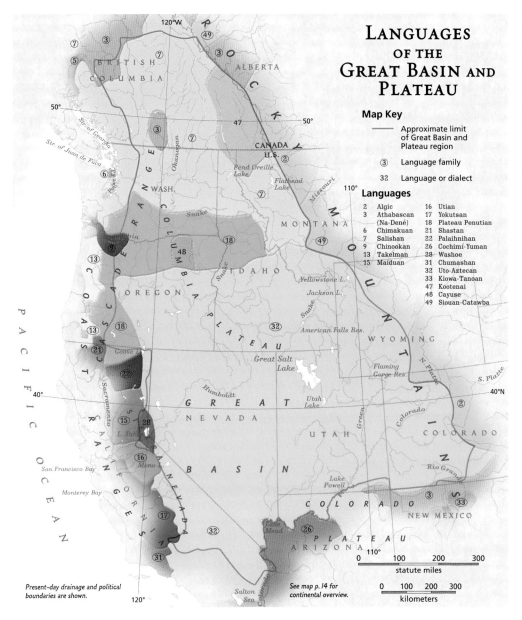

LANGUAGES OF THE GREAT BASIN AND PLATEAU

Map Key

— Approximate limit of Great Basin and Plateau region

③ Language family

32 Language or dialect

Languages

2 Algic	16 Utian
3 Athabascan	17 Yokutsan
(Na-Dené)	18 Plateau Penutian
6 Chimakuan	21 Shastan
7 Salishan	22 Palaihnihan
9 Chinookan	26 Cochimí-Yuman
13 Takelman	28 Washoe
15 Maiduan	31 Chumashan
	32 Uto-Aztecan
	33 Kiowa-Tanoan
	47 Kootenai
	48 Cayuse
	49 Siouan-Catawba

Present-day drainage and political boundaries are shown.

See map p. 14 for continental overview.

0   100   200   300
statute miles

0   100   200   300
kilometers

Three language families dominate the Great Basin and Plateau: Plateau Penutian, Salishan, and Uto-Aztecan. The Uto-Aztecan group includes both the Shoshone, with 20 federally recognized reservations today, and the Paiute, with 29. A few language isolates exist as well, such as the Kootenai and Cayuse, who were independent from the larger groups for a long period.

and Colville, for example, people from the many different tribes married one another. And they married the non-Native people who enveloped their communities, too. But this intertribal harmony had unintended consequences: It soon became very difficult to maintain tribal languages when every tribe was a minority on its own reservation. Many tribal languages faded away or were spoken only in certain contexts, and increasingly only by elders. However, hunting, fishing, and certain cultural activities superseded language barriers and remained vibrant through the treaty period and even today.

SURVIVAL

The Native nations of the Great Basin and Plateau endured many horrible chapters in their collective histories,

went to school as tribal language speakers, never to use those languages again. Adoption and foster care programs also funneled many children out of tribal communities.

Throughout the entire region, and especially on the Columbia Plateau, the government often tried to consolidate many tribes onto the same reservations, confederating their old political structures into unified political identities. For the government, it was a simple and effective way to manage the tribes. For the tribes, it posed new challenges on every level.

Most tribes managed to forge ahead politically, even when the government put enemy tribes on the same reservations. At Yakama

but they also showed incredible resilience. Although many people remark about what they lost—land, language, culture—it is astounding to see all that they still have. The tribal populations are growing very fast. Many retain knowledge of hunting, fishing, gathering, and ceremonial traditions.

Through the generations, many tribal leaders—including prominent Indian women—helped steward their people through the transitions. Sarah Winnemucca was a diplomat, speaker, and cultural force. Born about 1844, the daughter of a Paiute chief, she received formal English education in Nevada. Her band of Paiute was concentrated on the Malheur Reservation after the

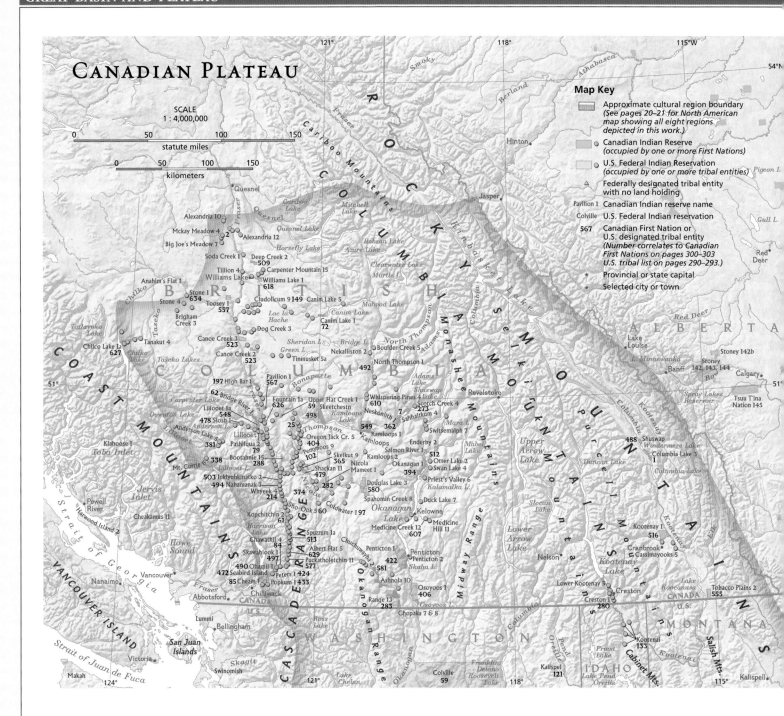

CANADIAN PLATEAU

Map Key

Approximate cultural region boundary
(See pages 20–21 for North American map showing all eight regions depicted in this work.)

Canadian Indian Reserve
(occupied by one or more First Nations)

U.S. Federal Indian Reservation
(occupied by one or more tribal entities)

Federally designated tribal entity with no land holding

Pavilion 1 Canadian Indian reserve name

Colville U.S. Federal Indian reservation

567 Canadian First Nation or U.S. designated tribal entity
(Number correlates to Canadian First Nations on pages 300–303 U.S. tribal list on pages 290–293.)

● Provincial or state capital

○ Selected city or town

SCALE
1 : 4,000,000

statute miles

kilometers

Civil War. Winnemucca worked cooperatively with the first Indian agent there, serving as his interpreter. That led to more translation work for other Indian agents and the Army. Winnemucca actively spoke out against corrupt Indian agents who stole tribal annuities and expropriated tribal land for white settlement—a common problem on Paiute reservation lands.

Her people descended into abject poverty when relocated

In Canada, the Native peoples of the Plateau suffered less physical dislocation than their American counterparts. Native villages in the region cluster around waterways because salmon was a staple food source.

to Yakima. In 1879–1880, she traveled to Washington, D.C., with her father to plead their case and successfully obtained permission for them to return to Malheur, only to be denied by the Indian agent at Yakama Reservation. It was a bitter disappointment. In 1883, Winnemucca traveled east again, where she gave 300 public lectures and wrote and published *Life Among the Paiutes: Their Wrong and Claims*, making her the first Indian woman to secure a copyright and publish in English. She returned home and built a school that promoted the tribal language until it was closed in 1887 as the U.S. developed a compulsory English-only education policy for Indian youth.

Christal Quintasket (1888–1936) was an Okanogan Indian from the Colville Reservation. One of her grandparents was a respected chief, but her own ambitions were entirely apolitical. Quintasket, who sometimes went by the name Mourning Dove as an adult, was a successful author and one of the very first female Indian authors in the world. Her novel *Cogewea the Half-Blood: A Depiction of the Great Montana Cattle Range* was published in

This Shoshone vest incorporates the floral and symmetrical geometric designs typical of Plateau tribal beadwork.

1927. It featured a strong female protagonist from the Flathead Reservation who grappled with the issues of being a mixed-blood, living in two worlds, and trying to claim agency in a world dominated by men, and white men at that.

The struggle was one that Quintasket was quite familiar with, both because of the racial issues in her personal life and because of her experience attending the Sacred Heart School near Kettle Falls, where she lost whatever knowledge she had of her tribal language through the punitive structure of the curriculum. She also published *Coyote Stories* in 1933, a collection of tribal stories. Posthumously, her unpublished notes and writings were collected and

Indians on the Great Plains and Plateau love to compete in games of chance and skill. Pictured here are gamblers from the Colville Reservation around 1911.

Today numerous tribes belong to the Plateau Penutian, Salishan, and Uto-Aztecan language families, descendants of the original settlers thousands of years ago of the American Plateau region. The region's abundant natural resources, especially the salmon and wild game, generated stability and allowed the reservation lands shown here to support the same families for innumerable generations.

edited into *Tales of the Okanogans* (1976) and *Mourning Dove: A Salishan Autobiography* (1990). Quintasket was married twice—first to a Flathead man and then a Wenatchee. She died of the flu in 1936 at age 48.

The cultures of the tribes in the Great Basin and Plateau are incredibly diverse. Their ceremonial and religious lives revolved around their environments and livelihoods. Some tribes thrived on fishing and gathering, others relied primarily on hunting, and still others were successful farmers. But there were common historical experiences and cultural evolutions that united the tribes of the region, as well.

The modern powwow, common to other regions besides Great Basin and Plateau, is one of those unifying cultural developments. Powwow customs, especially those related to war rituals, continue to evolve. The use of eagle feathers, for example, was common in the Great Plains and Plateau, although in the 19th century each feather had to be earned in battle. Today, the rules have changed and each feather need not be earned the same way, although they are still afforded great respect. The powwows of the

This spindle whorl kept wool from slipping during the spinning process. The thunderbird motif, common in many Native cultures, has a distinct Salish style.

"Everything on the earth has a purpose, every disease an herb to cure it, and every person a mission. This is the Indian theory of existence."

—Christal Quintasket (Salish)

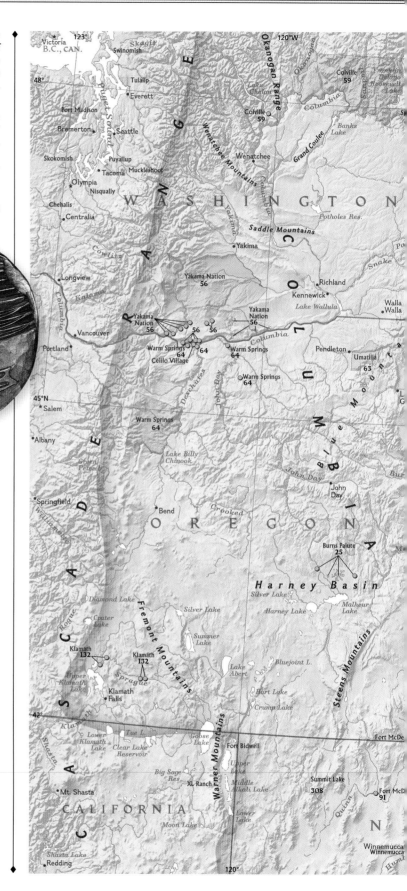

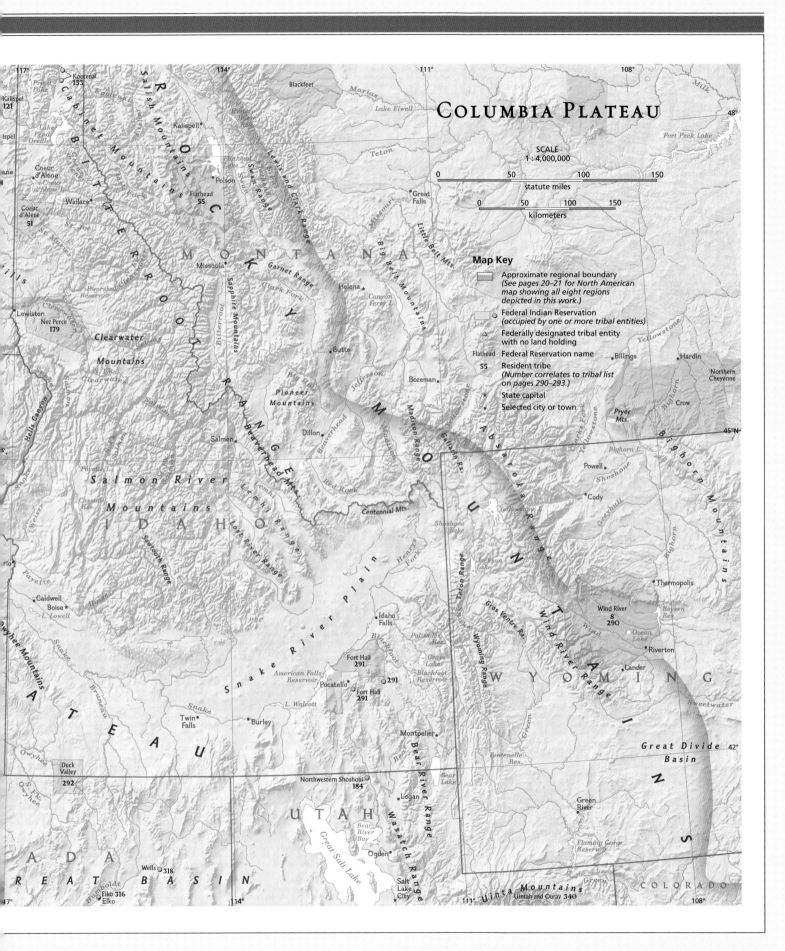

COLUMBIA PLATEAU

SCALE
1 : 4,000,000

| 0 | 50 | 100 | 150 |
statute miles

| 0 | 50 | 100 | 150 |
kilometers

Map Key

Approximate regional boundary
(See pages 20–21 for North American
map showing all eight regions
depicted in this work.)

Federal Indian Reservation
(occupied by one or more tribal entities)

Federally designated tribal entity
with no land holding

Flathead Federal Reservation name

55 Resident tribe
(Number correlates to tribal list
on pages 290–293.)

★ State capital

• Selected city or town

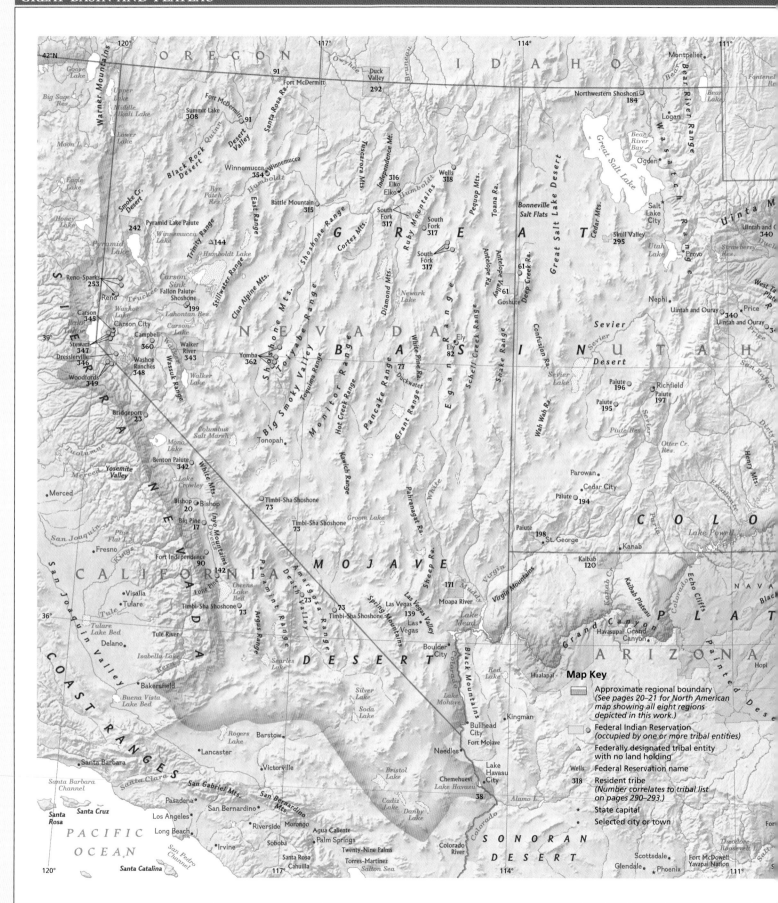

Map Key

Approximate regional boundary
(See pages 20–21 for North American map showing all eight regions depicted in this work.)

Federal Indian Reservation
(occupied by one or more tribal entities)

Federally designated tribal entity with no land holding

Wells   Federal Reservation name

318   Resident tribe
(Number correlates to tribal list on pages 290–293.)

★   State capital

•   Selected city or town

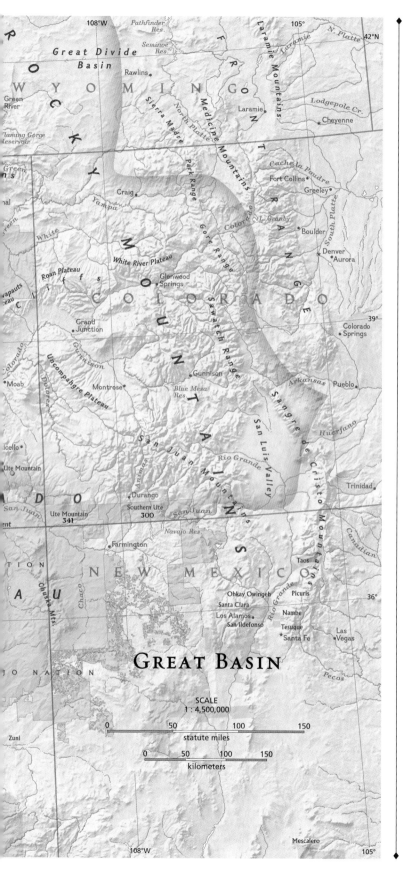

GREAT BASIN

SCALE
1 : 4,500,000

0   50   100   150
statute miles

0   50   100   150
kilometers

Tobacco was a sacred plant across the Great Basin and Plateau with many uses, including as an offering for prayers, like those of this Shoshone man.

Great Basin and Plateau have also been influenced by the regalia of the grass dance societies of the southern Plains, where the dancer and his outfit are meant to mimic the motion of tall grass in the wind. As the powwow spread throughout the Great Basin and Plateau, this style of dance became especially popular there. Likewise, the jingle dress has now become a major component of modern tribal powwow regalia.

Powwows are open to participation from people from all tribes and even non-Native visitors. Tribal communities take pride in their hospitality and good treatment of visitors. A living institution of the first peoples of the region, the powwow has brought the tribes of the Great Plains and Plateau together in a largely secular but distinctly native way. ✈

The mineral-rich mountains and hills of the Great Basin eventually brought miners and settlers, but the geographic isolation of many tribal communities in the region helped preserve ancient cultures and critical pieces of land.

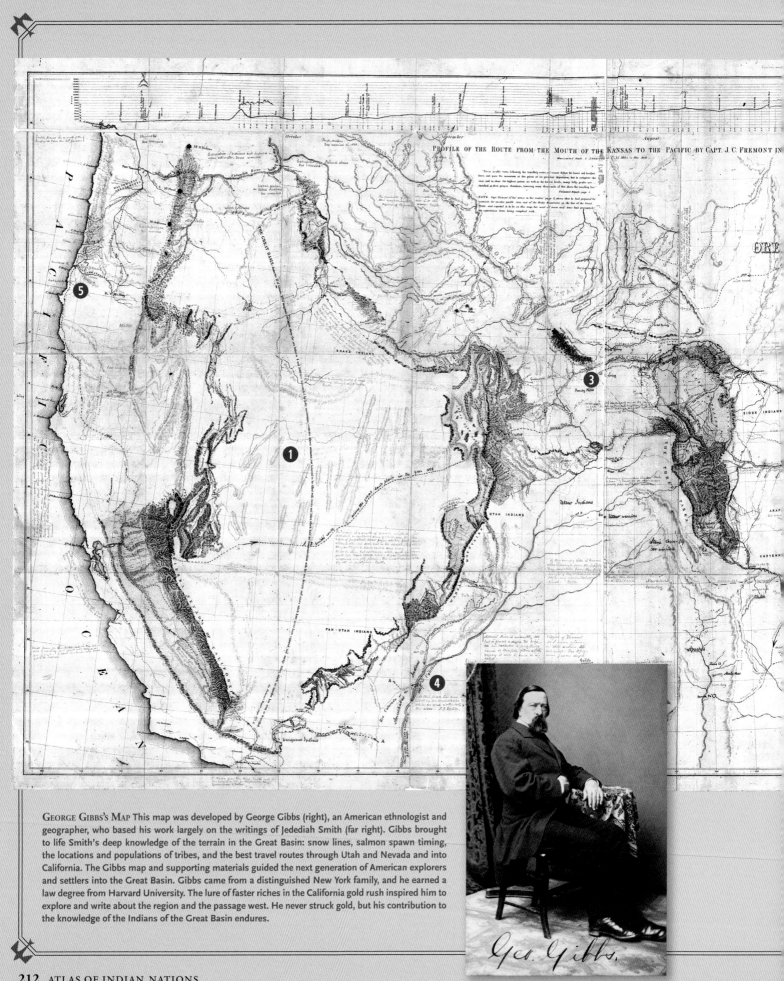

PROFILE OF THE ROUTE FROM THE MOUTH OF THE KANSAS TO THE PACIFIC BY CAPT. J. C. FREMONT IN

GEORGE GIBBS'S MAP This map was developed by George Gibbs (right), an American ethnologist and geographer, who based his work largely on the writings of Jedediah Smith (far right). Gibbs brought to life Smith's deep knowledge of the terrain in the Great Basin: snow lines, salmon spawn timing, the locations and populations of tribes, and the best travel routes through Utah and Nevada and into California. The Gibbs map and supporting materials guided the next generation of American explorers and settlers into the Great Basin. Gibbs came from a distinguished New York family, and he earned a law degree from Harvard University. The lure of faster riches in the California gold rush inspired him to explore and write about the region and the passage west. He never struck gold, but his contribution to the knowledge of the Indians of the Great Basin endures.

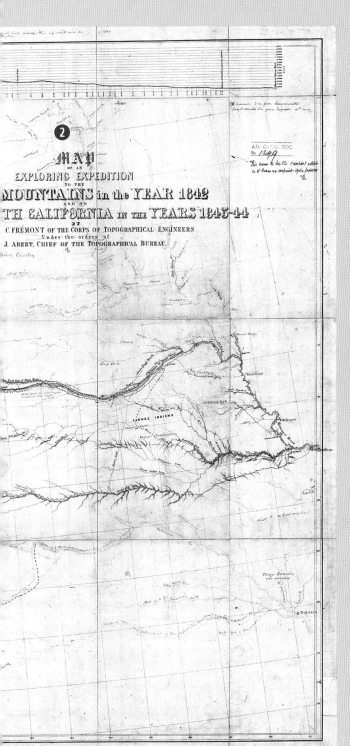

JEDEDIAH SMITH
First American in the Great Basin

Jedediah Smith was a fur trader, explorer, cartographer, and author who became the first American to explore and document the land and peoples of the Great Basin ❶. When he was 22, Smith received a commission to work for the American Fur Company in 1821. Through his role as fur trader, he came into contact with many tribes in the Plains and Great Basin. He was not a belligerent man, but he did view Natives as an inferior race. He directed his men to trade and charm first when meeting a new group of Indians, but to shoot one or two if they did not respond warmly. In 1823, his company fought the Arikara in South Dakota ❷, losing 13 men and gaining Smith a promotion to captain.

In 1824, Crow Indians drew Smith a map on a buffalo hide that detailed the South Pass ❸ through the Rocky Mountains to California. Smith explored the pass and later received credit for its discovery. Smith went into private business as a fur trapper and trader

Jedediah Smith

after that, taking two trips to California in 1826–28 and acquiring thousands of pounds of beaver furs, making a small fortune. His troop attacked the Mohave on each trip through their territory ❹. In Oregon ❺, he was chastised by the fur traders for attacking the Umpqua, who were usually friendly to whites. Smith continued to trap and trade without permission from the Americans, Mexicans, or Indians, inspiring the anger of all. He fought the Blackfoot in 1829. In 1831, he tried the same tactics with the Comanche, but got lanced and died, at age 32. ■

In 1824, Jedediah Smith was mauled by a grizzly bear, which tore off most of his scalp and an ear and broke several ribs. He wore his hair long afterwards to cover the scars.

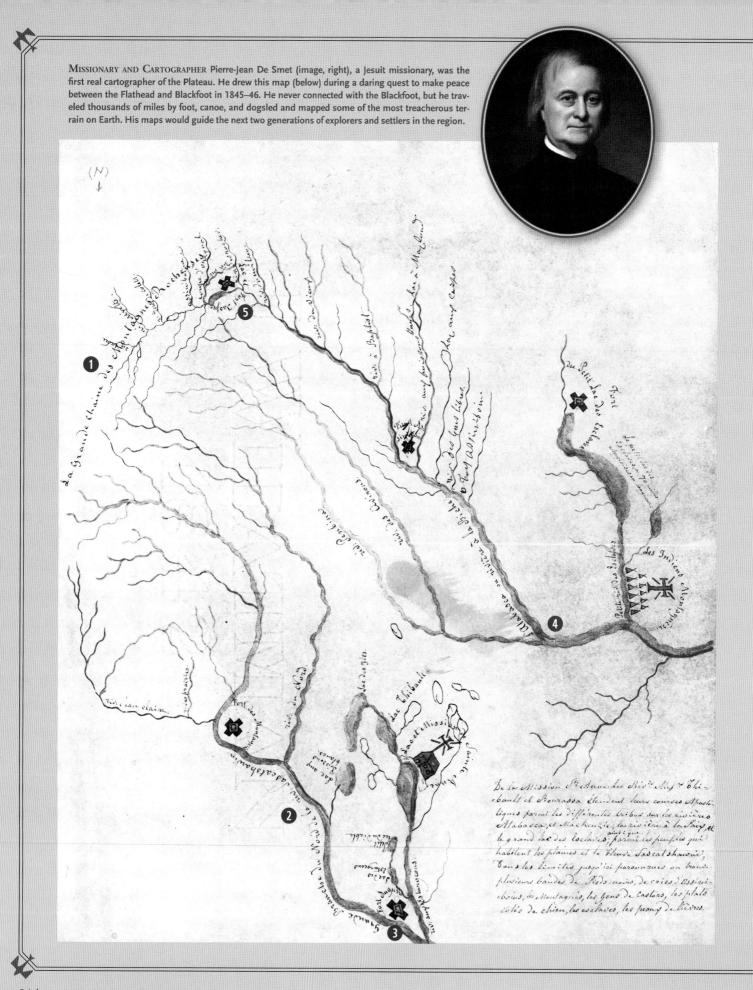

MISSIONARY AND CARTOGRAPHER Pierre-Jean De Smet (image, right), a Jesuit missionary, was the first real cartographer of the Plateau. He drew this map (below) during a daring quest to make peace between the Flathead and Blackfoot in 1845–46. He never connected with the Blackfoot, but he traveled thousands of miles by foot, canoe, and dogsled and mapped some of the most treacherous terrain on Earth. His maps would guide the next two generations of explorers and settlers in the region.

FATHER PIERRE-JEAN DE SMET

First Cartographer of the Plateau

Pierre-Jean De Smet was a Jesuit priest from Belgium who spent much of his adult life on the American Plateau, especially in the Bitterroot Valley in Montana with the Flathead Indians. De Smet first came to the United States in 1821, when he was 20 years old, to train for fieldwork in Indian missions. In 1838–39, he was deployed to Council Bluffs, Iowa, where he helped Joseph Nicollet. De Smet struggled to gain converts among the Potawatomi, and he was caught several times secretly baptizing children without parental consent. He worked among the Flathead, Kaw, and Nez Perce tribes, as well. De Smet's Flathead mission in the Bitterroot Valley (near present-day Missoula, Montana) was established in 1841.

De Smet believed he could broker peace between the Blackfoot and Flathead, who had been warring off and on for decades. His epic journey in 1845–46 to arrange that peace would end in failure—ironically, he got lost and never found the Blackfoot—but his writings and maps from his travels offer some of the most detailed early cartography and ethnological information of the Plateau. De Smet mapped much of the Kootenai and Vermillion Rivers, traveled north, crossed the Continental Divide, and mapped parts of the Canadian Rockies ❶ and the Saskatchewan River ❷. (Note that

north is on the right.) He wintered at Edmonton, Alberta ❸, and then pushed on by snowshoe and dogsled, mapping parts of the Athabasca ❹ and Saskatchewan Rivers, staying at Jasper House ❺, and plotting the locations of forts, posts, and Indian villages. He then went back down the Columbia River and eventually returned to the Flathead.

In the end, De Smet's mission work was less successful than his maps, which were indispensable to American settlers. But he gained the respect of many tribal leaders, including Sitting Bull, whom he helped convince to parley with the government over the Treaty of Fort Laramie in 1868. ∎

A number of Colville men, including Kalispel, Skitswish, and Salish, are pictured here with Father Pierre-Jean De Smet after his journey to Vancouver in 1859. The painting to the left shows Takumakst, the Salish village at Kettle Falls on the Columbia River in Washington.

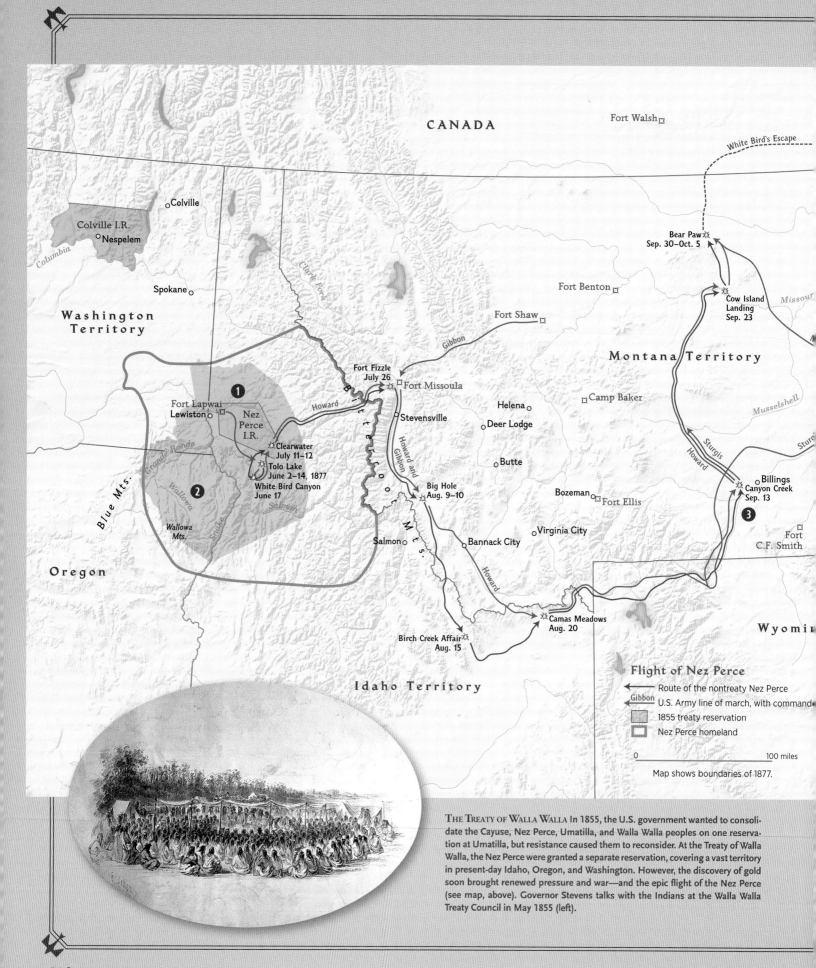

CANADA

Fort Walsh □

White Bird's Escape

○ Colville

Colville I.R.
○ Nespelem

Columbia

Spokane ○

**Washington
Territory**

Fort Lapwai
Lewiston ○

①

Nez
Perce
I.R.

☆ Clearwater
July 11–12
☆ Tolo Lake
June 2–14, 1877
White Bird Canyon
June 17

Grande Ronde

Blue Mts.

②

Wallowa

Wallowa
Mts.

Salmon

Snake

Oregon

Salmon ○

Birch Creek Affair
Aug. 15 ☆

Idaho Territory

Clarke Fork

Fort Fizzle
July 26
☆ Fort Missoula

Howard

Stevensville ○

Bitterroot

*Howard and
Gibbon*

Mts.

Big Hole ☆
Aug. 9–10

Bannack City ○

Camas Meadows
Aug. 20 ☆

Fort Shaw □

Gibbon

Helena ○

○ Deer Lodge

Butte ○

Howard

Bozeman ○ □ Fort Ellis

Virginia City ○

Fort Benton □

Montana Territory

□ Camp Baker

Bear Paw ☆
Sep. 30–Oct. 5

Cow Island
Landing
Sep. 23

Missouri

Musselshell

Sturgis

Howard

Billings ○
Canyon Creek
Sep. 13 ☆

③

Sturgis

Fort
C.F. Smith

Wyomi

Flight of Nez Perce

← Route of the nontreaty Nez Perce

Gibbon ← U.S. Army line of march, with command

▨ 1855 treaty reservation

▢ Nez Perce homeland

0 ——————— 100 miles

Map shows boundaries of 1877.

THE TREATY OF WALLA WALLA In 1855, the U.S. government wanted to consolidate the Cayuse, Nez Perce, Umatilla, and Walla Walla peoples on one reservation at Umatilla, but resistance caused them to reconsider. At the Treaty of Walla
Walla, the Nez Perce were granted a separate reservation, covering a vast territory
in present-day Idaho, Oregon, and Washington. However, the discovery of gold
soon brought renewed pressure and war—and the epic flight of the Nez Perce
(see map, above). Governor Stevens talks with the Indians at the Walla Walla
Treaty Council in May 1855 (left).

FLIGHT FOR FREEDOM
The Nez Perce War

The Nez Perce were extremely diplomatic with the U.S. government, and that got them favorable terms in the Treaty of Walla Walla in 1855, whereby they kept a large reservation in Idaho, Oregon, and Washington. But the discovery of gold on the reservation in 1860 brought more than 5,000 prospectors, ranchers, settlers, and soldiers. An extremely controversial treaty in 1863, signed by only two Nez Perce leaders, ceded the lands of all Nez Perce bands and called for their removal to a small reservation in Lapwai, Idaho ❶. Nez Perce chief Joseph advocated peace and even obtained permission to stay in the Wallowa Valley, Oregon ❷. But then the government reversed its position, jailed a prominent chief, refused to investigate the murders of Indians, and sent the Army to force their relocation in 1877.

White Bird, Joseph, and several other Nez Perce chiefs led the Nez Perce and a small band of allied Palus on a fighting retreat over 1,170 miles of mountains, hills, and frozen streams, seeking sanctuary first among the Crow in Montana ❸ and then with Sitting Bull and the Lakota in Canada ❹. Around 800 Indians, mainly children, women, and elders, faced off against 2,000 soldiers in 18 separate engagements and 4 major battles. White Bird and a small group made it to Sitting Bull's camp. Over 150 Indians were killed. The remaining 418 surrendered with Chief Joseph on October 5, 1877. Joseph said, "My heart is sick and sad. From where the sun now stands, I will fight no more forever." ■

CHIEF JOSEPH

Chief Joseph (1840–1904) was a prominent Nez Perce leader, who assumed the position from his father in 1871. In 1873, he convinced the government to allow his people to stay in Wallowa, but it was a short reprieve. When Gen. Oliver Howard came to forcibly relocate his people, Joseph continued to argue for accommodation, but after some of his young men killed four white settlers, there was no way to hold back the Army.

Joseph showed true mettle as a military leader during the epic flight of his people. He amazed Howard with clever battle tactics, including the deployment of advance and rear guards, skirmish lines, and field fortifications. In the end, Chief Joseph could not safely get all of his people to Canada. At the Bear Paw Mountains, only 40 miles from Canada, he surrendered. He and his people were imprisoned at Fort Leavenworth, Kansas, where this picture was taken of Joseph and five unidentified tribal members.

After an initial eight months in jail, they were held in Oklahoma for an additional seven years. In 1885, they returned to the Plateau, where most of the Nez Perce were concentrated on a reservation at Kooskia, Idaho; Joseph, however, lived the rest of his days in exile at the Colville Reservation in Okanogan, Washington, nearly 300 miles to the northwest, along with a small band of followers and among 11 other tribes on the reservation there.

Two warriors from the Nez Perce tribe pose for photographer Edward S. Curtis in the late 19th or early 20th century. A wool Nez Perce horse hood (inset, above) was decorated with appliqué, beadwork, and feathers.

Chief Sitting Bull's Camp

Miles City
Fort Keogh

wstone

ritory

CONFLICTS IN THE GREAT BASIN AND PLATEAU
Land and Mineral Speculation Culminating in Tragedy

In 1838, American missionaries Marcus and Narcissa Whitman arrived in Cayuse country, soon to be followed by numerous travelers with the opening of the Oregon Trail in 1842 ❶. With them came tragedy. A measles outbreak in 1847 devastated the tribal population, and some Indians held the missionaries responsible for bringing the whites among them and spreading the disease. They massacred the Whitmans and 12 other whites, igniting the Cayuse War of 1847–1855.

At first, the Cayuse hid in remote areas and raided. However, by 1849, with Cayuse lands awash in miners from the California gold rush, both peace and evasion were difficult. In 1850, the Cayuse turned over five of their tribesmen for the murder of the Whitmans, and they were summarily executed. Raids by the Cayuse and attacks by local militia continued until 1855.

In 1864, the Klamath, Modoc, and Yahooskin tribes, overwhelmed by the influx of white settlers and miners, agreed to settle on the newly established Klamath Reservation ❷ as a single confederated political entity. But the rapid impoverishment of the tribes at Klamath drove some residents to escape.

Modoc chief Captain Jack and a small band made a break for the Modoc ancestral homeland on the California border ❸. The U.S. Army and local militias fought them in a brutal struggle known as the Modoc War. The band surrendered in 1865 and returned to Klamath, only to escape again, avoiding capture from 1865 to 1873. Ultimately, they surrendered unconditionally and received no mercy from the U.S. government. All the Modoc leaders were hanged.

The Pend d'Oreille ❹ were diplomatic in their dealings with the government, but their treaty-stipulated rights to hunt and fish off the reservation were often rejected by non-Indians. In 1908, a group of eight Pend d'Oreille left the Flathead Reservation to hunt around Flathead Lake ❺. Confronted by the state game warden, three of the Pend d'Oreille men and one boy were shot and killed. The pregnant wife of one of the men then killed the game warden. Tensions remained high for several years and curtailed the tribe's ability to exercise its treaty-guaranteed rights. ∎

Buckskin Charley

OURAY AND BUCKSKIN CHARLEY Sometimes the rapid encroachment on tribal lands resulted in horrible violence. In 1879, the Ute at White River (left) rebelled against mistreatment by Indian agent Nathaniel Meeker and local settlers, killing several whites and bringing the wrath of the government. The Ute won their first battle against U.S. troops, but were eventually outnumbered by a larger troop deployment. Ouray of the Ute negotiated the release of white hostages for the government and tried to make a peace without retribution. He was acknowledged as a chief by the government for doing so, and that mantle later passed to Buckskin Charley, who kept the peace for the tribe. Their interventions were widely credited with saving many Ute lives and finding a diplomatic solution that avoided a crushing defeat.

A group of Bannock hunters (right) fords the Snake River in the Tetons, as painted by Frederic Remington in about 1895. A Ute warrior and his bride (left) pose astride horses in northwest Utah in 1874.

British Columbia

North-West Territories

Little Fort □

Ntlakyapamuk

Fraser Canyon War
※ 1858

□ Fort Langley

Fort Steele □

□ Fort MacLeod

Conflicts in the Great Basin and Plateau

※ Battle
□ Fort

0 _____ 200 miles
Map shows boundaries of 1870.

Victoria ○
Fort Townsend □
Port Gamble □ 1856
Seattle 1856
Seattle ○

Washington Territory

Kalispel
Spokane Fort Plains Colville
1858 1858 ※ Four Lakes 1858
※ Pine Creek 1858

Marias Massacre 1870 ※

Bear Paw 1877 ※

Missouri

Fort Steilacoom □
Yakama
Union Gap 1855

Spokan
Palouse

④
Coeur d'Alene
Flathead Lake
Fort Benton □

⑤
Fort Shaw □

Cow Island Landing 1877 ※

Montana Territory

Nisqually
Fort Simcoe □
Cayuse
※ Toppenish Creek 1855

Fort Lapwai □
Fort Fizzle ※ 1877
Fort Missoula □
Camp Baker □

Fort Vancouver □
Fort Walla Walla □
Portland ○
Cascades Massacre 1856
Salem ○
Fort Dalles □
Walla Walla
Grande Ronde Valley 1856
※ Tolo Lake 1877
Clearwater ※ 1877
White Bird Canyon 1877 ※
Nez Perce
Big Hole ※ 1877

Canyon Creek 1877 ※
Yellowstone
Manuel's Fort
Fort Keogh □

Dakota Territory

Umatilla

Oregon

①
Fort Harney □

Sheepeater War ※ 1879

Fort Ellis □
Fort C.F. Smith □

Camas Meadows ※ 1877

Fort Phil Kearny □

Fort Klamath □
②
Steen's Mountain 1867 ※
Sheepeater
Fort Boise □
Idaho Territory
Owyhee River 1866 ※

Fort Reno □

The Stronghold 1873 ※
③ ※ Willow Creek 1873
Three Forks 1866
Bannock

Fort Caspar □
Fort Fetterman □

Dry Lake 1873 ※
Modoc
Fort McDermitt □
Shoshone

Wyoming Territory
Fort Laramie □
Oregon Trail
Nebraska

Infernal Caverns 1867 ※

Bear River ※ 1863

Fort Fred Steele □
Platte

Fort Halleck □
Fort Douglas □
Salt Lake City ○
Fort Bridger □

Paiute
Pyramid Lake 1860 ※
Williams Station Massacre 1860 ※
Virginia City ○
Fort Ruby □
Walkara War 1853 ※
Fort Utah ※ Springville
Nephi ○
Green
Milk Creek 1879 ※
White River Agency ○ Meeker Massacre 1879

Gunnison Massacre 1853 ※
Ute ※ Fountain Green Massacre 1853
□ Fort Deseret

Colorado Territory

Sacramento ○
Fort Churchill □
Nevada

Central
Overland Trail

Utah Territory
Ute
Fort Cameron □
Fort Crawford □
Bent's Old Fort □
Arkansas
□ Fort Lyon

San Francisco ○

Circleville Massacre 1866 ※

Fort Lewis □
Fort Garland □

California

Paiute

Monterey ○

Pipe Spring 1866 ※

Colorado

White Massacre 1849 ※
Taos ○
Ojo Caliente Canyon 1854 ※ Cieneguilla 1854

Arizona Territory

New Mexico Territory

Fort Bascom □

Although all tribes were pressured to give up land, some in the Great Basin like the Ute clashed less with the U.S. government than others in the Plateau, such as the Bannock (left), Nez Perce, Shoshone, and Yakama.

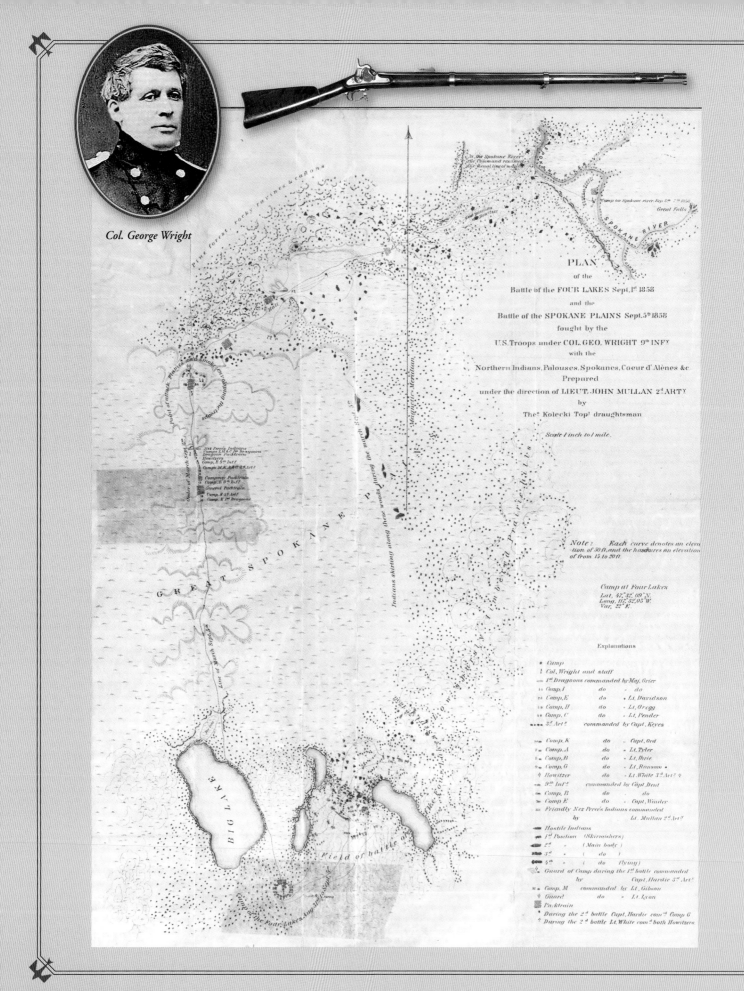

Col. George Wright

PLAN
of the
Battle of the FOUR LAKES Sept. 1st 1858
and the
Battle of the SPOKANE PLAINS Sept. 5th 1858
fought by the
U.S. Troops under COL. GEO. WRIGHT 9th INFY
with the
Northern Indians, Palouses, Spokanes, Coeur d'Alènes &c.
Prepared
under the direction of LIEUT. JOHN MULLAN 2d ARTY
by
Thos Kolecki Topl draughtsman

Scale 1 inch to 1 mile.

Note: Each curve denotes an elevation of 50 ft, and the hachures an elevation
of from 15 to 20 ft.

Camp at Four Lakes
Lat. 47°.32'.09" N.
Long. 117°.32'.05" W.
Var. 22° E.

Explanations

* Camp
1 Col. Wright and staff
1st Dragoons commanded by Maj. Grier
Comp, I   do   do
Comp, E   do   · Lt. Davidson
Comp, H   do   · Lt. Gregg
Comp, C   do   · Lt. Pender
3d Art.   commanded by Capt. Keyes

Comp, K   do   · Capt. Ord
Comp, A   do   · Lt. Tyler
Comp, B   do   · Lt. Ihrie
Comp, G   do   · Lt. Ransom
Howitzer   do   · Lt. White 3d Art. ✦
9th Infy   commanded by Capt. Dent
Comp, B   do   do
Comp, E   do   · Capt. Winder
Friendly Nez Percés Indians commanded
by   Lt. Mullan 2d Art.
Hostile Indians
1st Position   (Skirmishers)
2d   (Main body)
3d   (do   )
4th   (do   flying)
Guard of Camp during the 1st battle commanded
by   Capt. Hardie 3d Art.
Comp, M   commanded by Lt. Gibson
Guard!   do   · Lt. Lyon
Packtrain
✦ During the 2d battle Capt. Hardie comd Comp G
✦ During the 2d battle Lt. White comd both Howitzers

GREAT SPOKANE PLAINS

BIG LAKE

Field of battle of

BATTLE OF FOUR LAKES
The Painful Conclusion to the Yakama War

The Yakama War was one of the most painful conflicts in the entire Plateau region. The Yakama (Yakima) are really 14 different distinct tribal groups from the Sahaptian branch of the Plateau Penutian language family. Indigenous to the Yakima and Columbia River Valleys, they fished, hunted, and gathered in the region for countless generations.

The California gold rush of 1848–1855 brought prospectors and settlers into tribal lands along the Columbia River. Within a few years, the settlers were eager to claim the rich valleys in Oregon as their own. The Walla Walla Council of 1855 established three separate treaties to consolidate the tribal populations on the Nez Perce, Umatilla, and Yakama Reservations.

At Yakama, the Kah-milt-pay, Klikatat, Kow-was-say-ee, Li-ay-was, Linquit, Ochechotes, Palus (Palouse), Pasquouse, Se-ap-cat, Shyiks, Skin-pah, Wenatshapam, Wish-ham, and Yakama were consolidated and confederated as a single political entity. The transition was painful because it involved so much land loss, but the tribes made it with relative peace. However, the very same year the government concentrated the tribes at Yakama, gold was discovered within the boundaries of the reservation. The Indians were still trying to get used to being confined to a much

Chief Kamiakin

smaller space with less access to salmon and other critical foods. Now they were overrun with white settlers in the very same space.

From 1855 to 1858, the 14 tribes at Yakama and their neighbors, especially the Coeur d'Alene, engaged settlers and the U.S. Army in a number of battles and raids. On September 1, 1858, Chief Kamiakin led an attack on U.S. troops under the command of Col. George Wright near present-day Spokane, Washington. The soldiers had just been equipped with Springfield Model 1855 rifles, which were accurate up to 500 yards; the Indians had smoothbore muskets accurate up to 100 yards. In the Battle of Four Lakes, many Indians died from long-range rifle and sniper fire before they could even close ranks with the soldiers. The Indians retreated with heavy casualties, and then watched in horror as Colonel Wright led U.S. troops up the river valley, capturing 800 Indian horses. Wright kept 100 and killed the rest, leaving their bones to bleach in the sun.

The Army proceeded to finish the job with a scorched-earth military campaign directed at the Plateau tribes. Many Indian villages were looted and destroyed. The conflict did not end well for the tribes, who eventually surrendered. The government summarily executed Yakama chief Qualchan and 23 other chiefs. ∎

SCORCHED EARTH Col. George Wright (opposite, top left) led a scorched-earth military campaign against the Plateau tribes after the Battle of Four Lakes. The battle was widely viewed in the non-Native world as a major victory because no soldiers were killed, thanks to the Springfield Model 1855 rifle (opposite, top right), which was accurate up to 500 yards. Soldiers mowed down Indian warriors before they could get close enough to shoot back. Chief Kamiakin, who had united many of the Plateau tribes in common resistance, called for a retreat, and U.S. troops commanded the field (map, opposite). As the warriors scattered, the soldiers looted and destroyed tribal villages along the river valley, capturing 800 horses and killing most of them (right).

NATIVE TRIBES OF
THE GREAT BASIN AND PLATEAU

The tribes of the Great Basin and Plateau lived in extraordinarily isolated and treacherous terrain.
Following are brief histories of select tribes in the region.

■ BANNOCK

Current Locations: Idaho
Language Family: Uto-Aztecan

The Bannock are an offshoot of the Paiute and speak a language from the Numic branch of the Uto-Aztecan language family. They were big-game hunters and relied on antelope, bighorn sheep, deer, and, after acquiring horses from the Nez Perce, buffalo. The Bannock and their allies the Shoshone signed the Fort Bridger Treaty in 1868, which ceded much of their land and established a reservation for them at Fort Hall. A large group of Shoshone, led by Pocatello, were settled at Fort Hall as well. The two groups later merged and became known as the Shoshone-Bannock.

■ CAYUSE

Current Locations: Oregon
Language Family: Isolate

The Cayuse are a small tribe from a language isolate, unrelated linguistically to other tribes. They were nomadic hunters who also fished and gathered. After horses were introduced to the region, the Cayuse became adept in their use, training and breeding them. They developed a distinct breed known as the Cayuse pony. In 1855, the tribe signed a treaty and relocated to the Umatilla Reservation at Pendleton, Oregon. They were consolidated there with the Umatilla and Walla Walla as the Confederated Tribes of the Umatilla Indian Reservation. By 1904, the Cayuse had dwindled to 404 people. Today, they are rebounding and maintain an active sense of community.

■ COEUR D'ALENE

Current Locations: Idaho
Language Family: Salishan

The Coeur d'Alene are from the Interior Salish branch of the Salishan language family. They fished for salmon, trout, and

This Southern Ute men's shirt incorporates loomed beadwork in a geometric design, ermine hide tassels, and appliqué porcupine quillwork.

whitefish and moved as needed to augment their food supplies. The Coeur d'Alene tried to isolate themselves from the white traffic heading west across the Oregon Trail, which opened in 1842, and especially after the gold rush of 1849. The gold rush of 1860–63 on the Plateau itself proved more difficult to deal with. In 1873, an executive order reduced Coeur d'Alene land to 600,000 acres. Later, in 1894, the tribe was

forced to cede a strip to accommodate the Washington and Idaho Railway.

Due to environmental damage caused by lead, silver, and zinc mining, the Coeur d'Alene Reservation is today the second largest superfund cleanup site in the United States. The tribe has successfully asserted its sovereign authority over the land in recent years, including the land on the bottom of the lake in the Supreme Court case *Idaho v. the United States.*

■ COLVILLE (CONFEDERATED TRIBES)

Current Locations: Washington
Language Family: Various

The Confederated Tribes of the Colville Reservation evolved out of the U.S. government's consolidation of 12 distinct tribes from the Plateau region: the Arrow Lakes, Chelan, Colville, Entiat, Methow, Moses-Columbia, Nespelem, Nez Perce, Okanogan, Palus, Sanpoil, and Wenatchi. All 12 tribes hunted mountain goat, sheep, deer, moose, and elk. They also gathered food and fished for salmon and trout. The Colville lived right at Kettle Falls on the Columbia River and were largely sedentary fishermen. The name Colville came from their association with the Hudson's Bay Company trading post of that name.

All of the tribes on the Colville Reservation shared common linguistic roots as members of the Interior Salish branch of the Salishan language family except for the Nez Perce and Palus, who were moved there after the conflict between the Nez Perce–Palus alliance and the U.S. government. Both the Nez Perce and Palus are from the Sahaptin branch of the Plateau Penutian language family.

In 1781, the Salishan tribes were hit by smallpox brought into the region by fur traders. By 1846, Jesuit missionaries were firmly established among the Colville at Kettle Falls. Over time, all of the Colville and most of the other tribes converted to Christianity. The reservation at Colville was established in 1872 by executive order and pushed together the original ten tribes. The Nez Perce and Palus peoples joined them a few years later.

The Grand Coulee Dam on the Columbia River, built by the government in 1933, destroyed Kettle Falls and the salmon run there, a loss still felt by the tribes. The missionary work at Colville and the mixing of the tribes loosened their hold on tribal languages, although tribal members have worked hard to maintain hunting and fishing traditions and strengthen their government for the benefit of their people.

The Salish at Colville Falls flourished on one of the richest salmon fisheries on the planet. Many tribes relied on salmon, especially on the Plateau, but Colville Falls was coveted and considered sacred ground.

■ GOSHUTE

Current Locations: Nevada, Utah
Language Family: Uto-Aztecan

The Goshute are an offshoot of the Shoshone, a tribe from the Uto-Aztecan language family. Although they took big game when they could find it, the Goshute subsisted primarily on small game and also gathered.

When the first Mormons settled in the Tooele Valley in 1855, their livestock destroyed the region's fragile ecosystem. The Goshute soon turned to raiding livestock to compensate for the loss of natural food sources. In 1860, the U.S. Army, under Patrick Connor, attacked the Goshute. By 1863, the tribe had no choice but to surrender and sign a treaty. The government later consolidated many of the Goshute together with bands of Paiute and Bannock as a single political entity—the Confederated Tribes of the Goshute Reservation.

This Freemont arrowhead was the product of fine craftsmanship whose essential purpose was not beauty but survival.

Another smaller group was established as the Skull Valley Band of Goshute Indians.

■ KLAMATH

Current Locations: Oklahoma, Oregon
Language Family: Plateau Penutian

The Klamath are from the Plateau Penutian language family and are indigenous to southern Oregon. They are closely related to the Modoc, and both the Klamath and Modoc had continual contact with an unrelated tribe, the Yahooskin, an offshoot of the Shoshone. In 1826, all three tribes—the Klamath, Modoc, and Yahooskin—traded with Peter Skene Ogden, their first sustained American contact.

In 1954, the U.S. government terminated the tribal government at Klamath, a devastating blow to the people. The Klamath termination legislation and the earlier Klamath treaty of 1864 both had strong language protecting tribal water rights, an ongoing source of friction with regard to the dams on tribal rivers. In 1986, the tribe was reinstated as a recognized tribal entity. Today, the Klamath continue to fight for the ecological and cultural survival of the reservation.

■ KOOTENAI

Current Locations: British Columbia; Montana
Language Family: Isolate

The Kootenai are indigenous to present-day British Columbia, Idaho, Montana, and Washington. Their language is classified as a language isolate. The Kootenai had vibrant ceremonial life, with many well-known ceremonies and societies. The arrival of Jesuit missionary Pierre-Jean De Smet in 1845 brought profound change to the Kootenai. Many converted to Christianity and adopted Euro-American practices. The Hellgate Treaty of 1855 brought the first land cessions and confederated the Kootenai with the Salish and Pend d'Oreille. The encroachment on Kootenai land continued with the Plateau gold rushes of 1860–63.

Successive executive orders by U.S. Presidents further consolidated Kootenai populations. On the Flathead Reservation,

This Shoshone scene shows the Plateau as a cultural crossroads. As in the Plains, many tribes used tepees, kept herds of horses, and hunted. But like Northwest tribes, they also fished and gathered.

the Kootenai were confederated with the Salish as a single political entity. A small group of Kootenai was embedded with the Arrow Lake Band among the Confederated Tribes of the Colville Reservation, although the Kootenai were not designated as one of the 12 tribes legally represented there.

■ NEZ PERCE

Current Locations: Idaho, Washington
Language Family: Plateau Penutian

The Nez Perce people are descended from the Sahaptian branch of the Plateau Penutian language family and are closely related to the Palus. The Nez Perce were the largest tribe on the Columbia Plateau, with more than 6,000 members in a massive territory of 17 million acres. They hunted, gathered, fished, and bred horses, including the famous Appaloosa.

In 1855, the U.S. government tried to consolidate four tribes—the Cayuse, Nez Perce, Umatilla, and Walla Walla—on one reservation, but the Nez Perce balked. But they eventually signed the Treaty of Walla Walla, which created a separate reservation for them in much of present-day Idaho, Oregon, and parts of Washington and included terms supporting their hunting and fishing rights even on lands they sold to the government.

The Plateau gold rushes of 1860–63 brought so many whites to Nez Perce land that the government pressured the tribe for additional land cessions. Ultimately, the government convinced two Nez Perce chiefs to sign a treaty that ceded all Nez Perce lands and called for their removal to a small reservation in Lapwai, Idaho.

When the U.S. Army was sent to force the relocation of the Nez Perce in 1877, Chief Joseph and other chiefs led the Nez Perce and a small band of Palus on a 1,170-mile fighting retreat that became known as the Nez Perce War. They ultimately decided to seek refuge with Sitting Bull in Canada, but only a small group made it. The remaining 418 surrendered with Chief Joseph on October 5, 1877, just 40 miles from Canada. Joseph famously told them, "My heart is sick and sad. From where the sun now stands, I will fight no more forever." In 1885, most of the Nez Perce settled on a reservation at Kooskia, Idaho, but Joseph and a small group of followers lived in exile at Colville.

■ PAIUTE

Current Locations: Arizona, California, Idaho, Nevada, Oregon, Utah
Language Family: Uto-Aztecan

The Paiute, one of the largest tribes in the Great Basin and Plateau, come from the Numic branch of the Uto–Aztecan language family. Within the vast Paiute population, there were three major linguistic and cultural divisions: the Northern Paiute, Southern Paiute, and Owens Valley Paiute. The Bannock, Coco, Kawaiisu, and Timbisha have sometimes also been called Paiute, although they are distinct. The Paiute acquired horses from the Nez Perce and Shoshone and transformed hunting, travel, and war throughout the region.

The Great Basin's mountain ranges kept the Paiute isolated from Spanish, Mexican, and early American contact. However, conflict came to Paiute territories by 1860 with the arrival of white settlers. The Pyramid Lake War, Owens Valley Indian War, Snake War, and Bannock War all engulfed many bands of Paiute. Each was settled with substantial Indian casualties and calls for land cession. The reservations at Duck Valley, Malheur, and Pyramid Lake were soon crowded as the tribal population grew ever more concentrated. The Paiute adapted and survived, however. In 1980, two more Paiute communities regained federal recognition.

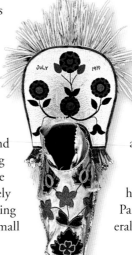

This Salish cradleboard from the early 1900s has a beaded buckskin apron and backboard with a floral design.

■ PEND D'OREILLE (KALISPEL)
Current Locations: Montana, Washington
Language Family: Salishan

The Pend d'Oreille are from the Salishan language family, indigenous to present-day Idaho, western Montana, and eastern Washington. The name Pend d'Oreille is a French term meaning "hang from the ears," a reference to the shell earrings commonly worn by adults in the tribe. Two main groups of the tribe—the Upper and Lower Pend d'Oreille—had separate political relations with the U.S. government.

The Pend d'Oreille were expert hunters, trappers, gatherers, and fishermen. The arrival of missionaries in 1844 did not immediately disrupt tribal life, but the stream of white settlers that ran through Pend d'Oreille land after the California gold rush changed everything. The Hellgate Treaty of 1855 consolidated most of the Upper Pend d'Oreille with a large group of Salish and most of the Kootenai into one confederated political entity on the Flathead Reservation. The government tried to concentrate the Lower Pend d'Oreille on a reservation in 1872, but could not get tribal leaders to agree to terms. It has since created the Kalispel Indian Reservation in Washington and worked hard to strengthen the political and economic infrastructure there for the benefit of the tribal population.

■ SALISH
Current Locations: British Columbia; Idaho, Montana, Washington
Language Family: Salishan

Salish is the name of a language family as well as one tribe within that language family. Many of the tribes on the Plateau come from the Salishan language family, a common people that diverged and diversified over time. The Interior Salish, a large and diverse tribe from the Salishan language family, are indigenous to present-day British Columbia, Idaho, Montana, and Washington. In the Pacific Northwest, the Coast Salish are closely related in terms of language, although significant cultural differences between the two groups of Salish emerged over time. The Salish people were fishermen, expert trappers, hunters, and gatherers.

Starting in the 1840s, Jesuit missionaries, including Pierre-Jean De Smet, worked extensively with the Salish, especially around Flathead Lake. As with the Pend d'Oreille and other tribes, the arrival of white settlers during the California gold rush prompted the government to pursue Salish land and mineral wealth.

Pictured here are Minnie Patawa (Walla Walla), Esther Motanic (Cayuse), and Melissa Parr (Umatilla), prizewinners in the "first real American beauty contest" at Pendleton, Oregon, in 1924.

The Hellgate Treaty of 1855 consolidated many Salish with the Upper Pend d'Oreille and most of the Kootenai into one confederated political entity on the Flathead Reservation.

The Colville Reservation, established in 1872 by executive order, combined ten Salishan-speaking tribes: the Arrow Lakes, Chelan, Colville, Entiat, Methow, Moses-Columbia, Nespelem, Okanogan, Sanpoil, and Wenatchi. The related but distinct Salishan-speaking Coeur d'Alene, Pend d'Oreille (Kalispel), and Spokane each had a distinct culture and story of their own (see separate tribal entries for each).

In the U.S., the Salish dealt peacefully with the government. But their treaty-guaranteed rights to harvest fish and hunt off the reservation were rarely supported. In Canada, the British Columbia Treaty Commission was created in 1993 to address the retained treaty rights of the First Nations peoples of British Columbia. Forty-seven First Nations participated, but the Salish distrusted the process and have remained intentionally unengaged. However, diplomatic efforts continue and the door is open for potential remedies for the Salish in British Columbia.

■ SHOSHONE
Current Locations: California, Idaho, Nevada, Oregon, Utah, Wyoming
Language Family: Uto-Aztecan

The Shoshone come from the Numic branch of the Uto-Aztecan language family. They are among the largest and the most diverse tribes in the region, with bands in the driest deserts in the southern Great Basin, the wide-open eastern Great Basin, and the lush valleys of the western Plateau. The Shoshone traveled extensively prior to European contact, often fighting the Arapaho, Blackfoot, Cheyenne, Crow, and even Lakota. As many moved onto the southern Plains, the Comanche separated from the rest of the Shoshone and grew exponentially in power and numbers.

While each band of Shoshone had very different experiences with the various waves of white settlement, some common themes emerged. The 1849 California gold rush brought trails and settlers to Shoshone lands. When gold was discovered on the Plateau in 1860, the ensuing gold rush lasted three years and multiplied the white population many times over. Mormons also established enclaves in the Great Basin during this period. When conflict arose, the U.S. government used the Army to suppress tribal resistance, and local militias and even posses played a major role in Shoshone life as well.

The Shoshone were wrongly accused of theft in 1862 in the Cache Valley, and four chiefs were executed, igniting a series of counterattacks. Shoshone chief Pocatello escaped with his band in 1863, barely avoiding the Bear River Massacre, in which witnesses say the U.S. Army killed almost 500 Indians, the single worst act of violence in the history of their tribe. The Bear River Massacre crushed any thoughts of further resistance from the Shoshone in the area.

Many of the Eastern Shoshone were settled on the Wind River Reservation in 1868 with their hereditary enemies the Arapaho. In the Snake River Valley that same year, the Shoshone and their allies the Bannock signed the Fort Bridger Treaty, which ceded much of their land and established a reservation for them at Fort Hall. After the government mismanaged the rations at Fort Hall in 1878, many left the reservation to harvest camas bulbs. When they discovered the nearby camas crop ravaged by hogs brought by white settlers, desperate Bannock, Shoshone, Paiute, and even some Umatilla started to raid white ranches and settlements. Defeat in battle brought the tribes back to Fort Hall Reservation. Pocatello's band of Shoshone was settled at Fort Hall as well. Over time the two groups merged and became known as the Shoshone-Bannock.

Tensions continued for many decades. In 1879, the U.S. and a band of about 300 Western Shoshone clashed in the Sheepeater Indian War. In 1911, a Shoshone man named Mike Daggett got into an altercation with white ranchers encroaching on tribal land and killed four of them. A white posse found and killed Daggett and all eight members of his family, including children. Their remains were donated to the Smithsonian Institution and eventually repatriated to the tribe in 1994.

■ SPOKANE
Current Locations: Idaho, Montana, Washington
Language Family: Salishan

The Spokane are from the Salishan language family indigenous to the northern Plateau.

Spokane art forms are heavily influenced by Salishan cultures from the Northwest, but their subsistence economy more closely resembles the hunters, gatherers, and fishermen of the Plains and Plateau.

As with other Plateau tribes, Spokane tribal life was disrupted by the white travelers and settlers who encroached on Spokane land after the California gold

For Indians across the Plateau and Great Basin, like the Yakama pictured here, horses were a critical part of daily life for hunting, travel, and war.

rush of 1849. In 1858, the Spokane and their allies the Coeur d'Alene and Palus fought the U.S. Army. In 1877, the Lower Spokane agreed to a new reservation, and an executive order in 1881 established the Spokane Indian Reservation. The Upper and Middle bands of Spokane were dissolved in 1887, and the tribal population was divided among the Coeur d'Alene, Colville, and Flathead Reservations.

On the Spokane Reservation, the U.S. government operated an open-pit uranium mine from 1956 to 1982. Today, it is a superfund cleanup site and a contentious issue for tribal members who have to live with the site's ongoing health and environmental effects.

■ UMATILLA
Current Locations: Oregon
Language Family: Plateau Penutian

The Umatilla speak Sahaptin, a language from the Sahaptian branch of the Plateau Penutian language family. Linguistically and culturally, they are closely related to the Nez Perce, Palus, Walla Walla, and Yakama. The Umatilla were expert hunters, fishermen, traders, and trappers. They quickly incorporated the horse into their travel and work life.

Pressure mounted for the Umatilla to cede land in the 1850s and 1860s as the gold rushes, the Oregon Trail, and settlement interest brought numerous whites to the Plateau. In 1855, the Umatilla, along with the Cayuse and Walla Walla, signed a treaty with the U.S. government that established a reservation at Pendleton, Oregon, ceded the remaining tribal land, and consolidated and confederated the tribes as a single political unit—the Confederated Tribes of the Umatilla Indian Reservation. Unlike many tribes, the Umatilla maintained peaceful relations with the government throughout the treaty period.

■ UTE
Current Locations: Colorado, Utah
Language Family: Uto-Aztecan

The Ute are from the Numic branch of the Uto-Aztecan language family. Their precontact economy focused on hunting, gathering, and limited agriculture. A powerful tribe, they sometimes raided smaller tribes nearby. The government slowly chipped away at their land base through treaties in 1849, 1863, and 1868. Today there are three Ute reservations in the Great Basin.

■ WALLA WALLA
Current Locations: Oregon
Language Family: Plateau Penutian

The Walla Walla speak Sahaptin, a language

from the Sahaptian branch of the Plateau Penutian language family. Linguistically and culturally, they are related closely to the Umatilla and more distantly to the Nez Perce, Palus, and Yakama. The Walla Walla were excellent hunters, fishermen, traders, and trappers. They encountered the Lewis and Clark expedition in both 1805 and 1806. Before the opening of the Oregon Trail in 1842 and the California gold rush in 1849, their first sustained contact with Europeans came when the British established a Northwest Company trading post in their territory in 1811.

In 1855, the Walla Walla signed a treaty with the U.S. government that established a reservation for themselves and the Cayuse and Umatilla tribes at Pendleton, Oregon, consolidating and confederating the tribes as a single political unit—the Confederated Tribes of the Umatilla Indian Reservation.

■ WARM SPRINGS (CONFEDERATED TRIBES)

Current Locations: Oregon
Language Family: Various

The Confederated Tribes of Warm Springs are really three distinct linguistic and cultural groups: four bands of Tenino, who speak Sahaptin, a language from the Sahaptian branch of the Plateau Penutian language family; two bands of Chinookan-speaking Wasco; and a group of Uto-Aztecan-speaking Paiute. The Tenino and Wasco were consolidated at Warm Springs in 1855; the government moved the Paiute there in 1879.

Numerous government-built dams on area rivers, including the Bonneville Dam (1938) and the Dalles Dam (1957), did tremendous damage to the fish populations, a longtime staple of the tribes. In recent years, however, a number of successful lawsuits have quantified some of the damage and yielded the tribe reparations, which they reinvested in tribal businesses.

Indians of the Plateau and Great Basin found many innovative ways to protect and store food for winter. Pictured here are two Salish women drying meat on a wooden frame.

■ YAHOOSKIN

Current Locations: Oregon
Language Family: Uto-Aztecan

The Yahooskin are an offshoot of the Shoshone, a tribe from the Numic branch of the Uto-Aztecan language family. The Yahooskin are indigenous to the Snake River and were sometimes called Snake Indians by settlers. The Yahooskin's first sustained American contact was with trader Peter Skene Ogden in 1826. In spite of their connection to the larger Shoshone group, the Yahooskin had more in common politically with their unrelated neighbors the Klamath and Modoc.

By 1864, the Klamath, Modoc, and Yahooskin faced constant encroachment by white settlers and miners and soon signed a treaty, which required them to settle on the Klamath Reservation as a single confederated political

These Ute-made moccasins are typical of the region, with the seamless face and tongue, and exquisite appliqué beadwork.

entity. The Yahooskin rapidly descended into poverty. In 1954, the Klamath were terminated as a federally recognized tribe, and a long political struggle followed until the tribe was finally reinstated in 1986.

■ YAKAMA (YAKIMA)

Current Locations: Washington
Language Family: Plateau Penutian

The Yakama are really 14 different distinct tribal groups from the Sahaptian branch of the Plateau Penutian language family: the Kah-milt-pay, Klikatat, Kow-was-say-ee, Li-ay-was, Linquit, Ochechotes, Palus (Palouse), Pasquouse, Se-ap-cat, Shyiks, Skin-pah, Wenatshapam, Wishham, and Yakama. Indigenous to the Yakima and Columbia River Valleys, they fished, hunted, and gathered in the region for countless generations. The Walla Walla Council of 1855 established three separate treaties with numerous tribes to consolidate the tribal populations on the Nez Perce, Umatilla, and Yakama Reservations.

NORTHWEST
COAST

CHAPTER SEVEN

CHEHALIS

CHINOOK

COOS

COQUILLE

COWLITZ

GRAND RONDE
(CONFEDERATED
TRIBES)

HOH

LOWER UMPQUA

LUMMI

MAKAH

MUCKLESHOOT

NISQUALLY

NOOKSACK

PUYALLUP

QUILEUTE

QUINAULT

SAMISH

SAUK-SUIATTLE

SILETZ

SIUSLAW

S'KLALLAM

SKOKOMISH

SNOQUALMIE

SQUAXIN ISLAND

STILLAGUAMISH
(STOLUCKWAMISH)

SUQUAMISH

SWINOMISH

TLINGIT

TULALIP

UMPQUA

UPPER SKAGIT

The Native nations of the Northwest Coast
developed in one of the most abundant fisheries
in the world. Salmon, whales, seals, and sea life
of all kinds sustained a high population density
and cultural values that stressed generosity to
a fault. The arts permeated every facet of life,
and the peoples there developed numerous
languages and traditions.

INDIAN NATIONS
OF THE NORTHWEST COAST

The Pacific Northwest is an area with incredibly diverse ecosystems, climates, and human histories. The Olympic, Coast, and Cascade Mountains have a cold, alpine climate. The coast has an oceanic climate with verdant plant life on land and abundant marine life in the water. It is rich in fish, especially salmon, and myriad species of marine life. Fish, furbearing animals, large and small game, and humans thrived here in large numbers. Every part of the region is close to the ocean, but hard to access by land from the east. This gave early inhabitants of the Northwest Coast protection from powerful outside groups and easy access to food. The human population in the Northwest Coast grew quickly and remained denser than most parts of the world.

Clovis points in the Northwest have been dated to 13,000 years ago, and an ongoing excavation at Paisley Caves, Oregon, has convinced many archaeologists that Indians were in the Northwest at least 14,500 years ago. Since England was completely covered in ice until around 12,000 years ago, the land tenure of the Northwest tribes and their status as indigenous peoples, and not immigrants, is beyond reproach.

POLITICAL AND SOCIAL HIERARCHY

Most tribes in the Northwest were highly stratified. There were nobles, commoners, and slaves. In some communities, the children in noble families were strictly sequestered from the main population and could not play with common children. Noble families kept separate residences and even in many social functions had limited interaction with other members of their tribe. Sometimes people ascended to more prestigious positions through their skills as warriors or traders. For some tribes, nobles marked their special status with unique and restrictive clothing, regalia, totem poles, symbols, jewelry, or, in the case of the Flathead, with intentional flattening of the forehead in infancy.

Many of the tribes in the Northwest placed a high value on the accumulation of wealth, and they imbued wealth with a singular purpose: it allowed the individuals who possessed it to enhance their prestige through ritualized giving. Trade, raiding and warfare, the taking of captives as slaves, and an elaborate culture of gifting—all were opportunities

Respect for position was reinforced in Northwest art forms. Pictured (left) is Taku chief Ano-Tlosh, who displays the colors, regalia, and sigil for his kin group. Above, a Haida totem pole. Totem poles symbolized the power, wealth, and prestige of Northwest families and kin groups.

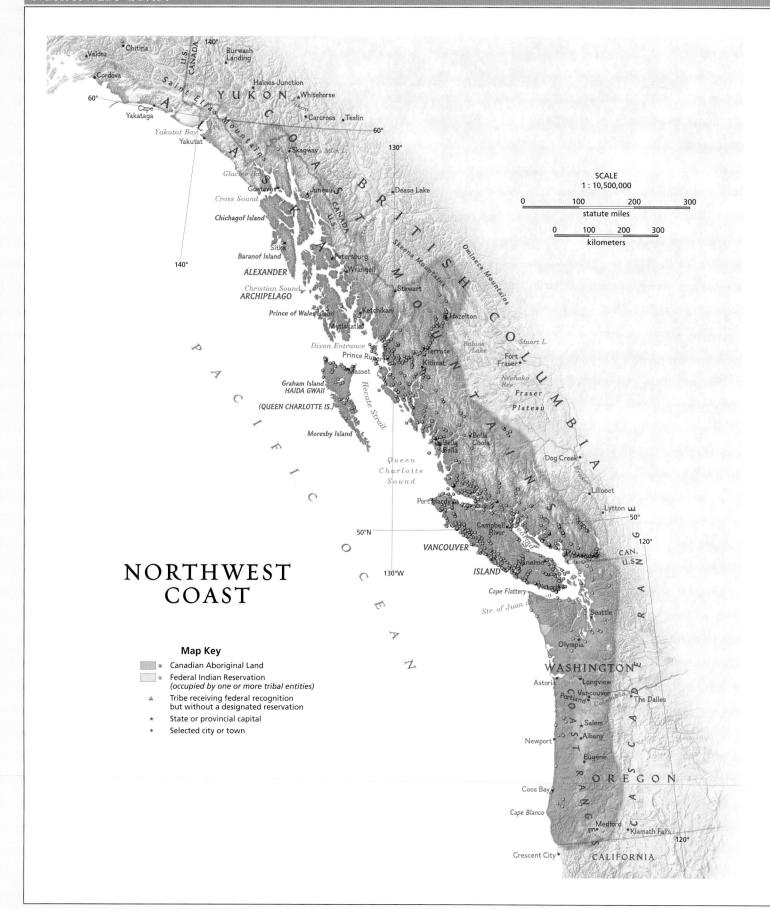

SCALE
1 : 10,500,000

0   100   200   300
statute miles

0   100   200   300
kilometers

NORTHWEST COAST

Map Key

▨ ∘ Canadian Aboriginal Land
▢ ∘ Federal Indian Reservation
(occupied by one or more tribal entities)
△ Tribe receiving federal recognition
but without a designated reservation
✦ State or provincial capital
• Selected city or town

for the powerful to become even more power-ful and exert their influence to maintain the social order.

The most common ritualized giving was the potlatch. At a potlatch, the host family or fami-lies might give away slaves, food, blankets, and trade items. Prestige went not to those who could accumulate the most wealth but those who were able to redistribute the most wealth.

After European contact, most Pacific Northwest tribes embraced the fur trade, and the gift items presented at potlatch ceremo-nies shifted with the shifts in tribal cultures. Eventually in both the United States and Canada, the potlatch was attacked by mis-sionaries who could not compete with wealthy tribal families in gifting and thus could not generate traffic to their missions. Ultimately, they worked with the U.S. and Canadian gov-ernments to formally ban potlatch ceremo-nies. In the U.S., government Indian agents were instructed to suppress tribal dances and giveaway ceremonies of all kinds. One such directive, designated Circular 1665, stayed an active mandate through 1933. In Canada, Parliament formally banned the potlatch in 1884. It took decades for the tribes of the Northwest to success-fully reassert their rights to carry on the ancient custom of potlatch.

DIVERSITY IN THE NORTHWEST

Common geology, geography, and food supplies like the ubiqui-tous salmon unified all the peoples of the Northwest. But diver-sity abounded there as well. The Pacific Northwest contains more tribes than most other regions of North America. Their languages come from several language families. Salishan, Penutian, Wakashan, and Athabascan dominate the lists, but there are a number of language isolates as well. Warfare and raiding were part of Northwest Coast tribal culture, but people were not regularly displaced en masse, and

CHRONOLOGY

9000 B.C.
Undisputed evidence of growing human habitation in the Northwest

A.D. 1794
Treaty of London (Jay Treaty) establishes U.S.–Canadian border

1795
Russian-American Company establishes presence in Northwest; colonization begins

1804
Battle of Sitka: Russian presence in Northwest solidified

1805
Lewis and Clark expedition reaches Northwest

1836–1869
400,000 white settlers come to Northwest via the Oregon Trail

1850–1899
26 Northwest gold rushes bring many new settlers, miners, and prospectors to Northwest

1854
Medicine Creek Treaty: Northwest tribes start ceding large amounts of land

1855
Quinault, Point Ellis, and Neah Bay Treaties strip massive land holdings from many tribes

1855–56
Puget Sound Indian War and Rogue River Indian War: Tribes resist relocation and confederation

The Native nations of the Northwest span from the sand dunes of the Oregon coast northward through Washington and British Columbia to parts of the Yukon and Alaska. The tribes are diverse, but common threads of culture have shaped each one as well, including the high value placed on wealth and ritual generosity.

that stability enabled linguistic diversity to deepen over time.

The treaty period proved to be a spe-cial challenge. The U.S. government tried repeatedly to move numerous tribes into single reservations, confederating their polit-ical systems. This accelerated the language shift and loss beyond the efforts of mission-aries and boarding-school policies. In spite of the number of diverse languages in the Northwest, most are now spoken only by elders; others are completely extinct.

Most Northwest tribes were quite seden-tary, although for major events like salmon spawning and whale migrations, they might temporarily move to seasonal camps. Some, like the Samish, had a defined territory but moved frequently within that territory, mak-ing them more nomadic than many other tribes. Most tribes built permanent cedar-plank longhouses. In many cases, these were large structures that accommodated extended family networks, but in some tribes, basic family units and dwellings were much smaller.

Natural resource gathering also varied sig-nificantly. Whales migrate all along the Northwest coast, and for some tribes, like the Makah, whale was a staple food and whaling a ritual practice. Other tribes, such as the Tlingit, were extremely adept at trapping and became inextricably linked to British and Russian fur trade networks.

THE RUSSIAN ERA

The Northwest and the Arctic were the only regions in North America that endured a sustained Russian colonial effort, but the impact was tremendous. In 1795, the Russian-American Company established a presence in the Northwest. Prior to this, the tribes of the region had seen Spanish, British, and even Japanese ships and

The tribes of the Northwest Coast held fairly consistent territories for long periods of time, which helps explain the region's linguistic diversity. With access to abundant salmon and protected by natural barriers such as the mountain ranges close to the coast and the ocean, the tribes had few reasons to move and many to stay right where they always were.

exploration attempts. They had sustained contact with British and even French trade networks in some places. But the Russian experience was decidedly more colonial—with missionaries, military forces, conscripted labor, and brutal retaliation for any kind of resistance. In 1804, Tlingit resistance to Russian subjugation, conscripted labor practices, and forced marriages culminated in the Battle of Sitka. The Tlingit repelled the Russian advance, but they could not sustain the war and soon came under Russian control. That era would not end until after Russia sold its land holdings and withdrew its trade networks in 1869.

THE BRITISH AND AMERICAN ERA

The United States and Great Britain sparred with one another over trade, taxation, tariffs, and territory many times, including during the American Revolution and the War of 1812. As they fought for control and rights to colonize, the fact that the tribes of the Northwest had ceded nothing to either of those countries mattered little to the would-be colonists. In 1794, the Treaty of London, also known as the Jay Treaty, set a border between the U.S. and Canada that divided tribal communities with no consideration for their sovereignty. Both the British and American governments

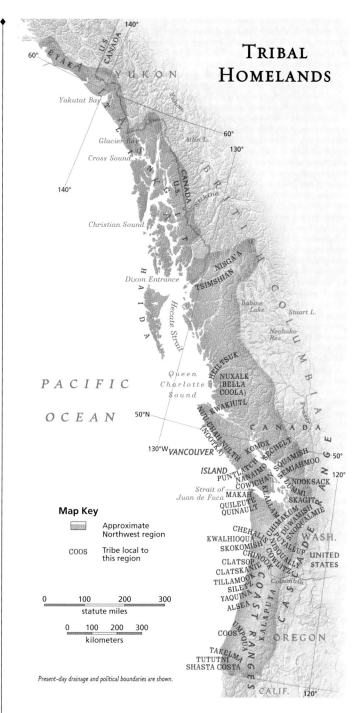

TRIBAL HOMELANDS

Map Key

Approximate Northwest region

COOS   Tribe local to this region

0   100   200   300
statute miles

0   100   200   300
kilometers

Present-day drainage and political boundaries are shown.

This painting shows Coast Salish women spinning and weaving. The blanket is fashioned from hair sheared from dogs, since few tribes in the Northwest kept herd animals.

then started to isolate tribal communities and pursue formal land acquisitions. Tribal language, culture, and tradition paid a heavy price during these power grabs.

It took the Americans just a few decades after the Revolution to assert a lasting presence in the tribal communities of the Northwest. In 1805, the Lewis and Clark expedition wintered in the Northwest. News traveled fast, and from 1836 to 1869 an

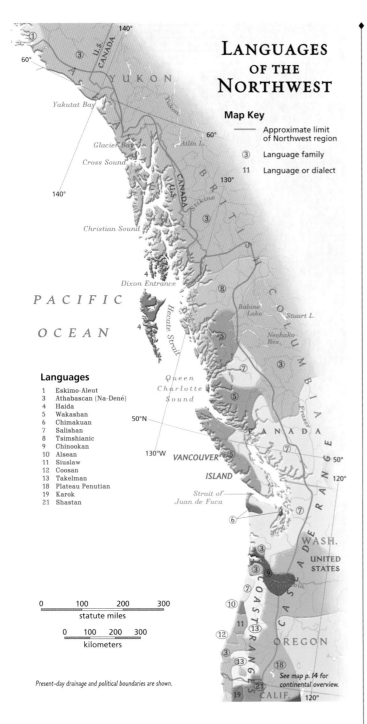

LANGUAGES OF THE NORTHWEST

Map Key

——	Approximate limit of Northwest region
③	Language family
11	Language or dialect

Languages

1   Eskimo-Aleut
3   Athabascan (Na-Dené)
4   Haida
5   Wakashan
6   Chimakuan
7   Salishan
8   Tsimshianic
9   Chinookan
10   Alsean
11   Siuslaw
12   Coosan
13   Takelman
18   Plateau Penutian
19   Karok
21   Shastan

0   100   200   300
statute miles

0   100   200   300
kilometers

Present-day drainage and political boundaries are shown.

that brought many new settlers, miners, and prospectors to the Northwest. Some ignited conflicts between tribes in British Columbia and prospecting parties. Some tribal peoples also tried prospecting themselves.

In the United States, most of the major land cession treaties were signed in the 1850s. The Medicine Creek Treaty of 1854 was one of the first really massive land cessions. The next year saw the Quinault, Point Ellis, and Neah Bay Treaties. Most tribes were soon minority populations and minority landholders in their own land. Conflict broke out over the attempts to relocate and consolidate some of the tribes. In 1855–56, the Puget Sound Indian War and the Rogue River Indian War saw several tribes try to fend off the assault on their ways of living and land. The tribes lost the battles, but they did hold onto their sense of community and deep knowledge of place. The establishment of reservations transferred most of the region out of Native control. That limited access to resources needed for food and shelter, which exacerbated the growing poverty of the tribal peoples there. Further complicating matters was the nature of the treaties themselves, some of which combined different tribes with distinct languages and cultural traditions into single political entities. Retaining tribal languages was more challenging than ever before. People had to adapt to new political, economic, linguistic, and cultural environments, and it was a painful process.

This Tlingit eagle mask shows both the artistic talent common throughout the region and the high value placed on kin networks and symbols.

THE NORTHWEST IN THE 20TH CENTURY

The tribes of the Pacific Northwest survived the treaty period, but pressure on their lands and lifeways did not end with the end of treatymaking. After the Dawes Act in 1887, many of the tribes in the U.S. experienced allotment, by which reservation land that had previously been held in common for the benefit of all tribal

estimated 400,000 white settlers came to the Northwest via the Oregon Trail. Tribal communities were overrun. Pressure grew on tribes to cede land, consolidate and confederate with one another, and make room for the white settlers, most of whom received free land grants to establish their families on what was undisputed tribal land a few years before.

From 1850 to 1899, there were 26 Northwest gold rushes

See map p. 14 for continental overview.

In British Columbia, First Nations and tribal villages are scattered along the coast. Many are concentrated heavily around the Queen Charlotte Islands and the adjacent mainland. The tribal communities lost direct control over much of the land there, but they retained harvest rights to the fish throughout the region—something not always supported by the government.

members now became private. Some reservation land was allotted to tribal members; the rest was labeled "surplus" and immediately opened for white settlement. Before long, even the tribal allotments started to flow out of tribal hands through every kind of swindle and resource speculation scheme imaginable.

The potlatch ceremony continued to be actively suppressed in both the United States and Canada until the 1930s. Throughout British Columbia, Oregon, and Washington, tribal potlatches, ceremonies, dances, and other traditions started to deteriorate and die out.

In the 1950s, the U.S. government developed a new policy toward tribes called termination. The government developed lists of tribes that it felt were sufficiently assimilated to have their citizens rely exclusively on their U.S. citizenship as a social safety net. Terminated tribes lost funding from the Bureau of Indian Affairs, as well as their special tax status and their unique position relative to state governments, and many descended into abject

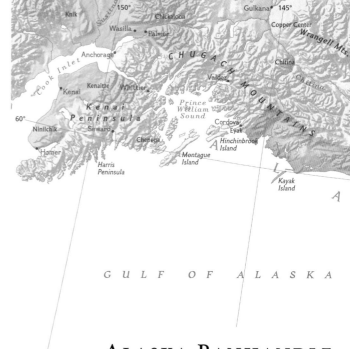

GULF OF ALASKA

ALASKA PANHANDLE AND COASTAL BRITISH COLUMBIA

SCALE
1 : 6,000,000

0   50   100   150   200
statute miles

0   50   100   150   200
kilometers

Map Key

Approximate cultural region boundary
(See pages 20–21 for North American map showing all eight regions depicted in this work.)

Canadian Indian Reserve
(occupied by one or more First Nations)

U.S. Federal Indian Reservation or Alaskan native land
(occupied by one or more tribal entities)

△ Federally designated tribal entity with no land holding

Masset I   Canadian Indian reserve name

Yakutat   U.S. Federal Indian reservation or Alaskan native land

396   Canadian first nation or U.S. designated tribal entity
(Number correlates to Canadian First Nations on pages 300–303 U.S. tribal list on pages 290–293.)

221   Alaska resident tribe
(Number correlates to tribal list on pages 296–297)

✳   Provincial or state capital

•   Selected city or town

These three brothers, photographed in 1907, were headmen of the Kak-Von-Tons of the Chilkat tribe. Their lineage and age gave them positions of respect in the tribal culture. The Chilkat lived in the Alaska–British Columbia border region.

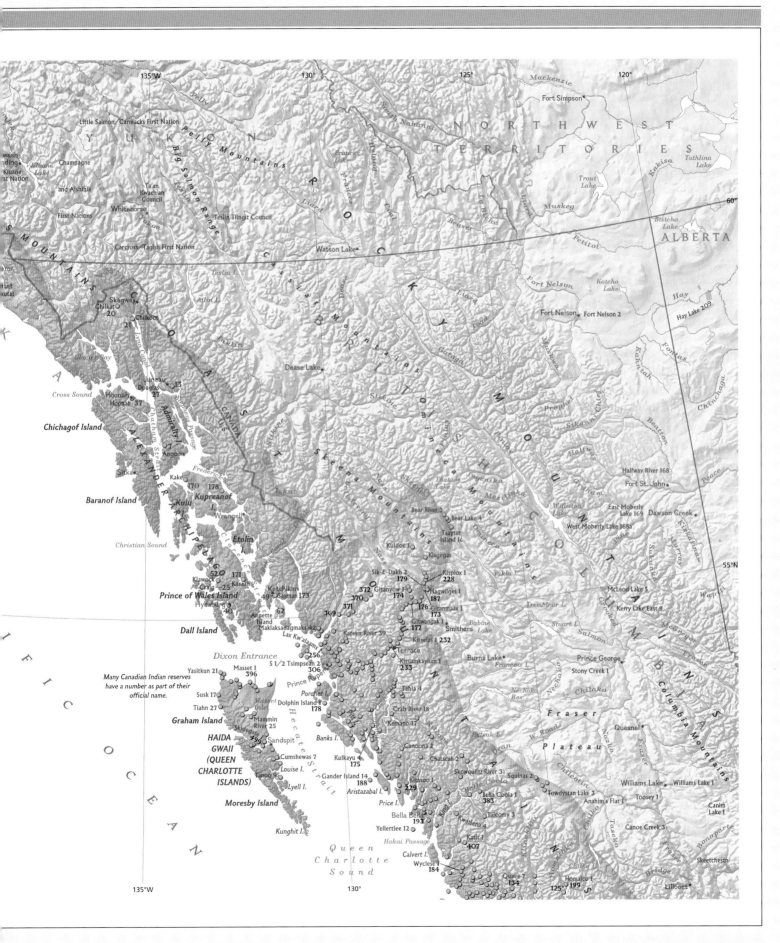

VANCOUVER ISLAND AND THE NORTHWEST U.S. COAST

Many Canadian Indian reserves have a number as part of their official name.

SCALE
1 : 6,000,000

| 0 | 50 | 100 | 150 | 200 |

statute miles

| 0 | 50 | 100 | 150 | 200 |

kilometers

Map Key

Approximate cultural region boundary
(See pages 20–21 for North American map showing all eight regions depicted in this work.)

Canadian Indian Reserve
(occupied by one or more First Nations)

U.S. Federal Indian Reservation
(occupied by one or more tribal entities)

△ Federally designated tribal entity with no land holding

Yuquot 1   Canadian Indian reserve name

Siletz   U.S. Federal Indian reservation

57   Canadian first nation or U.S. designated tribal entity
(Number correlates to Canadian First Nations on pages 300–303 U.S. tribal list on pages 290–293.)

★ Provincial or state capital

• Selected city or town

---

poverty. Some were later reinstated, and others continue to press their claims for federal recognition. Whether terminated and reinstated, terminated and not yet reinstated, or never terminated at all, the peoples of the Northwest are wary of the U.S. government because of the treaty abuses and pernicious policies like termination.

Vancouver Island is home to an incredibly diverse ecosystem, from a sheltered sound on the east to a temperate rain forest in the west. Indians there found salmon in great numbers as well as berries, wild game, and birds.

As in other areas of the U.S. and Canada, residential boarding-school policies were developed to advance the assimilation of Indian peoples of the Northwest Coast region. The schools used harsh physical punishment, isolation from home communities and families, and strict English-only language instruction to eradicate tribal languages and customs.

> "It is a strict law that bids us dance.
> It is a strict law that bids us distribute our property
> among our friends and neighbors. It is a good law.
> Let the white man observe his law; we shall observe ours."
>
> —CHIEF O'WAX̱ALAGALIS

The combined effect of the relocations and consolidations of the treaty period with the war on culture and the residential boarding-school policy was to destroy tribal languages in many places. In addition, those policies also did unspeakable harm to the basic social fabric.

The tribes of the Northwest pioneered a series of treaty rights cases, primarily around the salmon harvests that were, for some tribes, guaranteed in treaties. They rallied political support and successfully asserted their rights to the land and resources that their forebears had worked so diligently and sacrificed so much to keep for future generations. Those successes helped inspire tribes in the Great Lakes and other places to press their claims, as well. The Northwest led that charge across the United States. The tribes of the Northwest lost most of their land, and many lost their languages, but they all maintained connections to place and customs that set them apart from their non-Native neighbors.

Religious and cultural dances were common throughout the Northwest. Often masks were used to symbolize kinship groups or specific spirits whose help was sought for harvest, travel, or healing. Painted here is an entourage preparing for a medicine mask dance in the Strait of Juan de Fuca region of Vancouver Island.

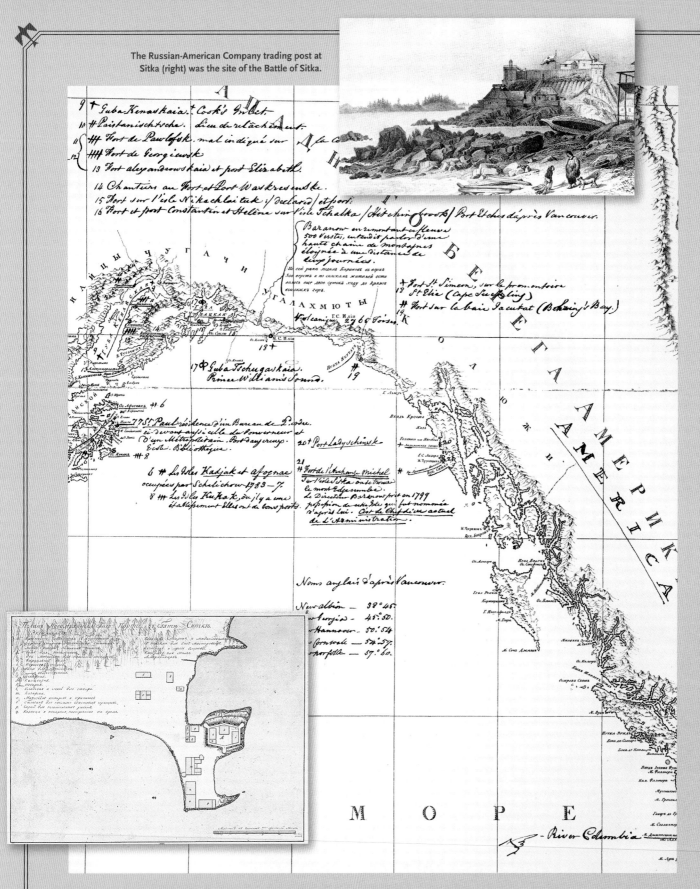

The Russian-American Company trading post at Sitka (right) was the site of the Battle of Sitka.

AUSPICIOUS LOCATION The high ground on the bay at Sitka is not just a beautiful location for a tribal village or a trading post (see map above). It also has a commanding view of the water—critical for defense and for spotting whales and shipping. Sitka is an auspicious location, prized by the Tlingit for its spiritual importance and by the Russians for its close proximity to the Tlingit, whom they wanted to exploit for labor and furs. Recent archaeological excavations have revealed that human use of the area extends back 11,000 years.

THE BATTLE OF SITKA
Russians Defeat Tlingit, Move Base to Sitka

The Battle of Sitka was the last battle between Alaskan Natives and Europeans, and it changed the indigenous Tlingit in many ways. The Tlingit had occupied the Alaska panhandle for more than 11,000 years. They fought sporadically with and raided other tribes and sometimes other Tlingit clans and villages, but their prosperity and autonomy were never seriously challenged until the Russian-American Company arrived in 1795. The Tlingit, especially those living at Sitka, endured several years of Russian efforts to coerce their labor. Alexander Baranov, who was in charge of Russian operations at Sitka, exerted tight and uncompromising control over the Natives there. Tlingit women were forced to marry Russian fur traders and were sometimes raped.

In 1802, the Tlingit had had enough. They attacked 20 Russians and more than 100 of their Aleut allies, killing all of them. Some British traders supplied the Tlingit with gunpowder, but most of the British, French, Spanish, and American merchants who often traveled the Inside Passage for trade and exploration were unwilling to support the Tlingit or offer refuge.

This eagle badge represents the peace forged between the Tlingit and the Russians after the Battle of Sitka.

In October 1804, Baranov came back to Sitka from Kodiak with a large force. The Tlingit were ready, though, and waited for the Russians in a heavily reinforced wooden fort they had constructed. As the Russians landed, the Tlingit warriors trapped them in a pincer movement and then closed ranks and repelled them. Baranov was seriously wounded in the melee. The Russians retreated and then spent a few days bombarding the tribal fort from their ships. The Tlingit, meanwhile, secretly evacuated Sitka, moving the entire tribal population to a different area.

With the town abandoned, the Russians moved their American base from Kodiak to Sitka, where they reinforced their buildings and showed little interest in diplomacy with the Tlingit for many years. Although the Russians eventually traded with the Tlingit and brought some of the tribe into their workforce, their fur empire suffered an irreparable blow. The Tlingit suffered even worse, as the tribe was denied access to sacred sites, natural resources, and its homeland for generations. ■

The Tlingit warriors at Sitka pinned down the Russians as they advanced from the beach and then engineered a pincer movement that forced the Russians to fight on two sides. The Russians' Aleut allies fled as the Tlingit swarmed the Russian position. The Russians retreated but their heavy naval bombardment drove the Tlingit inland.

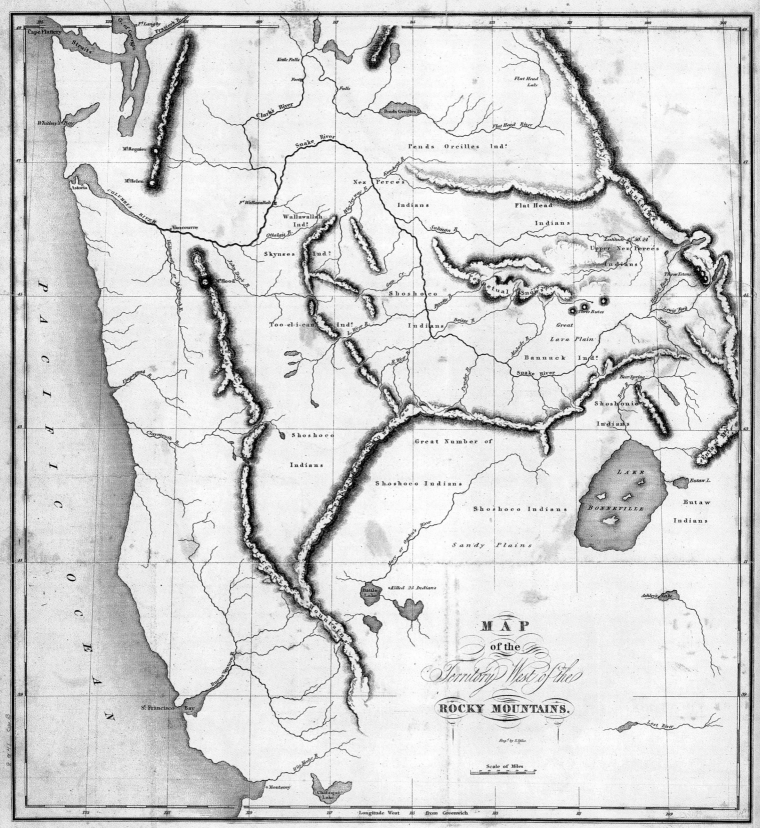

MAP
of the
Territory West of the
ROCKY MOUNTAINS.

Eng.d by S. Stiles.

Scale of Miles

BORDERS AND BOUNDARIES Most tribes in the Northwest defined their territories by such natural geographic features as the Pacific Ocean; the Coast and Cascade Ranges; major rivers, bays, and sounds; and land breaks. Europeans created new borders, often based on entirely different criteria. One was a straight line between the United States and Canada that crossed the Rocky Mountains and ran through the middle of many Native territories. Indians didn't cross the border—the border crossed them.

CREATING BORDERS
International and Tribal Boundaries

When Great Britain and the United States ended the Revolutionary War, Britain pulled troops out of the U.S., but left them in Canada. Britain did not acknowledge American independence officially until the Treaty of London in 1794, commonly called the Jay Treaty after John Jay, the principal U.S. negotiator. The Jay Treaty set the U.S.–Canadian border as it is today, which created many problems for tribes in the Northwest and elsewhere along the border.

The boundary went through the middle of tribal lands. Some tribes ended up with numerous villages on both sides of the border. Some were displaced, and others voluntarily moved to avoid dealing with the U.S. settler and military presence. The treaty provided some consideration of Native rights and land use, stating in Article III: "It is agreed, that it shall at all times be free to His Majesty's subjects, and to the citizens of the United States, and also to the Indians dwelling on either side of the said boundary line, freely to pass and repass, by land or inland navigation into the respective territories and countries of the two parties on the continent of America . . . and freely carry on trade and commerce with each other."

In spite of the language in the Jay Treaty, Indians had a difficult time passing through the border unharrassed—and they still do. Both the U.S. and Canada have strong immigration laws, tax and duty policies, security protocols, drug laws, and agricultural transport laws. Northwest Indians wanting to bring salmon to family members on the other side of the border were frequently denied entry, had their catch confiscated, or were even imprisoned. Free tribal trade was rarely permitted. Sometimes sacred items were confiscated in the name of drug enforcement. Security concerns after the 9/11 terrorist attacks have only magnified the issues at the border, which have been the subject of court cases in both countries. ∎

The Treaty of London, usually called the Jay Treaty, was signed in 1794. It averted a war between the United States and Britain and defined the U.S.–Canadian border as it is today. Article III of the treaty provided for the free trade and travel of Indians across the border. Surveying the border was an enormous undertaking. Pictured left, the British North American Boundary Commission clear and survey the boundary line. Above, Spokane Indians holding weapons sit in a doorway.

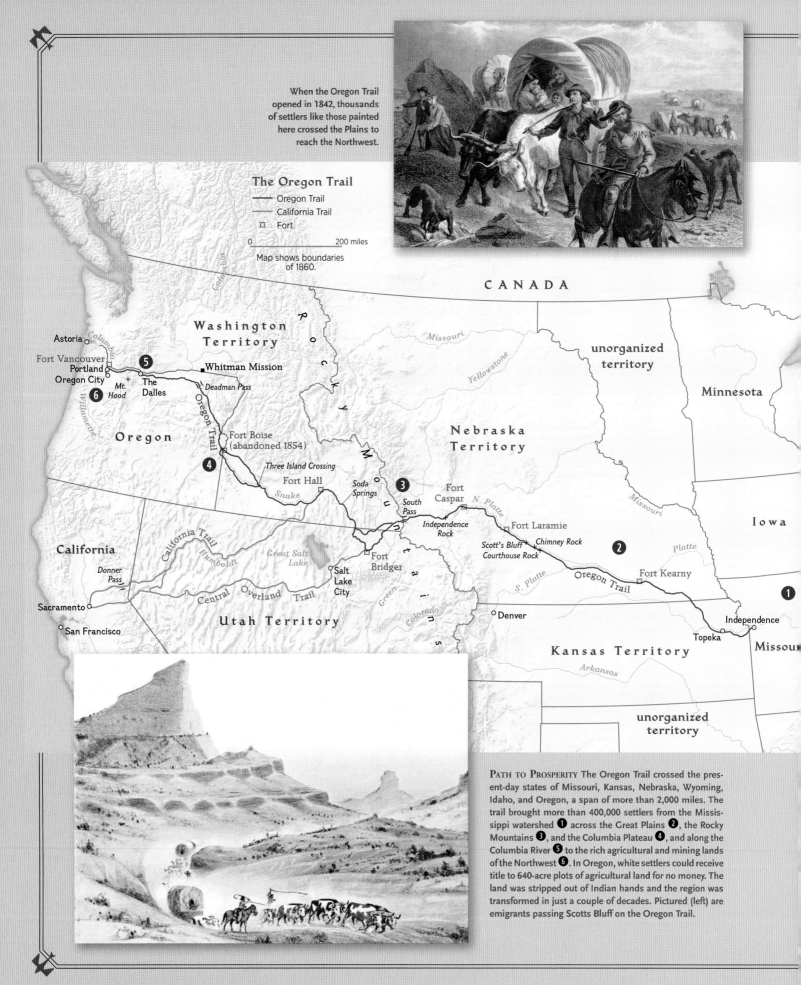

When the Oregon Trail opened in 1842, thousands of settlers like those painted here crossed the Plains to reach the Northwest.

The Oregon Trail

—— Oregon Trail
—— California Trail
⊡ Fort

0 |————————| 200 miles

Map shows boundaries of 1860.

CANADA

Columbia

Washington Territory

Astoria
Fort Vancouver
Portland
Oregon City
Mt. Hood
The Dalles
Deadman Pass
Whitman Mission

⑤

Oregon
Oregon Trail
Fort Boise (abandoned 1854)

④
Three Island Crossing
Fort Hall
Snake
Soda Springs
South Pass

③

Rocky Mountains

Missouri
Yellowstone

unorganized territory

Minnesota

Nebraska Territory

Fort Caspar
N. Platte
Independence Rock
Scott's Bluff
Courthouse Rock
Chimney Rock
Fort Laramie

②

Platte
Missouri

Iowa

Oregon Trail
Fort Kearny

California Trail
Humboldt
Great Salt Lake
Fort Bridger
Green

California

Donner Pass
Central Overland Trail
Salt Lake City

Utah Territory

Colorado

S. Platte

Denver

Kansas Territory

Arkansas

Sacramento

San Francisco

Topeka

Independence

Missouri

①

unorganized territory

PATH TO PROSPERITY The Oregon Trail crossed the present-day states of Missouri, Kansas, Nebraska, Wyoming, Idaho, and Oregon, a span of more than 2,000 miles. The trail brought more than 400,000 settlers from the Mississippi watershed ❶ across the Great Plains ❷, the Rocky Mountains ❸, and the Columbia Plateau ❹, and along the Columbia River ❺ to the rich agricultural and mining lands of the Northwest ❻. In Oregon, white settlers could receive title to 640-acre plots of agricultural land for no money. The land was stripped out of Indian hands and the region was transformed in just a couple of decades. Pictured (left) are emigrants passing Scotts Bluff on the Oregon Trail.

THE OREGON TRAIL
Northwest Tribes Overrun

The Oregon Trail is a difficult, 2,000-mile-long overland wagon road across the Plateau and Northwest. Although many offshoots and alternate trails were eventually created, the original trail stretched across the present-day states of Missouri, Kansas, Nebraska, Wyoming, Idaho, and Oregon. The idea for an overland route had evolved over many years. From 1803 to 1811, Meriwether Lewis and William Clark, John Jacob Astor, the North West Company, and the Hudson's Bay Company all explored, traded, mapped, and planned paths west. Whether for politics or commercial gain, all sought ways to gain access to the natural resources of the Northwest, and eventually they succeeded, creating a barely passable foot and horse trail across most of the distance.

In 1836, the first large group traversed the Oregon Trail. Although they had to clear huge stands of timber, separate their herd animals from the flow of human traffic, and float down the Columbia River for part of their journey, they made it. The trickle of white traffic to Indian lands in the Northwest started to flow more heavily after that.

Throughout the 1830s and 1840s, the U.S. government refused to give white settlers land grants in the Plains, believing that the area was not fit for human habitation. But in Oregon, it offered 640-acre allotments to white immigrants for free, with the simple requirement that they settle on and farm it. The Oregon Trail was wide open by 1842, and with the discovery of gold in California in 1848, it was soon flooded with prospectors, travelers, settlers, and ranchers traversing and encroaching on tribal lands across the Plains, Plateau, and Northwest, as well as California.

Between 1836 and 1869, an estimated 400,000 white settlers traversed the Oregon Trail. Indians in the Northwest became minorities in their own land. Missionaries from several denominations came en masse. Traders, miners, and farmers put down roots. Indians were obstructions in the eyes of many newcomers. There were conflicts in many areas, although the Northwest did not see widespread warfare. Even without it, the dispossession and pain of cultural shift and language loss permeated tribal peoples. ■

JOEL WALKER

Joel Walker was the first white settler to cross the Oregon Trail to the Northwest with his entire family. The trail had developed slowly over a period of years, beginning in the early 1800s with the Lewis and Clark expedition and the exploratory trip commissioned by John Jacob Astor. But the route was so arduous and dangerous that many families never dared try. However, in 1840, Walker, the brother of well-known mountain man Joseph Walker, packed up his four children, his wife Mary Walker, and her sister Martha Young, and headed west with a small wagon train.

Walker's entourage included about 60 people, including five missionaries. At Fort Hall, the trail became so narrow and rough that they had to abandon their wagons and journey the rest of the way on foot and by mule. After their arrival in Oregon, the news of their successful journey had widespread impact. Missionaries were excited by the opportunity to establish new missions among the Indians and settlers alike. The trip's success also inspired expeditions west across the trail by John Charles Frémont in 1842 and 1843. The opening of the route changed the tribes there forever.

Pictured here are emigrants heading west on the Oregon Trail in the mid-1800s. More than 400,000 white settlers traveled to the Northwest on the trail.

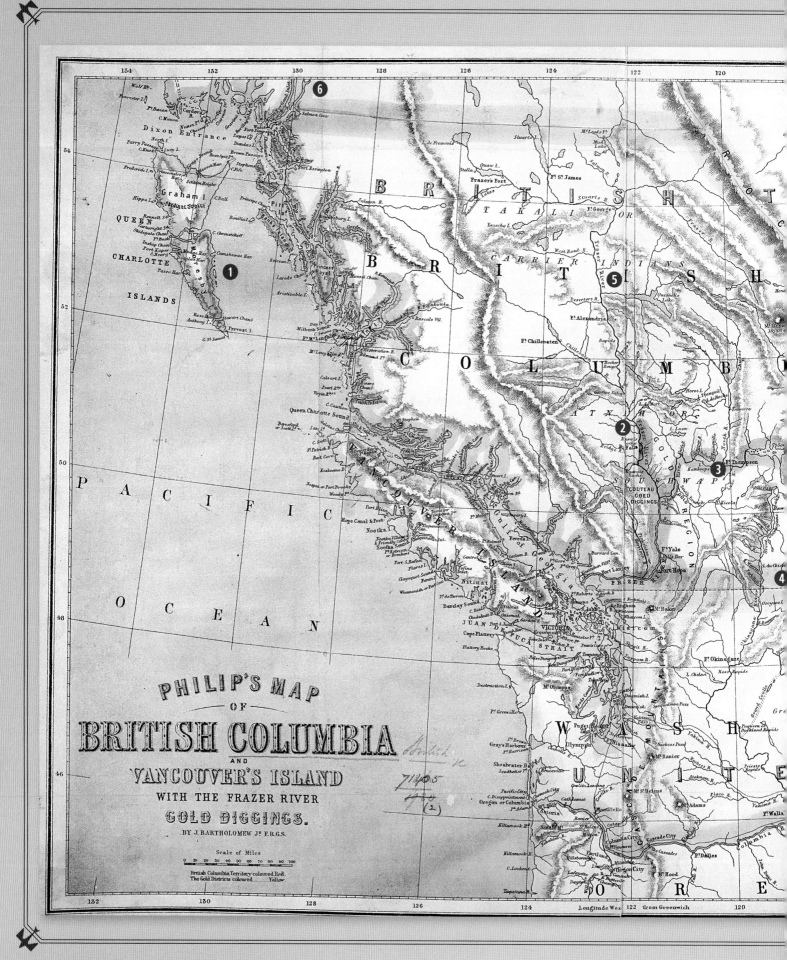

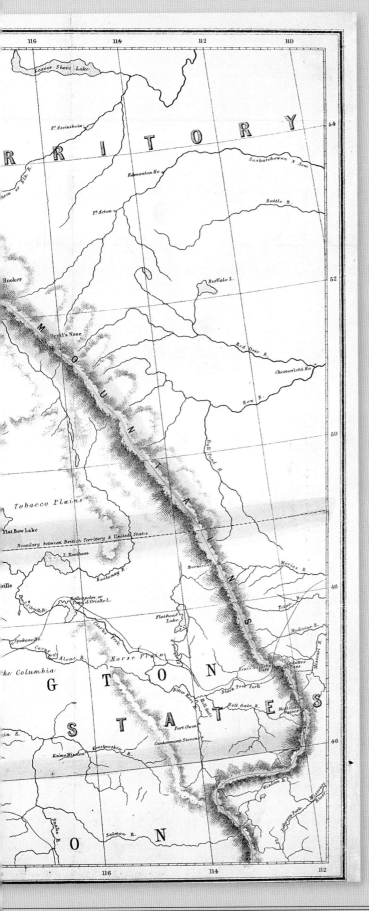

NORTHWEST GOLD RUSHES

Prospecting Overwhelmed Indian Country

The California gold rush in 1849 and the Klondike gold rush in Alaska in 1896 both brought many people through the Northwest en route to prospecting in adjacent regions. But from 1850 to 1899, there were 26 documented gold rushes in the Northwest as well—most in British Columbia, although Oregon saw some, too. The gold rushes did more than open mining and prospecting operations all over the Northwest; they also brought thousands of white settlers and prospectors, many of whom had little respect for tribal land tenure, rights, or life. It was a time of conflict and tension.

The Queen Charlottes gold rush ❶ started in 1851 when a group of Haida sold a 27-ounce gold nugget for 1,500 blankets at a trading post. The next major rush was the Fraser Canyon gold rush ❷, from 1858 to 1861. Over 30,000 people came to Victoria in 1858 alone, many from the now waning California gold fields. A very young Salish girl from the Thompson River area ❸ known as Nlaka'pamux was raped by prospectors, and tribal members then killed the prospecting party; their decapitated bodies were found floating down the river. That prompted the British government to send in the Royal Marines. British Columbia was officially declared a British colony, and Indians were besieged by prospectors who had the full support of the British military.

Two dozen other gold rushes broke out across British Columbia in the next few decades, including the Rock Creek gold rush ❹ (1859–1866), the Cariboo gold rush ❺ (1862–1865), and the Stikine gold rush, off the map near ❻ (1863). Following the prospectors came the fortune seekers who fed, clothed, and served them—ranchers, farmers, entrepreneurs, politicians, and missionaries. ■

INDIAN GOLD RUSHERS The Northwest gold rushes brought a wave of settlement to the region. But Indians were not passive players in their own history. They adapted to the gold rushes even if it seemed bizarre that white people could go crazy over shiny rocks. Pictured here are Indian miners on the Thompson River. The areas marked in gold on the adjacent map show the greatest concentrations of gold in British Columbia.

WHALING IN THE NORTHWEST
New Tests for Tribal Customs

Several tribes in the Northwest have long-standing traditions of whaling. The Makah ❶ stand out as especially skilled; gray and humpback whales were principal foods for their people. The Makah built massive cedar canoes that they paddled far from shore to intercept whales en route from mating and calving grounds off the coast of Mexico ❷ to feeding grounds in the Arctic ❸. They used simple harpoons of yew with mussel-tipped points, about 16–18 feet in length. Whaling could be extremely dangerous. A damaged boat could end in the death of every member of a whaling party. Tribal whalers had to know their prey, count each breath, gauge distance distorted by water and waves, and time the strike when the whale was 3 or 4 feet under the water to minimize damage from its tail. It was a practice that required incredible skill.

Once a whale was killed, a diver would cut around the whale's jaw so that it didn't fill up with water and sink as it was being towed to shore. The Makah believed that the spirit of the whale traveled with its body when it was brought to the village. They prepared songs

Every part of a whale was harvested. Pictured here are tribal whalers piecing up a whale in Neah Bay, Washington.

for the whale, welcoming and thanking the animal for its sacrifice to the people. The entire village came out at harvest, but certain families had predetermined rights to specific parts of the whale.

When the U.S. government came after Makah land in the 1850s, tribal leaders insisted on the right of the people to continue to harvest whales, seals, and other marine life as they had for thousands of years. The treaty of Neah Bay in 1855 included a massive land cession by the Makah but also stated, "The right of taking fish and of whaling or sealing at usual and accustomed grounds and stations is further secured to said Indians." The Makah have always fought for this right, but after the gray whale was listed as endangered—not because of tribal activity but because commercial overharvesting had decimated the whale population—the sustainability of the Makah harvest was legitimately called into question. The tribal hunt was suspended in the 1920s. The gray whale recovered and was delisted from the endangered species list in the late 20th century. In 1999, the Makah resumed traditional whale harvesting of one whale per year. ∎

RECIPROCITY AND RESPECT The Makah harvested gray and humpback whales for thousands of years before European contact. The painting to the left shows a diver cutting a whale under the jaw to ensure it did not sink while being towed. The migration routes (opposite) of the gray whale show their passage through tribal waters in the Northwest. Unlike the humpback, whose migratory route involves a northeasterly route from deeper waters toward Alaska, the gray whale closely hugs the coast in this area. The right and sperm whale range areas can also be seen.

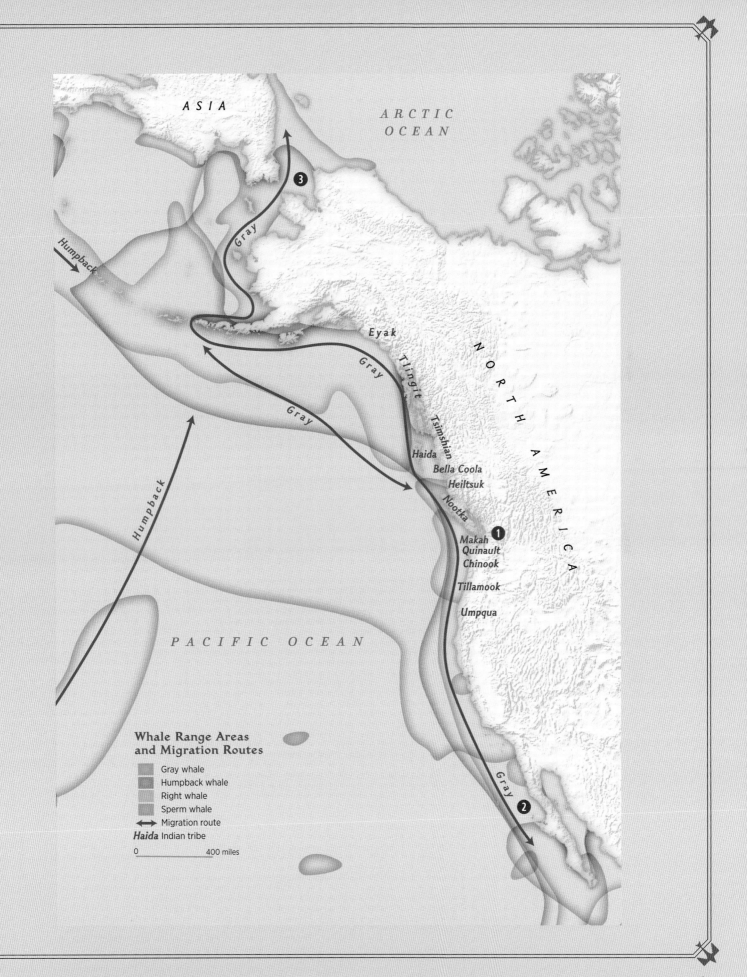

ASIA

ARCTIC
OCEAN

3

Gray

Humpback

Eyak

Gray

Tlingit

Gray

Tsimshian

Haida

Bella Coola

Heiltsuk

Nootka

NORTH AMERICA

Humpback

1

Makah
Quinault
Chinook

Tillamook

Umpqua

PACIFIC OCEAN

Gray

2

**Whale Range Areas
and Migration Routes**

Gray whale
Humpback whale
Right whale
Sperm whale
→ Migration route
Haida Indian tribe

0   400 miles

TRIBES OF THE NORTHWEST COAST

The Northwest Coast was a bountiful land of forests, fish, and richly furred animals. Customs of the diverse tribes include potlatches, making totem poles, fishing, and whaling. Following are brief histories of select tribes of the region.

▦ CHEHALIS

Current Locations: British Columbia; Washington
Language Family: Salishan

Many tribal groups in Canada and the United States speak languages from the Salishan language family. A few have been called Chehalis, although the term is misleading, because not all communities referred to as Chehalis had political, social, or even immediate language uniformity. The Halqemeylem Chehalis peoples currently reside in three distinct First Nations in Canada—Chehalis First Nation #5, Chehalis First Nation #6, and Peckquaylis First Nation. In the U.S., four major Salish groups in two subdivisions—the Upper and Lower Chehalis—were confederated together on one reservation in Washington State. The Upper Chehalis were comprised of the Satsop and the Lower Chehalis the Copalis, Humptulips, and Wynoochee. In 1860, when the tribes were confederated, their separate political structures and tribal members were combined under one political unit.

▦ CHINOOK

Current Locations: Oregon, Washington
Language Family: Chinookan

There are 16 distinct tribal groups of varying size in the Chinookan language family. When the Lewis and Clark expedition came to the Northwest, these were the tribes they encountered on the Lower Columbia River. The Chinookan peoples had a highly stratified society in which upper castes—spiritual leaders, warriors, traders—took great care to isolate themselves from lower castes. Often, their children were not even allowed to play together. To further distinguish the castes, some upper-caste Chinook slowly flattened the foreheads of their infants from 3 to 12 months of age by tying a board firmly to the child's head in a daily ritual. As a result, some of the Plateau Chinook were called Flathead. Throughout the coastal Chinookan territory, tribal members were excellent hunters of elk and small game. They also fished for salmon in the Columbia River.

Pictured here is a mask frontlet with the image of a man holding his prey (a whale) and the image of a sea monster that protected a family ancestor.

▦ COOS

Current Locations: Oregon
Language Family: Coosan

The Coos were a large tribal group of about 40–50 villages along the Oregon coastline. Lewis and Clark encountered them in 1806. They thrived on a mixed subsistence economy of hunting, fishing, gathering, and trapping. The Coos language is classified as a member of the Coosan language family, although some linguists believe it is really an offshoot of the Penutian family. Coos territory was the focus of some of the most intense white settlement during the height of westward movement across the Oregon Trail. In 1855, tribal leaders signed a treaty and relinquished most of their land in Oregon. They were eventually confederated with the Lower Umpqua and Siuslaw. The U.S. relocated the tribe to Port Umpqua in 1857 and then again, in 1876, to the Siletz Reservation. Missionary activity and white settlement engulfed the tribe and eventually its language died out, although the tribe maintains a distinct political identity and many members continue fishing and hunting traditions.

▦ COQUILLE

Current Locations: Oregon
Language Family: Athabascan

The Coquille are really 11 distinct tribes from the Athabascan language family, indigenous to the Coos River and Coos Bay in southwestern Oregon. Their language is now extinct. The Coquille got their name from the French word for "shell," because they ate lots of shellfish, mussels, and clams and used a variety of shells in art and jewelry. In 1855, as part of a major regional treaty effort, the Coquille surrendered most of their land to the U.S. government. Most of the 11 bands were confederated together on the Siletz Reservation. Today, there are two primary federally recognized Coquille groups—the Coquille Indian Tribe and the Confederated Tribes of the Siletz Reservation.

▦ COWLITZ

Current Locations: Washington
Language Family: Salishan

The Cowlitz comprise two distinct groups indigenous to western Washington along the Cowlitz and Lewis Rivers and near Fort Vancouver. The Upper Cowlitz, also known as Taidnapam, spoke the Cowlitz language, one of many in the Salishan language family. The Lower Cowlitz, also known as Kawlic, spoke Cowlitz as well, although many also spoke Sahaptin, a transplant from other tribes along the Cascades that eventually became more dominant among the Lower Cowlitz. Both the Upper and Lower Cowlitz maintained vibrant art and cultural traditions, including knowledge of gathering, hunting, and basketmaking. The tribes struggled to gain formal recognition from the U.S. government, which was eventually granted in 2000 when both groups were recognized as the Cowlitz Indian Tribe.

Animals, fish, and birds—like the kingfisher in this stylized Kwakiutl wood carving—were often represented in totem poles and ceremonial and secular arts in the Northwest.

GRAND RONDE (CONFEDERATED TRIBES)

Current Locations: Oregon
Language Family: Various

The Confederated Tribes of the Grand Ronde Community of Oregon is a federally recognized reservation and removal location. Twenty-seven different tribes speaking 27 different languages from a number of language families (Athabascan, Chinookan, Kalapuyan, Penutian, Salishan) were moved to Grand Ronde in the mid-1800s. Through six treaties in 1853 and 1854, the U.S. government acquired land from the member tribes, relocated them to Grand Ronde, and confederated them on a single reservation as a single political entity. Many forgot their native languages, but Chinook Jargon—a widely spoken trade language in the Northwest—proliferated at Grand Ronde. In time, Chinook Jargon speakers dwindled, but in the 21st century the tribe has worked to revive the language on the reservation.

HOH

Current Locations: Washington
Language Family: Salishan

The Hoh are an offshoot of the Quinault, and their heritage language is Quinault, one of many in the Salishan language family. Indigenous to the Olympic Peninsula in western Washington, the Hoh were salmon people who also gathered and hunted along the coast and inland. They were small in number and frequently intermarried with the neighboring Quileute tribe. For many decades, most of the tribal population was bilingual in Quinault and Quileute, but the Quileute speakers eventually dominated and Quinault died out among the Hoh. The Hoh signed the Quinault Treaty of 1855, which established a reservation for them and ceded most of their land. The tribal population continued to decline to its current level of fewer than 100 people.

LOWER UMPQUA

Current Locations: Oregon
Language Family: Isolate

The Umpqua are a group of several different tribes, some related to one another in language and all related in culture. There were at least three primary heritage languages for the Umpqua, although Takelma, a language isolate, was the primary language at the time of European contact. The Umpqua signed the first treaty between an Indian tribe and the U.S. government in Oregon in 1853. In 1855, government efforts to relocate many tribes in the Northwest led to the outbreak of the Rogue River Indian War, which drove most Umpqua from their traditional villages and into the hills nearby. Some eventually returned to the Cow Creek village site and were later recognized as the Cow Creek Band of Umpqua, a federally recognized reservation. The Lower Umpqua were relocated in two groups: One settled at Grand Ronde with 26 other tribes; the other was settled separately with a couple of other tribes as the Confederated Tribes of Coos, Lower Umpqua, and Siuslaw.

LUMMI

Current Locations: Washington
Language Family: Salishan

The Lummi are a Coast Salish tribe from the Puget Sound area in western Washington. They thrived on salmon fishing, picking berries, and harvesting camas bulbs. Influenced by Catholic missionaries, most

For tribes in the Northwest, wealth was a path to power, but never if it was simply hoarded. The purpose of wealth was to give it away in ritualized ceremonies, especially the potlatch ceremony, pictured here.

converted to Catholicism in the 1800s, and traditional activities like the potlatch eventually died out. In 1855, the Point Elliott Treaty forced the Lummi to cede most of their territory and concentrate on the new reservation. The tribe survived and adapted, and in 2007, the community revived the potlatch for the first time since the 1930s.

■ MAKAH

Current Locations: Washington
Language Family: Wakashan

The Makah are a Wakashan-speaking tribe from Neah Bay, Washington, on the Olympic Peninsula. Their language has sometimes been called Quileute because of the linguistic parallels between Quileute and Makah, in spite of political and cultural differences between the Quileute and Makah tribes. The tribal language is sometimes classified as being from the Chimakuan language family, likely an offshoot of the larger Wakashan language family. The language has since become extinct, but cultural traditions, including whaling, continue.

The Makah have lived at Neah Bay for at least 3,800 years. They built large cedar-plank houses and massive cedar canoes and thrived on a diet heavy in salmon, halibut, whale, seal, and shellfish. The Makah were especially skilled at whaling and harvested gray and humpback whales. The Treaty of Neah Bay in 1855 greatly reduced the tribal land base, but enabled the Makah to keep some of their homeland without being forced to relocate. In recent years, the tribe has revitalized its traditional whaling practice, but with a limited ceremonial harvest of only one whale per year.

This Tsimshian headdress shows a sea lion with a human figure on top, a common depiction of the link between the human and animal worlds.

■ MUCKLESHOOT

Current Locations: British Columbia; Washington
Language Family: Salishan

The Muckleshoot are an amalgamation of several Coast Salish peoples of the Puget Sound and Cascades, including the Duwamish, Skopamish, Smulkamish, Snoqualmie, Stkamish, Tkwakwamish, and Yilalkoamish tribes. They hunted, fished, and gathered. Their society was highly stratified, with the nobility, a middle class, and slaves (usually captives from raids of other tribes). During the Puget Sound Indian War of 1855–56, the Muckleshoot allied with other tribes in the Puget Sound area. They lost their land, but have kept some of their traditions alive, especially salmon fishing. The Muckleshoot ended up at the center of the Northwest fishing rights controversies in the 1960s and 1970s, in which the tribe successfully asserted its treaty-stipulated rights to fish for salmon in public waters.

■ NISQUALLY

Current Locations: Washington
Language Family: Salishan

The Nisqually are closely related to the Muckleshoot and Puyallup, in that they speak a dialectical variation of Lushootseed, a language in the Salishan language family. The Nisqually are indigenous to the Nisqually River delta. According to their oral history, the people came to the Puget Sound area thousands of years ago after a long migration from the Great Basin. The Nisqually signed the Medicine Creek Treaty in 1854, which sold much of the tribal land and required the tribe to relocate key villages. In the Puget Sound Indian War of 1855–56, Chief Leschi helped lead the Nisqually and several other tribes who lived in the Puget Sound area, but the tribal force was defeated.

■ NOOKSACK

Current Locations: Washington
Language Family: Salishan

The Nooksack are a Coast Salish people whose reservation is located in Deming, Washington. Salmon fishers, the Nooksack are also knowledgeable hunters and gatherers. Treaty-based land cessions and unapproved land squatting by white settlers eroded the tribe's land holdings. In 1971, the tribe received a one-acre land grant from the federal government as part of a formal recognition and reconciliation process. Since then, the tribe has worked hard to rebuild its land base to the current size of about 2,500 acres.

In a ritual rarely seen by outsiders, Kwakiutl dancers kick up smoke during a lunar eclipse to force the monster that ate the moon to sneeze and spit it back out.

PUYALLUP

Current Locations: Washington
Language Family: Salishan

The Puyallup are a Coast Salish tribe indigenous to western Washington, closely related to the Nisqually and Muckleshoot. Salmon and other fish, shellfish, wild game, berries, and camas all featured in their traditional diet. After the Medicine Creek Treaty of 1854, tribal members settled in the Edgewood, Federal Way, Fife, Milton, Puyallup, Tacoma, and Waller communities. When Nisqually chief Leschi helped lead a tribal force in the Puget Sound Indian War of 1855–56, the Puyallup rallied behind his leadership, but the conflict was a major defeat for the allied tribes. Today, the Puyallup operate the Chief Leschi School and a casino.

QUILEUTE

Current Locations: Washington
Language Family: Chimakuan

Indigenous to western Washington, the Quileute were salmon people who fished, gathered, and hunted along the coast and inland. Their language is one of two in the Chimakuan language family and is distinguished by its extremely rare absence of nasal consonant sounds. Their neighbors the Hoh frequently intermarried with the Quileute tribe. The Quileute signed the Quinault Treaty of 1855, which ceded most of their land and brought a number of missionaries to their community, including A. W. Smith in 1882. The impact on tribal customs, names, and language was profound. It was not until 1889 that President Grover Cleveland established a reservation for them at La Push. In recent years, the Quileute tribal population has been stable at around 2,000. Quileute folklore about wolves helped influence and inspire Stephenie Meyer's *Twilight* series.

QUINAULT

Current Locations: Washington
Language Family: Salishan

The Quinault are indigenous to western Washington, and the Quinault language is one of many in the Salishan language family. The Quinault are salmon people who fished, gathered, and hunted along the coast and inland. The Hoh split off from the main body of Quinault hundreds of years ago. The tribe signed the Quinault Treaty of 1855, which established a reservation for them but ceded most of their land, reducing access to fish and other resources in many places. Much of the tribal population lives in Taholah.

In this painting, a Tlingit chief displays a killer whale staff, an official badge of his office and a symbol of his power and position.

SAMISH

Current Locations: Washington
Language Family: Salishan

The Samish are a small tribe whose language, Straits Salish, was from the Coast Salishan language family, but was different from that of their Lushootseed Salish cousins. They relied on salmon and other marine fish and wildlife, hunted inland, and gathered. The Samish, more than most Northwest coastal tribes, moved season by season within a defined territory to best access food sources. In 1847, there may have been as many as 2,000 Samish people. However, over the next ten years, smallpox and measles epidemics claimed numerous lives, and Samish were also killed or taken captive in raids by the Haida and Tsimshian.

At the time of the Point Elliott Treaty, in 1855, there were only 150 documented Samish left. The Samish fractured after the treaty; most were relocated to Lummi or Swinomish communities, while some squatted on traditional lands. In the 20th century, Samish people from Lummi and Swinomish and from unrecognized tribal lands pursued land claims and formal recognition by the U.S. government, which was granted in 1996.

SAUK-SUIATTLE

Current Locations: Washington
Language Family: Salishan

The Sauk-Suiattle tribe's heritage language is Lushootseed, from the Salishan language family. They are closely related to the Skagit. The tribe relied primarily on fishing, augmented with hunting and gathering like most tribes in the Northwest. Prior to the Point Elliott Treaty in 1855, the tribe had not only been self-reliant but also fairly numerous, with an estimated population of around 4,000. The treaty and early settlement period was hard on the Sauk-Suiattle. In 1884, white settlers burned down all of the community's massive cedar-plank longhouses, leaving most tribal members homeless. Disease took a terrible toll, as did out-migration. By 1924, only 18 tribal members were left. Today, that number has rebounded to 200, and the tribe was formally recognized by the U.S. government in 1973. The Sauk-Suiattle work closely with the neighboring Swinomish on natural resource and fishery management.

SILETZ

Current Locations: Oregon
Language Family: Salishan

The Siletz are from the central Oregon coast along the Siletz River. Their heritage language was Tillamook, a language from the Salishan language family. Tillamook is now long extinct. The U.S. government established the Confederated Tribes of Siletz by executive order in 1855. The reservation of the same name was home to the Siletz and 26 other tribes. Today, the Siletz are not counted as a distinct tribal identity

The environment is remarkably varied in the Northwest—snowcapped mountains, fertile valleys, an ocean teeming with tribe-sustaining life. Pictured here are Chinook Indians near Mount Hood.

since all of the arrivals on the reservation merged over time politically, linguistically, and socially.

SIUSLAW

Current Locations: Oregon
Language Family: Penutian

The Siuslaw are a small tribe with a now-extinct language that was likely from the Oregon Coast Penutian language family. They fished for salmon, steelhead, halibut, and shellfish and also hunted and gathered. In 1855, government efforts to relocate many tribes in the Northwest led to the outbreak of the Rogue River Indian War. During those conflicts, the Siuslaw tried to defend their land and way of life. The tribe lost the conflict and was eventually combined with the Coos and some of the Umpqua as the Confederated Tribes of Coos, Lower Umpqua, and Siuslaw.

S'KLALLAM

Current Locations: British Columbia; Washington
Language Family: Salishan

The S'Klallam or Klallam (with numerous other spellings) are a Coast Salishan-speaking tribe from western Washington and Vancouver Island, British Columbia. The tribe was large, with anywhere from 10 to 30 permanent villages and at least one village shared with the Makah. The tribe expanded its domain and political influence with other tribes not by conflict but through arranged marriages and careful diplomacy. They relied primarily on fishing and a mixed hunting, fishing, and gathering economic structure; some S'Klallam harvested whales, as well. Today, the S'Klallam population is divided between four primary tribal communities, each with its own distinct political structure. They are the Lower Elwha Tribal Community (Washington), Jamestown S'Klallam Tribe (Washington), Port Gamble Indian Community (Washington), and Scia'new First Nation, sometimes called the Becher Bay Indian Band (Vancouver Island).

SKOKOMISH

Current Locations: Washington
Language Family: Salishan

The Skokomish are one of the largest tribes among the Twana, a group of nine primary tribes: the Dabop, Dosewallips, Duckabush, Duhlelap, Hoodsport, Quilcene, Skokomish, Tahuya, and Vance Creek. They are all from the Salishan language family. The Twana further divide into 33 different settlements, mainly on the Kitsap Peninsula in the Puget Sound Basin. The Skokomish are salmon people, but live in an area rich in medicines, root vegetables, and small and large game. With the mentorship of tribal elders, such as Bruce Miller (1944–2005), today's Skokomish have retained their distinct artistic traditions, food and medicinal knowledge, and customs.

SNOQUALMIE

Current Locations: Washington
Language Family: Salishan

The Snoqualmie are from the Coast Salishan language family, indigenous to western Washington. They fished, hunted, and gathered over an extensive region and had a pre-contact population of around 4,000. After the signing of the Point Elliott Treaty in 1855, some of the Snoqualmie were moved to the Tulalip Reservation. Most stayed in their ancestral homeland, but on a reservation with small acreage in the Snoqualmie Valley and Lake Sammamish area. In 1953, the Snoqualmie reservation was terminated by the federal government, a move that eliminated federal recognition and Bureau of Indian Affairs funding. The Snoqualmie were eventually reinstated in 1999.

SQUAXIN ISLAND

Current Locations: Washington
Language Family: Salishan

The Squaxin Island Tribe in western Washington comprises several bands of Lushootseed-speaking peoples from the Coast Salishan language family: the Noo-Seh-Chatl, Sa-Heh-Wa-Mish, S'Hotle-Ma-Mish, Squawksin, Squi-Aitl, Steh-Chass, and T'Peeksin. They were consolidated there after signing a treaty in 1855.

STILLAGUAMISH (STOLUCKWAMISH)

Current Locations: Washington
Language Family: Salishan

The Stillaguamish number fewer than 300 tribal members today and were not federally recognized until 1979. Since then, they have built a tribal fisheries program to develop jobs for tribal members.

■ SUQUAMISH

Current Locations: Washington
Language Family: Salishan

The heritage language of the Suquamish is Lushootseed, one of many in the Coast Salishan language family. The Suquamish signed the Point Elliott Treaty in 1855, which established their reservation. Chief Seattle, for whom the city of Seattle is named, was from the Suquamish tribe.

■ SWINOMISH

Current Locations: Washington
Language Family: Salishan

The Swinomish heritage language is Lushootseed, in the Coast Salishan language family. After signing the Point Elliott Treaty in 1855, most of the Swinomish were moved to the Swinomish Indian Reservation along with some Samish. In recent years, the Swinomish have collaborated with the Sauk-Suiattle on natural resource management.

■ TLINGIT

Current Locations: Alaska; British Columbia
Language Family: Athabascan (Na-Dené)

The Tlingit are a large tribe that lived in numerous villages all along the northern third of British Columbia's coastline and part of Alaska. They are from the Athabascan (Na-Dené) language family, but their culture is classic Northwest Coast. Their tribe is divided into moieties (cultural halves)—Raven and Eagle, and further structured into numerous clans, usually represented on elaborate totem poles in front of each house. The Tlingit mastered cedar-plank house construction and maximized harvests of salmon, herring, seal, and wild berries. They had to contend with a concerted military and colonial effort from the Russians. From 1886 to 1895, a series of devastating smallpox epidemics greatly reduced the tribal population and stressed the social fabric of their communities. The Russian and later British Presbyterian missionaries gained many converts during that time, although

This Nisga'a mask shows the deep spiritual perspective that permeates the arts in the Northwest.

some Tlingit retained traditional religious beliefs.

■ TULALIP

Current Locations: Washington
Language Family: Salishan

The Tulalip come from the Coast Salishan language family, and their heritage language is Lushootseed. They signed the Point Elliott Treaty in 1855, which ceded most of their land and consolidated them on their current reservation in Washington along with some of the Snoqualmie people. The Lower Skagit were relocated to Tulalip in 1873 by executive order.

■ UMPQUA

Current Locations: Oregon
Language Family: Isolate

The Umpqua are a group of several different tribes, some related to one another in language and all related in culture. There were at least three primary heritage languages for the Umpqua, although Takelma, a language isolate, was the primary language at the time of European contact. The Umpqua signed the first treaty between an Indian tribe and the U.S. government in Oregon in 1853. In 1855, government efforts to relocate many tribes in the Northwest led to the outbreak of the Rogue River Indian War. During those conflicts, most Umpqua retreated from their traditional villages and hid in the nearby hills. Many were eventually relocated to the Grand Ronde Reservation, but some continued to hide and eventually returned to the Cow Creek village site. They were later recognized as the Cow Creek Band of Umpqua, a federally recognized reservation. The other Umpqua were settled at Grand Ronde and among the Confederated Tribes of Coos, Lower Umpqua, and Siuslaw.

■ UPPER SKAGIT

Current Locations: Washington
Language Family: Salishan

The Skagit are members of the Coast Salishan language family; their heritage language is Lushootseed. The Skagit signed the Point Elliott Treaty in 1855, which established two separate reservations for the Upper and Lower Skagit. In 1873, the Lower Skagit were relocated to the Tulalip Reservation by executive order. Much of the tribal population is Catholic due to the influence of Roman Catholic missionaries.

In the Northwest, a family's lineage could determine its prestige and power within the tribe. Pictured here is a Lummi family, whose clothes display symbols specific to their kinship group.

CALIFORNIA

·CHAPTER EIGHT·

CAHTO (KATO)

CAHUILLA

CHEMEHUEVI

CHUMASH

CUPEÑO

HUPA (HOOPA)

KARUK (KAROK)

KUMEYAAY
(DIEGUEÑO, KAMIA,
TIPAI-IPAI)

LUISEÑO

MAIDU

MATTOLE
(BEAR RIVER
INDIANS)

MIWOK (ME-WUK)

MONO
(CALIFORNIA
PAIUTE)

PIT RIVER

POMO

ROUND VALLEY
(COVELO INDIAN
COMMUNITY)

SERRANO

SHASTA (CHASTA)

TOLOWA

WAILAKI

WASHOE

WINTUN
(NOMLAKI,
PATWIN)

WIYOT

YOKUT
(INCLUDING
CHUKCHANSI)

YUROK

Although tribes in California were often smaller than their neighbors in the Northwest and the Great Basin, there was a large number of them. As a result, California's population density was at least as high as other regions in North America. That demography required careful diplomacy. Albert Bierstadt painted this picture of an intertribal council in 1872.

INDIAN NATIONS OF CALIFORNIA

California is a place of astounding ecological and human diversity. The Sierra Nevada are harsh, rugged mountains, difficult to traverse. The northern coast has lush redwood forests and rivers full of salmon. In the south, the climate is hot, dry, and sparsely vegetated in many places—including blistering deserts like the Mojave. The Indians who settled in California are as diverse as the region in which they live. Some tribes numbered over 20,000 people prior to contact, but most were in the hundreds. California was densely populated, but in most places the tribal units were relatively small—compared to the large tribes of the Plains, for example. The abundant natural resources of the region sustained dense populations without debilitating wars over territory or food sources.

The Native peoples of California had to adapt to profound and continual change with the arrival of Spanish and, later, American settlers. From intertribal peace and occasional war to the colonial regimes of the Spanish mission system along the coast and the Russian fur empire in northern California, to the horrors of genocidal warfare during the gold rush years—the tribes of California survived it all, adapted, and forged new paths to prosperity. Even today, California has the largest Indian population of any state in the U.S. and more federally recognized tribes than any state in the U.S.—more than 100 distinct, recognized tribal entities. The story of the tribes of California is one of survival and perseverance.

California's abundant food resources and hospitable climate allowed numerous and diverse tribal languages and cultures to flourish. Pictured are an elaborate Chumash cave painting (above) and a Hupa man at the Sugar Bowl near Donner Pass in the Sierra Nevada Mountains (opposite).

THE ANCIENT ONES

Indians have been in California for a very long time. Archaeologists argue about specific dates and sites, but data from some excavations in California suggest that Indians occupied the region as early as 17,000 years ago. To put this in a global context, Indians were possibly in California 5,000 years before there were any human beings living in Great Britain, and 12,000 years before the famous ancient civilizations of Egypt, Israel, Phoenicia, and China. Unlike the Anasazi, Aztec, and Maya, the ancient Californians did not build massive structures of stone, nor did they change the landscape with fire or cultivation like tribes in the Northeast. But they did build and evolve complex cultures and artistic traditions, deep knowledge of the land, and highly specialized and unique ways of knowing.

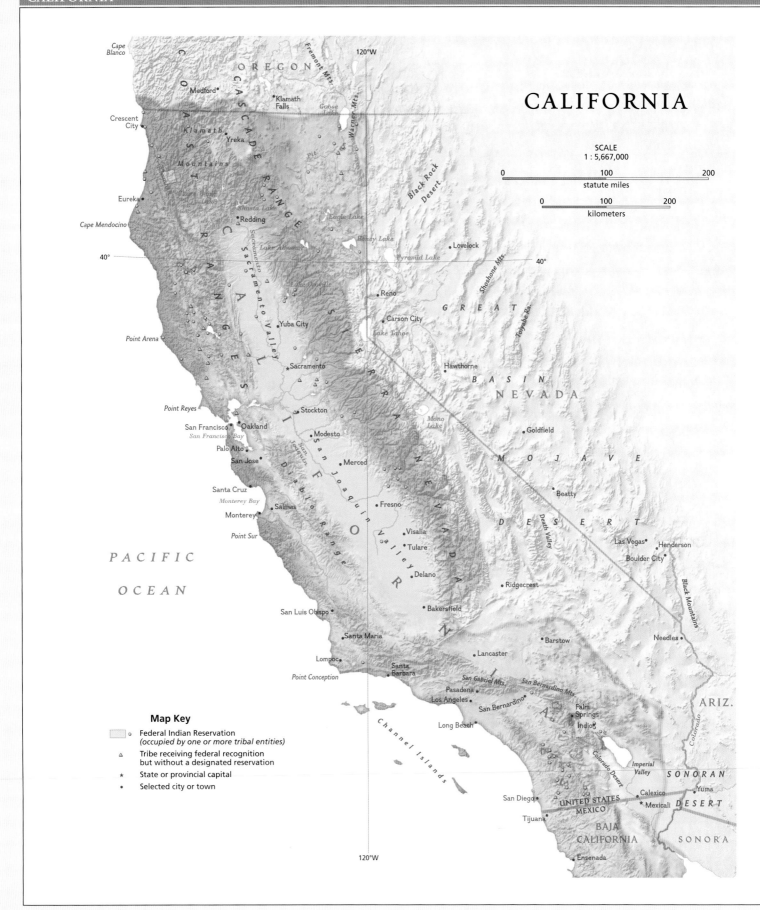

CALIFORNIA

SCALE
1 : 5,667,000

0   100   200
statute miles

0   100   200
kilometers

Map Key

Federal Indian Reservation
(occupied by one or more tribal entities)

△ Tribe receiving federal recognition
but without a designated reservation

★ State or provincial capital

• Selected city or town

PACIFIC

OCEAN

Cape Blanco
OREGON
Medford
Klamath Falls
Goose Lake
120°W
Crescent City
Klamath
Yreka
Mountains
CASCADE RANGE
Pit
Fremont Mts.
Warner Mts.
Black Rock Desert
Eureka
Shasta Lake
Redding
Eagle Lake
Cape Mendocino
Lake Almanor
Honey Lake
Lovelock
40°
Sacramento
Sacramento Valley
Lake Oroville
Pyramid Lake
Shoshone Mts.
40°
Point Arena
Yuba City
Reno
GREAT
Carson City
Lake Tahoe
Toiyabe Ra.
Sacramento
Hawthorne
BASIN
NEVADA
Point Reyes
Stockton
Mono Lake
San Francisco
Oakland
Goldfield
San Francisco Bay
Modesto
Palo Alto
San Joaquin
MOJAVE
San Jose
Merced
Santa Cruz
Monterey Bay
Salinas
Beatty
Fresno
Monterey
Diablo Range
San Joaquin Valley
DESERT
Point Sur
Visalia
Death Valley
Tulare
Las Vegas
Henderson
Delano
Boulder City
Ridgecrest
San Luis Obispo
Bakersfield
Black Mountains
Santa Maria
Barstow
Needles
Lompoc
Lancaster
Santa Barbara
Point Conception
San Gabriel Mts.
San Bernardino Mts.
ARIZ.
Pasadena
Los Angeles
San Bernardino
Palm Springs
Channel Islands
Long Beach
Indio
Colorado
Imperial Valley
SONORAN
Calexico
San Diego
UNITED STATES
Yuma
MEXICO
Mexicali
DESERT
Tijuana
Colorado Desert
BAJA
CALIFORNIA
SONORA
Ensenada

By the time Europeans first arrived in California, there were seven major language families represented, speaking 300 distinct dialects of more than 100 different languages. It was a place of amazing linguistic diversity, with language isolates as well as some small, specialized language families, such as the Yukian and Chumashan. California had also attracted Native immigrants, including four tribes from the Athabascan language family, who had migrated south from the Pacific Northwest. There were even two tribes from the Algonquian language family, which originated on the Atlantic Coast. The Hokan-, Penutian-, and Uto-Aztecan-speaking peoples of California, however, were truly ancient and indigenous.

The diverse peoples of California traded materials, food, and ideas and had done so for centuries prior to the arrival of the Europeans. The Wintun appear to have introduced the bow and arrow to other tribes in California. The southern tribes developed specialized skills in gathering and basketmaking. The northern tribes had salmon in abundance. California was a place rich in innovation and human exchange.

Spanish and Russian Aspirations

When Europeans came to California, they were astounded by the numbers and diversity of the Native people, the variety of the landscape, and the potential for new colonial experiments. Few of California's small tribes had any significant military experience, allies, or support when faced with conquest. The peacetime advantages of the California tribes turned out to be disadvantages when the Spanish and Russians descended on California.

The Spanish had enormous experience in running colonial regimes and an international empire. They had developed and refined their knowledge of how to conquer and control tribal communities through more than 200 years of conquest in Mexico

---

CHRONOLOGY

17,000 B.C.
Evidence of early Indian habitation in California

A.D. 1769–1834
Spanish mission system colonizes coastal California tribes

1812–1841
Russians use Fort Ross as base to colonize northern Pomo

1821
Mexico wins independence from Spain and claims colonial rights to California

1842
John C. Frémont and Kit Carson reach California via Oregon Trail

1848
Treaty of Guadalupe Hidalgo: U.S. claims colonial rights to California

1848–1855
California gold rush overwhelms tribes with flood of settlement

1891
Act for the Relief of Mission Indians confirms sovereignty of mission Indians

1934
Indian Reorganization Act bolsters tribal sovereignty nationwide

1987
California v. Cabazon Band of Mission Indians opens door for tribal gaming nationwide

---

The Spanish mission system reorganized many tribes around missions, coerced labor programs, and planned settlements. Even today, the human landscape in California shows the impact of this history, as seen in the locations and organization of California's tribal communities on this map.

---

and South America. A key component was the Catholic Church.

In California, King Charles III recalled the Jesuit missionaries in 1767 and sent in the Franciscans two years later. It would be a new chapter in an old game for the Spanish, who had perfected tactics for coerced labor and subjugation. They established 21 formal missions in California, most near the coast, where they could be easily fortified, supplied, and linked by a system of inland roads and naval communications. Father Junípero Serra, who founded the early Spanish missions in California, was not just in charge of the missions—he was also in charge of the Spanish military in California. The Spanish came not just to convert Indians to Christianity but also to convert the Natives into a labor force for the Spanish Empire.

Inevitably, the Spanish brought diseases to which the tribes of California had no natural immunity, and throughout the mission system era, the tribal population was ravaged by one epidemic after another. Mortality rates were very high, ranging from 50 to 95 percent. The Spanish mission system also systematically demolished tribal governance structures, cultural forms, and economies.

When Mexico gained independence in 1821, the Mexican government continued the system until 1834, when the missions were secularized. But secularization of the missions did not end the brutality experienced by mission Indians. Most were forced to live and work in a state of serfdom—disempowered and landless in their own land.

The Russians maintained Fort Ross in northern California from 1812 to 1841, and their subjugation of the northern Pomo was especially harsh. The Russians were interested in building a fur empire and did not pursue colonization farther south than San Francisco because they did not find abundant sea otters or other prized furbearing animals there.

The lands and governments of California Indians, as recognized today. Although tribes in California occasionally warred, the region was far more peaceful than the Northeast or Plains. The absence of conflict allowed many tribes to remain small and sedentary and to develop cultures distinct from their immediate neighbors.

While the coastal tribes reeled from decades of Spanish and Russian colonization, many of the inland tribes in California still had yet to see a white man. That would change in the 1840s. The opening of the Oregon Trail in 1842 and then the discovery of gold in California brought a calamity upon the California tribes beyond anyone's imagining.

THE AMERICAN PERIOD

Many Americans believed in manifest destiny—that it was God's plan for the United States to expand from Atlantic to Pacific. Any Indians who lived in the lands to be settled were simply obstacles to be dealt with during the white expansion across the continent. The Lewis and Clark expedition created an awareness of the potential of the West Coast. Jedediah Smith made two trips to California between 1826 and 1828, coming back loaded with furs and trade goods via the South Pass. John C. Frémont and Kit Carson made the trip to California from Missouri in 1842. Soon the Oregon Trail created a viable route to California for white Americans.

When it won its independence in 1821, Mexico had acquired California from the Spanish, and it still claimed control of California until the Mexican–American War of 1846–48 wrested it from their hands. The Treaty of Guadalupe Hidalgo in 1848 transferred jurisdiction to the United States, but the tribal population was still far from liberated. Tribal people still occupied all of California in 1848 and outnumbered whites ten to one. But

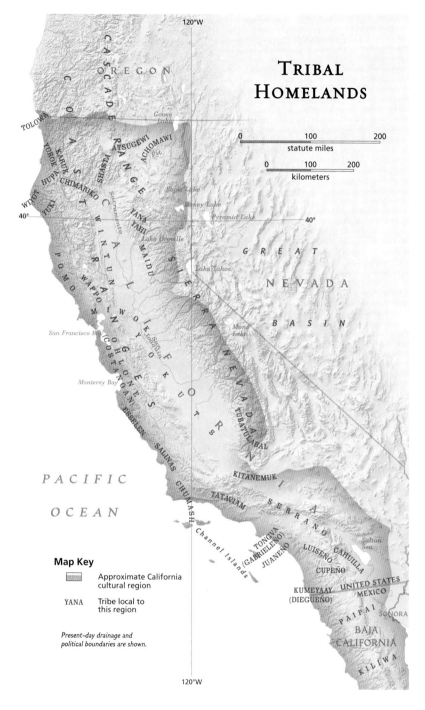

An elaborate woven basket made from natural fibers and dyes, exemplifying the Modoc weaving style. It is part of an exhibit at Lava Beds National Monument.

TRIBAL HOMELANDS

the discovery of gold in California changed that almost overnight. Within two years, Indians were a minority population and the victims of horrific genocide.

America's treatment of the Indian is a story full of betrayals, misunderstandings, tragedies, and violence. But California saw some of the most pernicious, pervasive, and inexcusable acts of genocide in American history. Beginning in the 1840s, tens of thousands of

Map Key

Approximate California cultural region

YANA   Tribe local to this region

Present-day drainage and political boundaries are shown.

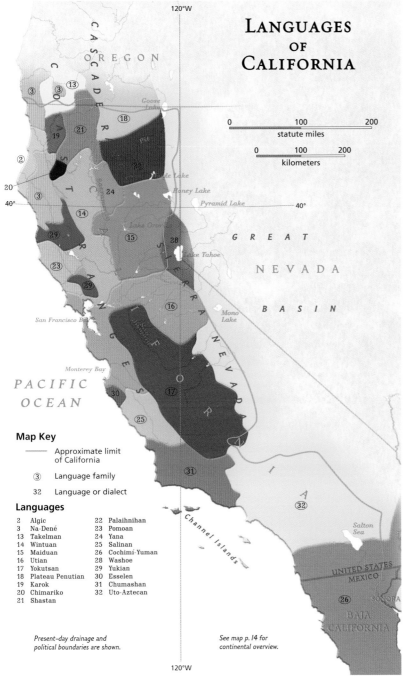

LANGUAGES
OF
CALIFORNIA

Map Key

— Approximate limit of California

③ Language family

32 Language or dialect

Languages

2 Algic	22 Palaihnihan
3 Na-Dené	23 Pomoan
13 Takelman	24 Yana
14 Wintuan	25 Salinan
15 Maiduan	26 Cochimí-Yuman
16 Utian	28 Washoe
17 Yokutsan	29 Yukian
18 Plateau Penutian	30 Esselen
19 Karok	31 Chumashan
20 Chimariko	32 Uto-Aztecan
21 Shastan	

Present-day drainage and political boundaries are shown.

See map p. 14 for continental overview.

The indigenous peoples of California spoke over 300 distinct dialects of more than 100 different languages before European contact. Most of those languages are from the Hokan, Penutian, and Uto-Aztecan language families; the oldest language families in California—Chumashan and Yukian—no longer have any viable spoken languages left.

California, driving tribal members into caves and massacring men, women, elders, and children. The Yahi were completely exterminated. Ishi, the last Yahi, died in 1911, sole survivor of the genocidal period who came out of the woods to share his story in the twilight of his life. The Yahi had not organized a major military resistance, attack, or massacre of white settlers. They just occupied land that white settlers wanted in the heart of the gold rush region. The Wiyot at Humboldt Bay were massacred by the hundreds in 1860 by white civilian militia, who timed their attacks when the men left the villages to hunt so they could more readily kill the children, elders, and women. Many other tribes suffered terribly throughout the 19th century.

The U.S. government supported the actions of its white citizens. Reservations were created by treaties, acts of Congress, and executive orders. Ostensibly, the reservations were to protect Indians from further genocide, but more importantly they served to protect the land interests of the white settlers and miners who came to California. Many Indians worked in a state of serfdom on rancherias—mission sites converted to private land with white ownership—and various enterprises around the state. The tribal population, already devastated by European disease pandemics, was reduced again by more than half.

Subsequent U.S. interactions with California Indians were a complicated series of steps both forward and backward. The Act for the Relief of Mission Indians, passed in 1891, was an attempt to provide a measure of support for the tribes who had been subjugated by the Spanish mission system, relegated to servitude, and made landless. It provided a path to formal recognition by the U.S. government and the appropriation of funds to establish reservation homelands. But at the same time as this effort to address the plight of the mission Indians, the government decided to allot

gold seekers descended on California. Some tribes had never seen white men, and most inland tribes had had no sustained contact with whites. But suddenly, many tribes were displaced from their lands, with prospectors, settlers, and the U.S. Army forcibly evicting them from their homes, herding them onto small rancherias, and killing anyone who resisted and many who did not.

Local militia attacked the Yana and the Yahi in northern

Hunters from the Tscholovoni Band near San Francisco in 1848. The San Francisco Bay area supported abundant wildlife and fisheries. The California gold rush, however, completely overwhelmed the Native population and the regional environment. Neither would be the same afterward.

many of the other California reservations. Through allotment, the federal government took reservation land that was held in trust for the benefit of all tribal members and chopped it up into individual parcels, giving some to tribal members, and opening the rest to further white settlement. Most of the land, including that allotted to Indians, left tribal hands in a short period of time. Indians even became minorities on their own reservations in some places.

Some tribes were disavowed altogether by the U.S. government through the 1950s policy of termination. Without a land base or federal recognition, the tribal population descended into poverty and often dispersed. Some terminated tribes were never reinstated; others were reinstated only after prolonged political battles.

In the 1950s, the U.S. government also developed a policy called relocation, which provided tribal members in California with one-way transportation to Oakland or other urban areas

Northern and central California contain nearly every form of natural topography, including snowcapped mountains, arid deserts, and lush microclimates. Not surprisingly, the people were equally diverse in language and culture. Their descendants have maintained distinct cultural and political groups (see areas on map marked in purple, opposite).

and a first month's rent payment in an effort to get Indians off of reservations. The belief was that reservations were bad places, pulling Indians down, and that disconnecting tribal members from the reservations would be a service to them. Even today, about half of California's Indian population lives off reservations, in large part because of this policy. But like most government policies where non-Native people claim to know better than Native people what was best for them, relocation, like termination, was a disaster. Relocated tribal people became even more impoverished than their reservation counterparts—but now the cultural safety net and extended family networks were harder for them to access. The government was evolving its policy and finding new ways to disconnect Indians from the land.

Concurrent with the attack on tribal land, the government established a residential boarding school system for Indians that would profoundly impact the California tribes. Starting

NORTHERN CALIFORNIA

Map Key

Approximate regional boundary
(See pages 20–21 for North American
map showing all eight regions
depicted in this work.)

Federal Indian Reservation
(occupied by one or more tribal entities)

△ Federally designated tribal entity
with no land holding

Karuk Federal Reservation name

122 Resident tribe
(Number correlates to tribal list
on pages 290–293.)

★ State capital

• Selected city or town

SCALE
1 : 3,500,000

0   50   100   150
statute miles

0   50   100   150
kilometers

OREGON

NEVADA

PACIFIC
OCEAN

CALIFORNIA

Smith River 296
Point St. George
Crescent City 81
Elk Valley
Karuk 122
Resighini 254
Yurok 364
16
Trinidad 39
Arcata
Blue Lake 22
Eureka
Table Bluff 355
14
Cape Mendocino

Medford
Upper Klamath Lake
Klamath Falls
Quartz Valley
Karuk 244
Karuk 122
Hoopa Valley 105
Big Bend 211
Roaring Creek 215
Montgomery Creek 214
Redding 251

Lower Klamath Lake
Tule L.
Clear Lake Reservoir
Mt. Shasta
Pit River 314

XL Ranch 216
XL Ranch
Big Sage Res.
XL Ranch 216
Cedarville
Middle Alkali Lake 37
Pit 6
Lookout 213
Moon L. 212

Fort Bidwell 89
Fort McDermitt
Summit Lake
Fort McDermitt
Winnemucca

Eagle Lake
Susanville 310
Honey Lake
Greenville 97
Susanville 310

Smoke Cr. Desert
Pyramid Lake Paiute
Pyramid Lake

Black Rock Desert
Desert Valley
Rye Patch Res.
Winnemucca Lake

40°

Round Valley 258

Laytonville 29
Sherwood Valley 286
Mendocino
Coyote Valley 70 222
Pinoleville 210
Ukiah
Redwood Valley 252
Upper Lake 100
Robinson 256
Clear Lake
Sulphur Bank 80
Guidiville 99
Point Arena
Manchester-Point Arena 152
Hopland 107
49
19 Big Valley
276
Stewarts Point 123
76 163
Dry Creek
Middletown
147
361
85
Santa Rosa

Paskenta 202
Grindstone 98
Chico 157
Lake Oroville
Berry Creek 15
Enterprise 83
Mooretown 174
Berry Creek 15
Colusa 27
Cortina 66
Rumsey
Lake Berryessa

PACIFIC
OCEAN

Lake Almanor
Reno
Truckee
Washoe Lake
Carson City
Lahontan Res.
Carson Sink
Falon Paiute-Shoshone
Washoe Ranches
Lake Tahoe

Auburn 336
Folsom Lake 287
Shingle Springs
352
112
24 Camanche Res.
31
Stockton
Calaveras
Chicken Ranch
150
San Pablo Bay
Vallejo
Berkeley
Oakland
San Francisco
San Mateo
Golden Gate
San Francisco
Farallon Islands
Point Reyes

Sacramento
Jackson 115
Tuolumne 332
44
Modesto
Don Pedro Res.
Yosemite Valley
Hetch Hetchy
Mono Lake

Merced
Picayune 209
Table Mountain 313
North Fork 183
18 Big Sandy
Cold Springs 52
Pine Flat L.
Fresno
Kings Canyon

San Jose
Santa Cruz Mountains
Santa Cruz
Monterey Bay
Salinas
Monterey
Point Sur

San Joaquin
Santa Rosa 271
Visalia
Tulare
Lake Success
Tule River 330

Bishop
Owens Lake Bed

Delano
Isabella Lake

37°N

124°
121° W
118°

SOUTHERN CALIFORNIA

SCALE
1 : 3,500,000

statute miles

kilometers

Map Key

Approximate regional boundary
(See pages 20–21 for North American
map showing all eight regions
depicted in this work.)

Federal Indian Reservation
(occupied by one or more tribal entities)

Federally designated tribal entity
with no land holding

Rincon   Federal Reservation name

255   Resident tribe
(Number correlates to tribal list
on pages 290–293.)

★   State capital

•   Selected city or town

---

in the late 19th century and continuing until World War II, Indian children were removed from their homes and placed in residential boarding schools run by the federal government. The schools enforced harsh physical discipline for the speaking of tribal languages, and students spent half of the school day working. Children were completely dislocated from their families and home communities—many did not see home for 12 years. Upon completion of schooling, racial barriers prevented many young Indians from finding jobs in mainstream America. Often they returned home, sometimes not recognizing their own parents or even speaking the same language. The residential boarding school system rent a giant tear in the social fabric of Indian life.

As tribal life, language, land, and politics continued to be

Present-day tribal communities in California (see map, above). Southern California was populated by numerous tribes when the Spanish first arrived. The smaller size of the tribes and their peaceful disposition made it difficult for many to resist or avoid the mission labor system.

pressured from many angles in California, the tribes there found a way to rise from the ashes, like the legendary phoenix central to many of their oral histories and legends.

CHARTING A NEW PATH

From 1769 to 1934, the tribes of California endured a steady, unrelenting attack on their religions, languages, and political systems. Federal recognition in the late 1800s gave the tribes a few minor protections, as did some acts of Congress designed to affirm their status as distinct political and cultural entities. But in 1934, the passage of the Indian Reorganization Act cleared the way for California tribes to exert greater political power, and in that window of opportunity, a new era opened in California Indian history. The

> "The following day after my baptism,
> they took me to work with the other Indians, and
> they put me to work cleaning a milpa [cornfield] of maize."
> —Janitin (Kamia)

Indian Reorganization Act changed the function of the Office of Indian Affairs (soon to be renamed the Bureau of Indian Affairs) from a micromanaging, supervisory agency into an advisory agency and bureaucratic funding mechanism. Modern tribal governments were created, revised, and developed. They were not perfect, but they were a big step forward. Tribal leaders had greater ability to exercise agency—to be more powerful players in their own history.

The tribes eventually worked at the forefront of the national movement to establish casino gaming on reservations. The court case *California* v. *Cabazon Band of Mission Indians* in 1987 removed the final obstacles to gaming development. The Pechanga Band of Luiseño Mission Indians became one of the wealthiest gaming tribes in the country. They used their new revenues to build tribal-language revitalization programs and exert a voice in American politics. There could be no return to the way things were before European contact, but there was a way forward—one that preserved the values and culture and ushered in a new era where the California tribes could shape their own future for the benefit of all.

McCloud River Indians dressed in war dance costume were captured on film in 1882 by San Francisco photographer Thomas Houseworth. Warriors prepared for battle by invoking spiritual protection through face painting, praying, and dancing.

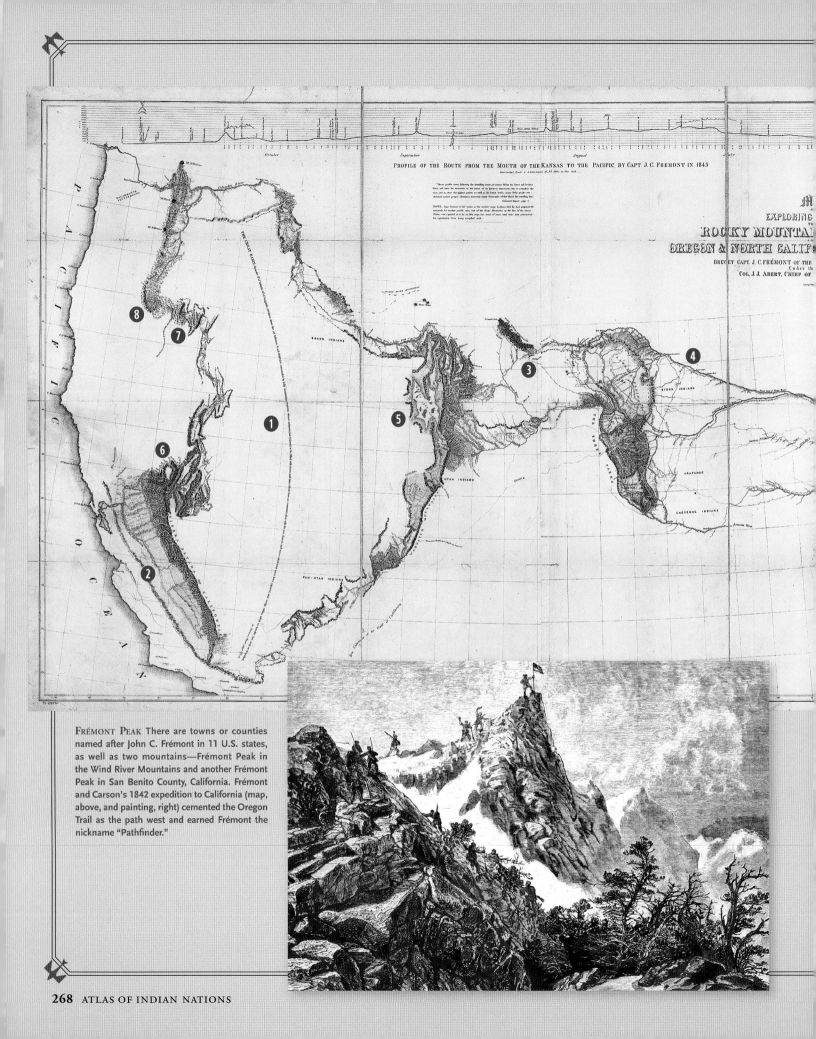

PROFILE OF THE ROUTE FROM THE MOUTH OF THE KANSAS TO THE PACIFIC BY CAPT. J. C. FREMONT IN 1843

EXPLORING
TO
ROCKY MOUNTAI
OREGON & NORTH CALIF
BREVET CAPT. J. C. FREMONT OF THE
Under the
COL. J. J. ABERT, CHIEF OF

FRÉMONT PEAK There are towns or counties named after John C. Frémont in 11 U.S. states, as well as two mountains—Frémont Peak in the Wind River Mountains and another Frémont Peak in San Benito County, California. Frémont and Carson's 1842 expedition to California (map, above, and painting, right) cemented the Oregon Trail as the path west and earned Frémont the nickname "Pathfinder."

FRÉMONT EXPEDITIONS
American Expansion Into California

John C. Frémont was an early American explorer, Army officer, and political figure who significantly contributed to America's expansion throughout the Great Basin ❶ and California ❷, primarily on four major western expeditions. In 1842, Frémont met Kit Carson on a steamship near St. Louis and hired Carson to help guide him west through South Pass ❸ to California. Frémont and Carson became fast friends, and together they led four major exploratory missions to California over the Oregon Trail ❹, branching off near Salt Lake ❺. In the course of those expeditions, Frémont identified the Great Basin as an endorheic geological feature (one with no river or ocean outlets). He was also the first American to see Lake Tahoe ❻.

Frémont nearly provoked a war with Mexico in 1846, when his small expeditionary force called for widespread attacks in California against the much larger Mexican military. He and Carson then retreated to northern California and Oregon ❼, attacking the Klamath and other tribes. They annihilated a Klamath village at the Williamson River outlet on Klamath Lake ❽.

Frémont went on to take a central role in orchestrating the American settlement of California, fighting Indians, advocating on political fronts, and litigating land claims after the Treaty of Guadalupe Hidalgo. He was the first elected senator from California when it became a state. Although he lost his bid for President of the United States, his sometimes controversial political and military career continued for many years. His expeditionary work in California earned him the nickname "Pathfinder." ■

JOHN C. FRÉMONT AND KIT CARSON

John C. Frémont's four western expeditions to California solidified the path west across the Oregon Trail and blazed the route for countless gold rushers and settlers. Frémont was a controversial figure in his own day, known to be hot-tempered, impulsive, and even reckless, but his impact on history is beyond question.

Throughout his exploratory and settlement efforts, Frémont worked in close contact with Kit Carson. Carson was initially hired by Frémont to guide his first expedition through South Pass on the Continental Divide. The success of that mission inspired several Mormon migrations to the Great Basin and further traffic west to California. Carson accompanied Frémont on other westward expeditions as well. In 1846, they attacked several Native communities in northern California and Oregon, completely destroying the village at the Williamson River outlet on Klamath Lake. Carson was nearly killed by a Klamath Indian there, only to be rescued at the last minute by Frémont, who trampled the Klamath man with his horse. Carson claimed from then on that he owed Frémont a life debt.

Frémont later became one of California's first two U.S. senators and was also a presidential contender. Carson moved to other areas in the West, working as a military officer and Indian fighter in the campaigns against the Navajo and in the Mexican–American War.

Frémont's fourth major expedition in 1848 was a disaster (above). Heavy snow diverted the group south, and ten people died. Frémont (inset, above left) suffered a great deal of criticism and lost some key friends and allies, but his reputation did not suffer enough to derail his political ambitions in California.

THE CALIFORNIA GOLD RUSH
Tribal Communities Overwhelmed

In 1848, Indians still outnumbered whites ten to one in California. But that would change dramatically in the span of just two years. The expeditions of John C. Frémont and Kit Carson in 1842–48 had already started a process of white American migration to California. Most of the land in California was unceded Indian land prior to 1848, or land that had been ceded to Spanish authorities between 1769 and 1821. The Mexican government inherited those claims when it won independence from Spain.

But neither Mexican nor Indian land rights were on the minds of white Americans as they sought to expand into California. The Mexican–American War in 1846–48 ended with the Treaty of Guadalupe Hidalgo and a formal American claim to California. The land tenure of Mexicans was addressed, but tribes were not consulted in the treaty. Then James W. Marshall discovered gold at Sutter's Mill in Coloma, California ❶. The convergence of military events, treaties, white settlement pressure, and the hopes of hundreds of thousands of miners and settlers for quick riches overwhelmed and devastated California tribes from 1848 to 1855. Major mining areas were opened near Shasta ❷, along the Feather River Valley ❸, and along the Sacramento River ❹.

Gold rushers and settlers killed Indians or chased them off their home-lands. Entire villages were wiped out. Many Native families were forced into slavery. Homicides and rapes of Indian people were common. Although the tribal population of California was large and dense, the tribes in California were small and not steeped in military tradition. There was resistance, but it usually ended in disaster. In 1850, American settlers Charles Stone and Andrew Kelsey enslaved hundreds of Pomo Indians, and when the Indians killed Stone and Kelsey, the Army slaughtered 130 Pomo at Clear Lake ❺. In 1860, 188 Indians were massacred at Humboldt Bay. The newspaper reporter who printed the story on the massacre was forced to leave town. ∎

The gold rush brought instant change to California. Some tribal people were enslaved. Others tried to pan for gold on their own and make their way in the new economy. Panning for gold was especially common during the early stages of the gold rush (left). Mining, a more labor-intensive method, became common in the latter years of the rush. It involved pulverizing the mined minerals, washing and sifting, and sorting (above).

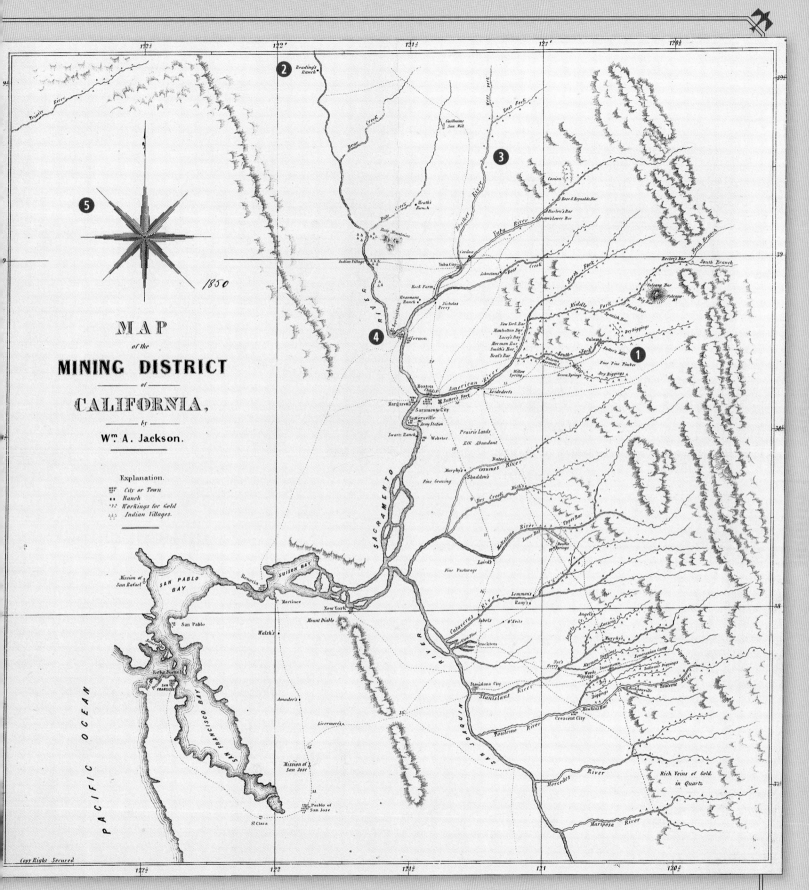

MAP
of the
MINING DISTRICT
of
CALIFORNIA,
by
Wm. A. Jackson.

Explanation.
City or Town
Ranch
Workings for Gold
Indian Villages.

PROSPECTORS OVERRUN INDIAN LANDS Shortly after James W. Marshall first discovered gold in the American River Valley (map, above), new prospecting and mining areas opened farther north along the Feather and Sacramento Rivers and in the northern California goldfields. Native Americans who lived in these gold-producing areas stood little chance of keeping their land or even their lives.

TRIBES OF THE KLAMATH RIVER Most of the tribes in California were overwhelmed and dislocated by the time anyone thought to document their cultures or villages. The Klamath River tribes (see map, left) withstood the surge of white settlement better than many other tribes. Kau-weh was destroyed by a mudslide in 1862, and some villages were consolidated by the U.S. government. But many have been inhabited in these locations for hundreds of years. The photos show a Hupa fisherman in 1923 (above) and a Klamath Indian (below, left).

KLAMATH RIVER TRIBES
Portraits of Survival

When the Spanish first established missions in southern California, they conscripted Indian labor and worked not just to convert the tribal population but also to relocate them and shape their culture to one of service to the Spanish crown. In northern California, the tribes of the Klamath River had early Spanish encounters, too, starting around 1775; they met British, French, and Russian explorers and fur traders, as well. But the Hupa, Karuk, Modoc, Yurok, and other tribes in the Klamath River region of northern California avoided the full might of European colonization in part because of their relative geographic isolation, and also because of their greater numbers and combined political and military strength.

Once the California gold rush began in 1848, it didn't take long for hordes of white American prospectors, entrepreneurs, and opportunists to make it to northern California. When they did, the discovery of more gold along the Feather, Klamath, Sacramento, and Shasta Rivers brought a massive

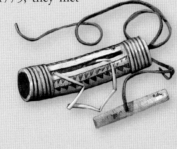

The Hupa and Yurok were and remain two of the largest tribes in California. A leather and tusk shell purse (above) display the fine artistic craftsmanship of the Yurok. Below is a Hupa dance ceremony.

surge of white settlement. It was a devastating development for the tribes there. Happy Camp was established on the Klamath River, so named because of the abundance of easily accessed gold. The newcomers had no regard for tribal people or their land rights. The Klamath and other rivers were dammed and diverted for mining, disrupting the salmon runs, the primary food source for the tribes of the region.

The Klamath River tribes had to develop new strategies for survival. Their population was reduced an estimated 75 percent by massacres and disease during the gold rush years. Conflict between Indians and miners led to the Klamath and Salmon River Indian War of 1855. The miners were supported by the full might of the U.S. Army, and tribal resistance was crushed. Some of the tribes were consolidated by treaty in 1855. Others hung on in their traditional homelands and live there yet today. Although tribal languages are spoken primarily by elders, if at all, traditional harvesting and cultural forms remain vibrant. ∎

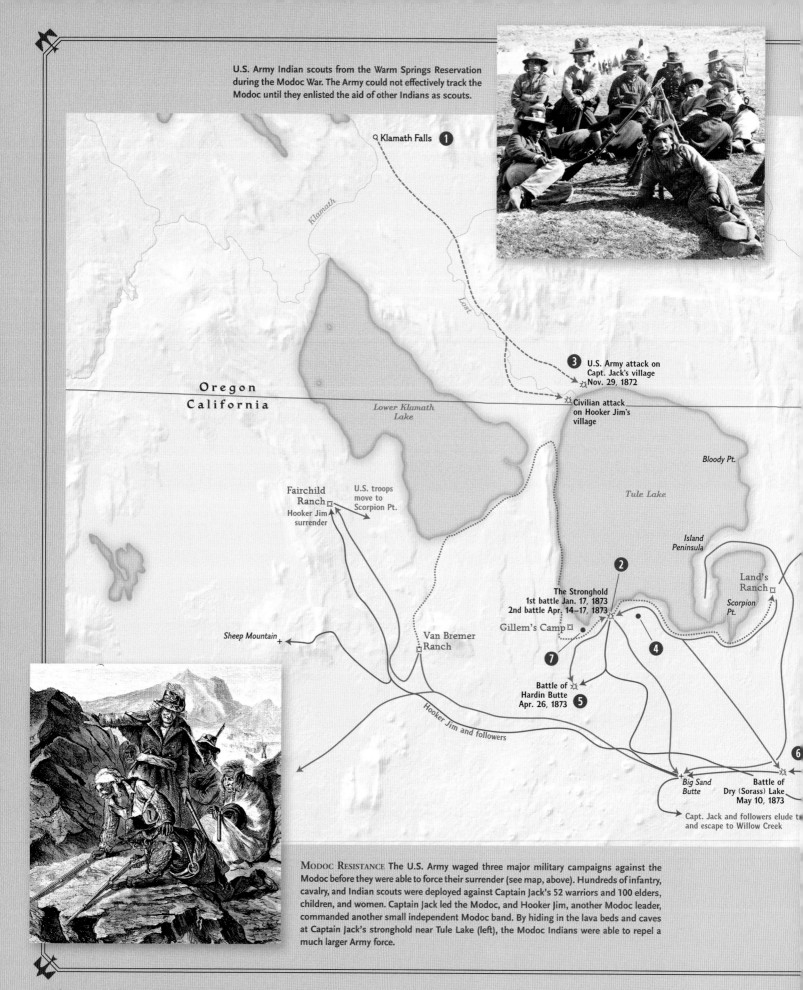

U.S. Army Indian scouts from the Warm Springs Reservation during the Modoc War. The Army could not effectively track the Modoc until they enlisted the aid of other Indians as scouts.

Klamath Falls **1**

Klamath

Lost

3 U.S. Army attack on Capt. Jack's village Nov. 29, 1872

Civilian attack on Hooker Jim's village

Oregon
California

Lower Klamath Lake

Bloody Pt.

Tule Lake

Fairchild Ranch

U.S. troops move to Scorpion Pt.

Hooker Jim surrender

Island Peninsula

Land's Ranch

2

The Stronghold
1st battle Jan. 17, 1873
2nd battle Apr. 14–17, 1873

Scorpion Pt.

Gillem's Camp

Sheep Mountain

Van Bremer Ranch

7

4

Battle of Hardin Butte Apr. 26, 1873 **5**

Hooker Jim and followers

6

Big Sand Butte

Battle of Dry (Sorass) Lake May 10, 1873

Capt. Jack and followers elude t~ and escape to Willow Creek

MODOC RESISTANCE The U.S. Army waged three major military campaigns against the Modoc before they were able to force their surrender (see map, above). Hundreds of infantry, cavalry, and Indian scouts were deployed against Captain Jack's 52 warriors and 100 elders, children, and women. Captain Jack led the Modoc, and Hooker Jim, another Modoc leader, commanded another small independent Modoc band. By hiding in the lava beds and caves at Captain Jack's stronghold near Tule Lake (left), the Modoc Indians were able to repel a much larger Army force.

THE MODOC WAR
California Tragedy

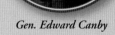

The Modoc are a small tribe from the Penutian language family, related to the Klamath. Originally from what is now the Oregon–California border region, the Modoc followed a seasonal round of gathering, fishing, and hunting. They are related to the Klamath, but when Europeans first came to their region, the Modoc and Klamath were occasional enemies.

After European settlers arrived, tribal members made many adaptations, acquiring European clothing and even adopting European names. In 1864, the now very large non-Native population demanded formal acquisition of the entire 5,000 square miles of Modoc land. The tribe, vastly outnumbered, had no choice but to sign a treaty in 1864 that required them to settle with their former enemies on the newly established Klamath Reservation, north of Klamath Falls ❶.

The rapid impoverishment of the Modoc at Klamath eventually frustrated Captain Jack, the Modoc chief. With a small band of followers, he left the reservation and took refuge in the lava beds south of Tule Lake ❷. The brutal struggle that ensued with the U.S. Army became known as the Modoc War and lasted until 1873. Major battles were fought at Lost River ❸, Hospital Rock ❹, the Stronghold (in the lava beds), Sand Butte(now called Hardin Butte) ❺, and Dry Lake ❻. A parley between U.S. military leaders and the Modoc leaders Captain Jack and Hooker Jim fell apart in 1873, and the Modoc killed Gen. Edward Canby at the

Gen. Edward Canby

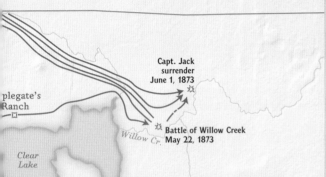

Capt. Jack
surrender
June 1, 1873

plegate's
Ranch

Battle of Willow Creek
May 22, 1873

Willow Cr.

Clear
Lake

Modoc War

←--- U.S. Army, 1st campaign
←······ U.S. Army, 2nd campaign
←— U.S. Army, 3rd campaign
←— Modoc routes after the
2nd battle of the Stronghold

0 _____ 5 miles

On April 11, 1873, peace negotiations disintegrated and the Modoc killed Gen. Edward Canby (above). When the Modoc surrendered, most of their leaders were hanged and the bulk of the tribal population relocated to Oklahoma.

CAPTAIN JACK

Captain Jack, whose Indian name was Kintpuash, was a chief among the Modoc people of the California–Oregon border region. His people lived by hunting, gathering, and fishing in the Tule Lake area. Captain Jack, born in 1837, became a chief as a young man, and sometimes his age and peaceful demeanor encouraged other Modoc to challenge or even shame him. He initially cooperated with the U.S. government through the early treaty period, including the 1864 treaty that called for the relocation of his people from their ancestral homeland to a confederated reservation with the Klamath and Yahooskin.

The Modoc were unhappy at Klamath, however, and Captain Jack agreed to lead them back to Tule Lake, but they were again rounded up and returned to Klamath. In 1869, he led around 150 Modoc off the reservation and back to the Tule Lake lava beds, where they fought off three major military excursions by the U.S. Army. Captain Jack's band at Tule Lake was joined by Hooker Jim and another band of Modoc. Hooker Jim's contingent had attacked white civilians, but Captain Jack refused to compel them to surrender to white authorities.

When the Modoc finally surrendered, Hooker Jim was convinced to testify against his friend and chief in return for amnesty. Captain Jack, Black Jim, John Schonchin, and Boston Charley were hanged. Their bodies were decapitated and their skulls preserved by the U.S. Army Medical Museum until they were transferred to the Smithsonian in 1898. Captain Jack's descendants pursued a repatriation claim from 1970 to 1984, and eventually the Modoc skulls and other skeletons were returned.

peace conference ❼. The Modoc eventually surrendered unconditionally. Hooker Jim testified against Captain Jack for amnesty; all other Modoc leaders were hanged.

The remnants of Captain Jack's band were absorbed into the Quapaw Agency in Oklahoma. A tract of land was set aside for them in 1874 in Oklahoma, but it was ill suited for agriculture and largely devoid of fish or game. The tribal population dwindled to 68 people by the time their lands were allotted in 1891.

The Modoc who were not part of Captain Jack's resistance remained in Klamath, Oregon, where they were confederated with the Klamath and Yahooskin. Many married into and were absorbed by the larger Klamath community. As living conditions in Oklahoma improved in the early 1900s, some Modoc migrated to Oklahoma to be with relatives, although the U.S. government refused to acknowledge them as Modoc rather than Klamath.

In the 1950s, the Modoc experienced more difficulties, losing their tribal status. In 1978, after a long legal battle, the Modoc of Oklahoma were reinstated as a federally recognized tribe. There are no remaining speakers of the historic tribal language, but the group of about 200 enrolled members retains its tenacious spirit of community. ∎

Frank and Tobey Riddle with an Indian agent (above, back row) and four Modoc women. Tobey Riddle, whose Modoc name was Winema, served as an interpreter in peace negotiations between her tribe and the U.S. government.

When the Modoc resistance was crushed, the U.S. Army forcibly relocated Captain Jack's band of Modoc (above) from their stronghold near Tule Lake in the lava beds of northern California to Oklahoma.

After Gen. Edward Canby was killed during peace negotiations, the Army brought all its resources to bear on the
Modoc, forcing a final confrontation at Captain Jack's stronghold in the lava beds (above). Many factors contributed to
the Modoc resistance—from unfair treaty terms to poverty
and mistreatment by their Klamath enemies on their new
reservation—but in American perceptions of the Modoc
War, the Indians were instigators. Wanted posters of Captain
Jack and other Modoc people active in the resistance (left)
portrayed them as criminals.

CALIFORNIA MISSIONS
Religious, Political, and Economic Attack

King Charles III of Spain recalled the Jesuit missionaries from California in 1767 and sent in the Franciscans to convert the indigenous population there. From 1769 to 1833, the Spanish mission system was the mechanism Spain used to dominate the Native people in Alta California, Spain's northernmost colony in the Americas.

Junípero Serra, who founded dozens of Franciscan missions in California with Gaspar de Portola, was also put in charge of the local Spanish army. The missions were established not just to convert the Indians but also to conscript them as a labor force. The Chumash, Kumeyaay, and other tribes were immediately targeted. Indians brought under the rule of the missions were considered slaves and treated as such, with mission discipline enforced by cruel punishments.

The Mission San Diego de Alcalá in San Diego ❶ anchored the southern tier of Spanish missions in Alta California. The northern boundary of the missions was at Mission San Francisco Solano in Sonoma ❷. Many present-day California

Fr. Junípero Serra

cities and towns were established on Indian village sites where the missions exerted their heaviest influence, including San Jose ❸, Santa Clara ❹, Santa Cruz ❺, San Miguel ❻, and Santa Barbara ❼. Military resistance by the Kumeyaay and other tribes was brutally suppressed. In 1824, the Chumash rebelled and captured two missions. Eventually, Chumash leaders agreed to a cease-fire, but the terms of the parley were ignored and the Chumash were immediately returned to slavery at the missions.

Mexico inherited the mission system from the Spanish after winning independence in 1821. It secularized the system in 1834 and abolished slavery. But after 65 years in the mission system, most of the subdued tribes had population declines of 90 percent from violence and disease. Most tribes ended up working for the Mexican and mission authorities for poverty wages until the American period. Even in the American period, many California Indians ended up working in feudal conditions for white ranchers, landless in their own land.■

The Chumash village of Chutchui was colonized by the Spanish, who built a large mission on the site and conscripted the Chumash population as slave labor. At first, the Chumash followed their traditions and even performed a tribal dance for the Spanish (above). But soon such dances were outlawed and the Chumash effectively controlled.

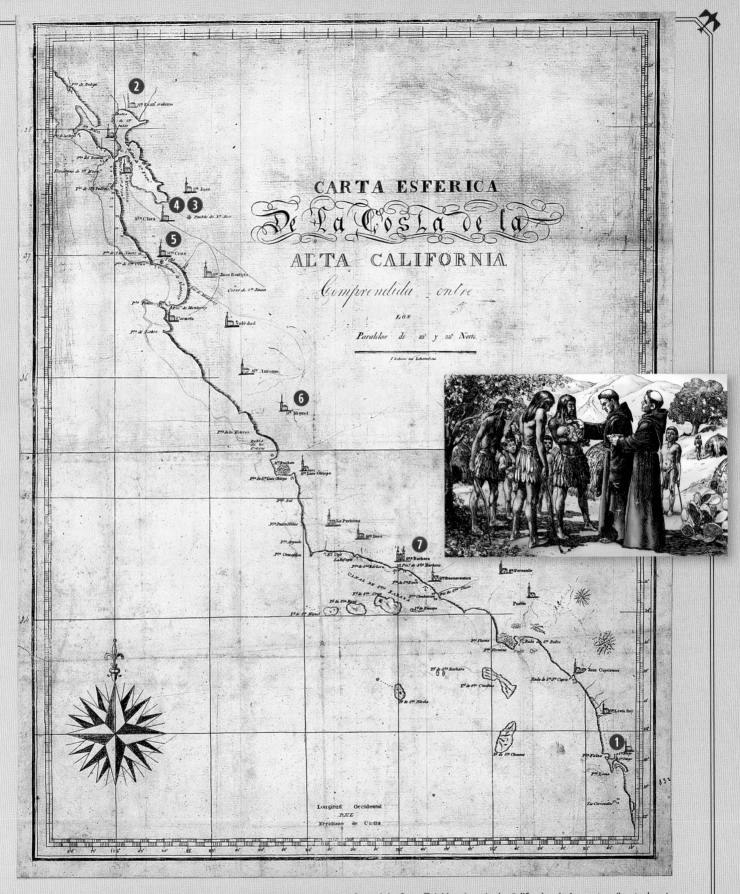

MISSION BUSINESS In 1769, Franciscan priests Francisco Gómez and Juan Crespi performed the first official baptisms in the California mission system (inset, above). With missions, presidios, pueblos, and public works up and down California (map dating to about 1839, above), the mission system was big business for the Spanish, producing enough food to feed the Spanish army, clergy, and slave population and paying for most of the wages of Spanish officials.

TRIBES OF CALIFORNIA

The Native people of California developed amazingly diverse tribal languages, cultures, and strategies for dealing with Spanish, Russian, and American invaders. Following are brief histories of select tribes of the region.

■ CAHTO (KATO)

Current Locations: California
Language Family: Athabascan

The Cahto language is one of four in California from the Athabascan language family. Many tribal members were bilingual in Cahto and Pomo prior to European contact. Tribal culture was heavily influenced by other tribes in north-central California, including the practice of body and face tattooing. The Cahto relied on hunting, fishing, and gathering prior to contact with Europeans. The Spanish and American periods forced many adaptations on the Cahto, who took up ranching and farming as well. Today, most Cahto are members of the Cahto Indian Tribe of the Laytonville Rancheria, although some were incorporated into another political structure at Round Valley, California.

■ CAHUILLA

Current Locations: California
Language Family: Uto-Aztecan

The Cahuilla, from the Uto-Aztecan language family, are indigenous to inland southern California, primarily south of the San Bernardino Mountains. The Cahuilla were one of the larger and more powerful tribes in the region and avoided sustained colonial advances from the Spanish during the mission system. Some Cahuilla had limited contact with Europeans prior to the Mexican–American War. The Cahuilla sometimes warred with the neighboring Luiseño, and during the Mexican–American War, a combined force of Mexican Californians and Cahuilla attacked and massacred a group of Luiseño.

After the Mexican–American War, the tribe struggled to adapt to the rapid influx

Hupa White Deerskin Dance headdress from the late 19th century, fashioned from iris fibers, grouse and blue jay feathers, and deerskin

of white settlers, but the California gold rush pushed tribal tolerance to the breaking point, and there were a number of attacks on tribal members by rushers. Eventually, the government intervened, and the tribe was pressured to cede land and concentrate on several tribal reservations. They include the Agua Caliente Band of Cahuilla Indians, the Augustine Band of Cahuilla Indians, the Cabazon Band of Mission Indians, the Cahuilla Band of Mission Indians, the Los Coyotes Band of Cahuilla and Cupeño Indians, the Morongo Band of Cahuilla

Mission Indians, the Ramona Band of Cahuilla Mission Indians, the Santa Rose Band of Cahuilla Indians, and the Torres-Martinez Desert Cahuilla Indians.

■ CHEMEHUEVI

Current Locations: California
Language Family: Uto-Aztecan

The Chemehuevi are from the Numic branch of the Uto-Aztecan language family, the southernmost group of Paiute. Most of the Chemehuevi-related tribal groups are from the Great Basin area. The Chemehuevi traditionally lived in the Mojave Desert and the Chemehuevi Valley along the Colorado River in southeastern California.

Chemehuevi country has an extremely hot and arid climate and is sparse in natural resources. The Chemehuevi, however, were adept at gathering plants and tubers, hunting small game, fishing in the Colorado, and trading crafts with other tribes and later with Europeans. The harsh climate in their territory discouraged European colonization throughout much of the Spanish period. Later, however, the U.S. government pressured the Chemehuevi for land cessions and concentrated the tribal population at the Chemehuevi Indian Tribe (in California) and another group at the Colorado River Indian Tribes (straddling the California–Arizona border) along with small groups of Hopi, Mohave, and Navajo.

■ CHUMASH

Current Locations: California
Language Family: Isolate

The Chumash are one of the larger tribes in California, indigenous to what is now

San Luis Obispo, Santa Barbara, Ventura, and Los Angeles counties from Morro Bay to Malibu, and also living on three of the large Channel Islands off the California coast. Their land tenure there was so long that their language is really a language family of its own, with several Chumash dialects; today, just a handful of speakers remain. The natural resources in Chumash land were vast, and tribal members thrived on fish, shellfish, seaweed, and other plants and animals harvested along the coast. The Chumash cultivated rich artistic traditions in many forms, from rock paintings to the still vibrant handcrafts of weaving and basketmaking.

The precontact Chumash population may have been as high as 20,000, but disease brought by the Spanish devastated tribal numbers. The Spanish worked to subjugate the Chumash through the mission system, and the resultant conflict, labor conscription, and forced adaptations challenged traditional Chumash politics, language, and culture.

Yokut Indians gather peaches near the Tule River in California. After the Spanish introduced cattle, sheep, goats, peaches, and wheat to the tribes, ranching and farming grew rapidly among the indigenous population.

■ CUPEÑO

Current Locations: California
Language Family: Uto-Aztecan

The Cupeño language is from the Takic branch of the Uto-Aztecan language family, closely related to Cahuilla and Luiseño. A 1990 language census recorded just five speakers, and most have died since then. The tribe historically lived in southwestern California. The Cupeño had early and sustained contact with the Spanish through the mission system, which eroded the tribal language and culture. During the American period, most Cupeño still worked in a state of serfdom on large ranches in their former territory. The tribe fractured, and some of the Cupeño were embedded in several different recognized tribal communities, including the Los Coyotes Band of Cahuilla and Cupeño Indians, Mesa Grande Band

This 19th-century Karuk basket exemplifies the fine weaving tradition of tribes in Humboldt County.

of Diegueño Indians, Morongo Band of Cahuilla Mission Indians, Pala Band of Luiseño Mission Indians, Santa Ysabel Band of Diegueño Mission Indians, and San Ygnacio Band of Mission Indians.

■ HUPA (HOOPA)

Current Locations: California
Language Family: Athabascan

The Hupa (Hoopa) migrated south into northwestern California around 1,200 years ago, making them one of the more recent tribal arrivals to this region. Their language is part of the Athabascan language family. The Hupa's cedar-plank houses, dugout canoes, and woven hats are more closely related to their Pacific Northwest forebears than to neighboring tribes in California. The Hupa avoided sustained colonial contact with Europeans throughout the Spanish era, but the 1849 California gold rush brought countless settlers to their lands. The government

pressured them for a land cession in 1864, which created the Hoopa Valley Reservation. Today, the Hupa are established in three distinct tribal communities: the Cher-Ae Heights Indian Community of the Trinidad Rancheria, the Elk Valley Rancheria, and the Hoopa Valley Tribe.

■ KARUK (KAROK)

Current Locations: California
Language Family: Hokan

The Karuk language, a member of the Hokan language family, is highly endangered; a language census in 2000 found just 55 speakers with any proficiency. The tribe is indigenous to northern California, and both oral records and archaeological evidence confirm their habitation along the Klamath River for thousands of years. The population was small, numbering a few thousand at most. But they were self-sufficient, fishing for salmon, hunting deer and small game, and harvesting acorns, berries, and tubers. The Karuk were also small-scale farmers and may have been the only California tribe to grow tobacco plants. Like most tribes in northern California,

Indians gather acorns in a traditional Pomo village, with thatched lodges and hive-like granaries and storage structures in the background.

the Karuk were overwhelmed by gold rushers in 1849 and succumbed to government pressure for land sales. Today, most Karuk are enrolled at the Karuk Tribe, but some were relocated to the Cher-Ae Heights Indian Community of the Trinidad Rancheria, as well.

■ KUMEYAAY (DIEGUEÑO, KAMIA, TIPAI-IPAI)

Current Locations: California; Mexico
Language Family: Yuman

The Kumeyaay are from the Delta-California branch of the Yuman language family. They are indigenous to the southern California–Baja California (Mexico) border region, with tribal populations on both sides of the border even today. Although their ancestors may have lived in the San Diego River Valley for as long as 12,000 years, the Kumeyaay emerged as a distinct people.

From 1769 to 1834, the Spanish sought to subjugate the Kumeyaay through the Spanish mission system. When the missions were secularized in 1834, the tribal population essentially worked as serfs for wealthy landowners who had usurped tribal control of their territory. In 1875, President Ulysses Grant created reservations for the Kumeyaay. Additional lands were added to the reservations via the 1891 Act for the Relief of Mission Indians. Nevertheless, American settlers relentlessly encroached on tribal lands from 1870 to 1910. The Kumeyaay live on 13 separate federally recognized reservations in California and 5 recognized tribal communities in Mexico.

■ LUISEÑO

Current Locations: California
Language Family: Uto-Aztecan

The Luiseño lived in more than 30 distinct villages in present-day Los Angeles and San Diego Counties at the time of Spanish contact. The Spanish exerted the full might of their military to bring the tribe

Kumeyaay condor feather dance apron, featuring a tied cordage technique unique to the region

into the Spanish mission system in the late 18th century. In 1798, they established the Mission San Luis Rey de Francia and used it as a base of operations throughout the region. The name Luiseño stems from the centrality of this mission in the colonial regime. The tribal language for the Luiseño is from the Cupan group of Takic languages in the Uto-Aztecan language family. Today, there are six recognized Luiseño tribes: the La Jolla Band of Luiseño Indians, the Pala Band of Luiseño Indians, the Pauma Band of Luiseño Indians, the Pechanga Band of Luiseño Indians, the Rincon Band of Luiseño Indians, and the Soboba Band of Luiseño Indians. The San Luis Rey Band of Luiseño Indians has not been federally recognized.

■ MAIDU

Current Locations: California
Language Family: Penutian

The Maidu are indigenous to northern California in the central Sierra Nevada range, between the Feather and American Rivers. Their language is from the Penutian language family and includes five distinct dialects. The Maidu never farmed, but were hunters and expert at all types of foraging and gathering. Their knowledge of edible plants and tubers earned them the often derisively applied nickname "diggers." The basketry and art traditions of the Maidu were and remain of great renown. After major gold finds on both the Feather and American Rivers during the gold rush period, the Maidu were coerced in a series of treaties and agreements to cede most of their land. Today there are eight federally recognized Maidu tribes in California and another eight unrecognized tribal communities.

■ MATTOLE (BEAR RIVER INDIANS)

Current Locations: California
Language Family: Athabascan

The Mattole spoke a language from the Athabascan language family and lived for countless generations in what is now Humboldt County, along the Bear River.

They relied on gathering, fishing, and small game hunting. Early Spanish and American colonial efforts damaged the tribal language and culture, and the language has since become extinct. Unlike neighboring tribes, both men and women in Mattole culture used to tattoo their faces.

During the Spanish mission period, the Mattole lost much of their traditional land, and as the tribe adapted to the Mexican and then American regimes, recovering use of their traditional land proved impossible. They became a federally recognized tribe and were confederated with a small group of Wiyot as the Bear River Band of the Rohnerville Rancheria. The Wiyot were always a separate entity, even speaking a language from the Algonquian language family, quite distinct from the Mattole.

MIWOK (ME-WUK)
Current Locations: California
Language Family: Penutian

The Miwok are from the Utian branch of the Penutian language family and include four distinct subdivisions: the Bay Miwok, Coast Miwok, Lake Miwok, and Plains and Sierra Miwok. The combined tribal population for all groups may have been as high as 11,000 prior to European contact, but devastating disease epidemics, especially smallpox, decimated the tribal population. The Spanish mission system also claimed many lives, especially among the Coast Miwok, who were forced into the San Francisco de Asís, San José, and San Rafael missions. There were fewer than 500 Miwok in all four bands by 1920 and just 20 Lake Miwok. Today, there are 11 federally recognized Miwok reservations in California and 6 more unrecognized Miwok tribal communities.

MONO (CALIFORNIA PAIUTE)
Current Locations: California
Language Family: Uto-Aztecan

The Mono are an offshoot of the Paiute, from the Numic branch of the Uto-Aztecan language family. The Mono are indigenous to the eastern side of the Sierra Nevada, where two main bands of Mono diverged and differentiated in language dialect and geographic range. Both groups of Mono were resourceful gatherers, hunters, and occasional fishermen. Many of the rich artistic traditions developed by the Mono thrive today.

The Mono were geographically isolated

A Cahuilla tribal member, photographed at the Agua Caliente Indian Reservation in Palm Springs, California

from other Paiute groups and had few encounters with other tribes or outsiders despite contact with Spanish explorers in the 18th century. Sustained engagement with Europeans came with the opening of the Oregon Trail and other paths west, and accelerated after the California gold rush began.

Today, the Eastern Mono, sometimes called the Owens Valley Paiute, are represented by six communities: the Big Pine Band of Owens Valley Paiute Shoshone Indians, Bridgeport Paiute Indian Colony, Fort Independence Indian Community of Paiute, Paiute-Shoshone Indians of the Bishop Community, Paiute-Shoshone Indians of the Lone Pine Community, and Utu Utu Gwaitu Paiute Tribe. The Western Mono, sometimes called the Monache or Mono Lake Paiute, are represented by five reservations: the Big Sandy Rancheria, Cold Springs Rancheria, Northfork Rancheria, Table Mountain Rancheria, and Tule River Indian Tribe. The Northfork Rancheria has 1,800 tribal members, making it one of California's most populous rancherias. Both the western and eastern dialects of Mono are extremely endangered, with only a dozen first speakers of each still alive.

PIT RIVER
Current Locations: California
Language Family: Hokan

The 11 distinct bands of the Pit River Tribe spoke two different but related languages: Achumawi and Atsugewi. Both languages are from the Palaihnihan branch of the Hokan language family. The tribe hunted deer, using staked pits and ambush tactics, but relied more on fishing and gathering. The neighboring Klamath and Modoc often raided the Pit River people for slaves prior to European contact. The California gold rush brought enormous pressure from white prospectors and settlers, forcing many cultural and political accommodations.

Today, the Pit River people live on eight reservation communities: the Alturas, Big Bend, Likely, Lookout, Montgomery Creek, Roaring Creek, and Susanville rancherias and the XL Ranch (in Modoc County). Six of these communities have a single confederated tribal political system, federally recognized in 1976, and based in Burney, California. Each of these communities is represented in the tribal government.

POMO
Current Locations: California
Language Family: Hokan

The Pomo settled in the Clear Lake region of northwestern California where the coastal redwoods meet the mixed inland forest and diversified into seven distinct linguistic and cultural groups. Their language is from the Hokan language family, but each of the seven major dialects is quite distinct and not mutually intelligible. The Kashaya dialect has just 100 speakers left, northern Pomo is entirely extinct, and the other dialects have only a small handful of speakers each. Many Pomo practiced the Kuksu religion, which involved elaborate dance, acting, and puberty rites and an annual mourning ritual.

The Spanish tried to colonize the Pomo in the 18th and 19th centuries, moving many of the southern Pomo to the San Rafael Mission from 1821 to 1828. The Russians, from a nearby base at Fort Ross, traded and occasionally tried to subjugate the Pomo as well from 1812 to 1841.

Smallpox, which was introduced by the Russians in 1837, devastated the tribal population. The California gold rush brought violence and displacement. In 1850, the U.S. Cavalry massacred as many as 400 Pomo at Clear Lake in an effort to evict them from their land and punish the tribe, which was mistakenly blamed for depredations against gold rushers.

The precontact Pomo population of 20,000 was reduced to 1,143 by 1930. Today, the Pomo are spread out among 20 different federally recognized tribes in the region.

ROUND VALLEY (COVELO INDIAN COMMUNITY)

Current Locations: California
Language Family: Various

The Round Valley Indian Tribes, also known as the Covelo Indian Community, comprise several different tribal groups, largely unrelated in language and culture—some even former enemies. The represented tribes are the Cahto, Concow, Nomlaki, Pit River, Pomo, and Yuki tribes. They were confederated as a single political entity in 1852.

Historically, the land where the Round Valley Tribes are located in present-day Mendocino County was Yuki territory. The California gold rush brought crushing pressure on the Yuki and their neighbors. In 1852, the U.S. government established the Nome Lackee Reservation, along with four others as designated multitribal relocation spots. The Yuki, Concow, and some of the Pomo and other tribes were relocated there at that time. Hoping to stem conflict between gold rushers and tribal members, the U.S. government built Fort Wright in 1862. In 1870, President Ulysses Grant redefined Nome Lackee as the Round Valley Indian Reservation, the designated relocation reservation for several tribes.

In spite of the incongruous collection of tribes at Round Valley, the people there

The Chumash wove intricate baskets using a variety of natural fibers and dyes.

slowly converged politically and culturally. In 1894, the government decided to allot the reservation, which ultimately shifted much of the land out of Indian hands. Land still held by Indians was now held privately rather than in common, and much of that land was sold or weighed down by debt or tax forfeitures. In 1934, the tribe created a modern political structure under the auspices of the Indian Reorganization Act.

SERRANO

Current Locations: California
Language Family: Uto-Aztecan

The Serrano are from the Takic branch of the Uto-Aztecan language family, indigenous to the territory between the San Gabriel and San Bernardino Mountains in southern California, extending east to the Mojave Desert. The name Serrano, meaning "Highlander," refers to the tribe's occupation of the high ground along the edge of these mountain ranges.

The Spanish established Mission San Gabriel Arcangel in 1771 and directed it to colonize the Serrano. After decades of inhumane treatment, the Serrano revolted against the missions, in alliance with the Cahuilla and the Quecha, in 1812. The Spanish brutally suppressed the tribal resistance and redoubled their efforts to bring more Serrano into the mission system. The U.S. government created two reservations for the Serrano—the Morongo Band of Mission Indians and the San Manuel Band of Mission Indians—with additional Serrano people embedded as minorities in the tribal population of the Sobobo Band

Chumash Indians head out to sea in a canoe, or *tomol*, to set nets. The Chumash relied on fishing before first contact, but shifted to ranching and farming as conscripted labor under the mission system.

of Luiseño Indians. While no living first speakers of the Serrano language remain, the tribe has attempted to rebuild basic language knowledge using audio and text materials created while the last Serrano speakers were still alive.

SHASTA (CHASTA)

Current Locations: California, Oregon
Language Family: Hokan

The Shasta are a Hokan-speaking tribe from northern California and southern Oregon, next to the traditional Wintu, Pit River, and Modoc territories. The Shasta population includes the Konomihu and Okwanuchu, who spoke Shasta but maintained independent political identities and territories. Shasta territory included gold-bearing land, and the tribe was battered by violence and land encroachment during the California gold rush. The treaties and executive orders that created reservations in northern California carved up Shasta lands without tribal consent, and the tribe lost much of its land in the region. Most of the Shasta stayed in California, where they remain an unrecognized tribal community. In Oregon, many Shasta, along with a number of other tribes in the area, were incorporated as the Confederated Tribes of the Grand Ronde Community of Oregon.

TOLOWA

Current Locations: California, Oregon
Language Family: Athabascan

The Tolowa language is from the Athabascan language family. The tribe is indigenous to northwestern California and southern Oregon. The remote and rugged terrain in Tolowa territory limited their contact with early Spanish and Russian colonial efforts. In 1828, Jedediah Smith became the first white man known to have established contact with the tribe. The gold rushes brought white settlers and rushers to Tolowa lands. They committed many depredations on the tribal population, including the infamous Achulet and Yontoket massacres.

The U.S. government established the Confederated Tribes of Siletz in Oregon by executive order in 1855. The Siletz reservation was home to the Tolowa and 26 other tribes. In 1860, a number of tribes in the California–Oregon border region joined forces in a conflict that would become known as the Rogue River Indian War. In the aftermath, about 600 Tolowa were relocated to Siletz in Oregon and others to the

A Hupa man poses in regalia for the White Deerskin Dance, one of the pre-Columbian ceremonies that thrived throughout the early contact period.

Hoopa Valley Reservation in California. Some embraced the Ghost Dance in the late 19th century. Today, the Tolowa population is divided between the Smith River, Elk Valley, and Trinidad Rancherias; the Hoopa Valley Indian Reservation; and the Confederated Tribes of Siletz.

WAILAKI

Current Locations: California
Language Family: Athabascan

The Wailaki are an Athabascan-speaking people native to the northern California coast from Fortuna to Fort Bragg, and inland along the Eel River. The Wailaki population numbered fewer than 1,000 at the time of first European contact, and they had sustained engagement with the Spanish during the mission system years. They suffered significant loss of life from European disease pandemics and the suppression of the mission system, and their tribal land was flooded with white settlers and gold rushers in the early American period. From 1858 to 1864, the Wailaki joined forces with several other tribes in a sometimes sporadic conflict known as the Bald Hills War. The U.S. Army crushed tribal resistance by 1863 and moved most of the pan-Indian tribal population to various reservations shortly after that. The Wailaki today are divided primarily between the Scotts Valley Band of Pomo Indians and the Grindstone Indian Rancheria of Wintun-Wailaki Indians in California.

WASHOE

Current Locations: California, Nevada
Language Family: Isolate

The Washoe are indigenous to the Carson Valley region and the surrounding area on both sides of the California–Nevada border. Their language, Washoe, sometimes classified as being from the Hokan language family, is considered a language isolate because it is distinct from other tribal languages. The Washoe sometimes warred with the Paiute and in general interacted more with Great Basin tribes than their California neighbors prior to European contact. The gold rush era brought their first sustained contact with whites, and a number of conflicts broke out, including the Potato War of 1857. Some of the Washoe were amalgamated with the Paiute and Shoshone at the Reno-Sparks Indian Colony, and others were folded into the Susanville Indian Rancheria along with members of several other tribes. The bulk of the remaining Carson Valley Washoe were reorganized in 1934 as the Washoe Tribe of Nevada and California, one of many tribal reconfigurations that accompanied the Indian Reorganization Act.

■ WINTUN (NOMLAKI, PATWIN)

Current Locations: California
Language Family: Wintuan

The Wintun language is one of four in the Wintuan language family. The closely related Nomlaki and Patwin are usually classified as dialects of Wintun. The Wintun tribes all lived in a long stretch of territory in northern California from Lake Shasta near the Oregon border to San Francisco. Early archaeological evidence suggests that the Wintun came to California from Oregon and may have introduced the bow and arrow to other California tribes.

The Wintun had early contact with the Spanish and Russians in California. The Spanish pulled some Wintun into the mission system, and the Russians traded occasionally with the tribe. Most Wintun were able to avoid colonization during this time. The American period was unavoidable for all California tribes, however, and within a few years of the gold rush, the Wintun were forced onto ever smaller remnants of their traditional land. They were eventually split between seven federally recognized communities throughout northern California.

■ WIYOT

Current Locations: California
Language Family: Algonquian

The Wiyot are the southwesternmost Algonquian-speaking tribe in the United States, indigenous to the brackish tidal marshlands around Humboldt Bay in California. The Spanish did not extend the mission system much farther north than San Francisco, and the Russians did not colonize farther south than historic Pomo territory, which allowed the Wiyot to avoid colonization and settlement efforts until the American period. Americans built Fort Humboldt in 1853 to subjugate Indians and protect prospectors. In 1860, local militia and vigilante squads began a war against the Wiyot. In one instance, later called the Humboldt Bay Massacre, they ambushed sleeping Wiyot villagers and indiscriminately killed most of the elders, women, and children. Several other attacks raised the casualties into the hundreds.

A spiritual leader from the Winnemem-Wintu tribe uses smoke to transmit prayers. The Winnemem are one of nine bands of Wintu indigenous to Redding, California.

Although precise numbers are not known, the Wiyot population was estimated to be around 3,300 prior to European contact. Many Wiyot died from diseases during the early contact period and the population dwindled as low as 100 during the reservation period. Today, most Wiyot are part of the Wiyot Tribe, although some are also embedded with the Bear River Band of the Rohnerville, Blue Lake, and Cher-Ae Heights Indians Community of the Trinidad rancherias as well.

■ YOKUT (INCLUDING CHUKCHANSI)

Current Locations: California
Language Family: Penutian

The Yokut are one of the larger tribal groups in California, with a precontact population of around 20,000. From the Penutian language family, the Yokut divided into six major bands—the Casson, Choinumni, Chukchansi, Lakisamni, Tachi, and Wukchumni—and occupied a vast territory in central California that included most of the San Joaquin Valley and surrounding areas.

The Yokut bands fared better than their coastal neighbors during most of the Spanish mission period, but most were overwhelmed after the California gold rush. Violence by miners and unrelenting pressure from the government did a great deal of damage to tribal languages and lifeways. Eventually, the entire Yokut population was concentrated on six major reservations. The Chukchansi band was divided between the Picayune Rancheria of Chukchansi Indians and the Table Mountain Rancheria. The Tachi were settled at the Santa Rosa Rancheria. The others were concentrated and settled as the Tejon Indian Tribe of California, the Tule River Indian Tribe, and the Tuolumne Rancheria.

■ YUROK

Current Locations: California
Language Family: Algonquian

The Yurok form one of the largest tribes in California, with more than 5,500 enrolled members at last count. A peaceful people, the Yurok historically subsided on fishing and the other bounties of the rich lands along the Klamath River as well as the northern California coast. They interacted well with the surrounding tribes, such as the Hupa, Wiyot, Tolowa, and Karuk, but until about 1828, there was virtually no contact between the Yurok and non-Natives. Gold brought outsiders onto Yurok lands and the subsequent resistance led by the Red Cap Indians—thought to have comprised a mix of tribes—ultimately failed. The federal government was in control by 1855 and eventually the Yurok were established on the 87-square-mile Yurok reservation in parts of Del Norte and Humboldt Counties on a 44-mile section of the Klamath River.

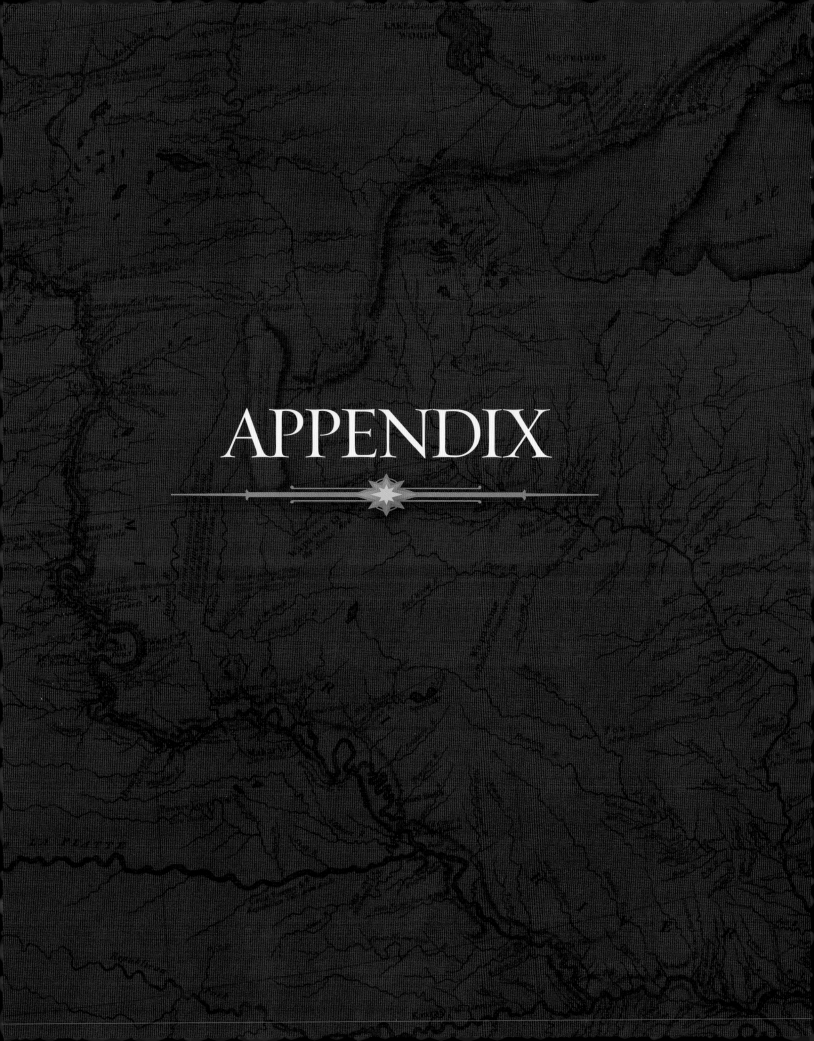

APPENDIX

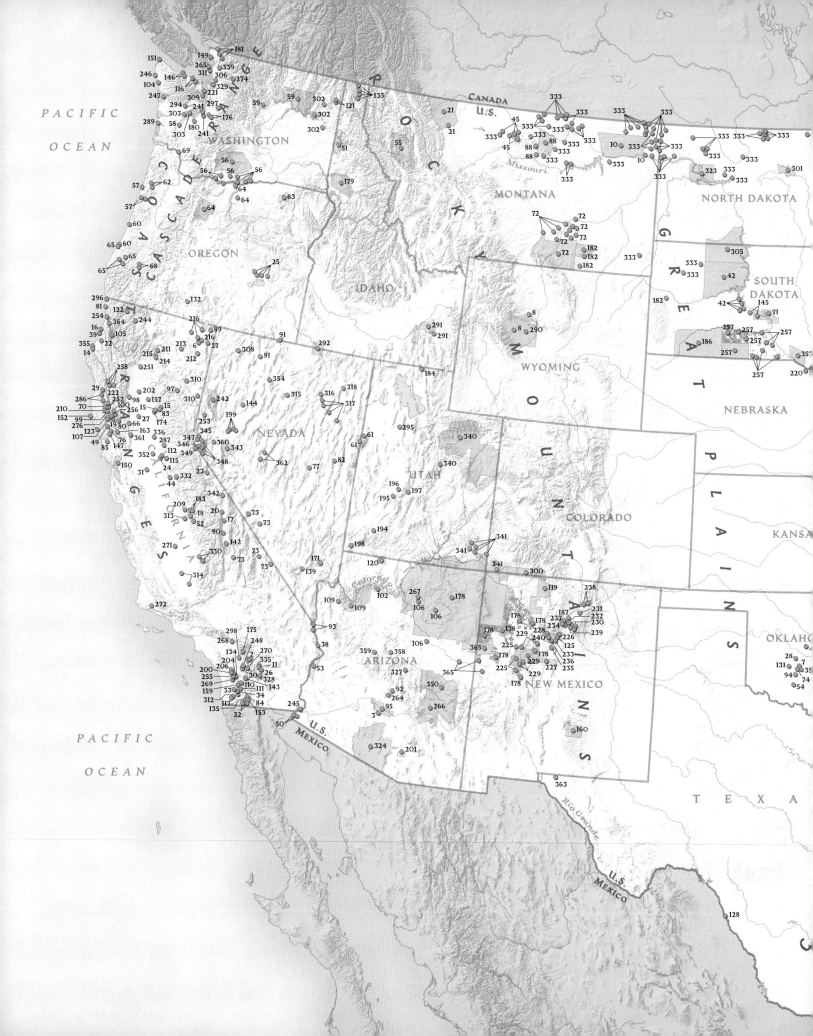

FEDERALLY RECOGNIZED INDIAN RESERVATIONS AND TRIBES

Lake Superior

Lake Huron

Lake Michigan

Lake Ontario

Lake Erie

Gulf of Maine

ATLANTIC OCEAN

Gulf of Mexico

CANADA
U.S.

MAINE

NEW YORK

VT.

N.H.

MASS.

CONN.

R.I.

PENNSYLVANIA

N.J.

MD.

DEL.

Washington, D.C.

W. VA.

OHIO

INDIANA

ILLINOIS

CENTRAL LOWLAND

IOWA

MINNESOTA

WISCONSIN

MISSOURI

KENTUCKY

VIRGINIA

TENNESSEE

NORTH CAROLINA

SOUTH CAROLINA

ARKANSAS

MISSISSIPPI

ALABAMA

GEORGIA

LOUISIANA

APPALACHIAN MOUNTAINS

COASTAL PLAIN

FLORIDA

BAHAMAS

SCALE
1 : 11,000,000

0   200   400
statute miles

0   200   400
kilometers

Map Key
Federal Indian Reservations

77 ● Federally recognized Indian tribe
(Number correlates to tribal list on pages 290–293.)

USING THE MAPS
An important distinction needs to be considered when utilizing this atlas. Our style is to label, on the large-scale regional maps, particular reserves in Canada and reservations in the U.S. The lists at the back of this book are of tribal entities. Reserves or reservations represent the modern geographic situation of a people, in many cases far from an ancestral homeland. A tribe embodies their cultural, linguistic, and traditional heritage. Our methodology in presenting this daunting subject, in a way befitting the scope of this book, was to limit our map coverage to those tribal entities given formal recognition by the governments of Canada or the United States.

INDIAN TRIBAL ENTITIES WITHIN THE CONTIGUOUS 48 STATES RECOGNIZED AND ELIGIBLE TO RECEIVE SERVICES FROM THE UNITED STATES BUREAU OF INDIAN AFFAIRS

1 Absentee-Shawnee Tribe of Indians of Oklahoma PLAINS

2 Agua Caliente Band of Cahuilla Indians of the Agua Caliente Indian Reservation, California CALIFORNIA

3 Ak Chin Indian Community of the Maricopa (Ak Chin) Indian Reservation, Arizona SOUTHWEST

4 Alabama-Coushatta Tribe of Texas SOUTHEAST

5 Alabama-Quassarte Tribal Town PLAINS

6 Alturas Indian Rancheria, California CALIFORNIA

7 Apache Tribe of Oklahoma PLAINS

8 Arapaho Tribe of the Wind River Reservation, Wyoming PLAINS

9 Aroostook Band of Micmacs NORTHEAST

10 Assiniboine and Sioux Tribes of the Fort Peck Indian Reservation, Montana PLAINS

11 Augustine Band of Cahuilla Indians, California CALIFORNIA

12 Bad River Band of the Lake Superior Tribe of Chippewa Indians of the Bad River Reservation, Wisconsin NORTHEAST

13 Bay Mills Indian Community, Michigan NORTHEAST

14 Bear River Band of the Rohnerville Rancheria, California CALIFORNIA

15 Berry Creek Rancheria of Maidu Indians of California CALIFORNIA

16 Big Lagoon Rancheria, California CALIFORNIA

17 Big Pine Paiute Tribe of the Owens Valley GREAT BASIN

18 Big Sandy Rancheria of Western Mono Indians of California CALIFORNIA

19 Big Valley Band of Pomo Indians of the Big Valley Rancheria, California CALIFORNIA

20 Bishop Paiute Tribe CALIFORNIA

21 Blackfeet Tribe of the Blackfeet Indian Reservation of Montana PLAINS

22 Blue Lake Rancheria, California CALIFORNIA

23 Bridgeport Indian Colony GREAT BASIN

24 Buena Vista Rancheria of Me-Wuk Indians of California CALIFORNIA

25 Burns Paiute Tribe GREAT BASIN

26 Cabazon Band of Mission Indians, California CALIFORNIA

27 Cachil DeHe Band of Wintun Indians of the Colusa Indian Community of the Colusa Rancheria, California CALIFORNIA

28 Caddo Nation of Oklahoma PLAINS

29 Cahto Tribe CALIFORNIA

30 Cahuilla Band of Mission Indians of the Cahuilla Reservation, California CALIFORNIA

31 California Valley Miwok Tribe, California CALIFORNIA

32 Campo Band of Diegueno Mission Indians of the Campo Indian Reservation, California CALIFORNIA

33 Capitan Grande Band of Diegueno Mission Indians of California: Barona Group of Capitan Grande Band of Mission Indians of the Barona Reservation, California CALIFORNIA

34 Capitan Grande Band of Diegueno Mission Indians of California: Viejas (Baron Long) Group of Capitan Grande Band of Mission Indians of the Viejas Reservation, California CALIFORNIA

35 Catawba Indian Nation (aka Catawba Tribe of South Carolina) SOUTHEAST

36 Cayuga Nation NORTHEAST

37 Cedarville Rancheria, Cafifornia CALIFORNIA

38 Chemehuevi Indian Tribe of the Chemehuevi Reservation, California GREAT BASIN

39 Cher-Ae Heights Indian Community of the Trinidad Rancheria, California CALIFORNIA

40 Cherokee Nation PLAINS

41 Cheyenne and Arapaho Tribes, Oklahoma PLAINS

42 Cheyenne River Sioux Tribe of the Cheyenne River Reservation, South Dakota PLAINS

43 Chickasaw Nation PLAINS

44 Chicken Ranch Rancheria of Me-Wuk Indians of California CALIFORNIA

45 Chippewa-Cree Indians of the Rocky Boy's Reservation, Montana PLAINS

46 Chitimacha Tribe of Louisiana SOUTHEAST

47 Choctaw Nation of Oklahoma PLAINS

48 Citizen Potawatomi Nation, Oklahoma PLAINS

49 Cloverdale Rancheria of Pomo Indians of California CALIFORNIA

50 Cocopah Tribe of Arizona SOUTHWEST

51 Coeur D'Alene Tribe PLATEAU

52 Cold Springs Rancheria of Mono Indians of California CALIFORNIA

53 Colorado River Indian Tribes of the Colorado River Indian Reservation, Arizona and California CALIFORNIA

54 Comanche Nation, Oklahoma   PLAINS

55 Confederated Salish and Kootenai Tribes of the Flathead Reservation PLATEAU

56 Confederated Tribes and Bands of the Yakama Nation PLATEAU

57 Confederated Tribes of Siletz Indians of Oregon NORTHWEST COAST

58 Confederated Tribes of the Chehalis Reservation NORTHWEST COAST

59 Confederated Tribes of the Colville Reservation PLATEAU

60 Confederated Tribes of the Coos, Lower Umpqua and Siuslaw Indians NORTHWEST COAST

61 Confederated Tribes of the Goshute Reservation, Nevada and Utah GREAT BASIN

62 Confederated Tribes of the Grand Ronde Community of Oregon NORTHWEST COAST

63 Confederated Tribes of the Umatilla Indian Reservation NORTHWEST COAST

64 Confederated Tribes of the Warm Springs Reservation of Oregon PLATEAU

65 Coquille Indian Tribe NORTHWEST COAST

66 Cortina Indian Rancheria of Wintun Indians of California CALIFORNIA

67 Coushatta Tribe of Louisiana SOUTHEAST

68 Cow Creek Band of Umpqua Tribe of Indians NORTHWEST COAST

69 Cowlitz Indian Tribe NORTHWEST COAST

70 Coyote Valley Reservation CALIFORNIA

71 Crow Creek Sioux Tribe of the Crow Creek Reservation, South Dakota PLAINS

72 Crow Tribe of Montana PLAINS

73 Death Valley Timbi-sha Shoshone Tribe CALIFORNIA

74 Delaware Nation, Oklahoma PLAINs

75 Delaware Tribe of Indians PLAINS

76 Dry Creek Rancheria Band of Pomo Indians, California CALIFORNIA

77 Duckwater Shoshone Tribe of the Duckwater Reservation, Nevada GREAT BASIN

78 Eastern Band of Cherokee Indians SOUTHEAST

79 Eastern Shawnee Tribe of Oklahoma PLAINS

80 Elem Indian Colony of Pomo Indians of the Sulphur Bank Rancheria, California CALIFORNIA

81 Elk Valley Rancheria, California CALIFORNIA

82 Ely Shoshone Tribe of Nevada GREAT BASIN

83 Enterprise Rancheria of Maidu Indians of California CALIFORNIA

84 Ewiiaapaayp Band of Kumeyaay Indians, California CALIFORNIA

85 Federated Indians of Graton Rancheria, California CALIFORNIA

86 Flandreau Santee Sioux Tribe of South Dakota PLAINS

87 Forest County Potawatomi Community, Wisconsin NORTHEAST

88 Fort Belknap Indian Community of the Fort Belknap Reservation of Montana PLAINS

89 Fort Bidwell Indian Community of the Fort Bidwell Reservation of California CALIFORNIA

90 Fort Independence Indian Community of Paiute Indians of the Fort Independence Reservation, California GREAT BASIN

91 Fort McDermitt Paiute and Shoshone Tribes of the Fort McDermitt Indian Reservation, Nevada and Oregon GREAT BASIN

92 Fort McDowell Yavapai Nation, Arizona SOUTHWEST

93 Fort Mojave Indian Tribe of Arizona, California & Nevada SOUTHWEST

94 Fort Sill Apache Tribe of Oklahoma PLAINS

95 Gila River Indian Community of the Gila River Indian Reservation, Arizona SOUTHWEST

96 Grand Traverse Band of Ottawa and Chippewa Indians, Michigan NORTHEAST

97 Greenville Rancheria CALIFORNIA

98 Grindstone Indian Rancheria of Wintun-Wailaki Indians of California CALIFORNIA

99 Guidiville Rancheria of California CALIFORNIA

100 Habematolel Pomo of Upper Lake, California CALIFORNIA

101 Hannahville Indian Community, Michigan NORTHEAST

102 Havasupai Tribe of the Havasupai Reservation, Arizona SOUTHWEST

103 Ho-Chunk Nation of Wisconsin NORTHEAST

104 Hoh Indian Tribe NORTHWEST COAST

105 Hoopa Valley Tribe, California CALIFORNIA

106 Hopi Tribe of Arizona SOUTHWEST

107 Hopland Band of Pomo Indians, California CALIFORNIA

108 Houlton Band of Maliseet Indians NORTHEAST

109 Hualapai Indian Tribe of the Hualapai Indian Reservation, Arizona SOUTHWEST

110 Iipay Nation of Santa Ysabel, California CALIFORNIA

111 Inaja Band of Diegueno Mission Indians of the Inaja and Cosmit Reservation, California CALIFORNIA

112 Ione Band of Miwok Indians of California CALIFORNIA

113 Iowa Tribe of Kansas and Nebraska PLAINS

114 Iowa Tribe of Oklahoma PLAINS

115 Jackson Rancheria of Me-Wuk Indians of California CALIFORNIA

116 Jamestown S'Klallam Tribe NORTHWEST COAST

117 Jamul Indian Village of California CALIFORNIA

118 Jena Band of Choctaw Indians   SOUTHEAST

119 Jicarilla Apache Nation, New Mexico SOUTHWEST

120 Kaibab Band of Paiute Indians of the Kaibab Indian Reservation, Arizona GREAT BASIN

121 Kalispel Indian Community of the Kalispel Reservation PLATEAU

122 Karuk Tribe CALIFORNIA

123 Kasbia Band of Pomo Indians of the Stewarts Point Rancheria, California CALIFORNIA

124 Kaw Nation, Oklahoma PLAINS

125 Kewa Pueblo, New Mexico SOUTHWEST

126 Keweenaw Bay Indian Community, Michigan NORTHEAST

127 Kialegee Tribal Town PLAINS

128 Kickapoo Traditional Tribe of Texas SOUTHWEST

129 Kickapoo Tribe of Indians of the Kickapoo Reservation in Kansas PLAINS

130 Kickapoo Tribe of Oklahoma PLAINS

131 Kiowa Indian Tribe of Oklahoma PLAINS

132 Klamath Tribes PLATEAU

133 Kootenai Tribe of Idaho PLATEAU

134 La Jolla Band of Luiseno Indians, California CALIFORNIA

135 La Posta Band of Diegueno Mission Indians of the La Posta Indian Reservation, California CALIFORNIA

136 Lac Courte Oreilles Band of Lake Superior Chippewa Indians of Wisconsin NORTHEAST

137 Lac du Flambeau Band of Lake Superior Chippewa Indians of the Lac du Flambeau Reservation of Wisconsin NORTHEAST

138 Lac Vieux Desert Band of Lake Superior Chippewa Indians, Michigan NORTHEAST

139 Las Vegas Tribe of Paiute Indians of the Las Vegas Indian Colony, Nevada GREAT BASIN

140 Little River Band of Ottawa Indians, Michigan NORTHEAST

141 Little Traverse Bay Bands of Odawa Indians, Michigan NORTHEAST

142 Lone Pine Paiute-Shoshone Tribe GREAT BASIN

143 Los Coyotes Band of Cahuilla and Cupeno Indians, California CALIFORNIA

144 Lovelock Paiute Tribe of the Lovelock Indian Colony, Nevada GREAT BASIN

145 Lower Brule Sioux Tribe of the Lower Brule Reservation, South Dakota PLAINS

146 Lower Elwha Tribal Community NORTHWEST COAST

147 Lower Lake Rancheria, California CALIFORNIA

148 Lower Sioux Indian Community in the State of Minnesota PLAINS

149 Lummi Tribe of the Lummi Reservation NORTHWEST COAST

150 Lytton Rancheria of California CALIFORNIA

151 Makah Indian Tribe of the Makah Indian Reservation NORTHWEST COAST

152 Manchester Band of Pomo Indians of the Manchester Rancheria, California CALIFORNIA

153 Manzanita Band of Diegueno Mission Indians of the Manzanita Reservation, California CALIFORNIA

154 Mashantucket Pequot Indian Tribe NORTHEAST

155 Mashpee Wampanoag Indian Tribal Council, Inc. NORTHEAST

156 Match-e-be-nash-she-wish Band of Pottawatomi Indians of Michigan NORTHEAST

157 Mechoopda Indian Tribe of Chico Rancheria, California CALIFORNIA

158 Menominee Indian Tribe of Wisconsin NORTHEAST

159 Mesa Grande Band of Diegueno Mission Indians of the Mesa Grande Reservation, California CALIFORNIA

160 Mescalero Apache Tribe of the Mescalero Reservation, New Mexico SOUTHWEST

161 Miami Tribe of Oklahoma PLAINS

162 Miccosukee Tribe of Indians SOUTHEAST

163 Middletown Rancheria of Pomo Indians of California CALIFORNIA

164 Minnesota Chippewa Tribe, Minnesota: Bois Forte Band (Nett Lake) NORTHEAST

165 Minnesota Chippewa Tribe, Minnesota: Fond du Lac Band NORTHEAST

166 Minnesota Chippewa Tribe, Minnesota: Grand Portage Band NORTHEAST

167 Minnesota Chippewa Tribe, Minnesota: Leech Lake Band NORTHEAST

168 Minnesota Chippewa Tribe, Minnesota: Mille Lacs Band NORTHEAST

169 Minnesota Chippewa Tribe, Minnesota: White Earth Band NORTHEAST

170 Mississippi Band of Choctaw Indians SOUTHEAST

171 Moapa Band of Paiute Indians of the Moapa River Indian Reservation, Nevada GREAT BASIN

172 Modoc Tribe of Oklahoma PLAINS

173 Mohegan Indian Tribe of Connecticut NORTHEAST

174 Mooretown Rancheria of Maidu Indians of California CALIFORNIA

175 Morongo Band of Mission Indians, California CALIFORNIA

176 Muckleshoot Indian Tribe NORTHWEST COAST

177 Narragansett Indian Tribe NORTHEAST

178 Navajo Nation, Arizona, New Mexico & Utah SOUTHWEST

179 Nez Perce Tribe PLATEAU

180 Nisqually Indian Tribe NORTHWEST COAST

181 Nooksack Indian Tribe NORTHWEST COAST

182 Northern Cheyenne Tribe of the Northern Cheyenne Indian Reservation, Montana PLAINS

183 Northfork Rancheria of Mono Indians of California CALIFORNIA

184 Northwestern Band of Shoshoni Nation GREAT BASIN

185 Nottawaseppi Huron Band of the Potawatomi, Michigan NORTHEAST

186 Oglala Sioux Tribe PLAINS

187 Ohkay Owingeh, New Mexico SOUTHWEST

188 Omaha Tribe of Nebraska PLAINS

189 Oneida Nation of New York NORTHEAST

190 Oneida Tribe of Indians of Wisconsin NORTHEAST

191 Onondaga Nation NORTHEAST

192 Otoe-Missouria Tribe of Indians, Oklahoma PLAINS

193 Ottawa Tribe of Oklahoma PLAINS

194 Paiute Indian Tribe of Utah: Cedar Band of Paiutes GREAT BASIN

195 Paiute Indian Tribe of Utah: Indian Peaks Band of Paiutes GREAT BASIN

196 Paiute Indian Tribe of Utah: Kanosh Band of Paiutes GREAT BASIN

197 Paiute Indian Tribe of Utah: Koosharem Band of Paiutes GREAT BASIN

198 Paiute Indian Tribe of Utah: Shivwits Band of Paiutes GREAT BASIN

199 Paiute-Shoshone Tribe of the Fallon Reservation and Colony, Nevada GREAT BASIN

200 Pala Band of Luiseno Mission Indians of the Pala Reservation, California CALIFORNIA

201 Pascua Yaqui Tribe of Arizona SOUTHWEST

202 Paskenta Band of Nomlaki Indians of California CALIFORNIA

203 Passamaquoddy Tribe NORTHEAST

204 Pauma Band of Luiseno Mission Indians of the Pauma & Yuima Reservation, California CALIFORNIA

205 Pawnee Nation of Oklahoma PLAINS

206 Pechanga Band of Luiseno Mission Indians of the Pechanga Reservation, California CALIFORNIA

207 Penobscot Nation NORTHEAST

208 Peoria Tribe of Indians of Oklahoma PLAINS

209 Picayune Rancheria of Chukchansi Indians of California CALIFORNIA

210 Pinoleville Pomo Nation, California CALIFORNIA

211 Pit River Tribe, California: Big Bend Rancheria CALIFORNIA

212 Pit River Tribe, California: Likely Rancheria CALIFORNIA

213 Pit River Tribe, California: Lookout Rancheria CALIFORNIA

214 Pit River Tribe, California: Montgomery Creek Rancheria CALIFORNIA

215 Pit River Tribe, California: Roaring Creek Rancheria CALIFORNIA

216 Pit River Tribe, California: XL Ranch Rancheria CALIFORNIA

217 Poarch Band of Creeks SOUTHEAST

218 Pokagon Band of Potawatomi Indians, Michigan and Indiana NORTHEAST

219 Ponca Tribe of Indians of Oklahoma PLAINS

220 Ponca Tribe of Nebraska PLAINS

221 Port Gamble Band of S'Klallam Indians NORTHWEST COAST

222 Potter Valley Tribe, California CALIFORNIA

223 Prairie Band Potawatomi Nation PLAINS

224 Prairie Island Indian Community in the State of Minnesota PLAINS

225 Pueblo of Acoma, New Mexico SOUTHWEST

226 Pueblo of Cochiti, New Mexico SOUTHWEST

227 Pueblo of Isleta, New Mexico SOUTHWEST

228 Pueblo of Jemez, New Mexico SOUTHWEST

229 Pueblo of Laguna, New Mexico SOUTHWEST

230 Pueblo of Nambe, New Mexico SOUTHWEST

231 Pueblo of Picuris, New Mexico SOUTHWEST

232 Pueblo of Pojoaque, New Mexico SOUTHWEST

233 Pueblo of San Felipe, New Mexico SOUTHWEST

234 Pueblo of San Ildefonso, New Mexico SOUTHWEST

235 Pueblo of Sandia, New Mexico SOUTHWEST

236 Pueblo of Santa Ana, New Mexico SOUTHWEST

237 Pueblo of Santa Clara, New Mexico SOUTHWEST

238 Pueblo of Taos, New Mexico SOUTHWEST

239 Pueblo of Tesuque, New Mexico SOUTHWEST

240 Pueblo of Zia, New Mexico SOUTHWEST

241 Puyallup Tribe of the Puyallup Reservation NORTHWEST COAST

242 Pyramid Lake Paiute Tribe of the Pyramid Lake Reservation, Nevada GREAT BASIN

243 Quapaw Tribe of Indians PLAINS

244 Quartz Valley Indian Community of the Quartz Valley Reservation of California CALIFORNIA

245 Quechan Tribe of the Fort Yuma Indian Reservation, California & Arizona CALIFORNIA

246 Quileute Tribe of the Quileute Reservation NORTHWEST COAST

247 Quinault Indian Nation NORTHWEST COAST

248 Ramona Band of Cahuilla, California CALIFORNIA

249 Red Cliff Band of Lake Superior Chippewa Indians of Wisconsin NORTHEAST

250 Red Lake Band of Chippewa Indians, Minnesota NORTHEAST

251 Redding Rancheria, California CALIFORNIA

252 Redwood Valley or Little River Band of Pomo Indians of the Redwood Valley Rancheria California CALIFORNIA

253 Reno-Sparks Indian Colony, Nevada GREAT BASIN

254 Resighini Rancheria, California CALIFORNIA

255 Rincon Band of Luiseno Mission Indians of the Rincon Reservation, California CALIFORNIA

256 Robinson Rancheria Band of Pomo Indians, California CALIFORNIA

257 Rosebud Sioux Tribe of the Rosebud Indian Reservation, South Dakota PLAINS

258 Round Valley Indian Tribes, Round Valley Reservation, California CALIFORNIA

259 Sac & Fox Nation of Missouri in Kansas and Nebraska PLAINS

260 Sac & Fox Nation, Oklahoma PLAINS

261 Sac & Fox Tribe of the Mississippi in Iowa PLAINS

262 Saginaw Chippewa Indian Tribe of Michigan NORTHEAST

263 Saint Regis Mohawk Tribe NORTHEAST

264 Salt River Pima-Maricopa Indian Community of the Salt River Reservation, Arizona SOUTHWEST

265 Samish Indian Nation NORTHWEST COAST

266 San Carlos Apache Tribe of the San Carlos Reservation, Arizona SOUTHWEST

267 San Juan Southern Paiute Tribe of Arizona GREAT BASIN

268 San Manuel Band of Mission Indians, California CALIFORNIA

269 San Pasqual Band of Diegueno Mission Indians of California CALIFORNIA

270 Santa Rosa Band of Cahuilla Indians, California CALIFORNIA

271 Santa Rosa Indian Community of the Santa Rosa Rancheria, California CALIFORNIA

272 Santa Ynez Band of Chumash Mission Indians of the Santa Ynez Reservation, California CALIFORNIA

273 Santee Sioux Nation, Nebraska PLAINS

274 Sauk-Suiattle Indian Tribe NORTHWEST COAST

275 Sault Ste. Marie Tribe of Chippewa Indians of Michigan NORTHEAST

276 Scotts Valley Band of Pomo Indians of California CALIFORNIA

277 Seminole Tribe of Florida SOUTHEAST

278 Seminole Tribe of Florida SOUTHEAST

279 Seminole Tribe of Florida SOUTHEAST

280 Seminole Tribe of Florida SOUTHEAST

281 Seminole Tribe of Florida SOUTHEAST

282 Seneca Nation of Indians NORTHEAST

283 Seneca-Cayuga Tribe of Oklahoma PLAINS

284 Shakopee Mdewakanton Sioux Community of Minnesota PLAINS

285 Shawnee Tribe PLAINS

286 Sherwood Valley Rancheria of Pomo Indians of California CALIFORNIA

287 Shingle Springs Band of Miwok Indians, Shingle Springs Rancheria (Verona Tract), California CALIFORNIA

288 Shinnecock Indian Nation NORTHEAST

289 Shoalwater Bay Indian Tribe of the Shoalwater Bay Indian Reservation NORTHWEST COAST

290 Shoshone Tribe of the Wind River Reservation, Wyoming GREAT BASIN

291 Shoshone-Bannock Tribes of the Fort Hall Reservation GREAT BASIN

292 Shoshone-Paiute Tribes of the Duck Valley Reservation, Nevada GREAT BASIN

293 Sisseton-Wahpeton Oyate of the Lake Traverse Reservation, South Dakota PLAINS

294 Skokomish Indian Tribe NORTHWEST COAST

295 Skull Valley Band of Goshute Indians of Utah GREAT BASIN

296 Smith River Rancheria, California CALIFORNIA

297 Snoqualmie Indian Tribe NORTHWEST COAST

298 Soboba Band of Luiseno Indians, California CALIFORNIA

299 Sokaogon Chippewa Community, Wisconsin NORTHEAST

300 Southern Ute Indian Tribe of the Southern Ute Reservation, Colorado GREAT BASIN

301 Spirit Lake Tribe, North Dakota PLAINS

302 Spokane Tribe of the Spokane Reservation PLATEAU

303 Squaxin Island Tribe of the Squaxin Island Reservation NORTHWEST COAST

304 St. Croix Chippewa Indians of Wisconsin NORTHEAST

305 Standing Rock Sioux Tribe of North & South Dakota PLAINS

306 Stillaguamish Tribe of Indians of Washington NORTHWEST COAST

307 Stockbridge Munsee Community, Wisconsin NORTHEAST

308 Summit Lake Paiute Tribe of Nevada GREAT BASIN

309 Suquamish Indian Tribe of the Port Madison Reservation NORTHWEST COAST

310 Susanville Indian Rancheria, California CALIFORNIA

311 Swinomish Indians of the Swinomish Reservation of Washington NORTHWEST COAST

312 Sycuan Band of the Kumeyaay Nation CALIFORNIA

313 Table Mountain Rancheria of California CALIFORNIA

314 Tejon Indian Tribe CALIFORNIA

315 Te-Moak Tribe of Western Shoshone Indians of Nevada: Battle Mountain Band GREAT BASIN

316 Te-Moak Tribe of Western Shoshone Indians of Nevada: Elko Band GREAT BASIN

317 Te-Moak Tribe of Western Shoshone Indians of Nevada: South Fork Band GREAT BASIN

318 Te-Moak Tribe of Western Shoshone Indians of Nevada: Wells Band GREAT BASIN

319 The Muscogee (Creek) Nation PLAINS

320 The Osage Nation PLAINS

321 The Seminole Nation of Oklahoma PLAINS

322 Thlopthlocco Tribal Town PLAINS

323 Three Affiliated Tribes of the Fort Berthold Reservation, North Dakota PLAINS

324 Tohono O'odham Nation of Arizona SOUTHWEST

325 Tonawanda Band of Seneca NORTHEAST

326 Tonkawa Tribe of Indians of Oklahoma PLAINS

327 Tonto Apache Tribe of Arizona SOUTHWEST

328 Torres Martinez Desert Cahuilla Indians, California CALIFORNIA

329 Tulalip Tribes of Washington NORTHWEST COAST

330 Tule River Indian Tribe of the Tule River Reservation, California CALIFORNIA

331 Tunica-Biloxi Indian Tribe SOUTHEAST

332 Tuolumne Band of Me-Wuk Indians of the Tuolumne Rancheria of California CALIFORNIA

333 Turtle Mountain Band of Chippewa Indians of North Dakota PLAINS

334 Tuscarora Nation NORTHEAST

335 Twenty-Nine Palms Band of Mission Indians of California CALIFORNIA

336 United Auburn Indian Community of the Auburn Rancheria of California CALIFORNIA

337 United Keetoowah Band of Cherokee Indians in Oklahoma PLAINS

338 Upper Sioux Community, Minnesota PLAINS

339 Upper Skagit Indian Tribe NORTHWEST COAST

340 Ute Indian Tribe of the Uintah & Ouray Reservation, Utah GREAT BASIN

341 Ute Mountain Tribe of the Ute Mountain Reservation, Colorado, New Mexico & Utah SOUTHWEST

342 Utu Utu Gwaitu Paiute Tribe of the Benton Paiute Reservation, California GREAT BASIN

343 Walker River Paiute Tribe of the Walker River Reservation, Nevada GREAT BASIN

344 Wampanoag Tribe of Gay Head (Aquinnah) NORTHEAST

345 Washoe Tribe of Nevada & California: Carson Colony CALIFORNIA

346 Washoe Tribe of Nevada & California: Dresslerville Colony CALIFORNIA

347 Washoe Tribe of Nevada & California: Stewart Community CALIFORNIA

348 Washoe Tribe of Nevada & California: Washoe Ranches CALIFORNIA

349 Washoe Tribe of Nevada & California: Woodfords Community CALIFORNIA

350 White Mountain Apache Tribe of the Fort Apache Reservation, Arizona SOUTHWEST

351 Wichita and Affiliated Tribes (Wichita, Keechi, Waco & Tawakonie), Oklahoma PLAINS

352 Wilton Rancheria, California CALIFORNIA

353 Winnebago Tribe of Nebraska PLAINS

354 Winnemucca Indian Colony of Nevada GREAT BASIN

355 Wiyot Tribe, California CALIFORNIA

356 Wyandotte Nation PLAINS

357 Yankton Sioux Tribe of South Dakota PLAINS

358 Yavapai-Apache Nation of the Camp Verde Indian Reservation, Arizona SOUTHWEST

359 Yavapai-Prescott Indian Tribe SOUTHWEST

360 Yerington Paiute Tribe of the Yerington Colony & Campbell Ranch, Nevada GREAT BASIN

361 Yocha Dehe Wintun Nation, California CALIFORNIA

362 Yomba Shoshone Tribe of the Yomba Reservation, Nevada GREAT BASIN

363 Ysleta Del Sur Pueblo of Texas SOUTHWEST

364 Yurok Tribe of the Yurok Reservation, California CALIFORNIA

365 Zuni Tribe of the Zuni Reservation, New Mexico SOUTHWEST

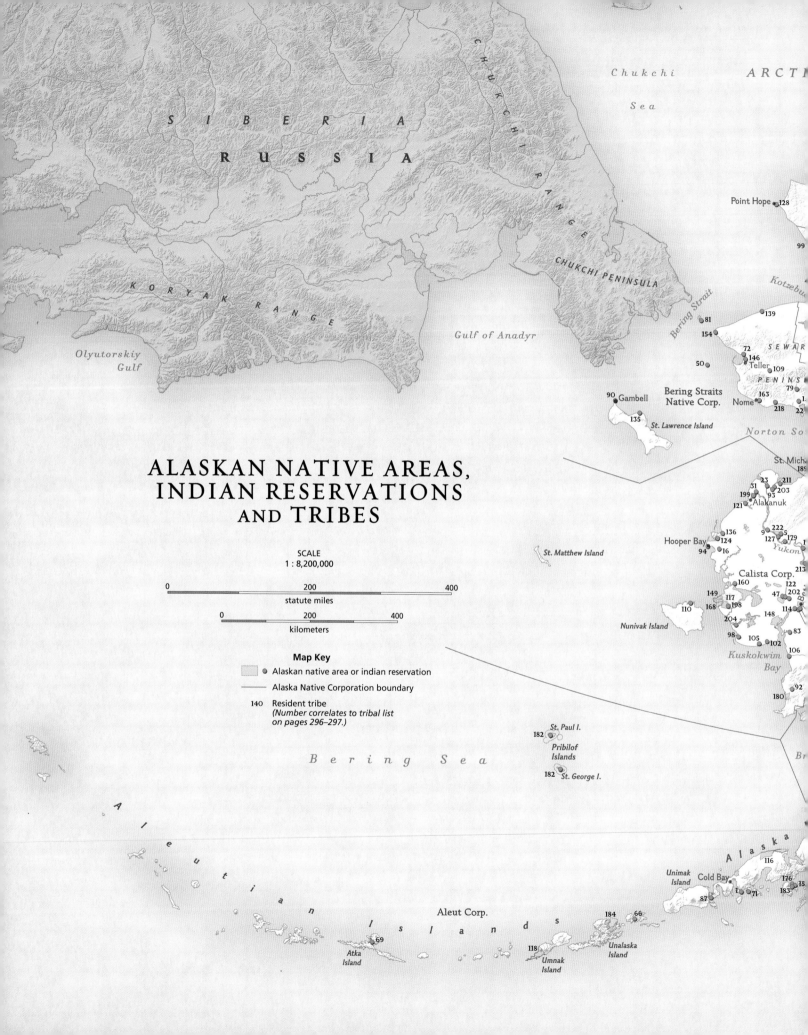

ALASKAN NATIVE AREAS, INDIAN RESERVATIONS AND TRIBES

SCALE
1 : 8,200,000

0   200   400
statute miles

0   200   400
kilometers

Map Key

Alaskan native area or indian reservation

Alaska Native Corporation boundary

140   Resident tribe
*(Number correlates to tribal list
on pages 296–297.)*

*Chukchi
Sea*

ARCTI

S I B E R I A

R U S S I A

CHUKCHI RANGE

CHUKCHI PENINSULA

Point Hope ● 128

99

Kotzebu

Bering Strait

Gulf of Anadyr

● 81

139

154

K O R Y A K   R A N G E

72   SEWAR

146   Teller   109

*Olyutorskiy
Gulf*

50 ●

79   PENINS

90   Gambell

163

Bering Straits
Native Corp.

Nome   218   22

135   *St. Lawrence Island*

Norton So

St. Mich

189

23   211

31   199   93   203

121   Alakanuk

St. Matthew Island

136   222
124   9   127   179
Hooper Bay   16   5   213
94

Calista Corp.   122   202
160   47   114
149   117   198   83
110   168   204   106
Nunivak Island   98   105   102   180   92

*Kuskokwim
Bay*

B e r i n g   S e a

182   St. Paul I.
*Pribilof
Islands*

182   St. George I.

A

A l e u t i a n

Alaska

116

Unimak
Island   Cold Bay   176   15
87   71   183

Aleut Corp.

184   66

59

118

*Atka
Island*   *Umnak
Island*   *Unalaska
Island*

I s l a n d s

OCEAN

Beaufort Sea

NUNAVUT

Barrow 70
42

Wainwright
220
10

Teshekpuk
Lake

120 Prudhoe
Bay

46

N O R T H   S L O P E

Colville

Sagavanirktok

Arctic Slope
Regional Corp.

UNITED STATES
CANADA

N O R T H W E S T

T E R R I T O R I E S

B R O O K S   R A N G E

Arctic Village
200
153

NANA
Regional
Corp.

97 68

Selawik
137
140 101

Chandalar

Porcupine

153

88   14
Fort Yukon

Y U K O N

Kobuk

32

4
6

Beaver
11
12

Circle
24

Koyukuk

38

Huslia
39

141

Doyon Ltd.

185

82

143
58   111

55
167
33 Galena
133

Yukon

156

Fairbanks

A L A S K A

Tanana

210

alakleet

35

207
Tanacross
142   147 166

Mt. McKinley
(Denali)
20,320 ft
(6194 m)

193

K U S K O K W I M   M O U N T A I N S

74

R A N G E

61

187 Iditarod
191 60
161

15
Gulkana 89
34
145
100

B R I T I S H
C O L U M B I A

206 91
78 215
113 217 219

57

53

17

77

AHTNA
Inc.

UNITED STATES
CANADA

Kuskokwim

95 Palmer
Cook Inlet
Region Inc.
29
Anchorage

150

Valdez

144
Cordova
86

221

20
21

Bristol Bay
Native Corp.

48 Kenai
216 Peninsula
Kenai
162

Seward
75

Juneau
27 13

37

157

164
208 177
159

Homer
112 130
186

Chugach Alaska
Corp.

7

67 158 30
181 41
84 56
63
188 51

54

Sealaska
Corp.

170 178

Wrangell

Afognak Island

126
197
28

64
132 123
192 190 Kodiak
107
96

Shelikof Strait

Gulf of Alaska

A l e x a n d e r   A r c h i p e l a g o

171 49 173
52 25
40   62

214 Kodiak
65 45 Island

Koniag
Inc.

USING THE MAPS
An important distinction needs to be considered when utilizing this atlas.
Our style is to label, on the large-scale regional maps, particular reserves in
Canada and reservations in the U.S. The lists at the back of this book are of
tribal entities. Reserves or reservations represent the modern geographic
situation of a people, in many cases far from an ancestral homeland. A tribe
embodies their cultural, linguistic, and traditional heritage. Our methodology
in presenting this daunting subject, in a way befitting the scope of this book,
was to limit our map coverage to those tribal entities given formal recognition
by the governments of Canada or the United States.

PACIFIC OCEAN

NATIVE ENTITIES WITHIN THE STATE OF ALASKA RECOGNIZED AND ELIGIBLE TO RECEIVE SERVICES FROM THE UNITED STATES BUREAU OF INDIAN AFFAIRS

1   Agdaagux Tribe of King Cove
2   Akiachak Native Community
3   Akiak Native Community
4   Alatna Village
5   Algaaciq Native Village (St. Mary's)
6   Allakaket Village
7   Angoon Community Association
8   Anvik Village
9   Asa'carsarmiut Tribe
10 Atqasuk Village (Atkasook)
11 Beaver Village
12 Birch Creek Tribe
13 Central Council of the Tlingit & Haida Indian Tribes
14 Chalkyitsik Village
15 Cheesh-Na Tribe (previously listed as the Native Village of Chistochina)
16 Chevak Native Village
17 Chickaloon Native Village
18 Chignik Bay Tribal Council (previously listed as the Native Village of Chignik)
19 Chignik Lake Village
20 Chilkat Indian Village (Klukwan)
21 Chilkoot Indian Association (Haines)
22 Chinik Eskimo Community (Golovin)
23 Chuloonawick Native Village
24 Circle Native Community
25 Craig Tribal Association (previously listed as the Craig Community Association)
26 Curyung Tribal Council
27 Douglas Indian Association
28 Egegik Village
29 Eklutna Native Village
30 Ekwok Village
31 Emmonak Village
32 Evansville Village (aka Bettles Field)
33 Galena Village (aka Louden Village)
34 Gulkana Village
35 Healy Lake Village
36 Holy Cross Village
37 Hoonah Indian Association
38 Hughes Village
39 Huslia Village
40 Hydaburg Cooperative Association

41 Igiugig Village
42 Inupiat Community of the Arctic Slope
43 Iqurmuit Traditional Council
44 Ivanoff Bay Village
45 Kaguyak Village
46 Kaktovik Village (aka Barter Island)
47 Kasigluk Traditional Elders Council
48 Kenaitze Indian Tribe
49 Ketchikan Indian Corporation
50 King Island Native Community
51 King Salmon Tribe
52 Klawock Cooperative Association
53 Knik Tribe
54 Kokhanok Village
55 Koyukuk Native Village
56 Levelock Village
57 Lime Village
58 Manley Hot Springs Village
59 Manokotak Village
60 McGrath Native Village
61 Mentasta Traditional Council
62 Metlakatla Indian Community, Annette Island Reserve
63 Naknek Native Village
64 Native Village of Afognak
65 Native Village of Akhiok
66 Native Village of Akutan
67 Native Village of Aleknagik
68 Native Village of Ambler
69 Native Village of Atka
70 Native Village of Barrow Inupiat Traditional Government
71 Native Village of Belkofski
72 Native Village of Brevig Mission
73 Native Village of Buckland
74 Native Village of Cantwell
75 Native Village of Chenega (aka Chanega)
76 Native Village of Chignik Lagoon
77 Native Village of Chitina
78 Native Village of Chuathbaluk (Russian Mission, Kuskokwim)
79 Native Village of Council
80 Native Village of Deering
81 Native Village of Diomede (aka Inalik)
82 Native Village of Eagle
83 Native Village of Eek
84 Native Village of Ekuk

85   Native Village of Elim
86   Native Village of Eyak (Cordova)
87   Native Village of False Pass
88   Native Village of Fort Yukon
89   Native Village of Gakona
90   Native Village of Gambell
91   Native Village of Georgetown
92   Native Village of Goodnews Bay
93   Native Village of Hamilton
94   Native Village of Hooper Bay
95   Native Village of Kanatak
96   Native Village of Karluk
97   Native Village of Kiana
98   Native Village of Kipnuk
99   Native Village of Kivalina
100 Native Village of Kluti Kaah (aka Copper Center)
101 Native Village of Kobuk
102 Native Village of Kongiganak
103 Native Village of Kotzebue
104 Native Village of Koyuk
105 Native Village of Kwigillingok
106 Native Village of Kwinhagak (aka Quinhagak)
107 Native Village of Larsen Bay
108 Native Village of Marshall (aka Fortuna Ledge)
109 Native Village of Mary's Igloo
110 Native Village of Mekoryuk
111 Native Village of Minto
112 Native Village of Nanwalek (aka English Bay)
113 Native Village of Napaimute
114 Native Village of Napakiak
115 Native Village of Napaskiak
116 Native Village of Nelson Lagoon
117 Native Village of Nightmute
118 Native Village of Nikolski
119 Native Village of Noatak
120 Native Village of Nuiqsut (aka Nooiksut)
121 Native Village of Nunam Iqua (previously listed as the Native Village of Sheldon's Point)
122 Native Village of Nunapitchuk
123 Native Village of Ouzinkie
124 Native Village of Paimiut
125 Native Village of Perryville
126 Native Village of Pilot Point
127 Native Village of Pitka's Point
128 Native Village of Point Hope
129 Native Village of Point Lay

130 Native Village of Port Graham

131 Native Village of Port Heiden

132 Native Village of Port Lions

133 Native Village of Ruby

134 Native Village of Saint Michael

135 Native Village of Savoonga

136 Native Village of Scammon Bay

137 Native Village of Selawik

138 Native Village of Shaktoolik

139 Native Village of Shishmaref

140 Native Village of Shungnak

141 Native Village of Stevens

142 Native Village of Tanacross

143 Native Village of Tanana

144 Native Village of Tatitlek

145 Native Village of Tazlina

146 Native Village of Teller

147 Native Village of Tetlin

148 Native Village of Tuntutuliak

149 Native Village of Tununak

150 Native Village of Tyonek

151 Native Village of Unalakleet

152 Native Village of Unga

153 Native Village of Venetie Tribal Government (Arctic Village and Village of Venetie)

154 Native Village of Wales

155 Native Village of White Mountain

156 Nenana Native Association

157 New Koliganek Village Council

158 New Stuyahok Village

159 Newhalen Village

160 Newtok Village

161 Nikolai Village

162 Ninilchik Village

163 Nome Eskimo Community

164 Nondalton Village

165 Noorvik Native Community

166 Northway Village

167 Nulato Village

168 Nunakauyarmiut Tribe

169 Organized Village of Grayling (aka Holikachuk)

170 Organized Village of Kake

171 Organized Village of Kasaan

172 Organized Village of Kwethluk

173 Organized Village of Saxman

174 Orutsararmuit Native Village (aka Bethel)

175 Oscarville Traditional Village

176 Pauloff Harbor Village

177 Pedro Bay Village

178 Petersburg Indian Association

179 Pilot Station Traditional Village

180 Platinum Traditional Village

181 Portage Creek Village (aka Ohgsenakale)

182 Pribilof Islands Aleut Communities of St. Paul & St. George Islands

183 Qagan Tayagungin Tribe of Sand Point Village

184 Qawalangin Tribe of Unalaska

185 Rampart Village

186 Seldovia Village Tribe

187 Shageluk Native Village

188 South Naknek Village

189 Stebbins Community Association

190 Sun'aq Tribe of Kodiak (previously listed as the Shoonaq' Tribe of Kodiak)

191 Takotna Village

192 Tangirnaq Native Village (formerly Lesnoi Village (aka Woody Island))

193 Telida Village

194 Traditional Village of Togiak

195 Tuluksak Native Community

196 Twin Hills Village

197 Ugashik Village

198 Umkumiut Native Village (previously listed as Umkumiute Native Village)

199 Village of Alakanuk

200 Village of Anaktuvuk Pass

201 Village of Aniak

202 Village of Atmautluak

203 Village of Bill Moore's Slough

204 Village of Chefornak

205 Village of Clarks Point

206 Village of Crooked Creek

207 Village of Dot Lake

208 Village of Iliamna

209 Village of Kalskag

210 Village of Kaltag

211 Village of Kotlik

212 Village of Lower Kalskag

213 Village of Ohogamiut

214 Village of Old Harbor

215 Village of Red Devil

216 Village of Salamatoff

217 Village of Sleetmute

218 Village of Solomon

219 Village of Stony River

220 Village of Wainwright

221 Yakutat Tlingit Tribe

222 Yupiit of Andreafski

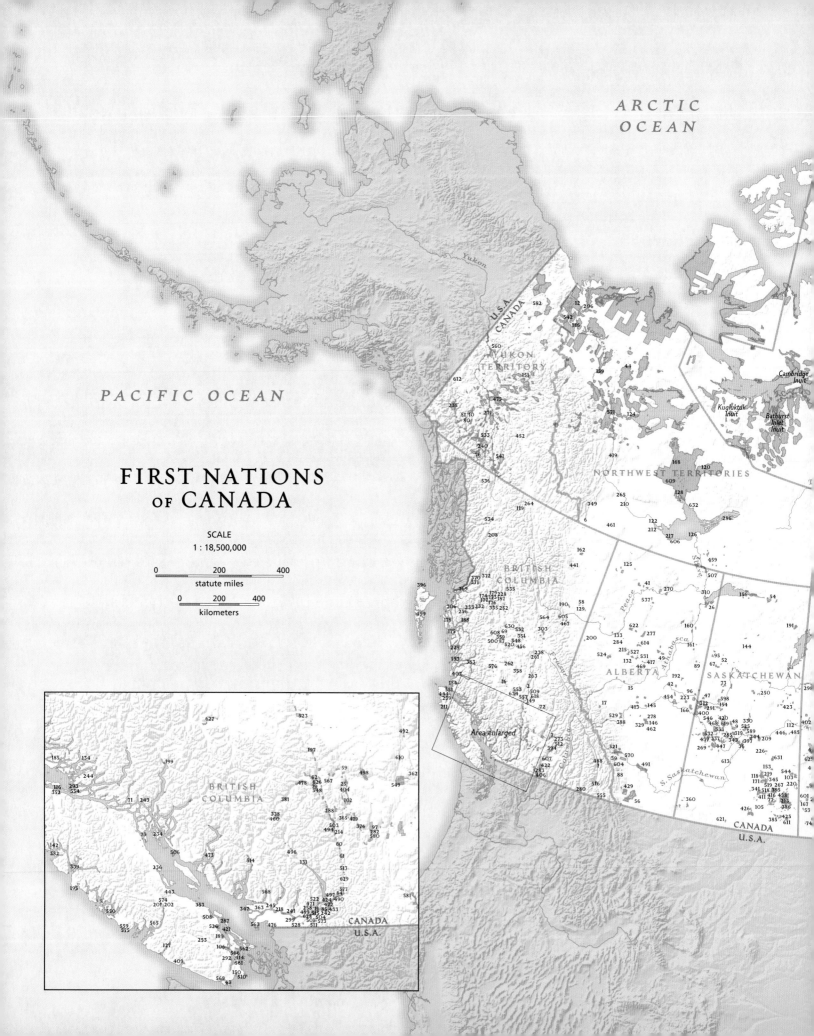

Map Key

Indian Reserves, Indian Lands, and Land Claim Settlement Lands

77 First Nation
(Number correlates to tribal list on pages 300–303.)

USING THE MAPS

An important distinction needs to be considered when utilizing this atlas. Our style is to label, on the large-scale regional maps, particular reserves in Canada and reservations in the U.S. The lists at the back of this book are of tribal entities. Reserves or reservations represent the modern geographic situation of a people, in many cases far from an ancestral homeland. A tribe embodies their cultural, linguistic, and traditional heritage. Our methodology in presenting this daunting subject, in a way befitting the scope of this book, was to limit our map coverage to those tribal entities given formal recognition by the governments of Canada or the United States.

In contrast with the adjacent lists for Alaska and the U.S. contiguous states, the numbers on this map correlate to the Aboriginal peoples—i.e., First Nations, Indian Bands, or Aboriginal communities—rather than to individual land parcels. A single Aboriginal group may be associated with multiple individual reserve areas; in these cases, that group's number is placed roughly in the geographic center of the multiple reserves or locations with which it is associated.

* The ?Akisq'nuk speak the Kutenai language, in which "?" represents a laryngeal stop. The ?Esdilagh speak the Chilcotin language, in which "?" represents a glottal ejective.

1 ?Akisq'nuk First Nation GREAT BASIN
2 ?Esdilagh First Nation GREAT BASIN
3 Aamjiwnaang NORTHEAST
4 Abegweit NORTHEAST
5 Acadia NORTHEAST
6 Acho Dene Koe First Nation ARCTIC/SUBARCTIC
7 Adams Lake GREAT BASIN
8 Ahousaht NORTHWEST COAST
9 Ahtahkakoop PLAINS
10 Aishihik ARCTIC/SUBARCTIC
11 Aitchelitz NORTHWEST COAST
12 Aklavik ARCTIC/SUBARCTIC
13 Albany ARCTIC/SUBARCTIC
14 Alderville First Nation NORTHEAST
15 Alexander PLAINS
16 Alexis Creek ARCTIC/SUBARCTIC
17 Alexis Nakota Sioux Nation PLAINS
18 Algonquins of Barriere Lake NORTHEAST
19 Algonquins of Pikwakanagan NORTHEAST
20 Animbiigoo Zaagi'igan Anishinaabek NORTHEAST
21 Anishinabe of Wauzhushk Onigum ARCTIC/SUBARCTIC
22 Anishnaabeg of Naongashiing ARCTIC/SUBARCTIC
23 Annapolis Valley NORTHEAST
24 Aroland NORTHEAST
25 Ashcroft GREAT BASIN
26 Athabasca Chipewyan First Nation ARCTIC/SUBARCTIC
27 Atikameksheng Anishnawbek NORTHEAST
28 Atikamekw d'Opitciwan ARCTIC/SUBARCTIC
29 Attawapiskat ARCTIC/SUBARCTIC
30 Aundeck-Omni-Kaning NORTHEAST
31 Bande des Innus de Pessamit ARCTIC/SUBARCTIC
32 Barren Lands ARCTIC/SUBARCTIC
33 Batchewana First Nation NORTHEAST
34 Bay of Quinte Mohawk NORTHEAST
35 Bear River NORTHEAST
36 Beardy's and Okemasis PLAINS
37 Bearfoot Onondaga NORTHEAST
38 Bearskin Lake ARCTIC/SUBARCTIC
39 Bearspaw PLAINS
40 Beausoleil NORTHEAST
41 Beaver First Nation ARCTIC/SUBARCTIC
42 Beaver Lake Cree Nation ARCTIC/SUBARCTIC
43 Beecher Bay NORTHWEST COAST
44 Behdzi Ahda First Nation ARCTIC/SUBARCTIC
45 Berens River ARCTIC/SUBARCTIC
46 Big Grassy ARCTIC/SUBARCTIC
47 Big Island Lake Cree Nation ARCTIC/SUBARCTIC

48 Big River PLAINS
49 Bigstone Cree Nation ARCTIC/SUBARCTIC
50 Biinjitiwaabik Zaaging Anishinaabek NORTHEAST
51 Bingwi Neyaashi Anishinaabek NORTHEAST
52 Birch Narrows First Nation ARCTIC/SUBARCTIC
53 Birdtail Sioux PLAINS
54 Black Lake ARCTIC/SUBARCTIC
55 Black River First Nation ARCTIC/SUBARCTIC
56 Blood PLAINS
57 Bloodvein ARCTIC/SUBARCTIC
58 Blueberry River First Nations ARCTIC/SUBARCTIC
59 Bonaparte GREAT BASIN
60 Boothroyd GREAT BASIN
61 Boston Bar First Nation GREAT BASIN
62 Bridge River GREAT BASIN
63 Brokenhead Ojibway Nation ARCTIC/SUBARCTIC
64 Brunswick House NORTHEAST
65 Buctouche NORTHEAST
66 Buffalo Point First Nation ARCTIC/SUBARCTIC
67 Buffalo River Dene Nation ARCTIC/SUBARCTIC
68 Bunibonibee Cree Nation ARCTIC/SUBARCTIC
69 Burns Lake ARCTIC/SUBARCTIC
70 Caldwell NORTHEAST
71 Campbell River NORTHWEST COAST
72 Canim Lake GREAT BASIN
73 Canoe Lake Cree First Nation ARCTIC/SUBARCTIC
74 Canupawakpa Dakota First Nation PLAINS
75 Cape Mudge NORTHWEST COAST
76 Carcross/Tagish First Nations ARCTIC/SUBARCTIC
77 Carry The Kettle PLAINS
78 Cat Lake ARCTIC/SUBARCTIC
79 Cayoose Creek GREAT BASIN
80 Champagne ARCTIC/SUBARCTIC
81 Champagne and Aishihik First Nations ARCTIC/SUBARCTIC
82 Chapleau Cree First Nation NORTHEAST
83 Chapleau Ojibway NORTHEAST
84 Chawathil GREAT BASIN
85 Cheam GREAT BASIN
86 Chemawawin Cree Nation ARCTIC/SUBARCTIC
87 Cheslatta Carrier Nation ARCTIC/SUBARCTIC
88 Chiniki PLAINS
89 Chipewyan Prairie First Nation ARCTIC/SUBARCTIC
90 Chippewas of Georgina Island NORTHEAST
91 Chippewas of Kettle and Stony Point NORTHEAST
92 Chippewas of Nawash First Nation NORTHEAST
93 Chippewas of Rama First Nation NORTHEAST
94 Chippewas of the Thames First Nation NORTHEAST
95 Clearwater River Dene ARCTIC/SUBARCTIC
96 Cold Lake First Nations ARCTIC/SUBARCTIC
97 Coldwater GREAT BASIN
98 Communauté anicinape de Kitcisakik NORTHEAST
99 Conseil de la Première Nation Abitibiwinni ARCTIC/SUBARCTIC
100 Conseil des Atikamekw de Wemotaci ARCTIC/SUBARCTIC
101 Constance Lake NORTHEAST
102 Cook's Ferry GREAT BASIN
103 Cote First Nation 366 PLAINS
104 Couchiching First Nation ARCTIC/SUBARCTIC
105 Cowessess PLAINS
106 Cowichan Tribes First Nation NORTHWEST COAST
107 Cree Nation of Chisasibi ARCTIC/SUBARCTIC

108 Cree Nation of Mistissini ARCTIC/SUBARCTIC
109 Cree Nation of Nemaska ARCTIC/SUBARCTIC
110 Cree Nation of Wemindji ARCTIC/SUBARCTIC
111 Cross Lake First Nation ARCTIC/SUBARCTIC
112 Cumberland House Cree Nation ARCTIC/SUBARCTIC
113 Curve Lake NORTHEAST
114 Dakota Plains PLAINS
115 Dakota Tipi PLAINS
116 Da'naxda'xw First Nation NORTHWEST COAST
117 Dauphin River ARCTIC/SUBARCTIC
118 Day Star PLAINS
119 Dease River ARCTIC/SUBARCTIC
120 Dechi Laot'i First Nations ARCTIC/SUBARCTIC
121 Deer Lake ARCTIC/SUBARCTIC
122 Deh Gáh Got'ie Dene First Nation ARCTIC/SUBARCTIC
123 Delaware NORTHEAST
124 Deline First Nation ARCTIC/SUBARCTIC
125 Dene Tha' ARCTIC/SUBARCTIC
126 Deninu K'ue First Nation ARCTIC/SUBARCTIC
127 Ditidaht NORTHWEST COAST
128 Dog Rib Rae ARCTIC/SUBARCTIC
129 Doig River ARCTIC/SUBARCTIC
130 Dokis NORTHEAST
131 Douglas NORTHWEST COAST
132 Driftpile First Nation ARCTIC/SUBARCTIC
133 Duncan's First Nation ARCTIC/SUBARCTIC
134 Dzawada'enuxw First Nation NORTHWEST COAST
135 Eabametoong First Nation ARCTIC/SUBARCTIC
136 Eagle Lake ARCTIC/SUBARCTIC
137 Eagle Village First Nation - Kipawa NORTHEAST
138 Eastmain ARCTIC/SUBARCTIC
139 Ebb and Flow PLAINS
140 Eel Ground NORTHEAST
141 Eel River Bar First Nation NORTHEAST
142 Ehattesaht NORTHWEST COAST
143 Elsipogtog First Nation NORTHEAST
144 English River First Nation ARCTIC/SUBARCTIC
145 Enoch Cree Nation #440 PLAINS
146 Ermineskin Tribe PLAINS
147 Esgenoopetitj First Nation NORTHEAST
148 Eskasoni NORTHEAST
149 Esk'etemc GREAT BASIN
150 Esquimalt NORTHWEST COAST
151 First Nation of Nacho Nyak Dun ARCTIC/SUBARCTIC
152 Fisher River ARCTIC/SUBARCTIC
153 Fishing Lake First Nation PLAINS
154 Flying Dust First Nation ARCTIC/SUBARCTIC
155 Flying Post NORTHEAST
156 Fond du Lac ARCTIC/SUBARCTIC
157 Fort Alexander ARCTIC/SUBARCTIC
158 Fort Folly NORTHEAST
159 Fort Good Hope ARCTIC/SUBARCTIC
160 Fort McKay First Nation ARCTIC/SUBARCTIC
161 Fort McMurray #468 First Nation ARCTIC/SUBARCTIC
162 Fort Nelson First Nation ARCTIC/SUBARCTIC
163 Fort Severn ARCTIC/SUBARCTIC
164 Fort William NORTHEAST
165 Fox Lake ARCTIC/SUBARCTIC
166 Frog Lake PLAINS
167 Gamblers PLAINS
168 Gameti First Nation ARCTIC/SUBARCTIC
169 Garden Hill First Nations ARCTIC/SUBARCTIC
170 Garden River First Nation NORTHEAST

171 George Gordon First Nation PLAINS
172 Ginoogaming First Nation NORTHEAST
173 Gitanmaax NORTHWEST COAST
174 Gitanyow NORTHWEST COAST
175 Gitga'at First Nation NORTHWEST COAST
176 Gitsegukla NORTHWEST COAST
177 Gitwangak NORTHWEST COAST
178 Gitxaala Nation NORTHWEST COAST
179 Glen Vowell NORTHWEST COAST
180 Glooscap First Nation NORTHEAST
181 God's Lake First Nation ARCTIC/SUBARCTIC
182 Grassy Narrows First Nation ARCTIC/SUBARCTIC
183 Gull Bay NORTHEAST
184 Gwa'Sala-Nakwaxda'xw NORTHWEST COAST
185 Gwawaenuk Tribe NORTHWEST COAST
186 Gwichya Gwich'in ARCTIC/SUBARCTIC
187 Hagwilget Village NORTHWEST COAST
188 Haisla Nation NORTHWEST COAST
189 Halalt NORTHWEST COAST
190 Halfway River First Nation ARCTIC/SUBARCTIC
191 Hatchet Lake ARCTIC/SUBARCTIC
192 Heart Lake ARCTIC/SUBARCTIC
193 Heiltsuk NORTHWEST COAST
194 Henvey Inlet First Nation NORTHEAST
195 Hesquiaht NORTHWEST COAST
196 Hiawatha First Nation NORTHEAST
197 High Bar GREAT BASIN
198 Hollow Water ARCTIC/SUBARCTIC
199 Homalco NORTHWEST COAST
200 Horse Lake First Nation ARCTIC/SUBARCTIC
201 Hupacasath First Nation NORTHWEST COAST
202 Huu-ay-aht First Nations NORTHWEST COAST
203 Indian Island NORTHEAST
204 Innu Takuaikan Uashat Mak Mani-Utenam
    ARCTIC/SUBARCTIC
205 Innue Essipit ARCTIC/SUBARCTIC
206 Inuvik Native ARCTIC/SUBARCTIC
207 Iskatewizaagegan #39 Independent First Nation
    ARCTIC/SUBARCTIC
208 Iskut ARCTIC/SUBARCTIC
209 James Smith PLAINS
210 Jean Marie River First Nation ARCTIC/SUBARCTIC
211 Ka:'yu:'k't'h'/Che:k:tles7et'h' First Nations
    NORTHWEST COAST
212 Ka'a'gee Tu First Nation ARCTIC/SUBARCTIC
213 Kahkewistahaw PLAINS
214 Kanaka Bar GREAT BASIN
215 Kapawe'no First Nation ARCTIC/SUBARCTIC
216 Kasabonika Lake ARCTIC/SUBARCTIC
217 K'atlodeeche First Nation ARCTIC/SUBARCTIC
218 Katzie NORTHWEST COAST
219 Kawacatoose PLAINS
220 Keeseekoose PLAINS
221 Keeseekoowenin PLAINS
222 Kee-Way-Win NORTHEAST
223 Kehewin Cree Nation PLAINS
224 Kingfisher ARCTIC/SUBARCTIC
225 Kingsclear NORTHEAST
226 Kinistin Saulteaux Nation PLAINS
227 Kinonjeoshtegon First Nation ARCTIC/
    SUBARCTIC
228 Kispiox NORTHWEST COAST
229 Kitasoo NORTHWEST COAST
230 Kitchenuhmaykoosib Inninuwug ARCTIC/
    SUBARCTIC
231 Kitigan Zibi Anishinabeg NORTHEAST
232 Kitselas NORTHWEST COAST
233 Kitsumkalum NORTHWEST COAST

234 Klahoose First Nation NORTHWEST COAST
235 Kluane First Nation ARCTIC/SUBARCTIC
236 K'ómoks First Nation NORTHWEST COAST
237 Konadaha Seneca NORTHEAST
238 Kwadacha ARCTIC/SUBARCTIC
239 Kwakiutl NORTHWEST COAST
240 Kwanlin Dun First Nation ARCTIC/SUBARCTIC
241 Kwantlen First Nation NORTHWEST COAST
242 Kwaw-kwaw-Apilt GREAT BASIN
243 Kwiakah NORTHWEST COAST
244 Kwikwasut'inuxw Haxwa'mis NORTHWEST
    COAST
245 Kwikwetlem First Nation NORTHWEST COAST
246 La Nation Innu Matimekush-Lac John ARCTIC/
    SUBARCTIC
247 La Nation Micmac de Gespeg NORTHEAST
248 Lac Des Mille Lacs NORTHEAST
249 Lac La Croix NORTHEAST
250 Lac La Ronge ARCTIC/SUBARCTIC
251 Lac Seul ARCTIC/SUBARCTIC
252 Lake Babine Nation ARCTIC/SUBARCTIC
253 Lake Cowichan First Nation NORTHWEST COAST
254 Lake Manitoba ARCTIC/SUBARCTIC
255 Lake St. Martin ARCTIC/SUBARCTIC
256 Lax Kw'alaams NORTHWEST COAST
257 Lennox Island NORTHEAST
258 Leq' a: mel First Nation NORTHWEST COAST
259 Les Atikamekw de Manawan ARCTIC/SUBARCTIC
260 Les Innus de Ekuanitshit ARCTIC/SUBARCTIC
261 Lheidli T'enneh ARCTIC/SUBARCTIC
262 Lhoosk'uz Dene Nation ARCTIC/SUBARCTIC
263 Lhtako Dene Nation ARCTIC/SUBARCTIC
264 Liard First Nation ARCTIC/SUBARCTIC
265 Liidlii Kue First Nation ARCTIC/SUBARCTIC
266 Listuguj Mi'gmaq Government NORTHEAST
267 Little Black Bear PLAINS
268 Little Grand Rapids ARCTIC/SUBARCTIC
269 Little Pine PLAINS
270 Little Red River Cree Nation ARCTIC/SUBARCTIC
271 Little Salmon/Carmacks First Nation ARCTIC/
    SUBARCTIC
272 Little Saskatchewan ARCTIC/SUBARCTIC
273 Little Shuswap Lake GREAT BASIN
274 Long Lake No.58 First Nation NORTHEAST
275 Long Plain ARCTIC/SUBARCTIC
276 Long Point First Nation NORTHEAST
277 Loon River Cree ARCTIC/SUBARCTIC
278 Louis Bull PLAINS
279 Lower Cayuga NORTHEAST
280 Lower Kootenay GREAT BASIN
281 Lower Mohawk NORTHEAST
282 Lower Nicola GREAT BASIN
283 Lower Similkameen GREAT BASIN
284 Lubicon Lake ARCTIC/SUBARCTIC
285 Lucky Man PLAINS
286 Lutsel K'e Dene First Nation ARCTIC/SUBARCTIC
287 Lyackson NORTHWEST COAST
288 Lytton GREAT BASIN
289 Madawaska Maliseet First Nation NORTHEAST
290 Magnetawan NORTHEAST
291 Makwa Sahgaiehcan First Nation PLAINS
292 Malahat First Nation NORTHWEST COAST
293 Mamalilikulla-Qwe'Qwa'Sot'Em NORTHWEST
    COAST
294 Manto Sipi Cree Nation ARCTIC/SUBARCTIC
295 Marcel Colomb First Nation ARCTIC/SUBARCTIC
296 Martin Falls ARCTIC/SUBARCTIC
297 Matachewan NORTHEAST

298 Mathias Colomb ARCTIC/SUBARCTIC
299 Matsqui NORTHWEST COAST
300 Mattagami NORTHEAST
301 McDowell Lake ARCTIC/SUBARCTIC
302 M'Chigeeng First Nation NORTHEAST
303 McLeod Lake ARCTIC/SUBARCTIC
304 Membertou NORTHEAST
305 Metepenagiag Mi'kmaq Nation NORTHEAST
306 Metlakatla NORTHWEST COAST
307 Miawpukek NORTHEAST
308 Michipicoten NORTHEAST
309 Micmacs of Gesgapegiag NORTHEAST
310 Mikisew Cree First Nation ARCTIC/SUBARCTIC
311 Millbrook NORTHEAST
312 Ministikwan Lake Cree Nation PLAINS
313 Mishkeegogamang ARCTIC/SUBARCTIC
314 Misipawistik Cree Nation ARCTIC/SUBARCTIC
315 Missanabie Cree NORTHEAST
316 Mississauga NORTHEAST
317 Mississauga's of Scugog Island First Nation
    NORTHEAST
318 Mississaugas of the Credit NORTHEAST
319 Mistawasis PLAINS
320 Mitaanjigamiing First Nation NORTHEAST
321 Mohawks of Akwesasne NORTHEAST
322 Mohawks of Kahnawá:ke NORTHEAST
323 Mohawks of Kanesatake NORTHEAST
324 Mohawks of the Bay of Quinte NORTHEAST
325 Montagnais de Natashquan ARCTIC/SUBARCTIC
326 Montagnais de Pakua Shipi ARCTIC/SUBARCTIC
327 Montagnais de Unamen Shipu ARCTIC/
    SUBARCTIC
328 Montagnais du Lac St.-Jean ARCTIC/SUBARCTIC
329 Montana PLAINS
330 Montreal Lake ARCTIC/SUBARCTIC
331 Moose Cree First Nation ARCTIC/SUBARCTIC
332 Moose Deer Point NORTHEAST
333 Moosomin PLAINS
334 Moravian of the Thames NORTHEAST
335 Moricetown ARCTIC/SUBARCTIC
336 Mosakahiken Cree Nation ARCTIC/SUBARCTIC
337 Mosquito, Grizzly Bear's Head, Lean Man First
    Nati PLAINS
338 Mount Currie GREAT BASIN
339 Mowachaht/Muchalaht NORTHWEST COAST
340 Munsee-Delaware Nation NORTHEAST
341 Muscowpetung PLAINS
342 Mushuau Innu First Nation ARCTIC/SUBARCTIC
343 Muskeg Lake Cree Nation #102 PLAINS
344 Muskoday First Nation PLAINS
345 Muskowekwan PLAINS
346 Muskrat Dam Lake ARCTIC/SUBARCTIC
347 Musqueam NORTHWEST COAST
348 Nadleh Whuten ARCTIC/SUBARCTIC
349 Nahanni Butte ARCTIC/SUBARCTIC
350 Naicatchewenin ARCTIC/SUBARCTIC
351 Nak'azdli ARCTIC/SUBARCTIC
352 Namgis First Nation NORTHWEST COAST
353 Nanoose First Nation NORTHWEST COAST
354 Naotkamegwanning ARCTIC/SUBARCTIC
355 Naskapi Nation of Kawawachikamach ARCTIC/
    SUBARCTIC
356 Nation Anishnabe du Lac Simon ARCTIC/
    SUBARCTIC
357 Nation Huronne Wendat NORTHEAST
358 Nazko First Nation ARCTIC/SUBARCTIC
359 Nee-Tahi-Buhn ARCTIC/SUBARCTIC
360 Nekaneet PLAINS

361 Neskantaga First Nation ARCTIC/SUBARCTIC
362 Neskonlith GREAT BASIN
363 New Westminster NORTHWEST COAST
364 Nibinamik First Nation ARCTIC/SUBARCTIC
365 Nicomen GREAT BASIN
366 Nigigoonsiminikaaning First Nation NORTHEAST
367 Niharondasa Seneca NORTHEAST
368 Nipissing First Nation NORTHEAST
369 Nisga'a Village of Gingolx NORTHWEST COAST
370 Nisga'a Village of Gitwinksihlkw NORTHWEST COAST
371 Nisga'a Village of Laxgalt'sap NORTHWEST COAST
372 Nisga'a Village of New Aiyansh NORTHWEST COAST
373 Nisichawayasihk Cree Nation ARCTIC/SUBARCTIC
374 Nooaitch GREAT BASIN
375 North Caribou Lake ARCTIC/SUBARCTIC
376 North Spirit Lake ARCTIC/SUBARCTIC
377 Northlands ARCTIC/SUBARCTIC
378 Northwest Angle No.33 ARCTIC/SUBARCTIC
379 Northwest Angle No.37 ARCTIC/SUBARCTIC
380 Norway House Cree Nation ARCTIC/SUBARCTIC
381 N'Quatqua NORTHWEST COAST
382 Nuchatlaht NORTHWEST COAST
383 Nuxalk Nation NORTHWEST COAST
384 Obashkaandagaang ARCTIC/SUBARCTIC
385 Ocean Man PLAINS
386 Ochapowace PLAINS
387 O-Chi-Chak-Ko-Sipi First Nation PLAINS
388 O'Chiese PLAINS
389 Ochiichagwe'babigo'ining First Nation ARCTIC/SUBARCTIC
390 Odanak NORTHEAST
391 Ojibway Nation of Saugeen NORTHEAST
392 Ojibways of Onigaming First Nation ARCTIC/SUBARCTIC
393 Ojibways of the Pic River First Nation NORTHEAST
394 Okanese GREAT BASIN
395 Okanese PLAINS
396 Old Massett Village Council NORTHWEST COAST
397 One Arrow First Nation PLAINS
398 Oneida NORTHEAST
399 Oneida Nation of the Thames NORTHEAST
400 Onion Lake Cree Nation PLAINS
401 Onondaga Clear Sky NORTHEAST
402 Opaskwayak Cree Nation ARCTIC/SUBARCTIC
403 O-Pipon-Na-Piwin Cree Nation ARCTIC/SUBARCTIC
404 Oregon Jack Creek GREAT BASIN
405 Oromocto NORTHEAST
406 Osoyoos GREAT BASIN
407 Oweekeno/Wuikinuxv Nation NORTHWEST COAST
408 Pabineau NORTHEAST
409 Pacheedaht First Nation NORTHWEST COAST
410 Paqtnkek Mi'kmaw Nation NORTHEAST
411 Pasqua First Nation #79 PLAINS
412 Pauingassi First Nation ARCTIC/SUBARCTIC
413 Paul PLAINS
414 Pauquachin NORTHWEST COAST
415 Pays Plat NORTHEAST
416 Peepeekisis Cree Nation No.81 PLAINS
417 Peerless Trout First Nation ARCTIC/SUBARCTIC
418 Peguis ARCTIC/SUBARCTIC
419 Pehdzeh Ki First Nation ARCTIC/SUBARCTIC
420 Pelican Lake PLAINS

421 Penelakut Tribe NORTHWEST COAST
422 Penticton GREAT BASIN
423 Peter Ballantyne Cree Nation ARCTIC/SUBARCTIC
424 Peters GREAT BASIN
425 Pheasant Rump Nakota PLAINS
426 Piapot PLAINS
427 Pic Mobert NORTHEAST
428 Pictou Landing NORTHEAST
429 Piikani Nation PLAINS
430 Pikangikum ARCTIC/SUBARCTIC
431 Pinaymootang First Nation PLAINS
432 Pine Creek PLAINS
433 Popkum GREAT BASIN
434 Poplar Hill ARCTIC/SUBARCTIC
435 Poplar River First Nation ARCTIC/SUBARCTIC
436 Potlotek First Nation NORTHEAST
437 Poundmaker PLAINS
438 Première nation de Whapmagoostui ARCTIC/SUBARCTIC
439 Première Nation des Abénakis de Wôlinak NORTHEAST
440 Première Nation Malecite de Viger NORTHEAST
441 Prophet River First Nation ARCTIC/SUBARCTIC
442 Qalipu Mi'kmaq First Nation NORTHEAST
443 Qualicum First Nation NORTHWEST COAST
444 Quatsino NORTHWEST COAST
445 Rainy River First Nations NORTHEAST
446 Red Earth PLAINS
447 Red Pheasant PLAINS
448 Red Rock NORTHEAST
449 Red Sucker Lake ARCTIC/SUBARCTIC
450 Rolling River PLAINS
451 Roseau River Anishinabe First Nation Government ARCTIC/SUBARCTIC
452 Ross River ARCTIC/SUBARCTIC
453 Sachigo Lake ARCTIC/SUBARCTIC
454 Saddle Lake Cree Nation PLAINS
455 Sagamok Anishnawbek NORTHEAST
456 Saik'uz First Nation ARCTIC/SUBARCTIC
457 Saint Mary's NORTHEAST
458 Sakimay First Nations PLAINS
459 Salt River First Nation #195 ARCTIC/SUBARCTIC
460 Samahquam GREAT BASIN
461 Sambaa K'e (Trout Lake) Dene ARCTIC/SUBARCTIC
462 Samson PLAINS
463 Sandy Bay PLAINS
464 Sandy Lake ARCTIC/SUBARCTIC
465 Sapotaweyak Cree Nation PLAINS
466 Saugeen NORTHEAST
467 Saulteau First Nations ARCTIC/SUBARCTIC
468 Saulteaux PLAINS
469 Sawridge First Nation ARCTIC/SUBARCTIC
470 Sayisi Dene First Nation ARCTIC/SUBARCTIC
471 Scowlitz NORTHWEST COAST
472 Seabird Island GREAT BASIN
473 Sechelt NORTHWEST COAST
474 Seine River First Nation NORTHEAST
475 Selkirk First Nation ARCTIC/SUBARCTIC
476 Semiahmoo NORTHWEST COAST
477 Serpent River NORTHEAST
478 Seton Lake GREAT BASIN
479 Shackan GREAT BASIN
480 Shamattawa First Nation ARCTIC/SUBARCTIC
481 Shawanaga First Nation NORTHEAST
482 Sheguiandah NORTHEAST
483 Sheshatshiu Innu First Nation ARCTIC/SUBARCTIC

484 Sheshegwaning NORTHEAST
485 Shoal Lake Cree Nation ARCTIC/SUBARCTIC
486 Shoal Lake No.40 ARCTIC/SUBARCTIC
487 Shubenacadie NORTHEAST
488 Shuswap GREAT BASIN
489 Shxwhá:y Village NORTHWEST COAST
490 Shxw'ow'hamel First Nation GREAT BASIN
491 Siksika Nation PLAINS
492 Simpcw First Nation GREAT BASIN
493 Sioux Valley Dakota Nation PLAINS
494 Siska GREAT BASIN
495 Six Nations of the Grand River NORTHEAST
496 Skatin Nations NORTHWEST COAST
497 Skawahlook First Nation GREAT BASIN
498 Skeetchestn GREAT BASIN
499 Skidegate NORTHWEST COAST
500 Skin Tyee ARCTIC/SUBARCTIC
501 Skowkale NORTHWEST COAST
502 Skownan First Nation ARCTIC/SUBARCTIC
503 Skuppah GREAT BASIN
504 Skwah NORTHWEST COAST
505 Slate Falls Nation ARCTIC/SUBARCTIC
506 Sliammon NORTHWEST COAST
507 Smith's Landing First Nation ARCTIC/SUBARCTIC
508 Snuneymuxw First Nation NORTHWEST COAST
509 Soda Creek GREAT BASIN
510 Songhees First Nation NORTHWEST COAST
511 Soowahlie NORTHWEST COAST
512 Splatsin First Nation GREAT BASIN
513 Spuzzum GREAT BASIN
514 Squamish NORTHWEST COAST
515 Squiala First Nation NORTHWEST COAST
516 St. Mary's GREAT BASIN
517 St. Theresa Point ARCTIC/SUBARCTIC
518 Standing Buffalo PLAINS
519 Star Blanket Cree Nation PLAINS
520 Stellat'en First Nation ARCTIC/SUBARCTIC
521 Stoney PLAINS
522 Sts'ailes NORTHWEST COAST
523 Stswecem'c Xgat'tem First Nation GREAT BASIN
524 Sturgeon Lake Cree Nation ARCTIC/SUBARCTIC
525 Sturgeon Lake First Nation PLAINS
526 Stz'uminus First Nation NORTHWEST COAST
527 Sucker Creek ARCTIC/SUBARCTIC
528 Sumas First Nation NORTHWEST COAST
529 Sunchild First Nation PLAINS
530 Swan Lake PLAINS
531 Swan River First Nation ARCTIC/SUBARCTIC
532 Sweetgrass PLAINS
533 Ta'an Kwach'an ARCTIC/SUBARCTIC
534 Tahltan ARCTIC/SUBARCTIC
535 Takla Lake First Nation ARCTIC/SUBARCTIC
536 Taku River Tlingit ARCTIC/SUBARCTIC
537 Tallcree ARCTIC/SUBARCTIC
538 Tataskweyak Cree Nation ARCTIC/SUBARCTIC
539 Taykwa Tagamou Nation ARCTIC/SUBARCTIC
540 Temagami First Nation NORTHEAST
541 Teslin Tlingit Council ARCTIC/SUBARCTIC
542 Tetlit Gwich'in ARCTIC/SUBARCTIC
543 The Crees of the Waskaganish First Nation ARCTIC/SUBARCTIC
544 The Key First Nation PLAINS
545 Thessalon NORTHEAST
546 Thunderchild First Nation PLAINS
547 Timiskaming First Nation NORTHEAST
548 T'it'q'et GREAT BASIN
549 Tk'emlúps te Secwépemc GREAT BASIN

550 Tla-o-qui-aht First Nations NORTHWEST COAST
551 Tlatlasikwala NORTHWEST COAST
552 Tl'azt'en Nation ARCTIC/SUBARCTIC
553 Tl'etinqox-t'in Government Office ARCTIC/SUBARCTIC
554 Tlowitsis Tribe NORTHWEST COAST
555 Tobacco Plains GREAT BASIN
556 Tobique NORTHEAST
557 Toosey GREAT BASIN
558 Tootinaowaziibeeng Treaty Reserve PLAINS
559 Toquaht NORTHWEST COAST
560 Tr'ondëk Hwëch'in ARCTIC/SUBARCTIC
561 Tsartlip NORTHWEST COAST
562 Tsawout First Nation NORTHWEST COAST
563 Tsawwassen First Nation NORTHWEST COAST
564 Tsay Keh Dene ARCTIC/SUBARCTIC
565 Tseshaht NORTHWEST COAST
566 Tseycum NORTHWEST COAST
567 Ts'kw'aylaxw First Nation GREAT BASIN
568 Tsleil-Waututh Nation NORTHWEST COAST
569 T'Sou-ke First Nation NORTHWEST COAST
570 Tsuu T'ina Nation PLAINS
571 Tulita Dene ARCTIC/SUBARCTIC
572 Tuscarora NORTHEAST
573 Tzeachten NORTHWEST COAST
574 Uchucklesaht NORTHWEST COAST
575 Ucluelet First Nation NORTHWEST COAST
576 Ulkatcho ARCTIC/SUBARCTIC
577 Union Bar GREAT BASIN
578 Upper Cayuga NORTHEAST
579 Upper Mohawk NORTHEAST

580 Upper Nicola GREAT BASIN
581 Upper Similkameen GREAT BASIN
582 Vuntut Gwitchin First Nation ARCTIC/SUBARCTIC
583 Wabaseemoong Independent Nations ARCTIC/SUBARCTIC
584 Wabauskang First Nation ARCTIC/SUBARCTIC
585 Wabigoon Lake Ojibway Nation ARCTIC/SUBARCTIC
586 Wagmatcook NORTHEAST
587 Wahgoshig ARCTIC/SUBARCTIC
588 Wahnapitae NORTHEAST
589 Wahpeton Dakota Nation PLAINS
590 Wahta Mohawk NORTHEAST
591 Walker Mohawk NORTHEAST
592 Walpole Island NORTHEAST
593 Wapekeka ARCTIC/SUBARCTIC
594 War Lake First Nation ARCTIC/SUBARCTIC
595 Wasagamack First Nation ARCTIC/SUBARCTIC
596 Wasauksing First Nation NORTHEAST
597 Waswanipi ARCTIC/SUBARCTIC
598 Waterhen Lake ARCTIC/SUBARCTIC
599 Wawakapewin ARCTIC/SUBARCTIC
600 Waycobah First Nation NORTHEAST
601 Waywayseecappo First Nation Treaty Four - 1874 PLAINS
602 Webequie ARCTIC/SUBARCTIC
603 Weenusk ARCTIC/SUBARCTIC
604 Wesley PLAINS
605 West Moberly First Nations ARCTIC/SUBARCTIC
606 West Point First Nation ARCTIC/SUBARCTIC
607 Westbank First Nation GREAT BASIN

608 Wet'suwet'en First Nation ARCTIC/SUBARCTIC
609 Wha Ti First Nation ARCTIC/SUBARCTIC
610 Whispering Pines/Clinton GREAT BASIN
611 White Bear PLAINS
612 White River First Nation ARCTIC/SUBARCTIC
613 Whitecap Dakota First Nation PLAINS
614 Whitefish Lake ARCTIC/SUBARCTIC
615 Whitefish River NORTHEAST
616 Whitesand NORTHEAST
617 Wikwemikong NORTHEAST
618 Williams Lake GREAT BASIN
619 Witchekan Lake PLAINS
620 Wolf Lake NORTHEAST
621 Wood Mountain PLAINS
622 Woodland Cree First Nation ARCTIC/SUBARCTIC
623 Woodstock NORTHEAST
624 Wunnumin ARCTIC/SUBARCTIC
625 Wuskwi Sipihk First Nation PLAINS
626 Xaxli'p GREAT BASIN
627 Xeni Gwet'in First Nations Government GREAT BASIN
628 Yakweakwioose NORTHWEST COAST
629 Yale First Nation GREAT BASIN
630 Yekooche First Nation ARCTIC/SUBARCTIC
631 Yellow Quill PLAINS
632 Yellowknives Dene First Nation ARCTIC/SUBARCTIC
633 York Factory First Nation ARCTIC/SUBARCTIC
634 Yunesit'in Government ARCTIC/SUBARCTIC
635 Zhiibaahaasing First Nation NORTHEAST

MAP SOURCES

Aboriginal Affairs and Northern Development Canada: www.aadnc-aandc.gc.ca.

Beck, Warren A., and Ynez D. Hasse. *Historical Atlas of California.* University of Oklahoma Press, 1975.

Bureau of Indian Affairs: www.bia.gov.

Canadiana.org.

Collins, Charles D., Jr. *Atlas of the Sioux Wars,* 2nd ed. Fort Leavenworth: Combat Studies Institute Press, 2006.

Encyclopedia of Saskatchewan (online). http://esask.uregina.ca.

Indian Land Cessions in the United States, 1784–1894: United States Serial Set, Number 4015. H.R. Doc. No. 736, 56th Cong., 1st Sess. (1899).

Kantner, John. "Chaco Roads." www.colorado.edu/Conferences/chaco/roads.htm.

National Geographic. *Historical Atlas of the United States.* Washington, D.C.: National Geographic Society, 1993.

———. *The Great Whales: Migration and Range* (map). Washington, D.C.: National Geographic Society, 1976.

National Park Service. *Chaco Culture National Historic Park* (map). National Park Service, 2006.

———. Little Bighorn Battlefield Historical Handbook: www.cr.nps.gov/history/online_books/hh/1a/hh1c.htm.

———. *Nez Perce Map* (online). www.nps.gov/nepe/index.htm.

———. *Oregon National Historic Trail* (map). National Park Service, 2007.

———. *Sand Creek Massacre Map* (online): www.nps.gov/sand/historyculture/massacre.htm.

———. *Sand Creek Massacre Project: Site Location Study.* Denver: National Park Service, Intermountain Region, 2000.

———. *Santa Fe National Historic Trail* (map).

———. *Trail of Tears* (map). National Park Service, 2012.

Natural Resources Canada: www.nrcan.gc.ca.

Royce, C. C. *Map of the former territorial limits of the Cherokee "Nation of" Indians.* 1884. g3861e np000155. http://hdl.loc.gov/loc.gmd/g3861e.np000155.

Sofaer, Anna, Michael P. Marshall, and Rolf M. Sinclair. "The Great North Road: a Cosmographic Expression of the Chaco Culture of New Mexico." www.solsticeproject.org/greanort.htm.

U.S. Department of Agriculture—Forest Service. *Nez Perce Outbreak and War* (map). 2004. https://fs.usda.gov/Internet/FSE_MEDIA/fsbdev3_055022.jpg.

Waldman, Carl. *Atlas of the North American Indian,* 3rd ed. New York: Facts on File, 2009.

ABBREVIATION KEY: BAL = Bridgeman Art Library; **LOC** = Library of Congress
NGC = National Geographic Creative; **SI** = Smithsonian Institution

Front Cover: Top Row (Left to Right), LOC, Edward S. Curtis Collection, LC-USZ62-46963; LOC, Edward S. Curtis Collection, LC-USZC4-8918; LOC, Edward S. Curtis Collection, LC-USZ62-110961; LOC, Edward S. Curtis Collection, LC-USZ62-125926; Bottom, Smithsonian American Art Museum, Washington, DC/Art Resource, NY; Back Cover (Left to Right): American Photographer, (20th century)/Private Collection/Peter Newark American Pictures/BAL; NGS Image Collection/The Art Archive at Art Resource, NY; Universal History Archive/Getty Images; Universal History Archive/UIG/BAL; Hulton-Deutsch Collection/Corbis; Dust Jacket Background Map (and Chapter Openers): LOC, Geography and Map Division; Back Flap Author Photo: John Swartz.

2–3, Courtesy Royal Ontario Museum; 4, Smithsonian American Art Museum, Washington, DC/Art Resource, NY; 6, LOC, Geography and Map Division; 8, Edward S. Curtis; 9, Werner Forman Archive/BAL; 10, Norbert Rosing/NGC; 13, National Museum of the American Indian, SI (18/9306); 22–3, Art Gallery of Ontario; 24, Smithsonian American Art Museum, Washington, DC/Art Resource, NY; 25, Sisse Brimberg & Cotton Coulson/NGC; 30 (LE), Wisconsin Historical Society, WHS-3058; 30 (RT), SI, Washington, DC/BAL; 33, Universal History Archive/UIG/BAL; 35, American Photographer, (20th century)/Private Collection/Peter Newark American Pictures/BAL; 36–7, Mashantucket Pequot Museum and Research Center; 37 (LE), Trolley Dodger/Corbis; 37 (RT), Mashantucket Pequot Museum and Research Center; 38 (LE), Musée McCord - McCord Museum, Montréal/Art Resource, NY; 38 (RT), The New York Public Library/Art Resource, NY; 39 (UP), English School, (19th century)/Private Collection/BAL; 39 (LOLE), English School, (20th century)/Private Collection/Ken Welsh/BAL; 39 (LORT), George Catlin/De Agostini Picture Library/BAL; 40 (RT), Superstock/Alamy; 40–1, Mashantucket Pequot Museum and Research Center; 41, bpk, Berlin/Art Resource, NY; 42, English School/Private Collection/Peter Newark American Pictures/BAL; 43 (LE), Merian, Matthaus, the Elder (1593–1650)/Virginia Historical Society, Richmond, Virginia/BAL; 43 (RT), French School, (18th century)/Private Collection/Peter Newark American Pictures/BAL; 44, The Art Archive at Art Resource, NY; 44–5, Mashantucket Pequot Museum and Research Center; 45 (UP), American School, (19th century)/American Antiquarian Society, Worcester, Massachusetts/BAL; 45 (LO), Picture Collection/The New York Public Library/Astor, Lenox and Tilden Foundations; 46, National Museum of the American Indian, SI (256676). Photo by NMAI Photo Services; 46–7, Courtesy William H. Marr; 47 (LE), Universal History Archive/UIG/BAL; 47 (RT), Musée de la Civilisation, Collection du Séminaire de Quebec, 1993.16462; 48 (UP and LO), Gilcrease Museum, Tulsa, OK; 49, Photo Courtesy of Great Lakes Digital Collection, Rudy Lamont Ruggles Collection, The Newberry Library, Chicago; 50, (E6938) Department of Anthropology, SI; 51, Irene Abdou/Stock Connection/Aurora Photos; 52, Smithsonian American Art Museum, Washington, DC/Art Resource, NY; 53, Buffalo Bill Historical Center/The Art Archive at Art Resource, NY; 54 (UP), American School, (19th century)/Detroit Institute of Arts, USA/Founders Society purchase and Flint Ink Corporation funds/BAL; 54 (LO), McCord Museum; 55, Phil Schermeister/Corbis/Aurora Photos; 56 (UP), Smithsonian American Art Museum, Washington, DC, Hemphill/Art Resource, NY; 56 (LO), Krista Rossow/NGC; 57, Christian Heeb/Aurora Photos; 58–9, Smithsonian American Art Museum, Washington, DC/Art Resource, NY; 60, Smithsonian American Art Museum, Washington, DC/Art Resource, NY; 61, Christian Heeb/Aurora Photos; 66 (UP), National Portrait Gallery, SI/Art Resource, NY; 66 (LO), Courtesy American Antiquarian Society; 69 (UP), Wimar, Charles Ferdinand (1829–1863)/Saint Louis Art Museum, Missouri, USA/Museum purchase/BAL; 69 (LO), bpk, Berlin/Ethnologisches Museum, Staatliche Museen, Berlin, Germany/Art Resource, NY; 70, Chris Johns/NGC; 72 (UP), Richard A. Cooke/Corbis; 72 (LOLE), Courtesy The Art Institute of Chicago; 72 (LORT), H. Tom Hall/NGC; 73, Archive of Moundville Archaeology/Research Laboratories of Archaeology/The University of North Carolina at Chapel Hill; 74 (LE and RT), ©The Trustees of the British Museum. All rights reserved; 75, ©The Trustees of the British Museum. All rights reserved; 76, Universal History Archive/UIG/BAL; 76–7, From the American Geographical Society Library, University of Wisconsin–Milwaukee Libraries; 77 (UP), Marilyn Angel Wynn/NativeStock Pictures; 77 (LO), National Anthropological Archives, SI [00217100]; 78 (UP), Courtesy Clements Library, University of Michigan; 78 (LO), Edwin L. Jackson/cherokeephoenix.org; 78–9, NGS Cartographic Division; 79, Victor R. Boswell, Jr./NGC; 80 (UPLE Inset), LOC, LC-USZC4-3156; 80 (UPRT), U.S. National Archives; 80 (LO), Courtesy of the University of Texas Libraries, The University of Texas at Austin; 81 (UP), Bettmann/Corbis; 81 (LO), Courtesy Special Collections, The University of Texas at Arlington Library, Arlington, Texas; 82, Clifton R. Adams/NGS; 83 (UP), Waterhouse, C.H. (fl.1812)/Private Collection/Peter Newark American Pictures/BAL; 83 (LO), National Portrait Gallery, SI/Art Resource, NY; 84, Victor Krantz, National Anthropological Archives, SI [240915]; 85, MPI/Stringer/Getty Images; 86 (UP), American School, (19th century)/© Peabody Essex Museum, Salem, Massachusetts/BAL; 86 (LO), The Mariners' Museum/Corbis; 87, Otis Imboden/NGC; 88–9, Historical Picture Archive/Corbis; 90, Carl Lomen; 91, Tom Thulen/Alamy; 93, Gordon Wiltsie/NGC; 97, (E45503) Department of Anthropology, SI; 98, Corbis; 101 (UP), National Anthropological Archives, SI [01457000]; 101 (LO), Werner Forman/Corbis; 102, The Trustees of the British Museum/Art Resource, NY; 102–3, Yale University Library; 103, Hulton-Deutsch Collection/Corbis; 104, Robert E. Peary Collection, NGS; 104–5, From the American Geographical Society Library, University of Wisconsin–Milwaukee Libraries; 105 (UP), Robert E. Peary Collection, NGS; 105 (LO), LOC, LC-USZC4-9011; 106 (UP), NFB/Getty Images; 106 (LO), © 2013 Stock Sales WGBH/Scala/Art Resource, NY; 106–7, LOC, Geography and Map Division; 107, Krieghoff, Cornelius (1815–1872)/Hudson Bay Company, Canada/BAL; 108 (UP), LOC Prints & Photographs Division; 108 (LO), Fine Art Images/SuperStock; 108 (Inset Flag), Wikipedia; 108–9, David Rumsey Map Collection, www.davidrumsey.com; 109, Alaska State Library, Louis Choris Collection, ASL-PCA-139-48; 110, Mingei International Museum/Art Resource, NY; 111 (UP), Michael Melford/NGC; 111 (LO), Werner Forman/Art Resource, NY; 112 (UP), (E286446) Victor E. Krantz, Department of Anthropology, SI; 112 (LO), Edward S. Curtis; 113, Michael DeYoung/Alaska Stock LLC/Corbis; 114–5, George Catlin/BAL/Getty Images; 116, Smithsonian American Art Museum, Washington, DC/Art Resource, NY; 117, Brian A. Vikander/Corbis; 120, Corbis; 121, Buffalo Bill Historical Center/The Art Archive at Art Resource, NY; 122, Buffalo Bill Historical Center/The Art Archive at Art Resource, NY; 125 (UP), Werner Forman/Art Resource, NY; 125 (LO), Anderson, John Alvin (1869–1948)/Private Collection/BAL; 126, C. J. Blanchard; 129 (LE), Shoshone Katsikodi School/BAL/Getty Images; 129 (RT), Universal History Archive/UIG/BAL; 130, Buffalo Bill Historical Center/The Art Archive at Art Resource, NY; 130–1, Hudson's Bay Company Archives/Archives of Manitoba/HBCA Maps; 133 (UP), Cross, Henry H. (1837–1918)/© Chicago History Museum, USA/BAL; 133 (LO), Kappes, Alfred (1850–1894) (after)/Private Collection/BAL; 135 (UP), American School, (19th century)/Private Collection/Peter Newark American Pictures/BAL; 135 (CTR), DEA Picture Library/Getty Images; 135 (LO), Denver Public Library, Western History Collection/BAL; 136 (UP), James Peters/Library and Archives of Canada/C-03464; 136 (LO), O.B. Buell/Library and Archives Canada/PA-118760; 137 (UP), Canadian Photographer (19th Century)/Private Collection/Peter Newark American Pictures/BAL; 137 (LO), McCord Museum; 138 (LE), LOC, LC-DIG-cwpbh-03110; 138 (RT), Corbis; 138–9, Amos Bad Heart Buffalo/BAL/Getty Images; 139, Buffalo Bill Historical Center/The Art Archive at Art Resource, NY; 140 (UP), Denver Public Library, Western History Collection, B-544; 141 (UP), Amos Bad Heart Buffalo/BAL/Getty Images; 141 (LO), LOC, John C. H. Grabill Collection, LC-DIG-ppmsc-02554; 142 (UP), American Photographer, (19th century)/Private Collection/Peter Newark Western Americana/BAL; 142 (LO), Schmidt, Harold von (1893–1982)/Private Collection/Peter Newark American Pictures/BAL; 143 (UP), American School, (19th century)/Brooklyn Museum of Art, New York, USA/Henry L. Batterman Fund and the Frank Sherman Benson Fund/BAL; 143 (LO), Bell, Charles Milton (c.1849–93)/Private Collection/Peter Newark Western Americana/BAL; 144 (UP), LOC, Brady-Handy Photograph Collection, LC-DIG-cwpbh-00883; 144 (LO), Marilyn Angel Wynn/NativeStock Pictures; 145 (UP), Denver Public Library, Western History Collection, Z-1549; 145 (LO), LOC, LC-DIG-ppmsca-15849; 146 (BACK), LOC, Geography and Map Division; 146 (INSET), Art Resource, NY; 147 (LE), LOC, Geography and Map Division; 147 (RT), Ted Wood/Aurora Photos; 148, Werner Forman/Corbis; 149, Underwood & Underwood/Corbis; 150 (UP), Phil Schermeister/Corbis; 150 (LO), Brooklyn Museum/Corbis; 151, Werner Forman/Corbis; 152, Universal Images Group/Getty Images; 153 (UP), Corbis; 153 (LO),

Marilyn Angel Wynn/Nativestock Pictures/Corbis; 154, Buffalo Bill Historical Center/The Art Archive at Art Resource, NY; 155, William Henry Jackson/Stringer/Hulton Archive/Getty Images; 156, National Museum of the American Indian, SI (P21885). Photo by Ravenswood Photo Shop; 157 (UP), Buffalo Bill Historical Center/The Art Archive at Art Resource, NY; 157 (LO), Smithsonian American Art Museum, Washington, DC/Art Resource, NY; 158 (UP), American School, (19th century)/© Peabody Essex Museum, Salem, Massachusetts/BAL; 158 (LO), Bettmann/Corbis; 159, Edward S. Curtis/Stapleton Collection/Corbis; 160 (UP), Denver Public Library, Western History Collection, X-31670; 160 (LO), Buffalo Bill Historical Center/The Art Archive at Art Resource, NY; 161, Richard A. Cooke/Corbis; 162, American School/BAL/Getty Images; 163 (UP), Aaron Huey/NGC; 163 (LO), Science & Society Picture Library via Getty Images; 164–5, Smithsonian American Art Museum, Washington, DC/Art Resource, NY; 166, Franklin Price Knott; 167, Ric Ergenbright/Corbis; 172, Werner Forman/Art Resource, NY; 175 (UP), Universal History Archive/UIG/ BAL; 175 (LO), SSPL/Science Museum/Art Resource, NY; 176 (LE), William Henry Jackson/George Eastman House/Getty Images; 176 (RT), Dixon, Maynard (1875–1946)/Private Collection/Peter Newark American Pictures/BAL; 177, Texas Archeological Research Laboratory (TARL)/The University of Texas at Austin; 178, LOC, Geography and Map Division; 179 (UP), Courtesy Palace of the Governors Photo Archives (NMHM/DCA), 011409; 179 (RT), South West Museum, Los Angeles, CA, USA/BAL; 179 (LO), Peter Newark American Pictures/BAL: 181 (LE), LOC, Geography and Map Division; 181 (RT), LOC, LC-USZ62-78976; 182, George H.H. Huey/Corbis; 183 (UP), Werner Forman Archive/BAL; 183 (CTR), Vincent Laforet; 183 (LO), Peter V. Bianchi/NGC; 184 (LE), Time & Life Pictures/US Signal Corps/Getty Images; 184 (RT), LOC, LC-USZC4-2631; 184–5, Courtesy of Sharlot Hall Museum Library and Archives, Prescott, Arizona/Secretary of War/U.S. National Archives; 185, Bettmann/Corbis; 186, Nicholas Philip Trist Papers, Manuscript Division, LOC; 186–7, LOC, Geography and Map Division; 187 (UP), LOC, Brady-Handy Photograph Collection, LC-DIG-cwpbh-02914; 187 (LO), Graham Ker; 188 (UPLE), Adoc-photos/Art Resource, NY; 188 (LO CTR LE), Buffalo Bill Historical Center/The Art Archive at Art Resource, NY; 188 (LO CTR RT), American Photographer, (19th century)/Private Collection/Peter Newark American Pictures/BAL; 189 (UP), American Photographer, (19th century)/Private Collection/Peter Newark American Pictures/ BAL; 189 (LO), LOC, LC-USZ62-86461; 190 (UP), Denver Public Library, Western History Collection, X-32995; 190 (LO), Art Resource, NY; 191 (UPLE), Fotosearch/Getty Images; 191 (UPRT), Courtesy Palace of the Governors Photo Archives (NMHM/DCA), 022938; 191 (LO), U.S. National Archives; 192, George H.H. Huey/Corbis; 193 (UP), Carpenter, William J. (b.1861)/Private Collection/BAL; 193 (LO), National Museum of the American Indian, SI (8003). Photo by NMAI Photo Services; 194 (UP), Werner Forman Archive/BAL; 194 (LO), Franklin Price Knott; 195, William Belknap Jr.; 196, Edward S. Curtis/Stapleton Collection/Corbis; 197 (UP), Franklin Price Knott; 197 (LO), Brooklyn Museum/Corbis; 198–9, Shoshone/The Walters Art Gallery, Baltimore; 200, Courtesy Royal Ontario Museum; 201, Marilyn Angel Wynn/NativeStock Pictures; 207, The Walters Art Gallery, Baltimore; 208, Werner Forman/Art Resource, NY; 211 (UP), Buffalo Bill Historical Center/The Art Archive at Art Resource, NY; 211 (LO), LOC, LC-USZ62-95590; 212, National Portrait Gallery, SI/Art Resource, NY; 212–3, From the American Geographical Society Library/Digital Map Collection/University of Wisconsin–Milwaukee; 213 (UP), Everett Collection Inc/Alamy; 213 (LOLE), Kansas State Historical Society; 213 (LORT), American School, (19th century)/Private Collection/Peter Newark American Pictures/BAL; 214 (UP), Collection of the Western Jesuit Missions/The Saint Louis University Art Museum; 214 (LO), Manuscripts, Archives, and Special Collections, Washington State University Libraries (WSU003); 215 (UP), Saint Louis University Libraries Special Collections; 215 (LO), Courtesy Royal Ontario Museum; 216, Washington State Historical Society/Art Resource, NY; 217 (UPRT), Washington State Historical Society, Tacoma; 217 (LOLE), Buffalo Bill Historical Center/The Art Archive at Art Resource, NY; 217 (LORT), Edward S. Curtis; 218 (UP), Jackson, William Henry (1843–1942)/ Private Collection/J. T. Vintage/BAL; 218 (LO), Denver Public Library, Western History Collection, X-30699; 219 (UP), Wikimedia Commons; 219 (CTR), U.S. National Archives; 219 (LO), LOC, LC-USZ62-106050; 220 (UPLE), Wikimedia Commons; 220 (UPRT), From the collections of Armémuseum (Swedish Army Museum), Stockholm, Sweden/Digital Museum/Wikimedia Commons; 220 (LO), Washington State Library/

Courtesy of the Office of the Secretary of State; 221 (UP), Washington State Historical Society, Tacoma; 221 (LO), Nona Hengen Studio; 222, Buffalo Bill Historical Center/The Art Archive at Art Resource, NY; 223 (UP), Courtesy Royal Ontario Museum; 223 (LO), Ira Block/NGC; 224 (UP), The Walters Art Gallery, Baltimore; 224 (LO), Buffalo Bill Historical Center/The Art Archive at Art Resource, NY; 225, Bettmann/Corbis; 226, SuperStock/Getty Images; 227 (UP), Getty Images; 227 (LO), Gift of the Coe Foundation/Courtesy Buffalo Bill Historical Center; 228–9, Courtesy Royal Ontario Museum; 230, LOC, LC-USZ62-93694; 231, Frans Lanting/NGC; 234, Courtesy Royal Ontario Museum; 235, Werner Forman/Art Resource, NY; 236, LOC, LC-USZ62-101169; 239, Courtesy Royal Ontario Museum; 240 (UP), Three Lions/Hulton Archive/Getty Images; 240 (CTR BACK), Smithsonian Libraries/Image Courtesy of Biodiversity Heritage Library (http://www.biodiversitylibrary.org); 240 (LO), Courtesy of the Bancroft Library, University of California, Berkeley; 241 (UP), Courtesy of the Alaska State Museum, Juneau, ASM-III-R-150; 241 (LO), Illustration by Louis S. Glanzman/National Park Service/Sitka Park Collection; 242, LOC, Geography and Map Division; 243 (LE), LOC, LC-DIG-ppmsca-03146; 243 (RT), LOC, LC-DIG-ppmsca-03400; 244 (UP), LOC, LC-USZC4-2634; 244 (LO), William Henry Jackson Collection/L. Tom Perry Special Collections/Harold B. Lee Library/Brigham Young University, Provo, Utah; 245, Church History Library; The Church of Jesus Christ of Latter-day Saints; 246–7, © The British Library Board. All Rights Reserved; 247, Courtesy City of Vancouver Archives; 248 (UP), Asahel Curtis; 248 (LO), Richard Schlecht/NGC; 250, Seattle Art Museum/91.1.82/Sakii.id (headdress frontlet)/Albert Edward Edenshaw/ca. 1870/Maple wood, paint, and abalone shell/Seattle Art Museum, Gift of John H. Hauberg; 251 (UP), Frans Lanting/NGC; 251 (LO), Washington State Historical Society/Art Resource, NY; 252 (UP), Canadian Museum of Civilization/Corbis; 252 (LO), Edward S. Curtis; 253, W. Langdon Kihn/NGC; 254, National Gallery of Canada (no. 6918); 255 (UP), Gary Fiegehen/All CanadaPhotos.com/Corbis; 255 (LO), Leslie Corbett/Buyenlarge/Getty Images; 256–7, Smithsonian American Art Museum, Washington, DC/Art Resource, NY; 258, LOC, Edward S. Curtis Collection, LC-USZ62-47020; 259, Marilyn Angel Wynn/Nativestock/Getty Images; 262, Tom Bean/Corbis; 264, HIP/Art Resource, NY; 267, National Anthropological Archives, SI [01519500]; 268, North Wind Picture Archives; 268–9, LOC, Geography and Map Division; 269 (UP), Courtesy of Picture History; 269 (LOLE), Courtesy of the Colorado Historical Society (Scan #10033520); 269 (LORT), The Philadelphia Print Shop; 270 (UP), Courtesy of the California History Room/California State Library/Sacramento, California; 270 (LO), Courtesy of the Bancroft Library, University of California, Berkeley; 271, LOC, Geography and Map Division; 272 (UP), Universal History Archive/UIG/BAL; 272 (BACK), National Anthropological Archives, SI [Manuscript 552-a]; 272 (LO), LOC, Edward S. Curtis Collection, LC-USZ62-123299; 273 (UP), Victor R. Boswell, Jr./NGC; 273 (LO), Kihn, William Langdon (1898–1957)/Haussmann, Zurich, Switzerland/BAL; 274 (UP), Eadweard Muybridge/George Eastman House/Getty Images; 274 (LO), MPI/Getty Images; 275 (UP), LOC, LC-DIG-cwpb-07417; 275 (LO), MPI/Getty Images; 276 (UPLE), Southwest Museum of the American Indian/Braun Research Library Collection/Autry National Center, Los Angeles; p.482; 276 (UPRT and LO), Corbis; 277 (UP), De Agostini/Getty Images; 277 (LO), LOC, LC-USZ62-130779; 278 (UP), San Juan Capistrano Historical Society; 278 (LO), Courtesy of the Bancroft Library, University of California, Berkeley; 279 (LE), LOC, Geography and Map Division; 279 (RT), California Missions Resource Center/Pentacle Press; 280, National Museum of the American Indian, SI (1215). Photo by NMAI Photo Services; 281 (UP), Reproduced by permission of The Huntington Library, San Marino, California (Pierce 02526); 281 (LO), National Museum of the American Indian, SI (246951). Photo by NMAI Photo Services; 282 (UP), W. Langdon Kihn/NGC; 282 (LO), National Museum of the American Indian, SI (217690). Photo by NMAI Photo Services; 283, Edward S. Curtis; 284 (UP), bpk, Berlin/Ethnologisches Museum, Staatliche Museen/Dietrich Graf/Art Resource, NY; 284 (LO), Seagoing Tomol. Created in 1992 by a team of artists in Lompoc. Photograph by David J. McLaughlin © 2005 Pentacle Press; 285, LOC, Edward S. Curtis Collection, LC-USZ62-101260; 286, Lynn Johnson/NGS.

LIST OF THE MAPS

KEY: (A) Archival map, (P) Physical map, (R) Large-scale regional map

6 American Indians

11 Paleo-Indian Migration and Sites

12 Mississippian Moundbuilders, 900–1450

14 Native Languages

15 Estimated Number of Inhabitants
per 100 Square Miles at the Time of Contact

15 European Settlement at a Glance

16 Epidemics Among Indians, 16th–20th Centuries

17 Religious Movements,
17th–20th Centuries

18–19 Shrinking Indian Territories

20–21 Atlas of Indian Nations Cultural Regions

CHAPTER 1: NORTHEAST
26–27 The Northeast (P)

28 Northeast Tribal Homelands

29 Languages of the Northeast

31 Great Lakes (R)

32 Atlantic Coast (R)

34–35 Maritime Canada (R)

36–37 Natives and Puritans (A)

38 Dutch and French Claims

40–41 The Fur Trade

42 East Coast Settlement and Conflicts

44–45 Battle of the Monongahela (A)

46–47 The Iroquois League (A)

49 The Black Hawk War (A)

CHAPTER 2: SOUTHEAST
63 The Southeast (P)

64 Southeast Tribal Homelands

65 Languages of the Southeast

67 Southern Appalachians and the Coastal Plain (R)

68 Florida (R)

71 Tennessee Valley to the Gulf Coast (R)

73 Map of Mound Park, Alabama (A)

74 The Secotan and the Lost Colony (A)

76–77 The Five Civilized Tribes (A)

78–79 The Trail of Tears (A)

80 Cherokee Country (A)

81 Emigrant Indians (A)

82 Territorial Cessions by the Cherokee

CHAPTER 3: ARCTIC AND SUBARCTIC
94–95 The Arctic and Subarctic (P)

96 Arctic and Subarctic Tribal Homelands

97 Languages of the Arctic and Subarctic

98 Alaska Native Corporations

99 Western Arctic and Subarctic (R)

100 Eastern Arctic and Subarctic (R)

102–103 First Arctic Encounters (A)

104–105 The Polar Regions (A)

106–107 Hudson Bay Fur Trade (A)

108–109 Colton's Map of the Territory of Alaska (A)

CHAPTER 4: PLAINS
119 The Plains (P)

120 Plains Tribal Homelands

121 Languages of the Plains

122–123 Northern Plains (R)

124–125 Central Plains (R)

127 Southern Plains (R)

128 The Horse in North America

130–131 Mapping Indian Lands (A)

132 Conflicts on the Great Plains

134 The Sand Creek Massacre

136 The Riel Rebellions

138–139 Battle of the Little Bighorn (A)

140 Map of Custer Battlefield (A)

142–143 The Sioux Wars

144 The Massacre at Wounded Knee

145 Battle of Wounded Knee (A)

146 The American Bison (A)

CHAPTER 5: SOUTHWEST

169 The Southwest (P)

170 Southwest Tribal Homelands

171 Languages of the Southwest

172–173 Arizona and New Mexico (R)

174–175 Southern Texas and Northern Mexico (R)

177 The Pueblo Revolt of 1680 (A)

178 Hopi Resistance (A)

180 The Santa Fe Trail

181 Hand-drawn Pike map (A)

182 Chaco Canyon

184–185 Territory and Military Department of New Mexico (A)

186–187 The Treaty of Guadalupe Hidalgo (A)

189 Conflicts in the Southwest

190–191 Long Walk of the Navajo

CHAPTER 6: GREAT BASIN AND PLATEAU

203 Great Basin and Plateau (P)

204 Great Basin and Plateau Tribal Homelands

205 Languages of the Great Basin and Plateau

206 Canadian Plateau (R)

208–209 Columbia Plateau (R)

210–211 Great Basin (R)

212–213 Jedediah Smith (A)

214 Father Pierre-Jean de Smet (A)

216–217 Flight of the Nez Perce

219 Conflicts in the Great Basin and Plateau

220 Plan of the Battle of Four Lakes (A)

CHAPTER 7: NORTHWEST COAST

232 Northwest Coast (P)

234 Northwest Coast Tribal Homelands

235 Languages of the Northwest

236–237 Alaska Panhandle and Coastal British Columbia (R)

238 Vancouver Island and the Northwest U.S. Coast (R)

240 The Battle of Sitka (A)

242 Map of the Territory West of the Rocky Mountains (A)

244 The Oregon Trail

246–247 Philip's Map of British Columbia (A)

249 Whale Range Areas and Migration Routes

CHAPTER 8: CALIFORNIA

260 California (P)

262 California Tribal Homelands

263 Languages of California

265 Northern California (R)

266 Southern California (R)

268–269 Map of the Frémont Expeditions (A)

271 Map of the Mining District of California (A)

272 Klamath River Tribes (A)

274–275 Modoc War

279 California Missions (A)

APPENDIX

288–289 Contiguous U.S. Federally Recognized Indian Reservations and Tribes Map

290–293 Contiguous U.S. Federally Recognized Indian Tribes List

294–295 Alaskan Native Lands Map

296–297 Alaskan Native Tribes List

298–299 Canadian First Nations and Reserves Map

300–303 Canadian First Nations List

Boldface indicates illustrations.

A

Abenaki 35
Ackomock-Ki (Blackfoot chief) 130
Acoma Pueblo **195**
Act for the Relief of Mission Indians
 (1891) 263
Adams, John Quincy 86
Agriculture 16, 37, 47, 167, 168
Ahhu (Inuit seamstress) **105**
Ahwelah (Inuit guide) 105
Alabama (Creek) 148
Alabama, Indians of see Creek
 (Muscogee)
Alaska
 Alaskan Natives 98, 101,
  294–297
 Aleut (Unangan) 96, **101**, 109,
  109, 110, **112**, 241
 Alutiiq 110
 Athabascan **97,** 110
 boarding schools 98, 101
 Chugach 110–111
 Eyak 111
 Holikachuk 111
 Inupiat **112**, 112–113
 list of all Alaskan Native entities
  296–297
 map of Alaskan Natives areas,
  reservations, and tribes
  294–295
 map of panhandle 236–237
 Russian colonization 109
 Tlingit 234, **235,** 240, 241, **241,**
  253, 255
 Yup'ik (Eskimo) **101, 110,** 113
 see also Inuit (Eskimo)
Alaska Native Claims Settlement Act
 (1971) 98, 101
Alberta, Canada
 Blackfoot (Blackfeet) **126, 149,**
  149–150, **162,** 213, 214, 215
 Cree (Plains Cree) 122, 123,
  152–153
 Cree (subarctic) 96, 101, 107,
  111, 113
 Sioux (Dakota, Lakota, Nakota)
  139, 152, 157, 158, 162–163
Aleut (Unangan) 110
 basket **112**
 fur trade **109**
 Russian era 96, 109, 241
 seal harvest **101**
Algonquian language family 7,
 28–29, 97, 261
 Arapaho 15–16, 134, 138, **142,**
  148, **153**

Blackfoot (Blackfeet) **126, 149,**
 149–150, **162,** 213, 214,
 215
Cheyenne 15–16, 134, 138, 141,
 142, 150, 151
Cree (Plains Cree) 122, 123,
 152–153
Cree (subarctic) 96, 101, 107,
 111, 113
Delaware (Lenape) **50,** 154
Gros Ventre 154–155, **159**
Innu (Montagnais-Naskapi)
 111–112
Kickapoo 50
Maliseet (Malicite) 35, 50–51
Menominee **2–3, 4,** 5, **24,** 51
Miami 157–158
Micmac 35, **51,** 51–52
Mohegan 52
Narragansett 52–53
Oji-Cree (Severn Ojibwe and
 James Bay Cree) 107, 113
Ottawa (Odawa) 27, 45, 54
Passamaquoddy 35, 54
Penobscot 35, 54–55
Peoria 160–161
Potawatomi 30, 40, 45, 55
Powhatan **43,** 55–56, **56**
Sac and Fox 48, **48,** 49, **157,**
 161–162
Shawnee 162
Shinnecock 56
 see also Ojibwe (Chippewa);
  Pequot; Wampanoag
Allotment 17, 235–236, 263–264
Alutiiq 110
Amadas, Philip 75
American bison **114–115,** 117
 extermination 126, **146,**
  146–147
 extermination map 146
 hunting on horseback 129
 protection **147**
 skulls **125, 146**
American era 16–17
 California 262–264, 266
 Northwest Coast 234–235
American Horse (Oglala Lakota
 chief) 144
Anasazi 167, 168, 182, 183, 194
Anián, Strait of 102, 103
Ano-Tlosh (Taku chief) **230**
Apache 192
 cradleboards **175**
 horses **188**
 hunting and fishing 167
 medicine man's amulet **175**
 raids 187, 188
 reservations 184

resistance 16, 165, 170, 184–185,
 188, 188–189, **189**
 tribal homelands map 189
Appalachian Mountains
 map 67
Arapaho 148
 Battle of the Little Bighorn 138
 Fetterman Fight **142**
 Ghost Dance **153**
 resistance 15–16
 Sand Creek Massacre 134
Arctic and subarctic 88–113
 Alutiiq 110
 art **106**
 Athabascan **97,** 110
 chronology 92
 Chugach 110–111
 Cree (subarctic) 96, 101, 107,
  111, 113
 environmental issues 101
 European encounters 96–98, **102,**
  102–103, **103**
 Eyak 111
 Holikachuk 111
 Hudson Bay fur trade **106,** 106–
  107, **107**
 hunting and fishing 91, 92, 96,
  111
 Innu (Montagnais-Naskapi)
  111–112
 Inupiat **112,** 112–113
 map 94–95
 map of Eastern Arctic and
  subarctic 100
 map of Lake Superior-Hudson
  Bay region 106–107
 map of languages 97
 map of north of Greenland
  104–105
 map of tribal homelands 96
 map of Western Arctic and
  subarctic 99
 migration 92
 North Pole expeditions **104,**
  104–105, **105**
 Oji-Cree (Severn Ojibwe and
  James Bay Cree) 107, 113
 politics 97
 redressing wrongs 98, 101
 Russian America **108,** 108–109,
  109
 sports and recreation **98**
 Yup'ik (Eskimo) **101, 110,** 113
 see also Aleut (Unangan); Inuit
  (Eskimo)
Arikara **8,** 148–149, 213
Arizona
 Cocopah 192
 Havasupai 175, 192–193

Hualapai 193–194
Maricopa 194
Mohave (Mojave) **172,** 194, 213
Navajo 167, 170, **190,** 190–191,
 191, 192, 193, 194–195
Paiute 205–206, 224
Pima **193,** 195
Quechan (Yuma) 196
Tohono O'odham (Papago) 196
Yaqui 197
Yavapai 167, 184, 197
Zuni 167, 168, 197, **197**
 see also Apache; Hopi
Arrowmaker (Ojibwe man) **35**
Asia
 map of migration pattern to the
  Americas 11
Assiniboine 149, **151**
Athabascan (nation) **97,** 110
Athabascan (Na-Dené) language
 family 7, 92, 97, 110, 235, 261
 Athabascan **97,** 110
 Cahto (Kato) 280
 Coquille 250
 Eyak 111
 Holikachuk 111
 Hupa (Hoopa) **258, 272, 273,**
  280, 281, **285**
 Mattole (Bear River Indians)
  282–283
 Navajo 167, 170, **190,** 190–191,
  191, 192, 193, 194–195
 Tlingit 234, **235,** 240, 241, **241,**
  253, 255
 Tolowa 285
 Wailaki 285
 Wiyot 263, 286
 see also Apache
Atlantic Coast
 map 32
Awatovi (Aguatuvi) 179

B

Bad Axe River, Battle of the 48, **48**
 map 49
Baishan (Chiricahua Apache war
 leader) **164–165**
Bandelier National Monument, New
 Mexico **182**
Bannock 219, **219,** 222
Baranov, Alexander 241
Barboncito (Navajo chief) 190, 191
Barlowe, Arthur 75
Baskets **61, 69, 112, 262, 281, 284**
Batoche, Battle of (1885) **136,** 137
Báxoje (Iowa, Ioway) 156
Bear River Indians (Mattole)
 282–283

Bear River Massacre (1863) 202, 204, 226
Beauty contest **225**
Beaver Wars (1641–1701) 38, 40
Becknell, William 180
Belts **46, 47, 86**
Benteen, Frederick 138, 140, 141
Bierstadt, Albert
painting by **256–257**
Biloxi 84
Birchbark canoes 25, 27, **33, 54**
Bison **114–115,** 117
extermination 126, **146,** 146–147
extermination map 146
hunting on horseback 129
protection **147**
skulls **125, 146**
Black Coyote (Lakota man) 144
Black Elk (Oglala Lakota medicine man) 144
Black Hawk (Sac and Fox leader) 48, **48,** 49, 162
Black Hawk War (1832) 48–49, 161–162
map 49
Black Hills, wars for **142,** 142–143, **143**
Black Horse (Hidatsa-Mandan) **150**
Black Jim (Modoc) 276
Black Kettle (Cheyenne chief) **133,** 134, 151
Blackfoot (Blackfeet) 149–150
brave and tepee **162**
conflicts with Flathead 214, 215
conflicts with J. Smith 213
family and tepee **126**
Winter Counts (pictographs) **149**
Bloody Brook, Battle of (1675) **39**
Boarding schools 16–17
Arctic and subarctic 98, 101
California 264, 266
Great Basin and Plateau 204–205
Northwest Coast 238
Bodmer, Karl
painting by **85**
Borders, international and tribal 242–243
map 242
Bosque Redondo Reservation, New Mexico 190, 191, **191**
Boston Charley (Modoc) 276
Bowlegs, Billy **69, 83**
Braddock, Edward 45
British Columbia, Canada
Athabascan **97,** 110
Chehalis 250
Cree (Plains Cree) 122, 123, 152–153
Kootenai 205, 223–224

map 236–237
Muckleshoot 252
Salish 208, **215, 223, 224,** 225, **227, 234**
S'Klallam 254
Tlingit 234, **235,** 240, 241, **241, 253,** 255
British era
alliances 15, 39
Arctic and subarctic exploration 96, 107
Battle of Fish Creek **137**
Battle of Monongahela 45, **45**
Chesapeake 43
genocide 33
legacy 39
Natives and Puritans 37
Northeast 25
Northwest Coast 234–235
reliance on indigenous population 74
search for Northwest Passage 102
slave trade 62–64
tribal conflicts 37, **43**
British North American Boundary Commission **243**
Brown, Dee 144
Buckskin Charley (Ute chief) 218, **218**
Buffalo **114–115,** 117
extermination 126, **146,** 146–147
extermination map 146
hunting on horseback 129
protection **147**
skulls **125, 146**
Burnham, Thomas Mickell
painting by **130**

C
Cabot, John 102
Caddo 150–151
Caddoan language family
Arikara **8,** 148–149, 213
Caddo 150–151
Pawnee **155,** 160
Wichita 163
Cahokia (site), Illinois 13, **13**
Cahto (Kato) 280
Cahuilla 280, **283**
Cajuns 39
California 256–287
allotment 263–264
American era 262–264, 266
ancient ones 259, 261
boarding schools 264, 266
Cahto (Kato) 280
Cahuilla 280, **283**
Chemehuevi 280

chronology 261
Chumash **259,** 278, **278,** 280–281, **284**
Cupeño 281
Frémont expeditions **268,** 268–269, **269**
genocide 262–263
gold rushes 262–263, **270,** 270–271, 273
Hupa (Hoopa) **258, 272, 273,** 280, 281, **285**
Indian Reorganization Act 266–267
intertribal council **256–257**
Karuk (Karok) **281,** 281–282
Klamath River tribes **272,** 272–273, **273**
Kumeyaay (Diegueño, Kamia, Tipai-Ipai) 278, 282, **282, 286**
languages 261, 263
Luiseño 267, 282
Maidu 282
map 260
map of gold rush 271
map of languages 263
map of mission system 279
map of tribal communities 265–266
map of tribal homelands 262
Mattole (Bear River Indians) 282–283
mission system 13, 261, **278,** 278–279, **279**
Miwok (Me-wuk) 283
Modoc War **274,** 274–277, **275, 276, 277**
Mono (California Paiute) 283
Paiute 205–206, 224
Pit River 283
Pomo 261, 270, **282,** 283–284
Quechan (Yuma) 196
relocation 264
Round Valley (Covelo Indian Community) 284
Serrano 284–285
Shasta (Chasta) 285
Shoshone **198–199, 201,** 202, 204, 205, **207, 224,** 225–226
Spanish and Russian aspirations 261–262
termination 264
Tolowa 285
Wailaki 285
Washoe 285–286
Wintun (Nomlaki, Patwin) 261, **267,** 286
Wiyot 263, 286
Yana 263, 286

Yokut (including Chukchansi) **281,** 286
California Paiute (Mono) 283
California v. *Cabazon Band of Mission Indians* (1987) 267
Calumet (pipe) **160**
Calusa **84**
Canada
border with United States 234, 243, **243**
list of all First Nations 300–303
map of First Nations 298–299
map of linguistic stocks 6
Canadian Plateau
map 206
map of Native villages 208–209
Canby, Edward 275, **275,** 277
Canoes
birchbark 25, 27, **33, 54**
dugout 27, 74
Captain Jack (Modoc chief) 158, 218, **274,** 275, 276, **276, 277**
Caribou 92, 96
Caribou Inuit **10**
Carleton, James H. **191**
Carolina Indians **74**
Carson, Kit **184,** 190, **190,** 262, **268,** 269, **269**
Catawba 84
Catlin, George
encounter with Otoe-Missouria 160
paintings by **58–59, 60, 116, 157**
Cayuga 46, 50, 216
see also Iroquois Confederacy
Cayuse 205, 218, 222
Cayuse War (1847–1855) 218
Central Plains
map 124–125
Chaco Canyon, New Mexico 10, 167, **182,** 182–183, **183**
map 182
Champlain, Samuel de 39, **39,** 40–41, **47,** 111
Charbonneau, Toussaint 202
Charles III, King (Spain) 261, 278
Chasta (Shasta) 285
Chehalis 250
Chemehuevi 280
Cherokee 84–85
assimilation plan 65
cabin **82**
cessation of land 69–70, 80, 82
citizenship 66
clashes over territory 64
in Five Civilized Tribes 76
language family 65
map of lands 80, 82

relocation 69–70, 78–80, **79**
slavery 66
Southeast 67
syllabary (writing system) 66, **66**
Trail of Tears 78–80, **79**
Treaty of New Echota **78**
Chesapeake region
  British colonies 43
Cheyenne 151
  Battle of the Little Bighorn 138, 141
  Fetterman Fight **142**
  moccasins **150**
  resistance 15–16
  Sand Creek Massacre 134
Chickasaw 65, 76, **77,** 151
Chilkat **236**
Chimakuan language family
  Quileute 251, 253
Chinook 250, **254**
Chinookan language family
  Chinook 250, **254**
Chippewa (Ojibwe) 53
  birchbark canoe 25, 27, **33, 54**
  clans 30–31
  fur trade 40, 96, 107
  harvesting wild rice **55**
  language 35
  shirt **53**
  territorial expansion 28
  Thirsting Dance 118
  as trade middlemen 35
  Turtle Mountain Reservation, North Dakota 153
  see also Three Fires Confederacy
Chiricahua Apache 188
Chitimacha 85
Chivington, John M. 134, **135**
Choctaw **77,** 85
  assimilation plan 65
  basket **69**
  citizenship 66
  current status 70, 77
  in Five Civilized Tribes 76, 77
  housing **77, 85**
  relocation 78
  stickball game **58–59**
Chugach 110–111
Chukchansi (Yokut) **281,** 286
Chumash **259,** 278, **278,** 280–281, **284**
Chumashan language family 263
Churchill, Frank 153
Citizenship 66
Civil War, U.S. 70, 80
Clans 29, 30–31
Clark, William 130
Clovis (site), New Mexico 10
Coast Salish **234**

Coastal Plain
  map 67
Cochise (Apache) 184, **185,** 189
Cocopah 192
Coeur d'Alene 222
Colonial regimes 13, 15–16
Colorado
  Ute 201, **218, 219, 222,** 226, **227**
Columbia Plateau
  map 210
Colville (Confederated Tribes) **215,** 222–223
Colville Falls **223**
Colville Reservation 205, **207,** 225
Comanche 129, 151–152, 180, 187, 213
Comanche (horse) **141**
Confederated Tribes
  Colville **215,** 222–223
  Grand Ronde 251
  Warm Springs 227
Connecticut
  Mohegan 52
  see also Pequot
Connor, Patrick 223
Cook, Frederick 105
Cook, James 102
Coos 250
Coosan language family
  Coos 250
Coquille 250
Corps of Discovery Expedition (Lewis and Clark expedition) **130,** 130–131, 202
  map 130–131
Cortés, Hernán 103
Coushatta 85–86
Covelo Indian Community (Round Valley) 284
Covenant Chain (British-Iroquois alliance) 47
Cowlitz 250–251
Cradleboards **175, 224**
Crazy Horse (Lakota leader) **133,** 139, 141, 142, **142**
Cree (Plains Cree) 122, 123, 152–153
Cree (subarctic) 96, 101, 107, 111, 113
Creek (Alabama) 148
Creek (Muscogee) 86
  agriculture 76
  ancestors 61
  assimilation plan 65
  cession treaties 66
  citizenship 66
  civil war 69, 83
  in Five Civilized Tribes 76

resistance 68–69
  trade in deerskins 64
  woven beaded belt **86**
Crespi, Juan **279**
Crook, George **189**
Crow 153–154, 213, 217
Cupeño 281
Curtis, Edward
  photographs by **112, 159, 217**
Custer, George Armstrong **133,** 138, **138,** 139, 140, 141, 142, 147

D
Daggett, Mike 226
Dakota 27, 48, **48, 153**
  see also Sioux
Dawes Act (1887) 17, 19, 235
De Bry, Theodore 75
De Smet, Pierre-Jean 202, 204, **214,** 214–215, **215**
De Soto, Hernando 61, 62, 70, 72
De Ulloa, Francisco 103
De Vargas, Diego 179, **179**
Delaware (Lenape) **50,** 154
Diegueño (Kamia, Kumeyaay, Tipai-Ipai) 278, 282, **282, 286**
Disease epidemics 10, 13
  California 261
  maps 16
  Northeast 25
  Plains 126
  Southeast 61–62
Dogsledding 91, **91**
Domínguez, Francisco Atanasio 201–202
Drake, Sir Francis 75
Du-cur-re-a (Ho-chunk chief) **52**
Dugout canoes 27, 74
Dutch era 15, 39
Dutch West India Company **38**

E
Eastern Arctic and subarctic
  map 100
Eastman, Charles A. **156**
Eastman, Seth
  painting by **158**
Egingway (Inuit guide) 105, **105**
Elk, Stanley Goodvoice **163**
Escalante, Silvestre Vélez de 201–202
Eskimo see Inuit; Yup'ik
Eskimo-Aleut language family 92, 97
  Aleut (Unangan) 96, **101,** 109, **109,** 110, **112,** 241
  Alutiiq 110
  Chugach 110–111

Inupiat **112,** 112–113
Yup'ik (Eskimo) **101, 110,** 113
  see also Inuit (Eskimo)
Etukishook (Inuit guide) 105
European contact
  Arctic and subarctic 96–98, **102,** 102–103, **103**
  convergence map 15
  disease introduction 13, 25, 61–62
  Great Basin and Plateau 202
  Northeast 38–39, 42–43
  Plains 126
  population map 15
  resistance 31, 33–34
  Southwest 168, 170–171
Eyak 111

F
Farming 16, 37, 47, 167, 168
Federally designated tribal entities 290–293
Federally recognized Indian reservations and tribes
  map 288–289
Fetterman Fight 142, **142**
First Nations of Canada
  list of all First Nations 300–303
  map 298–299
Fish Creek, Battle of 137, **137**
Five Civilized Tribes 65–66, **76,** 76–77, **77,** 78
  see also Cherokee; Chickasaw; Choctaw; Creek (Muscogee); Seminole
Flathead 214, 215, 231
Florida
  map 68
  Miccosukee 68, 70, 86–87, **87**
  slave raid 62–63
  see also Seminole
Florida Seminole 17, 69, 70, **70, 83**
Forsyth, James 144, **144**
Fort Abraham Lincoln State Park, North Dakota **161**
Fort Berthold Indian Reservation, North Dakota 149, **150**
Fort Bowie **184**
Fort Bridger Treaty (1868) 204
Fort Defiance, Arizona **191**
Fort Duquesne 45
Fort Phil Kearny **142**
Four Lakes, Battle of **220,** 220–221, **221**
  map of battle plan 220
Fox 15, 33
  see also Sac and Fox
Freemont arrowhead **223**

Frémont, John Charles 245, 262, **268,** 268–269, **269**
map of expeditions 268–269
French and Indian War **44,** 44–45, **45**
French era
alliances 13, 39, 44
Arctic and subarctic 96
Battle of Monongahela **44,** 45
fur trade 27, 96
genocide 15, 33
legacy 39
missionaries 13
Northeast 25
search for Northwest Passage 102
Frobisher, Martin 96, 102, **102,** 112
Fur trade
Arctic and subarctic 96–97, 107, **107, 109**
birchbark canoes 27
Great Basin 213
Hudson Bay 107, **107**
map 40
Northeast 40–41

G
Gadsden Purchase (1853) 187
Gall (Hunkpapa Lakota chief) 138, 139, 140, 141
Gaming development 267
Garfield (Jicarilla Apache chief) **196**
Gatewood, Charles 184
Genocide 15, 16
British era 31, 33, 43
California 262–263
French era 33
Georgia
distribution of Cherokee lands 82
Geronimo (Apache warrior) 184, 188, **188**
Ghost Dance 121–122, 144, 150
Gibbs, George 212, **212**
Gloucester Harbor, Massachusetts map 40–41
Gold rushes
California 262–263, **270,** 270–271, 273
Great Basin and Plateau 202
Indian miners **247**
map of California 271
map of Northwest Coast 246–247
Northwest Coast 235, 246–247, **247**
Gomes, Estêvão 102
Gómez, Francisco **279**
Goshute 223

Grand Ronde (Confederated Tribes) 251
Great Basin and Plateau 198–227
assimilation 202, 204–205
Bannock 219, **219,** 222
Battle of Four Lakes **220,** 220–221, **221**
Cayuse 205, 218, 222
chronology 202
Coeur d'Alene 222
Colville (Confederated Tribes) **215,** 222–223
conflicts **218,** 218–219, **219**
European encounters 201–202
Father Pierre-Jean De Smet **214,** 214–215, **215**
gambling **207**
Goshute 223
Great Basin map 211
Jedediah Smith 212–213, **213**
Klamath 218, 223, 269, **272,** 275
Kootenai 205, 223–224
map 203
map drawn by de Smet 214
map drawn by Gibbs 212–213
map of conflicts 219
map of languages 205
map of tribal homelands 204
Nez Perce **117,** 129, **200,** 216, **217,** 224
Nez Perce War **216,** 216–217, **217**
Paiute 205–206, 224
Pend d'Oreille (Kalispel) **215,** 218, 225
Spokane 226, **243**
survival 205–208, 211
tribal beadwork **207**
Umatilla 216, 226
Ute 201, **218, 219, 222,** 226, **227**
Walla Walla 216, 226–227
Warm Springs (Confederated Tribes) 227
Yahooskin 218, 227
Yakama (Yakima) 221, **226,** 227
see also Salish; Shoshone
Great Lakes region
map 31
reservations 31
resistance 15, 33
Great Plains *see* Plains
Great Sioux Reservation 138, 143
Greeneville, Ohio 34
Greenland Inuit 92, 98, 112
see also Inuit (Eskimo)
Gros Ventre 154–155, **159**
Gwich'in 92

H
Haida **231,** 247
Handsome Lake (Iroquois prophet) 47
Harrison, William Henry 33–34, 162
Haudenosaunee (People of the Longhouse) *see* Iroquoian tribes
Havasupai 175, 192–193
Hawkins, Benjamin 65, 76, 86
Headdresses **148, 156, 252, 280**
Hearne, Samuel 102
Henson, Matthew **105**
Hicks, Charles 69, **78**
Hidatsa 155, 202
Ho-chunk (Winnebago) 30, **30,** 48, **52,** 155–156
Hoffman, William 194
Hoh 251
Hokan language family 261, 263
Karuk (Karok) **281,** 281–282
Pit River 283
Pomo 261, 270, **282,** 283–284
Shasta (Chasta) 285
Yana 263, 286
Holikachuk 111
Hooker Jim (Modoc leader) 274, 275, 276
Hoopa (Hupa) **258, 272, 273, 280,** 281, **285**
Hootch, Molly 98, 101
Hopi 193
agriculture 10, 167
ancestors 194
dwelling **194**
kachinas **9,** 168
perseverance 172, 175
Pueblo Revolt 179, 193
religion 179
resistance 178–179, **179**
Snake Clan priest **166**
Horses
Plains **117,** 118, **128,** 128–129, **129**
Southwest 167
Howard, Oliver 217
Hualapai 193–194
Hudson, Henry 107
Hudson Bay
fur trade 96–97, **106,** 106–107, **107**
Hudson's Bay Company 107, **107**
Hunkpapa Lakota 140, 141, 144
Hupa (Hoopa) **258, 272, 273, 280,** 281, **285**
Huron 28, **38**

I
Idaho
Bannock 219, **219,** 222

Coeur d'Alene 222
Nez Perce **117,** 129, **200,** 216, **217,** 224
Paiute 205–206, 224
Salish 208, **215, 223, 224,** 225, **227, 234**
Shoshone **198–199, 201,** 202, 204, 205, **207, 224,** 225–226
Spokane 226, **243**
Indian Removal Act (1830) 68, 78
Indian Reorganization Act (1934) 266–267
Indian reservations
map of Alaskan Native areas, Indian reservations, and tribes 294–295
map of federally recognized Indian reservations and tribes 288–289
map of Southwest 172–173
Indian territories
map of Indian territories (1775–1819) 18
map of Indian territories (1820–1864) 18
map of Indian territories (1865–1894) 19
map of Indian territories (1895–2013) 19
Indian Territory 78, 80, 81, 124–126
see also Oklahoma
Indian Wars 170–171
Innu (Montagnais-Naskapi) 111–112
Intertribal religious movements
maps 17
Inuit (Eskimo) 112
art **106**
artist with daughter **106**
Canadian Inuit with kayak and igloo **88–89**
Caribou Inuit woman with children **10**
domestication of dogs **91**
European contact 102
fur trade 107
Greenland 92, 98, 112
hunter on ice **93**
man near igloo **113**
North Pole expeditions **104,** 105
Nunavut 97–98
in rainproof parka of walrus intestine **90**
traditional diet and lifestyle 101
Inupiat **112,** 112–113
Iowa (Báxoje, Ioway) 156
Iowa (state)
Ho-chunk (Winnebago) 30, **30,** 48, **52,** 155–156
Sac and Fox 48, **48,** 49, **157,** 161–162

Iroquoian language family
  Cayuga 46, 50, 216
  Mohawk 35, 46, 52
  Oneida 46, 53
  Onondaga 46, **47,** 53–54
  Seneca 46, 56
  Tuscarora 46, **56,** 57
  Wyandotte 163
Iroquoian tribes
  agriculture 47
  alliance with British 43
  artistic designs **56**
  conflict with Europeans **43**
  conflict with Innu 111–112
  dugout canoes 27
  mask **30**
  matrilineal clans 29, 30
  moccasins **54**
  village defenses **47**
Iroquois Confederacy 15, 38, 39,
    47, 52
Iroquois League 46–47, **47,** 50, 56
  map 46–47
  see also Cayuga; Mohawk; Oneida;
    Onondaga; Seneca
Iroquois Wars (1641–1701) 38, 40
Ishi (Yahi) 263
Isleta Pueblo **179**

J

Jackson, Andrew 69, 76, 78, **78,**
    83, 86
Jackson, William Henry
  photograph by **155**
James Bay Cree *see* Oji-Cree
Jamestown (colony), Virginia 43
Jamestown Settlement (living-history
    museum), Virginia **56**
Jay Treaty (1794) 51, 234, 243
Jefferson, Thomas 130
Joseph (Nez Perce chief) 217, **217,**
    224

K

Kachinas **9,** 168, **194**
Kalispel (Pend d'Oreille) **215,** 218,
    225
Kamia (Diegueño, Kumeyaay, Tipai-
    Ipai) 278, 282, **282, 286**
Kamiakin (Yakama chief) 221, **221**
Kansa (Kanza, Kaw) 156
Kansas (state)
  Iowa (Báxoje, Ioway) 156
  Kickapoo 50
  Potawatomi 30, 40, 45, 55
  Sac and Fox 48, **48,** 49, **157,**
    161–162

Karuk (Karok) **281,** 281–282
Kato (Cahto) 280
Kaw (Kansa, Kanza) 156
Kelsey, Andrew 270
Kickapoo 50
King Philip's War (1675) 37, **39,**
    42, 43, 53
Kintpuash (Captain Jack) 158, 218,
    274, 275, 276, **276, 277**
Kiowa 117, 156–157
Kiowa-Tanoan language family
  Kiowa 117, 156–157
Klamath 218, 223, 269, **272,** 275
Klamath and Salmon River Indian
    War (1855) 273
Klamath Reservation 158–159, 218,
    275, 276
Klamath River tribes **272,** 272–273
  map 272
Knight, Arlie **150**
Kohl, Johann Georg 106
Kootenai 205, 223–224
Kumeyaay (Diegueño, Kamia, Tipai-
    Ipai) 278, 282, **282**
Kwakiutl **251, 252**

L

La France, Joseph 96–97
La Salle, René-Robert Cavelier de
    39
La Vérendrye, Pierre Gaultier de
    Varennes, Sieur de 106
Labrador, Canada
  Innu (Montagnais-Naskapi)
    111–112
  Micmac 35, **51,** 51–52
  see also Inuit (Eskimo)
Lacrosse **158**
Lakota
  Battle of the Little Bighorn 133,
    138, 139, 140, 141
  Black Hills 142
  expansion of territory 123
  Fetterman Fight, Fort Phil Kearny
    142
  horse culture 129, **129**
  Nez Perce and 217
  resistance 15–16
  Sun Dance 118
  Winter Counts 117
  Wounded Knee Massacre 144,
    144
  see also Sioux
Lane, Ralph 75
Language families 7, 9, 15
  see also Algonquian language
    family; Athabascan (Na-Dené)
    language family; Caddoan

language family; Chimakuan
  language family; Chinookan
  language family; Chumashan
  language family; Coosan
  language family; Eskimo-
  Aleut language family; Hokan
  language family; Iroquoian
  language family; Kiowa-
  Tanoan language family;
  Muscogean language family;
  Penutian language family;
  Plateau Penutian language
  family; Salishan language
  family; Siouan language
  family; Tanoan language family;
  Uto-Aztecan language family;
  Wakashan language family;
  Wintuan language family;
  Yukian language family; Yuman
  language family
Language isolates
  Cayuse 205, 218, 222
  Chitimacha 85
  Chumash **259,** 278, **278,** 280–
    281, **284**
  Kootenai 205, 223–224
  Lower Umpqua 251
  Tonkawa 163
  Tunica 84, 87
  Umpqua 213, 251, 255
  Washoe 285–286
  Zuni 167, 168, 197, **197**
Languages
  California 261
  language families 15
  language isolates 65, 235
  map of Arctic and subarctic 97
  map of California 263
  map of Great Basin and Plateau
    205
  map of linguistic stocks 6
  map of Native languages in North
    America 14
  map of Northeast 29
  map of Northwest Coast 235
  map of Plains 121
  map of Southeast 65
  map of the Southwest 171
  number of distinct languages 7,
    9, 15
  number of language families 7,
    9, 15
Lava Beds National Monument,
    California **262**
Leech Lake Indian Reservation,
    Minnesota 17, **55**
Lenape (Delaware) **50,** 154
Leschi (Nisqually chief) 252, 253
Lewis, Meriwether 130

Lewis and Clark expedition **130,**
    130–131, 202
  map 130–131
Lincoln, Abraham 48, 204
Lindneux, Robert
  painting by **79,** 135
Linguistic stocks
  map 6
Little Bighorn, Battle of the 121,
    133, **138,** 138–141, **139, 140,**
    141
  maps 138–139, 140
Lone Dog **120**
Long Walk of the Navajo **190,**
    190–191, **191**
Looking Horse, Arvol 121
Lost Colony, Roanoke Island, North
    Carolina 74–75
Louisiana
  Biloxi 84
  Chitimacha 85
  Coushatta 85–86
  Tunica 84, 87
Loup, Nebraska **155**
Lower Creek 69
Lower Umpqua 251
Luiseño 267, 282
Lummi 251–252, **255**

M

MacKenzie, Alexander 102
Maidu 282
Maine
  Maliseet (Malicite) 35, 50–51
  Micmac 35, **51,** 51–52
  Passamaquoddy 35, 54
  Penobscot 35, 54–55
Makah 248, **248,** 252
Maliseet (Malicite) 35, 50–51
Mandan 157
Mandan-Hidatsa **161**
Mangas Coloradas (Apache chief)
    165, 188, **189**
Manhattan, purchase of **38**
Manifest Destiny 16, 181, 262
Manitoba, Canada
  Cree (Plains Cree) 122, 123,
    152–153
  Cree (subarctic) 96, 101, 107,
    111, 113
  Oji-Cree (Severn Ojibwe and
    James Bay Cree) 107, 113
  Sioux (Dakota, Lakota, Nakota)
    139, 152, 157, 158, 162–
    163
  see also Ojibwe (Chippewa)
Manuelito (Navajo chief) 190,
    190, 191

Maps
  Alaska panhandle and coastal British Columbia 236–237
  Alaskan Native areas, Indian reservations, and tribes 294–295
  Alaskan Native corporations 98
  Apache tribal homelands 189
  Arctic and subarctic 94–95
  Arctic and subarctic languages 97
  Arctic and subarctic tribal homelands 96
  Atlantic Coast 32
  Battle of Four Lakes 220
  Battle of Monongahela 44–45
  Battle of the Bad Axe River 49
  Battle of the Little Bighorn 138–139, 140
  Black Hawk War 49
  buffalo extermination 146
  California 260
  California gold rush 271
  California languages 263
  California mission system 279
  California tribal communities 265–266
  California tribal homelands 262
  Canadian Plateau Native villages 208–209
  Central Plains 124–125
  Chaco Canyon 182
  Cherokee lands 80, 82
  Columbia Plateau 209
  disease epidemics 16
  Eastern Arctic and subarctic 100
  European contact 15
  federally recognized Indian reservations and tribes 288–289
  First Nations of Canada 298–299
  Florida 68
  Frémont expeditions 268–269
  fur trade 40
  Gloucester Harbor, Massachusetts 40–41
  Great Basin 211
  Great Basin (Gibbs) 212–213
  Great Basin and Plateau 203
  Great Basin and Plateau conflicts 219
  Great Basin and Plateau languages 205
  Great Basin and Plateau tribal homelands 204
  Great Lakes region 31
  Indian territories, shrinking 18–19
  Indian Territory land allocations 81
  intertribal religious movements 17
  Iroquois League 46–47

Klamath River tribes 272
Lake Superior to Hudson Bay 106–107
languages 14
Lewis and Clark expedition 130–131
linguistic stocks 6
Maritime Canada 34–35
migration from Asia 11
Mississippian culture 12
Modoc War 274–275
Moundville, Alabama 73
New England 32
New Mexico 184–185
Nez Perce War 216–217
north of Greenland 104–105
Northeast 26–27
Northeast conflicts 36–37, 42
Northeast language 29
Northeast tribal homelands 28, 38
Northern Plains 122–123
Northwest Coast 232
Northwest Coast gold diggings 246–247
Northwest Coast languages 235
Northwest Coast tribal homelands 234
Northwest Passage 103
Oregon Trail 244
Plains 119
Plains settlements and forts 132
Plains tribal homelands 120
population at time of European contact 15
Pueblo country, New Mexico 177
Riel rebellions 136
Russian America 108–109
Sand Creek Massacre 134
Santa Fe Trail 180
Southeast federally recognized tribes 63
Southeast languages 65
Southeast watercolor map 74
Southern Appalachians and Coastal Plain 67
Southern Plains 127
Southwest 169, 181
Southwest Indian reservations 172–173
Southwest languages 171
Southwest tribal lands 170
Texas 174–175
Trail of Tears 78–79
Treaty of Guadalupe Hidalgo 186–187
Vancouver Island and Northwest U.S. Coast 238
Western Arctic and subarctic 99

whale range and migration routes 249
Wounded Knee Massacre 144, 145
Maricopa 194
Maritime Canada
  map 34–35
  see also Labrador, Canada; New Brunswick, Canada; Newfoundland, Canada; Nova Scotia, Canada
Marriage, clan restrictions 30
Marshall, James W. 270
Massachusetts see Wampanoag
Massasoit (Wampanoag chief) 37
Matrilineal clans 29
Mattole (Bear River Indians) 282–283
McDougall, William 137
Me-wuk (Miwok) 283
Meeker, Nathaniel 218
Menchero, Fray Juan Miguel 179
  map 178
Menominee 2–3, 4, 5, 24, 51
Mescalero Apache 190, 191
Metacom (King Philip) 37
Métis 136, 136–137, 137
Mexican–American War 170
  see also Treaty of Guadalupe Hidalgo
Mexico
  Apache and Comanche raids 187, 188
  colonial transition in Southwest 184–185
  independence 170
  Kickapoo 50
  Kumeyaay (Diegueño, Kamia, Tipai-Ipai) 278, 282, 282, 286
  map of linguistic stocks 6
  Sac and Fox 48, 48, 49, 157, 161–162
  Tohono O'odham (Papago) 196
  Treaty of Guadalupe Hidalgo 186
  tribal languages 7
  Yaqui 197
  Yavapai 167, 184, 197
Miami 157–158
Miccosukee 68, 70, 86–87, 87
Michif (language) 137
Michigan
  Ottawa (Odawa) 27, 45, 54
  Potawatomi 30, 40, 45, 55
  see also Ojibwe (Chippewa)
Micmac 35, 51, 51–52
Migration from Asia 9–10, 92
  map 11
Miles, Nelson 184, 188
Miniconjou 144

Minnesota
  Sioux (Dakota, Lakota, Nakota) 139, 152, 157, 158, 162–163
  see also Ojibwe (Chippewa)
Minuit, Peter 38
Mission system 261, 273, 277–278, 278, 279
  map 279
Mississippi see Choctaw
Mississippi River Valley
  map 71
Mississippian culture (moundbuilders) 13, 62, 72, 72, 73
  map 12
Miwok (Me-wuk) 283
Moccasins 54, 150, 227
Modern era 17
Modoc 158–159, 218, 262, 276, 276
Modoc War 218, 274, 274–277, 276, 277
  maps 274–275
Mohave (Mojave) 172, 194, 213
Mohawk 35, 46, 52
  see also Iroquois Confederacy
Mohegan 52
Mono (California Paiute) 283
Monongahela, Battle of (1755) 44, 44–45, 45
  map 44–45
Montagnais-Naskapi 111–112
Montana
  Assiniboine 149, 151
  Blackfoot (Blackfeet) 126, 149, 149–150, 162, 213, 214, 215
  Cheyenne 15–16, 134, 138, 141, 142, 150, 151
  Cree (Plains Cree) 122, 123, 152–153
  Crow 153–154, 213, 217
  Gros Ventre 154–155, 159
  Kootenai 205, 223–224
  Pend d'Oreille (Kalispel) 215, 218, 225
  Salish 208, 215, 223, 224, 225, 227, 234
  Sioux (Dakota, Lakota, Nakota) 139, 152, 157, 158, 162–163
  Spokane 226, 243
  see also Ojibwe (Chippewa)
Moore, James 62
Motanic, Esther 225
Moundbuilders (Mississippian culture) 13, 62, 72, 72, 73
  map 12
Moundville, Alabama 72, 72–73
  map 73

Muckleshoot 252
Muscogean language family
    Alabama (Creek) 148
    Chickasaw 65, 76, **77,** 151
    Coushatta 85–86
    Miccosukee 68, 70, 86–87, **87**
    see also Choctaw; Creek
        (Muscogee); Seminole
Muscogean-speaking peoples 64, 65
Muscogee (Creek) 86
    agriculture 76
    ancestors 61
    assimilation plan 65
    cession treaties 66
    citizenship 66
    civil war 69, 83
    in Five Civilized Tribes 76
    resistance 68–69
    trade in deerskins 64
    woven beaded belt **86**
Mystic Massacre (1637) 37, 55

N
Na-Dené language family *see*
    Athabascan (Na-Dené) language
    family
Naiche (Apache chief) 184, 188
Nakota 129, 149
    see also Sioux
Narragansett 52–53
Naskapi 101
Native Alaskans *see* Alaska
Navajo 194–195
    colonization 170
    Long Walk **190,** 190–191, **191**
    ranching 167
    silversmith **193**
    weaving **192**
Nebraska
    Ho-chunk (Winnebago) 30, **30,**
        48, **52,** 155–156
    Iowa (Báxoje, Ioway) 156
    Omaha 159
    Ponca 161
    Sac and Fox 48, **48,** 49, **157,**
        161–162
    Sioux (Dakota, Lakota, Nakota)
        139, 152, 157, 158, 162–163
Neiosioke 75
Nevada
    Goshute 223
    Paiute 205–206, 224
    Shoshone **198–199, 201,** 202,
        204, 205, **207, 224,** 225–226
    Washoe 285–286
New Brunswick, Canada
    Maliseet (Malicite) 35, 50–51
    Micmac 35, **51,** 51–52

New England
    early contact with British 43
    Indian-British conflict 37
    map 32
    map of conflicts 36–37
New Mexico
    map 177
    Navajo 167, 170, **190,** 190–191,
        191, 192, 193, 194–195
    territory map 184–185
    see also Apache; Pueblo
New York
    Cayuga 46, 50, 216
    Mohawk 35, 46, 52
    Oneida 46, 53
    Onondaga 46, **47,** 53–54
    Seneca 46, 56
    Shinnecock 56
    Tuscarora 46, **56,** 57
Newfoundland, Canada
    Micmac 35, **51,** 51–52
Nez Perce **117,** 129, **200,** 216, **217,**
    224
Nez Perce War **216,** 216–217, **217**
    maps 216–217
Nicollet, Joseph 215
Nisga'a **255**
Nisqually 252
Nixon administration 101
Nlaka'pamux (Salish girl) 247
Nooksack 252
North America
    map of disease epidemics 16
    map of intertribal religious
        movements 17
    map of linguistic stocks 6
    map of migration pattern from
        Asia 11
    map of Native languages 14, 15
    map of population collision 15
North Carolina
    Cherokee 82, **82**
    see also Cherokee
North Dakota
    Arikara **8,** 148–149, 213
    Cree (Plains Cree) 122, 123,
        152–153
    Hidatsa 155, 202
    Mandan 157
    Sioux (Dakota, Lakota, Nakota)
        139, 152, 157, 158, 162–163
    see also Ojibwe (Chippewa)
North Pole **104,** 104–105, **105**
Northeast 22–57
    alliances 27–28
    Battle of the Monongahela **44,**
        44–45
    Black Hawk War (1832) **48,**
        48–49

British-Indian conflicts **43**
Cayuga 46, 50, 216
chronology 27
clans 30–31
colonization and survival 34–35
conflicts 42
disease epidemics 25
economy 23
European contact **42,** 42–43, **43**
European invasion **38,** 38–39, **39**
family traditions **30**
fur trade 40–41
Ho-chunk (Winnebago) 30, **30,**
    48, **52,** 155–156
Iroquois League 46–47, **47**
Kickapoo 50
Lenape (Delaware) **50,** 154
Maliseet (Malicite) 35, 50–51
map 26–27
map of European-tribal conflicts 42
map of languages 29
map of tribal homelands 28
Menominee **2–3, 4,** 5, **24,** 51
Micmac 35, **51,** 51–52
Mohawk 35, 46, 52
Mohegan 52
Narragansett 52–53
Natives and Puritans 36–37, **37**
Oneida 46, 53
Onondaga 46, **47,** 53–54
Ottawa (Odawa) 27, 45, 54
Passamaquoddy 35, 54
Penobscot 35, 54–55
political and cultural diversity
    27–30
Potawatomi 30, 40, 45, 55
Powhatan **43,** 55–56, **56**
resistance 31, 33–34
Seneca 46, 56
Shinnecock 56
Tuscarora 46, **56,** 57
villages 27
waterways 25, 27
see also Iroquois Confederacy;
    Ojibwe (Chippewa);
    Pequot; Sioux (Dakota,
    Lakota, Nakota); Three Fires
    Confederacy; Wampanoag
Northern Cheyenne 133
Northern Plains
    map 122–123
Northwest Coast 228–255
    Battle of Sitka **240,** 240–241, **241**
    boarding schools 238
    British and American era 234–235
    Chehalis 250
    Chinook 250, **254**
    chronology 233
    Coos 250

Coquille 250
Cowlitz 250–251
diversity 233
fishing **228–229**
gold rushes 235, 246–247, **247**
Grand Ronde (Confederated
    Tribes) 251
Hoh 251
international and tribal borders
    242–243, **243**
land cession treaties 235
language map 235
Lower Umpqua 251
Lummi 251–252, **255**
Makah 248, **248,** 252
map 232
map of borders 242
map of tribal homelands 234
maps 238
mask frontlet **250**
Muckleshoot 252
Nisqually 252
Nooksack 252
Oregon Trail **244,** 244–245, **245**
political and social hierarchy 231,
    233
Puyallup 253
Quileute 251, 253
Quinault 251, 253
Russian era 233–234
Samish 253
Sauk-Suiattle 253
Siletz 253–254
Siuslaw 254
S'Klallam 254
Skokomish 254
Snoqualmie 254
Squaxin Island 254
Stillaguamish (Stoluckwamish)
    254
Suquamish 255
Swinomish 255
Tlingit 234, **235,** 240, 241, **241,**
    253, 255
treaty period 235
Tulalip 255
twentieth century 235–236,
    238–239
Umpqua 213, 251, 255
Upper Skagit 255
whaling **248,** 248–249
Northwest Passage 96, 102, **102,**
    103, 106
    map 103
Northwest Territories, Canada
    Athabascan **97,** 110
    Cree (subarctic) 96, 101, 107,
        111, 113
    see also Inuit (Eskimo)

Nova Scotia, Canada
  Micmac 35, **51,** 51–52
Nunavut, Canada 97–98
  Athabascan **97,** 110
  see also Inuit (Eskimo)

O

Odawa (Ottawa) 27, 45, 54
  see also Three Fires Confederacy
Oglala Lakota 141, **160, 163**
Ohkay Owingeh (San Juan Indian)
  176
Oji-Cree (Severn Ojibwe and James
  Bay Cree) 107, 113
Ojibwe (Chippewa) 53
  birchbark canoe 25, 27, **33, 54**
  clans 30–31
  fur trade 40, 96, 107
  harvesting wild rice **55**
  language 35
  shirt **53**
  territorial expansion 28
  Thirsting Dance 118
  as trade middlemen 35
  Turtle Mountain Reservation,
    North Dakota 153
  see also Three Fires Confederacy
Ojibwe (Severn Ojibwe) *see* Oji-Cree
  (Severn Ojibwe and James Bay
  Cree)
Okanogan 207
Oklahoma
  Alabama (Creek) 148
  Arapaho 15–16, 134, 138, **142,**
    148, **153**
  Caddo 150–151
  Cayuga 46, 50, 216
  Cheyenne 15–16, 134, 138, 141,
    142, 150, 151
  Chickasaw 65, 76, **77,** 151
  Comanche 129, 151–152, 180,
    187, 213
  Coushatta 85–86
  Delaware (Lenape) **50,** 154
  Iowa (Báxoje, Ioway) 156
  Kaw (Kansa, Kanza) 156
  Kickapoo 50
  Kiowa 117, 156–157
  Klamath 218, 223, 269, **272,** 275
  Miami 157–158
  Modoc 158–159, 218, **262,** 276,
    276
  Osage 159
  Otoe-Missouria 159–160
  Ottawa (Odawa) 27, 45, 54
  Pawnee **155,** 160
  Peoria 160–161
  Ponca 161

Potawatomi 30, 40, 45, 55
Quapaw 161
Sac and Fox 48, **48,** 49, **157,**
  161–162
Seneca 46, 56
Shawnee 162
Tonkawa 163
Wichita 163
Wyandotte 163
  see also Apache; Cherokee;
    Choctaw; Creek (Muscogee);
    Seminole
Oklahoma, removal to 68, 69
  see also Indian Territory
Omaha 159
Oñate, Juan de 176
Oneida 46, 53
  see also Iroquois Confederacy
Onondaga 46, **47,** 53–54
  see also Iroquois Confederacy
Ontario, Canada
  Cayuga 46, 50, 216
  Cree (subarctic) 96, 101, 107,
    111, 113
  Delaware (Lenape) **50,** 154
  Mohawk 35, 46, 52
  Oji-Cree (Severn Ojibwe and
    James Bay Cree) 107, 113
  Oneida 46, 53
  Onondaga 46, **47,** 53–54
  Ottawa (Odawa) 27, 45, 54
  Potawatomi 30, 40, 45, 55
  Seneca 46, 56
  Tuscarora 46, **56,** 57
  see also Ojibwe (Chippewa)
Ooqueah (Inuit guide) 105, **105**
Ootah (Inuit guide) 105, **105**
Opechancanough (Powhatan) 43
Oregon
  Cayuse 205, 218, 222
  Chinook 250, **254**
  Coos 250
  Coquille 250
  Grand Ronde (Confederated
    Tribes) 251
  Klamath 218, 223, 269, **272,**
    275
  Lower Umpqua 251
  Modoc 158–159, 218, **262,** 276,
    276
  Paiute 205–206, 224
  Shasta (Chasta) 285
  Shoshone **198–199, 201,** 202,
    204, 205, **207, 224,** 225–226
  Siletz 253–254
  Siuslaw 254
  Tolowa 285
  Umatilla 216, 226
  Umpqua 213, 251, 255

Walla Walla 216, 226–227
  Warm Springs (Confederated
    Tribes) 227
  Yahooskin 218, 227
Oregon Trail 202, 218, 235, **244,**
  244–245, **245**
  map 244
Osage 159
Osceola (Seminole chief) 69, 83
Otermín, Antonio de 176, 196
Otoe-Missouria 159–160
Ottawa (Odawa) 27, 45, 54
  see also Three Fires Confederacy
Ouray (Ute chief) 218
Outer Banks, North Carolina 74

P

Pacific Northwest *see* Northwest
  Coast
Paiute 205–206, 224
Paiute, California (Mono) 283
Palus 217
Papago (Tohono O'odham) 196
Parr, Melissa **225**
Passamaquoddy 35, 54
Patawa, Minnie **225**
Patrilineal clans 29
Patwin *see* Wintun
Pawnee **155,** 160
Peary, Robert E. **104,** 104–105
Pechanga Band 267
Pend d'Oreille (Kalispel) **215,** 218,
  225
Penobscot 35, 54–55
Penutian language family 235, 261,
  263, 275
  Maidu 282
  Miwok (Me-wuk) 283
  Modoc 158–159, 218, **262,** 276,
    276
  Siuslaw 254
  Yokut (including Chukchansi)
    281, 286
Peoria 160–161
Pequot 55
  colonization 34–35
  genocide 31, 33, 43
  King Philip's War 52
  Mystic Massacre 37
Pequot War (1637–1638) 37
Pima **193,** 195
Pine Ridge Reservation, South
  Dakota 144, **160**
Pit River 283
Plains 114–163
  Alabama (Creek) 148
  amulet **163**
  Arikara **8,** 148–149, 213

Assiniboine 149, **151**
Battle of the Little Bighorn **138,**
  138–141, **139, 140, 141**
beadwork dress **154**
Black Hills wars **142,** 142–143,
  143
buffalo **146,** 146–147, **147**
Caddo 150–151
Chickasaw 65, 76, **77,** 151
chronology 118
Comanche 129, 151–152, 180,
  187, 213
common struggles 126–127
conflicts with U.S. government
  132–133, **133**
Cree (Plains Cree) 122, 123,
  152–153
Crow 153–154, 213, 217
Delaware (Lenape) **50,** 154
disease epidemics 126
European settlers 126
Fox 15, 33
Gros Ventre 154–155, **159**
Hidatsa 155, 202
Ho-chunk (Winnebago) 30, **30,**
  48, **52,** 155–156
horses 118, **128,** 128–129, **129**
Indian reservations 124–125
intertribal conflict 122–124, 133
Iowa (Báxoje, Ioway) 156
Kaw (Kansa, Kanza) 156
Kiowa 117, 156–157
Lewis and Clark expedition **130,**
  130–131
Mandan 157
map 119
map of Central Plains 124–125
map of languages 121
map of Northern Plains 122–123
map of settlements and forts 132
map of Southern Plains 127
map of tribal homelands 120
Métis independence **136,** 136–
  137, **137**
Miami 157–158
Modoc 158–159, 218, **262,** 276,
  276
Omaha 159
Osage 159
Otoe-Missouria 159–160
Pawnee **155,** 160
Peoria 160–161
Ponca 161
pouch **158**
Quapaw 161
religion 118, 120–121
resistance 126
Sac and Fox 48, **48,** 49, **157,**
  161–162

Sand Creek Massacre 134–135, **135**
Shawnee 162
Tonkawa 163
Wichita 163
Wounded Knee Massacre **144,** 144–145, **145**
Wyandotte 163
see also Arapaho; Blackfoot (Blackfeet); Cheyenne; Sioux (Dakota, Lakota, Nakota)
Plains Cree 122, 123, 152–153
Plateau *see* Great Basin and Plateau
Plateau Penutian language family 205
  Klamath 218, 223, 269, **272,** 275
  Nez Perce **117,** 129, **200,** 216, **217,** 224
  Umatilla 216, 226
  Walla Walla 216, 226–227
  Yakama (Yakima) 221, **226,** 227
Pocahontas (Powhatan) 43
Pocatello (Shoshone chief) 204
Pomeyooc (Pomeiooc) 75
Pomo 261, 270, **282,** 283–284
Ponca 161
Pontiac (Ottawa chief) 15, 33, 54
Population
  maps 15
Portola, Gaspar de 278
Potawatomi 30, 40, 45, 55
  see also Three Fires Confederacy
Potlatch ceremony 233, 236, **251**
Powhatan **43,** 55–56, **56**
Powwows **51,** 208, 211
Procter, Henry 34
Prophetstown, Indiana 34, 162
Pueblo 195–196
  agriculture 167
  ancestors 194
  art **179**
  Catholicism 179
  map 177
  performing ceremony **197**
  perseverance 172, 175
  see also Hopi; Tigua; Zuni
Pueblo Revolt (1680) 170–171, **176,** 176–177, 179
Puritans 36–37, **37**
Puyallup 253

Q
Qualchan (Yakama chief) 221
Quapaw 161
Quapaw Agency, Oklahoma 276
Quebec, Canada
  Cree (subarctic) 96, 101, 107, 111, 113

Innu (Montagnais-Naskapi) 111–112
Maliseet (Malicite) 35, 50–51
Micmac 35, **51,** 51–52
Mohawk 35, 46, 52
Oji-Cree (Severn Ojibwe and James Bay Cree) 107, 113
  see also Inuit (Eskimo); Ojibwe (Chippewa)
Quebecois 39
Quechan (Yuma) 196
Quechua (language) 7
Quileute 251, 253
Quileute (language isolate) 235
Quinault 251, 253
Quintasket, Christal 207–208

R
Raleigh, Sir Walter 74, 75
Red Cloud 142, **143**
Red Stick (Upper) Creek 68–69, 83, 86
Religious movements, intertribal maps 17
Reno, Marcus 138, 139, 140, **140,** 141
Repatriation 276
Rhode Island
  Narragansett 52–53
Riddle, Frank **276**
Riddle, Tobey **276**
Ridge, John **78**
Ridge, Major 69–70, 78, 80
Riel, Louis 136, 137
  map of rebellions 136
Roanoke Island, North Carolina 75
Rolfe, John 43
Rolfe, Thomas 43
Romero, Joe 176
Ross, John 78, **80**
Round Valley (Covelo Indian Community) 284
Russia
  Yup'ik (Eskimo) **101, 110,** 113
  see also Inuit (Eskimo)
Russian-American Company **108,** 108–109, **109**
  Aleut relations 110
  Battle of Sitka 234, 241, **241**
  Northwest Coast 233–234
  Sitka trading post **240**
Russian era
  Arctic and subarctic **108,** 108–109, **109**
  brutality toward indigenous people 13, 96, 108, 110
  California 261–262

fur trade 13
  map of Russian America 108–109
  Northwest Coast 233–234

S
Sac and Fox 48, **48,** 49, **157,** 161–162
  see also Fox
Sacagawea (Shoshone guide) 130, 202
Salish **215,** 225
  cradleboard **224**
  drying meat **227**
  fishing **223**
  spinning and weaving **234**
  thunderbird motif 208
Salishan language family 205, 235
  Chehalis 250
  Coeur d'Alene 222
  Cowlitz 250–251
  Hoh 251
  Lummi 251–252, **255**
  Muckleshoot 252
  Nisqually 252
  Nooksack 252
  Pend d'Oreille (Kalispel) **215,** 218, 225
  Puyallup 253
  Quinault 251, 253
  Salish 208, **215, 223, 224,** 225, **227, 234**
  Samish 253
  Sauk-Suiattle 253
  Siletz 253–254
  S'Klallam 254
  Skokomish 254
  Snoqualmie 254
  Spokane 226, **243**
  Squaxin Island 254
  Stillaguamish (Stoluckwamish) 254
  Suquamish 255
  Swinomish 255
  Tulalip 255
  Upper Skagit 255
Samish 253
San Carlos Reservation 184, 188
Sand Creek Massacre 134–135, **135**
  map 134
Santa Fe, New Mexico 176
Santa Fe Trail 180–181, **181**
  map 180
Saskatchewan, Canada
  Assiniboine 149, **151**
  Cree (Plains Cree) 122, 123, 152–153
  Cree (subarctic) 96, 101, 107, 111, 113

Sioux (Dakota, Lakota, Nakota) **139, 152, 157, 158,** 162–163
  see also Ojibwe (Chippewa)
Sauk and Fox *see* Sac and Fox
Sauk-Suiattle 253
Scalping knife **143**
Scott, Thomas 137
Seal-oil lamp wick bag **111**
Secotan 74–75, **75, 86**
Seegloo (Inuit guide) 105, **105**
Seminole **76,** 87
  alliance with Red Stick Creek 69, 83, 86
  assimilation plan 65
  in Five Civilized Tribes 76
  Florida Seminole 17, 69, 70, **70, 83**
  harboring slaves 69, 83
  relocation to Indian Territory 83
  resistance 69
  success 70
Seminole Wars **69**
Seneca 46, 56
  see also Iroquois Confederacy
Sequoyah (Cherokee silversmith) 66, **66**
Serra, Junípero 261, 278, **278**
Serrano 284–285
Severn Ojibwe *see* Oji-Cree
Shasta (Chasta) 285
Shawnee 162
Sheepeater Indian War (1879) 226
Shelekhov, Grigory 108, **108**
Shinnecock 56
Shoshone **224,** 225–226
  beaded horse tackle **201**
  conflicts with settlers 204
  fording river on horseback **198–199**
  Lewis and Clark expedition 202
  reservations 205
  vest **207**
Siletz 253–254
Siouan language family 65
  Assiniboine 149, **151**
  Biloxi 84
  Catawba 84
  Crow 153–154, 213, 217
  Hidatsa 155, 202
  Ho-chunk (Winnebago) 30, **30,** 48, **52,** 155–156
  Iowa (Báxoje, Ioway) 156
  Kaw (Kansa, Kanza) 156
  Mandan 157
  Omaha 159
  Osage 159
  Otoe-Missouria 159–160
  Ponca 161

Quapaw 161
Sioux (Dakota, Lakota, Nakota) **139, 152, 157, 158,** 162–163
Siouan tribes 29–30
Sioux (Dakota, Lakota, Nakota) **139, 152, 157, 158,** 162–163
   Battle of the Little Bighorn **139**
   battle with Sac and Fox **157**
   doll **157**
   lacrosse **158**
   war dance **152**
   see also Dakota; Lakota; Nakota
Sitka, Alaska
   map 240
Sitka, Battle of **240,** 240–241, **241**
   map 240
Sitting Bull (Hunkpapa Lakota Sioux) 138, **138,** 142, **142, 143,** 215, 217
Siuslaw 254
Skitswish **215**
S'Klallam 254
Skokomish 254
Slaves and slavery
   British era 43, 62–64
   Five Civilized Tribes 65–66
   harbored by Seminole 69, 83
   Spanish era 13
Smith, Jedediah 212–213, **213,** 262, 285
Smith, John 43
Snoqualmie 254
Soule, Silas 134
South Carolina
   Catawba 84
South Dakota
   Sioux (Dakota, Lakota, Nakota) **139, 152, 157, 158,** 162–163
Southeast 58–87
   arts **61**
   Biloxi 84
   Catawba 84
   Chitimacha 85
   chronology 62
   Coushatta 85–86
   disease epidemics 58–87
   Five Civilized Tribes **76,** 76–77, **77**
   land grabs and resistance **82,** 82–83, **83**
   map of federally recognized tribes 63
   map of languages 65
   map of tribal homelands 64
   Miccosukee 68, 70, 86–87, **87**
   Moundville, Alabama **72,** 72–73
   resistance 62–66, 68–70, 83
   Secotan and the Lost Colony **74,** 74–75, **75**

Trail of Tears **78,** 78–81, **79, 80, 81**
Tunica 84, 87
watercolor map 74
see also Cherokee; Choctaw; Creek (Muscogee); Seminole
Southern Appalachians
   map 67
Southern Plains
   map 127
Southern Ute
   men's shirt **222**
Southwest 164–197
   agriculture 167
   American settlers 181, **181**
   Apache resistance **188,** 188–189, **189**
   art 167
   Chaco Canyon **182,** 182–183, **183**
   chronology 168
   Cocopah 192
   colonial transition 184–185
   European invasion 168, 170–171
   Havasupai 175, 192–193
   Hopi resistance 178–179, **179**
   Hualapai 193–194
   Indian wars 171–172
   indigenous foods 168
   kachinas 168
   Long Walk of the Navajo **190,** 190–191, **191**
   map 169
   map, settlers' 181
   map of languages 171
   map of reservations 172–173
   map of tribal homelands 170
   Maricopa 194
   Mexico, America, and the Apache **184,** 184–185, **185**
   Mohave (Mojave) **172,** 194, 213
   Pima **193,** 195
   Pueblo Revolt **176,** 176–177
   Quechan (Yuma) 196
   resistance 170–171, 185
   Santa Fe Trail 180–181, **181**
   Tigua (Ysleta del Sur) 196
   Tohono O'odham (Papago) 196
   Treaty of Guadalupe Hidalgo 186–187, **187**
   tribal languages 175
   tribal perseverance 172, 175
   Yaqui 197
   Yavapai 167, 184, 197
   Zuni 167, 168, 197, **197**
   see also Apache; Hopi; Navajo; Pueblo
Spanish era
   California 261–262

disease introduction 62
introduction of horse 128, 129
mission system 13, 261, 273, **278,** 278–279
reliance on indigenous population 74
search for Northwest Passage 102
slave labor 13
Spokane 226, **243**
Spotted Elk (Lakota) 144
Springfield Model 1855 rifle **220,** 221
Squanto (Tisquantum) 37
Squaxin Island 254
Stillaguamish (Stoluckwamish) 254
Stone, Charles 270
Stu-mick-o-sucks (Blackfoot chief) **116**
Subarctic see Arctic and subarctic
Sun Dance 10, 118, 120–121, **160**
Suquamish 255
Swinomish 255
Syncretism 172

T
Takumakst (Salish village) **215**
Tanoan language family
   Tigua (Ysleta del Sur) 196
Taos, New Mexico 175, **176**
Taza (Apache chief) 188
Tchow-ee-put-o-kaw (Creek woman) **60**
Tecumseh (Shawnee chief) 15, 33–34, 68–69, 86, 162
Tenskwatawa (Shawnee prophet) 33–34, 162
Tepees **156, 162**
Termination 17, 236, 238, 264
Teton, Randy'l Hedow **201**
Texas
   Coushatta 85–86
   independence 170, 187
   Kickapoo 50
   map 174–175
   territorial conflict 175
   Tigua (Ysleta del Sur) 196
Thames, Battle of the 34
Thanksgiving 37, **37**
Third Seminole War **69**
Three Fires Confederacy 27, 38, 39, 40, 53
Three sister crops 47
Tigua (Ysleta del Sur) 196
Tiguex 179
Timucua 62
Tipai-Ipai see Kumeyaay
Tippecanoe, Battle of (1811) 34
Tisquantum (Patuxet Indian) 37

Tlingit 234, **235,** 240, 241, **241, 253,** 255
Tobeluk v. *Lind* 98, 101
Tohono O'odham (Papago) 196
Tolowa 285
Tonkawa 163
Tonto Apache 184
Totem poles **231**
Trail of Tears 69, **78,** 78–80, **79, 80, 81**
   map 78–79
Treaty of Fort Laramie (1868) 142, 143, 153
Treaty of Guadalupe Hidalgo (1848) 170, 175, 186–187, **187,** 262, 270
   map 186–187
Treaty of London (1794) see Jay Treaty (1794)
Treaty of Neah Bay (1855) 248
Treaty of New Echota (1835) 70, 78, **78, 80**
Treaty of Payne's Landing (1832) 69, 83
Treaty of Walla Walla (1855) 216, **216,** 217
Tribal homelands, maps of
   Apache lands 189
   Arctic and subarctic 96
   California 262
   Great Basin and Plateau 204
   Northeast 28
   Northwest Coast 234
   Plains 120
   Southeast 64
   Southwest 170
Tribes
   federally designated tribal entities 290–293
   map of Alaskan Native areas, Indian reservations, and tribes 294–295
   map of federally recognized Indian reservations and tribes 288–289
   number of 7, 9
Trist, Nicholas Philip 187, **187**
Tscholovoni Band **264**
Tsimshian **252**
Tulalip 255
Tunica 84, 87
Turning Bear (Lakota warrior) **125**
Tuscarora 46, **56,** 57

U
Umatilla 216, 226
Umpqua 213, 251, 255
Unangan see Aleut

United States
  border with Canada 234, 243, **243**
  dispossession of Indians 16–17
  federally designated tribal entities 290–293
  map of federally recognized Indian reservations and tribes 288–289
  map of Indian territories (1775–1819) 18
  map of Indian territories (1820–1864) 18
  map of Indian territories (1865–1894) 19
  map of Indian territories (1895–2013) 19
  map of linguistic stocks 6
Upper (Red Stick) Creek 68–69, 83, 86
Upper Skagit 255
Utah
  Goshute 223
  Navajo 167, 170, **190**, 190–191, **191, 192, 193**, 194–195
  Paiute 205–206, 224
  Shoshone **198–199, 201**, 202, 204, 205, **207, 224**, 225–226
  Ute 201, **218, 219, 222**, 226, **227**
Ute 201, **218, 219, 222**, 226, **227**
Uto-Aztecan language family 7, 205, 261, 263
  Bannock 219, **219**, 222
  Cahuilla 280, **283**
  Chemehuevi 280
  Comanche 129, 151–152, 180, 187, 213
  Cupeño 281
  Goshute 223
  Luiseño 267, 282
  Mono (California Paiute) 283
  Paiute 205–206, 224
  Pima **193**, 195
  Serrano 284–285
  Shoshone **198–199, 201**, 202, 204, 205, **207, 224**, 225–226
  Tohono O'odham (Papago) 196
  Ute 201, **218, 219, 222**, 226, **227**
  Yahooskin 218, 227
  Yaqui 197
  see also Hopi

V
Vancouver, George 102
Vancouver Island
  map 238
  medicine mask dance **239**

Vann, James 69, **78**
Victorio (Apache) 184
Virginia
  Powhatan **43**, 55–56, **56**

W
Wabanaki Confederacy 35
Wabasha (Dakota leader) 48
Wahpeton Sioux **156**
Wahunsunacawh (Powhatan chief) 43
Wailaki 285
Wakashan language family 235
  Makah 248, **248**, 252
Walker, Joel 245
Walker, Joseph 245
Walker, Mary 245
Walla Walla 216, 226–227
Wallace, Minik 105
Wampanoag 57
  conflicts with British 37
  diplomacy 25
  genocide 31, 33
  hunting skills 25, **25**
  precontact lodge (replica) **57**
  Puritans and 37
Wampum belts **46, 47**
Wamsutta (Wampanoag chief) 37
War of 1812 34
Warm Springs (Confederated Tribes) 227
Warm Springs Reservation **274**
Washington
  Chehalis 250
  Chinook 250, **254**
  Colville (Confederated Tribes) **215**, 222–223
  Cowlitz 250–251
  Hoh 251
  Lummi 251–252, **255**
  Makah 248, **248**, 252
  Muckleshoot 252
  Nez Perce **117**, 129, **200**, 216, **217**, 224
  Nisqually 252
  Nooksack 252
  Pend d'Oreille (Kalispel) **215**, 218, 225
  Puyallup 253
  Quileute 251, 253
  Quinault 251, 253
  Salish 208, **215, 223, 224**, 225, **227, 234**
  Samish 253
  Sauk-Suiattle 253
  S'Klallam 254
  Skokomish 254
  Snoqualmie 254

Spokane 226, **243**
Squaxin Island 254
Stillaguamish (Stoluckwamish) 254
Suquamish 255
Swinomish 255
Tulalip 255
Upper Skagit 255
Yakama (Yakima) 221, **226**, 227
Washington, George 18, **44**, 45, 65, 86
Washita Creek **133**
Washoe 285–286
Watt-Cloutier, Sheila 101
Weroans (Secotan chief) **86**
Western Arctic and subarctic map 99
Whale range and migration routes map 249
Whaling **248**, 248–249
White, John 74, 75
  painting by **86**
White Antelope 134
White Bird (Nez Perce chief) 217
Whiteside, Samuel 144
Whitman, Marcus 218
Whitman, Narcissa 218
Wichita 163
Wild Cat (Seminole leader) 69
Wild rice harvest **55**
Wilson, Jack *see* Wovoka
Wilson, John 150–151
Winnebago (Ho-chunk) 30, **30**, 48, **52**, 155–156
Winnemem-Wintu **286**
Winnemucca, Sarah 205–207
Winter Counts (pictographs) 117–118, **120, 129, 149**
Wintuan language family
  Wintun (Nomlaki, Patwin) 261, 286
Wintun (Nomlaki, Patwin) 261, 286
Wisconsin
  Delaware (Lenape) **50**, 154
  Menominee **2–3, 4**, 5, **24**, 51
  Oneida 46, 53
  Potawatomi 30, 40, 45, 55
  see also Ojibwe (Chippewa)
Wiyot 263, 286
Wolastoqiyik (Maliseet, Malicite) 35, 50–51
Wooden Leg (Cheyenne warrior) **121**
Wounded Knee Massacre 122, **144**, 144–145, **145**
  maps 144, 145
Wovoka (Northern Paiute medicine man) 121–122, 144
Wright, George **220**, 221

Wyandotte 163
Wyoming
  Arapaho 15–16, 134, 138, **142**, 148, **153**
  Shoshone **198–199, 201**, 202, 204, 205, **207, 224**, 225–226

Y
Yahi 16, 263
Yahooskin 218, 227
Yakama (Yakima) 221, **226**, 227
Yakama Reservation 202, 205, 206
Yakama War 221
Yamassee War (1715–1717) 63
Yana 263
Yaqui 197
Yavapai 167, 184, 197
Yellow Calf (Arapaho chief) **148**
Yellowstone National Park **147**
Yokut (including Chukchansi) **281**, 286
Young, Brigham 204
Young, Martha 245
Ysleta del Sur (Tigua) 196
Yukian language family 263
Yukon, Canada *see* Inuit (Eskimo)
Yuma (Quechan) 196
Yuman language family
  Cocopah 192
  Havasupai 175, 192–193
  Hualapai 193–194
  Kumeyaay (Diegueño, Kamia, Tipai-Ipai) 278, 282, **282**, 286
  Maricopa 194
  Mohave (Mojave) **172**, 194, 213
  Quechan (Yuma) 196
  Yavapai 167, 184, 197
Yup'ik (Eskimo) **101, 110**, 113
Yurok **273, 286**

Z
Zuni 167, 168, 197, **197**

ATLAS OF INDIAN NATIONS
ANTON TREUER

PUBLISHED BY THE NATIONAL GEOGRAPHIC SOCIETY
JOHN M. FAHEY, Chairman of the Board
  and Chief Executive Officer
DECLAN MOORE, Executive Vice President;
  President, Publishing and Travel
MELINA GEROSA BELLOWS, Executive Vice President; Publisher
  and Chief Creative Officer, Books, Kids, and Family

PREPARED BY THE BOOK DIVISION
HECTOR SIERRA, Senior Vice President and General Manager
JANET GOLDSTEIN, Senior Vice President and Editorial Director
JONATHAN HALLING, Creative Director
MARIANNE R. KOSZORUS, Design Director
LISA THOMAS, Senior Editor
R. GARY COLBERT, Production Director
JENNIFER A. THORNTON, Director of Managing Editorial
SUSAN S. BLAIR, Director of Photography
MEREDITH C. WILCOX, Director, Administration and
  Rights Clearance

STAFF FOR THIS BOOK
SUSAN STRAIGHT, Editor
MARYANN HAGGERTY AND JOHN W. GLENN, Text Editors
CAROL FARRAR NORTON, Art Director
MATT PROPERT AND LINDA MEYERRIECKS, Illustrations Editors
JEFFREY WARANIAK, Researcher
CARL MEHLER, Director of Maps
MATTHEW CHWASTYK, Map Production Manager
SVEN M. DOLLING, MICHAEL MCNEY, GREGORY UGIANSKY,
  AND XNR PRODUCTIONS, Map Research and Production
MARSHALL KIKER, Associate Managing Editor
JOAN GOSSETT, Production Editor
GALEN YOUNG, Rights Clearance Specialist
KATIE OLSEN, Production Design Assistant

PRODUCTION SERVICES
PHILLIP L. SCHLOSSER, Senior Vice President
CHRIS BROWN, Vice President, NG Book Manufacturing
NICOLE ELLIOTT, Director of Production
GEORGE BOUNELIS, Senior Production Manager
RACHEL FAULISE, Manager
ROBERT L. BARR, Manager

The National Geographic Society is one of the world's largest nonprofit scientific and educational organizations. Founded in 1888 to "increase and diffuse geographic knowledge," the Society's mission is to inspire people to care about the planet. It reaches more than 400 million people worldwide each month through its official journal, *National Geographic,* and other magazines; National Geographic Channel; television documentaries; music; radio; films; books; DVDs; maps; exhibitions; live events; school publishing programs; interactive media; and merchandise. National Geographic has funded more than 10,000 scientific research, conservation and exploration projects and supports an education program promoting geographic literacy. For more information, visit www.nationalgeographic.com.

For more information, please call 1-800-NGS LINE (647-5463) or write to the following address:

National Geographic Society
1145 17th Street N.W.
Washington, D.C. 20036-4688 U.S.A.

Visit us online at www.nationalgeographic.com/books

For information about special discounts for bulk purchases, please contact National Geographic Books Special Sales: ngspecsales@ngs.org

For rights or permissions inquiries, please contact National Geographic Books Subsidiary Rights: ngbookrights@ngs.org

Copyright © 2013 National Geographic Society
All rights reserved. Reproduction of the whole or any part of the contents without written permission from the publisher is prohibited.

LIBRARY OF CONGRESS CATALOGING-IN-PUBLICATION DATA
Treuer, Anton
  Atlas of Indian nations. -- 1st edition.
    p. cm.
  Includes bibliographical references and index.
  ISBN 978-1-4262-1256-7 (hardcover (deluxe) : alk. paper) --
ISBN 978-1-4262-1160-7 (hardcover : alk. paper)
  1. Indians of North America--Maps. 2. Indians of North
America--History--Maps. I. Title.
  G1106.E1N3 2013
  970.004'97--dc23
                                        2013036634

Printed in China

14/RRDS/2

THE GREAT AMERICAN WEST

through the eyes of National Geographic

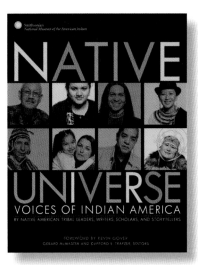

▲ Prodigious in scope and intimate in detail, this book, like the museum it celebrates, is a landmark.

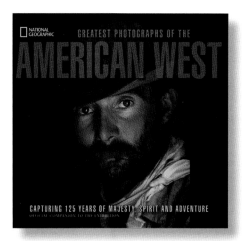

▲ Spectacular color photography and informative captions give a rich view of the enduring landscape that is the American West.

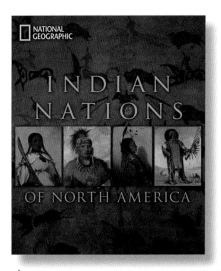

▲ Captivating and informative for all who appreciate history, diverse cultures, stunning images, and the artistry of maps.

▲ A vibrant adventure narrative, bringing Native American history and culture alive for young readers.

 Like us on Facebook.com: Nat Geo Books

 Follow us on Twitter.com: @NatGeoBooks

NATIONAL GEOGRAPHIC

Get closer to National Geographic explorers and photographers, and connect with other members around the globe. Join us today— it's free—at nationalgeographic.com/join.

AVAILABLE WHEREVER BOOKS ARE SOLD

nationalgeographic.com/books

Copyright © 2013 National Geographic Society